Cultural Atlas of the
RENAISSANCE

Project Manager Peter Furtado
Editor Chris Murray
Art Editor Adrian Hodgkins
Picture Editor Linda Proud
Cartographic Manager Olive Pearson
Cartographic Editor Sarah Phibbs
Index Ann Barrett
Production Clive Sparling
Typesetting Brian Blackmore,
Niki Moores
Advisory Editor Nicholas Mann

AN ANDROMEDA BOOK

Copyright © Andromeda Oxford
Limited 1993

Planned and produced by Andromeda
Oxford Limited
9-15 The Vineyard
Abingdon
Oxfordshire, England OX14 3PX

Published by Time-Life Books,
Amsterdam 1993

ISBN 0 7054 0869 8

Origination by Eray Scan Ltd, Singapore

Printed in Spain by Fournier A. Gráficas
S.A., Vitoria

30 29 28 27 26 25 24 23 22 21 20 19 18 17 16 15 14 13 12 11 10 9 8 7 6 5 4 3 2

Cultural Atlas of the
RENAISSANCE

C.F. Black, Mark Greengrass,
David Howarth, Jeremy Lawrance,
Richard Mackenney,
Martin Rady, Evelyn Welch

TIME
LIFE
BOOKS

CONTENTS

8   Chronological Table
11   Foreword

Part One: The Heartland of the Renaissance

14   What Was the Renaissance?
28   The Early Italian Renaissance
48   The Classical Renaissance
76   The High Renaissance

Part Two: The Renaissance and the Wider World

108   Italy, Venice and the Diffusion of the Renaissance
136   Germany and the Low Countries
164   France
184   Spain and Portugal
204   England and Scotland

225   List of Contributors
226   List of Illustrations
229   Bibliography
230   Gazetteer
234   Index

Special Features

18 Symbolism and Allegory
26 The Discovery of Antiquity
32 The Palazzo Pubblico, Siena
42 Dante and the Divine Comedy
44 Altarpieces
46 Giotto and the Arena Chapel
52 The Book Hunters
54 Medici Patonage
69 Brunelleschi: Perspective
70 Brunelleschi: Proportion
72 Urbino: The Ideal City
74 Florence in 1490
86 The Sistine Chapel Ceiling
92 The Rebuilding of Rome
100 Palladio and Neo-Classical Architecture
102 Leonardo and the Infinite Works of Nature
104 Ladies of Learning
116 The Printer–Publisher
120 The Venice Arsenal
128 Renaissance Music
132 Astrology and Astronomy
134 The Ottoman Empire
144 Alchemy and the Rosicrucians
148 Martin Luther
158 Van Eyck: The Ghent Altarpiece
160 German Wood Sculpture
162 The Northern Vision
168 Chambord
180 The Royal Collection of Francis I
182 Court Entertainments
194 The New Learning and the Inquisition
196 Philip II
200 The Escorial
202 Plateresque Architecture
208 Hampton Court
216 The Portrait in Miniature
218 The English Theater
222 New Colleges

List of Maps

11 Europe in 1993
15 Centers of artistic activity in Italy
16 Medieval western Christendom
23 Italian trade and the economy of Europe in the later Middle Ages
28 Italy in the early 14th century
34 Italian cultural centers c. 1300
41 The travels of Petrarch
49 The Florentine humanists, 1375–1460
52 The rediscovery of classical manuscripts
56 The expansion of Venice, Florence and Milan
58 Italy in the 15th century
66 Cultural centers of 15th-century Italy
77 The Italian Wars
79 Italy at the end of the Italian Wars
82 The travels of Leonardo da Vinci
91 The buildings of Palladio
94 The travels of Cellini
95 Italian cultural centers in the 16th century
108 European trade, c. 1500
110 European centers of learning
112 Venice as a cultural center
115 Centers of printing, 15th–17th centuries
119 Europe divided, c. 1560
122 Iberian exploration
125 Northern exploration, 1390–1570
138 Trade routes in northern Europe
140 The Holy Roman Empire: printing and education
142 The travels of Conrad Celtis
146 The travels of Erasmus
154 Religious changes in the 16th century
165 French expansion, 1453–1559
167 French Renaissance châteaux
170 The Valois Renaissance
177 The French Wars of Religion
184 Political divisions and centers of power in 15th-century Iberia
186 Spanish expansion in the Mediterranean
189 Religious and cultural centers in 16th-century Iberia
207 Political unrest in Britain, 1461–1509
212 Major buildings of Renaissance Britain

CHRONOLOGICAL TABLE

1300   1400

Head of Christ, Giotto   *Henry VII of England*   *St Matthew, Riemenschneider*   *Florence Cathedral*

ITALY	1302–10 Giovanni Pisano Pulpit, Pisa Cathedral 1305–6 Giotto Arena Chapel, Padua 1314–21 Dante *Divine Comedy* 1333 Martini *Annunciation* 1339 Lorenzetti *Good and Bad Government*	1342–43 Petrarch *My Secret* 1348–53 Boccaccio *Decameron*	c. 1400 Fra Angelico *Annunciation* 1404 Bruni begins his history of Florence 1416–20 Donatello *St George* 1427 Masaccio *Holy Trinity* 1440 Valla *Donation of Constantine*	1452–66 Piero della Francesca Arezzo cycle 1469-74 Ficino *Platonic Theory* 1474 Mantegna *Camera degli Sposi* c.1478 Botticelli *Primavera* c.1485 Giovanni Bellini *St Francis in Ecstacy*	1486 Poliziano *Miscellanea* 1490–95 Carpaccio *Legend of St Ursula*
GERMANY AND THE LOW COUNTRIES	1370s Communities based on the "modern devotion" formed 1395-1403 Sluter *Moses Fountain*		c.1430 Van der Weyden *Deposition* 1432 Van Eyck *Ghent Altarpiece*	1455 Ouwater *Raising of Lazarus* 1476 van der Goes *Portinari Altarpiece*	1494 Brant *Ship of Fools*
FRANCE			1400 Froissart completes *Chronicles* c. 1413 Limbourg Brothers *Duc de Berry Book of Hours*	c. 1450 Fouquet *Virgin and Child* 1461 Villon *Testament*	
SPAIN AND PORTUGAL			1420s First complete translation of the Aeneid into a modern language (Spanish)	1444 Mena *Labyrinth of Fortune* c.1465 Goncalves *St Vincent Polyptych*	1481 Nebrija *Latin Introductions* 1499 Rojas *La Celestina*
ENGLAND AND SCOTLAND	c. 1387 Chaucer begins *Canterbury Tales* 1395-9 *Wilton Diptych*			1476 Caxton sets up press in London 1491 Grocyn lectures on Greek in Oxford	1496 Colet lectures on scriptures at Oxford
HISTORICAL BACKGROUND	1309-1377 Avignon Papacy 1337 Hundred Years War begins 1347 Black Death 1353 Ottomans begin to invade Europe 1378 Beginning of Great Schism 1385 Gian Galeazzo unites Visconti lands in northern Italy		1431 Joan of Arc burned 1434 Cosimo de Medici returns to Florence 1453 End of the Hundred Years War, with defeat of England 1453 Constantinople falls to the Ottomans 1450s Gutenberg uses movable type 1454 Peace of Lodi	1455-85 Wars of the Roses in England 1458-64 Pius II pope 1471-84 Sixtus IV pope 1478 Spanish Inquisition established 1492 Columbus discovers the New World	1492 Ferdinand and Isabella drive the Moors from Spain 1492 Death of Lorenzo de Medici in Florence 1494 Spain and Portugal divide the New World 1494 Beginning of Italian Wars 1498 Savonarola burned

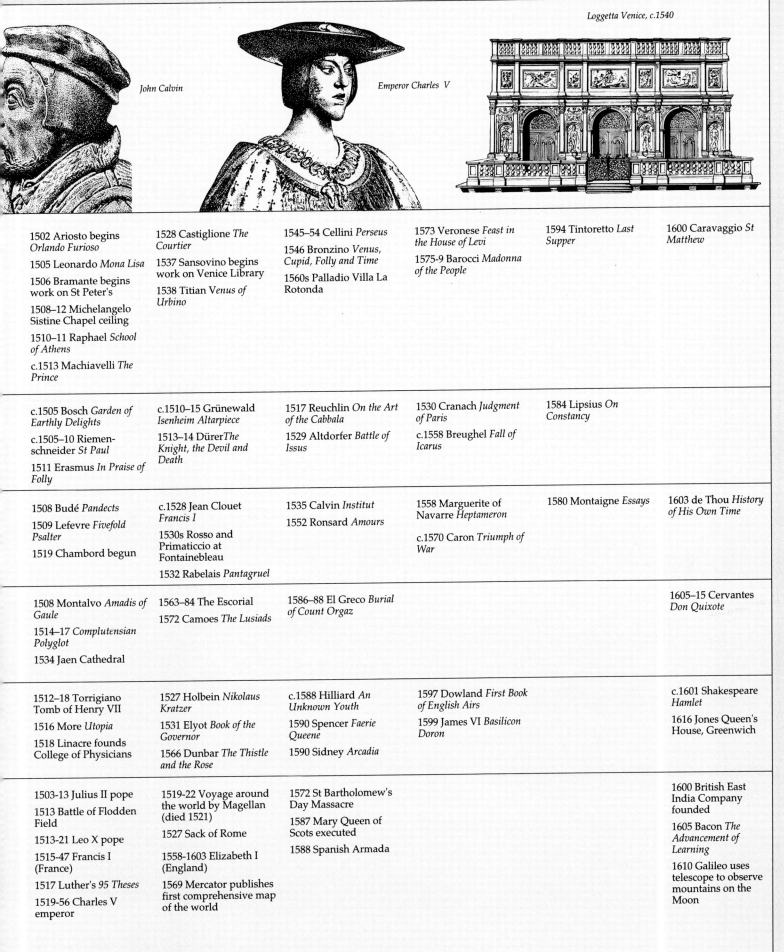

John Calvin

Emperor Charles V

Loggetta Venice, c.1540

1502 Ariosto begins *Orlando Furioso*

1505 Leonardo *Mona Lisa*

1506 Bramante begins work on St Peter's

1508–12 Michelangelo Sistine Chapel ceiling

1510–11 Raphael *School of Athens*

c.1513 Machiavelli *The Prince*

1528 Castiglione *The Courtier*

1537 Sansovino begins work on Venice Library

1538 Titian *Venus of Urbino*

1545–54 Cellini *Perseus*

1546 Bronzino *Venus, Cupid, Folly and Time*

1560s Palladio Villa La Rotonda

1573 Veronese *Feast in the House of Levi*

1575-9 Barocci *Madonna of the People*

1594 Tintoretto *Last Supper*

1600 Caravaggio *St Matthew*

---

c.1505 Bosch *Garden of Earthly Delights*

c.1505–10 Riemenschneider *St Paul*

1511 Erasmus *In Praise of Folly*

c.1510–15 Grünewald *Isenheim Altarpiece*

1513–14 Dürer *The Knight, the Devil and Death*

1517 Reuchlin *On the Art of the Cabbala*

1529 Altdorfer *Battle of Issus*

1530 Cranach *Judgment of Paris*

c.1558 Breughel *Fall of Icarus*

1584 Lipsius *On Constancy*

1508 Budé *Pandects*

1509 Lefevre *Fivefold Psalter*

1519 Chambord begun

c.1528 Jean Clouet *Francis I*

1530s Rosso and Primaticcio at Fontainebleau

1532 Rabelais *Pantagruel*

1535 Calvin *Institut*

1552 Ronsard *Amours*

1558 Marguerite of Navarre *Heptameron*

c.1570 Caron *Triumph of War*

1580 Montaigne *Essays*

1603 de Thou *History of His Own Time*

1508 Montalvo *Amadis of Gaule*

1514–17 *Complutensian Polyglot*

1534 Jaen Cathedral

1563–84 The Escorial

1572 Camoes *The Lusiads*

1586–88 El Greco *Burial of Count Orgaz*

1605–15 Cervantes *Don Quixote*

1512–18 Torrigiano Tomb of Henry VII

1516 More *Utopia*

1518 Linacre founds College of Physicians

1527 Holbein *Nikolaus Kratzer*

1531 Elyot *Book of the Governor*

1566 Dunbar *The Thistle and the Rose*

c.1588 Hilliard *An Unknown Youth*

1590 Spencer *Faerie Queene*

1590 Sidney *Arcadia*

1597 Dowland *First Book of English Airs*

1599 James VI *Basilicon Doron*

c.1601 Shakespeare *Hamlet*

1616 Jones Queen's House, Greenwich

1503-13 Julius II pope

1513 Battle of Flodden Field

1513-21 Leo X pope

1515-47 Francis I (France)

1517 Luther's *95 Theses*

1519-56 Charles V emperor

1519-22 Voyage around the world by Magellan (died 1521)

1527 Sack of Rome

1558-1603 Elizabeth I (England)

1569 Mercator publishes first comprehensive map of the world

1572 St Bartholomew's Day Massacre

1587 Mary Queen of Scots executed

1588 Spanish Armada

1600 British East India Company founded

1605 Bacon *The Advancement of Learning*

1610 Galileo uses telescope to observe mountains on the Moon

FOREWORD

Among the many value-laden terms that historians use to segment and to describe the past, "Renaissance" is perhaps the most powerful, and the most evocative. For the concept of rebirth applied to a civilization implies both a prior death and a prospective growth; it carries within it both the notion of dependence upon a pagan past and, in accordance with the potent Christian myth, the promise of a better life to come. That the beginnings of the modern world should now be characterized not just as a renaissance – for there had been others – but as *the* Renaissance, attests to a striking, and perhaps undue, optimism on the part of posterity as to the permanent potential of human society for self-improvement.

Yet this Renaissance is not purely the invention of modern historians, even if the term itself was not used in English until the early 19th century: 14th- and 15th-century Italians were already alert to changes in their society, and most especially in their culture, that they were anxious to promote as a bringing back to the light, or to life, of the values of an earlier age. They themselves believed that something was indeed being reborn. At the same time, and as a consequence of their determination to proclaim their own progress, they came slowly to view the past in unfavorable terms anticipating that other fundamental concept of modern historiography, the Middle Ages: a fallow period (which of course it was not) of perhaps a thousand years that lay between their own age and the glories of classical antiquity.

The 500th anniversaries celebrated in 1992 – of Columbus's voyage and the death of Lorenzo de' Medici – have tended to concentrate attention on two particular aspects of the Renaissance: exploration and the expansion of the known world, and the role of powerful statesmen not merely as politicians but also as patrons, or at least as focal points of cultural activity. But the widening horizons did not necessarily betoken a brave new Renaissance world across the seas, nor were all despots enlightened patrons of the arts and sciences. Fifteenth-century Florence was indeed a brilliant center for new developments in

Europe in 1993
Geography played an important role in determining the location and spread of the Renaissance, focused as it was initially in the trading cities of the Mediterranean and only later spreading north of the Alps. Yet the Renaissance also determined the geography of Europe in a very real sense. This was the great age of discovery and cartography, which literally put

Europe "on the map"; and, equally important, Renaissance ideas were critical to the consolidation of some of Europe's most enduring nation states, including England, France and Spain. Even Germany and Italy, which were not unified politically until the late 19th centuries, acquired a decisive national consciousness during the years of the Renaissance.

architecture and the arts, philosophy and literature, but it is important to remember that it was not the only center, and that progress was in one sense the product of regression. The dilemma of the new age had already been anticipated by a 12th-century classical scholar who compared his own position to that of a dwarf on the shoulders of a giant, raised on high by the achievements of the past, and yet able to see further than his predecessors. So also 14th- and 15th-century humanists grappled with the problem of how to acknowledge and benefit from all that had gone before, and yet still to make real progress. The giant was of course classical antiquity.

That the rebirth should first occur in Italy may well owe something to the particular political structures of the day: the multiplicity of autonomous city-states whose compact size and boundless sense of civic pride encouraged comparisons with republican Rome, and allowed the emulation of its values, ceremonies, art, architecture, literature and language in a new context. It undoubtedly also owes something to the efforts, for instance, of individual scholars and teachers who sought to rediscover and restore ancient texts and monuments, and to lawyers who in their daily work drew upon the conventions of classical rhetoric, and glossed the precepts of Roman law so as to apply them to 14th-century reality. By the middle of the 15th century, traces of the influence of the ancient world are to be found throughout Italian culture, not simply in the form of artistic or literary imitation, but also in the impact of its philosophy and its moral values on almost every aspect of social and political life. Venice and Padua, Milan and Bologna, Siena and Rome all had their individual roles to play in this remarkable evolution.

At the same time, however, profound changes in the economic and social structures of the Western world, and in the balances of political power, guaranteed that what was happening in Italy did not remain a purely Italian phenomenon. The expansion of trade, led in particular by the wealthy seafaring city-states of Genoa and Venice, ensured the diffusion of ideas and styles; the book-trade, encouraged by such major diplomatic gatherings as the various councils of the Church, and aided by the introduction from Germany of the new technology of printing in the 1460s, rapidly became international. So did the content of books: the sonnet, for instance, whose first great exponent was Petrarch, was over the course of the two centuries to become a pan-European genre. Artists and architects traveled and worked to commission far from their places of origin; scholars and intellectuals undertook diplomatic missions on behalf of their patrons; the foundation of new schools and universities increasingly encouraged a greater mobility and internationalism among students than we might encounter today, and the fall of Constantinople to the Turks in 1453 led to a significant exodus to the West of Greek scholars, who brought with them much of what remained of the culture of classical Athens and Byzantium.

Contacts with neighboring northern countries, and with Spain through the Aragonese kingdom of Naples, ensured the rapid, if uneven, diffusion of many of the features that we today associate with the Renaissance, and their gradual insertion, in sometimes strikingly different national forms, into the culture of the rest of Europe. In the 15th and 16th centuries, the Renaissance thus came to encompass divergences as great as those between Roman Catholicism and the German Reformation, Palladian villas and Hampton Court, Ronsard and Cervantes, Michelangelo and Dürer. The English Renaissance – to take but one example – needs to be understood in the context of developments in Italy, and yet evidently displays specific characteristics entirely different from any Italian models that one might perceive.

Thus a synoptic approach is barely possible today: we know too much, and are too aware of diversity. If the richness and excitement of the new culture are not to be lost in a welter of detail, broad divisions according to those ever-changing national frontiers which that culture transcended are still of value. We need to be able to observe what is specific to one region or state, while remaining aware of the constant flow of people and ideas between it and others, so as to understand the role of travel, exploration and trade in the diffusion of cultural change. Mapping these movements, and the constant shifts within the borders of a single political or geographical area, is a vital visual aid, in our increasingly visual age, to the interpretation of what might otherwise become a series of abstractions.

The multiple manifestations of the Renaissance call out for illustration: the revival of classical styles, the spread of learning, the complex interaction of pagan and Christian ideas, a rediscovered faith in the dignity of man, a sense of pomp and circumstance enhanced by the iconography and ceremonial of ancient Rome, the return of the pagan gods in all their significant splendor, and the delighted depiction of natural surroundings. Even if, as has been suggested, it is no longer possible to write cultural history on the grand scale, perhaps the careful scrutiny of plates and maps as adjuncts to historical narrative may enable readers to form in their own minds the synthesis that is denied to the historian: a synthesis no doubt as bright and idiosyncratic as are many of the products of the Renaissance themselves, and one that will constantly need to be checked against new sources, artifacts and monuments, always open to correction and completion. For in the late 20th century we are still dwarves perched on the shoulders of giants, torn between acknowledging our debt to the past, and our confidence that we can now look beyond it.

Nicholas Mann

PART ONE
THE HEARTLAND
OF THE
RENAISSANCE

WHAT WAS THE RENAISSANCE?

The term "Renaissance" is usually thought to be so well understood as not to require definition, but in fact it can be used in two quite different senses. Either it can denote a period of history, in the same way as for instance "the 15th century"; or, like the adjectives "medieval" and "Victorian", it can describe a set of quite distinct cultural ideas and values. A Renaissance artist, for instance, might simply be one who just happened to live during the Renaissance – for example Hieronymus Bosch, even though his nightmarish visions are often seen as essentially "medieval". Or he might be an artist who actively shared (and helped to form) the beliefs and outlook of Renaissance culture as a whole, such as Michelangelo or Botticelli. It is important to bear this distinction in mind because it was only late in the history of the Renaissance that the ideas with which we associate it most closely ceased to belong to a small group of individuals and acquired a more general currency.

The Renaissance is normally thought to have begun in Italy during the 14th century – perhaps as early as the painters Giotto (c. 1266–1337) or Cimabue (c. 1240–c.1302) – and to have ended in the late 16th century. Nevertheless, new cultural styles may exist side by side with the older ones they eventually replace. Many of the ideas we associate with the Renaissance may be discerned in the 12th century and there was much that was medieval in the Renaissance. It is clearly unwise to draw boundaries too sharply.

Although the word "Renaissance" may be found as early as 1829 in a novel by Balzac, it owes its first definition to the French historian Jules Michelet, writing in 1855. Michelet used it to describe the period of European history, running from roughly 1400 to 1600, that witnessed both "the discovery of the world" and "the discovery of man". Following the publication a few years later of the highly influential *The Civilization of the Renaissance in Italy* (1860) by the Swiss historian Jacob Burckhardt, the word became an accepted part of the historian's vocabulary. Burckhardt produced a romantically colored account of the Renaissance. Nevertheless, his achievement was to present the Renaissance not just as a period but as a cultural movement that marked a crucial point in the transition from the medieval to the modern world.

Michelet and Burckhardt may have invented the term "Renaissance", but they were hardly responsible for the creation of a myth. Scholars and artists living in the 15th and 16th centuries were themselves aware that they were living at a time of enormous cultural change. The Italian artist and art historian Giorgio Vasari (1511–74) wrote in 1550 of a second birth of the arts in Italy. He noted that the arts were moving toward perfection, and that a recovery of the ancient

Left The Procession of the Magi (c. 1460), by Gozzoli. This work unites many important aspects of Italian Renaissance art. In terms of technique, Gozzoli was one of the first to convey the illusion of spatial depth through perspective. The frequent depiction in his frescoes of Roman buildings and architecture indicates, furthermore, the extent to which he was inspired by classical models. Additionally, Gozzoli often included in his work portraits of the great patrons on whose munificence his generation of artists relied. This fresco shows Lorenzo de' Medici as one of the Magi. Lorenzo, who ruled Florence from 1469 until his death, was an avid collector of works of art and Italy's leading patron of scholars and painters.

Centers of artistic activity in Italy
Giorgio Vasari has provided perhaps the most vivid picture of the artistic life of the Renaissance era, but not a wholly complete one. In his *Lives of the Artists*, written in the mid 16th century, he described the artistic activities not only of his own day, but as far back as the 14th century. Based in Florence, his work overemphasizes the relative importance of Tuscany and the artistic poverty both of northern Italy and the south, which rates barely a mention in his work. Nevertheless, his book has colored perceptions of Renaissance Italy until modern times.

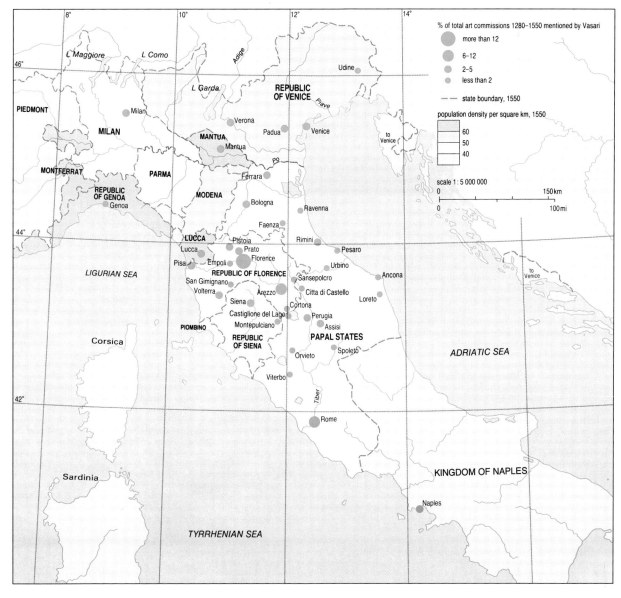

civilization of Greece and Rome was taking place. The humanist scholar Marsilio Ficino (1433–99) spoke of a new golden age in Florence that had "restored to life the liberal arts, which were almost extinct: grammar, poetry, rhetoric, painting, sculpture, architecture, music and the ancient singing of songs to the Orphic lyre". Even as early as the 14th century, the poet and humanist Petrarch (1304–74) suggested that a new period might be dawning as men "broke through the darkness to return to the pure, pristine radiance" of antiquity.

The few quotations given above provide a good definition of what the Renaissance actually was: a movement that affected all aspects of culture – literature and scholarship as well as painting, sculpture and architecture – and that consciously sought to recover and to revive the achievements of classical antiquity. The word "Renaissance" means "rebirth" and this was precisely how the leading scholars and artists of the 15th and 16th centuries interpreted the cultural milieu in which they lived and worked: as the rebirth of classical civilization after a long period of degeneration.

Medieval renaissances
It was a Renaissance scholar, Flavio Biondo (1392–1463), who first used the term *medium aevum* or "middle age" to describe the period between the fall

of the Roman Empire in the 5th century and the revival of the arts in his own day. For Biondo, and many of his contemporaries, the Middle Ages represented a millennium of decay during which the achievements of the preceding epoch had been either forgotten or allowed to languish. There is some justice in their beliefs. Nevertheless, it is now clear that classical culture had never completely disappeared from Europe during the Middle Ages, and that there had been several important attempts to revive it in the centuries preceding the Renaissance.

The earliest *renovatio* or "renewal" took place at the time of Charlemagne, during the late 8th and 9th centuries. After Charlemagne's coronation as emperor in AD 800, he sought to restore the Roman Empire in western Europe by sponsoring a revival of Roman architecture and literature. He rebuilt the royal palace at Aachen in the style of ancient Rome, authorized the copying and dissemination of classical texts, and gathered together a group of scholars dedicated to the study of Roman literature. Its members gave themselves classical names such as Horace and Homer; they referred to the palace at Aachen as the second Rome; and they planned for the establishment in Charlemagne's empire of "a new Athens, only much more excellent". Charlemagne, who participated wholeheartedly in this grand scheme, was himself illiterate.

It is easy to ridicule the pretentiousness of the Carolingian Renaissance. Nevertheless, this early revival kept alive classical ideas and models that might otherwise have been swept away. In particular, the copyists who worked at Charlemagne's court helped to preserve the texts of Latin manuscripts: many of the earliest versions of classical works come from Carolingian *scriptoria* (copying rooms). The clear, round hand in which these works were transcribed – Carolingian minuscule – was later thought by Renaissance scholars to be the authentic style of ancient Rome and was widely imitated. As a consequence, the "roman" print-type we have today is actually Carolingian in origin.

A second revival occurred in the 12th century and spread much more widely than its Carolingian predecessor. A renewed interest in Roman civilization was seen in the growth and spread of libraries and in a new interest in the purity of literary expression. Both classical sculpture and architecture were imitated. The fluted pilasters of the arcade of Autun cathedral deliberately recalled a nearby Roman gateway, the Porte d'Arroux, while the statue of Marcus Aurelius in Rome provided a model for several 12th-century equestrian reliefs.

The most important aspect of the 12th-century Renaissance, however, came through the Arab world. As a result of the Crusades and of contact with the Islamic civilization of Spain and southern Italy, scholars in western Europe obtained translations of some of the scientific and philosophical works of ancient Greece. The impact of Aristotle in particular was immense, for his works contained ideas on philosophy, physics, astronomy, logic, politics and ethics entirely unfamiliar to the scholars of the 12th century. Among the most important consequences of the rediscovery of Greek learning was the foundation of universities, most notably at Bologna, Padua, Paris and Oxford. The emphasis placed on the study of Aristotelian logic in the new universities, eventually to the virtual exclusion of all else, provoked a fierce reaction in the 14th and 15th centuries. The demand for more teaching of the "humanities" – poetry, literature and history – was a significant feature of the early Renaissance.

The Renaissance did not take place, therefore, against a background of complete cultural decay. There had been previous "renaissances", which in a number of respects had prepared the way for the achievements of the 15th and 16th centuries. Indeed, with the recent "discovery" of renaissances in the 10th and 13th centuries, the Italian Renaissance increasingly appears to be more the brilliant culmination of a series of earlier trends than a break with the past and a totally new beginning.

Pagan and Christian

One of the principal difficulties experienced both in the 12th and the 15th centuries was how to reconcile classical civilization with Christianity. The medieval world was an intensely religious one in which all phenomena were interpreted within a Christian framework. The Greek and Roman writers, however, were pagan and their accounts of the world were often contrary to the teachings of the Church. As late as the second decade of the 14th century, the poet Dante (1265–1321) consigned all classical writers to Hell in his *Divine Comedy* because they were unbaptized and "lived before the time of Christianity". For a time,

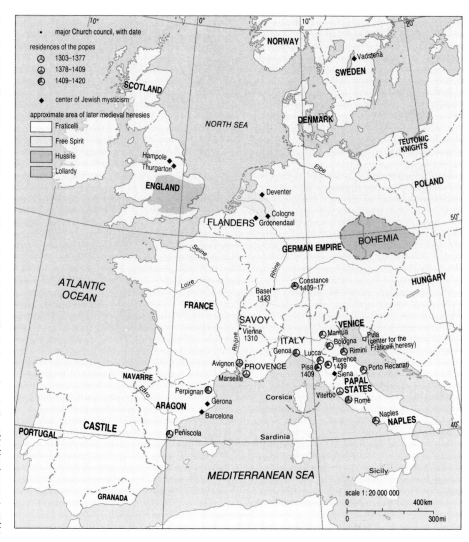

even Aristotelian philosophy was banned at the university of Paris because of its pagan associations. Aristotle was saved for posterity by two Dominican friars, Albertus Magnus (c. 1206–80) and Thomas Aquinas (c. 1225–74), who gave his ideas a Christian gloss.

In the Italian Renaissance there was a similar compromise between the classical and Christian traditions. Very few scholars became so absorbed in pagan literature as to reject Christianity. Although plenty of erotic verse was composed, the majority of artists and scholars employed the revived classical civilization in the service of the faith. Many of their most important commissions were undertaken on behalf of the Church, and the most common subject matter was found in the Bible and from the lives of the Church Fathers. Throughout the Renaissance artists continued to blend classical themes and techniques with a Christian iconography. Two of the most striking examples of this are Jan van Eyck's *Arnolfini Marriage* (1434) and Botticelli's *Primavera* (c. 1478), both of which have been shown to contain an elaborate Christian symbolism.

The humanist synthesis

The connection between the Renaissance and Christian belief is most apparent in the humanist literature of the period. "Humanism" is a term even harder to define than "Renaissance". The word *humanista* is first found in the 16th century as slang for a student who studied the liberal arts: it had its counterparts in *canonista* (a student studying canon law) and *legista* (a

Left and right above: Medieval western Christendom
Despite the overarching authority of the papacy over the western (Latin) Church, Christendom was far from being a monolithic bloc in the later Middle Ages. Heretical movements, such as the Hussites in Bohemia and the Lollards in England, combined a mild challenge to doctrinal orthodoxy with a blunt assertion of local pride that put great emphasis on the vernacular Bible. The prevalence of mystics in the Low Countries and England, men such as Meister Eckhardt and women such as Catherine of Siena, displayed a degree of free thought that was alarming to the Church hierarchy. Moreover, the political weakness of the papacy itself was thrown into high relief by its stay in Avignon under the sway of the French kings, and the need for Church councils to restore unity within a divided organization.

Right St. Augustine teaching Rhetoric and Philosophy by Gozzoli. Gozzoli's portrayal of the Early Church Father St Augustine as a teacher of classical learning symbolizes the artist's rejection of the traditional distinction between pagan scholarship and the Christian tradition.

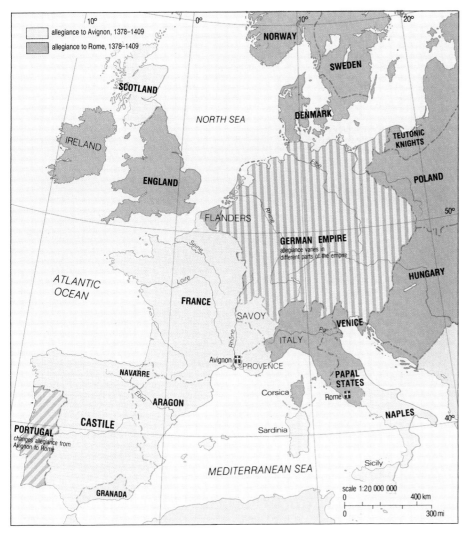

The term "humanism", though a late 18th- or 19th-century invention, is valuable, for it draws attention to some of the most important features of Renaissance thought and learning.

The *humanista* was so called because he was following a course in the humanities or, as they were then called, the *studia humanitatis*. This meant that he studied what was known at the time as grammar and rhetoric – which actually meant literature, poetry and history, and the skill of communicating clearly and convincingly. There was no "humanist program", no coherent humanist philosophy, beyond the study of these few subjects. Despite this apparent limitation, the implications of the study of the humanities for the period as a whole proved far reaching.

Firstly, study of the humanities marked a decisive break with the traditional university curriculum that was overwhelmingly concerned with teaching logic and with drumming dry intellectual formulas into students. Secondly, the humanities tended to emphasize secular rather than transcendental values. The *humanista*, either as student or scholar, was less concerned with studying metaphysics and theology than with trying to understand human action and striving to improve himself as a person. Classical literature provided a guide in the endeavor. Out of this arose the *humanista*'s preoccupation with reading the histories of Livy, the poetry of Horace, the speeches of Cicero, and the dramas of Terence and Plautus; and from this also arose books on conduct, most notably Castiglione's *The Courtier* (1528).

It is a cliché that the humanists sought "the perfectability of man". In fact, they aimed only at his improvement. The danger was, however, that the humanists tried to make man better without reference to the Church. In the Middle Ages it was overwhelmingly believed that man depended for goodness entirely upon God's grace, as taught and administered by the Church. Only by fixing heart and mind upon the contemplation of God's majesty, and by obeying the precepts of the Church, could man hope to rise above the level of a beast. The humanist, however, believed that man had the power of improvement within himself and that this talent could be released given the proper education and training. As Pico della Mirandola (1463–94) explained in his *Oration on the Dignity of Man* (1486), man, placed at the center of the universe, had the power "to degenerate into the lower forms of life, which are brutish . . . [or] to be reborn into the higher forms which are divine".

Mirandola's account of man's place in the world and of the capacity of his will was expressed, however, in profoundly Christian terms. He argued that it was God who had put man in the center of the universe and who had entrusted him with the power to become as an angel or as a beast. Molded in God's image, man possessed elements of divinity within himself that he could choose either to neglect or to nurture. Mirandola's ideas were thus hardly pagan; rather they represented a fusing of classical ideas with the traditional doctrines of Christianity derived from St Augustine. Nevertheless, by rejecting the paraphernalia of ceremonies and ritual cash-payments, which the Catholic clergy taught were necessary for salvation, both Mirandola and the study of the humanities as a whole challenged the primacy and importance of the Church.

A principal feature of Renaissance humanism was

Symbolism and Allegory

Much of the art both of the Middle Ages and of the Renaissance employed an elaborate symbolism. The bee, for instance, was frequently used as a sign for hard work; the basilisk or dragon represented the devil; and the bear denoted cruelty. Often a number of symbols were combined to make an allegorical representation of a more complex idea: as for instance in depictions of the contest between good and evil, or of the stages of life. Heraldic shields exemplify the relationship between symbol and allegory. Individual signs indicate the various qualities the bearer and his ancestors were thought to possess, such as bravery or loyalty; but taken together, these devices are an allegory of the family's history and pedigree. In the 8th century the use of symbol and allegory in art was supported by Pope Adrian I, who explained that "our mind may be stirred spiritually by the contemplation of an image", and that invisible concepts were best revealed "by means of the visible". The Bible, which is full of religious symbolism and parables, and the frequent depiction of Christ as a pelican, fish, lamb or shepherd, encouraged this type of artistic representation. At a time when most people were illiterate, symbols also performed an important educational function. Rather like a book, a picture could be "read" and a story teased out of its symbols and signs.

One of the most famous examples of symbolic and allegorical art is Jan van Eyck's *Arnolfini Marriage*. The picture, which was completed in 1434, portrays the marriage of Giovanni Arnolfini and Giovanna Cenami, wealthy Italians living in Bruges in the 1430s. The work contains a highly elaborate and mysterious religious symbolism, only a part of which is understood today. It acts not only as a kind of marriage certificate, but also as an allegory of marriage.

Above The *Arnolfini Marriage* depicts a couple exchanging their wedding vows. The two witnesses in the mirror (*left*) show the ceremony to be a valid one, and the signature of the artist below the candelabra, *Johannes de Eyck fuit hic. 1434* ("Jan van Eyck was here in 1434"), emphasize his own presence at the occasion. Some of the symbols refer to the nature of marriage itself: the dog in the foreground is a sign of fidelity; the carving of St Margaret on the back of the chair beside the bed represents childbirth; the bed itself represents the consummation of marriage. The whole scene is imbued with religious symbolism: roundels of Christ's Passion on the mirror; prayer beads; and a single candle, probably signifying the presence of Christ. As Erwin Panofsky, a leading historian of van Eyck, has explained, the room is a "nuptial chamber . . . hallowed by sacramental associations".

It is often thought that Giovanna must have been pregnant at the time of her marriage. It was common, however, for 15th-century artists to portray even virgins with swollen stomachs. Nevertheless, the way the bride holds herself is suggestive and it is indeed possible that van Eyck deliberately painted a pregnant Giovanna as both a symbol of the purpose of marriage and a prophecy. Thus the whole picture becomes an allegory not only of marriage itself but also of the future companionship of Giovanni and Giovanna. As a prediction, the *Arnolfini Marriage* failed: he died in 1470, she died 10 years later, and they left no children. As a portrait, however, the *Arnolfini Marriage* provides a powerful illustration of the use of symbol and allegory in Renaissance art.

Above A medallion portrait of Pico della Mirandola. Pico was a leading Italian neo-Platonist and the first Christian scholar to use the Hebrew cabbala in support of theology. Persecuted by the Church, Pico eventually settled in Florence and became a member of the Platonic Academy of humanist scholars centered on Lorenzo de' Medici.

Right This detail from Domenico Ghirlandaio's *Appearance of the Angel to Zaccharia* shows four of the greatest humanist scholars of 15th-century Florence gathered together. They are, left to right: Marsilio Ficino, the translator of Plato; the Dante scholar Cristoforo Laudino; Angelo Poliziano, who wrote the first musical drama, *Orfeo*; and Gentile de' Becchi. The *Appearance of the Angel* is typical of the work of Ghirlandaio (1449–94), who specialized in depicting imaginary meetings of well-known figures in impressive architectural settings.

its concern for accurate versions of classical texts. So a large part of the humanists' work involved the careful editing of Latin and Greek works, often for the benefit of students. The cross-matching of texts, which was facilitated by the development of printing, introduced new standards of historical research and literary criticism. The techniques employed by scholars were soon applied to nonclassical texts, however, and the discoveries these yielded also drew attention to the shortcomings of the Church. It was discovered, for example, that the papacy's claim to sovereignty over a large part of Italy rested on a document forged in the 8th century; and that the Vulgate, the "authorized" Latin version of the New Testament, was itself full of errors of translation. There is, therefore, a clear link between Renaissance humanism and the Protestant Reformation, the movement of religious criticism and renewal that took place in the 16th century.

Neo-Platonism

The first phase of Italian humanism – until roughly the middle of the 15th century – was chiefly concerned with Latin literature. The second phase was dominated by a new interest in classical Greek literature. Direction was given to this movement by increased contacts between Italian and Greek scholars. In 1453 Constantinople, the capital city of the Byzantine Empire, fell to the Ottoman Turks; as a result, many Byzantine Greek scholars fled to Italian cities.

Byzantine scholars introduced their Italian counter-parts to the works of Plato. The texts they brought with them were not pure ones, however, but commentaries composed in the main during the first centuries of the Christian era. These neo-Platonic commentaries presented Plato's philosophy as a complex allegory illustrating the hierarchical structure of the universe: God was the supreme principle of unity, the material world being linked to the heavens by an ascending series of intermediary realms. For the neo-Platonists, art, architecture, literature and music should seek to emulate the principles of perfection and harmony that governed the workings of God's creation.

By proclaiming an essential unity between the material and spiritual world, neo-Platonic philosophers were able to suggest that the scholar or "adept" had the power to manipulate the heavens and to transform nature. The adept, by studying the movement of the stars and by reciting incantations and hymns, could also ascend through the hierarchy of the universe and achieve a condition of spiritual perfection. These ideas were most powerfully expressed in Greek texts dating from the 2nd and 3rd centuries.

By insisting that man had the power to transform nature, neo-Platonism contributed to the study of both alchemy and astrology, and so indirectly prepared the way for the Scientific Revolution of the 17th century. Neo-Platonism also made the practice of magic fashionable and no longer the preserve of witches. By the 16th century the Renaissance scholar was as often a *magus* (magician) intent on the acquisition of magical powers as a man of letters committed to the humbler pursuit of knowledge. Translations of occult texts of the cabbala during the 15th and 16th centuries further encouraged the search for magical symbols and codes, and were largely responsible for the new interest in classical Hebrew works.

Neo-Platonism is frequently presented as an unfortunate diversion from the main path of the Renaissance. It is important to realize, however, that the importance placed in neo-Platonic philosophy upon the essential unity of the spiritual and material worlds greatly affected the art of the High Renaissance. The stress laid in the work of Leonardo da Vinci (1452–1519), Giovanni Bellini (c. 1430–1516) and Raphael (1483–1520) on harmony and symmetry, and the geometrical exactitude of their compositions, owed much to neo-Platonic ideas regarding the perfection of forms. The *Primavera* by Botticelli likewise included the common neo-Platonic equation of Venus and mankind, symbolizing the harmony of nature and civilization. For its part, the Ceiling of the Sistine Chapel (1508–12) by Michelangelo (1475–1564) is full of neo-Platonic imagery and has as its starting-point a vision of man's empowerment, the *Creation of Adam*: "And God created man in his own image . . . and breathed into his face the breath of life; and man became a living soul."

The Italian origins of the Renaissance
The 19th-century statesman Prince Metternich once referred to Italy as merely a "geographical expression"; the same comment might apply equally well to Italy during the 14th and 15th centuries. The Italian peninsula was politically divided. Sicily and southern Italy were separate principalities, belonging to Aragon and Naples respectively. Tuscany and Lombardy, however, consisted not of kingdoms but of a medley of independent and self-governing city-states. In the center of the peninsula lay the papal states, which were nominally subject to the pope. Papal rule was on the decline. During the 14th century, the popes had abandoned Rome and had set up their court at Avignon. The Avignon papacy (1309–77) was reviled by contemporaries as the "Babylonian Captivity". This was succeeded by a period of schism, when there was a pope in Rome and a rival one in Avignon. By the time the schism had ended, in 1449, the political and spiritual influence of the papacy had fallen to a low ebb and the popes were unable to take advantage of the confusion into which the cities of northern Italy had fallen.

From the 13th century onward, the cities of northern Italy were locked in conflict with one another. They were, moreover, internally unstable. Popular revolutions, bitter factional fighting, and successive *coups d'état* led by *condottieri* (mercenary captains), marked the history of the region's great cities. Usually it was only by appointing a "despot" and vesting him with supreme authority that a semblance of peace and order might be obtained. On occasions foreign predators stormed into Italy, drawn by the prospect of easy plunder. In 1494 Charles VIII of France invaded the peninsula and inaugurated the Italian Wars, a succession of conflicts that lasted until the middle of the next century.

Yet in many respects the violent passage of the 14th and 15th centuries in Italy differed little from what

Right A 16th-century panoramic view of the city of Genoa by Danti. Genoa was a city of seafarers and the home of Christopher Columbus. Genoa's walled fortifications, which ran a circuit of 19 kilometers, were constructed in the early 14th century. The government and commerce of Genoa was controlled by a small group of increasingly well-educated merchant patricians.

Below The *Primavera* or *Allegory of Spring* (c. 1478) by Botticelli. The *Primavera* contains a highly elaborate symbolism. It is an allegory on the harmony of nature and human civilization, which was a frequent theme of neo-Platonic philosophy. Nature is represented here by Spring, who is personified as the Roman goddess Flora bedecked with flowers. The Three Graces, performing an arabesque on the left of the picture, represent musical harmony and thus the civilization of mankind. Venus, in the center of the picture, is portrayed as a pagan Madonna who lifts up Man's mind to the contemplation of a divine beauty that transcends the distinction between nature and civilization.

was going on elsewhere in Europe. Between 1337 and 1453 England and France were locked in the Hundred Years War, and both countries were also wracked by periods of civil war. In 1327, 1399, 1471 and 1485, English kings were either deposed or slain by their political rivals. In France the powers of the crown were eroded by ambitious feudatories who had no misgivings about siding with the French king's English enemies. The same progress of war and civil strife marked the history of Spain, the Holy Roman Empire and the monarchies of eastern Europe: so much so that the 14th and 15th centuries have been called "the period of feudal anarchy".

Northern Italy differed from the rest of Europe in at least three important respects, however. *Firstly*, the Roman ruins that still dominated the urban landscape bore ample testimony to classical civilization. During the 14th and 15th centuries, a growing sense of the past prompted the study of these remains and the collection of artifacts from antiquity. It was by taking inspiration from the Pantheon in Rome that Brunelleschi (1377–1446), in designing the dome for the cathedral in Florence, managed to vault a wider space than had ever been spanned before. Succeeding generations of architects, including Alberti (1404–72), Bramante (c. 1444–1514) and Palladio (1508–80), were inspired by the buildings of ancient Rome and imitated in their own work the classical system of proportions. Likewise, Ghiberti (1378–1455) was influenced by surviving Roman models when designing the bronze reliefs for the Baptistery Doors in Florence (1425, 1452); and the *Gattamelata* (1453) by Donatello (1386–1466), the first bronze equestrian statue to be cast since Roman times, clearly derived its inspiration from Roman funerary busts and from the statue of Emperor Marcus Aurelius in Rome. It is well to recall that the exactitude, realism and concern for proportion that are among the distinctive features of Renaissance art were at first more apparent in sculpture than in painting. Similarly, it was the architects Brunelleschi and Alberti who by their use of perspective first showed how to make a two-dimensional surface convey the illusion of three dimensions.

Secondly, northern Italy was one of the wealthiest regions in Europe. Genoa and Venice, both with populations of roughly 100,000 in 1400, controlled much of the Mediterranean trade with the Levant; Florence and Milan, with populations of 55,000 and 90,000 respectively, were important centers of manufacture and distribution. In each of these cities, the middle class was large, entrenched and increasingly well educated. Many Italian noblemen considered it no affront to their status to move into the cities and to take part in urban life and politics. Eventually they sold their properties in the countryside to city-dwellers anxious to purchase a villa for the summer. The wars fought across the plain of Lombardy in the 14th and 15th centuries may even have added to the region's prosperity; for armies need to be provisioned and many mercenaries settled in Italy with plenty of booty to spend on luxuries.

Florence was the richest of the cities of northern Italy and dominated the earlier phases of the Renaissance. Its wealth was based on cloth-making, banking, and a trade in luxuries with the Levant. Florentine merchants and adventurers such as Buonacorso Pitti (1354–1432) engaged in a lucrative commerce throughout the continent. Florence's leading family, the Medici, who were the city's *de facto* rulers as well

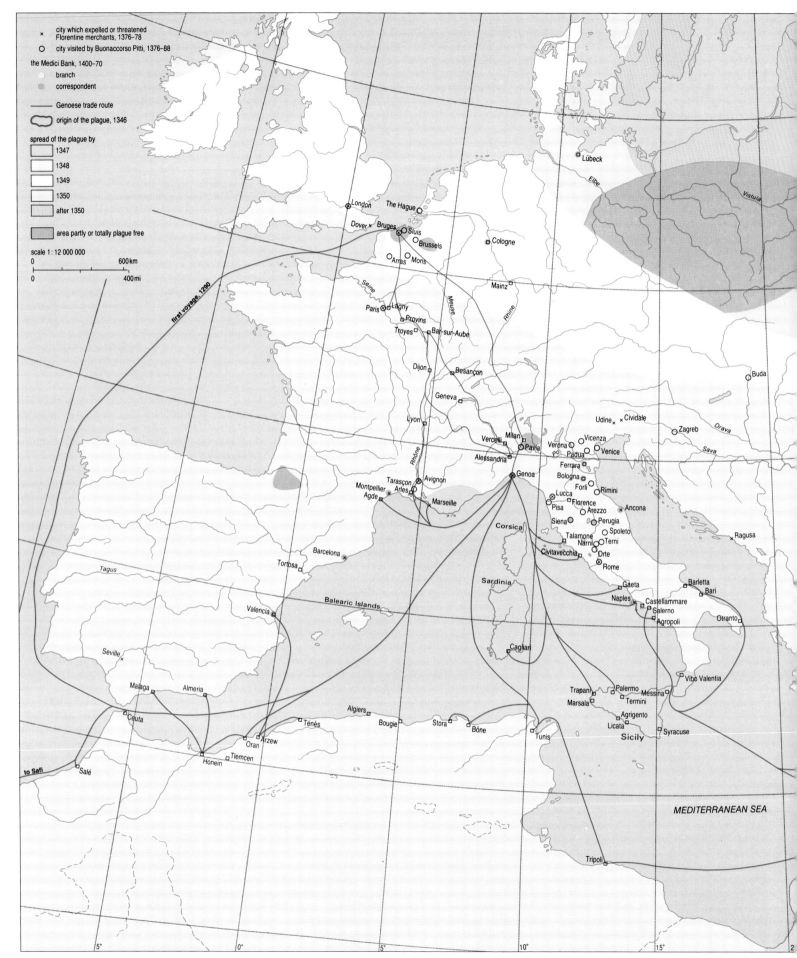

Key:

- ✕ city which expelled or threatened Florentine merchants, 1376–78
- ○ city visited by Buonaccorso Pitti, 1376–88

the Medici Bank, 1400–70
- ○ branch
- ● correspondent

— Genoese trade route
⬭ origin of the plague, 1346

spread of the plague by
- 1347
- 1348
- 1349
- 1350
- after 1350

▨ area partly or totally plague free

scale 1 : 12 000 000

0 ——— 600 km
0 ——— 400 mi

Italian trade and the economy of Europe in the later Middle Ages
Trade placed the city-states of Italy at the economic heart of Europe, wielding a powerful influence over a very wide area. The mainly maritime Genoese reached throughout the Mediterranean world and dealt no less effectively in northern Europe. Florentine merchants and bankers (such as the Medici and Pitti), building on the overland cloth trade, penetrated to many of the important trading centers of the Low Countries, Germany and England. They were not, however, universally welcomed, their wealth threatening the activities of local merchants. As the plague spread through Europe in the 1340s, town life, and long-distance trade, everywhere suffered a desperate slump.

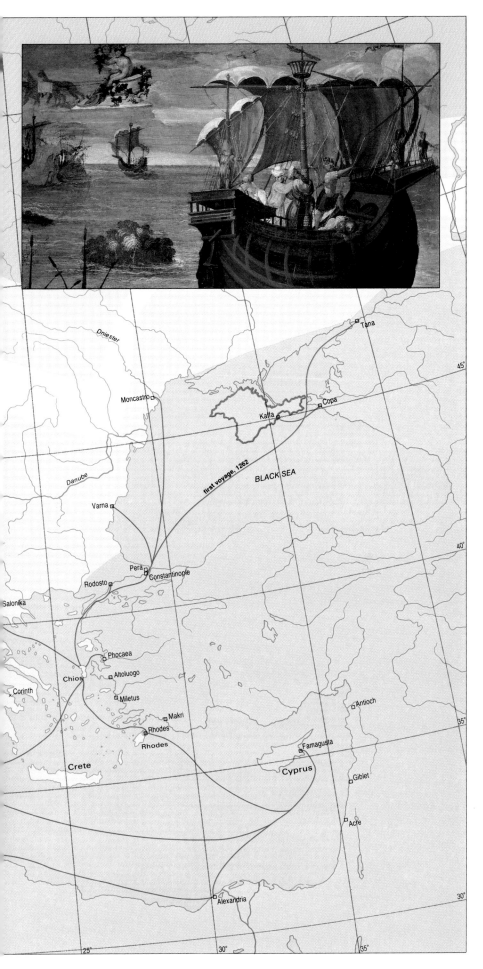

as bankers to the pope, were the most important source of patronage in the city, but there were several others. The competitiveness of the guilds and their control of many important institutions, including the cathedral, baptistery, and both the oratory and market of Orsanmichele, resulted in a large number of commissions for artists and architects. Merchants and financiers, fearful for their own salvation, invested heavily in works of devotional art, or left their wealth to the Franciscan friars, who, despite (or perhaps because of) their vows of poverty, were munificent patrons of the arts.

Thirdly, northern Italy differed from the rest of Europe in a unique and fundamental way: it was divided into city-states. The inspiration of classical civilization and the wealth of its cities provide important clues as to why the Renaissance began where it did. The existence of city-states allows us to understand why the Renaissance happened when it did.

The cities of northern Italy had much in common with the cities of ancient Greece and Rome. Not only were their populations of roughly the same size – between 25,000 and 100,000 – they also shared the same elements of civic pride and identity that Renaissance Italians called *campanilismo*, or love for the bell-tower (*campanile*) of one's birthplace. The bustle and tribulations of city life, described by the classical Roman writer Juvenal, were equally apparent to 14th and 15th century Italians – as was the conviction that living in a city was the most civilized form of existence. Aristotle's *Politics*, translated into Latin about 1260, was eagerly received in Italy. Its message that "he who is not a citizen is not a man, for man is by nature a civic animal" struck an immediate chord among the educated Italian audience of city dwellers who were used to participating in the hurly-burly of communal politics.

Following the establishment of Cola di Rienzo's short-lived republic in Rome in the mid 14th century, Italians became increasingly aware of the close resemblance between their own cities and those of the classical world. About 1400 in particular, political arguments using the vocabulary of Roman republicanism began to be put forward in Florence as a defense of urban freedoms against the "tyranny" of the Visconti family. The Visconti were the despots of contemporary Milan who had recently brought under their control a number of the smaller cities of northern Italy. The arguments used against the Visconti appealed to "the power, liberty, gifted minds and fame" of the Florentines, and presented the city of Florence as both the inheritor and repository of the classical values of ancient Rome. The influence of Florence was such as to inspire similar eulogies in neighboring cities also threatened by the Visconti – or even by Florence herself.

It may well be that these analogies with the Roman world were false and that in reality the government of Florence differed little from the government of Milan. Nevertheless, the political literature of the late 14th and 15th centuries consciously defined the Italian city by reference to the values and norms of ancient Rome.

Inset In his *Ariadne Abandoned*, the painter Gerolamo del Pacchia set a scene from the Greek myth of Ariadne and Theseus on a 15th-century trading ship typical of those that made Genoa and other Italian ports wealthy.

Once this historic connection had been made, it was only natural for scholars, patrons and artists to want to emulate the cultural achievements of antiquity. In short, it was the growth of a self-conscious civic culture in the cities of northern Italy that inspired the process of classical renewal known as the Renaissance.

The spread of the Renaissance

During the 15th century the civic culture of northern Italy was transformed into a princely one. The Medici of Florence, the Sforza of Milan (the successors of the Visconti family), the Gonzaga of Mantua, the Este of Ferrara and the Borgia popes in Rome became the leading patrons of the arts. The works they commissioned were intended to glorify their own dynasties and the authority they wielded. The artistic themes they preferred were those of the epic and of martial valor; their architectural commissions were for ostentatious palaces and temples. This transformation in the art of the period – most apparent in paintings of armor and triumphal arches by Mantegna (1431–1506) and in the monumental architecture of Alberti – proved to be of critical importance in helping the spread of the Renaissance.

Europe north of the Alps was dominated by powerful territorial rulers and a rural nobility. Its ethos of "hunting, women and banquets" was completely different from the civic values of Italy, and even educated northerners scorned urban pretensions and luxury. The transformation of Italian Renaissance culture from a predominantly civic one to one that was largely princely meant, however, that its innovations became more intelligible to northern society. Increasingly the artists and scholars of Italy were to be found in the retinue of a duke or pope rather than in a city council, and in the service of a court rather than that of a guild. The themes of their art and literature were likewise immediately recognizable to a society that was used to the glorification of dynasties and martial deeds. So it was now easier for Renaissance ideas to spread to the princely and aristocratic kingdoms of France, England and northern Europe. Both the passage of foreign invaders through Italy and the development of the printing press hastened the spread of the Renaissance north of the Alps.

The Italian Renaissance, once it had crossed the Alps, blended with older cultural trends. In the paintings of the French artist François Clouet (c. 1515–72), Italian styles merged with traditions deriving from French and Flemish painting. The course of the Renaissance in France was determined by the military campaigns of the Valois. In Spain the glorification of both the Catholic faith and the ruling Habsburg dynasty was sought. In Germany and the Low Countries the art and humanism of the Renaissance were affected by a deeper, northern spirituality that was entirely alien to Italy. This manifested itself not only in the disturbing images of Grünewald and Bosch, but also in the movement known as Christian humanism, which sought to use the techniques of Renaissance literary criticism on the Bible and early religious texts.

Concern for man's spiritual welfare led to an increased dissatisfaction with the dogma, luxury and corruption of the Church. Criticism of Catholic teaching and practices culminated in the early 16th century with the Protestant Reformation in Germany. Protestant theologians, led by Martin Luther (1483–1546), repudiated both papal authority and the traditional tenets of Catholic belief. They sought a purer form of religious observance, free of ritual and ceremony, and they based their religious convictions on the Bible rather than on the pronouncements of popes. During the course of the century, the Reformation spread from its birthplace in Germany to France, the Low Countries, England, Scotland, Scandinavia and a large part of eastern Europe.

The Reformation influenced the cultural life of a large part of Europe. Moral and religious themes strongly influenced the art and literature of the period, and religious partisanship began to hamper humanist learning. Moreover, as civil and religious war broke out across the continent the art of the Renaissance was increasingly employed to buttress the precarious authority of the ruling houses. The Catholic Counter-Reformation prompted in its turn a rejection of many humanist ideas. For these were now seen as a threat to the Church and as a potential source of heresy. In Spain, and to a lesser extent in France, the Renaissance was consumed in the fires of a militant Catholicism. Elsewhere, it was tamed and put to the service of church and state.

The history of the Renaissance outside Italy reflects in several respects the enormous political changes in Europe in the 16th century. In the late Middle Ages, Europe had still been united by a common adherence to the Catholic religion. Notions of a "universal empire" and a "universal peace among Christians" had been keenly embraced, though seldom realized. Even as late as the 15th century, large multinational armies had been gathered for the common purpose of crusading against the unbeliever. The institutions of the Church – its priesthood, religious orders and laws – being common to all parts of the continent, had lent medieval Europe its cultural identity and unity. Catholic Christendom had its secular counterpart in the vast dynastic empires that spread across a large part of the continent in the late Middle Ages.

As a consequence of the Reformation, however, Europe was riven by religious disputes that put an end to the idea of a united Christian commonwealth. More than half of the continent embraced Protestantism and a series of nationally organized churches took the place of the "Church Universal" of Roman Catholicism. International empires forged on the eve of the Reformation, such as the Habsburg empires of Catholic Spain and Austria, were challenged by rebellions among their subject nations: the Low Countries and Catalana, Bohemia and Hungary. In the political propaganda of the period, the claims of the nation-state were advanced with increasing confidence, not least in England and the Low Countries.

The Renaissance could not remain unaffected by the transition from Catholic universalism to the nation-state. Although a European movement affecting the entire continent, the Renaissance was shaped by the particular circumstances and conditions in each of the countries to which it spread. As a consequence, the Renaissance soon ceased to be as Jacob Burckhardt imagined it in the last century: an Italian phenomenon that other nations sought only to emulate. The diffusion of the Renaissance resulted not in cultural uniformity, but in a diversity of separate national movements. Its passage north of the Alps thus reinforced Europe's division into independent and competing national states, which has been a feature of the continent's history since the 16th century.

Right Campin's *Portrait of a Lady* (c. 1430) demonstrates the technical and compositional skill of the Flemish artists and the existence of an independent artistic tradition in northern Europe. Robert Campin (c. 1378–1444), who is probably to be identified with the Master of Flémalle, was strongly influenced by the art of the French and Flemish miniature painters. The strong features, incisive contours and shadows of the portrait suggest that Campin was also inspired by older traditions of Flemish sculpture.

The Discovery of Antiquity

Medieval scholars had only a very imperfect understanding of history and they looked at the past almost entirely from the point of view of their own age. Thus, it did not seem strange to one 13th-century Florentine writer to make a pre-Christian ruler attend Mass in church, or for Roman ruins to be uncritically regarded either as "marvels" or as "the work of giants". For their part, medieval artists frequently committed astonishing anachronisms by cladding Alexander in the armor of a knight or by setting ancient battles against the skyline of a medieval city.

During the course of the 14th and 15th centuries, scholars began to develop a more critical understanding of history and to appreciate the difference between themselves and the past. In his epic poem *Scipio*, Petrarch (1307–74) attempted an imaginative reconstruction of the Rome of Scipio's time based on his own researches among the Roman ruins. In the next century, an early generation of humanists copied inscriptions, collected antique coins and drew monuments of the Roman period. In his *Rome Restored* and *Italy Illustrated*, Flavio Biondo (1392–1463) provided a topographical description of the cities of ancient Italy based on his own visits to sites and on his own reading of classical sources. Biondo's work was an important source of inspiration both for Conrad Celtis (1459–1508) in Germany and for the antiquarian William Camden (1551–1623) in England.

The new sense of the past introduced by these researches influenced the art of the period. Painters were no longer content to clothe biblical and classical figures in modern dress, but sought instead to place them within an accurate historical context. Although Piero della Francesca (c. 1420–92) still put a Roman soldier and a 15th-century knight in the same battle, such anachronism became rare. The paintings of Andrea Mantegna (1431–1506), who was both a painter and a dedicated antiquarian, are powerful illustrations of the new sense of historical realism.

Below The *Apollo Belvedere*, a Greek statue discovered in Rome at the end of the 15th century, together with the Laocoon, unearthed in 1506, provided the core of the Vatican museum of antiquities established in Rome by Pope Julius II. According to the historian and painter Giorgio Vasari (1511–74), the generation of Leonardo, Michelangelo and Raphael owed much to Julius's collection and to its two most prized exhibits.

Bottom left The Tazza Farnese bowl, acquired by Lorenzo de' Medici in 1471, is an agate-sardonyx bowl carved in Egypt in the classical Greek style. The interior, representing "The Fertility of Egypt", shows the two Etesian winds, which ensured the flooding and thus the fertility of the Nile valley, flying above Egyptian divinities. An almost identical depiction of the Etesian winds is included by Botticelli in his *Birth of Venus* (*below*), completed c. 1485.

Right Andrea Mantegna was one of the earliest artists to seek to paint a subject from ancient history in a manner that was historically correct. His accurate representations of classical Roman architecture owed much to the many expeditions he undertook to inspect Roman ruins. The arch shown in the background of his *St James Before Herod*, completed c. 1454, is based upon the Arco dei Gavo at Verona.

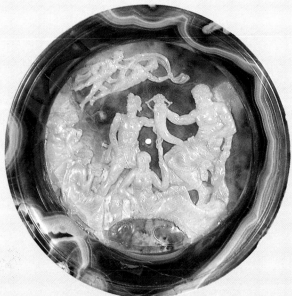

Below The classical style of architecture introduced by Brunelleschi (1377–1446) and Alberti (1404–72) was partly inspired by their study of the ruins of ancient Rome. The Roman ruins not only provided a source of artistic stimulation but they also helped to refine the art of drawing itself – in order for to make an exact geometrical representation, Brunelleschi and Alberti had to refine the technique of perspective. The greatest advocate of the art of drawing was Federico Zuccari (1543–1609) who regarded it as the most perfect form of expression.

Medieval artists and sculptors had often copied surviving examples of classical sculpture. It was not until the 15th century, however, that painters sought to emulate both the techniques and the subject-matter of Greek and Roman art. Whereas religious themes had predominated in the Middle Ages, mythological and classical scenes recalling the art of Ancient Greece and Rome became increasingly popular during the Renaissance. Sculptures, vases and marble friezes, discovered and displayed during the 15th and 16th centuries, were important sources of inspiration for the artists of the Renaissance. This interest in the art of the classical period resulted in a new variety of anachronism: the portrayal of contemporary people and events in an antique Roman setting. Architects were also affected by the revival of interest in the classical inheritance. The books of the Roman architect Vitruvius, who lived in the first century BC, strongly influenced the rebuilding of the Vatican area of Rome in the second half of the 15th century.

Below Petrarch's copy of Virgil, as illustrated by the Sienese artist Simone Martini (c. 1284–1344), is typical of the representation of the late Middle Ages. Aeneas shown on the far left is equipped as a medieval soldier, while the farmer and shepherd at the bottom, symbolizing Virgil's pastoral romances, are dressed as medieval peasants. Martini is known to have met Petrarch at the papal court in Avignon in 1339–40 and it is probable that the frontispiece was completed then. Petrarch later developed a new way of perceiving the past quite at variance with Martini's.

THE EARLY ITALIAN RENAISSANCE

The first faint signs of the profound intellectual, artistic and moral changes that eventually came to be known as the Renaissance appeared in the late 13th century in Italy. In order to understand why these changes began then, it is necessary to look at the political and social developments that formed their background.

In the central Middle Ages, Italy was divided into three main areas. In the south, Sicily and the adjacent part of the mainland formed the kingdom of Sicily, which had been constructed by Norman rulers from the late 11th century onward. Much of central Italy belonged to the papacy, an area often referred to as the Papal State. Northern Italy was part of the German Empire, having been joined to Germany in the 10th century.

From time to time German emperors had dreamed of establishing control over the whole of Italy and in effect establishing a new Roman Empire, if possible centered on Rome. Some emperors attempted to make their dreams a reality. One of the most determined was the Hohenstaufen ruler Frederick II, nicknamed *Stupor Mundi* ("wonder of the world"). Born in 1194, he became king of Sicily in 1197 and, after a struggle, king of Germany in 1212. By 1220 he had been elected king of the Romans and crowned emperor.

In the kingdom of Sicily the Norman rulers had built up a highly centralized state, based on the king's authority, and strong and efficient government. Frederick II sought to introduce such Sicilian methods and officers to northern Italy and to create a similarly strong government there. This alarmed the papacy, which feared that it could be reduced to dependence on a powerful ruler in Italy. Frederick's ambitions also threatened many cities in northern Italy – cities such as Florence, Pisa, Genoa, Milan and Venice. In the 11th and 12th centuries, several cities in Tuscany and Lombardy had become wealthy through their efficient control of trade between the eastern Mediterranean and northern Europe. They had also obtained some rights of self-government, which they were loath to lose.

Frederick's desire to govern northern Italy through his own officials had two main effects. Firstly, it stirred new opposition and resistance in some of the cities of Tuscany and Lombardy. Secondly, it exacerbated factional divisions within the cities. Italian cities had long been faction-ridden. Individuals gave their primary loyalty to their family; families interwined by marriages formed clans, which often signed oaths of allegiance against common enemies. There was little loyalty to city or state. During the reign of Frederick II the papacy tried to resist his ambitions to bring Italy under a strong imperial government. One of the papacy's ploys for undermining Frederick II was to seek support from the cities, or rather from a strong faction within each city. In Florence and then in other cities the pope's supporters became known as Guelphs (from the name of the German Welf family that had earlier challenged Frederick), while factions supporting the emperor were known as Ghibillines (from

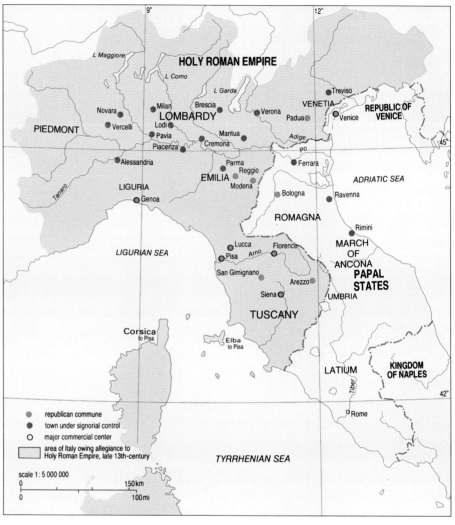

Italy in the early 14th century
Medieval Italy was riven by the dispute between two modes of civic government: the frequently factional communal, or republican model, exemplified by Florence or Venice, and the despotic or seigneurial, which often took over from the commune. The communes survived in some regions (Tuscany and Umbria) longer than in Lombardy. The authority of the Holy Roman Empire south of the Alps was on the wane and had little influence on the political decision-making of the rulers of the Italian cities.

Waiblingen, an important imperial center in Germany). Within cities Guelph and Ghibilline factions fought each other for supremacy. Sometimes, as one faction gained the upper hand, the other faction would be exiled.

In 1250 Frederick II died and his successors were unable to perpetuate his achievement: his son Conrad IV died in 1254; Frederick's illegitimate son Manfred established himself as king in Sicily, but was driven out – at the pope's invitation – by the French prince Charles of Anjou in 1266. In 1268 Frederick's grandson, Conradin, invaded Italy, but he was defeated and executed. The Hohenstaufen and their imperial dreams had been destroyed.

North Italian cities after the Hohenstaufen emperors

The defeat of the Hohenstaufen provided no respite to the quarrels and warfare within northern Italian cities. Factions continued to oppose each other under the names of Guelphs and Ghibillines. Sometimes these factions split, as in Florence in 1300 when the Guelph party became divided into the "whites" and the "blacks". The following year the two factions fought after youths cut off the nose of a member of a rival gang at a party.

Such internal divisions and conflict threatened to jeopardize the success of major Italian cities as trading centers, and some of their inhabitants sought ways of creating stronger government. One outcome was the principality. North of the Apennines, in Lombardy, cities such as Milan, Verona, Mantua and Ferrara sometimes invited a leading figure to become the senior municipal magistrate and act as peace-maker. In 1240, for example, Azzo VII d'Este, a representative of the Guelph party of Ferrara, was appointed captain of the people. When he died 24 years later his supporters gathered together to arrange for the appointment of his illegitimate grandson to the captaincy – the dynasty remained in power until the 17th century. Rulers were not always able to take power peacefully. In Milan two families, the Visconti and the Della Torre, fought for supremacy for almost 50 years.

These lords relied on alliances with other powerful families within the city and fearsome personal reputations. According to one chronicle, the first lord of Mantua, Pinamonte Bonacolsi, "expelled his fellow-citizens and occupied their property and destroyed the houses and towers of those whom he thought were his enemies. And he was feared like the devil." Tales were told of Bernabò Visconti's cruelty. Peasants found trapping game in the lord's hunting parks were forced to eat their catch alive, skin and all. He did not display

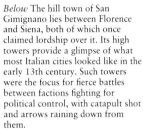

Below The hill town of San Gimignano lies between Florence and Siena, both of which once claimed lordship over it. Its high towers provide a glimpse of what most Italian cities looked like in the early 13th century. Such towers were the focus for fierce battles between factions fighting for political control, with catapult shot and arrows raining down from them.

favoritism in his punishments. When he discovered his daughter's affair with one of the palace courtiers, she was immediately imprisoned and starved to death. But for all the ferocity of such men, their suppression of violence did bring a measure of peace to beleaguered towns.

Rule by a single individual or family was not the only means of suppressing factionalism. Other important centers chose representative forms of self-government. In 1297, for example, Venice created an oligarchy of powerful noblemen by "closing" its ruling Great Council. Only families with members in that last government of the late 13th century could serve the city, creating a hereditary nobility of about 1,000 eligible citizens (about 2 percent of the population). It lasted until 1797. The doge, elected for life as head of the government from these patrician families, had the powers of a prince, but had to represent the city as well as his own interests.

Tuscan cities, equally desperate to bring an end to their conflicts, also flirted with the concept of a single leader. Florence was so exasperated by continuing violence that it introduced three temporary lordships: those of King Robert of Naples (1313–21), Carlo, duke of Calabria (1325–28), and Walter, duke of Athens (1342). But each in turn was expelled in favor of republican solutions. The city was run by legislative councils that operated under the supervision of nine

Bernabò was so great that he would never compete for power over Lombardy. He meant, instead, to devote himself to religion. But in 1385, in a carefully planned coup, he asked to pay homage to his uncle while journeying to a holy shrine outside Milan. Bernabò, who by this stage had little to fear from his nephew, went to meet him without an armed guard. His trust was misplaced. He was captured, imprisoned and died the following year. Gian Galeazzo immediately proclaimed himself lord of his uncle's dominion before assembling an army to march on northeastern Italy. Within a few years he had conquered Verona, Vicenza and Padua. By the 1390s his attention had turned south. Siena, Pisa, Perugia and, finally, Bologna all surrendered to the Visconti troops. It seemed as though all of Italy had recognized the superiority of a strong prince over the internal dissension of communal government. Florence, which considered itself the last bastion of republicanism, seemed completely isolated. The city reinforced its walls and armed its citizens, but at the turn of the century its fate looked dire.

Republican governments and public architecture.

The new institutions created in 13th- and 14th-century Italian cities required new buildings, both civic and religious. A 14th-century inscription on the facade of the Florentine palace known as the Bargello, built to house the city's judge, the *podestà*, indicates a pride bordering on arrogance:

Florence is full of all imaginable wealth. She defeats her enemies in war and in civil strife. She enjoys the favor of fortune and has a powerful population. . . . She reigns over the sea and the land and the whole of the world. Under her leadership, the whole of Tuscany enjoys happiness. Like Rome, she is always triumphant.

But the Bargello was a fortified palace, whose rough-hewn rusticated brown stones and high crenellations were designed to intimidate. The *podestà* could not rely on popular goodwill for protection: he needed strong walls and an armed guard. Florence's *Palazzo Pubblico* (town hall), built in 1299 to house the new communal government, also had to be constructed with defense in mind. It was placed next to the ruins of the homes of defeated Ghibellines – the Guelph government would not have its building touch the cursed site, which it had paved to destroy any hopes the enemy may have had of rebuilding their neighborhood.

This was a typically symbolic decision. Town halls were often built in positions designed to emphasize the primacy of public rights over private interest. In Siena the large central square, the *Campo*, was raised on meters of landfill to provide a site at the intersection of the city's three main districts. The main *piazze* were supposed to be clean, decorous places. Gambling was forbidden in most town centers and prostitutes were not allowed to ply for trade in them. The *piazze* also served political functions. When extra constitutional changes were required, eligible citizens were called to meetings in the main squares. The small narrow roads that led into these areas could be shut off by armed guards, trapping the throng until they agreed to elect new governments "popularly" or authorize change. The town halls themselves, designed with severe stone walls and fortified entrances, could be shut against unruly crowds gathering outside. Overlooking these squares the soaring towers of the town halls marked the victory of communal legislation over family in-

priors, a magistracy known as the *signoria*. These councillors were chosen from members of the city's main guilds. These were not workers' unions but associations of producers, owners and middle-class workers such as goldsmiths and doctors. Popular government did not, therefore, mean democracy. By insisting on guild membership as a criterion for involvement in government, Florentine citizens were able to exclude both the aristocracy, who they blamed for feudal violence, and also the poorer members of their society.

In Siena a similar form of government by wealthy professionals and merchants known as the Nine (after the number of its magistrates) was established in 1287. Election was dependent on stringent criteria: one had to be male, over 30, able to read and write, to have paid taxes and, most importantly, to own an expensive house in the city. As in Florence, these restrictions succeeded in excluding the less well-off.

The communal governments of Florence and Siena built some of Europe's most remarkable buildings. But their cultural achievements only disguised their underlying fragility. The Black Death of 1348 and the succeeding waves of plague severely disrupted traditional patterns of life. In Florence, a population of about 90,000 fell to about 50,000. The initial result was increased prosperity among the survivors. Wages rose as the supply of labor diminished and complaints about the arrogance and anarchy of once humble workers increased. There were political consequences as insurrection and rebellion became more common. In 1385 a mob, enraged by excessive tax demands, dragged the d'Este chancellor through the streets before lynching him. In Siena, the butchers tried to storm the town hall in protest over price-fixing. In Florence, the revolt of the *Ciompi* (wool-carders) in 1378 briefly brought lower-class wool workers to power. The wealthy families finally regained authority in 1382, only to face new threats.

In the late 1380s the lord of Milan, Gian Galeazzo Visconti (1351–1402), began assembling one of Europe's largest armies. Seen through Florentine eyes, Visconti was a tyrant in the mold of Nero and Caligula. He preferred to compare himself to Caesar and the other great imperial heroes of antiquity. Gian Galeazzo had had a remarkable rise to power. At his father's death in 1378 he had retreated to the town of Pavia, letting it be known that his fear of his Uncle

Below The *Campo* was Siena's main gathering place, a neutral zone in an otherwise fiercely territorial city. Here the main exercise of important civic duties was carried out in the town hall or *Palazzo Pubblico*, to whose design the surrounding palaces and shops had to conform.

terests. Under their shadow, publicly agreed laws had to be obeyed. Their bells and clocks ensured that citizens followed a uniform daily existence, rising, working and praying to an order determined by the commune. On the facades of town halls, rebels and traitors were painted hanging upside down as a warning to potential plotters.

Church and state were closely intertwined. Business contracts were signed in Florence's Baptistery and preaching regularly took place in the market place. Religion was the concern of the town council as well as of priests. As soon as Florence's new communal governments felt secure, attention was focused on the cathedral. Building a city's main church was the job of the secular authorities, one they used to demonstrate their prestige and prosperity. Italian towns were highly competitive. In the 11th century Pisa had marked its dominance over the Mediterranean by building a vast religious complex at the city's edge, the cathedral and the Campo Santo. Siena's growth was highlighted by the new cathedral it completed in 1264. When Florence's new government finally gained a measure of stability in the 1290s, it too laid the foundations of a greatly enlarged cathedral, Santa Maria del Fiore. The plan, larger and more ambitious than those of the cathedrals of either Pisa or Siena, involved destroying much of the ancient city center. Yet this only inspired the Sienese to commission yet another cathedral in 1316, an enormous undertaking that only came to a halt after engineers questioned the new project's stability and after economic collapse undermined civic confidence.

Siena

The Palazzo Pubblico, Siena

Below Sano di Pietro, *St Bernadino of Siena Preaching*. This picture of Siena's most important popular preacher provides a view of the *Palazzo Pubblico* and the *Campo* in the 15th century. The small chapel to the left, the *Cappella della Piazza*, was built as an offering to the Virgin after the Black Death of 1348.

Bottom Simone Martini's image of the Virgin and Child in Majesty was completed in 1315. Mary sits surrounded by a chorus of angels and martyrs under a canopy bearing Siena's coat-of-arms, the city's four patron saints presenting flowers. The entire picture is covered with inscriptions that invite onlookers to pray for the city.

The town hall in Siena, the *Palazzo Pubblico*, was the center of the city's political life. Here during the 14th century the four main elements of government – its chief magistrates, the *podestà*, the Nine, and the Great Council – met regularly to debate matters of public interest and to issue laws regulating citizens' daily lives. The town, divided into antagonistic families, neighborhoods and factions, had to ensure that its governors would put aside private interests and work toward the common good. Throughout the *Palazzo Pubblico* paintings such as Ambrogio Lorenzetti's *Good and Bad Government* (1339) reminded officials to act with justice and wisdom in order to ensure the city's prosperity. An important part of the image of a unified, well-ordered town concerned building regula-

Below The *Palazzo Pubblico* was begun in 1298 and the wings to either side were constructed between 1307–10. The marble crown on the bell tower, the Tower of the Mangia (1338–48), was designed by the painter Lippo Memmi (the brother-in-law of Simone Martini) in 1341.

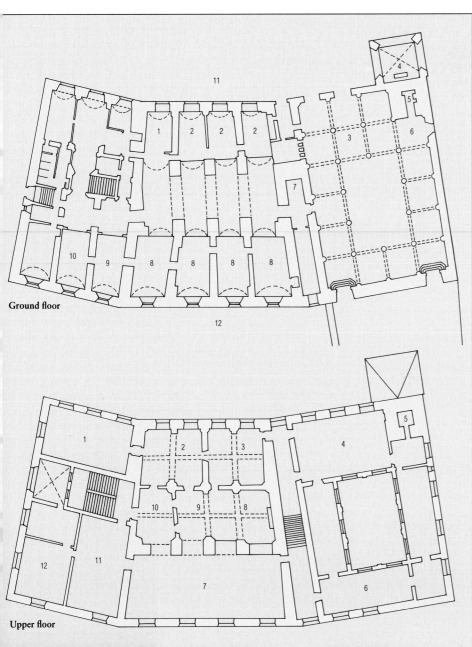

Ground floor

Upper floor

Ground floor plan	Upper floor plan
1. Chapel of the Council of Nine	1. Room of the Consistory
2. Administrative offices	2. Anteconsistory
3. Courtyard of the Podestà	3. Hall of the Balìa
4. Chapel of the Piazza	4. Chamber of the Podestà
5. Tower of the Mangia	5. Tower of the Mangia
6. Prison chapel	6. Rooms of the Podestà
7. Chapel of the Podestà	7. Room of the Mappamondo
8. State Rewards and Treasury offices	8. Chapel
9. Tax offices	9. Antechapel
10. Room of the Captain of the People	10. Sacristy
11. Piazza del Campo	11. Chamber of the Council of Nine
12. Market Square	12. Hall of the Pillars

tions. In 1297, for example, it was decided that all the palaces built facing the *Palazzo Pubblico* would have to use the same type of window openings and facades. Between 1327 and 1349, the owners of these same homes, and the city government, paid for the paving of Siena's main square, the *Campo*. The nine divisions in the brickwork are a reminder of the good government the Nine provided in the town hall. The *Palio*, the horse race that still takes place there, provided a chance for local neighborhoods, the *contrade*, to compete against one another without resorting to open violence, as in former years.

The Black Death of 1348 and the subsequent decline in population halted Siena's expansion, and work on the cathedral in Florence slowed down. But the tragedy also gave rise to a new group of monuments as dying men and women left money to shrines for their salvation. The small Florentine church of Orsanmichele, halfway between the cathedral and the town hall, was a prime beneficiary and a fine illustration of the impossibility of separating religion from other aspects of daily life. In the 14th century the arcades of Orsanmichele opened into the city's central grain market where food was sold at subsidized prices and stored against bad harvest and famine. Among the bustling market-stalls stood a curtained tabernacle marking the spot where, in 1299, a painted figure of the Virgin Mary had been seen to weep. As news of the miracle spread, pilgrims began to visit and stories of miraculous cures circulated. The picture would cure the sick and mad, and restore sight to the blind. A small group of devoted men and women, a confraternity, was established to look after the picture. To prevent her powers from diminishing, the image was kept veiled and only displayed at evensong when hymns of praise to Mary, known as *laude*, were sung and candles were sold to worshipers praying for her healing grace. As the confraternity's income grew, it was decided to build a better display. The painter Bernardo Daddi (c. 1290–c. 1348) was asked to provide a magnificent image of Mary, while the architect of Santa Maria del Fiore, Andrea Orcagna (c. 1308–68), was commissioned to enclose the image in a rich marble, mosaic and enamel shrine. He built an enormous stone monument with an octagonal cupola that mimicked the vault planned for the cathedral. Through the open market arcades the shrine's back could be seen, a large marble slab carved with a scene of the Virgin rising to heaven. Painted with gold leaf, the vivid image ensured that as the Florentine inhabitant hurried down this busy main street, his or her concern for shopping and business would be matched by an awareness of the need to prepare for the life hereafter.

Preaching and pulpits

The new cathedrals and the tabernacle of Orsanmichele were built in marble, a material that requires a highly organized and skilled labor force. From the workshops of Pisa cathedral emerged two of Europe's most brilliant sculptors, Nicola Pisano (active c. 1258–78) and his son Giovanni (active c. 1263–1314). Their most impressive carving was done on a single type of structure, the pulpit. Preaching was receiving renewed emphasis. The Church's involvement in power struggles with imperial forces in the 11th and 12th centuries had detracted from its traditional pastoral role. There were frequent complaints that bishops rarely visited their flocks and that parish priests were illiterate and uncaring. But the demand for religious guidance and concern for salvation did not disappear. Urban communities turned increasingly to wisemen who moved from town to town preaching and offering spiritual guidance. The sects they founded had views that could be quite extreme – Pope Boniface VIII (1294–1303) had to condemn one group who insisted on praying in the nude. All, however, shared a common belief that the Church was corrupt and cared only for earthly power.

The papacy could not allow such threats to its authority to continue. In the early 13th century, Pope

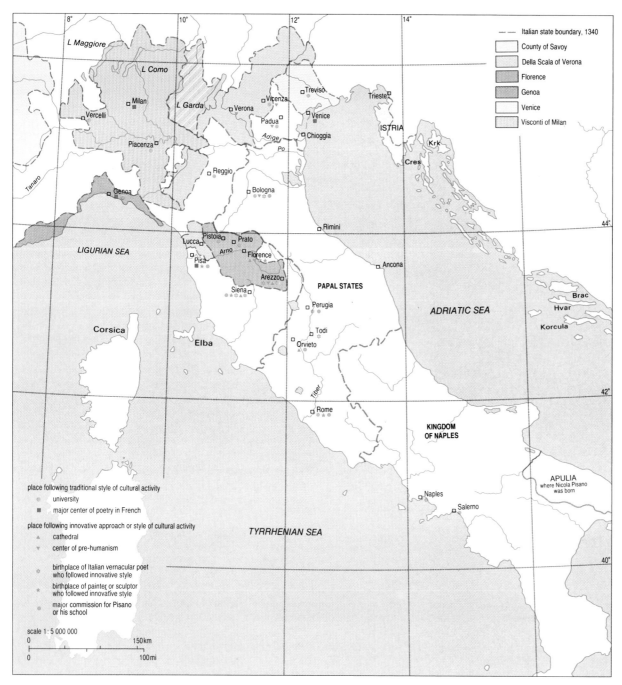

Italian state boundary, 1340
- County of Savoy
- Della Scala of Verona
- Florence
- Genoa
- Venice
- Visconti of Milan

place following traditional style of cultural activity
- ● university
- ■ major center of poetry in French

place following innovative approach or style of cultural activity
- ▲ cathedral
- ▼ center of pre-humanism
- ✿ birthplace of Italian vernacular poet who followed innovative style
- ★ birthplace of painter or sculptor who followed innovative style
- ● major commission for Pisano or his school

scale 1 : 5 000 000
0 — 150km
0 — 100mi

Innocent III decided to harness the energies of St Francis of Assisi. As a young man Francis had rejected his father's inheritance in favor of a life of extreme hardship. His humility, piety and intense devotion made a dramatic impact on the religious sensibility of the period. In time he formed a religious order, the Franciscans, who took vows of chastity, obedience and poverty. They refused to own property or goods and promised to travel and beg in order to spread the Gospel. Figures such as St Francis had been burnt as heretics in former times and the wealthy landowning Church was threatened by the Franciscans' beliefs that ownership was evil and that only the poor were truly virtuous. But the willingness of Francis to accept papal authority meant that his expanding influence could be of benefit to the Church.

Even before he died in 1226, the saint had become increasingly remote from his own order as new groups were set up throughout Europe. Although his original ideals were never fully lost, the rapid growth of his following required an administrative bureaucracy and permanence that he had never foreseen. His burial site,

Above: Italian cultural centers c. 1300
In the early 14th century, a sharp cultural divide can be seen between the south of Italy and the north, including Tuscany, where the bulk of cultural activity was located. The area of "traditional", or Gothic, culture again forms a distinct zone in the northwest. It was the points of overlap between the old and the new culture drawing its inspiration from the classical past (in which Nicola Pisano had shown the way) that were central to stimulating cultural change. Among the most important of these were Pisa, Bologna, Padua and Arezzo.

Right Florence at night. The Arno river winds its way through the city of Florence, providing water for its people and industry, energy for mills and transportation for its products. The bridges spanning the Arno are famous for the beauty of their construction, particularly the Ponte Vecchio, where goldsmiths' shops still line the sides. In this picture the dome of the cathedral dominates the city.

the Basilica of St Francis at Assisi, quickly became one of the largest and most lavishly decorated churches in Italy. Artists from Florence and Rome joined to fresco its churches (there are two churches, one above the other) and prominent figures commissioned chapels near the saint's body. By mid century the Franciscans, and the rival order of Dominican friars, had taken over the Inquisition, burning heretics (even the so-called "spiritual" Franciscans, the *fraticelli*, who claimed that their brothers were no longer following the true path of St Francis) and preaching the need for repentance to ever larger urban crowds.

Under the Franciscans' guidance sermons became more common. Witnesses testified to the power and efficacy of visiting friars who warned of the threat of eternal damnation and the need for salvation. It is no surprise, therefore, that one of the first commissions for Nicola Pisano was a pulpit. The monument he produced in 1260 for the Baptistery in Pisa represented the story of Christ's life in a startlingly novel fashion. Looking up at the lectern the congregation would have seen man's greatest sin, the Crucifixion of Jesus Christ, on the preacher's right, and to his left, the Last Judgment, when Christ will return to call each mortal to his or her final destiny. These scenes depicted the pain and suffering of the damned in awesome detail. In the other four panels of the story of Mary, however, Nicola provided a calmer vision, using classical sources taken from local Pisan antiquities as his model. His figure of a male virtue was a version of the ancient hero, Hercules. Even the figure of the Virgin Mary was modeled on a Roman sarcophagus visible in the nearby cemetery.

In the heated and competitive atmosphere of the cities of 13th-century Tuscany, Nicola's work made an immediate impression. In 1265 he and his workshop were invited to work for Pisa's rival, the city of Siena. In Siena Cathedral, he and his son Giovanni produced a larger and more complex structure. The calm visions of the Pisa Baptistery version may have proved unsuitable for the rhetoric of weekly sermons. The new pulpit was detailed and emotive. No space was left uncarved as the figures leant out into space to warn listeners of terrible fates. It is possible that the young Giovanni took a greater role in its production. Giovanni's first independent commission, for the church of Sant'Andrea in Pistoia (1297–1301), suggests that he ignored his father's earlier classicizing style in favor of Gothic drama. Twisting, mobile figures support the pulpit while the narrative scenes above are undercut and modeled with light and shadow using remarkably daring carving techniques. The Sant'Andrea pulpit was completed during the height of Pistoia's civil war between the White and Black Guelphs. It may not be too much to suggest that Giovanni reflected the violence within the city in his charged scene of the Massacre of the Innocents. He deliberately refrained from smoothing the faces of weeping mothers and agonized children, leaving the rough chisel-marks to suggest a highly personal response to the tragedy.

Thirteenth-century artists are often categorized as anonymous craftsmen with little sense of individuality. But Giovanni's pulpit in Pistoia bears an inscription recording the artist's self-conscious pride: "Giovanni carved it, who performed no empty work. The son of Nicola and blessed with higher skill. Pisa gave him birth and endowed him with mastery greater than any seen before." This is not the remark of an

unassuming artisan. Convinced of his own genius, proud of having outperformed his father, Giovanni Pisano is a reminder that many of the so-called "medieval" artists were as acutely aware of their individual ability as any sculptor of the High Renaissance.

Duccio and Giotto

Behind Nicola Pisano's pulpit in Siena Cathedral stood Duccio di Buoninsegna's great altarpiece the *Maestà* (1311), a double-sided image of the Virgin and Child in Majesty. The *Maestà* was a picture of tremendous religious and civic importance. In 1260 the citizens had walked barefoot to the Cathedral to ask the Virgin's help in their impending battle against the Florentines. They offered prayers and the keys of the city to a small Romanesque panel known as the *Madonna of the Big Eyes*, and were later convinced that the picture had brought them an unexpected victory. When the city council decided to replace the image, every care was taken to ensure that the new version was a worthy and impressive work. Duccio (c. 1260–c. 1318) was a local artist and the whole town followed his progress. Its completion was an occasion for celebration. A public holiday was declared when the picture, as one writer reported, "was carried through Siena with much devotion and around the *Campo* in procession, ringing all the bells for joy, and

Above Giovanni Pisano, *The Massacre of the Innocents*, a detail from the pulpit in the church of Sant' Andrea Pistoia (1297–1301). The rough and dramatic carving on this section of a pulpit emphatically reflects the highly charged nature of the scene itself. For congregations listening to sermons about hell and damnation, it presented a vivid and dramatic image of the horrors Herod had once inflicted on his innocent victims.

Right Duccio's *Maestà* (1311) once stood on the high altar of the cathedral of Siena. Now dismembered, its reconstruction has been the source of much controversy. The central panels, with an image of the Virgin in Majesty on the front and a lengthy cycle of Christ's Passion on the reverse, remain in Siena itself. Other episodes from the life of Christ and Mary once formed upper, lower and side tiers of the altarpiece.

this entire day the shops stayed closed for worship". The double-sided *Maestà* had been an enormous undertaking. From the nave, the congregation saw a huge image of the Virgin and Child on a throne surrounded by saints and angels. On the other side, the priests who sang the mass in the sacred enclosure of the choir could follow the story of Christ's passion. Duccio was immensely proud of the result. When he signed the work he asked the Virgin to look upon him and his city: "Holy mother of God bring peace to Siena and, because he painted you in this way, to the life of Duccio."

Mary had a very special place in Siena. She was not only its patron saint, she was its Queen and was expected to take a keen interest in civic welfare, protecting the town from earthquake, famine and social strife. In 1315, when another Sienese artist, Simone Martini (c. 1284–1344), frescoed the main meeting room of the city's town hall, he transformed Duccio's Madonna into a regal judge. Enthroned under a canopy emblazoned with the city's coat of arms, the Virgin counsels her viewers to judge wisely and fairly. Her son's scroll bears the words, "Love justice you who rule the earth", and inscriptions around the painting warn of the dire fate awaiting counselors who defraud the people. The rewards of just government are painted to either side. On the wall facing this fresco, Martini painted images of the towns and castles Siena had conquered in the name of Mary. A few years later, in 1339, Ambrogio Lorenzetti (active 1320–45) decorated the chamber of the Nine with explicit instructions for good government. On the wall under which the magistrates sat are the virtues of divine justice, concord and peace, which lead to civic harmony. The benefits of such rule appear on a long wall to the right: a prosperous town and well-tilled countryside. To the left, however, are the evils that bring strife and trouble, tyranny, discord, envy and hatred, and lead to violence, urban collapse and a desolate landscape.

Duccio's contemporary in Florence, Giotto di Bondone (c. 1266–1337), also painted an allegory of good government for the *podestà*'s palace. This, like much of the artist's work, has disappeared. What does remain of his work, however, shows the dramatic naturalism that immediately set Giotto apart from the other artists of his period. By introducing pictorial styles and techniques to create illusions of space, human drama and the textures of everyday life, he brought about a profound change in the nature of European painting. He enjoyed considerable fame in his own lifetime. At a time when most artists lived and worked within a small geographic area, he traveled widely, spreading his distinctive style from Padua to Naples. The greatest writers of the period sang his praises. Dante included him in his great poem, the *Divine Comedy*, as an example of the transience of worldly fame: "Cimabue thought to hold the field in painting, and now Giotto has the cry, so that the fame of the former is obscured." Boccaccio wrote stories recounting the artist's wit and practical jokes, and one of the proudest possessions of Petrarch was a picture of the Virgin by Giotto. When he bequeathed it to the lord of Padua, Francesco Carrara, he told the new owner that the "beauty of this painting the ignorant cannot comprehend, but masters of the art marvel at it".

Yet despite this attention, little is known about Giotto's early life. He seems to have been influenced by artists working in Rome in the mid 13th century, and by the sculptures of the Pisani. He may have worked at the Franciscan basilica in Assisi, but there is little agreement on which of its many remarkable frescoes are his. His allegorical fresco in Florence, described in the 16th century, has now vanished, together with his work in Naples for King Robert of Anjou and in Milan for Lord Azzone Visconti. Several panel paintings with his signature have confused art historians for decades, and are now thought to belong to his workshop.

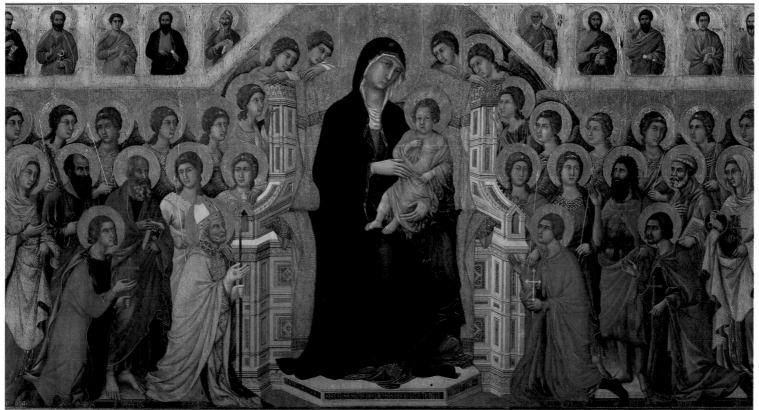

Above Giotto, *The Death of St Francis of Assisi* (c. 1315–1320). Giotto here depicted the moment when a friar, lifting the habit of St Francis, discovers that the saint had received the stigmata, the marks of Christ's crucifixion. This depiction of the personal and highly emotional response of each monk to both the death of their spiritual father and to the discovery of his affinity to Christ is one of the high points of Giotto's artistic vision.

Left Ambrogio Lorenzetti, *Good Government* (1339). The Palazzo Pubblico, Siena, was decorated with an extensive cycle of frescoes based on Aristotelian political philosophy. Good government was achieved when justice, wisdom, concord and unity guided men toward the common good. The ideal vision of the well-governed city of Siena shows numerous merchants going about their tasks and a bountiful supply of food imported from the rich countryside. Walls, towers and palaces are well maintained and the citizens well dressed. Here dancers wearing silk garments celebrate in the streets.

Giotto needed assistants because his new style and his outstanding skills as a story-teller were in great demand. Like the Pisani, whose work he knew well, Giotto could translate holy tales into compelling emotional moments. His Virgins were no longer remote queens of heaven; they were young girls facing difficult decisions or caring mothers concerned for their son's well-being. The work he performed in Florence for the bankers who financed civic growth can still be seen. The sin of money-lending could be cleansed by substantial donations to the Church and the poor. The Franciscans, with their vows of poverty, chastity and obedience, were particularly popular recipients of ill-gotten funds. The order's church in Florence, Santa Croce, became one of the city's largest buildings, with chapels whose names read like a roll call of the banking community. Here Giotto provided Europe's greatest bankers, the Bardi and the Peruzzi, with frescoes of saint's lives, frescoes that were part of their attempt to atone for the sins – usury and avarice – that had made them wealthy enough to commission chapels and frescoes.

His greatest surviving work was done in Padua for a nobleman concerned with his father's usury rather than his own life-style. Enrico Scrovegni was not modest about his needs. Instead of endowing a chapel within an existing monastery, he constructed a church (the Arena Chapel) next to his family palace. By 1305 the monks from the nearby Jeronimite monastery were complaining about the excessive luxury being invested in the chapel: Statues by Giovanni Pisano stood on the high altar and the walls were covered with frescoes. Spiraling around the viewer, the tragic

and glorious story of Christ's birth and death was played out in intimate detail. As visitors entered they were struck by an image over the high altar of the Annunciation of Christ's birth, the beginning of the Christian story. On the lowest level of the side walls, they saw images of the virtues and vices, and when they turned to leave, they walked out under a terrifying vision of the damnation awaiting those who sinned.

Giotto's travels did not loosen his ties with Tuscany. He was a shrewd businessman: he invested his profits in the weaving industry of his home town in the Mugello. Toward the end of his life he returned to Florence to dedicate his remaining years to the ultimate symbol of civic pride, the cathedral bell tower. In its official appointment of the artist in 1334, the city government expressed its pride in its appreciation:

It is said that in the whole world no one can be found who is more capable in these and other things than Maestro Giotto di Bondone, painter of Florence. He should be received therefore in his country as a great master and held dear in the city, and he should have cause to live permanently there. For many will profit from his knowledge and learning and the city's beauty will be enhanced.

Although Florence laid claim to Giotto, Italy as a whole benefited from his legacy. Earlier styles of painting did not disappear. Gilded Byzantine icons, remote and regal, still had a role to play in religious art, particularly after the Black Death. But Giotto's examples of human space and emotion, vividly depicted in strong, simple narratives, remained as a touchstone for later generations.

Literacy, literature and classical scholarship

Paintings such as those in the Arena Chapel were often called "bibles of the illiterate". The Bible itself was available only in Latin, its words too sacred to be made readily accessible. Women and children were expected to learn holy scripture from the images of saints' lives that decorated their churches and from sermons, prayers and catechisms. "Illiterate" did not, however, mean that viewers could not read, only that they could not understand Latin. Devotional texts written in Italian and French, such as the Franciscan *Meditations on the Life of Christ* and Jacopo da Voragine's *Golden Legend*, were extremely popular. These were books that told intimate nonbiblical stories about the daily lives of saints and martyrs, and invited readers to imagine themselves as present at holy events: young girls were to pretend that they were serving maids in the Virgin's house, young men that they watched Christ carrying the cross.

Nevertheless, Latin was still the primary means of communication for government, business and the Church. Along with rudimentary arithmetic, a basic understanding of Latin was essential for working in a mercantile culture. Most Italian towns had private or public grammar schools – Milan had 60 such schools in the late 12th century. About 1339, the Florentine chronicler Giovanni Villani could boast that between 8,000 and 10,000 Florentine boys and girls were being taught to read, and that of those a quarter went on to "abacus schools" to learn mathematics. Private tutors were also available and advanced students could listen to lectures given by Dominican and Franciscan friars or attend classes at newly established universities.

Padua, whose university was founded in 1222, was a particularly important center of learning. There scholars experimented with the styles and types of Latin literature of antiquity and reminded their fellow citizens that an ancient past was an important part of local identity. Symbols of the classical past could prove very effective in forging a modern civic consciousness. When the remains of an ancient skeleton were unearthed in Padua in the late 13th century, the poet Lovato dei Lovati (c. 1240–1309) immediately identified them as the bones of Padua's mythical founder, the Trojan Antenor. In Padua's main square in 1316 the scholar Alberto Mussato (1261–1329) presented a Latin play based on Seneca's tragedies. The performance was a warning against tyranny and his listeners had no difficulty in relating it to the ambitions of local lords who were trying to capture the city. It was a great success, even though Musato's prose was so difficult that few could understand it. The point had been made: antiquity was relevant to contemporary problems. The city's society of notaries petitioned him to write something about Paduan history that "notaries and humble clerics" could understand.

While Padua produced academics, Tuscany produced a generation of poets and writers who transformed the Italian language. In the 13th century there was no standard means of communication in Italy apart from Latin. Every region had its own local dialect and a Pisan merchant traveling north might have to carry a dictionary in order to understand his colleagues in Milan. By the 15th century the same well-educated individual would have been able to communicate in the Tuscan dialect, the forerunner of modern Italian. In the intervening period three writers – Dante, Petrarch and Boccaccio – had, in their own individual ways, ensured that Florentine speech had become the literary tongue of the entire peninsula. Yet ironically all three were, at various stages in their lives, rather ashamed of their Tuscan works, preferring to stress their skills in writing Latin.

Dante Alighieri, born in Florence in 1265, was embarrassed by the light offerings of his youth. In his early poetry he had used the traditions of Provençal love songs in devising his "sweet new style" (*dolce stil nuovo*) of poetry – verses that explored his passion for a young Florentine girl, Beatrice, and his despair at her death. Dante first saw his beloved in a Florentine church and much of his poetry has an urban setting. He was very much a man of his city, fighting in the Florentine army and serving on the *signoria*; as a White Guelph prior in the government of the late 13th century, he sat on the committee that determined the width and direction of city streets. But in 1302 his Black opponents gained the upper hand. Charged with misconduct and embezzlement, Dante, along with 300 others, was exiled from his native city. In the *Divine Comedy*, written between 1314 and his death in 1321, Dante took his opportunity to gain revenge on past and present enemies. Florentine people were full of avarice, envy, pride, "three fatal sparks have set the hearts of all on fire". His dearest ambition was that the emperor would take over Italy and restore imperial rule over the divided commune of Florence. But the lengthy three-part poem was much more than a political tract. Dante used the imaginary journey through Hell, Purgatory and Paradise, with his guides Beatrice and the Roman poet Virgil to explore many facets of human nature and experience. In doing so he provided an encyclopedic compendium of Christian and classical knowledge.

The other great lyricist who established the primacy of the Tuscan dialect was Francesco Petrarch (1304–74), though he wanted to be remembered for his long, rather ponderous epic *Africa*. He avoided Florence, preferring the peace that great lords of northern Italy and the papacy in Avignon could provide. When his friend Boccaccio accused him of supporting tyrants such as Archbishop Giovanni Visconti, he defended himself by saying that all he wished from them was "leisure, silence, serenity and freedom". Although his father had wanted him to study law, Petrarch, convinced of his own innate genius, had avoided civic involvement from an early age. Like Dante, he had hoped that an imperial figure – in his case Charles of Bohemia – would restore the greatness of ancient Italy. Unlike his predecessor, however, he did not actively campaign for political change. The poet felt isolated from his own age and closer to the ancients: "I write for myself and while I am writing I eagerly converse with our predecessors in the only way I can; and I gladly dismiss from mind the men with whom I am forced by an unkind fate to live." His works, introspective and self-absorbed, explore his own concerns and feelings in a way unfamiliar to his contemporaries. He held no university post and neglected the standard subjects of law and theology in favor of the private study of classical literature. His favorite Roman author was Cicero, following whose example he collected and circulated his own personal letters. His Christian guide was St Augustine, whose writings he used as a model for emotional introspection. He collected fine examples of ancient Greek and Latin texts, commissioning Simone Martini to decorate the frontispiece of one of his proudest possessions, a

Right: The travels of Petrarch
Petrarch, often called the first great humanist, trained as a lawyer but throughout his life derived his income from clerical posts with minor responsibilities, under the aegis of his patron Cardinal Giovanni Colonna. With his own family in exile from Florence, and the papacy exiled from Rome in Avignon, Petrarch was able to move with unusual freedom through north Italy and southern France, all the while devoting himself to his writing and scholarship. Ultimately he sought to create a home, build a library and tend his garden; he fulfilled this dream at Arquà, near Padua.

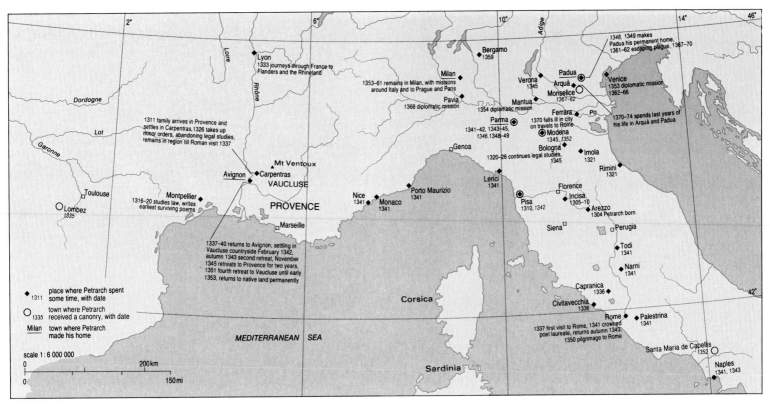

manuscript containing the works of the Roman poet Virgil. His supposed isolation did not prevent Petrarch from remaining remarkably well-connected and influential – his intellectual independence and all-consuming enthusiasm for the classics made him a model upon which future humanists would base their own careers.

Petrarch avoided Florence: his impact on the city came through his correspondence. In the city his greatest followers were the future chancellor Coluccio Salutati and the writer Giovanni Boccaccio. Like Petrarch, Boccaccio (1313–75) was first destined for commerce. But the effort was wasted, for as he wrote later: "If my father had dealt wisely with me I might have been among the great poets. But he forced me, in vain, to give my mind to money-making, and to a profitable career." Love poems and literature eventually took precedence. Dante had his Beatrice, Petrarch devoted his sonnets to Laura and Boccaccio found his muse in a young Neapolitan girl, Fiammetta. But the author found his most effective voice in prose, writing a lengthy, raucously funny, bawdy collection of short tales reflecting both contemporary Italian life and legends from many lands, the *Decameron* (composed 1348–53). The story was set in the plague of 1348, when a group of wealthy young men and women sought shelter from its ravages. Deploring the breakdown of society, they recalled pleasanter moments by exchanging tales of deceived husbands, unhappy wives and consoling moments of love. The *Decameron* enjoyed widespread popularity throughout Europe, though some of the stories were so explicit that early English editions often left the more salacious passages untranslated. Boccaccio, perhaps under the influence of a religious conversion, eventually rejected the light novella form, destroyed much of his early poetry and even disowned the *Decameron*. Under Petrarch's guidance, he turned to classical scholarship and his last years were spent searching for ancient texts in Naples and the Benedictine abbey at Monte Cassino. Responsible for ensur-

ing that Petrarch's humanistic influence was retained in Florence, Boccaccio also extended Dante's reputation, publishing a eulogistic biography in the mid 1350s. He also published two other biographical works, *On the Fates of Famous Men*, and *On Famous Women*. In 1373, the *signoria* asked him to lecture on the *Divine Comedy*, a task he undertook for 100 gold florins. But illness soon overtook him and he returned to his native town of Certaldo, where he died in December 1375, 18 monghs after Petrarch. For many, these two deaths meant the end of Italian poetry.

The final irony of the 14th century is that Dante, Petrarch and Boccaccio produced some of Italy's greatest literary masterpieces in a period they regarded as essentially bereft of cultural value. All three were eventually convinced that the men of their own day had little to offer in comparison to the great writers and thinkers of ancient times. Yet their very disillusionment gave rise to works which, along with the architecture, sculpture and painting of the period, has ensured that the very century they grew to despise is now seen as a time of extraordinary artistic achievement.

New directions in Italian culture

During the late 13th and 14th centuries leading sculptors, painters and writers in northern Italy had begun to look to antique models for source materials. Painters and sculptors, especially Giotto and Niccolò and Giovanni Pisano, continued to represent traditional Christian subjects, but their antique examples pointed them toward placing greater emphasis on the human qualities of the people they portrayed. Dante, Petrarch and Boccaccio sought examples and inspiration in the works of classical authors. Many of these people were connected with Florence, where some leading citizens took a keen interest in their work. However, at the end of the 14th century it was uncertain whether the new directions taken would be built upon, or, like the city of Florence itself, they would be consigned to the past.

Dante and the Divine Comedy

At the time this fresco in the cathedral of Florence was painted (1464), Dante Alighieri was celebrated as the city's foremost poet and writer. Lectures and readings of his work were held regularly within the church to familiarize Florentines with the "sweet new style" of poetry he is thought to have introduced into Italy in the 13th century. Yet the writer had actually lived much of his life outside the city in a bitter exile from the factional conflicts that had deprived him of his home. The *Divine Comedy* was written during this period of his life and he enjoyed castigating his fellow citizens for their greed and divisiveness: "Rejoice, O Florence, since you are so great that over sea and land you beat your wings and your name is spread through Hell." But the lengthy poem was much more than a retaliation for political rejection. An extraordinary compendium of 14th-century knowledge and philosophy, the *Divine Comedy* invited its readers to ponder the nature and variety of human existence and heavenly salvation.

For generations of Italian readers Dante's vision of Hell, Purgatory and Paradise was the quintessential vision of the after-life. The poem takes the form of a journey in search of goodness, truth and beauty.

Midway in the journey of our life I found myself in a dark wood, for the straight way was lost. Ah, how hard it is to tell what that wood was, wild, rugged, harsh; the very thought of it renews the fear! It is so bitter that death is hardly more so. But to treat of the good that I found in it, I will tell of the other things I saw there.

With his guide, the Latin poet Virgil, the writer passes through the gates of Hell to descend through the many layers of the underworld. Here he meets illicit lovers, gluttons, usurers and assassins, all of whom suffer cruel punishments specifically devised for their sins. Vats of boiling tar, snakes and monstrous devils and many other torments awaited those who had transgressed.

But there was hope. The second section described the slow ascent up the mountain of Purgatory. The concept that men and women could still cleanse their worldly sins even after death meant that God's mercy might yet bring salvation to the worst human being. Dante's readers were accustomed to purchasing papal and episcopal indulgences that guaranteed to free them from their sins. Prayers and masses said for their souls would also aid their progress through the multistoreyed Purgatory Dante described. Their goal was the vision of Paradise, which the poet provided in his final section. There Dante's beloved, the young Florentine girl Beatrice, awaited to guide him to a true understanding of faith and divine love.

Dante first met Beatrice when he was nine and she was eight. She became the single most important inspiration for his poetry, from his early love poems in *New Life* to the *Divine Comedy*, which he began after her death at the age of 24. In the final section of the *Divine Comedy* they are reunited, Beatrice leading him to the Virgin Mary.

Below Dante Standing Before the City of Florence (1465) by Domenico di Michelino. In the 15th century the city of Florence had hoped to transfer the bones of its most famous literary figures from their resting places to the cathedral. But the city of Ravenna, where Dante was buried, refused to give up the poet's remains. This fresco was commissioned instead, to commemorate the man the city of Florence had once sent into exile. The painter Domenico di Michelino, having carried out the designs given to him by a better known artist, Alessio Baldovinetti, was rewarded for having added more figures and for having produced the work in six months.

Altarpieces

The altarpiece became one of the primary forms of artistic expression in the Church in the 14th and 15th centuries. Originally placed on the front of the altars the paintings gradually assumed greater and greater importance as backdrops for the most critical part of the mass, the moment the host is consecrated. Along with a crucifix, candlesticks and fine linens, the altarpiece ensured that the site for this reenactment of Christ's sacrifice was dignified and worthy.

Each picture had to produce a sense of religious awe and devotion, and to provide a focus for prayer and meditation. Altars were usually dedicated both to God and to specific saints. As the mother of Christ, Mary was among the most popular, for worshipers believed that she held great influence and could ask for mercy and compassion on behalf of sinners. Other saints had special functions. St Appollonia, for example, was the patron saint of tooth-pullers, while Saint Sebastian provided protection from the plague.

Altarpieces usually focused on saints and there were a great many ways in which they and their stories could be depicted. The first altarpieces, *dossals* or *retables*, were simple rectangular panels transferred from the altar front to the altar table. These gradually became more elaborate. Individual figures were often portrayed in the upper panels and side buttresses, and narrative events were usually shown in the lower section, the *predella*. Small portable triptychs could be set up in the bedroom to encourage private devotion, while enormous multitiered polyptychs might act as screens between the nave of the church, where the laity stood, and the choir, where only the priests were permitted to stand. As the polyptych became less fashionable and the liturgy changed yet again in the 16th century, many were destroyed or sawn into their component parts. This has made it more difficult to appreciate the full impact of these works.

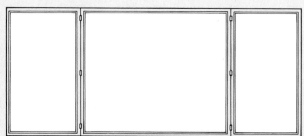

Left A diptych, or two-paneled altarpiece. Small altarpieces were made up of several planks of wood. These were joined together by nails or wooden dowels and often covered with a piece of linen and gesso in order to provide a smooth surface for painting. A layer of red bole (a sticky pigment) would then be covered with thin sheets of gold leaf and only then would the painter begin work.

Right The three-paneled altarpiece, the triptych, would usually be opened only during Mass or on special feast days. The two wings would cover and protect the central image, and their exterior would usually be painted, often with grisaille (two-toned) figures imitating sculpture, or, more simply, with the coats-of-arms of the patron who had commissioned the image.

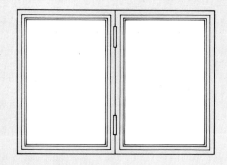

Left The triptych was often of an elaborate design. Here the two wings close to cover a domed central image.

Below The *Portinari Altarpiece* (c. 1476) by Hugo van der Goes was painted for Tommaso Portinari, who worked for the Medici – he and his sons appear in the left-hand panel, his wife and daughter in the right-hand panel. This Flemish altarpiece was greatly admired in Florence. Northern artists painted many of the finest altarpieces of the Renaissance. Outstanding are works by van Eyck, van der Weyden, Bosch and Grünewald.

Above In his *Deposition* (c. 1443) Fra Angelico spread the picture plane over the entire surface of the central panel rather than sub-dividing it into several individual images. This is more common with large works.

Right An outline of Duccio's *Maestà*, a large and complex polyptych that once stood in the cathedral of Siena. Like Fra Angelico's *Deposition*, the main image is painted on a broad central panel without wings. Smaller images appear both below (on the *predella*) and above, and also (unusually) on the reverse side, which faced the choir.

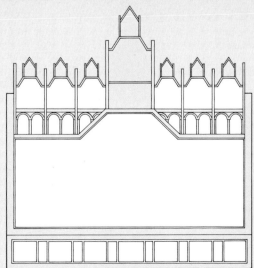

Below The triptych form was particularly suitable for small portable altarpieces. They could be easily erected to provide a ready-made focus for prayer while traveling. The wings could be angled to ensure that the viewer concentrated on the central image, which was usually a Virgin and Child. On the side panels special patron saints or even narratives of Christ's life gave additional material for devotional meditation.

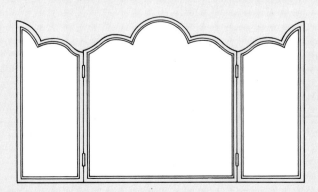

Giotto and the Arena Chapel

The Arena Chapel, which takes its name from an ancient Roman amphitheater nearby, was built by a wealthy nobleman, Enrico Scrovegni. He was given permission to erect the small private oratory next to his palace in 1302, and it was dedicated to the Virgin Annunciate the following year. His motivation was, in part, to atone for the sins of his father, who was so notorious a usurer Dante placed him in Hell in his *Divine Comedy*. The plan quickly became more elaborate and by 1305 monks living nearby complained about the inappropriate luxury displayed in Scrovegni's chapel: "He should not have built a large church there, and the many things which have been made there more for pomp, vainglory and wealth than for the praise, glory and honour of God."

Scrovegni chose Giotto to decorate the chapel, the subject being the lives of the Virgin Mary and Christ, and it is upon this extraordinary cycle of frescoes that Giotto's reputation is firmly based. Many episodes, particularly those relating to the infancy of Mary, were not taken from the Bible but from popular works such as Jacopo da Voragine's *Golden Legend*. Depicting his figures in a moving, humane fashion, Giotto fashioned a new visual language in which the emotional content of religious tales was conveyed through stark gestures and spare, careful composition. Through such means worshipers were encouraged to identify emotionally with those depicted in the scenes and thereby see the relevance of such holy stories to their own lives.

Right The *Flight into Egypt* illustrates Giotto's abilities as a story-teller. Placed against the bare background of a rocky, inhospitable terrain, the figure of Virgin wears a calm but determined expression. Joseph's look, as he turns to consider the fate of his wife and the infant she carries, is one of concern. It is this ability to tell stories through the convincing depiction of moments of drama or pathos that so deeply impressed Giotto's contemporaries.

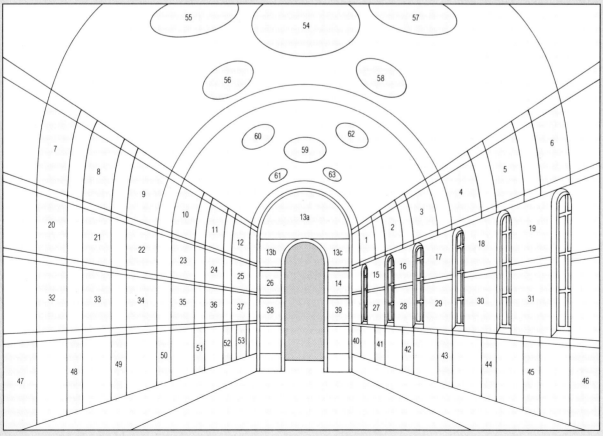

The Story of Mary
1. Expulsion from the temple
2. Joachim retires to the sheepfold
3. Annunciation to Anna
4. Sacrifice of Joachim
5. Joachim's dream
6. Meeting at the Golden Gate

The Story of madonna
7. Birth of Mary
8. Mary is taken to the temple
9. Presentation of the rods
10. The priests pray for guidance
11. Marriage of Mary and Joseph
12. Mary returns home
13a, b, c The Annunciation, with "the prologue in heaven" above the door, the Angel Gabriel to the left and the Virgin Mary to the right of the door.

The Story of Jesus
14. Meeting of Mary and Elizabeth
15. Nativity
16. Adoration of the Magi
17. Presentation at the temple
18. Flight into Egypt
19. Massacre of the Innocents
20. Christ diputing with the elders
21. Baptism of Christ
22. Marriage at Cana
23. Raising of Lazarus
24. Entry into Jerusalem
25. Expulsion from the temple
26. Treachery of Judas
27. Last Supper
28. Washing the feet

Below Viewers entering the chapel are immediately confronted with a powerful image of the Virgin Annunciate over the apse. This scene, which connects Mary's life before the birth of Christ to the episodes of His infancy and Passion, acts as the pivot for the multilayered stories on the walls. Giotto carefully balanced the images, arranging the narrative around all four walls so that viewers would be encouraged to see connections between the episodes. Allegories of human virtue and vice are depicted on the lowest level. Interestingly, the sin of avarice is not depicted. On the west wall above the entrance Giotto painted the culmination of the cycle, the *Last Judgment*. It is here, immediately over the door, that the kneeling figure of Enrico Scrovegni appears, presenting a model of the chapel to the Virgin.

29. Kiss of Judas
30. Christ before Caiaphas
31. The mocking of Christ
32. Road to Cavalry
33. Crucifixion
34. Lamentation
35. Resurrection
36. Ascension
37. Pentecost
38, 39 Architectural details

Allegories of the Virtues and Vices
40. Prudence
41. Fortitude
42. Temperance
43. Justice
44. Faith
45. Charity
46. Hope
47. Despair
48. Envy
49. Infidelity
50. Injustice
51. Anger
52. Inconstancy
53. Foolishness

The Vault – The Prophets
54. Virgin and Child
55. Malachi
56. Isaiah
57. Daniel
58. Baruch
59. Christ
60. Prophet
61. Prophet
62. John the Baptist
63. Prophet

THE CLASSICAL RENAISSANCE

September 1402 brought a long-awaited miracle to the city of Florence. With Milanese troops outside their walls poised to capture the city, their greatest enemy, Gian Galeazzo Visconti, ruler of Milan, died from a sudden illness. In the chaos that followed, towns such as Siena, Pisa, Perugia and Bologna, which had once accepted Visconti supremacy, declared their independence. Florence called for three days of feasting and festivities. The city was quick to use its new opportunities. From being the besieged victim, it became the aggressor, conquering surrounding lands and cities as it expanded toward the Apennines and the Mediterranean. But Florence was not alone: Venice, Naples and a rejuvenated Milan were all anxious to retake lands they claimed as their own.

The main beneficiaries of the territorial wars that engulfed the Italian peninsula in the early 15th century were the itinerant professional soldiers, the *condottieri*. These figures had played a crucial role in many 14th-century battles. The Englishman Sir John Hawkwood, for example, defended the Florentines during their conflicts with the Visconti and was rewarded by being portrayed in a fresco on the walls of the cathedral. Hawkwood was a rare example of reliable mercenary who dealt fairly with his employer. Most cities had a more ambiguous relationship with their hired armies. *Condottieri* were suspected of avoiding battle and drawing out sieges in order to earn more. Many were willing, for the right price, to change sides in mid conflict. The worst offender was Sigismondo Pandolfo Malatesta (1417–68), a brilliant tactician who angered his employers by continual defections. In the midst of the Neapolitan battles of the 1460s he switched sides from King Alfonso of Naples to the opposing forces (without, however, returning the money he had received from the king). But the most dramatic story of the 15th century was undoubtedly that of Francesco Sforza (1401–66). His service to the queen of Naples in the 1420s brought him wealth, and his invasion of the Marches in eastern Italy (taking advantage of a weak papacy) made him a minor ruler in the Papal State. Duke Filippo Maria Visconti of Milan, anxious to ensure that the Sforza army fought on his behalf, promised to betroth his only child to Francesco. By 1450, despite a series of upsets and setbacks, the impoverished minor nobleman from a country village in the Romagna had become duke of Milan.

Politicians, rulers and humanists

Soldiers were not the only group of skilled men called upon to serve the needs of the aggressively expanding Italian city-states and their rulers. Gian Galeazzo Visconti is reported to have claimed that the pen of the chancellor of Florence, Coluccio Salutati (1331–1406), had done more damage that 30 squadrons of Florentine cavalry. The chancellor appreciated the compliment, replying "does he think I am going to restrict my pen when, if the opportunity were given, I would not hold back the sword?" Battles were always accompanied by the grand speeches and poetry needed to convince allies and enemies alike of the just cause of each engagement. These were sometimes provided by university teachers or scholars of the *studia humanitatis* (the humanities), who studied grammar, rhetoric, poetry, history, and ethics. They became known as humanists, but like Petrarch professional scholars of the 15th century were no longer confined to academic or clerical institutions. Trained in classical techniques of rhetoric, they were happy to serve patrons of every political complexion. Despots had teams of secretaries at their disposal, ready to give literary debates a political twist. In the 1440s the scholar Lorenzo Valla (1407–57) discovered that the Donation of Constantine, which supposedly gave the pope full temporal control over imperial lands, was a forgery, a discovery that aided his patron King Alfonso of Naples, then in open conflict with the papacy. Salutati and his successors used the examples of ancient republics in Greece and Rome to define Florence's special nature.

But most humanists, although they used their skills to promote their employers' interests, were not primarily interested in contemporary issues. Their goal was the recovery of the language and literature of a past age. Latin was their fundamental obsession.

Above Sigismondo Malatesta, who took control of Rimini as a young man, was one of the most important *condottieri* of his age, his military skills widely recognized by the many Italian states and rulers who employed him as a soldier. But his reputation for treachery and double-dealing did not endear him to more powerful leaders. When Pope Pius II led the attack on Rimini in the 1460s, Malatesta found few allies willing to come to his aid.

Left Paolo Uccello, *Sir John Hawkwood* (1436). The Englishman John Hawkwood (or Giovanni Acuto, as he was known in Italian) was one of Florence's most celebrated mercenary soldiers in the late 14th century. Unlike many of his fellow *condottieri*, he served the city faithfully and rarely reneged on his contracts of service. In thanks, and as an incentive to *condottieri* acting for Florence in the 15th century, the city commissioned Uccello to paint this fictive equestrian monument of the soldier in Florence cathedral.

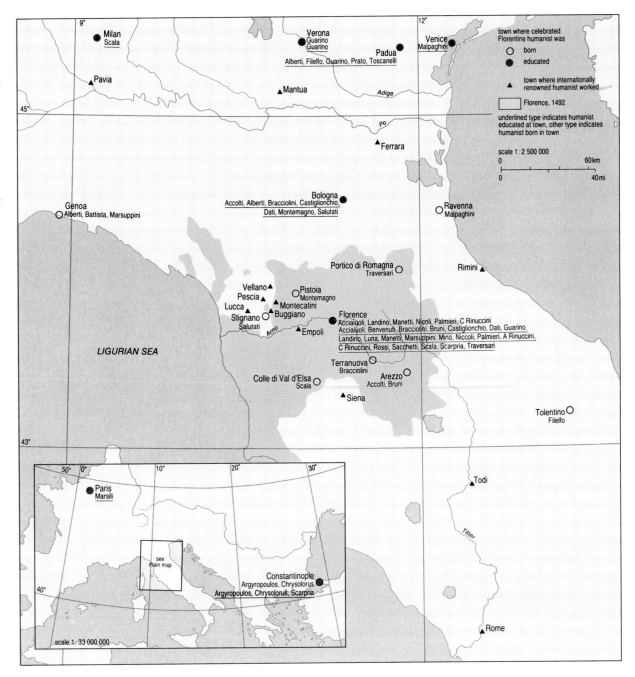

The Florentine humanists, 1375–1460
Of 36 well-known humanists working in Florence in the late 14th and early 15th centuries, slightly fewer than half were actually born in the city, and many of the rest came from lands then under Florentine control. (Interestingly, most of the renowned humanists of the day – men such as Alberti, Poggio Braccioloni, Leonardo Bruni, Coluccio Salutati – were born outside Florence.) Most were educated in Florence itself, though several studied in the university towns of Padua and Bologna, or at more distant centers, from Paris to Constantinople. It was only when Florence began to offer large numbers of its citizens a full education in the humanities – so that few needed to travel further afield for their studies – that the great flowering of Florentine humanism occurred.

Men such as Poggio Bracciolini (1380–1459), working first as a secretary to Henry Beaufort, Bishop of Winchester in England, and then for the pope, scoured Europe's monastic libraries for new or better texts of classical authors. Arranging for these works to be copied and sold through Florentine bookdealers such as Niccolo Niccoli and Vespasiano da Bisticci, Poggio ensured that his friends were able to fill their private libraries with fine copies of ancient writings. Fascinated with Roman monuments, he also kept a collection of busts in his study. But these were often unearthed not for their artistic qualities, but for inscriptions, which indicated how words should be spelled and conjugated. Poggio, in fact, restored Roman lettering to popular use while his close friend and correspondent, Niccoli, developed a new form, the italic script, still used today.

The interest in Latin literature was matched by a fascination with Greek culture. Petrarch had owned a copy of Homer's *Iliad* in the original Greek, but, much to his despair, was unable to read it. To remedy widespread ignorance of Greek, Salutati arranged for Manuel Chrysoloras (c. 1350–1415), a Greek diplo-mat and teacher from Constantinople, to teach the subject in Florence. He began teaching in 1396. In the 1420s the Sicilian humanist Giovanni Aurispa (c. 1370–1459) brought over 200 Greek manuscripts from Constantinople to Italy, including the complete works of Plato. The fall of Constantinople to the Turks in 1453 induced the migration of scholars and manuscripts. Knowledge of important Greek texts was quickly disseminated by translations into both Latin and Italian. The initial preoccupation was with accurate copies, editions and translations of major authors such as Plato, Plotinus and Aristotle. But in the later 15th century scholars such as Marsilio Ficino (1433–99) and Angelo Poliziano (1454–94) were able to move beyond linguistic inquiries to explore the problematic relationship between the wisdom of the ancients and Christian revelation. They found much of Plato's writings on the higher nature of truth and beauty particularly relevant to contemporary concerns with the nature of God and divine understanding.

Despite the high-minded nature of much of their inquiry, the 15th-century humanists were not dull

49

Right Malatesta Temple (1450–62), Rimini. Designed by Leon Battista Alberti and built under the supervision of the local architect and sculptor, Matteo de Pasti, the classicizing facade given to the Gothic church of San Francesco was based on an ancient arch of Augustus, which could still be seen on the outskirts of Rimini. With few local sources of stone, Sigismondo Malatesta imported marble and rare stones from all over Italy and Istria, and expropriated ancient slabs belonging to nearby monasteries. A lengthy Latin inscription on the cornice extolled the virtues of Rimini's ruler, while Greek verses on the side of the church told of his military victories and Christian piety.

Above A medallion self-portrait by Leon Battista Alberti. Alberti was a humanist writer whose passion for the visual arts led him to write several influential treatises on painting, sculpture and architecture. Though also a painter, he is best remembered as the designer of some of the most innovative buildings of the Italian Renaissance.

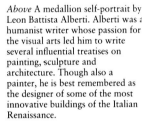

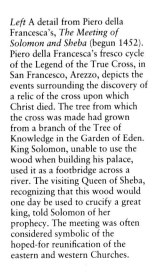

Left A detail from Piero della Francesca's, *The Meeting of Solomon and Sheba* (begun 1452). Piero della Francesca's fresco cycle of the Legend of the True Cross, in San Francesco, Arezzo, depicts the events surrounding the discovery of a relic of the cross upon which Christ died. The tree from which the cross was made had grown from a branch of the Tree of Knowledge in the Garden of Eden. King Solomon, unable to use the wood when building his palace, used it as a footbridge across a river. The visiting Queen of Sheba, recognizing that this wood would one day be used to crucify a great king, told Solomon of her prophecy. The meeting was often considered symbolic of the hoped-for reunification of the eastern and western Churches.

scholars working in academic isolation. Although Poggio wrote a number of moral and historical texts, his most popular work was a collection of 273 mildly pornographic short stories. Fascination with antiquity could veer to the eccentric. In Rome, Pomponio Leto (1428–98) founded an informal private academy for the study of ancient history. The members met for dinner regularly, discussed classical topics and gave each other classical nicknames. Leto, who wore Roman dress and kept a collection of marble inscriptions in his home, even attempted to garden according to the instructions of ancient authors.

The range of topics a humanist might cover can be seen in the career of the Florentine Leon Battista Alberti (1404–72). His family had been exiled by the Medici rulers of Florence and he spent much of his youth in Genoa and Bologna before gaining a position in the papal chancery. He finally returned to Florence with Pope Eugenius IV in the 1430s and there, in the company of artists such as Filippo Brunelleschi, began composing works that provided a theoretical underpinning for the city's remarkable artistic development. His writings on painting, sculpture and architecture were matched with treatises on moral philosophy, the family, a book on horses, a description of the ruins of Rome, a tract on secret codes and one on applied mathematics, and a grammar book designed to show that Tuscan was as elevated a language as Latin.

As Alberti's interests demonstrate, the issues that fascinated humanists were many. Their discoveries were meant to provide a new model for the ideal human existence. Moral inquiry, just balance and proper etiquette would become the concerns of both rulers and scholars. In 1373 Petrarch, adamant that "the task of restoring Padua to its former noble majesty consists not so much in large projects as in small details", had offered practical advice to the ruler of Padua, Francesco Carrara, telling him to repair the city streets and force pig-owners to keep their swine out of town. He had also warned his lord that "although soldiers can at times be useful to you and perform good services in time of war, it is only learned men who can provide the right advice at the right moment, and thus ensure your fame". Francesco Carrara's response is unknown, but other princes did take heed. The presence of humanist advisers at court or in the city became commonplace, giving their ideas a direct impact on Italian life. With the help of ancient wisdom, a well-educated man or the philosopher prince could serve his government and his people. Even aristocratic women needed such education if they were to guide their sons and daughters toward a life of virtue. In Mantua, Vittorino da Feltre (1378–1446) established a school at the Gonzaga court where he trained the children of the nobility. His star pupil was the marquis of Mantua's young daughter Cecilia, who at eight years of age astonished visitors with her knowledge of Greek. Vittorino's humanism was tinged with pragmatism. He was concerned about the children's health – one chubby child was put on a diet and all had to take plenty of exercise. Study always had to have a purpose: "Not everyone can excel in philosophy or the law, nor are all equally favored by nature; but all are destined to live in society and practice virtue."

Vittorino's legacy, the notion that scholarship and classical learning were critical components of a civilized society, has left its mark on the educational philosophy of the West. But the princes he served cared little for his posthumous reputation. Florentine governments were more magnanimous toward those scholars and civil servants who extolled the values of

The Book Hunters

With the revival of interest in Roman literature, it became necessary to find and bring together as many ancient texts as possible. The work of collecting and copying these texts formed the first phase of humanism. With the price of a professionally copied book being beyond the means of all but the very wealthy, men such as Salutati, Niccoli and Bracciolini made their own copies. Attention soon broadened to include Greek literature, and in the 1420s the entire corpus of Plato arrived in the West for the first time, brought by Giovanni Aurispa.

Poggio Bracciolini based the style of his writing on the lucid Carolingian miniscule. At the time this was called antica, today it is called roman. Niccolo Niccoli devised a speedier style of writing that became the basis for what we now call italic. Niccolo's enthusiasm for acquiring books was so great that he finally made himself bankrupt.

These books were copies, made treasures by the beauty of their miniatures and bindings. Many of the original texts found in this period failed to survive because collectors were more interested in the text than in the book as a collectable object.

Texts copied many times down the ages became peppered with errors. So the second phase of humanism is marked by the work of men such as Poliziano, who strived to produce standard correct texts.

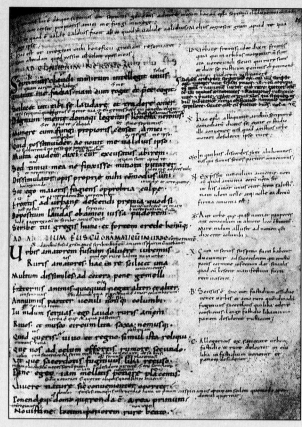

Left A page from a copy of Horace acquired by Petrarch in 1347. The notes in the margin are in Petrarch's own hand. Petrarch's friend and correspondent, Coluccio Salutati, was an enthusiastic book collector, making his own copies of texts and finding lost works. Among his pupils were Poggio Bracciolini and Leonardo Bruni, two of the leading figures in book hunting. In becoming chancellor of Florence, Salutati set the new standard of learning required for men of high office.

Right A detail from Ghirlandaio's *St Jerome* showing the kind of equipment used to copy books. Along with Augustine, Jerome became a popular subject in 15th-century art as both patriarchs symbolized the ideal of the humanist scholar: the man made wise by study.

The rediscovery of classical manuscripts
The classical texts lost to the West were more often than not rediscovered in the West in monastic libraries. Such libraries, however, which for centuries had protected ancient literature, had become places of decay and neglect. It is to Poggio Bracciolini (*above*) and Niccolo Niccoli that we owe a significant proportion of the classical texts now known to us. Like Bruni, Poggio obtained a post as an apostolic secretary, a position that entailed traveling with popes and cardinals and so gave ideal opportunities for seeking texts in the monasteries of France, the Rhineland and Switzerland.

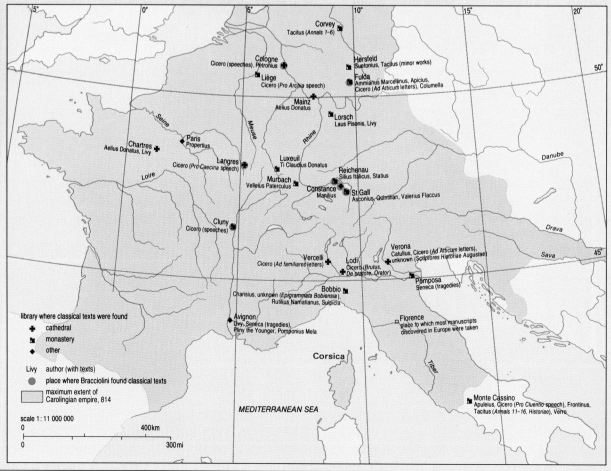

Corvey
Tacitus (Annals 1–6)

Cologne
Cicero (speeches), Petronius

Hersfeld
Suetonius, Tacitus (minor works)

Liège
Cicero (Pro Archia speech)

Fulda
Ammianus Marcellinus, Apicius,
Cicero (Ad Atticum letters), Columella

Mainz
Aelius Donatus

Lorsch
Laus Pisonis, Livy

Chartres
Aelius Donatus, Livy

Paris
Propertius

Langres
Cicero (Pro Caecina speech)

Luxeuil
Ti Claudius Donatus

Reichenau
Silius Italicus, Statius

Murbach
Velleius Paterculus

Constance
Manilius

St Gall
Asconius, Quintilian, Valerius Flaccus

Cluny
Cicero (speeches)

Verona
Catullus, Cicero (Ad Atticum letters),
unknown (Scriptores Historiae Augustae)

Vercelli
Cicero (Ad familiares letters)

Lodi
Cicero (Brutus,
De oratore, Orator)

Pomposa
Seneca (tragedies)

Bobbio
Charisius, unknown (Epigrammata Bobiensia),
Rutilius Namatianus, Sulpicia

Avignon
Livy, Seneca (tragedies),
Pliny the Younger, Pomponius Mela

Florence
place to which most manuscripts
discovered in Europe were taken

Corsica

Monte Cassino
Apuleius, Cicero (Pro Cluentio speech), Frontinus,
Tacitus (Annals 11–16, Historiae), Varro

MEDITERRANEAN SEA

Seine
Meuse
Rhine
Loire
Danube
Drava
Sava
Tiber

library where classical texts were found
✦ cathedral
✦ monastery
◆ other

Livy author (with texts)
● place where Bracciolini found classical texts
maximum extent of Carolingian empire, 814

scale 1 : 11 000 000
0   400km
0   300mi

republican government (the so-called civic humanists). Leonardo Bruni (c. 1370–1444), chancellor of Florence, was the author of a history of the city written in imitation of classical models. In his will he asked to be buried in a modest grave marked with a simple slab. Instead, in 1444 the city gave him a state funeral and commissioned an elaborate marble monument from the sculptor Bernardo Rossellino. The tomb, erected in the Franciscan church of Santa Croce, has young cherubs dangling thick garlands of fruit and vines over a triumphal arch. On the sarcophagus, the writer himself, dressed in robes of state, lies wreathed in laurel leaves, his history of Florence clasped to his chest.

The Medici and Florence

Bruni was given such honors because he, like Coluccio Salutati, had shown that scholarship could be a political force. By their example, the two writers had illustrated the integration of academic study with an active involvement in social and political life. They had spent much of their careers defining the nature of Florentine liberty and republicanism. But by Bruni's death much of what he described had disappeared. The forms of communal government continued, but they were now controlled by a single family – the Medici. In the 1420s warfare and high taxation had revived Florence's traditional divisions. In 1433 the leader of one group, Cosimo de' Medici, was exiled to Venice. But the victorious faction, which centered on the Albizzi and Strozzi families, committed a fatal error. Florentine governments were chosen by randomly selecting names from sealed pouches. The Albizzi did not change the slips placed in these bags and consequently, when a pro-Medici government was elected in 1434, Cosimo was recalled and his enemies overthrown. The returning patrician did not make the same mistake. He repacked the pouches, ensuring that every name drawn after his return owed allegiance to his faction. Cosimo himself refrained from taking power overtly, content to let the facade of republican elections conceal his influence. He was particularly careful to appear an ordinary citizen. He drank the local wine, dressed modestly and supposedly rejected Brunelleschi's model for a new palace on the grounds that it was too grand for a mere banker. But his authority and influence were visible throughout the city in many acts of public generosity. Most of Florence's great churches and monasteries contain some direct or indirect example of Medici patronage. He gave funds to Santa Croce to build the novices' chapel, sponsored an abbey in Fiesole and personally financed the entire Observant monastery at San Marco. His neighborhood church of San Lorenzo was another beneficiary. His father had commissioned Brunelleschi's Old Sacristy for the Cathedral; when funds for the nave ran out, Cosimo stepped in to ensure that it was completed.

Medici patronage was not based entirely on political expedience. Cosimo had long been interested in scholarship, assisting promising students and loaning funds to impoverished scholars. In 1427 he went to Rome, joining Poggio Bracciolini in his search for inscriptions. Even when he became deeply involved in politics, his fascination with the ancients did not diminish. In 1462, for example, he wrote from his villa inviting the young Marsilio Ficino to visit: "Yesterday I arrived at Careggi – not so much for the purpose of improving my fields as myself – let me see you,

Medici Patronage

In 1434, Cosimo de' Medici returned to his hometown from a year-long exile in Venice, ushering in almost half a century of Medicean dominance in Florence. Although he and his sons, Piero and Giovanni, rarely held public office, their power and influence could be felt throughout the city. By manipulating the voting system, they could place their friends, neighbors and associates in strategic positions. Few decisions in Florence's town hall were taken without a visit to the Medici palace. But Cosimo was very discreet in his exercise of political authority. While claiming to act as an ordinary citizen, he built up a reputation as a discriminating artistic and literary patron. He was celebrated for his understanding and appreciation of classical learning, and for supporting artists such as Donatello, whose works were housed in the family palace. The construction of this palace, which was designed by Michelozzo in 1444, was one of Cosimo's most important undertakings, but he also took personal responsibility for a large number of public projects. Family money ensured the completion of Brunelleschi's designs for the church of San Lorenzo (whose sacristy was begun by Cosimo's father), the library and Observant Dominican monastery of San Marco, the novice's chapel in the Franciscan church of Santa Croce, and the church of the Badia outside Fiesole. Cosimo's financial support for the city and its monuments earned him the name *pater patriae* ("father of his country") after his death, a title inscribed on his simple tombstone at the foot of the high altar of San Lorenzo. His wide range of public endeavors was not matched by the next generation of Medici. Although Piero and his son Lorenzo continued to support churches and monasteries, they preferred to concentrate on their private collections of precious objects, antiquities and lavishly illustrated classical manuscripts.

Above left The frontispiece of Marsilio Ficino's translation of Plato, one of several works of scholarship commissioned by Cosimo de' Medici.

Below The Annunciation (c. 1448–50) by Fra Filippo Lippi. This picture was originally painted for the Medici palace and may have been intended to go over a doorway or even to be part of a piece of furniture.

54

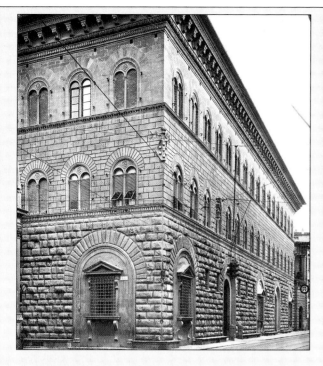

Left The Palazzo Medici, designed for Cosimo by the sculptor-architect Michelozzo, transformed the style of palace architecture in Florence. Taking its motifs from 14th-century rusticated buildings such as the city's town hall, the family palace clearly suggested that it, too, was an important public site.

Middle left Donatello's *Judith and Holofernes* (c. 1457) was originally cast as a fountain for the Medici palace. It shows Judith, a Jewish widow who seduced and then slew the Assyrian general, Holofernes, thereby saving her people. Piero de' Medici added an inscription that suggested the statue represented humility overcoming pride.

Below A marble relief of Cosimo de' Medici by Verrocchio (c. 1464). Cosimo was the founder of the family's political fortunes. Shrewd, careful and discreet, he ensured that the Medici and their allies had full control over Florence's taxation, diplomacy and justice.

Marsilio, as soon as possible, and do not forget to bring with you the book of our favorite Plato." His biographer and friend, the bookseller Vespasiano da Bisticci, could write a eulogy after his death: "Cosimo had a knowledge of Latin which would scarcely have been looked for in one occupying the station of a leading citizen engrossed with affairs. He was grave in temperament, prone to associate with men of high station who disliked frivolity and averse from all fools and actors and those who spent time unprofitably."

But political and financial responsibilities had to take precedence. As papal bankers, the Medici were already one of the wealthiest families in Florence. It has been estimated that Cosimo's father's personal wealth (80,000 florins) in 1427 could have paid the annual salaries of 2,000 laborers in the wool industry. Cosimo lent money to the Florentine government and, in turn, directed its internal politics and international diplomacy. He used his position to reverse the city's long-standing enmity with Milan. Medici money had financed Francesco Sforza's conquest of that city in 1450, and Medici loans kept the new ducal government afloat. Their alliance was directed against Venice, whose mainland territories had expanded over the century. But the fall of Constantinople to the Turks in 1453 encouraged Venice to sue for peace. In 1454 an agreement was signed whereby the peninsula's five major powers – Milan, Venice, Florence, Naples and the pope – recognized one another's boundaries and laid the ground for Italy's future stability.

The Peace of Lodi, as the treaty was known, governed diplomatic relations for the next 25 years. Although warfare was by no means a thing of the past, the battles were either confined to the south, where Neapolitan barons attempted to overthrow King Alfonso of Naples, or to minor skirmishes in the Papal State. For the first time in almost a hundred years, citizens in Florence were free from attack and invasion – a small price to pay, it seemed, for the acceptance of Medicean domination, particularly when it was so carefully disguised. Cosimo and his sons could be praised by humanists and poets alike as the defenders of a prosperity and tranquility that fostered learning and a love of the arts.

In Milan, peace brought security to the new Sforza regime. Having taken the city by force in 1450 from a republican government established after the death of the last Visconti duke in 1447, Francesco Sforza (1401–66) had no official title to the duchy. When the other major powers recognized his position, such legal niceties could be ignored. The duke and duchess were careful to appease their subjects by living modestly and providing generous public donations, such as the hospital they sponsored in 1456. Francesco, who had little education in his youth, hired the finest humanists to train his heir, Galeazzo Maria Sforza (1444–76), as the perfect Renaissance prince. The boy was taught to sing in French, write in Latin, read Greek, play the organ and the clavichord, dance, joust, ride and deliver lengthy classical speeches to visiting dignitaries. When Galeazzo Maria succeeded his father in 1466 he should have been well prepared for his new duties. Instead, he told all the humanists at court to leave, returned his Latin books to the library and set about leading a life of such debauchery and political ineptitude that three of his own courtiers murdered him a decade later.

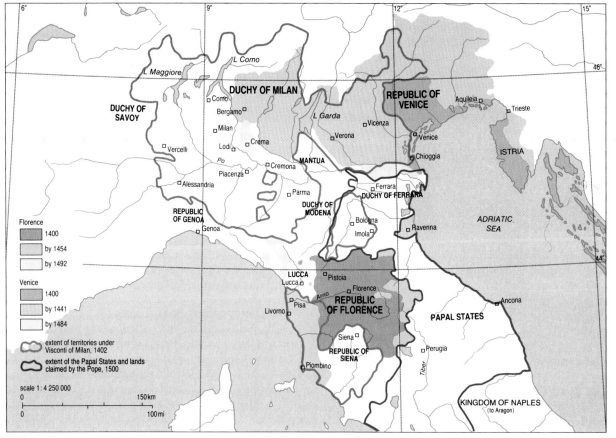

Left: The expansion of Venice, Florence and Milan
Through the 15th century, the politics of northern Italy were dominated by the increasing sway of these three states, which came into conflict on several occasions. Venice, which had long disdained expansion on the Italian mainland, challenged Visconti Milan by seizing Vicenza in 1404 and continued to build up its hinterland thereafter. This expansionism left smaller states such as Mantua and Ferrara poised uncomfortably between the major power blocs. The papacy formed a fourth major power bloc on the peninsula. The French invasion in 1494, followed later by armies from Spain and the Empire, brought a new, and ultimately disastrous, dimension to Italian politics; only Venice was to resist the invaders.

Right Bertoldo di Giovanni, medallion commemorating the Pazzi conspiracy. The greatest threat to the Medici regime came in 1478 when Pope Sixtus IV, angry at Florentine resistance toward his ambitions in the Papal States, conspired with local enemies of the Medici such as the Pazzi family to assassinate Giuliano and Lorenzo de' Medici. Giuliano was killed in the cathedral, while Lorenzo escaped by sheltering behind the heavy sacristy doors. Lorenzo both mourned his brother and celebrated his own escape. In this medallion Giuliano is seen within the octagonal choir of the cathedral.

Galeazzo Maria's assassination in 1476 brought dangers to the Medici regime, who by that stage were increasingly dependent on their Sforza alliance. The next generation of Florentine patricians had proved more ostentatious with their authority. Piero de' Medici (1416–69), Cosimo's oldest son, ignored the local Florentine aristocracy by arranging marriages with foreign nobles, betrothing his son Lorenzo (1449–92) to the daughter of a powerful Roman family, Clarice Orsini. Envy turned into internal discord. In 1466 the Pitti family conspired to overthrow the dynasty and in 1478 members of the Pazzi clan, with the connivance of the anti-Medicean Pope Sixtus IV, attempted to murder Lorenzo and his brother Giuliano during a service in the cathedral. Giuliano was killed but Lorenzo escaped by sheltering behind the bronze doors of the sacristy. The city rallied in support of the Medici and Jacopo dei Pazzi and several other conspirators were hanged from the windows of the Palazzo Vechio. The rest of the family were barred from office, imprisoned or exiled and all signs of their prestige within the city erased or defaced. Even the Piazza dei Pazzi had its name changed. Lorenzo ordered a medal commemorating the event and had wax portraits of his dead brother placed on every street corner in Florence.

Lorenzo's survival only encouraged him to act with greater firmness and determination. In his own memoirs he claimed that after his father's death he had taken over the role of leading Florence with little enthusiasm: "The chiefs of the city and the state came to our house to offer their condolences and to urge me to take over the affairs of the city as my grandfather and my father did. I accepted with reluctance, and only for the preservation of friends and family wealth." His statement makes little appeal to the public benefits his leadership would provide. It was in his and his allies' private interest to take control. Only by dominating the city could his fortune be preserved, because if the Medici did not run Florence, their enemies would. Although, like his grandfather, he still professed to be a private citizen, Lorenzo's acts were increasingly those of a prince. Although he never held senior office, few government decisions were taken without his authority, and his advice and opinions were asked on everything from new clerical appointments to new architectural styles. Like Cosimo, Lorenzo was fully involved with the scholars and artists of his city, but his patronage was very different.

Left Lorenzo de' Medici, who came to power in Florence in 1469, was a firm, determined and able leader – as this expressive bust by Verrocchio suggests. His fame, however, deserved or not, rests largely on his support for a brilliant circle of scholars, artists and poets, including Pico della Mirandola, Poliziano, Botticelli and Verrocchio. He himself was a fine poet. In this portrait he wears the garments of a Florentine man of government, clothes appropriate to a republican citizen rather than to the princely ruler he was.

Right A detail from the *Story of St. Francis* in the *Sassetti Chapel* (1485) by Ghirlandaio. In this chapel, designed to commemorate a financier with the Medici bank, Francesco Sassetti, the Medici tutor and poet Angelo Poliziano appears with the sons of Lorenzo de' Medici as well as with his fellow humanists Matteo Franco and Luigi Pulci. Relationships between scholars and patrons were often close.

Instead of spending his wealth on public building, he used it to build up a great private collection of antiquities, inscribing his name on Roman agate vases, gems and carnelians. The villa of Poggio a Caiano outside Florence, which he helped design and build, became a retreat where he could escape to listen to music, write poetry and converse with his friends and companions on philosophical topics such as the immortality of the soul. Poliziano and the poet Luigi Pulci (1432–84) acted as tutors to his children and, along with other young humanists, formed a group that exchanged letters, texts and poems, and praised their patron's achievements as a writer, musician and classical scholar. Thanks to their efforts and the later myths that accrued to his name, Lorenzo de' Medici is now bathed in a golden glow of popular legend in which his munificence and learning seem to epitomize Renaissance individualism. Certainly some of his contemporaries were anxious to promote his reign as a time of great achievements. A Medici associate, Giovanni Tornabuoni, had one of his new frescoes for his chapel in Santa Maria Novella inscribed with the boast: "In the year 1490, this most beautiful city, renowned for its power and wealth, for its victories, for the arts and its buildings, enjoyed great prosperity, health and peace." But when Lorenzo died at the comparatively early age of 43 two years later, these words seemed hollow. Lorenzo had not provided a stable future; he had carefully managed a period of decline. The Medici bank, the very foundation of the family's power, was in serious trouble. Loans had been made for political rather than monetary reasons

and the worst-hit branches, those of London, Bruges and Milan, had had to be closed. Four years after Lorenzo's death, his son Piero was forced to flee the city and a new republic was declared – one free of Medicean control.

The Medici position was also affected by the disintegrating alliance between the major Italian city-states. In 1480 Francesco Sforza's younger son Lodovico Maria (1451–1508) had taken power in Milan, ruling in the name of his nephew. When the prince died in 1494, Lodovico immediately proclaimed himself duke. But the legitimate heir had a powerful ally in his grandfather, the king of Naples. To protect his position, Lodovico encouraged the king of France to claim his ancient rights to southern Italy. In 1494 Charles VIII answered the invitation, marching through Italy to conquer Naples – the beginning of the Italian Wars, which dragged on until 1559. But the strategy proved disastrously destabilizing in the long term. Charles VIII's arrival near Florence gave the city an opportunity to overthrow Medici power. The French kings also had claims on Milan, through blood ties to the duke of Milan, Gian Galeazzo Visconti. Although Charles failed to establish a permanent base in Italy, his successor, Louis XII, continued his advances. Milan was now a target, and in 1500 Lodovico was captured and taken to France to die. With French armies north and south of the Apennines the history of Italy was no longer the study of local city-states but, once again, a story of European dimensions. The fate of Florence, Milan and Naples would now be decided by France and Spain.

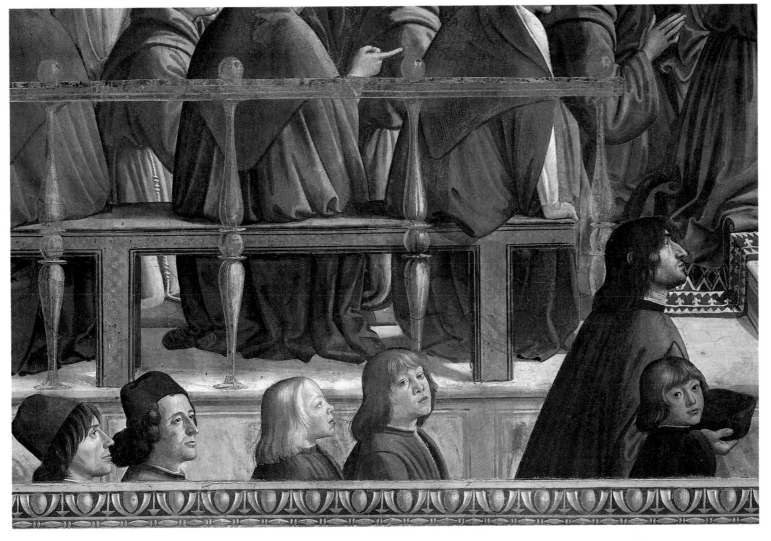

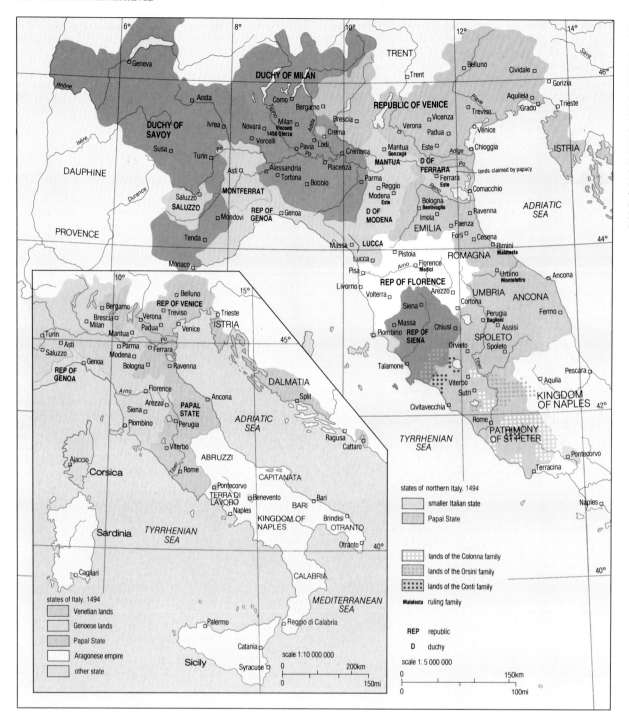

Italy in the 15th century
By the mid 13th century many Italian cities had established their independence of imperial authority, and were faced with a new form of squabbling politics. Few were able to preserve this independence in the face of the rising power of a few cities – notably Venice, Milan and Florence – and several powerful dynasties. Among the most powerful were the Visconti, who from Milan were able to dominate most of northern Italy in the last years of the 14th century. The Medici, despite the republican constitution of Florence, were another dynasty with enormous power. Other states, such as Venice and the papacy, had elected heads.

The impact of antiquity

If the history of 14th-century patronage usually focuses on public, communal commissions, the emphasis in the 15th century shifts to the private aristocratic world of the wealthy individual. The revival of antiquity was, therefore, closely linked to the powerful group of patrons and their humanist advisers. Although Cosimo de' Medici used his resources to found a monastic library in San Marco, most patrons of the period reveled in the personal possession of fine manuscripts, gems, cameos, medals and musical instruments, items that could be seen only within small but richly decorated private studios or *studioli*. Few of these remarkable rooms have survived intact. Only terracotta roundels with signs of the zodiac remain from Piero de' Medici's study in Florence. The best-preserved example is undoubtedly that of the duke of Urbino, Federigo da Montefeltro (1422–82).

His career was a typical Renaissance tale. The illegitimate son of the rule of a small provincial town in the Apennines, he had studied with the Gonzaga children at Vittorino da Feltre's school in Mantua. He then made his fortune as a mercenary soldier, losing an eye in a battle. When his half-brother was assassinated in 1444, Federigo was called to restore order and reestablish the family's control in Urbino. He proved an immensely popular ruler. His profits as a *condottiere* meant that taxes were low and his earnings could be invested in embellishing the town and his palace. His *studiolo* was filled with cupboards decorated with illusionistic intarsia work, depicting books, statuettes, scientific instruments and musical instruments as well as armor and weaponry. These illustrated his dual nature as a man of arms and a man of letters, a master of both the sword and the pen. Above the cabinets were portraits of famous men of letters: Plato, Aristotle, Homer and Virgil next to images of Petrarch, Dante and Federigo's own schoolmaster, Vittorino da Feltre. They surveyed the duke as he worked.

Rooms to which princes could retreat to contemplate the past were also used by a number of Italian women. The most famous female collector, was Isabella d'Este (1474–1539), the marchioness of Mantua. She grew up in the court of Ferrara, where she received a classical education. At 16 she married Francesca Gonzaga and moved to Mantua, where she lived 49 years, often acting as regent during the many absences of her husband, a *condottiere*. She was an avid collector of antiquities even though she lacked the resources to make major purchases. Isabella encouraged gifts – Cesare Borgia presented her with Michelangelo's *Cupid* – and was not averse to taking objects when an opportunity presented itself. She had no complaints when her Mantuan agent joined a mob sacking a patrician palace in Bologna in order to snatch two ancient busts. In 1506 she could write with satisfaction: "We have obtained both the agate vase and the Jan van Eyck... as well as Andrea Mantegna's Faustina [a bust of the Roman empress once owned by the artist Mantegna] and so – little by little – we are advancing our plans for the collection." When her estate was inventoried after her death she owned over 1,600 items, including precious stone vases, bronze and marble statues, gems, coins and medals. The objects required a suitable place for storage and display. In 1496 she began to commission paintings

for her study from the best available artists. Seven based on classical allegories of Christian virtues were eventually painted by Andrea Mantegna, Piero Perugino, Lorenzo Costa and Correggio. Eventually the collection grew so large that it expanded into a set of nearby rooms, known as the "Grotto". Here she gave musical recitals and kept gems, medals, busts and statuettes as well as natural curiosities such as a "unicorn" horn, amber and a fish tooth.

Isabella was happy to show her collection to distinguished visitors. The study and its objects demonstrated her prestige, wealth and learning. As the 15th century drew to a close, however, the study's original function, as a retreat from the cares of an increasingly violent world, became more important. The political philosopher Niccolò Machiavelli's words on his use of the study to visit the ancients come from a man deeply troubled with his own world:

When evening comes, I return home and go into my study. On the threshold I strip off my muddy, sweaty, workday clothes, and put on the robes of court and palace, and in this graver dress I enter the antique courts of the ancients and am welcomed by them, and there I taste the food that alone is mine, for which I was born. There I make bold to speak to them and ask the motives for their actions, and they, in their humanity, reply to me. And for the space of four hours

Below Andrea Mantegna, *Parnassus*. The first of a series of paintings produced for the *studiolo* of Isabella d'Este, *Parnassus* is a complex allegory of the cultural sophistication of the Mantuan court. Mars (war) and Venus (love) preside over Apollo and the Muses, whose dance reminds spectators that music and the arts are now able to flourish since war has been tamed by love. A poet who compared Isabella d'Este herself to Venus was, however, chided for suggesting that the marchioness would appear as a nude female whose husband, Vulcan, rages over the infidelity of his wife.

I forget the world, remember no vexations, fear poverty no more, tremble no more at death: I pass into their world.

Machiavelli had found, like Petrarch before him, that the past, as represented in ancient texts, coins and medals, could be a more pleasant place than the present. Antiquity might be a means of improving men's morals, but for many the study of the past was merely a measure of the disintegration of modern man.

Antiquity and the Church

Those fearful of the world's fate looked to the Church as well as to antiquity for guidance. Some believed that it was impossible for a humanist to be a good Catholic. One Florentine preacher railed against parents who taught their children the names of Venus, Jupiter and Saturn instead of the Father, Son and Holy Ghost. But the Christian and classical worlds were not irreconcilable. Marsilio Ficino's neo-Platonic writings were animated by his desire to find God through spiritual beauty. His close friend Pico della Mirandola (1463–94) was a follower of the radical Florentine preacher Savonarola. The Catholic Church was not, however, a haven of peace and tranquility in the early decades of the 15th century. There were three competing popes in 1414, one from France and two from Italy. The situation was only resolved the following year when two were deposed and the third resigned. In 1417 Martin V became pope. At the time of his election, however, his basilica was in the hands of a *condottiere*, Braccio da Montone, and it was not until 1420 that he was able to enter the city. Rome, according to most observers, was a desolate sight. Its small population, about 25,000, was concentrated near the river Tiber and away from the low-lying malaria infested plains. The stones of the Coliseum were being removed for lime-burning or building work. Weeds covered the antiquities, and abject poverty could be seen everywhere. The inhabitants were far from welcoming, and the warfare that followed the death of Martin V forced the new pope, the Venetian Eugenius IV, to flee in 1433, rowing across the Tiber disguised as a monk. He was not able to return for 10 years.

Eugenius and his successors had two conflicting purposes during the 15th century: to restore political authority in their Italian territories and spiritual authority in Europe. As in earlier centuries, the concern with land made it difficult to differentiate between the papacy and any other form of princely leadership. Martin V and his successors did not help matters by using their position to reward and enrich their family. The Borgia pope Alexander VI (1492–1503), who married his daughter Lucrezia to three of Italy's rulers and carved out a state for his son Cesare in the Romagna, was the most notorious example of papal corruption.

The need to reestablish Roman authority brought substantial benefits to the eternal city. In 1447, much to the surprise of many observers, the cardinals elected a humanist scholar, Tommaso Parentucelli, as pope – Nicholas V (1447–55). As an impoverished student the new pope had helped catalog the Medici library and been a tutor to the Strozzi children. As pope he immediately set about forming a collection of texts for the Vatican. His other major responsibility was the physical restoration of the decaying city. Alberti, by then a member of the papal secretariat, dedicated his

Left Adoration of the Magi (1438–45), by Fra Angelico. As the founder of the Observant Dominican monastery of San Marco, Cosimo de' Medici was given a double cell along one of the monastic corridors on the main floor. Fra Angelico frescoed each cell with simple scenes designed to encourage prayer and contemplation. Cosimo's main room was decorated with the *Adoration of the Magi*, the same narrative that filled the entire chapel within the Medici palace. As unofficial rulers of Florence, the family encouraged their association with this particular biblical story. They sponsored a religious confraternity devoted to the Magi and on the feast of Epiphany processed through the city dressed in the regal costume of Magi.

treatise on architecture to Nicholas V, and began laying plans for one of the largest schemes of urban regeneration of the period. Alberti provided designs for a new St Peter's, and ideas for the surrounding neighborhood would have transformed the crowded medieval streets into broad avenues and piazzas. The pope's death in 1455 cut short his grand plans, but in 1458 a new pope was able to bring some of Alberti's ideas to fruition. Like Nicholas V, Enea Silvio Piccolomini, Pope Pius II (1458–64), was a well-known humanist scholar. But he was more concerned with restoring his birthplace, the tiny town of Corsignano, than in changing Rome. He instructed one of Alberti's followers, Bernardo Rossellino, to transform the town from a small country village into a Renaissance city. Cardinals were encouraged to buy land and build palaces, while the pope built a new public square, cathedral, town hall and an enormous private palace.

Despite their short reigns, both Nicholas V and Pius II established an important precedent. The leader of the Catholic Church needed to use his princely patronage, not personal poverty, to display his power. In 1471 a pope from the northern town of Savona, Sixtus IV (1471–84), took advantage of this ideal to transform the city. Following Nicholas V's lead, he enriched the Vatican Library with over a thousand Greek and Latin manuscripts. The Sistine Chapel in the Vatican was also his creation. In the city he rebuilt ancient churches, new bridges, and issued statutes to improve public hygiene and regularize street cleaning.

The Renaissance papacy was well aware of the need to offer a spiritual as well as a temporal revival to the beleaguered Italian peninsula. Rome was the center of the Christian world as well as of the ancient Roman empire. Popes could argue that consolidating temporal power was crucial to the reestablishment of the universal Catholic Church. Eugenius IV had already tried in 1439 to bring together Eastern and Western Churches by hosting a year-long meeting with the Byzantine emperor, John Palaeologus, and his clergy in Florence and Ferrara. After the fall of Constantinople to the Turkish sultan, Mehmed the Conqueror,

in 1453, Nicholas V called on all Christian rulers to ignore their differences and join together in a holy war against the infidel, a plea later renewed by Pius II and Sixtus IV. Their efforts were, however, a resounding failure. Despite many promises, no troops were ever sent and only a Turkish landing in southern Italy at Otranto in 1480 brought home the full danger. Fortune, rather than planning, saved the peninsula as Mehmed's death in 1481 and the subsequent struggle for succession in the Ottoman empire prevented all-out war between Muslims and Christians on Italian soil.

To encourage devotion and fund the crusades against the Turks, Nicholas V and Sixtus IV both proclaimed jubilee years in Rome. These were occasions when pilgrims visited the city, made offerings and were rewarded with indulgences – papal guarantees that their sins (even murder) would be removed and that their time in purgatory would be shortened. These were very successful. The Jubilee of 1450 attracted over 100,000 visitors; so many that the main bridge across the Tiber collapsed. But for many of these pilgrims, their hopes for salvation lay not in the wealthy popes but, as in the previous century, in preachers who emerged to answer their religious anxieties. If the Borgia family was one image of the Italian church, St Bernardino of Siena (1380–1444) was the other. Born to an aristocratic Sienese family, his early life demonstrates the type of popular religion familiar to his contemporaries. He studied law and was fond of poetry. But as a youth he became a member of a confraternity whose members met in secret to whip themselves and to sing praises to the Virgin Mary. When he joined the Franciscans, his gift for preaching became apparent. As he traveled through Italy, the urban churches proved too small to hold his audiences and he gathered the crowds in town squares. The effects were dramatic. In Milan, businessmen gave up their jobs and gave away their wealth, warring families made peace, and, as one writer from Viterbo put it, "we were so full of piety after hearing him that we felt we had all become

Previous page Pinturricchio, *Scenes from the Life of Enea Silvio Piccolomini* (1503–08). Commissioned by Cardinal Francesco Piccolomini in the early 16th century, the frescoes in the library attached to the cathedral of Siena celebrate the deeds of his illustrious uncle, Enea Silvio Piccolomini, who became Pope Pius II. Ten frescoes recreate a flattering view of his career and successes. This scene shows him as bishop of Siena presiding over the marriage of the emperor Frederick III and Eleanor of Aragon.

saints". Bernardino, who refused to wear shoes and to accept any money, should have been, like St Francis before him, a scourge to the established Church. He was, indeed, accused of heresy on a number of occasions. But the wealthy Italian rulers and the papacy saw the benefits of harnessing his abilities. He was encouraged to help reform the Franciscans, which were now split between those who supported a more comfortable existence (Conventuals) and those who wanted to return to a harsher but purer age (Observants).

Pope Eugenius IV was a firm supporter of the new friars, the Observants, and encouraged Cosimo de' Medici to support their monasteries in Florence. In San Marco, the Observant Dominican church, Cosimo built new cloisters and invited a member of the order, Fra Angelico, to paint their walls. Fra Angelico (1387–1455) and his assistants decorated each monk's cell with a simple devotional image in clear, pure colors that were designed to assist meditation. The last cell in the long dormitory belonged to Cosimo himself, where he too could retire from the cares of Florentine politics and immerse himself in the contemplation of the life hereafter.

Fra Angelico's frescoes and St Bernardino's sermons were only a fraction of the many remarkable responses to the travails of 15th-century religious experience. For all the emphasis on the classical, pagan revival of the period, salvation remained an essential human concern of men and women throughout Italy.

The arts in Florence

Few Florentines were permitted inside the monks' cells in San Marco. Citizens could not, however, ignore the dramatic physical changes taking place all around them. Florentines in particular could judge the prestige of their wealthy patriciate by the large number of palaces built in the 15th century. Although they were still very mixed, philosophical attitudes toward wealth and its display had been changing for some time. Whereas once poverty had been held up as a superior state to riches, now a more moderate concept held that men of influence had a duty to display the virtues of magnificence. By building palaces and sponsoring public and religious institutions, they spread rather than hoarded their wealth to the benefit of the city and the Church. This rationale was used to justify increasing expenditure on lavish private estates. Cosimo de' Medici's home on the Via Larga, built in 1444, was only one of many fine buildings erected in the 15th century. Thirty were built between 1450 and 1470 alone. The Medici palace, designed by Michelozzo (1396–1472), with its solid, rusticated, fortress-like exterior, was imitated by many other patrician builders.

One patron, however, chose a very different format. Giovanni Rucellai (1403–81), who was married to a member of the Strozzi family (an anti-Medicean clan), had barely escaped exile in 1434. For 30 years the ruling faction kept him from political office, relenting only in the 1460s when Cosimo married his granddaughter to Giovanni's grandson. The isolation did not, however, prevent financial success. Rucellai, the third wealthiest man in Florence, used his riches to the benefit of his family, his neighborhood and the city. His purpose was clear: to ensure that he and his family were remembered in later years as generous, respectable aristocrats. He began with a new palace, designed by Leon Battista Alberti (or one of his followers). The facade was based on the orders of the Roman Coliseum and the friezes decorated with Rucellai's personal insignia. Alberti was also responsible for the design of the merchant's tomb in the local church of San Pancrazio, a remarkable monument built in imitation of the Holy Sepulcher in Jerusalem. Rucellai even wrote to the Levant to get its precise measurements. This combination of classical study and Christian belief characterized Rucellai's final commission for Alberti's skills, the unfinished facade of the Dominican monastery of Santa Maria Novella. There Alberti was careful to absorb the general style of the 14th-century lower storeys. But on the upper section, huge Roman letters told approaching worshipers that Giovanni Rucellai had paid for its completion.

Although wealthy individuals such as Rucellai took increasing responsibility for much of Florence's art, communal sponsorship did not entirely cease. Nevertheless, close examination of such commissions reveals that the Medici and their supporters were often to be found among the committee members who awarded public contracts. Their actions, however, were closely scrutinized by other leading citizens and their patronage remained a very public issue, hotly debated and assessed by all members of the community. The open nature of artistic competition was an important part of Florence's cultural preeminence, encouraging artists and patrons alike to greater efforts in return for public appreciation and prestige. In 1401, for example, the guild responsible for one of Florence's most important buildings, the Baptistery, decided to order a new set of bronze doors. Two goldsmiths, Lorenzo Ghiberti (1378–1455) and Filippo Brunelleschi (1377–1446) were invited to provide trial pieces based on the biblical story of Abraham and Isaac. The winner would be given the massive enterprise, estimated to take up to 10 years of full-time work. It took almost two years of debate before the winner was declared. The two panels, which now hang side by side in the Bargello Museum in Florence, are very different from each other and from the sculpture of contemporaries. Yet both sculptors used antique sources to illustrate their skills. With his figure of a boy examining his foot, Brunelleschi quoted a famous Roman bronze, *The Thorn Puller*. In his Isaac, Ghiberti produced one of the first classical nudes since antiquity.

Ghiberti, who cast his sample in a single piece, won the competition because of his technical superiority. It took him 25 years to complete the doors and as soon as he was finished he was asked to produce yet another set, the *Gates of Paradise*. His skill also resulted in commissions for large bronze statues to fill the niches on the exterior of Orsanmichele, which was owned by Florence's major guilds. The market had finally been moved from the building at the end of the 14th century and its walls enclosed. In 1406 the government, angered by the guilds' reluctance to fulfill their obligations to provide major shrines, threatened to take away their rights over the site unless they immediately erected altars. The threat led to an intense program of decoration. As they passed along the main street, Florentines could watch with fascination as each year brought yet another masterpiece of sculpture. Ghiberti produced three life-sized figures in metal; Donatello and Nanni di Banco (c. 1384–1421) attempted to outshine him with their mastery of marble. By the mid 15th century Orsanmichele had become an unrivaled advertisement for the wealth of the city's guilds and the talents of its artists.

The only major sculptor missing from the site was Brunelleschi. After his defeat in the Baptistery competition in 1402 he rarely attempted to work as a sculptor again. But he was compensated with the job of completing the Cathedral's cupola. The Cathedral's 14th-century architecture demanded a domed roof larger than any ever built before. The technical problems were daunting and Brunelleschi's solution, a double dome with a strong inner shell and a light high outer shell, was remarkably elegant in its simplicity. This and other examples of his engineering and design abilities led to further commissions from the government for fortresses and military defenses, and from private and ecclesiastical patrons for new chapels and churches. The Medici were among his earliest patrons. Cosimo's parents requested the employment of Brunelleschi on the sacristy they were sponsoring in their neighborhood church of San Lorenzo. Cosimo himself ensured that the rest of the building was constructed according to the architect's plans. The work Brunelleschi performed there and at the Innocenti Hospital had a dramatic impact. The familiar pointed arches, soaring vaults and brick columns of Gothic churches were replaced by the simple proportions and classical references Brunelleschi took from early Christian and antique models. Even the colors, the pale blue-grays of the soft *pietra serena* stone he introduced, changed the viewer's experience of a religious building.

Although he was closely connected to the Medici family, others were quick to recognize Brunelleschi's extraordinary abilities. Giovanni Rucellai wrote: "There has been no one since the days when the Roman ruled the world, so accomplished in architecture and geometry and sculpture; he is a man of much genius and imagination." Skill, charm and diplomacy gave him social advantages that Ghiberti, despite his attempts to write a treatise on painting, never achieved. In 1425, for example, Brunelleschi became the first sculptor and architect to join the Florentine government.

Brunelleschi's contemporary and friend, the sculptor Donatello (c.1386–1466), was equally successful in his work but loath to take such a public stage. He was the son of a wool-comber, and it was said that when Cosimo de' Medici gave him a red cloak (a garment worn only by the wealthy), the sculptor felt it inappropriate to his station and refused to wear it. But, like Giotto before him, his skills were in demand throughout Italy and he traveled widely, exploring and collecting antiques in Rome and working throughout central and northern Italy. Donatello did not have to seek work. He could pick and choose from a variety of patrons anxious for his services. Even the king of Naples had to flatter the artist in the hope that he might condescend to join his court, writing: "We have heard of the skill and subtlety of the master Donatello in making both bronze and marble statues. There has come upon us a great wish to have him at our court in our service for some time."

The king was unsuccessful in his request, for Donatello was notoriously independent. Even when he accepted a commission, he did not always bother to complete work ordered by his most illustrious clients. The lords of Mantua and Ferrara tried fruitlessly to persuade him to return to their cities to complete unfinished statues. But when his imagination and

interest were fully engaged, as it was in Padua between 1444 and 1453, Donatello's output was prodigious. For that university town he produced a monumental shrine to St Anthony and a large free-standing equestrian statue of the *condottiere* Erasmo da' Narni, better known by his nickname, Gattamelata ("Honey-Cat").

Donatello modeled the horse's head on antique prototypes in the Medici collection and his most original and disturbing pieces were done for Cosimo's enjoyment. The bronze *David* (c. 1430), which once stood in the Medici palace courtyard, has a sensuality that seems inappropriate for an Old Testament figure. An inscription on its base informed viewers that this was a symbol of Florentine liberty (Florence being a defenseless David against a Giant, Milan). But even this interpretation could not disguise its very personal nature. The deliberate evocation of republican ideology was used again to justify the production of Donatello's bronze *Judith and Holofernes* (c. 1457). Originally produced as a fountain for the Medici palace gardens, the Jewish heroine who murdered the Assyrian to save her people was meant to be a symbol of humility's victory over pride. Nevertheless, the powerful image of a woman decapitating her half-dressed would-be lover was too disturbing for many Florentines. When it was moved to the Piazza della Signoria after the Medici downfall in the 1490s, a petition was put forward to remove it from public view, since "it is not appropriate to show a woman killing a man". Donatello's close personal relationship with Cosimo de' Medici may have given him considerable freedom in his choice of subject matter and style of execution. Piero de' Medici placed Donatello's body in a tomb near Cosimo's in the church of San Lorenzo.

If Brunelleschi and Donatello are regarded as the leading architects and sculptors of their day, Masaccio (1401–28) is usually given the same prominence in the field of painting. Masaccio had a short career, dying before the age of 30. In his brief lifetime, however, he managed to make many of Brunelleschi's mathematical achievements more accessible to his fellow Florentines. Perspective, the technique of producing an accurate, measurable representation of three-dimensional space on a two-dimensional surface was one of Brunelleschi's major discoveries. Masaccio was quick to grasp its possibilities. He first used the concept in his narrative frescoes of the Life of St Peter for the Brancacci Chapel in Santa Maria del Carmine. Then, shortly before his death in 1429, he perfected the technique – in a frescoed version of the Hopy Trinity in Santa Maria Novella – by which he gave vivid reality to the complex religious subject of God the Father, the Son, and the Holy Ghost. Mary and St John the Evangelist, together with the two donors, stand firmly on their plinths, while the place of the mystical Trinity cannot be defined. The bottom of the cross sits toward the front of the picture but its top is at the back. Here perspective enforces the contrast between the "real" space of the human world and the immeasurable realm of the divine.

Brunelleschi, Donatello and Masaccio are often taken as the epitome of Renaissance achievement. Breaking the boundaries of convention, merging innovative techniques with centuries-old traditions of craftsmanship, they seem close to our view of the modern progressive artist. Yet they were all firmly bound within the social structure of their own period.

Left Donatello's statue of a prophet, popularly known as *Zuccone* or "pumpkin-head", was carved between 1423 and 1425. A dramatic figure, his twisting posture and compelling gaze would have been impressive even to viewers on the ground far below his niche on the belltower of Florence cathedral.

Right Masaccio's *Holy Trinity* (1427) was the last work he completed before he died in Rome in 1428. It is an extraordinary experiment in spatial depth. The donors, the Virgin, and Saint John the Evangelist stand in a concrete, mathematically definable space. The Trinity, however, is set within a different perspective. Masaccio was thus able to use the system of perspective to show how an important theological concept such as the Trinity cannot be confined or contained in an earthly world.

Below Masaccio, *Tribute Money* (c. 1424–25), The Brancacci Chapel, Florence. Commissioned by Felice Brancacci in the early 1420s from Masaccio and his older colleague, Masolino, the frescoes of the Brancacci Chapel first demonstrated on a large scale the new techniques made possible by linear perspective. The story of Christ's instruction to St Peter to pay the tribute demanded by Caesar (to the left of the picture the saint discovers the necessary coins in the mouth of a fish) had a particular relevance in Florence, where a new system of direct taxation was being introduced. The Brancacci were very influential in getting the *catasto*, a survey of the wealth and holdings of all local families, accepted by the Florentine government.

Strong personalities in their own right, Donatello and Masaccio actually spent much of their careers working in close collaboration with other artists. The sculptor set up a company with his fellow Florentine Michelozzo to produce tombs, tabernacles and pulpits for clients throughout Italy. Masaccio painted many of his altarpieces and the Brancacci Chapel itself alongside an older painter, Masolino, whose gentler style was very different from his own. The concept of the Renaissance artist as an emerging multitalented intellectual is not wrong, but it must be balanced with an understanding of the strength of Florence's workshop tradition and the continuity of craftsmanship.

The arts in Venice

In northern Italy artists' workshops were often made up of entire families. Brothers, sons, sons-in-law and occasionally even daughters ensured that styles and techniques were passed down from generation to generation. New ideas could also be quickly absorbed and spread. The vogue for perspective and measured drawing is first seen in a sketchbook from the 1430s by the Venetian painter Jacopo Bellini (c. 1400–c.1470). This shows the artist struggling to come to terms with the new mathematics. The rest of his family, particularly his sons Giovanni (c.1430–1516) and Gentile (c.1429–1507) had fewer difficulties and their patrons were quick to see the possibilities of this "modern" technique. This was not the only innovation to reach Venice. The use of oil-based paints, widely known in the Netherlands, was also pioneered in Italy by artists working in Venice.

The city provided numerous artistic opportunities and a wide range of potential patrons. The nobility who ran the senate never allowed a single family to gain control of their government. Their marble palaces, extravagant displays of wealth and prestige, still line the Grand Canal today. The city's leader, the doge, was a powerful figure, but he was expected to represent the rest of the patriciate and maintain a sense of community through lavish processions and ritual performances. Every year, for example, he married the sea, throwing a ring into the ocean in an elaborate ceremony designed to symbolize Venice's maritime powers. The doge's palace on the Piazza San Marco was both his personal residence and the site of

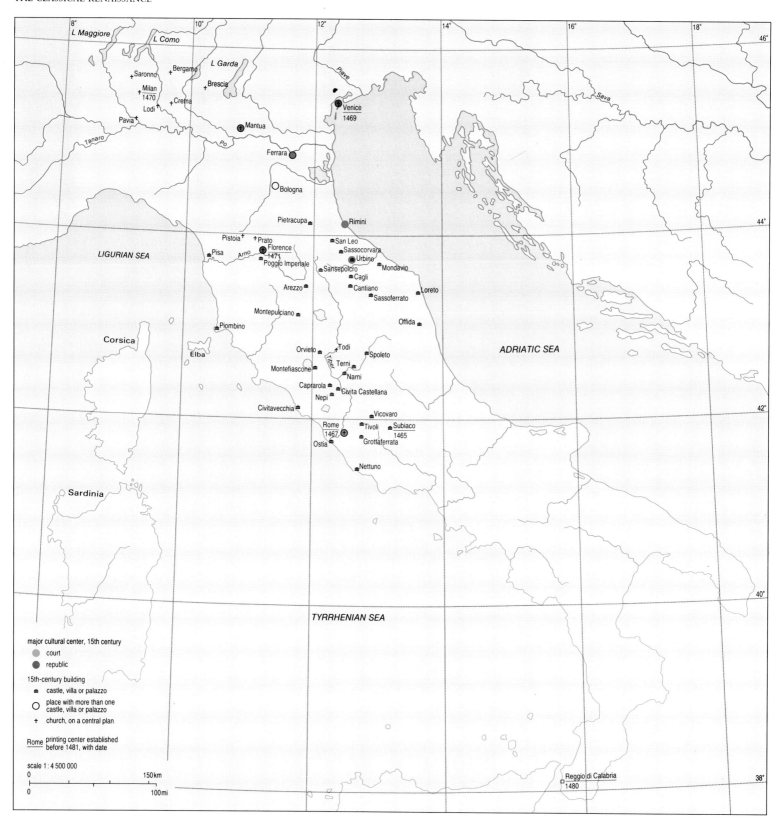

government. In the 15th century artists such as Gentile da Fabriano (c. 1370–c. 1427), Pisanello (1395–1455) and the Bellini brothers were invited to paint in the hall of the Great Council celebrations of military victories or important moments in Venetian history. Their work was destroyed by fire in the 16th century but some of their rich, theatrical narrative style can still be seen in the commissions of Venice's other corporate patrons, the lay brotherhoods or *scuole*. These confraternities offered wealthy citizens, particularly those not admitted to government, a chance to participate in public life. Men and women paid subscriptions to ensure a form of welfare service. In

return the *scuole* cared for their members and their families when they were ill, provided decent funerals and annuities for widows. They also served an important social function, with members meeting for religious festivals and public processions. Their halls and chapels were painted with canvases detailing the lives of their patron saints, such as those Vittore Carpaccio (c. 1457–c. 1522) provided for the confraternity of St Ursula. The artist's images of Ursula's life fuse a remarkably detailed impression of Venetian life with an imaginative vision that removes the event from any one time and place. He managed to achieve the same effect in his nonreligious paintings, such as his por-

Right The *Dream of St Ursula* (1490–95) by Carpaccio. The paintings of Carpaccio are remarkable for their meticulous representations of everyday life. In this picture every detail of the bedroom is observed – the wooden clogs under the bed, the hourglass near an open book, the mortar and pestle on the wall, the intricate carvings around the bed. Yet these very details, the open spaces and the subtle light effects lend an air of unreality to the scene. As the princess sleeps an angel brings her the palm of martyrdom.

Cultural centers of 15th-century Italy
The artistic life of the 15th century depended on the great patrons, whether in ducal courts such as at Mantua or Urbino, or civic patrons as at Venice. The emphasis on courtly living gave great importance to the palace and the villa as architectural forms. The Church, by comparison, was less important as a patron of the arts than would be the case in the following centuries. As the new technology of printing spread south of the Alps, its adoption in the great cities contributed to the intensity of intellectual life there; in the 1470s 40 percent of all printed books were Italian, and the proportion had fallen only slightly 20 years later.

trayal of two Venetian ladies, possibly courtesans, wearing low-cut dresses and fashionable hairstyles. While less well-known than his Florentine contemporaries, Carpaccio had the ability – one he shared with his contemporaries Giovanni and Gentile Bellini – of transforming the mundane detail of everyday life into a special, meditative moment has arrested the attention of viewers for centuries.

Artists at the princely courts

Florence and Venice had a large urban aristocracy interested in demonstrating their family position by sponsoring scholarship and the arts. Italy's other major centers also had a wide range of patrons, but there the main focus was often on the princely court. In Milan, Ferrara, Mantua, Urbino and Naples the ruler's image was stamped on coins, erected on homes and gates, worn as jewelry and painted on flags and banners. Unlike the republics, where a variety of private patrons competed to display their wealth, only the prince was permitted to flaunt his prestige and authority. State images had to reflect his personal qualities. In Ferrara the citizens "volunteered" to put up statues in honor of their lords Niccolò and Borso d'Este. After Alfonso of Aragon finally captured Naples in 1444, his supporters erected a triumphal arch to commemorate the victory. In Milan, partisans of the Sforza family put portraits of the ducal family on their palace facades.

Some towns were effectively extensions of the prince's court. Urbino and Rimini had been sleepy backwaters until their ruler's *condottiere* booty had brought a measure of wealth and sophistication. The ducal palace in Urbino dominated the small town, while under Sigismondo Pandolfo Malatesta, Rimini benefited from a major new Franciscan church, now known as the Malatesta Temple. The design by Alberti was meant to rival the Pantheon in Rome. The old

building was given a cladding of white marble and rare stones (many taken from a local monastery), and a monumental facade based on ancient triumphal arches. Greek inscriptions celebrated the patron's military prowess and piety, while the tombs on the exterior, modeled on ancient sarcophagi, held the bodies of poets such as Basinio da Parma, who had once praised the *condottiere*'s achievements.

Alberti was also involved in another small princely court in Mantua. For his friend and patron Lodovico Gonzaga he devised two innovative churches, Sant' Andrea and the centrally planned San Sebastiano, based on the principles of the Roman architect Vitruvius. Neither was completed during the 15th century, but Alberti's architectural experiments ensured that his theoretical concepts were taken seriously by later generations. Another artist permanently based at the Mantuan court, Andrea Mantegna (1431–1506), was also given considerable freedom to try new methods and styles of painting. In return, he ensured that the Gonzaga were remembered as celebrated patrons of the arts. Mantegna's most famous work, the painted chamber or *camera picta* in the castle of St George, recreates a family meeting against a luxurious background of golden drapery and lush scenery. Innumerable portraits of relatives, courtiers and friends were carefully painted there, including the king of Denmark, Christian I, who had recently visited Mantua, and the Holy Roman Emperor, who had given the ruler of Mantua the title of Count Palatine.

Not all princely commissions were so exalted. An artist who managed to attract the lord's attention would be required to undertake any number of tasks, from designing theatrical backdrops, sketching em-

broidery and costume designs, or taking portraits of prospective brides and bridegrooms to other courts. He was also expected to have a certain courtier-like facility. The high status of a skilled artisan was, of course, not a new phenomenon. Giotto had been a member of the king of Naples' household in the 14th century and the inscriptions on the Pisani pulpits suggest that personal modesty was not their strong point. But in an age when humanists such as Alberti practiced architecture and architects wrote treatises, the once firm distinctions between the practicing craftsman and the intellectual aristocrat began to blur.

The crystallization of Renaissance culture
During the 15th century the ideas and artistic achievements of the 14th century grew into a more forceful and more coherent set of attitudes. The interest in antiquity turned into a cult of antiquity, with scholars seeking to establish high-quality texts of antique writings and to understand and revive the full range of classical culture. Some scholars, such as Alberti, sought to systematize both ancient and modern knowledge in the form of treatises. Scholars found that their discoveries, particularly in the fields of political theory, history and morality, were of relevance to contemporary rulers. Renaissance ideas and arts were therefore taken up enthusiastically by town leaders and princes in many parts of Italy. Even the papacy, trying to revive its fortunes after the return to Rome from Avignon in 1420, joined in. By the end of the 15th century, though Italy remained "medieval" in many respects, its culture had become distinctly different from that found beyond the Alps.

Above Andrea Mantegna, *The Gonzaga Family and Court* (1472), the *camera picta*, Castello di San Giorgio, Mantua. Commissioned by the Marquis of Mantua, Ludovico Gonzaga, from his court painter Andrea Mantegna, the *camera picta* provides one of the most evocative scenes of 15th-century court life. Waited on by courtiers, the marquis reclines in a chair (with his favorite dog, Rubino, underneath the seat) and discusses a letter with one of his secretaries. Beside him are his wife, Barbera of Brandenberg, and his daughters. Other walls in the *camera picta* create illusions of the countryside, fictive tapestries, mosaic relief and, in the ceiling above, suggest that two potted plants are in danger of falling on the heads of viewers below.

Brunelleschi: Perspective

Filippo Brunelleschi's contemporary biographer, Antonio Manetti, has left a description of the artist's first attempts to create the illusion of real space on a two-dimensional panel. It appears that having taken careful measurements of one wall from the hexagonal Florentine baptistery (*below*), Brunelleschi painted an image of the building that, depending on the viewing angle (the account is not entirely clear), either incorporated the surrounding square, or only the baptistery itself, onto a wooden panel (*right*). He then drilled a hole through the back of the painting (through the vanishing point of the picture) and set up a mirror in front of it. Viewers could then stand in the main doorway of Florence cathedral (*bottom*) and, peering through the hole into the mirror, view the reflected picture. From this angle the viewer enjoyed the illusion that the painting and the actual baptistery were one and the same.

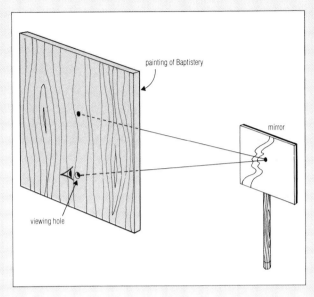

painting of Baptistery

mirror

viewing hole

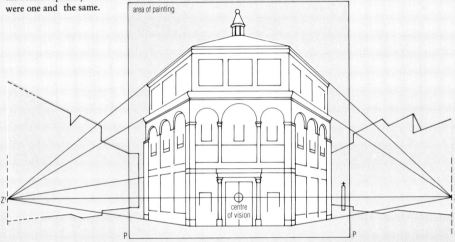

area of painting

Z¹

Z²

centre of vision

P   P

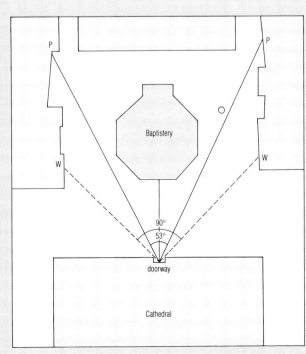

P   P

W   W

Baptistery

90°
53°

doorway

Cathedral

Linear perspective – the mathematical representation of three-dimensional space on a two-dimensional picture plane – is one of the lasting achievements of Renaissance art. Although there was a long history of interest in spatial representation, the precise technique needed was discovered by the sculptor and architect Filippo Brunelleschi during the second decade of the 15th century. Brunelleschi was educated in basic mathematics and Latin before pursuing an early career as a goldsmith. He used his learning to transform traditional surveying measurements into pictorial compositions. His first experiments resulted in two "perspective panels", one depicting the Florentine Baptistery and the other the city's town hall. Other artists were quick to see the possibilities of Brunelleschi's achievements. The sculptor Donatello began experimenting with spatial illusions in low-relief marble and bronze panels, while the painter Masaccio was able to incorporate Brunelleschi's ideas into his fresco of the Holy Trinity in Santa Maria Novella in 1427. Approximately 10 years later, the humanist Leon Battista Alberti wrote a theoretical treatise explaining the theories of perspective (the Italian translation of 1436 was dedicated to Brunelleschi). Alberti's example was followed by the sculptor Lorenzo Ghiberti, who used the new theories both in his work on the Gates of Paradise for the Florentine Baptistery and in his writings, the *Commentarii*. Paolo Uccello and Piero della Francesca, who wrote several treatises on mathematics, also managed to combine both the theory and the practice of perspective effectively.

Right Paolo Uccello, *Perspective Study of a Chalice* (c. 1430). In his life of the painter Paolo Uccello, the 16th-century writer Giorgio Vasari claimed that the artist's wife would invite Uccello to bed, only to be told that Uccello would not leave his "sweet mistress, perspective". In the 19th century, John Ruskin would claim that Uccello "went off his head with love of perspective". In his drawing of a chalice Uccello demonstrates the careful mathematics that lies behind his perspectival paintings.

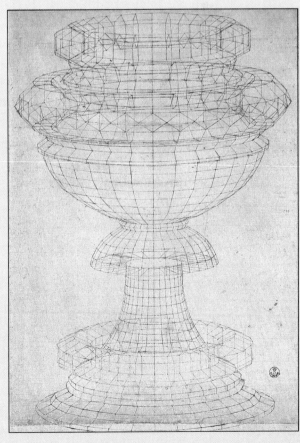

Brunelleschi: Proportion

In his 10 books on architecture, the Roman author Vitruvius laid out a system of mathematical building proportions based on the human body. The capital of a column was thought of as the head, the column as the torso, the base as the feet. Doric columns were masculine, corinthian columns female. That "man was the measure of all things" was a recognizable ancient motif taken up again in the 15th century by the architects and theorists engaged in the study of perspective, Brunelleschi and Alberti.

Geometric projections had long been the hallmark of the medieval masons' system of construction. But Brunelleschi's buildings did not hide their underlying structure. Made up of circles and squares, hemispheres and cubes, his buildings carefully articulated the principles of proportion that lay behind the design.

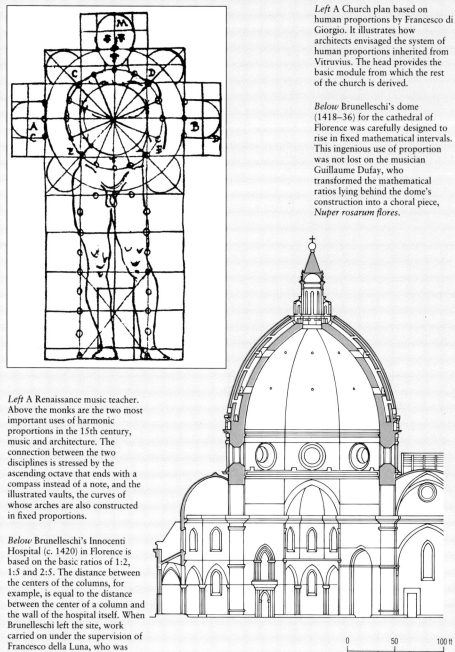

Left A Church plan based on human proportions by Francesco di Giorgio. It illustrates how architects envisaged the system of human proportions inherited from Vitruvius. The head provides the basic module from which the rest of the church is derived.

Below Brunelleschi's dome (1418–36) for the cathedral of Florence was carefully designed to rise in fixed mathematical intervals. This ingenious use of proportion was not lost on the musician Guillaume Dufay, who transformed the mathematical ratios lying behind the dome's construction into a choral piece, *Nuper rosarum flores.*

Left A Renaissance music teacher. Above the monks are the two most important uses of harmonic proportions in the 15th century, music and architecture. The connection between the two disciplines is stressed by the ascending octave that ends with a compass instead of a note, and the illustrated vaults, the curves of whose arches are also constructed in fixed proportions.

Below Brunelleschi's Innocenti Hospital (c. 1420) in Florence is based on the basic ratios of 1:2, 1:5 and 2:5. The distance between the centers of the columns, for example, is equal to the distance between the center of a column and the wall of the hospital itself. When Brunelleschi left the site, work carried on under the supervision of Francesco della Luna, who was later accused of misinterpreting Brunelleschi's plans.

0   50   100 ft
0   10   20   30 m

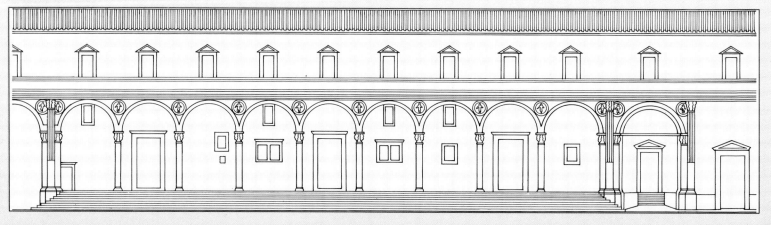

Brunelleschi's training in basic mathematics and his friendship with one of Florence's leading mathematical theorists, Paolo Toscanelli, gave him the background he required for his invention of perspective and the elaboration of his system of proportions. The Old Sacristy in San Lorenzo was the first formulation of the new style that would become so closely associated with the 15th-century Italian Renaissance. Responsible for many of the city's most prominent building projects, Brunelleschi was most renowned during his lifetime for his great feats of engineering. The erection of the dome of the cathedral of Santa Maria del Fiore proved particularly awe inspiring. Brunelleschi's achievements occurred within the heated atmosphere of Florence. He was a great rival of

the other major sculptor-architect within the city, Lorenzo Ghiberti, and entered into more friendly competition with Donatello.

Brunelleschi's system of perspective was his own remarkable discovery; his use of ornament and orders drew heavily on Romanesque models; and in his system of proportions he devised a rigorous refinement of medieval practices. It is the synthesis of these elements that gives his work its profound originality.

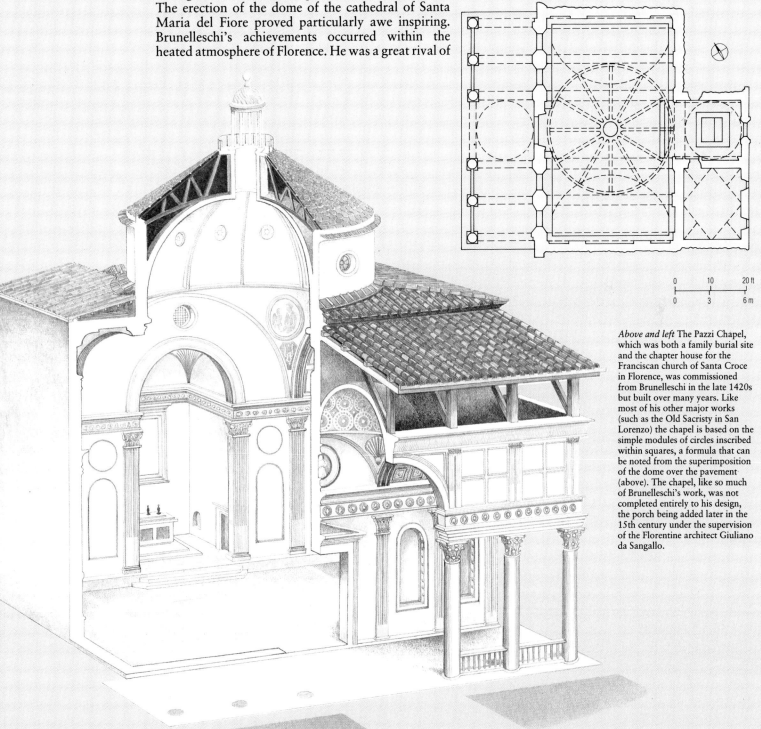

Above and left The Pazzi Chapel, which was both a family burial site and the chapter house for the Franciscan church of Santa Croce in Florence, was commissioned from Brunelleschi in the late 1420s but built over many years. Like most of his other major works (such as the Old Sacristy in San Lorenzo) the chapel is based on the simple modules of circles inscribed within squares, a formula that can be noted from the superimposition of the dome over the pavement (above). The chapel, like so much of Brunelleschi's work, was not completed entirely to his design, the porch being added later in the 15th century under the supervision of the Florentine architect Giuliano da Sangallo.

Urbino:
The Ideal City

Federigo da Montefeltro became duke of Urbino in 1444, his earnings as a professional soldier allowing him to spend lavishly as a patron. He was a successful but honorable and humane *condottiere*. He was also a man with a love of scholarship and the arts, having revived his education at the humanist school of Vittorino da Feltre in Mantua. Vittorino, he said, had instructed him in "all human excellence". It was this passion for human excellence that characterized his court.

When he appointed Francesco Laurana court architect in 1468, he emphasized that Laurana's role was "to make our city of Urbino a beautiful residence worthy of the rank and fame of our ancestors and our own status". Both the palace that was created and Montefeltro's generous support for artists and scholars made Urbino a model of the ideal city. Alberti was a regular visitor and Piero della Francesca dedicated his treatise on mathematics and perspective to the duke. Marsilio Ficino lent him his translation of Plato's *Republic*. By 1482 his library contained over a thousand manuscripts.

Federigo was succeeded by his son Guidobaldo who, along with his wife, Elisabetta Gonzaga, continued the tradition of supporting writers and artists such as Castiglione and Raphael. Castiglione's *The Courtier* evokes a colorful image of the urbane and civilized court of Urbino.

Left The *studiolo* of Federigo da Montefeltro. Portraits of famous literary figures from the classical and contemporary periods, including a painting of his old tutor, Vittorino da Feltre, lined the walls. The illusionistic intarsia work on the cupboards referred to the duke's pursuits and achievements as a man of both arms and letters.

Right Urbino was a major center of majolica ware, and Nicola da Urbino, who painted this bowl about 1520, was one of the finest majolica painters of the Urbino district.

Left Piero della Francesca's *Flagellation* is an enigmatic picture. The fact, for example, that it focuses on the unknown characters in the foreground instead of the scene of the flagellation in the rear has provoked numerous interpretations. It once bore the inscription, "They conspired together", and it has been suggested that the image alludes to both the conspiracy to kill Jesus Christ and the assassination of Federigo da Montefeltro's brother, Oddantonio.

Far left Federigo da Montefeltro with his Son, Guidobaldo, a painting attributed to Justus of Ghent (sometimes to Pedro Berruguete). This image of father and son wearing ducal regalia expresses Federigo's hopes that his only son, Guidobaldo, would follow his intellectual and political aspirations.

Below Portrait of Baldassare Castiglione (c. 1514) by Raphael. Castiglione, the author of *The Courtier*, was resident at the court of Urbino in the early 16th century, along with other important writers. His description of literary life under the duchess, Elisabetta Gonzaga, with its elegant wit and courtly behaviour, has profoundly influenced our understanding of the Umbrian court. Raphael grew up at the court, where his father Giovanni acted as poet and painter to both Duke Federigo and his son, Guidobaldo. Raphael and Castiglione remained close friends even after leaving Urbino.

Florence in 1490

When the painter Domenico Ghirlandaio finished work on the Tornabouni Chapel in Santa Maria Novella he dated the frescoes with a flourish: "In the year 1490, this most beautiful city, renowned for its power and wealth, for its victories, for the arts and its buildings, enjoyed great prosperity, health and peace."

Florence, indeed, seemed to be a town enjoying political stability and tremendous cultural excitement. The young aristocrats no longer fought street battles. They joined together to hear the lectures and discussions led by neo-Platonic philosophers and writers. Despite concern over the banking system and public finances, building work was still transforming the city's image. Lorenzo de' Medici was supervising a competition to replace the unfinished 14th-century facade on the cathedral, and encouraging his fellow citizens to straighten and widen streets and build modern palaces and villas.

This period of growth and prosperity would be looked upon with envy and nostalgia by later generations suffering from the warfare and the internal strife that followed the Medici's expulsion in 1495. The time of Lorenzo was Florence's "Golden Age".

1 Cathedral
2 Giotto's campanile
3 Baptistry
4 Palazzo Medici-Riccardi
5 San Lorenzo, Laurentian Library
6 Santa Maria Novella
7 SS. Annunziata
8 The Innocenti Hospital
9 San Marco Museum
10 Palazzo Vecchio
11 Bargello, National Museum
12 Orsanmichele
13 Santa Croce, Pazzi Chapel
14 Santa Maria del Carmine, Brancacci Chapel
15 Santa Spirito
16 Palazzo Spini
17 Palazzo Pitti, Museum
18 Palazzo Strozzi
19 Santa Trinitá
20 Uffizi Galleries (built 1560)

Right This map of Florence illustrates the city's prosperity during the 15th century. The town center was still dominated by the most important civic buildings, the town hall or *Palazzo della Signoria* at one end and the cathedral, and baptistery at the other. Orsanmichele, the shrine closely connected to the city's welfare, lay between them. The old 14th-century monastic churches, the Franciscans to the right and the Dominicans to the left, had both received significant new additions – the Pazzi Chapel based on Brunelleschi's earlier plans, and the completed facade of Santa Maria Novella designed by Leon Battista Alberti, respectively. Across the river another important Brunelleschian church, Santo Spirito, was finally nearing completion after more than half a century of delay and indecision. The most significant change, however, was the construction or modernization of almost one hundred new palaces within the town walls during the 15th century. Following the example of the Medici, aristocratic families sought to outdo each other in the size and scale of their new residences.

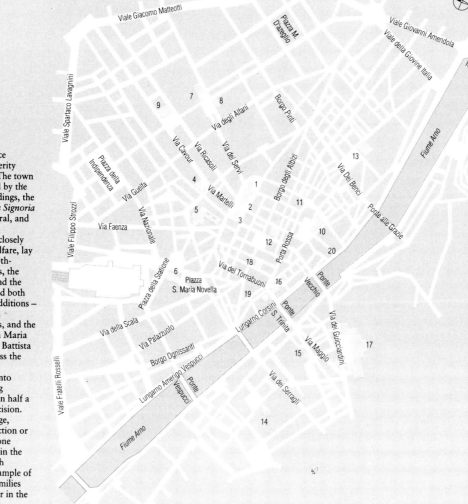

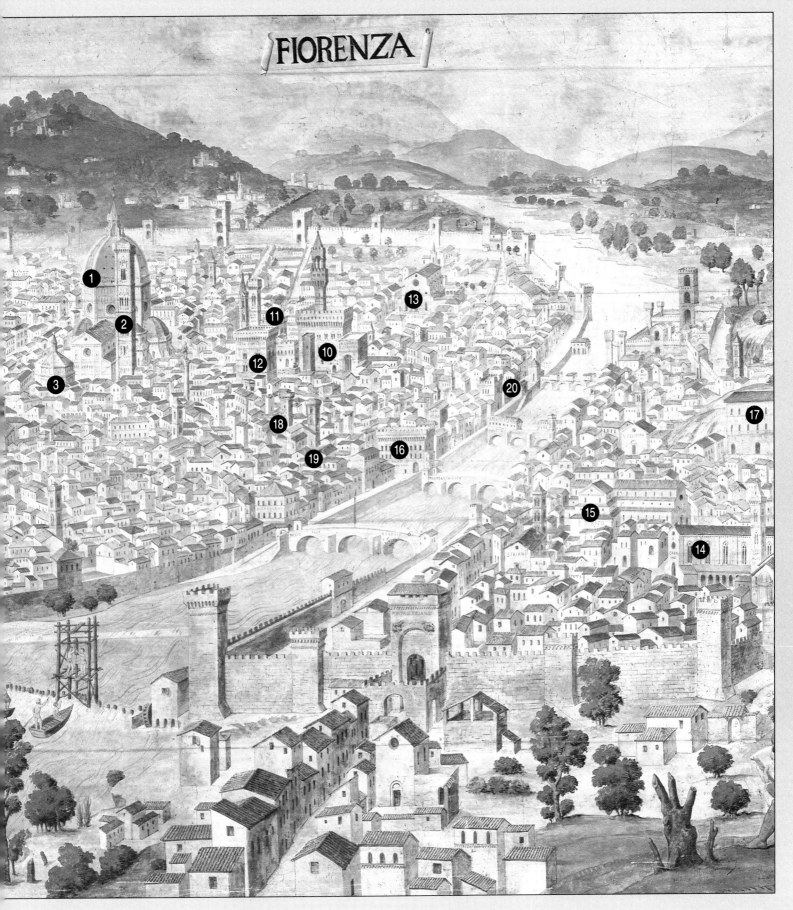

FIORENZA

THE HIGH RENAISSANCE

The High Renaissance was full of paradoxes. Seen by some as "absolutely secular", classical Roman and pagan, and presided over by worldly and immoral popes such as Alexander VI and Julius II, it yet produced some of the most effective works in Christian art – such as the Madonnas of Raphael and Andrea del Sarto and the Sistine Ceiling by Michelangelo. High Renaissance art may be seen as characterized by harmony, balance and gracefulness, and by proportion based on the perfect human form. Yet the background in Italy is one of war, destruction, epidemics, religious crisis and corruption – a background that both impeded and stimulated cultural production and change.

A major crisis began when King Charles VIII of France invaded the Italian peninsula in September 1494, claiming sovereignty over Naples. By February 1495 Milan had been occupied, the Medici family driven out of Florence, and Naples overcome. Charles's occupation did not last long; he was soon out of Italy. Peace, however, did not descend: this episode merely began a period of warfare in Italy, lasting until 1559, during which Italy was also a key center of European conflict.

The French (who reinvaded in 1499 under Louis XII and tended to dominate the north from Milan) and the Spanish (based in the south) contended for control. Swiss and German mercenary soldiers fought for various sides – or for themselves. The Ottoman Turks harried the shoreline and shipping, while Sultan Suleiman I discussed taking over Rome. Italian states formed and reformed leagues and alliances, for or against particular non-Italian invaders and each other. The larger Italian states with varying degrees of independence from non-Italian control – the Papal State, Florence-Tuscany, the Venetian Republic – jockeyed for position. They sought to consolidate their power, with the elimination of petty princes and tyrants, or by domination over the communal oligarchies of lesser cities and towns. By 1559, and the European peace of Cateau-Cambrésis, Spain (now under Philip II) was left as the dominant non-Italian influence, sovereign over the Kingdom of Naples and the Duchy of Milan. There were now, in effect, far fewer independent princedoms or republics than in 1494.

During the war, parts of Italy suffered considerable destruction and political and social dislocation. War had led to the sacking of cities, Brescia and Prato in 1512 and Rome in 1527 being the worst examples. There had been major sieges (of Pisa on and off through the 1490s, of Florence in 1529–30). But war was accompanied by, and triggered, other disasters: the spread of disease, starvation and economic recessions. Famine and plague raged throughout the 1520s, though the worst plague epidemic of the period came later, 1575–77 and particularly affected Venetia and Lombardy. There were typhus epidemics in 1505 and 1528. There was also the new curse of syphilis (variously called the French or Neapolitan disease). It became a major epidemic disease from the 1490s,

spread first by sailors, then soldiers and camp followers involved in the Italian Wars. It caused much fear and shock throughout Europe, as syphilis in the early decades had a high mortality rate.

An appreciation of this gloomy picture is important for understanding developments in high culture. Artists might be forced to move because of violence or because political changes removed key patrons; their new location might prove worse, or more profitable – as in the careers of Leonardo da Vinci or Benvenuto Cellini. The destruction could create major new opportunities. The Sack of Rome in 1527 by unpaid, rebellious, mainly Germanic soldiers, caused the loss of many portable and decorative art works: stained glass, jewelry, tapestries, relics in lavish containers. But within a generation it had helped to stimulate the redevelopment of Rome.

The Italian Wars saw armies on a grand scale, equipped with heavy and more destructive cannons for bombarding cities. This stimulated developments in the design and construction of defensive fortifications, castles and war machinery – providing work for Leonardo da Vinci in Milan and elsewhere; Michelangelo in Florence; Antonio Sangallo the Younger in Florence; and Fra Giocondo in Naples and Padua. Besides the practical works required of them, these men were stimulated intellectually: new ideas were fed from military architecture into civil and ecclesiastical architecture and engineering, and also into urban design and planning, affecting many cityscapes, in particular those of Rome, Florence, Perugia and (later) Turin.

The Italian Wars
In September 1494 a large French army led by Charles VIII crossed into Italy to claim Naples. This invasion was the opening of the Italian Wars, a series of conflicts that finally came to an end in 1559. The Italian Wars, invited by the rivalry among Italian states and their lack of any clear leadership came to involve Spain, the Holy Roman Empire, Switzerland and the papacy, as well as Italian states. The alignments of these foreign and Italian powers shifted constantly. The Ottoman Turks also launched attacks against the Italian peninsula during this period. Charles reached Naples in February 1495 but by October he was back in France, driven out of Italy by a coalition of Venice, Milan, Spain, the Holy Roman Empire and the papacy. In response to the fighting, Italian states employed architects to construct major fortifications – those by Fra Giocondo da Verona, and Guiliano and Antonio da Sangallo are the finest. One important consequence of the Italian Wars was that it brought European powers into direct contact with the Italian Renaissance. Ironically, this is particularly true of France, where Italian influences, brought back by returning armies, came to dominate French cultural life and had a profound effect on the development of the Renaissance there.

Left A woodcut from a book on warfare printed in 1521. It illustrates the siege of Padua (1509) by the Holy League in its campaign against Venice, and clearly shows the striking contrast between the old and the new in warfare, with mounted knights facing cannons. Wars played an important role in determining the course of the Renaissance.

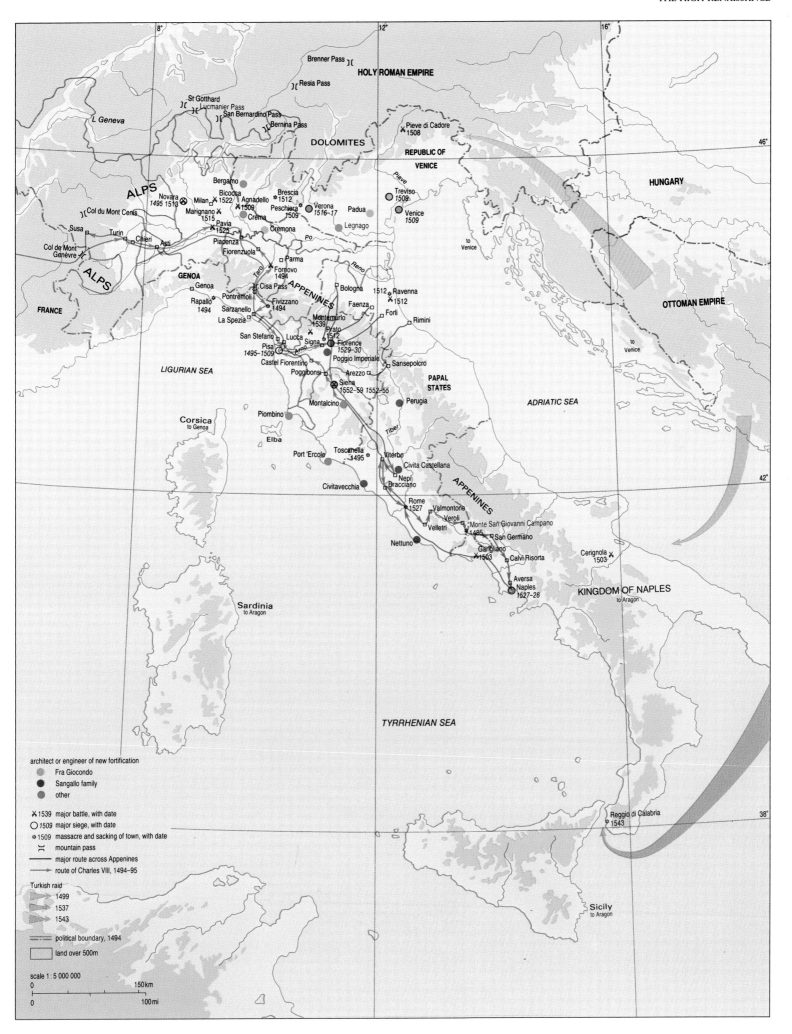

Brenner Pass)(

HOLY ROMAN EMPIRE

Resia Pass)(

St Gotthard)(
Lucmanier Pass)(
San Bernardino Pass)(
L Geneva
Bernina Pass)(

DOLOMITES

✗ Pieve di Cadore
1508

REPUBLIC OF

46°

VENICE

ALPS

Bergamo □

○ Treviso
1509

Plave

HUNGARY

Novara ⊗
1495 1513
Milan □ ✗ 1522
Bicocca
Marignano ✗
1515
Agnadello
✗ 1509
Crema □
Brescia
✤ 1512
Peschiera □
1509

Verona ○
1516-17

Padua ○

Legnago ●

Venice
1509

)(Col du Mont Cenis

Pavia
✗ 1525
Piacenza □
Fiorenzuola
Cremona ●

Po

to
Venice

OTTOMAN EMPIRE

Susa
Turin □
Chieri □
Asti □

ALPS

Parma □
Fornovo ✤
1494

Reno

FRANCE

Col de Mont
Genèvre

GENOA

Genoa □
Rapallo ✤
1494
Pontremoli □
Sarzanello ✤
La Spezia □

Cisa Pass)(
Fivizzano ✤
1494

APPENINES

Bologna □

1512 ✗ Ravenna
✗ 1512

Faenza □

Forli □

Montemurlo
1539
Prato
✤ 1512

Rimini □

San Stefano □
Signa
Pisa ⊗
1495-1509
Lucca □
Arno

Florence ●
1529-30

Poggio Imperiale

Sansepolcro □

PAPAL
STATES

ADRIATIC SEA

LIGURIAN SEA

Castel Fiorentino □
Poggibonsi □

Arezzo □

Siena ⊗
1552-59 1552-55

Perugia ●

Montalcino ●

Piombino □

Tiber

Elba

Corsica
to Genoa

Port 'Ercole □

Toscanella
1495 ✤

Viterbo □

Civita Castellana
Nepi □
Bracciano □

APPENINES

42°

Civitavecchia □

Rome ✤
1527

Valmontone
Veroli □

Nettuno ●

Velletri □

Monte San Giovanni Campano
✤ 1485
San Germano □

Gariglano
✗ 1503
Calvi Risorta □

Cerignola ✗
1503

Aversa ○
Naples
1527-28

KINGDOM OF NAPLES
to Aragon

Sardinia
to Aragon

TYRRHENIAN SEA

architect or engineer of new fortification
● Fra Giocondo
● Sangallo family
● other

✗ 1539 major battle, with date
○ 1509 major siege, with date
✤ 1509 massacre and sacking of town, with date
)(mountain pass
— major route across Appenines
→ route of Charles VIII, 1494-95

Turkish raid
1499
1537
1543

political boundary, 1494
land over 500m

scale 1 : 5 000 000
0   150km
0   100mi

Sicily
to Aragon

Reggio di Calabria
✤ 1543

38°

The experiences and challenges of war could also generate major intellectual argument and debate, especially on political theory. In 1509 the Venetian Republic was confronted by the League of Cambrai (an alliance between Pope Julius II, the Emperor Maximilian, France, Spain, Ferrara and Mantua) and lost control of most of its mainland territory – Venice even faced the possibility of being starved into submission and occupied. Salvation from this threat caused leading civic and Church figures to reassess the values of the Republic: they fostered a self-regarding "myth of Venice" to boost morale and to promote the virtues of their dedicated patrician class, the city's comparative liberty, Christian civic humanism, and major artistic achievement by both native Venetians and immigrants. This war-generated myth stimulated literature, such as the political dialogues and treatises of Cardinal Gasparo Contarini and Paolo Paruta, and propagandist paintings by, for example, Jacopo Sansovino. It also increased the impact of Venetian skills and taste on cultural centers elsewhere in Italy and in Europe.

The Sack of Rome in 1527 had numerous cultural effects outside Rome. It dispersed artists, patrons and religious leaders, and encouraged or discouraged their return. Venice was the chief beneficiary, partly through a conscious policy of Doge Andrea Gritti (1523–38), who wanted to make Venice a second Rome. The sculptor and architect Sansovino moved to Venice, where he had a major impact on the city's architecture. Pietro Aretino – poet, dramatist, journalist, wit, high-class pornographer – had already moved to Venice predicting the sack; its occurrence (and Venice's liberty) probably ensured that he stayed there. Once the military and political threats to Rome had diminished, papal patronage ensured urban renewal and the promotion of classical humanism in literature and the arts – in closer harmony with traditional Christian teaching, Rome was to become the center of a reformed Catholicism able to confront Protestant criticisms and heretical teaching.

The scope of the High Renaissance

The High Renaissance in Italy conventionally dates from the 1490s; there is little agreement over when it ended. During the earlier Renaissance writers and artists had sought to regain knowledge and standards lost since the height of classical Roman achievements. The "High" Renaissance is the period when – in the judgment of contemporaries – a new self-confidence emerged, achievements were comparable with those of the classical past, and leading figures were able to create new works based on classical models.

The High Renaissance shows a growing understanding of nature (as so clearly seen in the notebooks and sketches of Leonardo da Vinci). It exhibits a greater ability to reproduce nature in two- or three-dimensional art and to describe it in literature. But, crucially, there is the developing attitude that nature can – and should – be improved upon, should be exceeded by the use of human intellect, invention and imagination. With better understanding of human anatomy there are major breakthroughs in the portrayal of the human form, whether in Michelangelo's sculpture or Titian's painting. Developments in oil painting allow for more subtle uses of color, light and shade, and optical illusions. A better understanding of the laws of perspective, mathematics and optics leads to a fascination for painted perspectives and a greater

skill in creating them, and to the use and control of spatial relationships in architecture.

The concept of a "High" or perfect Renaissance in the visual arts owes much to Giorgio Vasari (1511–74), the first major art historian, who has dominated the way subsequent art historians have described, assessed and interpreted Italian art of the Renaissance. Vasari was a painter and architect, working in particular for the Medici dukes of Tuscany; but he is most noted for his *Lives of the Artists* (first published in 1550, with a major revised and expanded version in 1568). For Vasari the major arts of painting, sculpture and architecture had – under divine inspiration – reached a new state of perfection, rivaling and even surpassing classical models. This perfection was seen in particular in the work of the "divine" Michelangelo, though signs of perfection could be detected in the paintings of Leonardo da Vinci and Raphael. He saw other contemporary artists such as Giorgione, Giulio Romano and Titian as worthy contributors. Vasari's assessments and criteria have led historians to formulate the concept of a High Renaissance based on the chief works of these artists.

In literature the High Renaissance witnesses a greater confidence that a purified literary Italian language – building on both the old vernacular and the achievements of humanist philology – could produce poetry and prose to exceed the classical in its graceful and imaginative conveying of ideas, emotions and narrative. The interests of 15th-century humanism persisted – particularly neo-Platonic philosophy, classical rhetoric and Roman history (from which lessons might be drawn). There was also greater fascination with classical mythology, often seen through the eyes of Ovid, and classical theater, especially the comedies of Plautus. Platonic philosophy and antique mythology also influenced the content and meanings of painting and sculpture.

One explanation for the achievement and leading characteristics of the High Renaissance is the fruitful interchange of ideas between classical scholars, theologians and creative artists. Moreover, some academies and some universities (notably Bologna, Padua and Pisa) encouraged the cross-fertilization of ideas and carried High Renaissance attitudes, styles and ideas into the later 16th century.

Academies, as associations of the cultured elite, proliferated in the 16th century. Many may have been merely social gatherings of pretentious nobles and gentlemen reading poor poems to each other. But some were the basis for circulating new ideas in minor cities such as Casale, Cosenza and Lecce, while others played key roles internationally. A Venetian academy launched about 1500 by the printer and humanist Aldus Manutius was a crucial promoter of Greek studies. Florence had academies for teaching artists (the Accademia del Disegno, founded in 1562), and for promoting vernacular literature and purifying the language – culminating in the Accademia della Crusca, founded in 1582. Padua, besides having a lively university, boasted a vital private academy of the *Infiammati* (the "inflamed") for philosophers and humanists.

The High Renaissance has no clear end-point. Some of the ideals and characteristics exemplified by Vasari's art heroes (and literary contemporaries) persist through the mid 16th century – via Vasari's own imitations, and the work of Veronese and Palladio – and into the Counter-Reformation of the

Italy at the end of the Italian Wars The Italian Wars ended with the Peace of Cateau-Cambrésis in 1559. New cultural leadership came from several sources. Bishoprics, even in the poor, backward south of the peninsula, sponsored wider education and commissioned buildings and art works. Lay confraternities commissioned chapels, paintings, theater, music and pageantry. Innovative individuals also provided cultural leadership. Federico Barocci (c. 1535–1612), for example, used High Renaissance styles to produce religious pictures that were both sensitive and original.

late 16th and 17th centuries. Then – while reforming bishops and lay religious confraternities provide additional cultural leadership – certain aspects of the High Renaissance are given new religious meaning and emotion in the paintings of Federico Barocci, the music of the Gabrieli (Andrea and Giovanni) and Gesualdo, and the poetry of Torquato Tasso.

Republican Florence and its impact

One of the casualties of the 1494 French invasion of Italy was the political dominance of the Medici in Florence, long its ruling family. A more democratic republican regime took over, initially influenced by Fra Girolamo Savonarola (1452–98), a brilliant firebrand preacher, prophet and moral critic. Both repub-

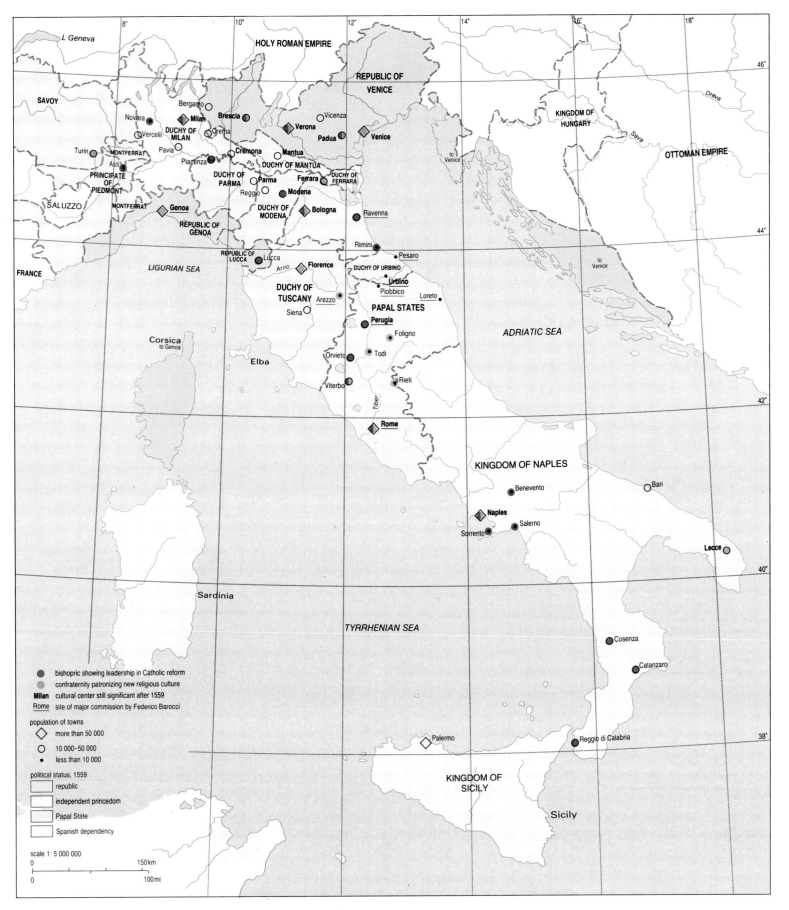

bishopric showing leadership in Catholic reform

confraternity patronizing new religious culture

Milan cultural center still significant after 1559

Rome site of major commission by Federico Barocci

population of towns

◇ more than 50 000

○ 10 000–50 000

• less than 10 000

political status, 1559

republic

independent princedom

Papal State

Spanish dependency

scale 1 : 5 000 000

0 ———— 150km

0 ———— 100mi

Left Madonna with the Yarn-Winder (c. 1501) by Leonardo da Vinci. Leonardo and his studio experimented with several versions of this picture, which was painted for a leading French official, Florimond Robertet. Whether Robertet received the Duke of Buccleuch's version (shown here) or another version now in New York, is unclear. Leonardo's hand is evident in both versions, particularly in the painting of the Child and the rocks; but both show signs of cooperation from assistants. (There are several other versions that are probably entirely by assistants.) Nevertheless, this version clearly illustrates Leonardo's expressive use of light and dark, and of *sfumato*, the subtle blending of one tone into another without clear outlines. It also illustrates Leonardo's principle that "figures ought to be painted in such a way that those who see them will be able to discern from their attitudes the thoughts of their minds".

lican leaders and Pope Alexander VI (whom he wanted deposed by a council of the Church) became embarrassed by his vehement political and moral criticisms. Under torture he was forced to confess to plots against the Church and to preaching pernicious innovations, and was burnt at the stake as a heretic and schismatic. Savonarola frequently attacked the lasciviousness of much art and ordered some works to be burned; Vasari says that one such burning in 1496 included profane paintings and sculptures, love songs and lutes.

The puritanical atmosphere he created in Florence might seem unhealthy for the arts and for culture generally. But Savonarola, contrary to common belief, was not hostile to the arts; his preaching encouraged new directions and attitudes within religious culture. The painter Bartolommeo della Porta offered his own nude paintings to be burned; he became a friar in 1500 (hence *Fra* Bartolommeo) and his paintings, becoming the foundation of Florentine religious art, influenced Raphael. This republican period in Florence (lasting till 1512) saw major achievements in painting and sculpture, though its longterm impact on political theory may be more important.

Right A terracotta bust of Niccolò Machiavelli, possibly based on his death mask. Machiavelli's *The Prince* (c. 1513), a frank analysis of the political realities of his period, is a landmark in political theory. His works are based on his own bitter experience of political life: "I hope, and hoping increases my torment ... hoping, I weep, laugh and burn; and I fear what I hear and see."

Below Michelangelo's *David* (1501–4) is one of the most familiar images of the Renaissance. A colossal figure, David stands confident and alert – a symbol of republican Florence. For Vasari, Michelangelo's *David* set a new standard in sculpture, surpassing the achievements of the ancients.

During this time Leonardo da Vinci moved between the Milan court and the Florentine Republic. In Florence he worked on major paintings, such as the *Madonna with the Yarn-Winder* (c. 1501), the *Mona Lisa* (1505), and *Madonna and Child with St Anne* (c. 1508). These introduced his new technique, called *sfumato*, in which colors and tones shift from light to dark gradually, without clear-cut demarcations – this often lands his painting on air of mystery. This signaled a major stage in the development of oil painting. In the interests of Florentine republican propaganda, emphasizing past victories, Leonardo was commissioned to paint in fresco *The Battle of Anghiari*, to accompany *The Battle of Cascina* painted by Michelangelo. While these paintings are lost, another republican symbol, Michelangelo's *David* (1501–04), one of the high points of Renaissance marble sculpture, has survived – a male nude figure of controlled power and dignity, standing against tyranny and fear.

Out of the republican experience – and its failure, when the Medici were returned in 1512 – also came the achievements of the notorious Niccolò Machiavelli (1469–1527). The son of a lawyer and keen humanist who gave his son a classical education, Machiavelli rose to some prominence as second chancellor to the Florentine Republic from 1498, acting as diplomat (within Italy and to France), and writer of letters and reports. (His dealings with the ruthless Cesare Borgia may well have colored his views.) Machiavelli lost his job soon after the return of the Medici in 1512; he suffered imprisonment and torture and then turned to writing works that were often aimed (unsuccessfully) at securing employment from the Medici. Machiavelli's experiences, and his knowledge of classical history, were fed into his major political writings: *The Prince* (written c. 1513, though not printed until 1532), *The Discourses* (c. 1513–19), and *The Art of War* (1519–20).

Consistency is not to be expected across the whole rang eof his political writings. At heart a republican and a deeply patriotic Florentine, loathing the invaders and particularly Swiss mercenaries, Machiavelli became best-known for his advice to princes – to be cunning and ruthless in facing the realities of power, divorcing political action from morality. His political writings, printed and translated after his death, or distortions of his ideas circulated through friendly or hostile authors, have ensured his place in the forefront of Western political thought – and sometimes practice.

Machiavelli was more than a politician: he stands out as a full High Renaissance cultural figure. He combined a humanist education, especially a love of ancient history, with a keen eye for the unpleasant realities of the human condition. His surviving letters show him as observant, erudite, witty and sociable. He wrote about Florentine history and the Italian language. He also wrote short stories and bawdy plays, two of which can still be successfully performed. The comedy *Clizia*, produced spectacularly in Florence in 1525, is seen as a considerable improvement on the works of the Roman Plautus, whose plays had inspired him. The more original *Mandragola* ("The Mandrake-root"), about sex and deception, was first performed in Venice also in 1525 and is one of the finest Renaissance comedies. Machiavelli the Renaissance dramatist is in many ways the key to the political Machiavelli.

Milan and Leonardo da Vinci

Milan is less known than it should be for its contribution to the High Renaissance. Though legally ruled by Duke Gian Galeazzo Sforza from 1476 to 1494, it was dominated by his uncle Lodovico "il Moro" ("the Moor"), who then usurped the dukedom and ruled until he was expelled by the French in 1499. Lodovico and his highly cultured wife Beatrice d'Este (from Ferrara's ruling family) created a highly civilized court in the midst of political turmoil.

In architecture Lodovico – aware of Brunelleschi's achievements in Florence – offered opportunities to Donato Bramante (c. 1444–1514) to become the founding father of High Renaissance architecture. He designed the small barrel-vaulted church of Santa Maria in San Satiro, where (lacking space) he created the mere illusion of a choir at the east end (1482–86). He also designed Santa Maria delle Grazie (begun 1493), with its play on real and fictive space (pretend pedimented windows, seeming roundels in the dome); and the new cloister for old Sant' Ambrogio, inspired by the classical architectural writer Vitruvius. Bramante was also a painter with a reputation for *trompe l'oeil*.

Bramante's architecture was influenced by his friend Leonardo da Vinci (1452–1519), who arrived in Milan in 1482 and came to be a central figure at court. In offering his services to Lodovico, Leonardo had boasted of his many talents: inventor of machines of war (for land or sea), expert in tunneling and in water engineering; and, he claimed, "I can carry out sculpture in marble, bronze and clay; and in painting can do any kind of work as well as any man". Although many works remained incomplete, and boasts unfulfilled, Leonardo did have remarkably wide talents with which he could win the support and affection of Lodovico and many at his court. He was prized for his technical abilities with machines – even if his flying machines and submersibles did not function. He amused and fascinated with his drawings – whether of grotesques, inventions or the manifold effects of nature. He became intrigued – and distracted from painting – by the work of another of Lodovico's

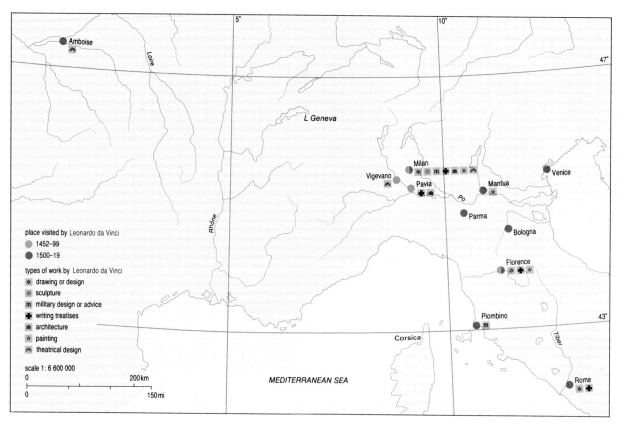

The travels of Leonardo da Vinci
Because their commissions came from churches and courts, Renaissance artists were expected to move from place to place. Leonardo da Vinci was based in Florence, then stayed at the Sforza court in Milan and Vigevano. After 1499 he traveled a great deal, seeking new patrons or escaping war – or benefiting from it, as when touring the Papal State in 1502 as Cesare Borgia's mapmaker and military engineer. He spent the last few years of his life at a château near the French court at Amboise, an honored guest of Francis I.

place visited by Leonardo da Vinci
● 1452–99
● 1500–19

types of work by Leonardo da Vinci
✺ drawing or design
◉ sculpture
m military design or advice
✱ writing treatises
m architecture
☆ painting
✺ theatrical design

scale 1 : 6 600 000
0   200km
0   150mi

protégés, the great mathematician Luca Pacioli (c. 1445–1517), for whose *Divine Proportion* (1509), a work on both mathematical and artistic proportion, he provided illustrations. Leonardo contributed to court theatrical entertainments in Milan and at country villas, with machinery and set designs – as for the *Masque of the Planets* during wedding celebrations in 1490, or for the performance of a play, *Danae*, by the poet and ducal chancellor Baldassare Taccone in 1496. For the latter there was a *trompe l'oeil* city scene, a forerunner of city-scene stage buildings in the Teatro Olimpico, Vicenza.

Leonardo's career at the Milan court emphasizes the point that the rising status and prestige of leading artists in the High Renaissance – Raphael, Michelangelo, Cellini and Titian are good examples – were based both on their great diversity of talents and on their willingness and ability to participate in court life alongside scholars and patrons.

Leonardo's more famous creations from his time in Milan are his two versions of the *Virgin of the Rocks* (c. 1483, Louvre; and the later copy, c. 1488, perhaps reworked c. 1507, National Gallery, London). Also painted at this time were *The Last Supper*, in the refectory of Santa Maria delle Grazie (1495–97); and portraits of Lodovico's mistresses, especially that of Cecilia Gallerani (a lutenist and poet), identified with the *Lady with an Ermine* (c. 1483–4). *The Last Supper* was for Lodovico and Beatrice's favorite convent, where they wished to be buried. Leonardo's experiments with paint mean that what survives is only a pale indication of the original, though its structure and proportions suggest the influence of Bramante and Pacioli. Leonardo wanted – in what he called the "silent poetry" of painting – to depict the drama of Scripture, capturing the attitudes, facial expressions and the gestures of the participants. The other paintings cited show Leonardo's maturing use of *sfumato* (the softening of outlines) and *chiaroscuro* (the blending of light and dark).

Leonardo's first *Virgin of the Rocks* was commissioned by the new confraternity of the Immaculate Conception. Confraternities (lay brotherhoods promoting the religious life of men and sometimes women) were major cultural patrons of altarpieces, processional banners, side chapels and religious music. Based on a detailed contract, this commission, which fostered the increasingly popular but controversial doctrine of the Immaculate Conception of the Virgin, is a reminder that the High Renaissance could

Below A portrait of the mathematician Luca Pacioli (c. 1495) by Jacopo de' Barbari. Pacioli's books were some of the first mathematics textbooks printed in the West. His work on proportion reflected his association with such artists as Piero della Francesca and Leonardo da Vinci (who provided illustrations for one of his books), and his work on double entry bookkeeping helped to maintain the success of Italian merchants.

be vibrantly and deeply Christian as well as anti-clerical, classical and pagan. Leonardo, in various paintings completed or projected, did much to revitalize the iconography of the Virgin, using both his own and his patrons' ideas.

Rome before the Sack of 1527

The mixtures of pagan and Christian aspects of humanism, of overt sensuality and sexuality with moral seriousness, of rational argument and of superstitious prophesying based on astrology or omens such as monstrous births, can all be found in High Renaissance Rome under Popes Alexander VI (1492–1503),

Pius III (1503), Julius II (1503–13), Leo X (1513–21), Adrian VI (1522–23), Clement VII (1523–34) and Paul III (1534–49). In high places there was certainly gross corruption – much of it connected with Alexander VI, his Borgia children and their associates. But the papal court could also display refined manners, listen to the most erudite sermons and discourses, sponsor new hospitals for the poor, commission the most harmonious and well-balanced altarpieces from Raphael and Giulio Romano, and issue documents and literary works in the most polished Latin or Italian.

The popes were campaigning on various fronts.

Right Leonardo's *Lady with an Ermine* (c. 1483–4) is usually taken to be a portrait of Cecilia Gallerani, the mistress of Lodovico Sforza. The ermine was a Sforza emblem, and its Greek name, *galee*, echoes the sitter's; according to Leonardo, the ermine signified moderation and purity. An accomplished lutenist, Italian poet and Latin letter-writer, Gallerani is depicted as the embodiment of courtly manners and gracefulness.

They wanted to consolidate their political control over Rome and the Papal State; to expand the population of Rome (about 55,000 in 1500) and rebuild toward the ancient Roman walls; to make Rome a fitting leader of the Church and Christendom; and, often, to enhance the prestige of the pope's family. Cultural patronage would assist in all this, as well as entertain and instruct. By taxing the consolidated Papal State or borrowing massively, popes would spend lavishly to promote their aims through the arts and literature. Rome, increasingly attracting the dominant cultural figures of the age, developed a court society in which classical scholars, theologians, artists and church administrators intermingled.

In 1499 Bramante moved from Milan to Rome as a war refugee. Soon (in 1502) he produced one of the gems of High Renaissance architecture, the little Tempietto at San Pietro in Montorio, in honor of St Peter. The Tempietto is a circular chapel surrounded by columns that used the full Doric order and a richly decorated frieze. When Julius II finally decided that the old Constantine basilica of St Peter (built c. 330) was too dilapidated – and old-fashioned – to be repaired, and launched the project for a new St Peter's, it was Bramante who provided the initial design. This was in the shape of a Greek cross (a cross with arms of equal length), which neo-Platonists and mathematicians considered to be an ideal, God-given form. In the event, many architects later, Michelangelo designed and built (from 1546) his Greek-cross structure for the dome, crossing and high altar area. Later still, the architect Carlo Maderno extended one arm of the cross, creating the existing long nave to accommodate large congregations.

Michelangelo's early periods in Rome, in 1496–1501 and 1505–15, were largely governed by the misfortunes in his native Florence and his difficult relationship with the Medici family. The early period produced the marble *Pietà* (1498–99), now in St Peter's, which shows an ever-youthful Virgin cradling the body of the dead Christ. This was commissioned by a French Cardinal, Jean Villiers, whose origins help explain why Michelangelo followed a northern European, not Italian, tradition of representing the Sorrows of the Virgin – with Christ cradled in Mary's arms rather than stretched across her lap. However, where his predecessors had Christ's body precariously overwhelming the Virgin, Michelangelo has a perfectly balanced relationship between the two figures. The group shows a perfect mastery of carving technique in the finest detail, anatomical observation, psychological insight and compassion. The humanist confidence in showing Christ as beautifully human, and the Virgin compassionate but not overwrought, contrasts strikingly with the increasing pessimism and retreat from perfect harmonies seen in Michelangelo's later, incomplete, sculptures of Christ – *The Deposition of Christ* (1547–55) and the *Rondanini Pietà* (1555–64).

The second period of Michelangelo's Roman career was dominated by two projects: the sculptured tomb for Pope Julius II, and the painted ceiling of the Sistine Chapel in the Vatican. The tomb project plagued Michelangelo's life and increased his bad temper, as the pope and his heirs continually changed their minds (and their funding) of the grandiose project. His famous *Slaves* (c. 1513), in various stages of release from their marble blocks, and the majestic seated *Moses* (1515–16), are the meager but fascinating and

influential testimonies of this attempt by Julius II to glorify himself through art.

The Sistine ceiling (1508–12) is a brilliant expression of the Christian humanism of the High Renaissance. It was based on Michelangelo's own ideas and on the scholarly erudition of a leading Augustinian prior, Egidio da Viterbo, Julius II's favorite court preacher. Despite Michelangelo's plea that he was not a painter, the Sistine Chapel ceiling is one of the great masterpieces of painting.

In 1508 Raphael had been attracted to Rome. A native of Urbino, Raphael had developed his style in Umbria (under Perugino) and in Florence. The varied influences on him (from Perugino, Fra Bartolomeo and Leonardo) are best seen in *The Entombment* (completed in 1507), which he painted for Atalanta Baglioni to commemorate her murderous son. He had died in her arms seeking forgiveness for his involvement in a failed but bloody attempt to overthrow other members of the Baglioni family who ruled Perugia. Pope Julius II, visiting Perugia in 1506 (to curb the Baglioni), saw works by Raphael and commissioned him to decorate major rooms in the Vatican palace. The aim was to display the authority, teaching and historical leadership of the papacy and the

Above Portrait of Leo X (c. 1518) by Raphael, which includes portraits of Leo's two cousins, Cardinals Giulio de' Medici and Luigi Rossi, is a powerful image of the Medici papacy. The picture is remarkable for its realism and psychological characterization.

Right An early work, and the only one he signed, Michelangelo's *Pietà* (1497–1500) displays a remarkable technical virtuosity and youthful confidence. It is an expression of both Christian piety and the neo-Platonic belief that physical beauty is a reflection of the soul. When asked why Mary was so youthful he said that God would have granted her youthfulness in order to "prove to the world the virginity and perpetual purity of the Virgin".

Below A medallion depicting Michelangelo (1560–1). Though this medal was minted by Leone Leoni, the design was largely Michelangelo's. Now principal architect of St Peter's in Rome, Michelangelo shows himself as a princely figure, recalling an earlier medal of Julius II commemorating the building of St Peter's. The reverse shows a blindman guided by a dog, an image of Michelangelo's growing pessimism.

Catholic Church. Initially Raphael was one of a team (including Perugino), but he soon became dominant. The *Stanze* (frescoes) told many stories and gave out many messages. The Stanza della Segnatura (originally Julius II's study, though named after a law court that later met there) was dedicated to the four faculties of knowledge according to scholastic teaching: theology, philosophy, jurisprudence and poetry. On one wall there is the *Disputa*, in which theologians debate the mysteries of Catholic faith, with the communion host in a monstrance on the altar. Facing it is *The School of Athens*, an allegory of secular learning: men thinking, debating, writing, calculating. It includes the two great pre-Christian philosophers Aristotle and Plato (the latter in Raphael's time was seen as the chief forerunner of Christian teaching), Pythagoras (dealing

with harmony), Euclid (with compasses), and Ptolemy (holding a starry sphere). Raphael painted his self-portrait behind the figure of Geometrym.

The titles of other paintings produced by Raphael for Julius's program give some idea of the variety of messages or propaganda that paintings could convey: *Parnassus* (a celebration of the Muses and famous poets); *The Justice Wall*; *The Expulsion of Heliodorus* (a violent scene, showing how heavenly intervention protected the treasures of the Temple in Jerusalem); *The Liberation of St Peter*; and *The Mass at Bolsena* (proving to a doubting priest that the communion host has become the true body and blood of Christ). The *Stanze* display Raphael's remarkable mastery of painting (a mastery acknowledged by his contemporaries), his control of perspective and composition and his

The Sistine Chapel Ceiling

The Sistine Chapel, the Vatican's principal chapel, was built in 1473 for Pope Sixtus IV; in 1508 Pope Julius II commissioned Michelangelo to paint the ceiling. A simple scheme based on the 12 Apostles gradually evolved into a complex spectacle depicting nearly 300 figures. Although some ideas came from others, possibly from Julius himself, the elaboration of the scheme was Michelangelo's, the content and its depiction changing as he progressed.

The basic narrative is clear, though there is much room for scholarly debate about deeper meanings, especially over neo-Platonic influences and biblical interpretation. The central scenes, which show the creation of the universe and man's story from the Fall to the Flood, vary considerably in mood and complexity. There is the humanist confidence in God's creation of Adam, the male ideal; and the fear, misery, resignation and compassion depicted in the Flood scene. In between is the Fall and Expulsion from the Garden of Eden, with its striking contrast between the beautiful, serene Eve about to accept the serpent's apple, and the ugly, cowed Eve being driven from Paradise.

Michelangelo complained that he was a sculptor, not a painter, and unskilled in fresco techniques. Judging by his letters and poems, he was miserable, frustrated and painfully uncomfortable, but he worked feverishly and by late October 1512 he had finished. It had taken him four agonizing years.

Below This diagram shows how the basic story unfolds. Above the altar Michelangelo depicted the beginning of all things, The Creation of Light (1); the creation of the universe continues in (2) and (3). The story of mankind begins with Adam (4), Eve (5) and the Expulsion from Eden (6); it continues with the story of Noah, and other Old Testament figures. At (25) above the west wall, Michelangelo painted Jonah (a story which was seen as prefiguring Christ's death and resurrection). On the west wall itself (40), he later painted the culmination of the Christian story, the Last Judgment.

The diagram also shows how many other artists were involved in painting the Sistine Chapel.

Other artists
A   Perugino and Pinturicchio
      Moses's Journey into Egypt
B   Sandro Botticelli
      Scenes from the Life of Moses
C   Cosimo Rosselli
      Crossing of the Red Sea
D   Cossimo Rosselli assisted by
      Piero di Cosimo
      Moses and the Tables of the
      Law
E   Sandro Botticelli
      Punishment of Korah, Datan
      and Abiram
F   Luca Signorelli
      Testament and Death of Moses
G   Matteo da Lecce
      Fight over the Body of Moses
H   Van den Broeck
      Resurrection of Christ
I   Cosimo Rosselli
      Last Supper
K   Perugino
      Handing Over of the Keys
L   Cosimo Rosselli and
      Piero di Cosimo
      Sermon on the Mount and
      Healing of the Leper
M   Domenico Ghirlandaio
      Calling of the First Apostles
N   Sandro Botticelli
      Temptations of Christ and
      Purification of the Leper
O   Perugino and Pinturicchio
      Baptism of Christ

Michelangelo's Ceiling
1. The Creation of Light
2. The Creation of the Stars
     and Planets
3. The Separation of Land and
     Water
4. The Creation of Adam
5. The Creation of Eve
6. The Fall and Expulsion from
     Paradise
7. The Sacrifice of Noah
8. The Flood
9. The Drunkenness of Noah
10. Judith and Holofernes
11. David and Goliath
12. The Brazen Serpent
13. The Punishment of Haman
14. Jeremiah
15. The Persian Sibyl
16. Ezechiel
17. The Erythrean Sibyl
18. Joel
19. Zechariah
20. The Delphian Sibyl
21. Isaiah
22. The Cumaean Sibyl
23. Daniel
24. The Libyan Sibyl
25. Jonah
26–39. Christ's Ancestors and
     Scenes from the Old Testament
40. Last Judgment

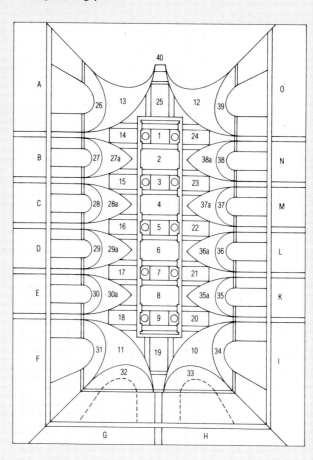

ability to portray the anatomy of the human body in violent or contemplative scenes.

From 1513 Raphael continued his work on the *Stanze* under Leo X. He also became involved in the new St Peter's project after Bramante's death (1514), and he worked for Agostino Chigi, the key financial figure in the papacy from Alexander VI to Leo X. Chigi (1465–1520) was a leading literary patron, the sponsor of the first Greek press in Rome, and the center of a lavish court of his own. Most notably he led a spectacular, sometimes scandalous, life-style in a suburban villa, later called the Villa Farnesina, which was also designed to serve as a retreat for Julius II. Renaissance popes and their leading cardinals and officials liked to withdraw from business and summer heat in central Rome to higher hills within the ancient walls or just outside, or farther afield to Frascati or Tivoli.

The Villa Farnesina was designed initially by Baldassare Peruzzi (1481–1536) and later developed by Antonio Sangallo the Younger (1483–1546). Peruzzi, also a painter, helped Chigi plan lavish decoration, mostly mythological scenes based on the *Metamorphoses* of the Latin poet Ovid. Chigi had a lively love life, which paintings in the villa were designed to encourage and celebrate. Raphael designed (and partially painted) a cycle of fresco paintings on the story of Cupid and Psyche (c. 1518). His most famous scene is his *Galatea*, showing the beautiful sea nymph, beloved of Polyphemus, pulled over the waves by dolphins, while other sea creatures play erotically. This work led to Vasari's praise of Raphael. The High Renaissance celebration of eroticism, the delight in depicting the male and female bodies, the use of illusionistic effects in two-dimensional paint were continued by others in this villa. Sodoma (Giovanni Bazzi) painted Chigi's bedroom with scenes from the life of Alexander the Great, including his marriage to Roxana. Later Pietro Aretino was fondly to recall this villa and its life: an ideal combination of sensual pleasure and scholarly erudition.

High Renaissance Venice

Venice would be claimed – by friend and foe alike – as *the* center for sensual high art (and low life) for much of the 16th century. We can see this in the writings of Pietro Aretino, the painted female nudes of his friend Titian, and in the love poetry and career of leading courtesan Veronica Franca.

Venice was arguably the most dynamic cultural center throughout the 16th century. The city itself (of about 100,000 people in 1500, and nearly 170,000 in 1563) had considerable wealth, widely spread among its inhabitants. The sources of that wealth were international trade, manufacturing, and progressive agriculture in its mainland territories, called the Terraferma. The Terraferma contained other vital cities with cultural and patronage links to the center – most notably Verona, Vicenza and the university city of Padua.

Within Venice there were many sources of patronage: the republican government; the leading patrician families that dominated the government, numerous lay confraternities (*scuole*), and competing religious orders. There was close cooperation between the republican state and the Venetian Church to make Venice, under the protection of the Virgin and St Mark, a rival to Rome and a purer exponent of Catholicism. In this image-building the arts were given

Left A view from the Piazza San Marco in Venice focusing on the Benedictine church and former monastery, San Giorgio Maggiore, Palladio's ecclesiastical masterpiece (begun 1565). On the left is the Doge's Palace, influenced by Moorish architecture. On the right is the Lion of St Mark, the emblem of Venice.

Above Portrait of a Lady (c. 1533) by Lorenzo Lotto. Lotto's troubled personality and enigmatic portraits puzzled his contemporaries. This portrait is probably of Lucrezia Pesaro at the time of her marriage. Her challenging look and the drawing of Lucretia, a Roman matron who committed suicide after being raped, are assertions of her virtue.

high priority. Like Rome, Venice was a major importer of cultural talent, given its eastern Mediterranean contacts and the influences of Constantinople and the Eastern Church – links with the East were culturally and economically vital.

Venice became preeminent in many artistic fields that were to prove influential: in printing and the dissemination of knowledge and images; in oil painting and the use of colors; in building, whether spectacular palaces on canals or modest well-organized housing for artisans; in choral music, madrigals, and the development of music for stringed instruments; in the creation of elaborate glassware; in vernacular theater, culminating in a public opera house in 1637; and in processions and in carnival entertainment.

As the leading printing center, Venice popularized and cheapened book production. Its printers issued

good inexpensive editions of Latin, Greek and Hebrew works for scholars (especially under the influence of the great humanist publisher Aldus Manutius). They also published romances, histories and dialogues in Italian for a wider cultural audience; elementary readers for those seeking literacy; printed music; atlases and maps (such as Jacopo de' Barbari's great print of Venice in 1500); and illustrations for anatomical or botanical texts.

From the early 16th century artists in Venice made major breakthroughs in the techniques and application of oil painting on canvas, introducing new approaches to the uses of color. Vasari was reluctant to give the greatest praise to Venetian artists (as opposed to the Florentine–Roman schools), because their oil-painting technique meant that there was less need for the careful thought, preliminary drawing and precise design required in fresco work and tempera painting.

Portraiture – notably under Lorenzo Lotto and Titian – was given new psychological depth and visual impact, both through color and structural composition There was new vitality and impact in narrative painting (now painted in oils on canvas, rather than in fresco), which were often to be found in confraternity chapels and meeting rooms. The finest examples are Jacopo Tintoretto's numerous and vast canvases telling Old and New Testament stories for the Scuola Grande of San Rocco, to which he devoted much of his life and work from 1564 to 1587 and which mark the transition from High Renaissance art to the art of the Catholic reform movement, the Counter-Reformation.

The giant of painting in the full High Renaissance style was undoubtedly Titian (Tiziano Vecellio, c. 1488–1576), whom Vasari eventually (overcoming concerns about Venetian "color") came to like and admire. Titian received patronage and highest honors from the Habsburg Emperor Charles V and later his son Philip II of Spain; to them he sent portraits, mythological stories and female nudes. Titian's colorful and sensual paintings of the female nude are major achievements, though their unashamed eroticism has embarrassed some critics. There has been much debate about how far Titian was influenced by classical writings (especially by Ovid) and mythology. In fact, his voluptuous paintings of Venus, Danaë, and Sacred and Profane Love frankly represent real women – the wives, servants or courtesans who were courted, admired and loved by Titian's friends and patrons. If Michelangelo set new standards for portraying the

male nude (in both sculpture and painting), Titian championed the female nude.

Titian had an equal impact on religious art. An important example can be cited from Venice's great Franciscan church that meant so much to leading families, Santa Maria dei Frari. This is the main altarpiece painting, *The Assumption of the Virgin* (or *Assunta*). Its impact, when unveiled in 1519, was – and remains to this day – considerable. Elongated figures are visible along the entire length of the nave and through the choir; the colors, especially the red of the Virgin's cloak, are bold and vibrant; and there is a dynamic sense of a sweeping movement upward, with God the Father coming down to meet the Virgin. The painting was a major contribution to the Counter-Reformation doctrine of the Virgin Mary, its composition and style having an impact that was felt well into the Counter-Reformation and Baroque.

Above Titian's *Bacchus and Ariadne* (1523), painted for Duke Alfonso d'Este in Ferrara, was based on the writings of the Roman poets Catullus and Ovid. It depicts Bacchus arriving on the island of Naxos to woo Ariadne, who had been abandoned by Theseus. While the energy of the gestures indicates Titian's – and Alphonso's – admiration for Raphael and Michelangelo, the brilliance of color and dynamic composition are Titian's masterly achievement.

Titian had many cultured friends in Venice, a fact that probably discouraged him from accepting invitations to serve the papacy and courts in Europe and elsewhere. He was especially friendly with fellow Venetians Pietro Aretino and Jacopo Sansovino. Aretino (1492–1556), one of the key literary figures of the High Renaissance, has also caused embarrassment to critics, particularly for his erotic sonnets (*Sonetti lussuriosi*, 1524). They were published with frank engravings by Giulio Romano, which were censored by Pope Clement VII. Similarly controversial were Aretino's dialogues, the *Ragionamenti* (1534–36), in which Roman prostitutes discuss clients and seduction techniques, and through which Aretino satirizes the literary dialogues and neo-Platonic theories of his more serious contemporaries. More significantly, Aretino wrote major plays, especially the comedy *The Courtesan* (1525), satirizing the papal courts, and a tragedy, *Orazia* (1546). He also wrote serious religious works (religion and sexuality mingled easily in Venice) and numerous letters, many of which were published in his day in the relatively safe haven of Venice; they remain eminently readable as satire, journalism and social comment.

Titian's other leading friend, the sculptor and architect Jacopo Sansovino (1486–1570), arrived in Venice in 1527. A refugee from the Sack of Rome, he brought to Venice his experience of the Florentine Renaissance and a knowledge of Roman remains. He transformed the styles of Venetian sculpture and architecture from their blend of medieval Gothic forms and Byzantine decoration into a Venetian version of the High Renaissance. His best known sculptures are the huge statues *Mars and neptune* (1554–56) on the Scala dei Giganti of the doge's palace. His impact on sculpture is seen in tombs and in the statues decorating the Loggetta, the arcade below the famous tall bell-tower or campanile in St Mark's square. The Loggetta was part of a major urban plan to systematize and beautify the squares in front of St Mark's and the adjacent Doge's Palace. Sansovino supervised the project as architect to the basilica of St Mark. He imported ideas from Rome, but adapted them to Venice by softening the architectural lines – indenting and patterning (rusticating) walls and classical columns, employing the play of light and rich decorative sculpturing. He also contributed to the replanning of Venice with designs for the Mint (begun 1535) and the Library (begun 1537), the latter being described by a succeeding great architect, Palladio, as "the richest, most ornate building since Antiquity". Sansovino also helped to classicize Venetian palace building and ecclesiastical architecture.

Rome after the Sack
In many ways Rome soon recovered from the Sack of 1527 and cultural patronage was again pursued with vigor. To some extent there was a changed mood – less confident and more anxious, less worldly and more concerned with the afterlife, less overtly pagan, more orthodoxly Christian. But the changes were slow and the cultural output full of paradoxes and contrasts.

The buildings of Palladio
Andrea Palladio was one of the most influential European architects, notably in Britain and colonial north America – both through his completed buildings and his designs in *The Four Books of Architecture* (1570). Influenced by humanist patrons and Roman ruins, his use of classical orders with pillars and pilasters, his porticos, loggias and mathematically proportioned rooms set new standards in town palaces (notably in Vicenza), churches (Venice) and country villas. Some of the villas be designed were soon enhanced by frescoes – mythologies, eulogies of rural life and witty illusionistic effects, notably by Paolo Veronese.

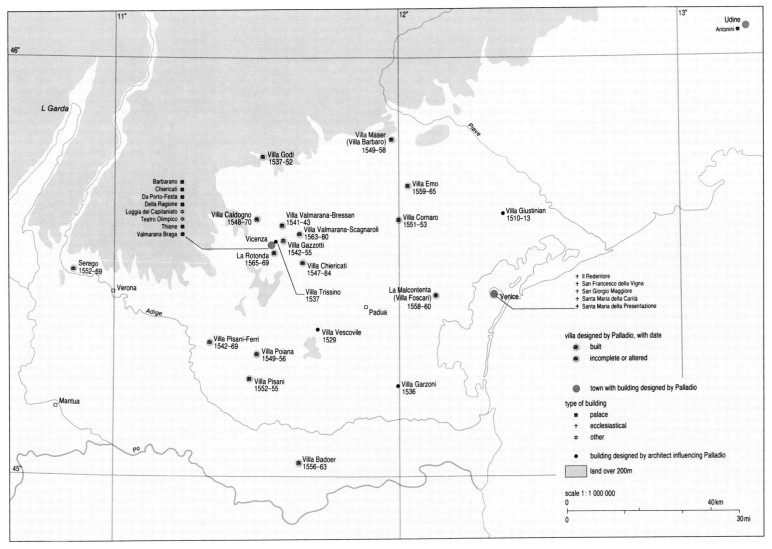

The Rebuilding of Rome

Rome grew rapidly during the 16th century, its population rising from 55,000 to 100,000, and more and more of the land within the ancient walls being developed. Essentially there were two cities: the Vatican, west of the Tiber, and the main – classical – city to the east. Under papal leadership from Alexander VI (1492–1503) to Sixtus V (1585–90) both cities were replanned and expanded, with some buildings being demolished to make way for imposing new buildings and monuments. Straighter roads were created between the major Christian churches and the important gates and bridges (such as Michelangelo's Porta Pia), so that religious processions, pilgrimages, commercial activity and policing were made easier. New housing was developed, and along the main routes orderly palace building was encouraged. This redevelopment reached its high point with the frenetic activity of Pope Sixtus V and his engineer-architect Domenico Fontana (1543–1607). Fontana set about the task with great enthusiasm. He erected obelisks in key locations, such as outside Santa Maria Maggiore, improved Rome's water supply by using both ancient and modern aqueducts, and completed Michelangelo's dome for St Peter's.

During the High Renaissance the new St Peter's slowly came to dominate the Vatican district, and the palace complex became a more regularly structured edifice, with ever more lavish decoration. The ancient Capitoline Hill, or Campidoglio, was the center of Roman civic government. Pope Paul III (1534–49) commissioned Michelangelo to turn this area into an orderly piazza with imposing civic buildings – at a time, ironically, when real civic power was declining under papal dominance.

Below Many architects were involved in the creation of St Peter's, but Michelangelo – modifying Bramante's designs – takes credit for the great dome, the apses and transept. The dome dominates the skyline. It is harder to see the lower exterior of the apse and transepts as these are partly hidden by secluded Vatican gardens.

Right This view of Rome emphasizes the dominant position of the Campidaglio. In 1536 Michelangelo embarked on a major piece of Renaissance urban planning around a piazza. This old view from Michelangelo's splendid double steps of the town hall (Palazzo Senatorio) shows the statue of Marcus Aurelius, the centerpiece of his plan (since removed). The balustrade has imperial Roman statues looking down over the great flight of steps. Later architects completed Michelangelo's planned palaces to the sides.

Above A 1589 print celebrating the achievements and buildings (completed or projected) of Sixtus V, including a new Vatican library, a hospital for the poor, and improvements in the water supply. Obelisks and classical columns (with Christian additions) marked the new routes and vistas.

Right Redecoration of the Vatican under Gregory XIII and Sixtus V included painted maps and views of Rome's recent development. This view by Ignazio Danti (pre-1586) shows St Peter's under construction, protected by fortifications facing the hillsides and the Castel Sant' Angelo next to the Tiber.

One of the figures who flitted in and out of Rome was Benvenuto Cellini (1500–71). Though his father wanted him to be a musician, he insisted on becoming a gold- and silversmith and became one of the most accomplished ever. Very few of his intricate works survive, but his gold and enamel saltcellar, presented to Francis I of France in the 1540s, is one of the major High Renaissance display pieces of craftsmanship and virtuosity.

Cellini is better known for his autobiographical *Life*, which he wrote between 1558 and 1566, partly in response to Vasari's first edition (1550) of his *Lives of the Artists*. In one of the most readable and enthralling books of the period, Cellini reveals himself as a complex and violent character – bisexual, ready to pick fights and even to kill in defense of his reputation or his friends. He spoke openly and frankly to popes and all others. Clement VII and Paul III admired his work, were violently angry with him when works were not delivered quickly, and forgave his crimes when they were. Cellini provided jewelry, silver basins and jugs, elaborate cope buttons, rings and crucifixes. He also designed medals and major coins (and controlled the papal mint for a while). With these he helped to boost the image of the popes and the papacy.

A leading contributor to the new image-building of the papacy was Giorgio Vasari, in his role as painter. He was responsible for fresco decorations in the Chancellery Palace (c. 1545–46), with such titles as *Paul III Inspecting the Rebuilding of St Peter's* and *Paul III Distributing Benefices*. They were painted for Pope Paul III's grandson, Cardinal Alessandro Farnese (1520–89), the vice-chancellor occupying the palace. One of the great Roman patrons of the period, his initial interest was in collecting medals, jewelry, majolica pottery, miniatures and illuminated manuscripts, with the *Farnese Hours*, illustrated by Giulio Clovio, as the most splendid example.

Cardinal Farnese became interested in larger paintings, including erotic works. The cardinal next made his mark as the commissioner of a splendid country villa-palace at Caprarola. The designer was Jacopo Vignola and it was lavishly decorated with frescoes by Taddeo and Federico Zuccaro, and others, combining recondite mythological scenes and depictions of the diplomatic successes of Farnese. Classical and Renaissance themes were taken up in the elaborate formal gardens of the villa. In the 1560s Cardinal Farnese became patron of Il Gesù, the Roman headquarters church for the new religious order of Jesuits, and employed Vignola as architect; Farnese and Vignola thus became major contributors to the Roman Catholic revival.

In the 1530s, Michelangelo underwent a profound change of mood. He grew more pessimistic about man and developed a growing sense of his own worthlessness before God. His art lost its classical confidence, balance and polish. His changing mood, and the deepening of his pessimistic Christian convictions, coincided largely with his intense friendship with the poet Vittoria Colonna (1490–1547), marchioness of Pescara. After the death of her young husband in 1525, Vittoria Colonna became the center of a literary and religious network of Catholic reformers including Cardinals Reginald Pole and Pietro Bembo, and the writers Aretino, Ariosto and Castiglione. She wrote poems, Petrarchan sonnets influenced by Bembo, about her late husband or on religious themes. Michelangelo, who met her in 1536, knew her well

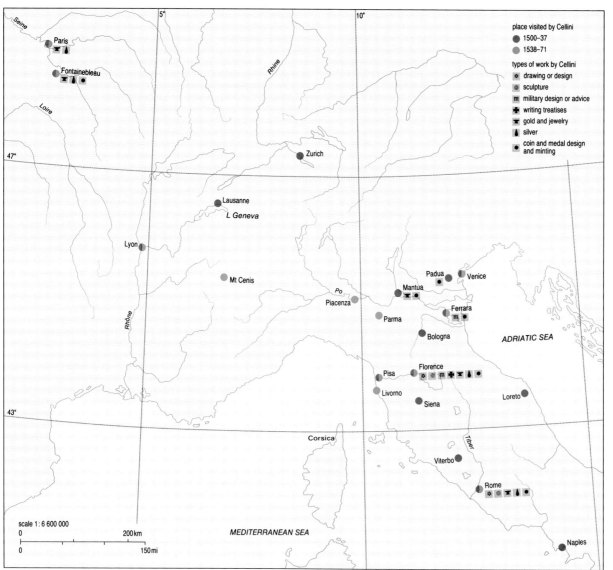

The travels of Cellini
The travels of Benvenuto Cellini, a passionate sometimes violent man of enormous vitality, were dictated as much by restlessness and expediency as by a need to find work. Banished from his native Florence after a duel, he moved to Rome, where he worked for several prominent patrons, including Clement VII. He left Rome after murdering a rival goldsmith, moving between Naples, Mantua and Florence. He was invited to England, but refused to travel with Pietro Torrigiano, who in a brawl had broken the nose of the "divine Michelangelo". In 1537 he moved to France to work for Francis I; suspected of stealing gold and gems, he fled back to Italy. He died in his home town of Florence in 1571.

Above In 1534 Cellini commemorated his patron, Pope Clement VII, with two medals. The common obverse is one of the finest Renaissance portraits. The second reverse has Moses striking the rock in the desert – a reference to this pope's initiative in creating a new civic well in Orvieto.

from her stay in Rome in 1538–41 and 1544–47. He also wrote moving poems for her, poems about his art, love and God. This was part of a deeply emotional, spiritual love affair, and a step toward his final period of devotion to God.

Michelangelo's poems, like his later sculpture, are rough hewn; not smooth and polished in language, but experimental and rule-breaking, at times moving, occasionally witty, and illuminating about his sculpture and paintings. Plans for publishing his poetry in the late 1540s came to nothing, though some were given publicity in lectures to academies and in publications by others, such as his literary friend Benedetto Varchi, and Vasari.

Michelangelo's involvement in the Colonna circle is the background to some influential paintings in Rome, most obviously the *Last Judgment* painted on the altar wall of the Sistine Chapel in the Vatican. Suggested by Clement VII just before his death in 1534, it was insisted on by Paul III. Cartoon designs were started in 1536, but the work was not completed until 1541. For Vasari it was the height of "the grand manner of painting, directly inspired by God . . . "we are shown the misery of the damned and the joy of the blessed . . . in it may be seen marvelously portrayed all the emotions that mankind can experience . . . Michelangelo's figures reveal thoughts and emotions that only he has known how to express."

By 1550 Michelangelo contributed two other highly influential frescoes to the Pauline Chapel in the Vatican: *The Conversion of St Paul* and *The Crucifixion of St Peter*. Because the figures in these works are shown without beauty, as puppets in the hands of God facing the inevitable, some critics see these paintings as totally anticlassical and so anti-Renaissance. Michelangelo's mood at this time is reflected in the poem *The Voyage of my Life*.

Lesser cultural centers and courts

In addition to the major urban centers and their cultural highlights during the High Renaissance, there were many lesser cultural centers in Italy. Many of them focused on small courts dominated by a single family. Out of this environment came the single most influential literary work on courtly culture: *The Courtier* (*Il Cortegiano*) by Baldassare Castiglione (1478–1529). Castiglione was a diplomat, with experience at the courts of Milan (under Lodovico Sforza), Mantua, the Vatican and Urbino. The court at Urbino was the setting for his famous book (finally published in Venice in 1528), which is written as a dialogue, or series of after-dinner discussions between courtiers, soldiers, and literary and artistic men and women of his day.

The Courtier can be read at many levels: as a mildly humorous discourse on courtly manners, as a collection of anecdotes, a contribution to moral philosophy, a manual on how to advise a princely ruler – and

Italian cultural centers in the 16th century
The towns and cities of 16th-century Italy can be divided into two broad categories: those that provided a single source of patronage, such as a court or villa; and those that provided several sources – courts, city governments, various competing patrician families and dominant religious and educational institutions. Some universities – in particular Bologna, Padua and Pisa – made significant contributions to the investigative sciences. Several cities had literary and artistic academies that spread humanist scholarship, new artistic theories, scientific information or a purer Italian language. A few minor localities produced majolica, an elaborately decorated pottery on which images from mythology, history and religion often appeared.

survive – and an easy introduction to the theory of Platonic love. *The Courtier* was also a major contribution toward civilizing society, both encouraging more humane behavior and linking the realism of Machiavelli to a concern for moral values. The courtier – and by extension all those wishing to be seen as gentlemanly and ladylike – should cultivate as many artistic achievements as possible, or at least be able to discuss them knowledgeably without causing others to feel uncomfortable. He or she should behave and talk with grace, and a certain nonchalance (*sprezzatura* is

Castiglione's famous word for it). He argued that women ought to be fully educated, and that the role of *donne di palazzo* (women of the court) was equal (even perhaps superior) to that of male courtiers.

Smaller courts in the High Renaissance played a decreasing role as cultural centers because political power – and so patronage – was concentrated more in the larger cities. Urbino itself did not maintain its earlier importance after 1508, when the duchy passed to the della Rovere family, though in the later 16th century the della Rovere dukes were good patrons of

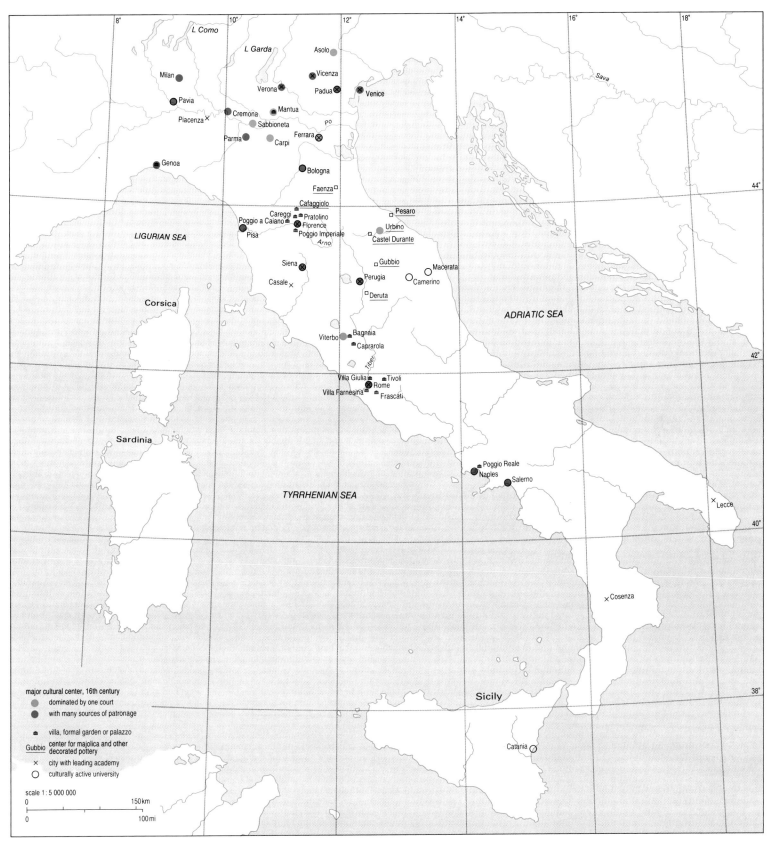

major cultural center, 16th century
● dominated by one court
● with many sources of patronage

▣ villa, formal garden or palazzo
Gubbio center for majolica and other decorated pottery
× city with leading academy
○ culturally active university

scale 1 : 5 000 000
0 _____ 150 km
0 _____ 100 mi

Federico Barocci. To High Renaissance techniques of composition Barocci (c. 1535–1612) added a new sense of color and the depiction of genuine, appropriate emotions and gestures to create an adventurous religious art, suitable for the reforming mood. Under ducal protection, fending off importuning patrons and clients, the hypochondriac Barocci could work in Urbino at his own slow pace and have his altarpieces transported to other parts of Italy.

Mantua under the Gonzagas remained a cultural center in the mid 16th century, surviving as such the deaths of Mantegna, Alberti and Isabella d'Este. To house the ever-growing collection of works of art, great and small, the Gonzagas continually developed their city-palace complex, with Giulio Romano (c. 1492–1546) as court architect and coordinator of decorations. There and in the Palazzo del Tè, an entertainment retreat just outside the city walls, Giulio and his team painted erotic scenes – and some splendid portraits of prized thoroughbred horses. More significantly, Mantua contributed to the development of Italian music (religious and chamber), especially as Duke Guglielmo was himself a composer. He failed, however, to persuade the great Giovanni Palestrina to settle in Mantua.

Ferrara likewise played a role as a musical center through the 16th century. The madrigalist Luzzasco Luzzaschi (c. 1545–1607) encouraged female singers and provided them with trios, and Carlo Gesualdo (c. 1561–1613) became renowned for his adventurous use of dissonances and emotional effects in madrigals and religious motets. Gesualdo, prince of Venosa, settled in Ferrara (after having his first wife murdered when caught in the act of adultery) and married into the d'Este family.

Ferrara was even more important as a literary court, particularly for fostering epic and pastoral poetry and plays. Ludovico Ariosto (1474–1533) was a poet and playwright. He wrote odes and epigrams in Latin and Italian, and for the court he provided comedies in Italian verse and directed entertainments. He is famous for his long epic poem *Orlando Furioso*, which he began in 1502 and completed a few months before he died. It updated a medieval romances about Charlemagne's period with the introduction of classical elements, contemporary topical allusions and the techniques of Italian poetry. He primarily deals with Orlando's unrequited love for Angelica, and with the pagan Ruggiero's conversion to Christianity in order to woo Bradamante – and, allegedly, to start the d'Este dynasty of Ferrara.

Ferrara and the d'Este family went on to foster the literary transition from High Renaissance to Counter-Reformation. Torquato Tasso (1544–95), having been in various courts (especially Urbino) was employed by Cardinal Luigi d'Este and went to Ferrara. In the 1560s he wrote for a local academy on the art of poetry, and then composed for the court a pastoral play *Aminta* (1573), a Renaissance idyll of Arcadia complete with nymphs and shepherds. It incorporates neo-Platonic ideas on love and beauty and attacks the corruption of urban life. Even more notably, Tasso created the massive epic poem *Jerusalem Delivered* (1575), turning the story of the crusaders' reconquest of Jerusalem, aided by God and His angels, into a literary masterpiece for the Catholic revival. From the vibrant narrative emerge major characters, notably Tancredi as a tormented lover; the warrior Rinaldo as a militant Christian facing up to the pagan female

warrior Clorinda; and the sensual Saracen temptress Armida. Tasso spent the years 1577 to 1586 in a hospital asylum in Ferrara. Not because of court intrigue (as often alleged) but at least initially as a result of a violent mental breakdown. He continued to write, revising his epic and producing much else. His role as a leading literary figure in the court of Ferrara was taken over by Giovanni Battista Guarini (1538–1612), whose long-lasting contribution was another pastoral play, *The Faithful Shepherd* (1589).

The courtly literature of Ariosto, Tasso and Guarini played a dominant role in Italian culture, not only enriching the literary language and providing good reading, but also providing material for painters and musicians. Niccolò dell'Abbate's painted fresco illustrations of *Orlando Furioso* in the Palazzo Poggi, Bologna; Gesualdo and Marenzio composed madrigals to his works; and Claudio Monteverdi wrote a dramatic and moving setting of Tasso's description of *The Battle of Tancredi and Clorinda*, first performed in 1624. The texts remained inspirational for later Baroque composers and painters such as Salvator Rosa and Giambattista Tiepolo.

Finally, there are some very small localities that played a cultural role. Deruta and Gubbio produced highly prized types of majolica, a glazed pottery that could be lavishly decorated. The finest examples were coveted at leading courts. They could convey the ideas of painters – directly or through prints – and contributed to the spread of clasical mythology and religious imagery. The involvement of some skilled and learned decorators, such as Giorgio Andreoli and his sons in Gubbio and Francesco Xanto Avelli (mainly working in Urbino), suggest that there were important contacts between major and minor localities.

Florence and the Medici dukes

The Medici family returned to rule Florence in 1512. They lost control to another republican regime in 1527, but regained their position in 1530 after a long siege. They then became powerful princely rulers of Tuscany as dukes and (after 1569) grand dukes. In the earlier years much artistic influence in Florence came from Rome because the Medici were popes: Giovanni as Leo X (1513–21) Giulio as Clement VII (1523–34). The Medici popes were inclined to see cultural activity in Florence as an extension of papal activity, which explains the movement of key figures such as Michelangelo and Cellini between Florence and Rome. Duke Alexander (1530–37) had an excessive interest in women, low life and intrigue. Although he was often generous, he is usually seen as richly deserving his gruesome assassination (while pursuing another beauty) at the hands of a disgruntled relative (and companion in escapades), Lorenzino. Alexander was a good patron to, among others, Bronzino and Vasari. Another patron was Cosimo I de' Medici, who emerged from obscurity to rule as duke (1537–74) and soon developed a high reputation as a clever politician, strong ruler, and beneficial cultural leader.

Medicean Florence made an important contribution to the High Renaissance. Michelangelo was central. He created the Medici Chapel in San Lorenzo (c. 1519–33) as a mausoleum for the family. With its harmonious combination of architecture and sculpture, it represents a high point in the Christian Renaissance and a deep-felt expression of Michelangelo's own devotion to Christianity. Within an architectural setting that (as Vasari stressed) broke away from the classical norms set by Vitruvius and Brunelleschi, the effigies of two Medici captains, Giuliano and Lorenzo, sit in niches ready to face the Madonna and eternity. Beneath are the nude marble figures of male Day and female Night, male Dusk and female Dawn. Michelangelo left Florence before the work was completed, and though the Madonna remained unfinished, "in the imperfect block one can recognize the perfection of the completed work".

During the same period Michelangelo designed and launched the construction of the Laurentian Library, the reading room for the Medici collection of manuscripts. The biggest problem for Michelangelo – and a resulting triumph – was the entrance staircase, which had to be inserted in a confined space, much smaller than it appears. Although the final design is not functionally ideal for a library entrance, it changed the whole notion of sculptured internal staircases.

The image and artistic reputation of the Medici were served by many other artists and writers. Cellini proved his ability in large sculptural work with a bronze portrait bust of Cosimo I, and his nude *Perseus* (1545–54) holding the severed head of snake-haired Medusa and standing over her naked body (modeled on Cellini's mistress, Dorotea). *Perseus* symbolized the heroic, youthful ruler calmly overcoming troubles and challenges. As their leading court painter the Medici employed Agnolo Bronzino (1503–72), who produced stylish formal portraits of the Medici and their courtiers. His other works are characterized by sensuality, contorted body postures and recondite allusions, sacred and profane. They include the famous allegory *Venus, Cupid, Folly and Time* (1546), and *Christ in Limbo* (1552), which shocked and embarrassed leading Counter-Reformation critics, though it delighted Vasari for its "most beautiful nudes" and for its portraits of contemporary Florentines.

Vasari himself was a leading contributor to the Florentine High Renaissance, and to the Medici court. For the growing governmental system – and to provide a theater and residences for artists – he designed the Uffizi (literally "Offices"), now housing the famous art gallery. Nearby he helped to organize the redecoration of the medieval Palazzo Vecchio, to be suitable for the Medici court. Much of the decoration was to celebrate Florentine victories and the virtues of Medici rule. Vasari was a prolific painter. He was often facile, displaying his cleverness at representing the human form, but incapable of portraying convincing emotions. Occasionally he reached the standards he admired in others – in some portraits, and in the *Perseus and Andromeda*, painted in 1570. But above all it was Vasari's *Lives* that contributed most: as propaganda for the values of the High Renaissance and for the role of Tuscans, and as a literary work in its own right.

Below The entrance hall of the Laurentian Library, Florence, by Michelangelo. Work on the library began in 1524 but stopped when the Sack of Rome in 1527 forced Pope Clement VII, who had commissioned the work, to go into hiding. Work began again soon after, but Michelangelo was no longer involved and it was as late as 1559 before he supplied a model for the staircase. This striking view of the entrance hall shows Michelangelo's mastery of decorative architecture – his use of columns and recesses being inspired by Bramante as well as by classical examples – and his success in making the staircase a major sculptural feature.

As one of the final expressions of the High Renaissance it is worth noting the *Intermedi* (or *Intermezzi*) for the wedding celebrations in 1589 for Grand Duke Ferdinando de' Medici (who had just given up being a cardinal) and Princess Christine of Lorraine. The six *Intermedi* were essentially musical interludes, performed between the acts of a comedy, but they were also impressive contributions to the festivities. They involved elaborate stage scenery and costumes by Bernardo Buontalenti, many of whose working designs survive. The music for singers and instrumentalists was composed by major musicians, such as Emilio de' Cavalieri, Luca Marenzio (one of the finest madrigalists of the day) and Cristofano Malvezzi. It owed something to current Florentine theorizing about classical music as well as to the practical developments of Netherlandish and Italian musicians. The Italian texts, mainly by the poet Ottavio Rinuccini, drew inspiration from Ovid and classical mythology. The 1589 Florentine *Intermedi* can be seen as opening the way to Baroque opera.

The High Renaissance in perspective

The high points of the Italian Renaissance came between the 1490s and the 1520s – the mastery in depicting the human form shown by Leonardo, Michelangelo and Titian; the confidence in handling perspective, and playing tricks with it, shown by Raphael and Bramante; new developments in the use of color pioneered by Leonardo and Titian; the confident assurance that the classical world had been mastered and improved upon, seen in the architecture of Bramante and Sansovino and in the literature of Castiglione, Machiavelli, and Ariosto.

The effects of these achievements were long-lasting, though the mood of supreme confidence soon waned. Christian pessimism returned, eroticism diminished. If Raphael and Michelangelo had achieved perfection through balanced and harmonious representation, their successors needed to find new styles and techniques. This often meant distortion, contorted gestures and dissonance.

The Catholic Counter-Reformation is often blamed

Below Veronese's *Feast in the House of Levi* (1573) was intended as a Last Supper, but the Inquisition thought that setting Christ among clowns, dwarfs, servants and animals trivialized the subject. Furthermore, the inclusion of two Germans receiving bread and wine suggested a concealed Lutheran message about the Eucharist. Refusing to change the picture in any way, Veronese merely changed the title. In its use of classical architecture, deep perspective, rich colors and close observation of life, the picture epitomizes the art of the Venetian Renaissance. It also strongly evokes the luxury and splendor of Venetian life.

for the curtailment of the High Renaissance, and a subsequent decline in Italian culture. Changing taste in favor of the later styles of Mannerism and the Baroque, and a better understanding of Church history have modified these criticisms. The Counter-Reformation did have some negative effects. The Council of Trent (meeting intermittently from 1545 to 1563) sought to define Catholic teaching and reform Church practices in response to the growth of Protestantism in northern Europe. Its decrees, printed in 1564, encouraged a puritanical and conservative approach to the arts. Unseemly, "lascivious" church art and music were attacked; artistic messages should follow the Bible and hallowed Church tradition; music should enhance the words of the liturgy, not obscure them in complicated polyphony.

In practice few artists or works of art suffered. Michelangelo's Sistine Chapel *Last Judgment* had some of its nudity covered. Some artists, notably Bronzino (one of the leading lascivious offenders), modified their approach to altarpieces. The Venetian

Inquisition investigated Veronese and one of his Last Supper paintings for possible Lutheran messages about the Eucharist. Writers were more vulnerable. Machiavelli was listed in the papal Index of prohibited Books in 1559 as a full heretic, and so new editions of his writings were not tolerated. Works by Boccaccio, Aretino and Castiglione could be published only in expurgated versions. But old editions circulated surreptitiously, and Machiavelli could still be studied. Aretino's salacious works were reissued under false imprints.

It can be argued, however, that by the later 16th century the openness, the visual and intellectual experimentation of the High Renaissance, were discouraged. The technical achievements were put to new uses in more overtly Christian art, and in more circumspect and seemly classical paganism. From the 1590s onward, however, a reassessment of the work of High Renaissance masters such as Raphael, Leonardo and Michelangelo contributed to the foundation of a new "Baroque" vitality.

Palladio and Neo-Classical Architecture

The neo-classical style of Andrea Palladio (1508–80) has had a longlasting impact on architecture, especially villas and country houses. He started as a humble stonemason, but was soon patronized by a Vicenza patrician, Giangiorgio Trissino, a leading classicist and amateur architect, at whose villa Palladio worked. Trissino introduced Palladio to the theory of classical architecture, enabled him to study ancient buildings in Rome and elsewhere, and put him in touch with other humanists in the Venetian Republic, who in the 1530s gave him several commissions.

Palladio studied Roman remains, absorbed the theories of Alberti and the classical writer Vitruvius, and observed the buildings and designs of High Renaissance contemporaries such as Raphael, Bramante, the Sangallos, Michelangelo and Sansovino. His designs were based on the novel use of classical columns, pilasters and pediments, of loggias and porticos, and he introduced the temple front into domestic architecture.

Palladio was a prolific designer and builder – of urban noble palaces, civic buildings, country villas and churches. His villas, however, are probably his most famous works. Most were not just country retreats from the city politics for Vicenza and Venice, but also working farms where noble landowners expected to supervise new enterprises. Their designs had to cater for family living, administration, storage, and for entertainment and salon life. Painters were brought in – with and without Palladio's approval – to decorate interiors with scenes celebrating the joys, work and wit of refined rural life.

Palladio had considerable success with secular patrons in Vicenza and the countryside; but not in Venice itself, possibly because his neo-classical style seemed not to fit in with contemporary notions of villa design. He produced ecclesiastical masterpieces, notably on the islands of the Giudecca. There he constructed monastic buildings and then the church (from c.1565) for the Benedictines at San Giorgio Maggiore. This was followed by Il Redentore from 1576 (an expression of the city's gratitude for deliverance from plague), and the church facade (1580) of Santa Maria della Presentazione for an institution helping poor girls (Le Zitelle). San Giorgio and the Redentore are notable for their temple-like facades, and for the harmonious relationship between facade and dome seen from afar. Internally, they are also notable for the sense of spaciousness and the relationships – solving both visual and functional problems – between presbytery, choir, nave and side-chapels.

Palladio's impact has come both from his actual buildings, and from his designs and writings, especially the prints in his *Four Books of Architecture* (1570). He particularly inspired British architecture through architects such as Inigo Jones, Colen Campbell, Lord Burlington and Robert Adam. His influence in America can be seen in the building designed by President Thomas Jefferson, particularly his Monticello house, his own home in Virginia.

Right Palladio closely studied classical remains as a preparation for his own work. Surviving drawings link his buildings and the designs in his *Four Books of Architecture*. The facade of the Venetian church of Il Redentore shows signs of his study of the Pantheon; the interior of the Villa La Malcontenta was clearly influenced by the Baths of Constantine. The Palazzo Valmarana in Vicenza was influenced both by Palladio's study of the Temple of Mars and his drawing of the temple facade surviving in Assisi (*right*). This drawing, showing Palladio's special interest in classical columns and their decoration, is one of many Palladio drawings that Inigo Jones and his associates brought back from Italy in the early 17th century.

Above The Villa Barbaro at Maser was built in the hills of the Trevigiano for the Barbaro brothers: Daniele, who with Palladio published a translation and comment on Vitruvius' *Ten Books of Architecture* (1556), and Marcantonio, who dabbled in sculpture and architecture. Their villa was the center of a very active farm, and the extended porticoed outbuildings were functional as well as splendid visually. Palladio and Daniele apparently disagreed over the final designs, and Paolo Veronese was brought to finish the project, producing splendid illusionist frescoes.

Right Palladio was a member of the Olympian Academy in Vicenza. Long interested in classical theaters, he had produced temporary theaters and sets. In 1580 he designed a permanent theater, the Teatro Olimpico, for the Academy. There is a small elliptical audience hall, and the elaborately decorated stage with its triumphal arch. In 1584 Vincenzo Scamozzi altered the design when, for a production of *Oedipus Rex*, he created street scenes behind the arch. These became permanent. It is fitting that Palladio ended his career with a classically inspired theater.

Left The Villa La Rotonda was built for a leading church official, Paolo Almerico, on a hill just outside Vicenza. Unlike most Palladian villas it was not a working farm, but a retirement home suitable for the relaxation after service in Rome. It is Palladio's only fully centralized design, with four porticos leading into the central domed interior room. The dome was influenced by the Roman Pantheon. Completion came, possibly by Vincenzo Scamozzi, after Palladio's death; fresco and stucco decoration followed through the 17th century. The plan and external design are seen as the perfection of Palladio's ideas.

Leonardo and the Infinite Works of Nature

Many Renaissance artists and philosophers wrote of nature and its value for art, but none was so observant or analytical as Leonardo da Vinci. The proof of both his insatiable curiosity and his deep understanding of nature is to be found in his many drawings and notebooks. Often delaying work on commissioned paintings, he recorded with meticulous care what he saw all around him, however commonplace.

Early drawings from the 1470s show his fascination with landscapes, with mountains, rocks and water, and with the effects of color and light in nature. "The colors of the shadows in mountains at a great distance take a most lovely blue, much purer than their illuminated portions." Such observations were often incorporated into his paintings. Increasingly, he became fascinated by the most intricate workings of nature, a fascination clearly evident in his drawings of plants and anatomical dissections – dissections he himself carried out.

Some studies were intended to improve his painting. Drawings of the Star of Bethlehem and other flowers enhance the natural setting and the image of nature's profusion in his painting *Leda and the Swan*. Studies of horses were preludes to his fresco *The Battle of Anghiari*, or his projected equestrian statue for his patron Lodovico Sforza. An accurate understanding of muscles and sinews was the key to realistic depic-

tions of men, women and animals in action; anatomical observations could also lead to ideas about engineering, including a flying machine. Even imaginative artistic creations depended on close observation of the real world.

Leonardo envisaged his drawings and notes forming an encyclopedic book of nature, with lesser treatises on such subjects as optics, anatomy and painting. His observations and thoughts developed into a natural philosophy based on the wholeness of nature. "The eye, the window of the soul, is the chief organ by which the understanding can obtain the most complete and magnificent view of the infinite works of nature." Carried away with detailed study, Leonardo completed no great encyclopedia or even treatise, and too few paintings.

> You cannot invent animals without limbs, each of which must itself resemble those of some other animal. So ... for a dragon take for its head that of a mastiff or hound, with the eyes of a cat ...

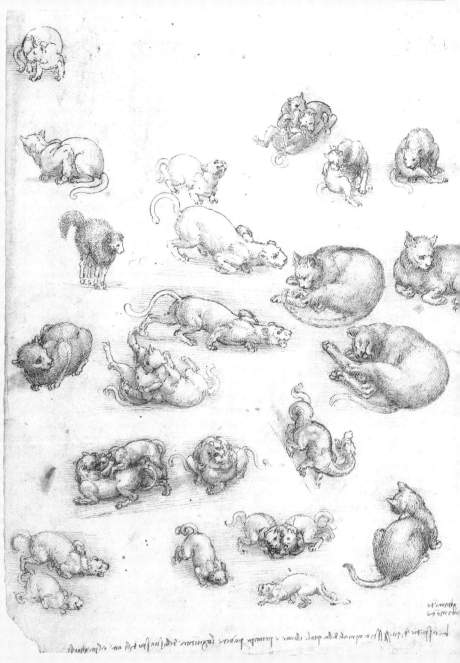

> You imitators of nature – be sure to attend to the many configurations of things.

Would that ... I were able to reveal the nature of man just as I describe his figure.

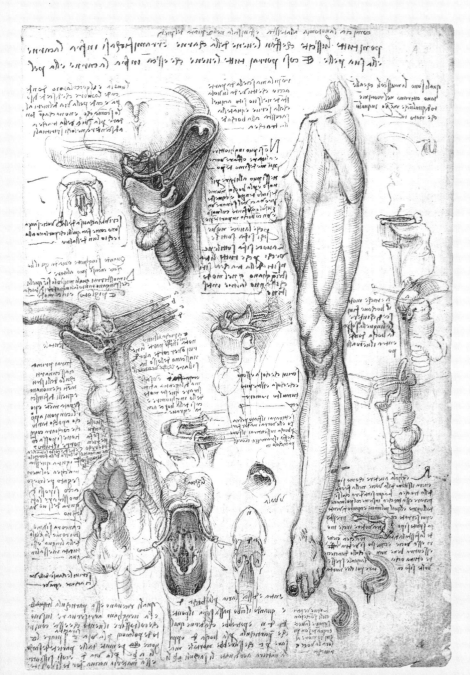

All visible things are produced by nature, and these her children gave birth to painting. So we may rightly call painting the grandchild of nature and related to God.

On the tops and sides of hills, foreshorten the shape of the ground and its divisions, but give proper shape to what is turned toward you.

Ladies of Learning

The idea that women could benefit from education was adopted by Western society along with other Greek ideas and values, and during the Renaissance the schools of humanists such as Vittorino da Feltre and Battista Guarino admitted girls as well as boys. Naturally, the only girls involved were the daughters of those inclined to a humanistic education.

As long as education was appreciated as a training of the mind, it made no difference whether the pupil was a boy or girl. When a girl grew devoted to study, however, she found herself facing enormous difficulties. There was no career open to her, and little chance of devoting her life to scholarship. Some, such as Isotta Nogarola and Cassandra Fedele, did try to enter the arena of humanist debate, but their reward was to be mythologized. Men could cope with the lofty concept of a learned virgin, but not with a competitive female.

Poliziano's trip from Florence to Venice in 1491 was prompted by his desire to see for himself the renowned Cassandra Fedele, with whom he had been corresponding. He wrote back to Lorenzo de' Medici that she was a miraculous phenomenon, "most modest, and to my eyes even beautiful. I departed stupefied". Whether from prolonged stupefaction, or from mere neglect, Poliziano did not reply to Cassandra's next letter and the goddess became an ordinary, hurt, woman. Guarino, faced with similar signs of humanity in his correspondent, Isotta Nogarola, told her firmly: "You show yourself so cast down, humiliated and truly womanish that I am able to perceive nothing which accords with my previous magnificent opinion of you."

The majority of women who refused marriage were consigned to the convent. Some of the educated ones opted to go voluntarily. It was not a choice, however, between study and the domestic life, for either way secular studies had to be abandoned. On the whole, the women who chose marriage fared better. The lady of the court, such as Lorenzo de' Medici's mother Lucrezia, or Elisabetta Gonzaga, was venerated, and in human rather than mythological terms. The affection in which Lorenzo's friends held his mother was marked and sincere. Lorenzo himself consulted her often in matters of politics. Elisabetta Gonzaga, the hostess of the debate in Castiglione's *The Courtier*, Marguerite of Navarre and Lady Margaret Beaufort, used their high positions to support humanist projects and endeavors. Henry II of France said of his aunt, Marguerite of Navarre: "If it were not for my aunt Margaret I should doubt the existence of such a thing as genuine goodness on the earth."

The scholarly woman, finding herself a rarity in her society, corresponded with like-minded women across Europe. Cassandra Fedele offered herself as an adornment to the court of Queen Isabella of Spain but was refused permission to leave her native city by the Venetian authorities. They considered her an ornament they wanted to keep. Marguerite of Navarre had in her court the young Anne Boleyn, and Anne's daughter, the future Queen Elizabeth, translated Marguerite's poems from French into English.

Above Lady Margaret Beaufort (c. 1441–1509) married Edmund Tudor at the age of 12 and was widowed at the age of 13. Her son, Henry VII, was the first Tudor monarch, and it was during his reign that Renaissance ideas first made a significant impact in England. Despite the turmoil of her times, Lady Margaret remained constant in her support of the new learning, was a keen patron of scholarship, and did much to reinvigorate the universities of Oxford and Cambridge.

Right One of the outstanding pupils of Vittorino da Feltre was the daughter of the Duke of Mantua, Cecilia Gonzaga (1426–51). Such was her passion for study that she refused an arranged marriage to the Duke of Urbino and chose instead to go into a convent. Her tutor supported her and on the day she entered the convent her brothers and a large crowd escorted her through the streets of Mantua.

Left Margaret Roper (1505–44) was the favorite daughter of Sir Thomas More. On the birth of Margaret's first child, Erasmus sent her, along with a kiss for the baby, his commentary on the *Christmas Hymn of Prudentius*. Margaret translated the work into English and published it in 1526. She corresponded tenderly with her father during the weeks leading up to his execution.

Right Marguerite d'Angouleme, Queen of Navarre (1492–1549) was the sister of Francis I and encouraged his support of humanist culture. A friend of Erasmus, she was a highly influential figure in Reformation circles. Her principal work, the *Heptameron* – a collection of 70 stories in the manner of Boccaccio's *Decameron* – was published in 1558.

Left Isabella d'Este's correspondence with Cesare Borgia. Isabella (1474–1539) and Beatrice d'Este (1475–97), the daughters of the Duke of Ferrara, were educated by the humanist Battista Guarino. After their marriages, Isabella reigned over a cultural flowering in Mantua while Beatrice, who married the Duke of Milan, encouraged Leonardo to visit the city.

Above The poet Vittoria Colonna (1490–1547) counted Pietro Bembo and Castiglione among her friends, and Michelangelo's adoration was made public in the several sonnets he composed in her honor. Her book of poems, *Rime Spirituali*, was published four times between 1538 and 1544.

PART TWO
THE RENAISSANCE AND THE WIDER WORLD

ITALY, VENICE AND THE DIFFUSION OF THE RENAISSANCE

Widening horizons

In Act II of William Shakespeare's *A Midsummer Night's Dream* (first performed in the 1590s), Oberon the fairy king sends Puck to fetch him "a little western flower called love-in-idleness" with which he wants to taunt Titania, the fairy queen. Puck departs, promising "I'll put a girdle round about the earth/In forty minutes". Puck's lines provide an attractive example of what the Renaissance had given Europeans by the late 16th century: that is, a new confidence in the way in which they could now think and speak of time and space. That confidence was derived from the investigations of humanists and the achievements of artists in Italy in the 15th century.

How were the innovations of the humanists and artists of Italy transmitted to the rest of Europe? One set of routes was provided by the commercial networks that medieval Italian merchants had established, and that gave Italy so many points of contact with other parts of Europe. Two other developments increased the speed with which the new ideas were to circulate: books and educational institutions. Printing joined the words of the humanists with the engravings of the masters in one of Europe's first mass-production processes. The humanists valued education, and there was increased demand for books and the ideas they contained in the new centers of learning established all over Europe in the 15th and 16th centuries.

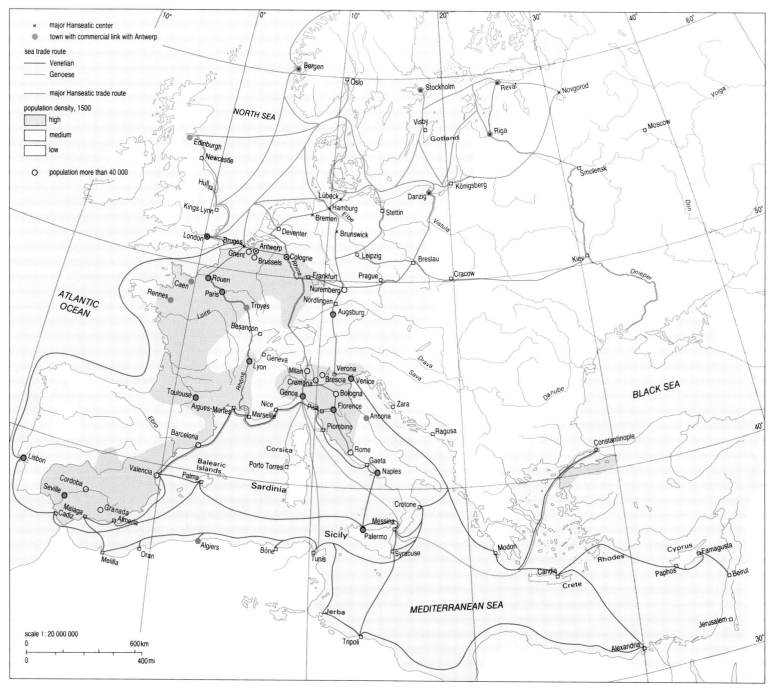

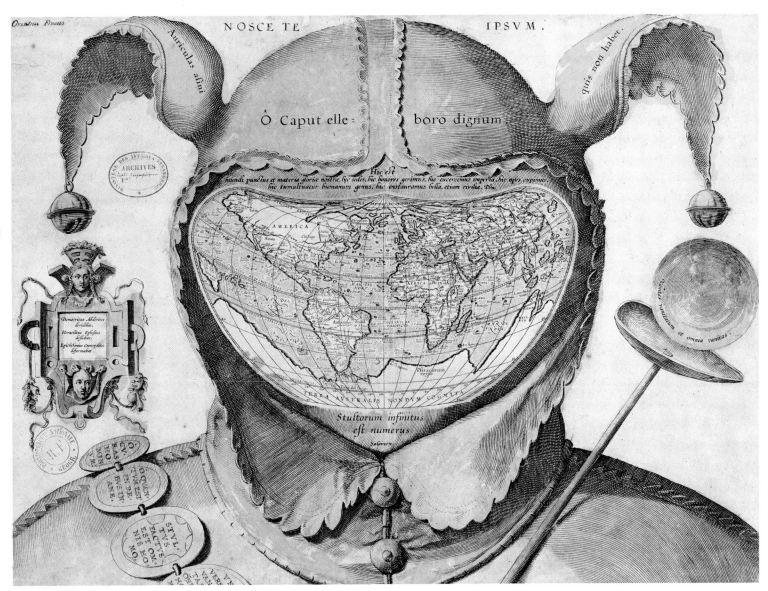

Above A world map within a fool's head (c. 1590). Accurate drawing and the technology of printing helped Europeans to record and understand the world they began to explore during the Renaissance. As in this remarkable instance, the delight in cartography was sometimes matched by an exuberance of wit and imagination.

Left: European trade, c. 1500
By the 14th century, European trade routes ran along east–west axes in the Baltic and the Mediterranean, and the two maritime zones were linked by another axis stretching from London in the north to Rome in the south. In the 16th century, the opening of new possibilities in the Atlantic produced a dramatic redefinition of Europe's commercial networks, and while many of the traditional centers continued to thrive, the economic boom was most marked in new centers, especially Antwerp, Lyon and Seville. Such cities were creating new economic possibilities, though they failed to develop a distinctive cultural identity to equal that of the Italian city-states of the 15th century.

The diffusion of the Renaissance can easily appear as an irresistible process that carried all before it in Europe after 1500. It might be argued, for instance, that the urban setting of the Italian achievements increased the creativity and the restlessness of the laity in towns elsewhere in Europe, making them impatient of the burdens placed upon them by the clergy, leading therefore to the Protestant Reformation. The Reformation, that is, was initially and fundamentally the outcry of urban societies in Germany and the Swiss Confederation. Then again, the "spirit of inquiry" or endless curiosity that characterizes "Renaissance man" can be seen as the mainspring of the exploring impulse that was to take European culture across the world. It scarcely needs restating that Christopher Columbus was a Genoese, and that he sought across the Atlantic Ocean the "Cipango" (Japan) that the Venetian Marco Polo had heard of on his Asian travels and had later written about. Indeed, the stamp of Renaissance man was left on the new continent. Michael Waldseemüller was so impressed with Amerigo Vespucci's account of his voyages in 1498–99 that when he produced his map of the world in 1507–09 he named the new continent America in honor of the Florentine pilot.

Other achievements might be traced to the Italian Renaissance, especially the Scientific Revolution of the late 17th and 18th centuries. This might first have gathered strength in Italy, following the scientific observations of Galileo and his confirmation that the Earth moved round the Sun. However, the Counter-Reformation Catholic Church forced Galileo to recant and discouraged scientific speculation in the Catholic countries of southern Europe. It was northern Europe – especially the Netherlands and England – that eventually led the way.

The danger of the interpretation outlined above is that it assumes that the Renaissance was a unified movement with a single direction, and that it was, above all, "modern" and "progressive". It *is* important to appreciate the originality and excitement of Renaissance culture and its importance for the development of modern Europe. On the other hand, however, it is dangerous to assume that other parts of Europe were somehow less advanced than Italy, and that the 16th century was a time when they tried – despite their backwardness – to catch up. Indeed, it is possible to argue that in some regions history and culture were pulling in directions that made the passive absorption of Italianate values undesirable or unacceptable. In Reformation Germany, for instance, the application of the humanist study of history revealed a distinctly *un*classical past. The Germans had not been conquered by the Romans: why should they then accept the rule of a Roman pope? A growing sense of national identity did much to intensify the aspiration for religious reform in Germany.

Correspondingly, the Counter-Reformation was, in

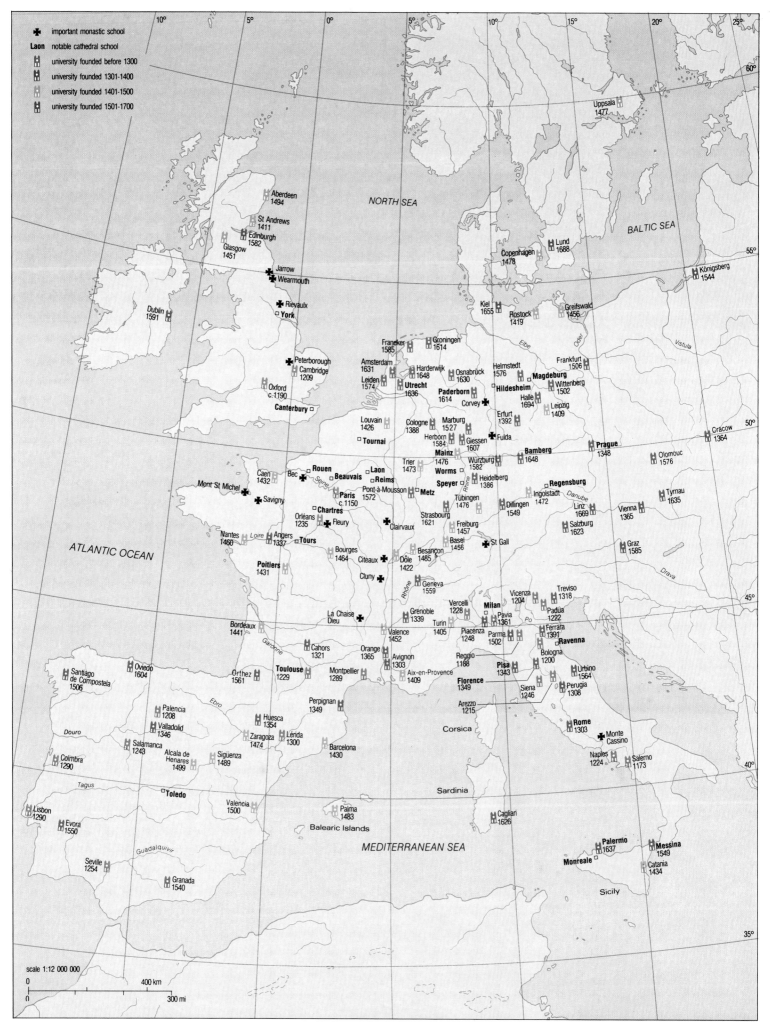

important monastic school

Laon notable cathedral school

university founded before 1300

university founded 1301-1400

university founded 1401-1500

university founded 1501-1700

NORTH SEA

BALTIC SEA

Uppsala
1477

Aberdeen
1494

St Andrews
1411

Edinburgh
1582

Glasgow
1451

Jarrow

Wearmouth

Rievaulx

York

Dublin
1591

Peterborough

Cambridge
1209

Oxford
c.1190

Canterbury

Copenhagen
1478

Lund
1688

Königsberg
1544

Kiel
1655

Rostock
1419

Greifswald
1456

Franeker
1585

Groningen
1614

Frankfurt
1506

Amsterdam
1631

Harderwijk
1648

Osnabrück
1630

Helmstedt
1576

Magdeburg

Leiden
1574

Utrecht
1636

Paderborn
1614

Corvey

Hildesheim

Wittenberg
1502

Halle
1694

Leipzig
1409

Louvain
1426

Cologne
1388

Marburg
1527

Erfurt
1392

Herborn
1584

Giessen
1607

Fulda

Prague
1348

Olomouc
1576

Cracow
1364

Tournai

Mainz

Bamberg
1648

Trier
1473

Würzburg
1582

Caen
1432

Bec

Rouen

Beauvais

Laon

Reims

Worms

Heidelberg
1386

Regensburg

Tyrnau
1635

Mont St Michel

Savigny

Pont-à-Mousson
1572

Metz

Speyer

Tübingen
1476

Ingolstadt
1472

Linz
1669

Vienna
1365

Paris
c.1150

Chartres

Orléans
1235

Fleury

Clairvaux

Strasbourg
1621

Dillingen
1549

Salzburg
1623

Nantes
1460

Angers
1337

Tours

Bourges
1464

Citeaux

Dôle
1422

Besançon
1485

Freiburg
1457

Basel
1456

St Gall

Graz
1585

Poitiers
1431

Cluny

Geneva
1559

Grenoble
1339

Vercelli
1228

Milan

Vicenza
1204

Treviso
1318

La Chaise
Dieu

Turin
1405

Pavia
1361

Piacenza
1248

Parma
1502

Padua
1222

Bordeaux
1441

Valence
1452

Orange
1365

Avignon
1303

Reggio
1188

Ferrara
1391

Ravenna

Cahors
1321

Aix-en-Provence
1409

Bologna
1200

Urbino
1564

ATLANTIC OCEAN

Oviedo
1604

Santiago
de Compostela
1506

Toulouse
1229

Orthez
1561

Montpellier
1289

Perpignan
1349

Pisa
1343

Florence
1349

Siena
1246

Perugia
1308

Palencia
1208

Huesca
1354

Arezzo
1215

Rome
1303

Monte
Cassino

Valladolid
1346

Zaragoza
1474

Lérida
1300

Salamanca
1243

Alcala de
Henares
1499

Sigüenza
1489

Barcelona
1430

Corsica

Naples
1224

Salerno
1173

Coimbra
1290

Toledo

Tagus

Sardinia

Lisbon
1290

Valencia
1500

Palma
1483

Cagliari
1626

Evora
1550

Balearic Islands

MEDITERRANEAN SEA

Palermo
1637

Messina
1549

Seville
1254

Monreale

Catania
1434

Granada
1540

Sicily

Ebro

Douro

Guadalquivir

Garonne

Loire

Seine

Rhine

Rhône

Po

Elbe

Oder

Vistula

Danube

Drava

scale 1:12 000 000

0   400 km

0   300 mi

certain respects, also a Counter-Renaissance. In Spain, as in Italy, Catholic ideology rejected humanism both intellectually and socially, and did so for the same reason in each case: the lack of certainty it caused. It rejected intellectual speculation for its uncertainty and it rejected uncertainty as a luxury of social elites. The Church could provide all the guidance that was needed. Not to obey was a symptom of pride, the sin of Lucifer. As the Catholic reformer and founder of the Jesuits, St Ignatius (1491–1556), put it in his *Spiritual Exercises*: "To arrive at the truth in all things, we ought always to be ready to believe what seems to us white is black, if the hierarchical Church so defines it." Once the Church had given a lead, it was the duty of the faithful merely to follow. Galileo's ideas placed him under suspicion of heresy because he said he could not be sure, which was a challenge to the dogmatic certainties of the Church.

Finally, there is nothing to suggest that the values of the Renaissance were opening up the New World, having been rejected, for the time being, in Europe itself. The Spanish conquerors of America were interested in material gain, in grants of Indians and gold, not in abstract values. The followers of Hernán Cortés in Mexico and of Francisco Pizarro in Peru were mercenaries in a frontier war, not the propagandists of humanism.

These negative considerations are of great importance, for they emphasize that the Renaissance was a complex phenomenon. The 16th century was an age of upheaval, not of smooth transition. Europe was divided by the Reformation and constantly menaced by the apparently unstoppable might of the Ottoman Empire. The diffusion of Renaissance culture could not escape those conflicts. This chapter looks at the fundamental stages of that diffusion. How did Renaissance culture spread in Italy itself? Why did Venice become so important in the transmission of that culture to other parts of Europe? What were the implications of Renaissance values for the Reformation and the Scientific Revolution? What, finally, did the Renaissance contribute to the identity of modern Europe?

Italy in the context of Europe

The diffusion of Renaissance culture from Italy into Europe was made possible partly by the way Renaissance culture had been diffused and changed within Italy itself. The artistic and humanist culture of 15th-century Florence had been closely identified with the city's republican politics and civic culture. It was unlikely therefore to attract the interest of princes who ruled elsewhere. In the late 15th and early 16th centuries Florence itself became less republican and its Medici governors more and more resembled the princely rulers and families of other Italian cities.

Parallel changes took place in Renaissance arts and ideas, which made Renaissance culture more appealing to princely courts. In the early 15th century there had been numerous patrons of the arts in Florence who had competed with each other for the services of different artists. Artists themselves had competed for patronage. This situation had encouraged tremendous vitality. In the later 15th century, however, the Medici had become leading patrons. This trend had considerable implication for ideas and artistic styles. In the early 15th century, Florentine humanists had developed a republican rhetoric during the city's conflict with the Visconti rulers of Milan. In the later 15th

century humanists were more absorbed in philosophy, especially neo-Platonism and its more detached view of the world. In painting in the early 15th century, the invention of perspective had produced compositions of breathtaking drama and realism. By the later 15th century, compositions were more allusive and indirect.

These changes meant that by the end of the 15th century Medicean Florence had conformed to the political structures found in many parts of Italy, which in turn resembled the political structures of most princely states of Europe. The argument must not be pressed too far, however, for there is no evidence that the states of Italy were particularly outward-looking. Theirs was an assured and elegant world, but in many respects it was self-contained. At the end of the 15th century that self-contained world was smashed open.

In 1494 France and Spain clashed over which dynasty had the stronger claim to Naples. Within a few years the contest had spread to Milan. Despite their name, the Italian Wars are most easily understood as the struggle for European predominance between the Habsburgs of Germany and the Valois of France. The wars brought European princes and European nobles into contact with Italian culture, but the outsiders had not come to learn about Italian culture: they had come to teach Italians how the rest of Europe now fought its wars. When the emperor's unpaid German mercenaries plundered Rome in 1527, it seemed to some that the Goths had returned – Luther's name was left in graffiti amid the frescoes of Raphael. It is not surprising that the Italians themselves saw the invaders as barbarians. But this reveals the isolation of Italy and its attitudes rather than its cultural supremacy.

A consideration of the main trade routes in Europe undermines any assumption of Italian dominance in trade as the 16th century opened. For example, the Baltic trading zone, which the Hanseatic League had largely controlled in the Middle Ages, was of great importance. Moreover, the opening of the Atlantic suddenly brought prosperity to Antwerp, though the paradox here is that the cultural repercussions of Antwerp's economic boom were so limited. This in turn raises doubts about any simple connection between the control of trade routes and the diffusion of ideas. Certainly Antwerp became Europe's great emporium before the conflicts of Protestant and Catholic powers brought about its eclipse in the later 16th century, and it was a major center of the European printing industry – the celebrated Plantin firm was one of more than 50 printing houses in the city. Yet it never became a great cultural center in the way some of the Italian states had been. Why, for example, was there no Antwerp school of painting?

There was no great flowering of arts and letters in the other economic success stories, such as Seville, Lyons or even London, at least before about 1600. These cities were unlike the centers of the Italian Renaissance, most obviously Florence and Venice, because they were not city-states. This reinforces the idea that the achievements of the independent Italian cities were not easily transferable to the boom-towns and capitals that were part of much larger political entities in the north and west of Europe.

The journeys of notable individuals provide more convincing evidence of how ideas moved from one place to another. The travels of Leonardo da Vinci were not untypical, as Vasari's *Lives of the Artists*

European centers of learning
The Renaissance was an age of revolution in education. Of crucial importance was the greater accessibility of learning to the laity. However, scholasticism – the old learning of the medieval clergy – was not wholly supplanted by humanism – the new learning of laymen. Many of the new university foundations aimed to provide the state with literate servants rather than to exalt the accurate study of the classical world. Moreover, traditional centers, such as the Sorbonne in Paris, resisted novelty and remained influential. Indeed, in some ways humanism was reabsorbed by scholasticism in the 16th century, and in some areas the old learning was only finally supplanted during the Scientific Revolution of the 17th century.

(1550) demonstrates. The printing press gave wide circulation to the ideas of Erasmus, but he also traveled extensively throughout the zone marked by Cambridge in the north and Rome in the south. Venice was an exotic center of creativity because of the human traffic that flowed through it. It is important to remember, also, that the process of cultural exchange in the Renaissance was by no means one-way – that is *from* Italy *to* everywhere else.

The idea of interaction rather than merely of Italian "export" in the development of Renaissance culture in Europe as a whole becomes still more persuasive when the parts played by printing and by institutions of learning are considered. The printing press was not, of course, an Italian invention, and centers of book production were not necessarily centers of the new learning. This point is obvious in the cases of Antwerp and Lyons, but it is also applicable to Venice, where the dominant social order did not need humanism for either ideological or historical purposes.

The chronology of university foundations questions any idea that Italy provided a lead for the rest of Europe in some simple way. Medieval foundations may or may not have welcomed the intellectual innovations of the humanists. The English humanist John Colet gave an airing to neo-Platonism in lectures in Oxford in the 1490s, yet it was Cambridge – where Erasmus stayed for a time (1509–14) and where the Strasbourg reformer Martin Bucer passed his later years (1548–51) – that provided the greater impetus for debate on matters of religion. On the other hand, the academics of the Sorbonne remained staunchly traditional in their intellectual stance – Luther called them "the moles and bats of Paris".

It is important to reflect on this feature, for though humanism is easily associated with scholarship, the Renaissance as a whole was by no means the product of academies. The great centers of the Renaissance were not the sites of ancient universities, such as Padua and Bologna. The university in Florence did not exert a decisive influence on the shaping of Florentine culture. It is more convincing to see the university foundations of the period 1400–1600 as providing trained servants of the state rather than full-time scholars. There was no university in Venice, the city that was to prove both an inspiration and a formative influence on the shape of modern European civilization. In Venice the Renaissance survived in a republican state; and it is from Venice that the new dimensions of the European Renaissance may be viewed most profitably.

Venice and Florence

Because Venice experienced no political revolution or violent social conflict in the late 15th and early 16th centuries, unlike other Italian cities, it is often treated as an exception in an age of religious war and rebellion. Why then did it play such an influential part in the development of Renaissance Europe? While the Florentine Renaissance exploded from a white-hot nucleus, the Venetian Renaissance reflected the city's capacity to absorb influences from outside. Venice had no historical connection with the classical past but celebrated a unique continuity in its own development. Stability and continuity were the key features of Venetian social life guaranteed by the constitution. This was an aristocratic constitution that denied magisterial office to people who were not members of a rigidly defined patriciate. Venice was an

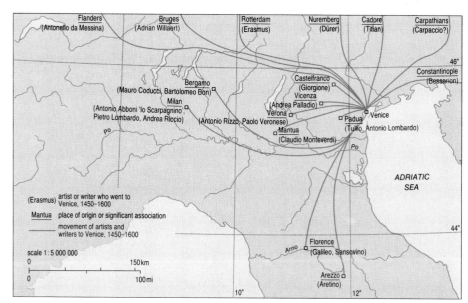

oligarchy. The constitution was less vulnerable than the Florentine constitution to the informal exercise of power networks of clients within the elite. Equally, there was no pretense of a broadly based political community, which in Florence, in principle at least, was guaranteed by membership of a guild. This emphasis on stability had its cultural repercussions. There was no profit in using history – as the Florentine rhetoricians had done – to draw attention to the degrading process by which ancient Rome had passed from republic to principate, and to consider therefore how that process might be avoided.

With regard to the visual arts, it is much harder than in the case of Florence to describe the Venetian Renaissance in terms of the interrelated achievements of famous painters, sculptors and architects. Only among the first of these is it helpful to make direct comparisons, and that is because contemporaries did so. Even then it is hard to compare like with like, for the fundamental strength of Florentine painting was the draftsmanship that underpinned the composition, while the Venetian "school" was distinguished by its use of color for pictorial effect. The Venetian achievement in sculpture and architecture can only appear markedly inferior – no Venetian sculptor compares, say, with Donatello or Michelangelo, and Venetian architecture (with the important exception of Palladio) was shaped by Gothic and Byzantine influences.

Paradoxically, in examining Venetian culture in terms of Renaissance humanism and Renaissance art, at least one vital component of the Venetian Renaissance is lost. For Venetian architecture and Venetian painting enjoyed a close relationship with Venetian music. Andrea Palladio (1508–80) took careful account of acoustics in the design of his Venetian churches, while many Venetian paintings are enriched – as was the public life of the city itself – by the inclusion of musicians and their instruments.

The profound cultural differences between Florence and Venice and the problems of comparison they cause cannot be brushed aside, yet they serve to emphasize two important similarities. First, the Renaissance in both Florence and Venice flowered under republican governments. Second, the material achievements of both cities owed much more to a highly skilled work force than to scholars and academicians.

The significance of Venice

So there were points of contact between Venice and Florence. What then does the history of Venice say about the nature of the Renaissance in Italy and in Europe as a whole? Although the Venetian Republic referred to itself as "La Serenissima" ("The Most Serene"), its civilization was no smooth amalgam but a taut reconciliation of many of the political and cultural tensions that existed in other cities and states. One of the books that spread the "myth" of Venice as the perfect state to other parts of Europe was Gasparo Contarini's *On the Commonwealth and Government of Venice*, which he wrote in the 1520s. It presents the Venetian constitution as a mixture of Aristotle's ideal forms: monarchy represented by the doge, aristocracy by the Senate, democracy by the Great Council. It emphasizes that judgments are always made collectively and that the wise ancestors of the Venetian aristocracy had made careful provision to ensure that there was no room for faction or tyranny. Yet this was a book written when Andrea Gritti was doge (1523–38). Gritti had defended Padua against the League of Cambrai, a European coalition engineered by Pope Julius II in 1508 to dismember the Venetian Republic and divide its territories among the signatories. As doge he stressed the princely authority of that office, for example in giving private audience to the ambassadors of foreign powers, which was against the Venetian constitution. Moreover, Gritti promoted the imperial theme in replanning Venice. Sansovino's work in the piazzetta at San Marco helped to persuade visitors that Venice was the new Rome. As the century

wore on, tensions grew between those who prized the austere traditional values of republicanism – sobriety, prudence, restraint – and those who stressed the imperial theme – opulence, power, glory. Like Florence, Venice experienced something of the conflict between republican virtue and princely magnificence that was so critical to the development of the Renaissance.

Some Venetians advocated that their churches should become independent from the papacy in Rome. Venice became antagonistic toward the Holy See: in 1482 the city was placed under papal ban and again during the crisis of the League of Cambrai. During another clash, in 1606, the English ambassador, Sir Henry Wotton, became convinced that with encouragement from abroad Venice might become a Protestant state. This was either exaggeration or wishful thinking, but there can be no doubt that the

Venetian State experienced something of the conflicts of the Reformation era.

Finally, the Venetians themselves became convinced that the Atlantic routes for the spice trade meant the end of their prosperity. They proved themselves wrong, and in so doing became the eastern outpost of what we might now call the West.

This extraordinary resolution of so many different facets of Europe's historical experience in the 15th and 16th centuries made Venice unique – but unique as a combination of typical features. Venice therefore provides a fascinating perspective on the great themes of the age. It shows that humanism and the visual arts had diverged, and that in spite of this rift the Atlantic discoveries were bringing about a new cultural coherence in Europe as a whole.

The social implications of humanism can be seen with great clarity. The explanation of this lies in the visits of "the prince of humanists", Erasmus, and his collaboration with the great printer-publisher Aldus Manutius (c. 1450–1515), that began in 1508 and made Erasmus's *Adagia* a best-seller. The ideas of Erasmus were informed by the intense spirituality of the "modern devotion", a lay religious movement that emerged in the Low Countries in the 14th century. He was impatient with a religion based on merely external observance. Much of the paraphernalia of such a religion, especially the cult of the saints, reinforced superstition and encouraged dependence on a priesthood that through its ignorance and impiety had sacrificed any claim to privileged status. Monks, abbots and friars were not mentioned in the Bible, which was the true source of Christianity. Such ideas expressed the spiritual dissatisfaction of an urban laity that had grown impatient with ceremonies that disrupted the working day, and tired of priests who demanded a share of the earnings. This was the essence of the anticlericalism that became so powerful a force in the urban Reformation.

Printing was to prove a powerful instrument of expression and propagation. Aldus was not the only printer Erasmus used. What attracted Erasmus to Aldus was the delightful italic script Aldus used, a script that made a book both attractive and handy. Aldus had created the pocket edition.

There is plenty of evidence to show that Erasmian

Left Andrea Gritti was not a popular choice as doge in 1523, perhaps because his imperious nature – caught majestically in Titian's portrait of about 1535 – was not entirely in keeping with Venetian traditions of collective rule. However, Gritti's patronage of artists such as Sansovino made Venice look all the more an imperial capital after the Sack of Rome in 1527.

Right: Centers of printing, 15th–17th centuries
The new technology of printing developed and spread within the old urban heartland of Europe. There can be no doubt that the new ideas of the Renaissance and of the Reformation spread with unprecedented speed and were particularly attractive to literate laymen. The images of Renaissance artists and the words of Renaissance writers and reformers could be mass-produced. Although the low level of literacy must always qualify generalization about the social impact of the book, the Reformation was, in its early stages, an urban phenomenon among the literate laity, while efforts to counter it were associated with relentless censorship.

Below In the absence of tension between the two opposites, Titian's enigmatic painting *Sacred and Profane Love* (c. 1515) serves as a symbol of the Venetian Renaissance. It also helps to explain why Venice made such an impact on the European imagination in the 16th and 17th centuries. Surprisingly, the naked figure represents sacred love, the clothed figure profane.

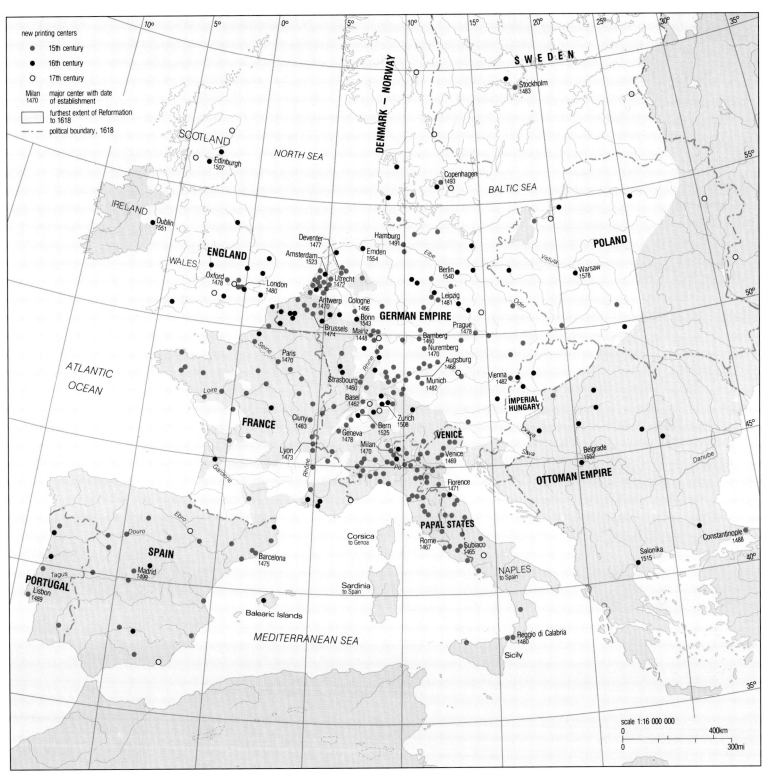

new printing centers
- 15th century
- 16th century
- ○ 17th century

Milan 1470 major center with date of establishment

☐ furthest extent of Reformation to 1618

–·– political boundary, 1618

SWEDEN

Stockholm 1483

SCOTLAND

NORTH SEA

DENMARK – NORWAY

BALTIC SEA

Copenhagen 1493

POLAND

Edinburgh 1507

IRELAND

Dublin 1551

ENGLAND

WALES

Deventer 1477

Hamburg 1491

Emden 1554

Warsaw 1578

Elbe

Vistula

Amsterdam 1523

Berlin 1540

Oxford 1478

London 1480

Utrecht 1472

Antwerp 1470

Cologne 1466

Leipzig 1481

GERMAN EMPIRE

Brussels 1474

Bonn 1543

Prague 1478

Oder

ATLANTIC OCEAN

Mainz 1448

Bamberg 1460

Nuremberg 1470

Seine

Paris 1470

Augsburg 1468

Vienna 1482

Strasbourg 1460

Munich 1482

IMPERIAL HUNGARY

Loire

Basel 1462

FRANCE

Cluny 1483

Zurich 1508

Geneva 1478

Bern 1525

VENICE

Drava

Milan 1470

Venice 1469

Belgrade 1552

Sava

Lyon 1473

Po

Rhône

Garonne

OTTOMAN EMPIRE

Danube

Florence 1471

Ebro

PAPAL STATES

Corsica to Genoa

Rome 1467

Subiaco 1465

Salonika 1515

Constantinople 1488

Douro

SPAIN

Barcelona 1475

NAPLES to Spain

Tagus

Madrid 1499

PORTUGAL

Lisbon 1489

Sardinia to Spain

Balearic Islands

MEDITERRANEAN SEA

Reggio di Calabria 1480

Sicily

scale 1:16 000 000

0   400km

0   300mi

ideas circulated freely among the Venetians: that they often doubted whether the Eucharist host was more than a piece of bread, that they found the observance of feast days an annoyance, that pilgrimages were laughable, that the oil for lamps at shrines might just as well go on salad – and that reading the Bible was the delight of the soul. Such beliefs are known, however, because so many Venetians found themselves before the tribunal of the Holy Office, which arrived in the city in 1547. Ultimately, Venice remained a Catholic city – for all the papal interdicts and the influence of Erasmus – and Venetian art supported the Catholic cause. The humanist emphasis on the significance of the word had pulled in one direction; the image, so important to the unlettered, was to move in another. Both Titian and Tintoretto reanimated Catholic art.

Concentration on the Venetian Renaissance, created from wealth accumulated in the Middle Ages, with elements of the Reformation cohabiting with the Counter-Reformation, is a reminder of the danger of convenient stereotypes. The culture of Renaissance Venice shows that a synthesis of apparently irreconcilable contradictions was possible. This has important general implications, for it helps us to understand that in the 15th and 16th centuries, whatever its internal conflicts, European culture was acquiring a new coherence in its relationship to the rest of the world. What is extraordinary is the emergence of such coherence at a time when divisions within Europe itself, a result of the Reformation, had never been deeper. Both the divisions and the coherence owed much to the culture of the Renaissance.

The Printer-Publisher

Printing with movable type was invented in Germany in the 1420s and by the 1450s had been perfected by Johannes Gutenberg at Mainz. One of the world's great technological revolutions, it was greeted cautiously by the scholars of the day.

Hand-written books had often been inexpertly copied and suffered from errors and omissions. Renaissance scholars who had been painstakingly correcting manuscripts were now faced with the prospect of corrupt texts being replicated over and over again. Moreover, they were faced with losing the income they earned through copying. Yet the invention gave them access to books never previously available and even the fiercest critics were soon adding printed books to their collections.

Printing was an expensive process and the great printers were entrepreneurs who could draw upon the resources of wealthy patrons. The best printers managed to combine scholarly integrity with beautiful craftsmanship. Froben in the Netherlands, Estienne in France and Caxton in England managed to set standards of printing and publishing rarely bettered since. While serving public demand with editions of romances, fables, bibles and religious works, they also printed Latin and Greek literature.

Aldus Manutius (1450–1515) became devoted to Greek studies during the two years he lived in the house of the humanist Pico della Mirandola. When he conceived of publishing Greek texts, he chose Venice as his location, for the city had an exceptional collection of Greek books and was the center of the Italian printing industry.

His scholarly background made him sensitive to the requirements of his humanist customers and he employed some of the finest scholars as editors. The best of these was the Cretan Marcus Musurus (1470–1517). The task of an editor was arduous. First he had to obtain a text to serve as copy for the typesetters, then he had to emend the text to the best of his ability.

The care Aldus took in producing accurate texts reflected the concerns of humanists such as Angelo Poliziano and Marsilio Ficino. Poliziano's *Miscellanea*, the notebooks of a scholar-editor with an enthusiasm for correct spellings and definitions, became required reading for scholars.

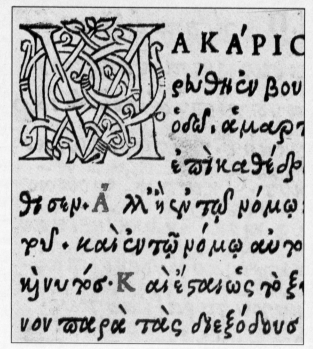

Above A medallion portrait of the printer Aldus Manutius, whose commitment to scholarly excellence and fine craftsmanship set the highest standards for publishing.

Right The Greek word *kolophon*, meaning "finishing touch", gave its name to the ornamental tailpiece with which scribes ended their labors. With the invention of printing, the name was extended to include printers' devices. Drawing on the traditions of heraldry and emblems, they were designed to inform the reader of themes dear to the printer. The dolphin and anchor represents the motto *festina lente* or "make haste slowly".

Top The printed book often tried to compete with the illuminated manuscript on its own terms, and artists were hired to paint decorated borders and capitals on printed pages. But printing required paper rather than vellum, and the results looked very different. Beauty in printing was found more in the font than in adornment. Aldus's sloping roman font was called Aldino in Italy and *italique* in France.

Above Greek type was far more complex than Latin because of its diacritical marks, used to indicate pronunciation. Aldus based his Greek font on the elaborate script

of Musurus and set a fashion that lasted centuries.

Right A modern reconstruction of the printing shop of Aldus. Gutenberg's process employed individual letters, cast in metal, that could be composed in "forms", blocks of type (of one or two pages) for printing at one impression. These were printed using an oil-based ink and a press adapted from that used by papermakers.

Below This depiction of a printing shop was one printer's reminder to himself and his staff that they were mortal. In the dance of death, skeletons are inviting the compositor, the inker, the press-operator and the bookseller to join them. It is clear from the picture that printing had turned the bookseller – who had once been a stationer and a go-between for copyists and their clients – into a publisher also.

Word and image: Renaissance, Reformation and Scientific Revolution

The Renaissance and the Reformation appear to have little in common. The Renaissance links the European experience to the classical past in one great continuum. The Reformation cuts across it as a unique divide. "Renaissance" is a term used of the Carolingian and Ottonian eras (8th to 9th and 10th centuries) and of the 12th century. These periods also showed strong interest in aspects of the classical past. The Reformation occurred only once, in the 16th century. The contrasts may be extended. The Renaissance of the 15th century was "secular" – or at least it acknowledged that the whole of human history could not be contained entirely within a Christian framework. The Reformation was first and foremost a religious phenomenon, expressing criticism of the Church and responding to ordinary believers' thirst for spiritual succor. The Renaissance was something to which all the regions of Europe could relate, albeit in different ways. To that extent the Renaissance tended to promote cultural unity. The Reformation demanded a stance for or against and so proved profoundly divisive, setting Protestant north against Catholic south.

Nevertheless, on closer inspection there is evidence of an important legacy of the "secular" Renaissance to the "religious" Reformation. The intellectual thrust of humanism was toward a pure original text, a return to sources. Although this tendency is often related to classical texts, the religious implications were never far removed. In the first instance, there was the matter of Church history. The great scholar Lorenzo Valla (1407–57) – who enjoyed papal patronage – was able to demonstrate in 1440 that the Donation of Constantine was an 8th-century forgery. This grant by Emperor Constantine was alleged to have established the authority of the papacy over Italy and the western Church. Valla showed that words used in the text could not have been applied to or employed by the emperor or his agent. Valla also produced a set of notes on the New Testament, writings that were to exercise a profound influence on the thinking of Erasmus. It was entirely consistent with Valla's approach to apply the principles of humanist scholarship to the text of the Bible. In doing so he demonstrated that many of the most obvious manifestations of ecclesiastical power – particularly those associated with the papacy and with monasticism – had little if any foundation in Scripture. Set in the context of the revival of Platonic philosophy, which encouraged the individual to seek God without recourse to a priestly intermediary, the potential of Renaissance humanism became explosive. It offered not only a systematic critique of ecclesiastical institutions, but also alternative versions of the spiritual life. It did so by returning to sources.

One of Luther's most durable and monumental achievements was the translation of the Bible into German so the ordinary man and woman could read the pure Word of God. The Protestant reformer John Calvin (1509–64) might seem a world away from the Italian Renaissance, yet his scholarship owed much to the techniques of the humanists. His earliest surviving work is a humanistic exercise, a commentary on Seneca's *On Clemency* (1532). Although Calvin was no slavish imitator of Italian learning, the monumental and systematic exposition of his *Institutes of Christian Religion* (1536) demonstrate his debt to the

Left Charles V on Horseback (1547) by Titian. In 1547, after the Battle of Mühlberg, Charles V seemed to have triumphed completely. German Protestantism had been defeated. Here, clad in the armor he wore at Mühlberg and seated on the horse he rode, Charles is depicted alone and supreme. In 1552, however, he was deserted by Maurice of Saxony, and a few years later, disillusioned, he abdicated. Handing most of his vast empire to his son, Philip II of Spain, he retired to a monastery.

Below One of the many illustrations from *On the Fabric of the Human Body* (1543) by Andreas Vesalius, a Flemish anatomist who lectured in Padua and later became physician to Philip II of Spain. His well-illustrated books gave the first comprehensive and wholly original description of human anatomy. The practice of dissection was controversial, however, and the Inquisition sentenced Vesalius to death for "body snatching", a sentence commuted to making a pilgrimage to the Holy Land.

scholarly techniques of the humanists. What is so exciting about the text of his most famous work is the conviction that the Scriptures enable Christians to get as close as possible to the Word of God.

It is somewhat surprising, but nonetheless significant, to recognize the intensely secular dimension of the *Institutes*. For in them Calvin makes much of the history of the papacy. Calvin tended to write human history as a parallel to the Bible: the history of the papacy was seen as the Old Testament of fallen man, with the Reformed Church promising a New Testament of redemption. All the same, his argument draws strength from the use of historical examples to demonstrate the corruption of the papacy through its involvement in worldly affairs. So even Calvin made use of the secular branches of Renaissance learning. The ancient Greeks and Romans had constructed secular states without knowledge of Christianity. The papal fraud was the creation of a secular state under the flag of Christianity. In a profoundly important way, humanist historical studies, by examining a non-Christian past, had exposed the worldliness of the papacy.

It is curious to think of Calvin in the same intellectual context as Niccolò Machiavelli (1469–1527),

until it is remembered that religious reform gave enormous impetus to the formation of sovereign secular states. When Machiavelli, in *The Prince* (c. 1513), asserted that he merely wrote of human affairs "as they really are", then it was perfectly logical to point to the worldly ambitions of the papacy. If the popes could use Christianity to reinforce their secular power, could not secular rulers do the same? This message was highly significant for Catholic and Protestant alike. The kings of France enjoyed rights of intervention in ecclesiastical appointments: this "Gallicanism" was reaffirmed in an agreement reached by Catholic monarch and Roman pope (the Concordat of Bologna, 1516). The Spanish Inquisition was responsible to the monarchs, not to Rome. Henry VIII became head of the Church of England – not as a Protestant, merely as a schismatic Catholic. When religious peace finally came to the states of Germany in 1555, its mainstay was the principle that the territorial ruler could determine whether his lands were to be Lutheran or Catholic, a principle later defined as *cuius regio, eius religio* ("to whom the kingdom, his the religion").

While princely authority was enhanced by claims to power in religious affairs, claims that owed a good

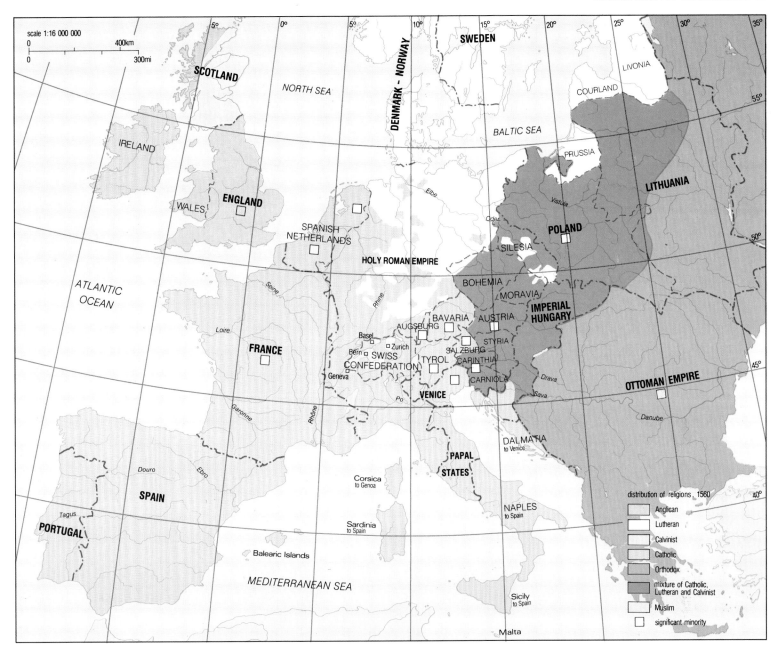

Europe divided, c. 1560
The Reformation spread outwards from its German heartland after Luther's protest, but it was forced back on itself by the Catholic reaction. Parts of the north remained Lutheran. In Italy and Spain Catholicism was secure. The divisions were exacerbated by the emergence of Calvinism. Following its sudden success in Scotland, there appeared to be the chance that a call to arms from Geneva might activate revolutionary cells all over Europe in a "Calvinist International". The outcome of civil wars in France and of the revolt of the Netherlands against Spain were in the balance throughout the later 16th century, but ultimately the reform took root only where it was sanctioned by the secular power.

deal to the ideas of the humanists, the stature of princes was enhanced by the use of Renaissance art. Princely magnificence found expression in pageants and ceremonies, and patronage at court. The French king Francis I appeared as a Gallic Hercules, Henry VIII of England as an imperial sovereign, Charles V of the German Empire as the supreme expression of knighthood.

The Reformation, then, derived something of its character from the secular and religious implications of humanism; the princes who gained power from the religious upheaval used the visual arts of the Renaissance to emphasize their secular authority. The religious potential of the visual arts, however, was also to serve the purposes of the Catholic revival, the Counter-Reformation. The Council of Trent met intermittently between 1545 and 1563 to reform abuses in the Catholic Church. Among many reaffirmations of traditional doctrine, it established that the targets of Protestant criticism – shrines, the cult of the Virgin and the saints, the sacramental role of the priesthood – should be extolled and exalted in the decoration of church interiors all over the world.

While the Reformation provoked something of a crisis in the Renaissance relationship of word and

image, that relationship recovered its energy in the presentation of new views of the natural world. What made possible the accuracy of Renaissance representation – the confident translation of what the mind envisages to what the hand can produce – was the science of perspective. The importance of this development may be grasped by considering the efforts modern scientists make to reconcile notions of the infinitely large, based on the theory of relativity, with notions of the infinitely small, based on quantum mechanics. In the course of the 16th century the notion of infinity had already progressed some way down this path. Certainly, by mid-century there was a powerful impulse to explore both the macrocosm and the microcosm. In this, 1543 is a symbolic year, for it saw the publication of Copernicus's book on heavenly bodies (*On the Revolutions of the Celestial Spheres*) and Vesalius's work on human bodies (*On the Fabric of the Human Body*). The worlds that lay within man and the worlds beyond him were almost literally opened up. The immediate impact of the ideas of Vesalius (1514–64) owed much to anatomical drawings, which the printing press could now reproduce from engravings. Once the telescope was in use, in the 17th century, Galileo (1564–1642) could

The Venice Arsenal

Below The Arsenal's symbolic roles are illustrated by its two adjacent gates. With its twin towers, the watergate, from which the war galleys emerged, was defensive. By contrast, the richly carved landgate (shown here) was modeled on the classical Roman arch at Pola. It was chosen as a civilizing image, a metaphor for the concept of Venice as "the new Rome", inheritor of the classical mantle and champion of the Christian West.

The Arsenal was the power-base behind Venice's great trading empire. It was at once a shipyard, naval base and armory, becoming the greatest industrial complex in the West.

To foreign visitors it was a marvel of largescale assembly-line techniques – techniques that anticipated those of the Industrial Revolution by three centuries. Within the walls, a ship's keel was transformed in methodical stages to emerge from the great gate as a fully fitted-out trading ship or war galley, ready to sail.

Equally significant was the Arsenal's role as the hub of a communications network linking Venice with the great ports of the eastern Mediterranean, Alexandria and Beirut, and thence overland to India and China. From these regular trading voyages came not only spices but news, information and cultural exchanges with the East. Westwards the galleys sailed regularly to Spain, England and the Low Countries.

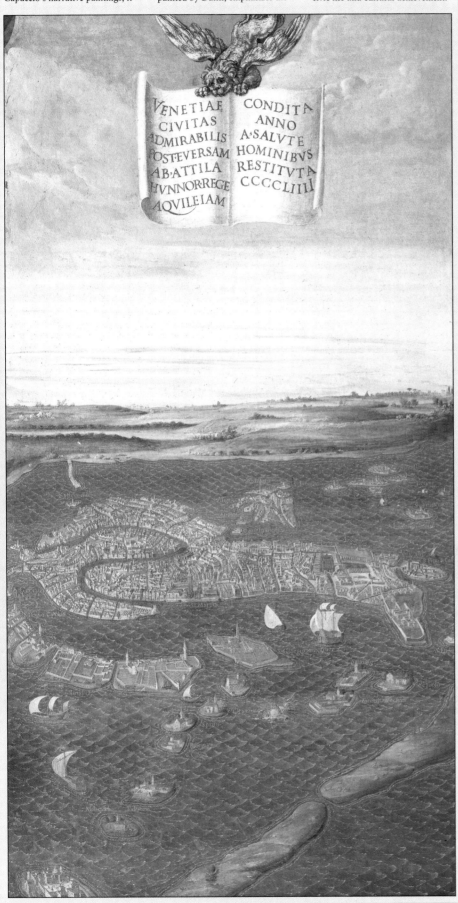

Bottom left Carpaccio's *Leavetaking of the Betrothed* from *The Legend of St Ursula* series (1490–95) incorporates two splendid castles, that on the right based on the walls and towers of the Arsenal. The picture also shows examples of contemporary Venetian shipping. Like many of Capaccio's narrative paintings, it brings together idealized images of his native city with imagined exotic foreign capitals, the latter often spiced with details obtained from well-traveled Venetian merchants.

Below Painted views of great cities became widespread in the 16th century. This view of Venice, painted by Danti, emphasizes the city's unique location between the Terraferma and the Adriatic. The rapid spread of printing, notably in Venice, ensured that similar images in the form of woodcuts or engravings became widely and cheaply available all over Europe. They all helped to foster the concept of Venice as the center of civic life and cultural achievement.

VENETIAE CONDITA
CIVITAS ANNO
ADMIRABILIS A·SALVTE
POSTEVERSAM HOMINIBVS
AB·ATTILA RESTITVTA
HVNNORREGE CCCCLIIII
AQVILEIAM

produce drawings of the stars and planets to take Copernicus's theories further. Observation and practice – not abstract speculation, not academic debate – produced theory. This generalization in many ways holds together the artistic and "scientific" achievements of the Renaissance; it links the everyday social milieu of Florence and Venice; and it spans the gap of the two centuries separating Brunelleschi from Galileo.

The Renaissance cannot be fully understood by reference to the world of scholars and connoisseurs alone. Leonardo da Vinci, the supreme "Renaissance man", could not be described as a "humanist". Both Brunelleschi and Ghiberti trained in goldsmiths' shops. The great building projects of the Renaissance in Florence certainly owed more to practice than to theory. Brunelleschi was clearly a capable site manager who always had an eye to improving the efficiency of a skilled work force. (In the building of the cupola at Santa Maria del Fiore, for instance, meals were taken to workmen on the scaffolding to save the time they were spending climbing down and up again.)

In a comparable way, Venetian workshops produced luxury goods made with outstanding skill, particularly books, furniture and glass. Most significantly of all, Venice had its Arsenal, an enormous industrial complex – modern tankers are easily accommodated – supported by the resources of the entire state, with a work force of several thousand – caulkers, carpenters, sailmakers, ironmongers, hemp twisters, oar-makers. It is immortalized in Dante's vision of hell (in the *Divine Comedy*), but a more measured and more significant assessment is provided by Galileo. His *Dialogue Concerning Two New Sciences* (1632) demonstrates the importance of the practical skills of the general population in creating the material culture of the Renaissance. In this work Galileo, so often presented as the supreme theoretician, pays tribute move his two speakers to the technological expertise of the Arsenal work force. In the Venice Arsenal, as on site at the cathedral in Florence, practice produced theory. It is perhaps no accident that building techniques applied to the construction of ships were to play so fundamental a part in propelling European culture across the globe.

The opening of the Atlantic

Beginning in the early 15th century, the Portuguese went by sea to the east, which involved the dogged exploration of the west coast of Africa: Fernão Gomes in 1469–75, Bartolomeu Dias in 1487–88, Vasco da Gama in 1497–99, and Pedro Cabral in 1500. The achievements of the Spaniards (or those in the employment of Spain) were logged toward the end of the century. They went westward, across the great open sea to America: Christopher Columbus in 1492, Amerigo Vespucci and Alonso de Ojeda in 1499–1500. Then, having crossed the sea, the Spaniards took control of the new lands, Cortes conquering Mexico in 1519, Pizarro establishing a Spanish foothold in Peru in 1531. The first circumnavigation of the earth (1519–21) had taken place by then. Appropriately, it was a Portuguese in the service of Spain, Ferdinand Magellan, who brought together the eastward and westward enterprises. Although Magellan himself was killed in the Philippines, his subordinate, Juan Elcano, brought home what was left of the fleet.

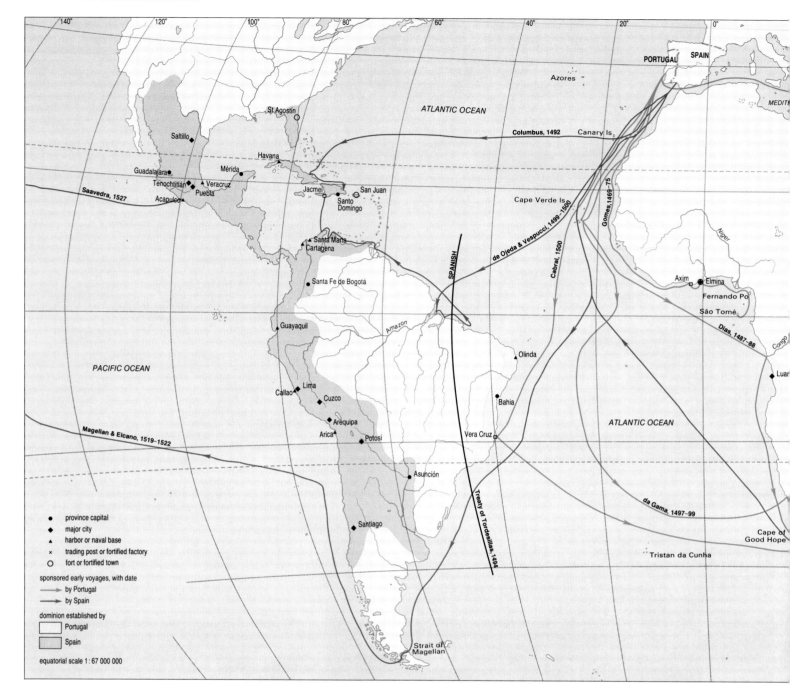

While the pattern of the expansion is clear enough, its character is more difficult to define. The implications were depressingly obvious in Venice: it ceased to be at the center of Europe's commerce. In their panic, the Venetians veered from fantastic explanations to fantastic remedies. One nobleman suggested that Venice had lost divine favor to the Portuguese as a result of tolerating the presence of Jews in the city. The Venetian government established a Commission on Spices with the specific brief of making agreements with the Sultan of Egypt to deprive the Portuguese of the trade. One proposal was to cut "with great ease and in a short time a channel from the Red Sea which would indeed connect to the sea on this side", though in the event the Venetians did not build a Suez canal and instead lamented the impoverishment of their markets.

The despondency of the Venetians has tended to exaggerate the proportions of the idea that "the rise of the Atlantic" spelled "the decline of the Mediterranean". Such an interpretation has obscured the interrelationship of the two theaters in the definition

of the modern West, with all that that has meant for the coherence of an identifiable civilization.

What inspired the expansion from Iberia was not so much an economic impulse as the ideology of the crusade. The Portuguese, having tried and failed to penetrate Muslim territories in north Africa, explored the west coast in the search for a weakness in the flank of Islam. In 1578 Prince Sebastian of Portugal attempted a new campaign of conquest in north Africa. It ended in defeat at Alcazarquivir in 1578. But this was no isolated act of folly. It was consistent with the extension of the frontier of Christian Iberia that the Spaniards had begun with victory over the Moors at Las Navas de Tolosa in 1212. Likewise, when the Spaniards reached as far west as Chile in 1541, they founded Santiago in Estrema, marking a new frontier that had once been defined by Santiago de Compostella in northwest Spain.

Viewed as an Iberian crusade, Atlantic expansion depended on security in the Mediterranean, which was only possible because the eastern flank could be held. That flank was subject to continuous pressure

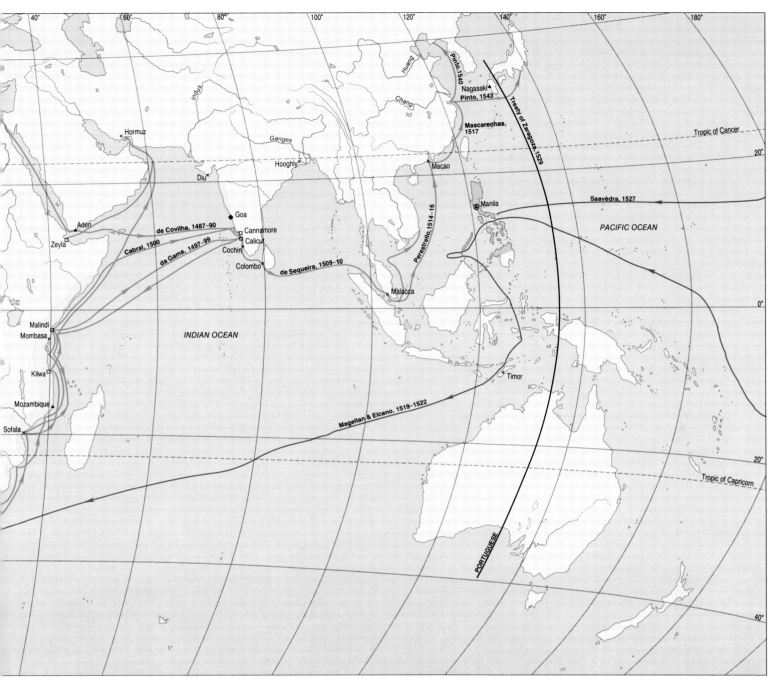

Iberian exploration
Having failed to penetrate Muslim power in north Africa, the Portuguese sailed south in a flanking action that was to take them to the Far East by the early 16th century. Despite the extraordinary length of their lines of communication, Portuguese tactics of artillery bombardment in the open ocean were to prove virtually invincible. There was a similar crusading zeal in Spanish exploration to the west, and early colonization had a feudal character – Spanish warriors exploited the labor of native populations with the sanction of the Church. Appropriately, it was a Portuguese in Spanish service, Magellan, who joined the eastward thrust of the Portuguese and the westward voyages of the Spaniards in the first circumnavigation of the world.

from the power of the Turk, pressure that accelerated the transmission of ancient Greek learning to Renaissance Italy. Contact with the Greek world as preserved in Byzantium had increased as the Turks threatened Constantinople during the 14th and 15th centuries and as Byzantium looked west for aid. A number of notable Byzantine scholars, such as Bessarion (c. 1395–1472) and Plethou (c. 1355–1450), were present at the Council of Florence, which met in 1439 and fleetingly achieved the reunion of the Latin and Orthodox Churches. This preoccupation with the Turkish threat reflects the strength of the crusading impulse during the Renaissance, a period too often assumed to be secular or even "pagan". The Peace of Lodi (1454) established an equilibrium of sorts among the five major powers of Italy – Florence, Venice, Milan, Naples and the Papal State. Yet its declared purpose was to coordinate resistance to the Turkish threat, which had become all the more menacing as a result of the fall of Constantinople a year before (1453). The humanist Enea Silvio Piccolomini, who became Pope Pius II (1458–64), spent his pontificate

exhorting the Christian powers to defend the Church against the infidel. The response at this stage was poor and the Turks ravaged Otranto in southeast Italy in 1480. By then the Venetians were only too aware of the Turkish advance. Within 10 years of the fall of Constantinople, the republic was at war with the Turks in Euboea. Samos fell in 1475. In 1499 a Venetian fleet failed disastrously to achieve victory at the Battle of Zonchio, a campaign that began to reveal the problems Venice would face in manning and supplying a sustained war effort to hold its overseas territories against the Turks. Its key strongholds of Coron and Modon fell in 1500, and there were further losses when war was joined again in the mid 16th century: the Turks captured Monemvasia and Nauplia in 1540, and Cyprus in 1571.

There had been one notable – and subsequently neglected – success. The Venetians had strengthened their defenses at Zadar, Catara, Khania, Cerines and Famagusta. Most important of all, extra money was allocated to the defenses of Corfu. In 1535 the great fortress architect Michele Sanmicheli inspected the

fortifications. (It is worth pausing to recall that carefully designed bastions, their fields of fire meticulously marked, also figure prominently among the drawings of Leonardo and Michelangelo.) In 1537 the Turks laid siege to Corfu. They failed to take it – at the cost of dreadful casualties, for many civilians were sent out of the citadel merely to starve to death between besiegers and besieged. The failure was critical, for had Corfu fallen it would have provided the Turks with a base from which to launch a fullscale invasion of Italy. The development of the design of fortifications in the Renaissance has been carefully studied, but the importance of the application of the new designs in the fortresses that withstood the Turkish onslaught – a list that includes Vienna in 1529, Guns in 1532 and most notably Malta in 1565 – has not received the attention it deserves.

Mention has already been made of the Venice Arsenal and of the technological know-how of its work force. One of the improvisations that emerged from the shipyards was the galeass, an armed merchantman. At one level its introduction to the war fleets is symptomatic of the Republic's desperate shortage of vessels. At the naval Battle of Lepanto in 1571, however, Don John of Austria, the Christian admiral and half brother of Philip II, divided his line into three sections, each of which was preceded by two galeasses. Their concentrated firepower is said to have been responsible for sinking some 70 Turkish ships in the battle. While fortresses and naval architecture are rarely central subjects in cultural

Right: Northern exploration, 1390–1570
By the end of the Renaissance, London had begun to occupy a central place in the east–west trade of northern Europe – a position similar to that occupied by Venice in the Mediterranean before the Atlantic discoveries. The voyages of the Cabots, John and Sebastian, met with mixed success, but after his father's death at sea, Sebastian showed himself to be an entrepreneur of visionary quality. He helped to make London – the political and commercial center of England – the basis for the nation's overseas enterprises. The extension of the commercial network by Anthony Jenkinson broadened still further the new horizons of English commerce.

Left The *Santa Maria*, a woodcut from Columbus's *Letter* of 1494.

Below The battle of Lepanto, fought in the Gulf of Corinth on Santa Giustina's Day in 1571, was the largest battle of the 16th century. More than 200 Christian ships and perhaps as many as 300 Turkish vessels fought an engagement that cost many thousands of lives. Although the significance of the Christian victory is often disputed, the Turks never again fought a naval battle on such a scale against their western foes.

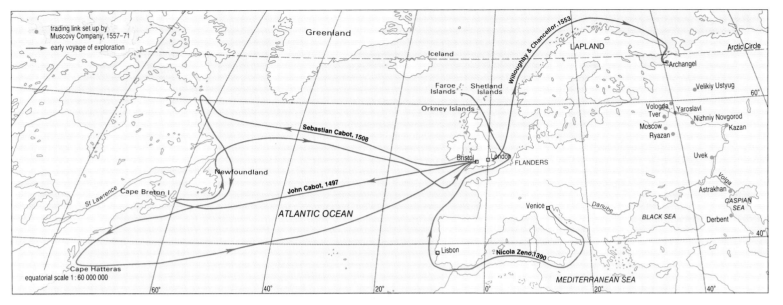

Key:
- trading link set up by Muscovy Company, 1557–71
- early voyage of exploration

Willoughby & Chancellor, 1553
Sebastian Cabot, 1508
John Cabot, 1497
Nicola Zeno, 1390

equatorial scale 1 : 60 000 000

Overleaf World Map (1641) by Willem Blaeu. Developments in exploration, depiction and printing during the Renaissance were to exert a decisive influence on the way in which modern Europeans perceive the world. The projection of the Flemish cartographer Gerhardus Mercator – despite its distortions at the poles – became the standard way of representing the round world on a flat surface.

considerations, the Battle of Lepanto was to leave its mark on Renaissance art. Veronese produced at least two depictions of Lepanto. One takes pride of place in the Sala del Collegio in the doge's palace; it shows Christ blessing the victorious admiral Sebastian Venier, who had become doge. The other (now in the Accademia, Venice) shows Santa Giustina (the battle was fought on her day, 7 October) interceding in heaven on Venice's behalf while cherubs rain fiery darts on the Turkish fleet. Once again a paradox emerges. These paintings celebrating the triumph of Catholicism in crusade are the work of an artist who in 1573 appeared before the Inquisition because of doubts about the orthodoxy of his portrayal of the Last Supper.

Appropriately, Lepanto was also commemorated at the Arsenal. The gateway constructed c. 1460 by Antonio Gambello is widely regarded as the first sign of classical revival in the buildings of Venice. After Lepanto it was further embellished with depictions of victory and of Santa Giustina to celebrate the role of the shipyards in the triumph of Christendom.

That triumph soon appeared hollow. The Venetians withdrew from the Holy League they had formed with Philip II of Spain, the Genoese and the papacy, and made a separate peace with the Turks in 1573. The Turks retained Cyprus and other conquests in the Adriatic, while Venice's losses were merely confirmed.

However lavishly they commemorated the Battle of Lepanto, the Venetians appear as miserly renegades. Yet theirs was a consistent approach. They had always fought hard for the defense or advancement of material interests. By contrast, Philip II of Spain (1556–98) was to bankrupt his empire several times in order to sustain a colossal war effort in the promotion of a religious cause. Spain became a great Atlantic power but applied little expertise to the exploitation of its empire.

The Venetians could never free themselves from the Mediterranean world, but within it they had created a mercantilist empire. The mercantilist system was embodied in a set of small colonies linked by sea routes, supervised by a state that used its naval and military power to protect maritime commerce and that engaged in war to advance or defend material interests. This type of thinking is often identified with the 17th century, particularly with the imperialism of the English and the Dutch. However, the Venetians,

the supreme exponents of Italian commercial enterprise, had set the pattern in the Middle Ages. Nor was this a slight resemblance or chance coincidence. Although they never developed commercial interests in the new Atlantic world that was developing, the Venetians had had a hand in opening up its possibilities. In the late 14th century the voyages of the Venetian patricians Antonio and Niccolò Zeno took the standard of St Mark to the Faroe Islands and to the Orkneys, to Iceland and to Greenland. They received word of America from fishermen they encountered. In the mid 15th century Venetian galleys bound for Flanders were delayed in Lisbon by a storm. One of the noblemen aboard, Alvise da Ca' da Mosto, took ship with the Portuguese and left a fascinating record of the journey to the Canary Islands and to Cape Blanco and Senegal. His is the first original account of the European exploration of Africa that has survived, and his penchant for the concrete rather than the fanciful puts him in the same tradition as Marco Polo.

Most important of all are the Cabots, John (1450–98) and his son Sebastian (1476–1557). John – Genoese by birth but recorded as having taken Venetian citizenship – sailed to Newfoundland in 1497 in the service of Henry VII of England. It was reported in Venice that Cabot had discovered "mainland 700 leagues away, which is the country of the Grand Khan", that he had "coasted it for 300 leagues and landed". Cabot had not, apparently, forgotten his homeland, for he "planted on the land which he has found a large cross with a banner of England and one of St Mark, as he is a Venetian, so that our flag has been hoisted very far afield".

According to one 16th-century commentator, Sebastian named the coast now known as Newfoundland "the Land of the Baccalai" – codfish. Another source records that codfish "on that coast are found in such quantity and so tightly packed together, that sometimes they prevent the passage of the caravels". Clearly there would be rich catches off these frozen coasts, and who would be better equipped to exploit the commercial possibilities of salted codfish than the Venetians? Pope Pius II reviled the Venetians as "the offscourings of fishermen" for their lack of commitment to his crusade. John Cabot himself invested in three salt works in the Venetian lagoon, so he may have had some interest in or even experience of the commercial potential of salting fish.

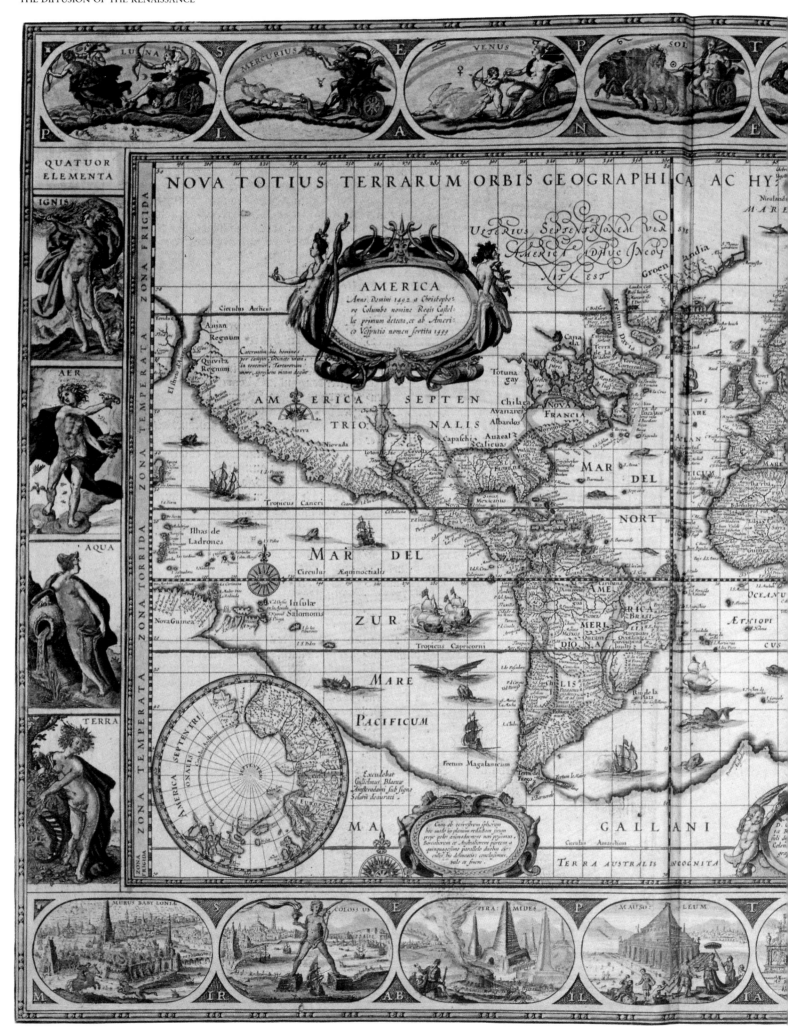

Sebastian Cabot enjoyed little success in the westward voyages he undertook, but he did much to foster English exploration in the northeastern waters of America. Perhaps the greatest achievement in his long career was the attachment of the business interests of London to overseas enterprise – shifting the home of English navigation from Bristol. Cabot was the inspiration of the voyage of Willoughby and Chancellor in search of a northeast passage in 1553. Although Willoughby perished, Chancellor reached Moscow via Archangel and helped to extend London's commercial sphere of interest as far as the Caspian Sea, a commercial network strengthened by the travels of Anthony Jenkinson between 1557 and 1570. London was becoming the center of a commercial world that stretched from Newfoundland to Samarkand, just as Venice had stood at the center of a Mediterranean world that lay between Lisbon and Damascus. One of the most significant aspects of the Renaissance was the transmission of the commercial culture of medieval Italy to the new European world that was taking shape around the globe, and that was to shape the globe itself.

Defining a world

Forts, armed merchantmen, factory ships plundering the oceans, joint-stock companies – these are subjects not often identified with the great burst of cultural creativity known as the Renaissance. Yet it is important to become aware not just of artistic and literary achievements but of the urban and commercial matrix in which those achievements took shape. This is a reminder that the culture of the Renaissance cannot be viewed in isolation from its social context. More specifically, such an approach confronts the paradox that though the Renaissance is so frequently identified with modernity and progress, with a break from the past, Italy's lasting impact on the wider world owed much to the culture of its "medieval" merchants.

The transmission of the Renaissance was only one strand of the relationship that bound Italy to the rest of Europe. There is no need to qualify the opening assertion that what was achieved in Italy in the 15th and 16th centuries was decisive in shaping Western culture because it gave a new sense of time and space to Europe as a whole. However, the second but scarcely secondary theme has been to highlight two other ways in which Italy helped to define "the West": first, its defense of Europe's eastern flank against the threat of a quite different civilization (the Ottoman empire); second, its contribution to the mentalities and techniques that were to take European values round the world.

It is important to emphasize that these achievements were closely intertwined. This can be done by referring again to the quotation from Shakespeare used to introduce the chapter, for it also serves by way of a conclusion. Puck's pledge to put "a girdle round about the earth" was no flight of fancy on Shakespeare's part. It appears to have been inspired by a picture of Sir Francis Drake's ship the *Golden Hind*, celebrating his circumnavigation of the world (1577–80). By the end of the 16th century Europeans had indeed put "a girdle round about the earth". More importantly, they had begun to conceive of doing so in a mere 40 minutes. Their ability both to go round the world and also to imagine doing so at such speed owed much to the culture of the Italian Renaissance and to the Italian commercial world that had nurtured it.

Renaissance Music

During the Renaissance music began to move from the sacred to the secular – from church to court. Gradually the medieval love of intellectual complexity in music gave way to a growing desire to employ a colorful, sensual array of new musical forms – such as the madrigal and instrumental fantasia – and new combinations of voices and instruments. The Renaissance brought about a dramatic increase in musical culture throughout Europe. Music was no longer used primarily in the service of God, but also for the sheer enjoyment of both performer and listener. The advent of printed music led to the spread of popular chamber music, while instruction books and theory manuals encouraged domestic music-making and high standards of performance.

Renaissance artists and scholars were seeking to recapture the spirit of the ancient world, and music played a crucial role in the humanist neo-Platonic vision of a unified cosmos. The aim of instrumental and vocal music was seen to be the imitation of the "music of the spheres", and the technical and musical skill of the individual performer was praised for allowing a glimpse of the divine on Earth, whether through the medium of a sacred motet or a virtuoso lute improvisation.

By the end of the 16th century, the emphasis on the dramatic expression of emotion in accompanied song had paved the way for the birth of opera.

Right Excerpt of a Mass by Jean Mouton, printed by Pierre Attaingnant in Paris (1532). Attaingnant was the first to use the technique of printing staff, notes and text in a single impression, and his vast output ensured that vocal and dance music was widely available.

Bottom left The unaccompanied vocal ensemble of eight to ten singers was the ideal early Renaissance medium. Church choirs would gather round a lectern to perform liturgical music, as depicted in this group of angels by van Eyck. Such a group may well have been employed by van Eyck's main patron, the Duke of Burgundy, at whose chapel elaborate religious and secular celebrations were performed.

Above In this 16th-century pastoral setting a group of lute, recorder, bass viol and virginals play an arrangement of a French *chanson*, the commonest genre of verse-setting before the madrigal.

Left Lorenzo Costa (c. 1500) here depicts three singers and lute performing a *frottola*, an Italian song popular at the court of Isabella d'Este in Mantua. In four parts, these rhythmic verse-settings could be adapted for voices or instruments.

Right A woodcut illustrating a 16th-century Mass being celebrated at court. Music played an integral part in religious services. Here the singers are shown gathered around a single music stand before the altar at the point when the host is elevated.

Following pages Jan Bruegel's *The Sense of Hearing* (c. 1600) illustrates a rich variety of musical instruments in use at the end of the Renaissance: a family or "consort" of three viols (fretted, bowed instruments held between the knees), two lutes, rebec (small bowed treble instrument on the floor), fiddle (lying on some music), trombone and assorted bows. The voice is represented by the open part-books of madrigals.

129

Astrology and Astronomy

Astrology entails the belief that events on this world are caused or affected by the powers of planets and stars. Plato, Aristotle and most classical authors were convinced that a link exists between the movement of the heavens and events on Earth – that the macrocosm of the universe influenced the microcosm of daily life. The beliefs of the Greek and Roman philosophers, together with the writings of Ptolemy of Egypt (c. AD 90–160), became widely known in western Europe after the 12th century and led to a revived interest in astrology. Works of neo-Platonism and hermeticism (bodies of mystical speculation dating from the first centuries AD) were first translated from the Greek in the late 15th and 16th centuries and helped to make astrology fashionable in the Renaissance.

The astrologers of the late 15th and 16th centuries generally believed, insofar as they could agree at all, that the world was a globe set in the heart of a spherical universe (even in the Middle Ages, few educated people believed the world to be flat). Around the Earth revolved seven crystalline spheres on which the planets and stars rested, making heavenly music as they turned. The signs of the zodiac united the stars and constellations in 12 separate images and 36 gods or "decans". Streaming down from the heavens was a continuous flow of invisible influences. By studying the movement of the heavens and by working out which influences were to be expected, the astrologer could predict the future. Many scholars also believed that the *magus* or adept could by the use of charms, invocations and talismans channel these celestial forces.

During the 16th and early 17th centuries, scholars gradually learned to reject the model of the universe inherited from Ptolemy and the ancient world, in which the Earth was at the center. Firstly, they needed an accurate scheme for measuring the movement of the stars in order to work out the correct date for movable Church feasts such as Easter. The notion that the universe revolved around the Earth had led to inaccuracies in the Church's calendar, and the need to remedy these deficiencies led to the more systematic observation of the celestial movements. Secondly, astrologers were convinced that the Sun stood metaphysically at the heart of the planetary system and was the principal influence on the Earth. A more accurate plotting of the movements of the stars, together with the speculations of philosophers trained in neo-Platonic and hermetic theory, forced a revolution in the understanding of the universe. In 1543 Nicholas Copernicus published his profoundly influential *On the Revolutions of the Celestial Spheres*, in which he argued that the Earth and the planets revolved around the Sun. His account was prefaced with a *Eulogy to the Sun* that is entirely characteristic of the speculative neo-Platonism of the 16th century. Although Copernicus believed that the planets were driven by "spirits" and "celestial intelligences", his Sun-centered model provided the basis for the achievements of Kepler and Galileo and for the modern science of astronomy.

Below Hermes Trismegistus standing beneath a model of the heavens and discoursing with astrologers. It was long believed that Hermes was a contemporary of Moses and that he was the most ancient teacher of wisdom known to man. The works attributed to Hermes, however, were composed in Egypt during the 2nd and 3rd centuries AD. These hermetic texts contained much on magic, astrology and alchemy, but were so obscure they were virtually unintelligible.

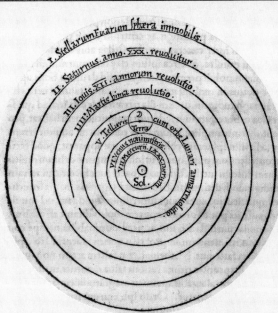

Left The astronomer Johann Kepler, who first discovered the laws of planetary motion, still believed that the planets made a heavenly music as they moved – from his *Harmony of the World* (1619).

Top left The Sun stands at the heart of the universe and of the revolving celestial spheres in this late 15th-century manuscript on astrology. Leo, the sign of the zodiac most closely associated with the Sun, stands between the figure's legs. The effect of the celestial influences of the Sun on mankind are demonstrated at the foot of the illustration.

Above Diagram of Copernicus's scheme of the universe, taken from *On the Revolution of the Celestial Spheres* (1543), showing the Earth and the planets revolving around the Sun, with the Moon completing an orbit of its own around the Earth. Copernicus still believed, however, that the planets were embedded in crystalline spheres. Furthermore, he mistakenly presumed that their movement was circular in accordance with the neo-Platonic principle of the harmony of the universe. Copernicus's theory of the universe was later refined by Kepler.

Above Although maps depicting the world were drawn with great accuracy even as early as the 14th century, the first terrestrial globe or *Erdapfel*, showing the earth rotating on a polar axis, was made by Martin Behaim of Nuremberg in 1492, the same year Columbus discovered the New World.

Left Constellations of stars, as symbolized by the 12 signs of the zodiac, were believed not only to influence events on Earth but also to affect parts of the human body. As this 16th-century print suggests, surgical operations on the head or the feet were thought to be best performed when Aries or Pisces respectively was in the ascendant.

Above Galileo Galilei, an instrument-maker who worked most of his life in Venice and Florence, was the first to use the telescope to explore the heavens. With the help of this recent invention, he described the mountains of the Moon, discovered four of Jupiter's planets, and found that the Milky Way contained a countless multitude of stars. In the *Starry Messenger* (1610), Galileo suggested that the universe might be infinite. Although his writings were later banned by the pope, Galileo demonstrated the superiority of the Sun-centered theory of planetary motion over the Earth-centered, and he laid the foundations of the sciences of dynamics and gravity.

The Ottoman Empire

By the end of the 16th century, the borders of the Ottoman Empire were some 10,000 kilometers in length. This vast territorial bulk exerted a pressure that helped to transform "Christendom" into "western Europe".

The origins of Ottoman power lay in an Anatolian principality uneasily located between Byzantium and the Seljuk Turks. As a result of the Mongol invasions of the 13th century, Seljuk power declined and the frontier state grew in importance under the Osman dynasty. The state was dedicated to holy war, which it pursued without regard to political considerations. That last characteristic, however, made the success of Ottoman campaigns seem all the more unstoppable. The armies of Mehmed the Conqueror took Constantinople – the "eastern Rome" in 1453. Thereafter, the autocracy extended its territorial power as a means of providing its victorious warriors with booty.

The Venetians were swept from the Morea between 1463 and 1479, and in 1480 the Turks threatened Otranto on the Italian coast. The Knights of St John won honorable withdrawal from Rhodes in 1522, but in 1526 Turkish armies destroyed the independence of Hungary at Mohacs. Alliance with Francis I against Charles V intensified the threat to Christendom, and the Turks scored another great naval success at Prevesa in 1538. By the 1550s, Ottoman power in north Africa was a threat to Iberia itself.

The Ottoman Empire was to survive for several centuries, even though in its latter stages it became the "sick man of Europe". Even by 1600, however, there were signs that Ottoman power was not invincible. Protracted sieges – most significantly at Malta in 1565 – exposed the need to achieve a lasting victory and emphasized the problems of communication in so vast an empire. Any delay in the successful completion of a campaign in the west could be compounded by a threat in the east from Persia. Moreover, in 1571 the Christian fleet of the Holy League inflicted a colossal defeat at Lepanto, which was the biggest battle of the 16th century. Although historians have tended to diminish the significance of the battle, the Turks never again took on a Christian fleet in an engagement of such a scale.

Below The siege of Constantinople. When Constantinople fell to the Turks in 1453 the Roman Empire finally came to an end. The eastern empire, of which Constantinople was the capital, had outlived the western empire by nearly 1,000 years. The impact on Christendom of the fall of Constantinople was enormous. On the one hand, there were calls for a new crusade, calls which served to revive medieval ideals. On the other hand, ancient Greek learning and scholarship were driven westward, giving new energy and purpose to the revival of classical learning we call the Renaissance.

Above The Horses of San Marco, Venice. Venetian commercial power had dictated the sack of Constantinople by the army of the Fourth Crusade in 1204 – and treasures such as the Horses of San Marco were part of the booty. The defeat of the Genoese in the late 14th century had apparently confirmed Venetian commercial supremacy in the Mediterranean. The Ottoman expansion challenged Venetian naval supremacy and thrust Venice on to the defensive in an area in which it had traditionally predominated – at a time when competitors were beginning to take advantage of opportunities opening up in the Atlantic.

Above Venetian Embassy in the East by Gentile Bellini. Although Christians and Turks were often involved in open conflict, the channels of communication through diplomacy and trade remained open. Venice's Jewish community provided a critical point of contact with the economy of the eastern Mediterranean, and merchants from the Ottoman Empire were often present in Venice itself in the ordinary course of business, and they had their own warehouse. Questions of religious separateness appear to have been overcome by a common recognition of the need to trade.

Left The sultan was expected to lead his armies in the field and so he was frequently away on campaign. At Constantinople, however, his public appearances were designed to emphasize the magnificence of the autocracy. The close identification of the state with militant Islam is a reminder that the Ottoman Empire did not experience that great tension of church and state so characteristic of Western societies in the 16th century.

GERMANY AND THE LOW COUNTRIES

During the course of the 16th century Germany and the Low Countries rivaled and even began to outpace Florence, Milan, Rome and Naples in the fields of classical scholarship, learning and art. In 1518 the German humanist and knight Ulrich von Hutten described in glowing terms the progress made by the new learning in Germany: "Oh Century! Oh Letters! It is a joy to be alive! Studies thrive and minds flourish. Woe to you, Barbarism! Accept the noose! Look forward to exile!" The humanist Nicolas Gerbel congratulated himself for living "in this glorious century when so many remarkable men have arisen in Germany".

The origin of the Northern Renaissance is, however, a vexed problem. It was common a century ago for historians to accept that the lands north of the Alps were a cultural wasteland until the late 15th century, and that the civilization that subsequently arose there was due entirely to Italian influence. Some scholars, however, rejected this interpretation. They argued instead that the Northern Renaissance owed much more to native traditions and German "folk culture", and that it would have come about even if there had been no Italian Renaissance.

Most scholars now try to steer a midway course. It is undeniable that the Northern Renaissance owed its main inspiration to Italy and that it was built upon foundations laid by Italian humanists and artists. Nevertheless it is equally clear that the lands north of the Alps were not a cultural blank sheet just waiting for the imprint of Italian learning. In the Low Countries and Germany there were traditions of scholarship and learning that made the region highly receptive to the ideas spreading from Italy. The fusion of the new learning with these traditions gave the Northern Renaissance its distinctive character as a cultural movement. The Northern Renaissance was thus more concerned with textual criticism than its Italian counterpart was, and far more occupied with issues of personal religion and morality. In particular, the humanists and artists in Germany and the Low Countries did not exult over the greatness and dignity of man. They dwelt instead on man's inherent worthlessness and the gulf that separated man from the majesty of God.

Forerunners of the Northern Renaissance

Two important centers of classical scholarship appeared north of the Alps during the 14th century: the Brethren of the Common Life in the Low Countries, and the court of Charles IV of Bohemia. Although quite separate in their geographical location and their

Below The Land of Cockaigne (1567) by Pieter Bruegel the Elder depicts the "paradise of gluttony" of popular Flemish tradition. Disquieting images, however, disturb the impression of calmness and somnolence. The egg walking on two legs with a knife protruding from its shell, for example, is a symbol of the devil also employed by Hieronymus Bosch. The picture is thought to be a satire on the indolence of Bruegel's countrymen and on their passion for feasting and sleeping. At the time this picture was painted the Low Countries had just been occupied by the Duke of Alva. Bruegel may be alluding here to the way in which a lack of moral strength among the population of the Low Countries had made Alva's oppression possible.

Ifula Flumin.

Above Deventer in the Netherlands was an important intellectual center because of the school there run by the Brethren of the Common Life. Founded by Gerard Groote of Deventer, the Brethren were a congregation of laymen dedicated to the education of the young. They laid stress on the study of the classics and the school at Deventer was the nursery for a generation of northern humanists. Deventer was also an important commercial center, the site of a major international fair, and a member of the north European trading association known as the Hanseatic League. This woodcut shows broad-beamed bulks, which were typical vessels of the period, moored in the river Ijssel. Just below the soldier is the church and boarding house of the Brethren of the Common Life where Erasmus probably stayed in the early 1480s.

cultural and social milieu, both demonstrate the significance of religious tradition and spiritual devotion in the making of the Northern Renaissance.

During the second half of the 14th century, Gerard Groote of Deventer (1340–84) established in Utrecht in the Low Countries communities of lay people and clergy who followed a common rule but who, unlike monks, took no vows and were free to leave when they wished. The purpose of the "modern devotion", as it was known, was to study and meditate upon the faith so as to live the Christian life more completely. The members of these communities, who were known as the Brethren of the Common Life, laid strong emphasis on the importance of education and reading, and a principal occupation of the Brethren in their communal lodgings was the copying of texts. They also established in many cities in the Low Countries schools where they introduced their pupils to classical writings. The school at Deventer was the first one north of the Alps to provide instruction in Greek. Three of the greatest of the northern humanists – Nicholas of Cusa, Jacob Wimpfeling and Desiderius Erasmus – were taught by the Brethren at Deventer. The education provided by the Brethren of the Common Life was rooted in the close study of Roman, Greek and early Christian texts, from which moral and spiritual examples were drawn. The Brethrens' repudiation of the conventional methods of medieval scholastic inquiry created a freer intellectual climate in northern Europe and helped prepare the way for the new learning. Through their involvement in education, the Brethren introduced many hundreds of northerners to the classics.

Charles IV of Bohemia (1346–78) was one of the greatest patrons of the 14th century. He gathered around him at his court in Prague many notable scholars and artists, including for short periods Petrarch and Cola di Rienzo. Charles was responsible for founding the university of Prague in 1348, which by the end of his reign had over a 1,000 students, and for the construction of St Vitus's Cathedral in Prague. He also composed his own autobiography, sponsored the writing of several chronicles of Bohemian history, and oversaw the translation of the Bible into Czech.

The foremost scholar at Charles's court was the chancellor, Johannes of Neumarkt (c. 1310–80),

under whose direction the language of state documents was made to conform more closely to classical models of expression. Neumarkt's library contained a great number of classical Latin texts as well as works by Dante. One of Neumarkt's disciples, Johannes of Štibor (c. 1350–c. 1413), was the author of the dialogue *The Bohemian Ploughman* (c. 1400), which records an imaginary conversation between a peasant and Death. Although composed in German prose, *The Bohemian Ploughman* was clearly influenced by Petrarch, Dante and Cola di Rienzo, and represents an important milestone in the passage from medieval to Renaissance literature.

Fourteenth-century Bohemian humanism had a powerful spiritual dimension. This aspect is seen most clearly in the writings of Milič of Krometříž (c. 1325–74), who was another of Neumarkt's disciples, and who served as a notary in the royal chancellery. Milič is commonly considered to have been an exponent of the modern devotion in Bohemia, placing a strong stress on the importance of man's direct relationship with God.

The Bohemian Renaissance was cut short, however, by the spread of the Hussite heresy in the early 15th century, when Bohemia became a battleground between Catholics and Hussites. The eventual triumph of the Hussite faith, an early version of Protestantism, meant that the kingdom was seldom visited by scholars and was for a long time cut off from the mainstream of European cultural life.

The early course of the Northern Renaissance

Neither the Brethren of the Common Life nor the court of Charles IV created the Northern Renaissance. The critical influence transforming medieval culture into Renaissance civilization came from Italy and in the contacts established across the Alps in the 15th century. Although there had always been traffic across the Alps during the Middle Ages, the exchange of ideas was slow until the early 15th century. The Church councils held at Constance (1414–18) and at Basel (1431–49), at which representatives from all Christendom were gathered, gave German churchmen one of the earliest opportunities to meet their fluent and educated Italian counterparts. Afterward there was a growing interchange of visitors between Italy and the northern countries. Italian humanists and artists journeyed north as emissaries, diplomats, secretaries and commercial agents. The Italian humanists Poggio Bracciolini and Pietro Vergerio traveled in Germany, and the latter, one of the first theorists of humanist education, went on to spend almost three decades in Hungary (1417–44); the poet Callimachus, a refugee from Rome, lived many years in Lemberg (Lvov) in Poland; the humanist Antonio Bonfini became court historian to King Matthias Corvinus of Hungary (1458–90); and Enea Silvio Piccolomini (1405–64), later Pope Pius II, served in the chancellery of Emperor Frederick III (1440–93).

On the whole Italian visitors to the north were scathing about what they saw. Enea Silvio Piccolomini commented in 1462: "Literature flourishes in Italy and princes there are not ashamed to listen to, and themselves to know, poetry. But in Germany princes pay more attention to horses and dogs than to poets – and thus neglecting the arts they die unremembered like their own beasts." Other Italians mocked the Germans for their lack of both "spirit" and a history (Tacitus's *Germania* was not yet discovered), and they compared the Danube unfavorably with the Tiber.

Such criticism from Italian visitors stimulated a curiosity and rivalry among their German hosts, and in the 15th century many thousands of students from Germany and the Low Countries journeyed to the universities of Padua and Bologna. Returning home, they passed on what they had learned to a wider audience. In their subsequent writings they frequently copied out whole sections of the works of Italian humanists. As lawyers and diplomats they often adorned their letters and papers with evidence of their knowledge of the classics. There is scarcely a single

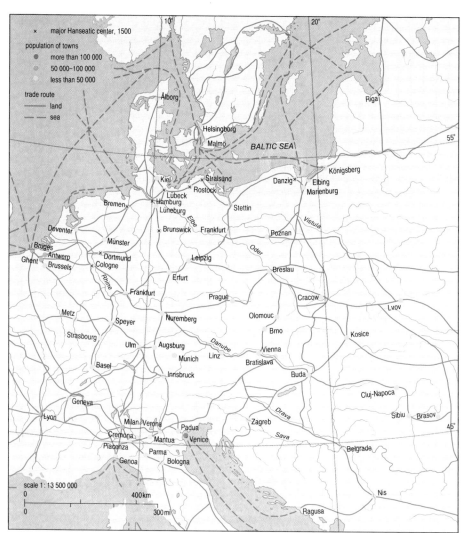

Left: Trade routes in northern Europe
Baltic commerce was dominated by the Hanseatic League, a loose confederation of more than 200 trading communities. During the 15th century, the cities of southern Germany acquired increased significance because of their connections with eastern Europe and northern Italy.

Bottom left The Stag Hunt (1544) by Lucas Cranach the Elder depicts the hunt laid on by the Elector of Saxony for Charles V, emperor of Germany and king of Spain. Hunting was the favorite pastime of the aristocratic courts of northern Europe.

Below King Matthias Corvinus of Hungary was one of the greatest royal patrons of the arts. He commissioned the copying and illumination of several thousand classical and religious texts. This psalter was originally part of the Corvina library.

northern humanist of any distinction who did not early on in his career spend at least a year in Italy.

It was in the princely and episcopal courts in Germany and east–central Europe that most northern scholars found employment. There were many of these courts, for the German Empire was made up of more than 300 semi-independent principalities. Rudolf Agricola (1444–85), one of the first German scholars to study in Italy, was supported in Heidelberg by the combined patronage of the prince and the bishop. Frederick the Wise of Saxony (1486–1525) invited poets and artists to his court, and in 1502 founded the university of Wittenberg. In Moravia a flourishing literary circle gathered round the court of Bishop Stanislas Thurzó of Olomouc (c. 1470–1540). Archbishop János Vitéz of Esztergom (c. 1408–72) played a similar role in Hungary both as the patron of humanists and as the author of texts composed in a strictly classical style. For their part, many of the Polish magnates and bishops were magnificent patrons of the arts, decorating their palaces with sculptures and paintings in Italian Renaissance styles. The

court of Sigismund I (1506–48) in Cracow was also an important center of patronage, particularly after his marriage in 1518 to a member of the Sforza family of Milan. During Sigismund's reign, the Wawel castle in Cracow was rebuilt in Renaissance style with the help of Italian architects.

Among secular rulers of the 15th and early 16th centuries, Emperor Maximilian I (1486–1519) and King Matthias Corvinus (1458–90) of Hungary deserve special mention. Maximilian was Archduke of Austria and ruler of the Low Countries as well as Emperor of Germany. He had a deep personal interest in art and letters, and his court in Vienna was a vibrant center of humanist culture. He composed (though with the help of ghost writers) two epic narratives, the *Teuerdank* and *Weisskunig*, and established a chair of rhetoric and poetry at the university of Vienna. The plans Maximilian later entertained for a triumphal arch in honor both of himself and of his own dynasty drew upon the combined expertise of humanist scholars Statius and Pirckheimer, the architect Kölderer, and the artist Albrecht Dürer.

In Hungary the court of Matthias Corvinus provided a notable center of scholarly and artistic patronage. Matthias commissioned the Italian humanist Antonio Bonfini to compose a detailed record of Hungarian history. He rebuilt the royal palaces at Visegrád and Buda, adding wings in the style of the 15th century, and he maintained one of the finest Renaissance libraries in late 15th-century Europe. With over 2,000 manuscript volumes, the Corvina Library in Buda was second only to the Vatican Library in Rome. An army of humanists, scribes, illuminators and bookbinders was employed in the workshops of Buda on the tasks of copying and emending classical texts. The library itself frequently provided a venue for learned meetings and debates modeled on the Florentine Platonic Academy of Lorenzo de' Medici and Marsilio Ficino. Matthias strove, as Bonfini put it, "to transform Pannonia into a second Italy". Unfortunately the humanist tradition in Hungary was cut short in the 16th century when the Ottoman Turks began pushing into Europe, and a Renaissance culture had no opportunity to flourish. Following the death in battle of the last king of Hungary in 1526, Louis II, who was also king of Bohemia, Bohemia and what was left of Hungary were acquired by Emperor Maximilian's grandson, Ferdinand, and became part of the Habsburg Empire.

Although many rulers and princes were sympathetic to humanism, their resources were too slender to provide much patronage. Accordingly, many humanists in Germany sought employment as teachers in the new universities. Higher education was at this time a growing industry. At the beginning of the 15th century there were only four universities in the whole of Germany: Vienna, founded in 1365; Heidelberg (1386); Cologne (1388) and Erfurt (1392). During the period from 1400 to 1502 an additional 10 were created. By the early 1500s the annual entry of students to these foundations was approximately 2,500 and the total number of enrolled students was almost three times that figure.

For most of the 15th century the curriculum for the bachelor of arts degree in German universities was remarkably narrow. Although the course was intended to teach the subjects of the *trivium* (grammar, logic and rhetoric), the strongest emphasis was on the study of Aristotelian logic. Even grammar had become a

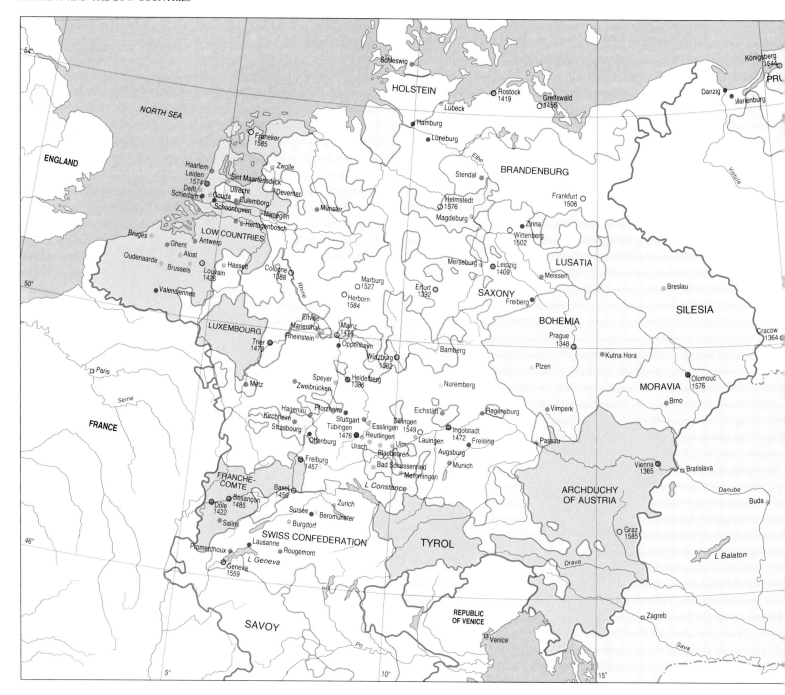

subdiscipline of logic. Courses in rhetoric, which was the study of style and expression through the vehicles of poetry, history and oratory, had in many universities been reduced to one lecture a year.

The German humanists who took up employment in the universities devoted much energy to reforming the curriculum. They endeavored to convince other teachers of the merit of including the new disciplines of the *studia humanitatis* in the curriculum. Peter Luder (c. 1415–c. 1474), giving an inaugural lecture at the university of Heidelberg in 1456, told his audience that history, oratory and poetry should be considered subjects as worthy of study as logic and grammar. History, Luder explained, was a guide to living, and its study enhanced intellectual and moral perceptions. Oratory inspired eloquence, and poetry not only improved powers of expression but also revealed moral and religious truths. Quoting Cicero, Luder concluded his address by asserting that the *studia humanitatis* "inspire youth, give pleasure in old age, embellish prosperity, offer escape and solace in adversity and give enjoyment at home".

Luder's theme was repeated by many other humanists. Not only did they reiterate in their writings and orations the importance of the *studia humanitatis* in the curriculum, they also produced a variety of teaching manuals and treatises on education. In their eagerness to introduce young people to the fluency and eloquence of classical writers, late 15th-century humanists edited and published texts by Ovid, Cicero, Seneca, Virgil, Terence and Plautus. In works advocating the reform of the curriculum they demonstrated how more traditional methods of teaching could be reconciled with the new disciplines of the *studia humanitatis*.

The interest of humanists in reforming education affected schools as well as universities. Although the German humanists encountered some opposition from older teachers, who had been brought up on traditional scholastic methods, their persistence had by the close of the 15th century transformed education. Now every university offered courses in the *studia humanitatis*, and many municipal and cathedral schools had adopted new methods of teaching.

The Holy Roman Empire: printing and education
During the 15th and 16th centuries, printing and education were of vital importance in spreading the new learning. At the beginning of the 15th century there were only four universities in Germany. By the end of the century there were 14, the curriculum in most of them being strongly influenced by humanist ideals. Printing also spread rapidly. Following the establishment of the first press in Mainz in the mid 15th century, the printing of religious, classical and humanist works made cheap texts available for the first time. During the Reformation, the printing presses printed many thousands of religious and political pamphlets each year and helped determine the course of religious debate in northern Europe.

Germany, or to give the region its proper title, the Holy Roman Empire of the German Nation, was a confederacy of more than 300 principalities. A substantial area comprised ecclesiastical lands that

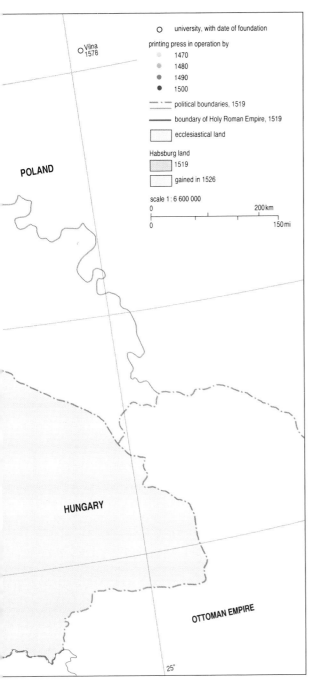

The cities of northern Europe played a vital role in the dissemination of humanist scholarship. In the Low Countries they were home to many of the region's leading schools, and also to the Chambers of Rhetoric, societies that organized not only debates but also festivals of drama and poetry. German towns, particularly those in the south, which were closer to Italian influences, also acted as important centers for the spread of humanist learning. Salaried positions in municipal administrations were often occupied by distinguished scholars.

The merchant aristocracy of the German cities introduced and fostered the new learning. The Pirckheimer family of Nuremberg sent their sons to study in Italy. Willibald Pirckheimer (1470–1530) studied at the universities of Padua and Pavia before returning to Nuremberg in 1496 to serve for the rest of his life on the city council. He acted as a notable patron of the arts, in particular of Albrecht Dürer. Having learned Greek, Pirckheimer translated editions of Xenophon, Aristophanes, Aristotle, Plutarch and Thucydides. In Augsburg the wealthy Fugger and Welser merchant-families commissioned important works of art, architecture and literature.

The coming together in cities of men, money and ideas often led to the foundation of "sodalities". As meeting places for cultured men and women sharing a common interest in classical antiquity, the sodality, or academy, was a feature of humanism both north and south of the Alps. Generally gathering in private homes, the members of a sodality would discuss literature and read from their own works in an atmosphere made convivial by food and wine. The sodalities not only acted as centers for the dissemination of the new learning, they also provided an opportunity for people of different occupation and background to exchange ideas freely. During the course of his own travels in Europe Conrad Celtis founded four such academies: at Heidelberg, Vienna, Lübeck and Cracow. He also encouraged the foundation of a number of smaller sodalities in other parts of Germany, their principal tasks being to sponsor new writing and to gather material for a topographical history of Germany.

During the second half of the 15th century printing presses were established first in the main commercial cities, and then in the university towns. Although to begin with printed works were in the main mystical texts and books of popular devotion, they rapidly came to include classical and humanist works. In the Low Countries, for example, almost half of all the works published before 1500 were editions of the classics, grammars and humanist texts, and by the 1520s all the major Latin authors had been published in Germany.

By the early 16th century there were presses in 250 German towns and in nearly all of the cities in the Low Countries. The leading German publishing centers were Nuremberg, Wittenberg, Strasbourg, Augsburg, Magdeburg, Frankfurt, Basel and Zurich. In the Low Countries, Utrecht, Delft, Gouda, Deventer, Zwolle, Nijmegen, the main publishing centers were Leiden, Louvain and Antwerp. During the second half of the 15th century, over 25,000 works were printed in Germany, excluding broadsheets and pamphlets. If the average edition numbered 250 volumes, which is probably an underestimate, then there must have been six million works published before 1500 in Germany alone.

Above Willibald Pirckheimer, shown here in a medallion designed by Albrecht Dürer, was a typical representative of the patrician elites who governed the great cities of the Empire. Pirckheimer's training in humanist studies, acquired while a student in Padua and Pavia, made him a suitable ambassador for the city, and in this capacity he visited Cologne, Innsbruck and Switzerland. He was particularly active in reforming Nuremberg's educational system.

belonged to the various bishops, archbishops and abbots of the Empire. A large number of these ecclesiastical lords were from the same aristocratic families as other prominent territorial princes. The nominal ruler of the Empire was the Emperor, who was elected by the princes of Brandenburg, Bohemia, the Palatinate and Saxony, and the archbishops of Mainz, Trier and Cologne.

In the Low Countries there were few opportunities for receiving a higher education. There were only two universities in the region, at Cologne and at Louvain (founded 1426), and both of these institutions proved particularly resistant to humanism. Besides the schools established by the Brethren of the Common Life, the main centers of learning until the close of the 15th century were monasteries. The abbey of Aduard, for instance, had two schools for the teaching of Latin, and under the abbacy of Henry van Rees (1449–85) became the focal point of a circle of scholars known as the Aduard Academy.

A similar role was played in the Rhineland by the abbey of Sponheim. The abbey had one of the finest libraries of the period, with over 2,000 volumes, 100 of which were Greek. Sponheim earned its reputation principally because of Abbot Johannes Trithemius. Trithemius (1462–1516) was one of the first humanists north of the Alps to combine an interest in the classics with the study of magic and sorcery. Appropriately, the abbey of Sponheim was later to become associated with the legendary Doctor Faustus.

The flowering of the Northern Renaissance

The principal concern of German humanists in the later 15th century was the reform of education and the creation of an intellectual climate sympathetic to the new learning. As it spread through individual contacts with Italy, the courts, universities and cities, so the humanists became bolder and more innovatory. The period from the 1490s until the onset of the Reformation in the 1520s represents the high point of northern humanism.

The most exuberant of the northern humanists was Conrad Celtis (1459–1508). Celtis's career straddled two periods. During his early life humanism was seeking to establish itself north of the Alps; during his later years, when he acquired his reputation as the greatest German lyricist of the Renaissance, humanism had become the dominant and most creative intellectual movement in Germany. Born the son of peasants in a village near Würzburg, Conrad Celtis ran away from home and received an education in the universities of Cologne, Heidelberg, Rostock and Leipzig. It was during the 1480s that he established his reputation, writing poetry, editing several editions of Seneca's tragedies, and preparing a treatise on the art of writing Latin verse. In recognition of his contribution to learning, Emperor Frederick III crowned him with a laurel wreath in Nuremberg in April 1487 and conferred on him the title of doctor of philosophy. From then on Celtis insisted that he be formally referred to as "poet laureate".

In the same year Celtis journeyed to Italy, where he was both inspired by what he saw and offended by Italian assumptions of superiority. Over the next decade he journeyed throughout northern Europe and taught at the universities of Cracow and Ingolstadt. As he traveled through Europe he established sodalities and ceaselessly urged his countrymen to embrace humanist ideals. Celtis commemorated his journeying in his greatest poetic work, *The Four Loves* (1502), in which he describes the cities of Mainz, Lübeck, Regensburg and Cracow and recounts his erotic adventures in each. In 1497 Celtis accepted the invitation of Emperor Maximilian to join the university of Vienna. There he founded the College of Poets, wrote poems and plays, directed plays by Terence and Plautus, and lectured while drunk. He died of syphilis at the age of 49. Celtis's gravestone in St Stephen's Cathedral in Vienna bears the simple inscription: VIVO ("I live").

The course of the Northern Renaissance rapidly became affected by the deeper stirrings of nationalist and religious sentiment that were to lead to the Reformation and to divide the Christian world between Protestants and Catholics. The start of the Reformation is usually put at 1517, when Martin Luther began his attack on the Roman Catholic church by calling for a radical reform of its government and practices. Nevertheless, Luther's protest was one of many and it was only his distinction as the leading theologian in the fashionable university of Wittenberg that lent a special significance to his criticisms.

The German humanists had long been critical of the Church and they were persistent advocates of the reform of clerical abuses. They employed their rhetorical techniques to heap scorn on ecclesiastical practices and they used their humanist knowledge to expose flaws in traditional Catholic scholarship and theology. During the early 16th century few humanists matched

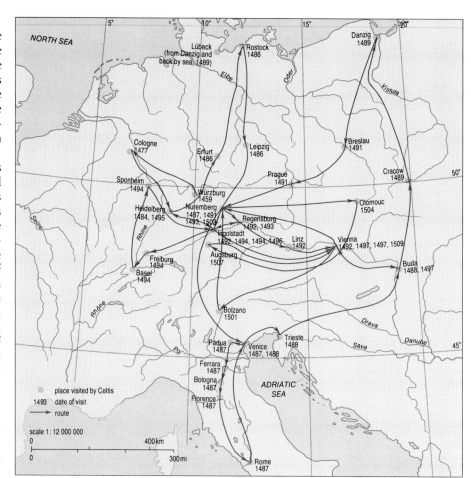

Left: The travels of Conrad Celtis
The humanists of the 15th and
16th century were part of an
international community of
scholars. In their search for new
ideas and sources of inspiration, as
well as of patronage, they were
prepared to spend much of their
lives in travel. Conrad Celtis was
one of the most colorful scholars of
his day.

Below This woodcut from 1518
depicting the triumph of Johannes
Reuchlin is typical of the polemical
art of the period. Reuchlin,
professor of Greek and Hebrew at
the universities of Ingolstadt and
Tubingen, is received with music
and laurel wreaths at the gateway
of his native Pforzheim. His
adversaries, the monks and
"obscure men" who had criticized
Reuchlin's interest in Jewish letters
and thought, proceed in chains
before him. At the bottom of the
print, Johannes Pfefferkorn, a
converted Jew who had led the
campaign against Reuchlin, is
shown prostrate and bound. In
1520, however, having been
condemned by both pope and
emperor, Reuchlin eventually
accepted the verdict of the Church
against his work.

the exuberance or Celtis's poetry of the extravagance of his own life. Most, instead, devoted an increasing share of their scholarly energies to the cause of the German nation and of religious reform.

Ulrich von Hutten (1488–1523), descended from an impoverished noble family, studied at the universities of Cologne, Erfurt, Frankfurt, Greifswald, Wittenberg and Vienna. Upon completing his education he went to Italy, where he studied law at Bologna and learnt Greek. To support himself in Italy he served for a time as a mercenary soldier. During this part of his life Ulrich von Hutten began composing poetry of sufficient distinction to win both praise from Erasmus and the title of poet laureate from Emperor Maximilian. Ulrich von Hutten was ready, however, to exchange the pen for the sword. In 1519 he embarked upon a private war against a robber baron, Duke Ulrich of Württemberg; later von Hutten attacked Church properties and participated in the Knights' Revolt of 1522. He died shortly afterwards of syphilis.

Unlike Conrad Celtis, Ulrich von Hutten was greatly influenced by the political and religious controversies of the period. In 1515 he contributed to the volume *Letters of Obscure Men*, a devastating satire aimed at the "obscurantist" theologians of Cologne who had sought to obstruct the pursuit of humanist learning. The work, consisting of fictitious letters, portrayed the "obscure" men of Cologne as idiots and knaves, who could not write Latin, were obsessed with trivial details and had no appreciation of good literature. Shortly afterward von Hutten published a new volume of *Letters* that was more political and

bitter than the first. In this edition he criticized the Church in Rome, the life of monks and the trade in relics and indulgences. In 1518 von Hutten edited Lorenzo Valla's *Donation of Constantine*, which had exposed the fraudulence of papal claims to temporal power, and he included in this edition a sarcastic dedication to the pope. In the same year von Hutten published four dialogues that poured scorn on Pope Leo X and the cardinals, and blamed the Roman church for destroying German virtue, robbing the Holy Roman Empire, and impeding the progress of learning. He also tracked down and published antipapal tracts written in Germany during the Middle Ages. Not surprisingly, Ulrich von Hutten was also one of Martin Luther's earliest supporters.

Johannes Reuchlin (1455–1522) sought to avoid controversy, but he still found himself drawn into the polemical debates of the years immediately preceding the Reformation. Reuchlin was educated at the universities of Freiburg, Paris and Basel. During the earlier part of his career he made three trips to Italy, where he came into contact with such leading humanists as Pico della Mirandola and Marsilio Ficino. He was greatly impressed with Pico's theses on cabbalistic knowledge and the stress he laid upon the study of Hebrew letters.

Indeed, although he published editions of Demosthenes, Hippocrates and Homer, Reuchlin's principal contribution was as a Hebraicist. Reuchlin was convinced that the Hebrew cabbala (a body of mystical writings) contained the most ancient wisdom and that cabbalistic letter mysticism could be united in a new

Alchemy and the Rosicrucians

Scholars had studied alchemy throughout the Middle Ages, but the discovery of ancient Greek and Hebrew texts during the 15th and 16th centuries suggested new ways of converting base metal into gold. These sources argued that the entire universe was bound together by hidden forces and inhabited by angels and demons. They also argued that the *magus* (magician) who grasped the structure of the universe had the power to control these forces and might uncover the secrets both of alchemy and of human destiny. The suggested methods of manipulation involved the use of invocations, charms, symbols and astrological charts.

Because their work might easily be confused with witchcraft, the alchemists and magicians of the 16th century concealed it behind confusing symbols and allegorical descriptions. One text on conjuring and astral projection masqueraded as a work on ciphers and codes. Many alchemists, however, believed that the search for the philosopher's stone – either the technique of transmutation, or the "prime matter" from which it was thought gold might be made – had an important moral and spiritual dimension. By transmuting "base" metal into "perfect" gold, a way of making human society perfect would also be revealed.

The addition of religion to alchemy led to some curious results. In the 16th century, a Catholic priest and alchemist in Hungary composed an "alchemical mass", celebrating Christ as the true elixir and philosopher's stone. In Germany, a spate of allegorical and alchemical publications proclaimed the imminent renewal of the world and the renewal of mankind.

Of these alchemical texts, the most famous were the Rosicrucian manifestos of the early 17th century. The manifestos were allegedly written by members of the Brotherhood of the Rosie Cross and promised "a general reformation, both of divine and human things". The anonymous authors claimed to have a wealth of secret knowledge and they invited those who were interested to "give their names . . . and be partakers with us of our treasures." Publication of the first manifestos was followed shortly after by an alchemical romance entitled *The Chymical Wedding of Christian Rosenkreutz*, the meaning of which is still much debated.

Although many sought to contact the Brothers of the Rosie Cross, they were never found and it is probable that the manifestos were an elaborate deception, the purpose of which is unknown.

Above right The Alchemist from Heinrich Khunrath's *Amphitheater of Eternal Wisdom* (1609). The alchemist kneels before an altar on which are texts inscribed with geometrical and magical symbols. To the right are the alchemist's furnace, and instruments used in chemical experiments. On the table are musical instruments that might be used to summon angels and to invoke magical forces.

Right The Monas or One, from Michael Maier's *Atalanta Fugiens* (1618). Alchemists and magicians frequently devised symbols intended to encapsulate in a single emblem the hidden unity of the world. The geometrical symbolism of alchemy, and much of its ritual, were later adopted in freemasonry which also owes much to the alchemical and Rosicrucian literature of the 17th century.

Below The search for hidden knowledge is demonstrated in *The Cave of the Illuminati*, published in Khunrath's *Amphitheater of Eternal Wisdom*. Those seeking illumination move through a dimly lit cave decorated with texts announcing the revelation of ancient mysteries. The Protestant courts of Germany were the principal centers of patronage for alchemists and magicians in Europe. The Rosicrucian manifestos were almost certainly composed in Württemberg and in a circle close to its Protestant duke. According to one theory, the marriage of Princess Elizabeth Stuart to the Calvinist Frederick of the Palatinate in 1613 inspired both the manifestos' promise of a reformation of the world and the allegorical *Chymical Wedding of Christian Rosenkreutz*. This wedding of the daughter of James I of England to the foremost Protestant ruler in Germany is shown here (*bottom*) in a contemporary engraving.

synthesis with the Pythagorean belief in the power of numbers. In two works, *On the Wonder-Making Word* (1494) and *On the Art of the Cabbala* (1517), he explained that the new synthesis supported and elucidated important elements of Christian theology. Reuchlin's belief in the significance of Hebrew letters led him not only to learn Hebrew but also to explain its grammar in a textbook published in 1506. Although as a theologian Reuchlin was more interested in the esoteric and abstruse than in issues of faith and salvation, he provided the means by which scholars could be introduced to the original language of the Old Testament. His contribution in this respect was no less than that of Colet, Lefèvre and Erasmus, all of whom laid stress on the Bible as a historical text that should be read and understood in the language in which it was first written.

Reuchlin's interest in Hebrew scholarship resulted in conflict with the Church authorities. It was in Reuchlin's defense that von Hutten composed the *Letters of Obscure Men* against the conservative Dominican theologians of Cologne. In 1513 Reuchlin was summoned to appear before the Inquisition. The polemical tracts he composed in his defense were subsequently confiscated and finally denounced as heretical by Pope Leo X in 1520. Although Reuchlin did not become a supporter of the Reformation, he welcomed Luther's protest. "God be praised", he explained, "that now the monks have someone else who will give them more to do than I."

German patriotism and a concern for the restoration both of true spirituality and of classical scholarship found their most complete expression in the Alsace school of humanists. Sebastian Brant (c. 1458–1521), who worked as city secretary in Strasbourg, enjoyed the friendship of Reuchlin, was a prolific poet of Latin devotional verses, and published editions of classical and Italian humanist texts. His greatest work, *The Ship of Fools*, published in 1494, was immensely popular and found a large readership. In well-turned verses Brant exposed the foibles and follies of mankind. He ridiculed ostentation and display, particularly in the Church and among merchants, and he called upon Emperor Maximilian to undertake the reform of clerical abuses.

Some modern scholars have suggested that *The Ship of Fools* should be seen as a work of medieval German literature. Brant, however, intended it to be a humanist work, and it has a classical rhetorical structure. Most importantly, it was the first modern work of poetry to be composed in German – as a mark of Brant's patriotism and his devotion to the cause of a restored Germany. In subsequent works he repeated his plea for Maximilian to reform the Church in Germany and urged him to rebuild Germany's lost greatness.

The most influential of the Alsatian humanists was Jacob Wimpfeling (1450–1528). Educated at Deventer by the Brethren of the Common Life, Wimpfeling studied at Freiburg, Erfurt and Heidelberg, but never visited Italy. During the 1480s he served as court poet to Duke Frederick of the Palatinate and as rector and vice-chancellor of the university of Heidelberg, before moving to Strasbourg. Much of his career was devoted to the typical tasks of the first generation of northern humanists – organizing a sodality and publishing educational works. Nevertheless, he could not remain unaffected by the patriotism and anticlericalism of the period. In his work *On Integrity* he attacked the morals of the priesthood and in 1510 he presented Emperor Maximilian with a list of complaints against the Church in Rome. In a work published five years later, Wimpfeling warned that if a reform of the Church was not undertaken, a revolt against Rome might be expected.

Wimpfeling's greatest contribution to humanist learning lay in history. The study of German history had become particularly important with the discovery and printing in 1473 of Tacitus's *Germania*. Germans now felt that they had a worthy and glorious history of their own that made them the equals of the French and Italians. In 1505 Wimpfeling published his *Epitome of German Affairs*, a history of Germany since the days of Tacitus. By way of a conclusion, Wimpfeling praised the cultural and technical achievements of the German people, pointing to the German discovery of printing as a unique contribution to civilization.

Desiderius Erasmus (c. 1467–1536) was the greatest humanist of the Northern Renaissance. In the course of his scholarly career he spent long periods in the Low Countries, France, Germany, Italy and England, and he maintained a substantial correspondence with humanists throughout Europe. The modern critical edition of his letters runs to 11 thick volumes, and includes recipients as far afield as Spain, Scandinavia and Moravia. Erasmus is an international figure, rather than a narrowly national one, and he cannot be portrayed simply as a representative of either Dutch or German humanism.

Nevertheless, Erasmus could not help but be influenced by the traditions of scholarship and learning in the Low Countries. For it was at the schools of the Brethren of the Common Life at Deventer and 's-Hertogenbosch that he received his education and, as a regular canon, spent the earlier part of his career. Only in his late twenties did he begin to travel abroad, first to Paris in 1495 and four years later to England. So it is not surprising that the bulk of his writings continued to be influenced by the particular concerns of the humanists in the Low Countries and, in particular, of the Brethren of the Common Life. He turned away from poetry and drama, except as models of style, and he was little influenced by the patriotic, polemical and anticlerical writings of the German humanists. He devoted himself instead to writing educational texts, to studying philology and to the establishing and promoting of deeper moral and spiritual truths. His overwhelming concern was to make people better Christians by providing them with moral examples and with a body of reliable texts on which to base their understanding of Christ's message.

Erasmus's early life is shrouded in mystery; even the year of his birth is uncertain. He was educated by the Brethren of the Common Life in the school in Deventer run by Alexander Hegius, a close acquaintance of Rudolf Agricola. Although Erasmus was later to write of schoolmasters as "the most unfortunate and wretched class of men, and the most hateful to the gods", he retained his admiration for Hegius.

In 1487 Erasmus entered the Augustinian monastery of canons regular at Steyn and was ordained as a priest five years later. It was at this time, in the early 1490s, that he composed his first major work, the *Antibarbari*, a defense of the ancient classics. Here Erasmus argued that work of pre-Christian literature should not be rejected as "pagan". For the spirit of Christ moved even then, revealing parts of the Christian message: "Everything in the pagan world that was

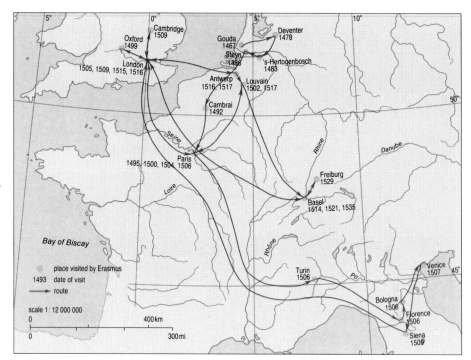

valiantly done, brilliantly said, ingeniously thought, and diligently transmitted, had been prepared by Christ for his society". In the *Antibarbari* Erasmus vindicated the study of the classics as both literature and as texts containing eternal moral and spiritual truths.

Between 1495 and 1499 Erasmus studied in Paris at the Sorbonne. To support himself he began to give private lessons and wrote several works on education and on style. He then paid a brief visit to England, after which he compiled the *Adagia*, which was in time to become one of the cornerstones of the revived classical culture of Europe. At the time of its publication the *Adagia* was described as a simple "collection of old and celebrated proverbs". Its actual purpose and significance were more profound. It was at the simplest level a volume of phrases that might be used to adorn and embellish literary works. Over and above this, it provided an introduction to classical scholarship, for each proverb was accompanied by references to ancient literature and authors. At the highest level, the *Adagia* performed a moral and religious function. By drawing parallels with the Scriptures and with other Christian texts, Erasmus was able both to guide his readers toward the practice of Christian charity and also to establish a new harmony between ancient literature and the teachings of the Church. The first edition of the *Adagia* was published in 1500 with 818 entries. In subsequent editions Erasmus added to the number of proverbs, until by the time of his death in 1536 there were over 4,000. Many of the stock phrases of today owe their survival and currency to Erasmus's work of compilations.

While staying in England Erasmus was introduced by John Colet to the idea of editing a Greek edition of the New Testament. Erasmus was later engaged for many years on this labor, in which he attempted to apply the methods of language analysis that Italian humanists had previously applied to classical texts. Erasmus's New Testament appeared with a prefatory piece entitled the *Paraclesis* or "Exhortation", in which he summarized the essentials of his beliefs and concerns. He repeated the message of the *Antibarbari*

Top: The travels of Erasmus Born probably at Gouda and educated at Deventer and 's-Hertogenbosch, Erasmus began studying at Paris in 1495. In 1499 he made his first trip to England, where he met Thomas More, John Colet and Archbishop Warham. For virtually all of his adult life he was constantly on the move. Although he spent most of his career traveling in France, the Low Countries and Switzerland, he often revisited England for long periods and was resident in Italy from 1506 to 1509. Between 1521 and 1529 he was in Basel. In 1535, after an interlude of six years in Freiburg, he returned to Basel where he died.

Above A doodled self-portrait taken from one of Erasmus's notebooks.

Right A portrait of Erasmus by Hans Holbein the Younger. Holbein was one of the greatest portrait painters of his age. He specialized in members of the middle-class and humanists, and later in leading figures of the English court. He completed this portrait of Erasmus in 1523, when Erasmus was in his mid fifties.

Below Erasmus's *Adagia*, his most popular work, was a collection of Greek and Latin proverbs. The title page from the 1523 edition has portraits of the classical authors from whose works the *Adagia* was compiled.

on the value of classical pre-Christian literature, and emphasized the importance of personal faith. He was particularly critical of the stress laid in Catholic devotion on ritual and in Catholic theology on logic, and he called upon his readers "to restore the philosophy of Christ not in ceremonies alone and in syllogistic propositions but in the heart itself and in the whole life".

Erasmus's career as a philologist, editor and moral theologian contrasts with his reputation as a radical satirist. In two works, *Colloquies* (1526) and *In Praise of Folly* (1511), Erasmus poked fun at the institutions of the day and at ordinary life in dramatic and iconoclastic fashion. The Virgin Mary thus thanks the reformer Ulrich Zwingli for having attacked her cult — now she has fewer petitioners to trouble her with their extravagant and immodest appeals.

Yet even in these satirical works Erasmus's concerns are much the same as in his texts on moral theology. As Erasmus explains, those with a reputation for wisdom, the philosophers and theologians, are the ones most in Folly's power, even though they refuse to admit it. Their vocations and their "petty ceremonies and silly absurdities" are contrasted with the religion of the New Testament. In the conclusion of *In Praise of Folly*, Erasmus suggests that only by surrendering intellectual pretense and by embracing Christian joy can man become truly happy as a "fool in Christ".

Erasmus's career draws together several of the more important themes and traditions of northern humanism. As a writer of grammars and educational texts he sought to make the classics accessible to a new generation of students; as the author of the *Antibarbari* and the *Adagia* he endeavored to make these same works acceptable objects of study. In his own work of editing the New Testament and the writings of the Church Fathers, he relied upon the techniques of criticism and of philological method previously developed in Italy. The satirizing methods he employed, particularly with regard to the clergy, may be compared to those used by Brant and von Hutten. But Erasmus was also influenced by the deeper currents of northern scholarship. Far more than the Italian humanists, Erasmus was preoccupied with issues of morality and with the Christian vocation. For Erasmus the inward life of the spirit was the proper goal of scholarly inquiry, and the proper practice of religion was the focus of his interest as a humanist. In these respects at least he may be considered a representative less of European humanism than of a specifically northern European spirituality.

The Art of the Northern Renaissance
Just as there is debate over the extent to which northern humanism is indebted to Italian humanism, so there is controversy over how much Northern Renaissance art owes to Italian art. It is clear that a

Martin Luther

In July 1505 the young Martin Luther was caught in a violent thunderstorm. He called upon God to save him and promised in return to become a monk. Two weeks later Martin obediently entered an Augustinian monastery at Erfurt.

Augustinian monks were permitted to study and teach theology and in 1511 Luther, who had rapidly become one of the leading academic theologians in Germany, joined the University of Wittenberg in Saxony. He found little solace in the monastic life, however, for he was convinced that whatever he did as a monk would still be insufficient to win him salvation.

Between 1515 and 1517 Luther reconsidered his beliefs. Previously he had thought that he was unfit for Heaven. Now he saw that the fault lay more with the Catholic Church. He was particularly critical of the Church's teaching that salvation could be obtained by performing rituals and by buying indulgences: according to Catholic teaching, a person could receive an "indulgence" or ticket to Heaven in exchange for giving money to the Church.

In 1517 he published a discussion pamphlet on indulgences, the Ninety-Five Theses. What might have been a purely academic dispute was inflamed by rivalries among the religious orders in Germany. For attacking the sale of indulgences he was accused of heresy, but refused to back down. By 1521 he had broken with the Catholic Church entirely and was forced to go into hiding. Not only did he refuse to acknowledge the spiritual leadership of the pope in Rome, he also denied the value of ritual as a means of salvation. He argued that man was saved by faith alone and that the Bible and not the pope should be the source of all theological authority.

Extreme left While in hiding Luther, shown here in an early portrait by his friend Lucas Cranach, translated the New Testament into German. The first edition (part of the title page appears *far left*) was published in 1522. Luther came out of hiding but was seldom able to travel. His message was therefore spread through print. *Above* A woodcut by Cranach (c. 1545) is typical of Protestant propaganda. On the right, God and St Francis watch in horror as the pope sells indulgences and a monk preaches easy salvation. On the left, Luther preaches that salvation depends upon faith. *Left* Catholics used similar techniques against Luther. In this woodcut from 1529 Luther is shown with seven heads. Such depictions had little effect, however, and by the time of Luther's death in 1546 most of the German people and princes were Protestant.

powerful artistic tradition existed in the Low Countries and Germany quite independently of the contemporary artistic movement in Italy. Equally, though, the growth of realism and naturalism in northern art was influenced to some degree by the Italian Renaissance. Just how and to what extent the art of Italy influenced the art of northern Europe, however, is harder to establish than is the case with humanist literature and scholarship. At the same time, northern art was plainly influenced by the same spiritual and religious concerns that lent northern humanism its distinctive character as an intellectual movement.

Thus on the one hand the art of the Northern Renaissance may be presented as a fusion of native and imported styles; on the other, it may be depicted as having been imbued with a uniquely northern quality. In short, while Dürer's technique as an engraver owed much to Italy, the subject matter of his work has few parallels south of the Alps; and with Hieronymus Bosch we have an artist whose themes and preoccupations are common enough in northern Europe but entirely alien to Italian art.

During the 15th century artists in Flanders began to break away from the traditional Gothic style of the Middle Ages. Such was their reputation that their work was much sought by Italian patrons, most notably by the banking families of the Medici, Arnolfini and Portinari. Indeed Bartolomeo Fazio, in his *Book of Famous Men*, composed in the mid 1450s at the court of Naples, identified two of the four greatest artists of his age as Flemish and described Jan van Eyck as "the leading painter of our time".

Flemish art of the 15th century achieved distinction through the work of the two artists identified by Fazio as "the greatest" of his age: Rogier van der Weyden (c. 1399–1464) and Jan van Eyck (c. 1390–1441). To these can be added a third, Albert Ouwater (active 1450–80). Their combined influence served to lend a new solidity and realism to the static and stylized forms of the period. Instead of communicating mainly by allegory and symbol, devices which required the intellectual engagement of the onlooker, these artists sought to appeal directly to the emotions by establishing a more convincing representation of the world.

The art of Rogier van der Weyden is notable for the solidity of its figures and for the sense of pathos they convey. Van der Weyden was probably influenced by the more realistic forms of sculpture that had already begun to influence Flemish art. Certainly the powerful rhythm of outlines, folds and drapery in his portraiture appears to owe much to the 14th-century sculptor Klaus Sluter, who had worked in Flanders and in the Burgundian court at Dijon. However, van der Weyden also visited Italy and the influence of Masaccio's style cannot be excluded.

Van der Weyden's most important work was the *Deposition of Christ*, painted about 1430. The restrained emotionalism of the picture, with its rich adornment and convincing depiction of Christ being lowered from the Cross, produced many imitators across northern Europe. Yet the picture is not wholly successful. The entire scene is confined to a box and though the figures may be placed in realistic poses the work as a whole lacks visual depth. Van der Weyden's *Deposition of Christ* has Renaissance portraits trapped within the unconvincing framework of the Gothic style.

If van der Weyden gave Flemish art solid figures, van Eyck was responsible for placing these figures

1500

Albertus Durerus Noricus
ipsum me proprijs sic effin-
gebam coloribus ætatis.
anno XXVIII.

against an effective background. He did this through the use of perspective and by the addition of landscape scenes. Van Eyck's figures are no less powerful than van der Weyden's, their drapery folds no less convincing. His settings, however, have a depth altogether lacking in the work of van der Weyden. The perspectives in *The Marriage of Arnolfini* (1434) and *The Madonna with Chancellor Rolin* (c. 1435) may be contrived, and the distancing of figures in *The Adoration of the Lamb* (part of the Ghent altarpiece, 1432) may be faulty, but the work of van Eyck exhibits a use and appreciation of space that is quite remarkable.

This new realistic treatment of space is exaggerated in his work by the frequency with which he resorts to *trompe l'oeil*. Some of his portraits are set in frames out of which hands, feet and heads protrude. In others a convex mirror in the background reflects objects at the front of the picture, or, as with *The Marriage of Arnolfini*, even some that are outside it. In the opinion of contemporary Italian critics, van Eyck was the equal of Apelles, the legendary master of *trompe l'oeil* in the reign of Alexander the Great.

During the second half of the 15th century Flemish art was influenced by the ideas of the Florentine humanist Leon Battista Alberti (1404–72). In Alberti's opinion it was the artist's task to construct a "stage" on which characters moved and involved the audience in the unfolding drama. This sense of a narrative relied upon postures and gestures derived from the rhetorical writings of the Latin authors Cicero and Quintilian, and had as its purpose to instruct, move and please the audience. Among the 15th-century Flemish artists, Albert Ouwater proved the finest exponent of narrative painting. In his *Raising of Lazarus*, executed in 1455 in Haarlem, Ouwater conveys not only the illusion of actual space but presents groups of figures gesticulating so as to tell a story. Thus there is an agitated group of onlookers, Christ giving His blessing, Martha at prayer, and Peter demonstrating the power of Christ. There is an attempt at accurate history as well, for the whole drama is located in what Ouwater understood to be an old building – though in fact a Romanesque church – and the onlookers are clad not as Flemish contemporaries but as orientals. The abstract symbolism of the Middle Ages was thus replaced by a more lifelike and historically accurate form of narrative realism.

But a more disturbing trend soon appeared in Flemish art. In the works of Ouwater's pupil, Geertgen tot Sint Jans (c. 1460–c. 1495), the drama of the narrative rapidly overtook the boundaries of reality. Thus while Geertgen's *The Holy Kindred* (c. 1485) conforms entirely to the style of his master, in *Nativity at Night* (c. 1490) the artist suspends the Virgin in eerie shadows among a swarm of shadowy angels. With Geertgen's torn and bleeding Christ in *The Man of Sorrows* (c. 1490) we have what is perhaps the first modern expressionist painting from the Low Countries. This trend in northern art was to find its culmination in the work of Hieronymus Bosch (c. 1450–1516), in which the art of the narrative supersedes realism entirely, giving way to fantastic images, macabre symbolism and nightmare visions. It was to be continued into the second half of the 16th century by Pieter Bruegel the Elder (c. 1525–69), who like Bosch combined the fantastic with images drawn from contemporary proverbs and tales.

German art in the 15th century was strongly influenced by Flemish traditions. For the most part, however, the German artists of the 15th century managed only pale imitations of the work of van der Weyden, and their technique remained far less rich and refined than that of the Flemish masters. Only in Austria, which was far more open to Italian influences, did the Tyrolean painter Michael Pacher (c. 1435–98) demonstrate an understanding of the use of shadows, perspective and landscape. Another exception was the Alsatian Martin Schongauer (c. 1450–91), whose copper engravings rivaled the achievement of the Italians Mantegna and Pollaiuolo.

About 1500, however, German painting soared to sudden and unexpected heights of achievement. Over the next 30 years Germany produced a group of remarkable artists, including Albrecht Dürer, Hans Holbein the Younger, Mathis Grünewald, Lucas Cranach and Albrecht Altdorfer. The extent to which these artists were inspired by Italian influences remains a matter of debate; of the list given above, only Dürer visited Italy. Nevertheless, Italian engravings and pattern books were in circulation in Germany and we know, for instance, that Altdorfer's first surviving work was taken from an engraving by Mantegna.

Yet the themes of the German artists and the way in which they represent them are far removed from the conventions of Italian Renaissance painting. The dynamism, expression, emotion and naturalistic qualities of German art are in complete contrast to the idealism, sense of balance and harmony shown by the neo-Platonists of Italy. In addition, there is a powerful and disturbed religious undercurrent to northern art: a premonition of the Reformation and an expression of the wider *Angst* afflicting the spirituality of Germany and the Low Countries. So while Albrecht Dürer (1471–1528) may have learned his skills as an engraver from Mantegna, and based his representation of the human form on anatomical descriptions found in Venice, the subject matter of his set of engravings *The Apocalypse of St John* (1498) and of *The Knight, the Devil and Death* (1513–14) reflects the particular religious tensions of northern Europe.

Religious emotionalism and a minute attention to detail were the hallmarks of northern art during the Renaissance. The former was based on a conception of man that stood at complete odds with the ideas of Italian artists. Instead of seeing man as the center of the divine work of creation, the northern artists saw him as being a trivial part of God's universe and dwarfed by the majesty of the natural world.

The emotionalism of German art finds its fullest expression in the achievement of Mathis Grünewald (c. 1474–1528). Grünewald specialized in the depiction of the Crucifixion and his paintings are unsurpassed as examples of the intensity of religious feeling in Germany on the eve of the Reformation. His brutal and repulsive depictions of Christ's sufferings, most notably on the Isenheim altarpiece (1515), provide some of the most powerful and compelling images in Western art. In *The Temptation of St Anthony*, on the same altarpiece, he painted horrific monsters and vividly colored creatures in a style reminiscent of Bosch.

The strange emotionalism of Grünewald was manifested in a dazzling use of color and with an expressionist's disregard for fine detail. Among his contemporaries, however, there was a far greater concern for accuracy and for realistic and minute depiction. Hans Holbein the Younger (c. 1497–1543) was the most distinguished portrait painter of his day, his work

Left Lucas Cranach, who spent most of his career as painter at the court of the Electors in Saxony, was frequently commissioned to paint portraits of his patrons and of other political and religious leaders of the period. It is improbable, however, that the portrait shown here represents a real person, for it lacks the sharp characterization typical of his work. The portrait is more likely to be of an idealized feminine type. Completed in 1526, it is probably one of a series of imaginary portraits Cranach painted in the 1520s.

characterized by strict attention to detail and accuracy of brush strokes. Among Holbein's subjects were Erasmus, Thomas More, Henry VIII and a number of Henry's wives. With a similar concern for accuracy, Dürer made engravings and drawings of extraordinary precision, including his remarkable watercolors *Hare* and *Great Piece of Turf*, both painted about 1503. The second is so accurate a depiction that botanists can easily identify dandelions, meadow grass, yarrow and plantains in the composition. Lucas Cranach (1472–1553), court painter to Frederick the Wise of Saxony, also executed portraits of great veracity, though his technique was more to capture a pose or a glance than to record every detail.

The tradition of landscape painting, which goes back to the 15th-century Flemish school, found its most complete expression in the work of the German artists. Panels on the Isenheim altarpiece are notable for their inclusion of alternately luxurious and menacing forests, of rocks, mysterious glens and mountain passes. During the course of the early 16th century depictions of the landscape became increasingly extravagant until they dwarfed entirely the subject matter of the picture. Thus in Albrecht Altdorfer's *St George and the Dragon* (1511) the struggle is fought out in miniature behind and beneath the spreading foliage of a forest. In his *Battle of Issus*, (1529), the landscape and cosmos are blurred. Vast skies, a setting sun, and the elemental conflict of fire and water overawe the human conflict shown at the foot of the picture.

These depictions of the landscape were intended not only to demonstrate the artist's skill but also to indicate the insufficiency of man. Humankind was but a small part of God's creation and the lives of individuals counted for little against the enormous and enduring quality of the natural world. This idea is expressed most vividly by Pieter Bruegel the Elder in his *Landscape with the Fall of Icarus* (c. 1558). While laborers work in a field against a luminous seascape, a tiny Icarus perishes unobserved, only his legs visible in the tide. The sense of human insignificance captured in

the *Fall of Icarus*, is further conveyed in Bruegel's art by his use of aerial space. *The Numbering at Jerusalem*, *Children's Games* and *The Massacre of the Innocents* are all seen from above, as if one were actually looking down on the scenes shown. Despite the vividness of his pictures of human life, mankind is depicted in Breugel's paintings on a reduced scale and is deliberately set against the vastness of the universe.

The Development of the Northern Renaissance

Although Cranach served as painter to the Saxon court until the middle of the century, German art entered a period of decline after 1530. In the Low Countries there were likewise few artists of distinction, apart from Pieter Bruegel, until the closing years of the century. There were two main reasons. Firstly, several major artists died about this time: Grünewald and Dürer both died in 1528, and Altdorfer in 1538. Secondly, Emperor Charles V (1519–56) gave most of his commissions to Spanish and Italian artists and in Germany did not retain the extravagant court of his predecessor, Maximilian I.

The Reformation and the growing religious conflict were also significant in this decline. Some artists, such as Grünewald, suffered because of their Protestant beliefs. Others saw their incomes reduced, for the Protestant churches were not notable patrons. The Protestant stress on preaching the word made the visual aspect of worship less important. Indeed, in areas under Zwinglian and later Calvinist control, art was considered idolatrous and there was a reaction against it. It was because of this intolerance that in the early 1530s Hans Holbein the Younger left Basel for England. In the 1560s in the Low Countries Calvinist zealots devastated church buildings, tearing out altarpieces and burning paintings.

German humanism also lost much of its vitality under the impact of the Reformation. The religious leaders of the Protestant Reformation prized eloquence, poetry, rhetorical skills and classical learning. However, they saw these not as ends in themselves, but as instruments to be used in the making of committed Christians. Thus the humanists of the Reformation were not involved in forming sodalities or in proclaiming the cause of cultural reform. Nor were they prepared to investigate pagan learning. The interest of the early German humanists in the cabbala, occult learning and neo-Platonism was thus allowed to languish. In the schools and universities of Protestant Germany, only "safe" classical texts were taught.

Reformation humanism achieved its most notable success in education. Luther's close colleague, Philipp Melancthon (1497–1560), undertook a major reform of education in Protestant areas. He reorganized the schools in Germany, equipping them to educate many thousands of pupils in classical learning and Protestant values. It was Melancthon's particular achievement to have transformed the educational system in Protestant Germany by moving it away from the elitism of early humanism toward compulsory and universal schooling. Johannes Sturm (1507–89), the principal of the grammar school in Strasbourg, was another important educator during the early phase of the Reformation. He was the author of a large number of works on education and his school served as an inspiration for Claude Baduel, reformer of the academy at Nîmes, for Roger Ascham, tutor of Elizabeth I of England, and for Catholic and Jesuit educators.

Below St George and the Dragon (1511) by Albrecht Altdorfer. The importance of Altdorfer lies in his establishment of landscape as a new genre. A fascination with nature can be seen in earlier northern artists; in Altdorfer nature becomes the very subject. In this picture the drama of St George defeating the dragon is subordinated to the depiction of the dense foliage of a primordial forest. Conrad Celtis, whose pastoral poetry may have inspired Altdorfer, wrote of his landscapes: "What delights me are the springs and green hills, the cool banks of the murmuring stream, the dense foliage of the shady woods and the rich vegetation of the fields."

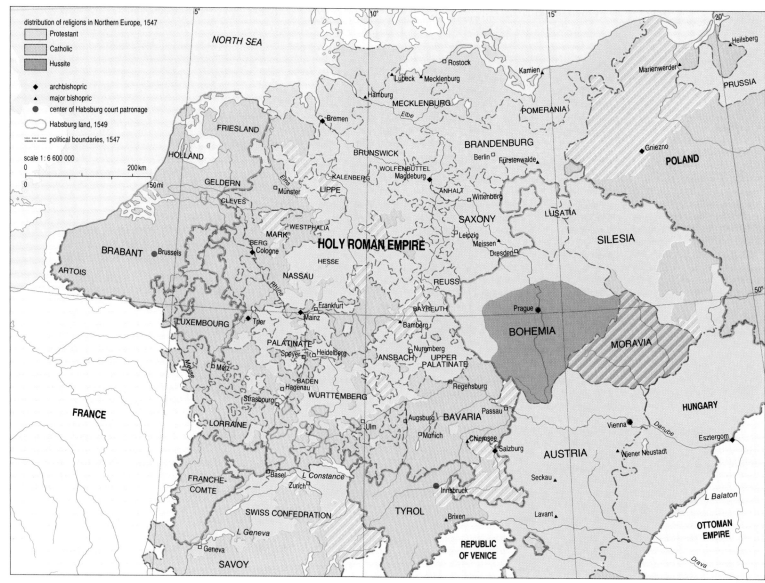

distribution of religions in Northern Europe, 1547

Protestant
Catholic
Hussite

◆ archbishopric
▲ major bishopric
● center of Habsburg court patronage
◯ Habsburg land, 1549
┅┅┅ political boundaries, 1547

scale 1 : 6 600 000
0   200 km
0   150 mi

The broadening of education certainly made more people literate and able to communicate in the classical style, and it is not surprising, therefore, that neo-Latin poetry flourished during the 16th century. It is possible to argue that in terms of sheer volume literary life became stronger under the aegis of the Reformation. The overall quality of these works, however, is not remarkable. Although there was some experimentation, biblical and religious themes predominated and acted as a restraint on lyrical expression. The eroticism, aggression and biting criticism of Celtis and von Hutten were also entirely missing.

In the Low Countries, however, humanist scholarship prospered and reached new heights during the second half of the 16th century. Under the influence of Erasmus and traditions he embodied, Dutch humanism retained its close connection with textual analysis. The printing house of Christopher Plantin in Antwerp poured out editions of the classics as well as legal and theological works. Even in the worst years of the Dutch Revolt in the 1570s and 1580s (when the Dutch were trying to drive the Spanish out of the Low Countries), and even after the sack of Antwerp in 1576, Plantin continued to publish such notable works as Ludovico Guicciardini's *Description of the Netherlands* (1557), Ortelius's book of maps, *Theatrum Orbis Terrarum* (1570), and French and Latin editions of the Bible.

The most remarkable work published by Plantin was the *Complutensian Polyglot*, a version of the Bible in the earliest languages of its composition – Latin, Greek, Hebrew, Syriac and Chaldean. The *Polyglot* was first published in Spain in 1514–17. Plantin's edition was sponsored by Philip II of Spain and edited by the king's chaplain, the Spanish humanist Benedictus Arias Montanus. Leading scholars from all parts of Europe collaborated in the project. Begun in August 1568, the complete work in eight folio volumes was finished in 1572. This edition of the *Polyglot* (the first edition had been published in Spain over 60 years before) represents the last great humanist achievement of the southern Low Countries.

The Dutch Revolt was caused by religious controversy. The Dutch, led by the Protestant Prince William of Orange, rebelled against the foreign rule of Catholic Spain and of its king, Philip II (1556–98). Although William of Orange (1533–84) managed to free the northern provinces of the Low Countries from Spain, he was unable to capture the southern part of the country and the cities of Antwerp and Brussels. As Spanish rule was consolidated in the south, so the scholarship of the southern part of the Low Countries became more constrained, serving principally the cause of militant Catholicism.

In the Protestant Low Countries, which became an independent state during the late 1570s, the study of the classics centered on the newly founded university

Religious changes in the 16th century
During the second and third decades of the 16th century, a large part of northern Europe embraced Protestant beliefs. Many Bohemians, however, remained loyal to the Hussite faith. In 1546–47 Charles V attempted to reimpose Catholicism in the Empire by force and defeated the Protestant princes at the battle of Mühlberg. Unlike the situation in the Low Countries, in Germany Charles lacked sufficient resources to consolidate his military victory. In large parts of northern Europe, Catholics and Protestants shared the same communities and a majority of the population seem to have adopted a religious position that was neither fully Catholic nor properly Protestant.

of Leiden. At a time of intense religious strife, Leiden was noted for its tolerance and for its breadth of vision. It employed some of the most outstanding scholars of the late 16th and 17th centuries. The first professor of Latin at the university was Justus Lipsius, whose masterpiece was his edition and notes on Tacitus's *Annals*. Lipsius (1547–1606) attempted to reconcile the teaching of the Stoics with the Christian faith and his work *On Constancy* (1584), in which he set out the philosophy of the Stoics, went through 80 editions in the next three centuries. Like Erasmus, he carried on a vast correspondence with humanists and scholars throughout Europe.

The university of Leiden also took over the traditions of the Collegium Trilinguale in Louvain, now in Spanish hands, and promoted the study of Oriental, Hebrew and Semitic languages as well as of classical literature. In the 17th century it numbered among its professors both Daniel Heinsius (1581–1655) and Hugo Grotius (1583–1645). The former, as Professor of Greek, edited Aristotle's *Poetics* and published texts by Horace, Seneca and Terence. Although Heinsius was also a versatile neo-Latin poet, some of his most notable verses were composed in the vernacular, in particular the *Nederduytsche Poemata* of 1616. The readiness of an international scholar to publish his verses in a language that was not classical aided the progress of the Dutch language toward literary respectability.

Hugo Grotius has been described as the typical representative of the Dutch Renaissance man. His interests included the writing of history, theology, biblical and classical scholarship. Although the bulk of his work deal with theological problems, in particular the question of whether or not man had a free will, he was a pioneer in the study of international law. In his *The Law of War and Peace* (1625) Grotius argued that there were laws of war and peace that could govern human affairs even in an age of indepen-

dent and sovereign states. The enormous range of Grotius's concerns, together with his interest in securing international harmony among Christian princes, puts him firmly in the Erasmian tradition of Flemish scholarship.

Only one other country in northern Europe shared with the Protestant Netherlands a tradition of religious and intellectual tolerance. In Poland Protestantism existed on an equal legal footing with Catholicism and the country provided a haven for both religious refugees and new ideas. Of all the branches of learning, astronomy was the first in Poland to speak out against the theological dogmas inherited from the Middle Ages.

Nicholas Copernicus (1473–1543) passed most of his life as a canon at the cathedral of Frauenburg on the Baltic coast. During his youth he spent eight years in Italy, where at the universities of Padua and Bologna he acquired a doctorate in law, studied medicine, and was introduced to the *studia humanitatis*. Copernicus's earliest work was a Latin translation of the Byzantine Greek writer Simocatta. But it was his *On the Revolutions of the Celestial Spheres*, published just after his death in 1543, that earned him his later reputation and provided the foundation of modern astronomy. Copernicus's discovery not only destroyed the belief that the sun revolved around the earth, it also undermined the work of theologians who had used religious arguments to prove the immovability of the Earth. Although the Church authorities succeeded in 1616 in having Copernicus's book banned, his heliocentric system continued to exercise an enormous influence through the work of Tycho Brahe, Galileo and Kepler.

Religious tolerance provided opportunities for intellectual innovation and fostered competition among the religious groups in Poland to improve education. Schools based on the curriculum and teaching methods of Johannes Sturm in Strasbourg were estab-

blished in the major Protestant cities and supported by noble patronage. In the second half of the century the Catholics set up Jesuit colleges for the education of the young and a network of seminaries for the training of priests. Nevertheless, these new centers of learning could not compete in terms either of prestige or of quality with foreign institutions, and the sons of Polish noblemen continued to frequent Italian universities, most notably the university of Padua, where Copernicus had studied.

Court patronage and Rudolf II

In the southern part of the Low Countries, the Spanish Netherlands, the restoration of peace with the Protestant north in 1609 ushered in a new period of prosperity. The court in Brussels, supported by the Catholic clergy, provided an important focus of artistic patronage. In the 17th century not only were the medieval buildings of Brussels, Antwerp and other leading cities cloaked in new decorative Baroque facades, but painting was sponsored to glorify the Catholic Church and the ruling Habsburg dynasty.

After the Reformation princely patronage in Germany was primarily concerned with architecture rather than with art. Buildings provided one obvious way in which a ruler might demonstrate his prestige, wealth and power. In the 1550s, therefore, Otto Heinrich of the Palatinate enlarged the castle at Heidelberg and remodeled it along classical lines. Columns, pediments and pilasters crowded the facade of the new castle, vying for space with medallions and sculptures. A more restrained style is evident in the Stadtresidenz at Landshut, built between 1536 and 1542 for Ludwig of Bavaria. Ludwig had been particularly impressed with the recently built Palazzo del Tè, which he had seen when visiting Mantua. He imported Italian architects and stonemasons to Landshut, where they built a copy of the Mantuan palace. For the most part, however, German princes were content to preserve the older Gothic structures and decorate them with Renaissance ornamentation.

The Habsburg emperors of Germany were the greatest patrons in central Europe and they retained in their courts some of the leading scholars of their day. Although by no means as magnificent and idiosyncratic as his father Maximilian, Emperor Ferdinand I (1558–64) assisted humanist studies by sponsoring, among much else, the publication of the Syriac New Testament of the orientalist Johann Widmanstetter. The emperor himself carried on a diversity of intellectual pursuits and was described by the Venetian ambassador as "a most curious investigator of nature, of foreign countries, plants and animals." His son and successor, Maximilian II (1564–76), gathered around him a wide collection of savants sufficiently talented to merit praise from Lipsius. Maximilian's favorite artist was the Milanese Giuseppe Arcimboldo (1527–93), "the prince of illusionists and most acrobatic of painters". Arcimboldo's present-day reputation derives from his grotesque compositions of human heads made from fruits, but in his own lifetime he was renowned for his skill in devising scenes of court pageantry and spectacle.

During the 16th century the courts of central Europe became increasingly preoccupied with the pursuit of arcane knowledge and wisdom. It was believed at this time that all branches of knowledge shared the same foundation and that their study would reveal the true nature and order of the cosmos.

Symbolism, magic and the examination of occult and cabbalistic texts were thought to provide a key to unraveling the divine mystery of the universe. In the Protestant courts of the Palatinate, Württemberg, Hesse and Brunswick, and in the castle of the Rožmberk family in Krumlov, magicians cooperated with neo-Platonic philosophers and with humanists in a common search for hidden knowledge.

The most remarkable patron of arcane knowledge was the son of Maximilian II, Emperor Rudolf II (1576–1612). Rudolf transferred the Habsburg court to Prague and during his long reign the Hradčany castle in Prague rather than the Hofburg in Vienna was the center of imperial patronage. Rudolf II's Prague attracted some of Europe's most notable scholars and artists, including the Flemish Mannerist Bartholomeus Spranger, the Dutch sculptor Adriaen de Vries, the astronomers Johannes Kepler and Tycho Brahe, both of whom were greatly influenced by Copernicus and by the English magician John Dee.

The intellectual world of Rudolf II's Prague was concerned primarily with the revelation of mystery. This might be achieved through the sinuous and lascivious forms of Spranger's painting, by the study of symbols, or by alchemy and necromancy. There was no difference between these diverse arts, it was thought, for all might offer a solution to problems that transcended human reason. In a similar way, it was thought that revelation might be obtained by indiscriminate collections of works of art, coins and freaks of nature. In the juxtaposition of such items clues might be given as to the hidden unity of the material world.

In Rudolf's court the techniques of classical scholarship were bent to the decipherment of arcane texts; humanist inquiry was directed toward the exploration of secret knowledge; painting reverted to an obscure allegorical style reminiscent of medieval iconography. In place of the Italian and classical letters preached so enthusiastically by Conrad Celtis a century earlier, Rudolf's court sought inspiration from the occult and mysticism.

Rudolf's 17th-century successors gradually gave up the search for occult meaning. They committed themselves instead to the cause of the Catholic faith and to the defeat of Protestantism. The triumph of the Habsburg emperors on the battlefields of central Europe during the Thirty Years War (1618–48) was followed by a revival in their lands of traditional forms of devotion and learning. Those elements of humanist learning and scholarship that survived the intolerance of the new century were harnessed to the service of Catholicism.

Conclusion

While obviously influenced by Italian scholarship and learning, the Renaissance north of the Alps demonstrated certain distinctive characteristics. These features, being common to the region as a whole, make it possible to consider the Northern Renaissance as a cultural movement in its own right. Northern humanism was thus far more concerned with issues of religion and of personal piety than was its Italian counterpart. The proper education of the young and the critical examination of religious texts formed an important part of scholarly activity from the late 15th century onward and both reached their high point in the work of Erasmus. After the onset of the Reformation in Germany, Renaissance scholarship became

Below The *Book of Great Alchemy*, composed in manuscript about 1560, contains a series of alchemical texts written in German and also includes several magical alphabets that may be used in invocations. The alphabet written at the bottom of the lefthand page was believed to be the devil's own alphabet. In the 16th century published collections of magical alphabets were frequently disguised as works on codes.

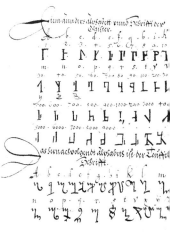

Right A portrait of Emperor Rudolf II as Vertumnus (the Roman god of the seasons) was completed in Prague by Giuseppe Arcimboldo about 1590 and is one of a series of allegorical works. The painting's use of symbolism and of the grotesque makes it typical of Mannerist art, but the composition also recalls the stress laid in the court masque and ceremonial on impersonation and transformation.

increasingly confined to philological inquiry and to the editing of texts for the purpose of moral and spiritual edification. Only in the Low Countries, and to a much lesser extent in Poland, did the scholarship of the post-Reformation period demonstrate any lasting achievement.

Like the northern humanists, northern artists were preoccupied with a religious theme: the magnificence of God's creation and, by extension, man's insufficiency and lack of merit. Unlike the Italian painters, they did not believe in the essential dignity of man. So there is a clear link between the Northern Renaissance and the Protestant Reformation, which taught that man, because of his complete lack of worth, depended for salvation upon divine grace. The court of Rudolf II in Prague partly rejected this notion, for its patron supposed that a higher form of understanding could be mastered without divine intervention through the study of arcane texts and sciences. Rudolf's court may have provided a welcome refuge for scholars and scientists who otherwise would have fallen foul of the ecclesiastical authorities. But the study of the occult proved an intellectual dead end and was largely abandoned by Rudolf's successors. By their determination to restore the Catholic faith to primacy in European politics and culture, the Habsburg emperors of the 17th century transformed the Renaissance into the Baroque.

Van Eyck: The Ghent Altarpiece

The Italian humanist Bartolommeo Fazio, writing in the 1450s, described Jan van Eyck, as "the prince of painters". Van Eyck's work was much collected in 15th-century Italy and was admired and imitated by later northern artists such as Dürer, Rubens and Rembrandt. Van Eyck's reputation lay in his astonishing use of color, in his attention to detail and in his use of space. His pictures not only pick out tiny details in the foreground but also unfold in slow stages toward a distant and luminous horizon. The art historian Erwin Panofsky has described van Eyck's eye as "at one and the same time a microscope and telescope". Although van Eyck was not, as was once thought, the earliest artist to use oil paints, he was the first to demonstrate the advantages of this medium. His technique was to apply layers of pigment and glaze to add both texture and depth to his colors. More than any other surviving work, the Ghent Altarpiece illustrates van Eyck's skill and originality as a painter – an originality that Italian painters were quick to recognize. Vasari wrongly credited him with the invention of oil paints.

Jan van Eyck was born in the Low Countries, probably near Maastricht. He was court painter first to the Count of Holland in The Hague and then to Duke Philip the Good of Burgundy, who entrusted him with diplomatic missions to Spain and Portugal. Most of his surviving works were completed during the last decade of his life, which he spent in Bruges. At first he worked with his brother Hubert (d. 1426), of whom little is known, except that Jan regarded him as "the greatest painter who ever lived".

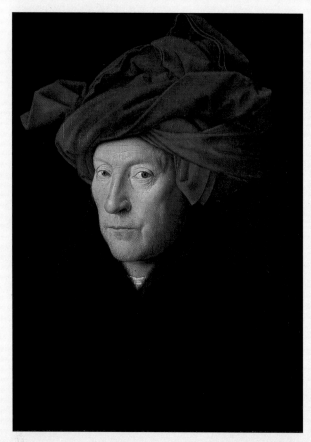

Below The Ghent Altarpiece was probably begun by Hubert van Eyck but completed (in 1432) by Jan. On the upper row of panels God the Father is shown sitting between the Virgin and John the Baptist. On the outer panels are a choir of angels and Adam and Eve. The lower row is a vision of the Adoration of the Lamb. The Heavenly City is on the horizon, but its skyline is that of a Dutch city and the church tower on the right is probably that of the cathedral of Utrecht. In its richness of detail and brilliance of color, the Ghent Altarpiece is a joyous expression of the Christian message of the Fall and Redemption.

German Wood Sculpture

German art of the 16th century owed much to earlier traditions of German woodcarving. The attention to fine detail, the angularity of the lines, and the exaggerated gestures that are typical of Dürer's work, for example, are anticipated in the German wood sculpture of the 15th and 16th centuries.

German sculpture itself was influenced by the art of the late medieval court of Burgundy, where animated and eloquent figures, distinguished by their long, flowing drapery folds, were sculpted in both wood and stone. This style was introduced into Germany by Nikolaus Gerhaert (active 1462–73), whose sympathetic and subtle characterization also had a lasting effect upon German wood sculpture.

The greatest German wood sculptures were carved in limewood in southern Germany. Being a more tractable hardwood than either oak or walnut, limewood favored detailed and expressive carving. To begin with, the German sculptors painted their works in vivid colors. In the 1490s, however, Tilman Riemenschneider (c. 1460–1531) and Veit Stoss (c. 1450–1533) broke with this tradition and began applying a monochrome glaze to their completed sculptures. This use of monochrome helps to explain the dynamism and vitality of German wood sculpture, for in dispensing with the expressive and decorative effects of color the sculptor was obliged to communicate solely through his chisel.

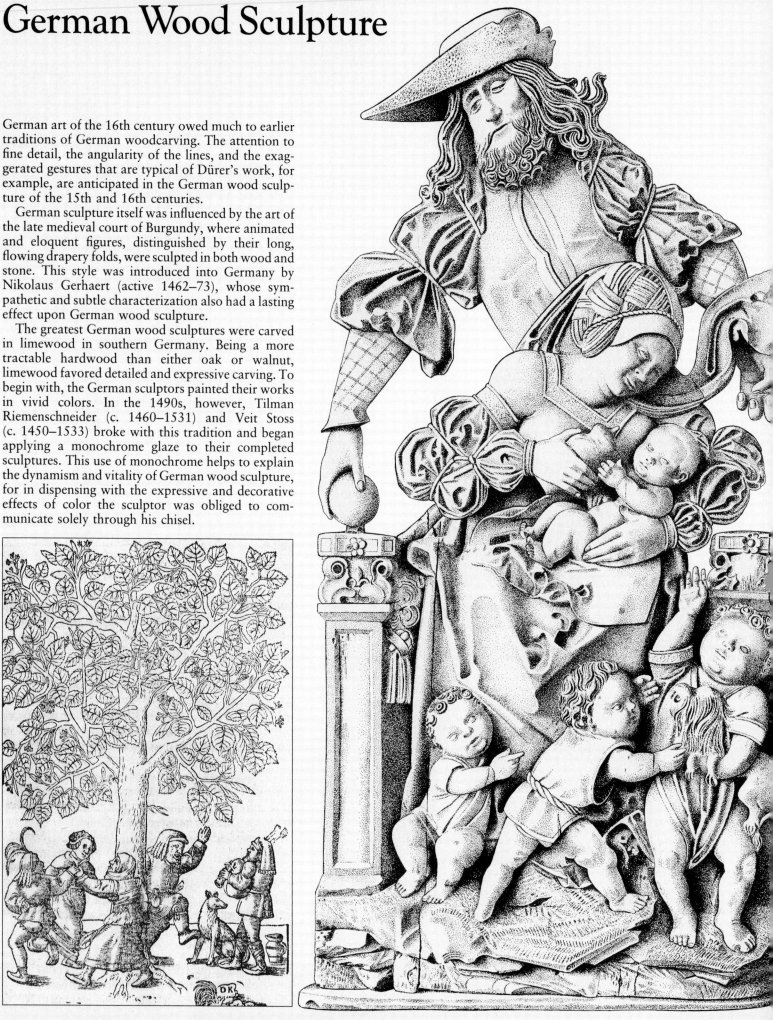

Left Bust of a Man (c. 1465) by Nikolaus Gerhaert. This striking bust, thought to be a self-portrait, is not in wood but in limestone – most of Gerhaert's works were destroyed during the Reformation. In both its expressiveness and its naturalism, however, it shows the strong influence of wood carving.

Below Statue of St Paul (c. 1505–10) by Tilman Riemenschneider, commonly considered the greatest of the south German wood sculptors.

Left St Roche (c. 1510–20) by Veit Stoss of Nuremberg. St Roche was the saint commonly invoked against the plague. According to legend, he had cared for victims of the plague before eventually succumbing to it himself. Shortly after its completion the statue was moved to Florence, where it was described by the Italian art-historian Vasari as having "drapery with most subtle carving, so soft and hollowed, and as it were paper-like, and with such a fine movement in the arrangement of the folds, that nothing more wonderful is to be seen".

Far left Mary Cleophas, Alpheus and their Children, from the *Altarpiece of the Holy Kindred* (1510). The altarpiece was carved in half-relief by Daniel Mauch of Ulm (1477–1540) and may have been commissioned by a wealthy merchant family from Augsburg. Its ornamentation shows strong Italian influences, though the figures are carved in a typically south German style.

Extreme left The Lime Tree (1551) by Hieronymous Bock. Lime trees were prized not only for their wood, which was excellent for carving, but also for their supposed magical properties. They were often hung with prayers against the plague and pilgrimages were made to limegroves – Bock recommended dancing around them.

The Northern Vision

By the late 15th century, the conviction was widespread in Northern Europe that society had gone wrong. A flood of publications complained of the "innovations" of the age – of the arrogant power of the princes; of the casual violence done by traveling bands of mercenary soldiers; of the corruption and wealth of the Church; and of the avarice of the rising merchant class. In a superstitious age, peasant rebellions, bad harvests and outbreaks of the plague confirmed the belief that God was angry with mankind and that the Day of Judgment was imminent. The publication in 1486 of the book *Hammer of Witches*, which described the ceremonies of witchcraft, contributed to the belief in a diabolic conspiracy to subvert the world and bring it under the rule of Satan. The demons in Bosch's paintings are thus not simply the product of imagination but attempts to visualize the currents of evil thought to be swirling through late medieval society.

Premonitions of the Apocalypse contributed to a resurgence of popular piety. Individuals sought to win a place in Heaven through worshiping relics, making pilgrimages, joining religious societies, and buying indulgences. A few tried to divert God's wrath and find relief from spiritual torment by scourging themselves on processions through the countryside or by frenzied dancing. Nevertheless, a conviction remained that all was not hopeless, that salvation could still be obtained by fastening on the love of Christ. This message of hope informed even the otherwise "pessimistic" art of Bosch and Grünewald.

Left Although Mathis Grünewald is best known for his depictions of Christ's Crucifixion, the side-panel of his Isenheim altarpiece (c. 1512–15) shows the Resurrected Christ ascending to Heaven in a halo of light. Christ still bears the marks of the nails, but His body is free of the wounds that disfigured it upon the Cross. The panel illustrates the redemptive nature of Christ's sacrifice and His promise to heal mankind of sin.

Right The fantastic imagery of Hieronymus Bosch drew not only on medieval bestiaries, tarot cards, gargoyles and descriptions of the Day of Judgment, but also on the symbolism of alchemy, magic and astrology. This fish in water, a detail taken from the *Temptation of St Anthony* (c. 1500–10), is a metaphor of sensual temptation and an illustration of the medieval proverb that man is surrounded by devils "as the swimmer is surrounded by water".

Left *The temptation of St Anthony* (c. 1485) by Matin Schongauer. St Anthony was the founder of monasticism. His solitary and ascetic life in the wilderness was disturbed by temptations that often took the form of hallucinations. St Anthony's "temptations" were either inducements to sexual pleasure or material wealth; sometimes they involved physical attacks by demons. Depictions of the temptation of St Anthony were common in northern art during the late Middle Ages.

Right *Melancolia* (1514) is considered one of the most complex of all Dürer's engravings. The winged figure probably represents Saturn, who in the 16th century was associated with high abstract contemplation, pure mathematics and a melancholy disposition – hence the sphere, the geometrically shaped stone, the dividers and scales, and the brooding face of the central figure. The engraving may in addition be a metaphor of the type of theoretical insight that thinks but is incapable of performing any decisive action. Whatever its precise interpretation, the engraving is profoundly pessimistic in its illustration of the limits and deficiencies of the human mind.

FRANCE

An age of expansion

Renaissance France in the first half of the 16th century was confident and expansionist. It hardly seems the same kingdom as that which, during the Hundred Years War only a century earlier, had needed miraculous signs from heaven and the leadership of Joan of Arc to prevent its territorial dismemberment at the hands of the English and Burgundians. Yet the experience of this exhausting war and the subsequent reconstruction helps to explain the distinctive features of the French Renaissance: its early hesitancy, its persistent royal focus, its ambiguity toward outside influences, and its introspective spirituality.

Unwelcome intervention in France's internal affairs by hostile neighboring dynasties had been a key feature of the Hundred Years War. In its aftermath the kings of France became obsessed with resuming the traditions of piecemeal annexation and integration that had originally created the powerful French state of the 13th century. Little by little neighboring principalities that had never formed part of the French domain were incorporated into it. The seizure of English Gascony in 1453 was followed by further substantial annexations in Burgundy (1477), Provence (1481) and Brittany (1491). At the same time many of the remaining feudal landed interests fell to the crown – first Armagnac (1473), then Anjou (1489) and finally, following the treason of the Constable, Charles de Bourbon, the substantial Bourbon inheritance (1527). With these the Valois, the ruling dynasty of France from 1328 to 1589, were able to reinforce their authority. By 1500 France had taken on its distinctive hexagonal shape.

The expansionist imagination of the Valois found it easy to justify intervention farther afield. Slender claims to Naples, Milan, the County of Artois and elsewhere were strengthened by marriage alliances, each carrying with it a possible justification of French involvement somewhere. Often the French court provided a refuge for political exiles eager to advance French interests (and their own) abroad. Neapolitan barons, exiled Genoese and Milanese, enemies of the Borgias in Rome, Florentine dreamers and schemers, all were drawn by the magnet of French ambition to propose cloudy schemes for a French king to invade Italy, unite it, reform the papacy and start a new crusade to the Holy Land.

Conquest had its cultural context, too. Charles VIII (1483–98), Louis XII (1498–1515) and Francis I (1515–47) were presented by their publicists as latter-day Hannibals crossing the Alps. Julius Caesar provided an even stronger comparison. Among the most fascinating illuminated manuscripts of the early 16th century is the remarkable three-volume commentary on Caesar's *Gallic Wars*. It was prepared for Francis I under the direction of his former tutor and grand almoner at his court, François Demoulins. The illustrations show the young French king meeting Caesar while hunting in the woods around Fontainebleau – two equals in mutual admiration of their skills in the arts of war. The great victories, especially that of Francis I at Marignano (Melegnano) in 1515, became the focus for the conquering, heroic theme. It was expressed in exquisite medallions (generally produced by Italian craftsmen), imperial statues, triumphal arches and even the vividly descriptive songs of the court composer Clément Jannequin (c.1485–1558).

French expansion 1453–1559
During the Renaissance France expanded rapidly, distant provinces such as Brittany, Picardy and Provence being brought within the orbit of the kingdom for the first time. By 1559 France was a third larger than it had been at the close of the Hundred Years War in 1453. The lure of Italy was particularly prominent in France's strategy of expansion, but this policy invited hostile alliances and retaliation, especially from the Habsburg dynastic coalition (the Italian Wars). France was still vulnerable to invasion, especially along its northern and eastern flanks. Internally, the story was one of consolidation. There was long-term investment in the legal and financial instruments of royal sovereignty, especially the *parlements*, or royal law courts. But France was far from being an absolute monarchy, despite its pretensions. There were still many regional representative assemblies and vigorous local traditions.

Left A medallion commemorating Francis I's famous victory at Marignano (1515) during the Italian Wars. The image-makers of his court were keen to show Francis equaling the military glories of ancient Rome. Here he is wearing a classical-style ornamental helmet. On the reverse side, the trophy of captured Swiss weapons is a reminder that the Swiss mercenaries had been defeated by the French *gendarmerie*. The legend around the trophy, "By God's protection and imperial virtue", is a further allusion to the imperial theme.

So France's Renaissance was closely linked to its military campaigns. Once engaged in the Italian Wars, during which they sought to establish control over the Italian peninsula, the French were at war in 43 of the 65 years from 1494 to 1559. In close collaboration with their generals, the Valois kings planned military campaigns carefully. Victories were the result of surprise attack (assisted by choosing the most appropriate route across the Alps) and the ability to sustain armies at a great distance.

But there was a price to pay for this military and political adventurism. It aroused fears among France's neighbors, fears symbolized from the 1490s onward by the conflict between the French royal house and the Habsburgs over Italy. There was also the increased cost of protecting an expanded landed frontier, which was especially vulnerable in the north and northeast. This entailed maintaining the only standing army in Europe, the famous *gendarmerie*, theoretically the preserve of the old nobility. Then there was the risk of military disaster. This occurred at Pavia in northern Italy in February 1525 when the French army was routed and Francis I captured and held for two years. In Picardy in August 1557 half the French army was

seized along with the Constable of France, Anne de Montmorency. Such defeats revealed the possibly fatal vulnerability of the French kingdom. Finally, there was the cost of integrating the newly incorporated lands into the French monarchy. Fundamentally different in linguistic background, legal traditions, customs and history, they were also less densely populated and less developed economically than the French heartland. Absorbing these lands into the French kingdom took enormous resources and effort. This perhaps helps to explain why it was in the French heartlands – in the Ile de France, the Loire Valley and Normandy – that the cultural investment in the Renaissance was concentrated. It also helps to explain why, despite the extensive French Atlantic coastline and the voyages of the explorer Jacques Cartier (1491–1557) from St Malo in the 1530s and 1540s, France's overseas expansion was so limited.

The "great monarchy of France"
French kings, their retinues and courts, and the broader world of royal officialdom were vital to French cultural life. The Valois knew the power of cultural patronage and in the hands of a dominant,

shrewd and intelligent king like Francis I patronage was employed to fashion both an image of monarchy and an elite's sense of identity.

The French court was a large and growing establishment during the Renaissance. On the eve of the first expedition to Italy in 1494 (the opening of the Italian Wars), the household had 318 officials on the payroll. By 1523 the *maison du roi* comprised 540 officials and the wagebill continued to rise throughout the first half of the 16th century. Yet this takes no account of the separate retinues of the queens, queen mothers and royal children as well as the councillors, notaries, royal secretaries, foreign legations and numerous hangers-on. Overall, it must regularly have exceeded 1,000 people.

Organizing the court, ensuring its supply, security and transport, was a major operation. Transportation was of particular importance as the French court traveled from place to place, its complex itinerary dictated by the political needs of governing a large and disparate state by means of local elites. Italian residents at the court were exhausted and bemused by it all. "This court is like no other", wrote the Bishop of Saluzzo to Cosimo I of Florence. "Here we are completely cut off from business, and if by chance there is any, no hour, day or month is set aside for certain to deal with it. Here one thinks of nothing but hunting, women, banquets and moving house..." Moving house was an operation requiring 18,000 horses. The baggage was vast, a testimony to the growing sophistication of French court taste. This showed in other ways too – in clothes, food, entertainment, etiquette and a greater role for women at court. Some of these changes were the result of increased Italian influences, though the impact of Burgundian court traditions was also important, as were indigenous pressures toward a more complex and civil society.

Housing an enlarged court influenced the architectural ambitions of the monarchy at least as much as the desire for ostentation. Part of the slow process of reconstruction of the realm after the Hundred Years War involved the French nobility in rebuilding its châteaux with defense no longer the primary consideration. Military features gradually began to take second place, or rather to be worked into buildings as surface decoration. At the same time the campaigns in Italy brought prominent members of the French nobility into direct contact with the classical architecture of the High Renaissance. The results may be measured in the surviving French Renaissance châteaux. At first classical motifs were added to fundamentally Gothic buildings. By the 1520s, however, classical forms began to dictate the overall structure of buildings, just as new patterns of courtly living determined their internal organization.

The process was particularly evident in royal palaces. Charles VIII returned from Naples in 1495 with a group of artists and craftsmen he put to work on the château at Amboise, already undergoing reconstruction. By Francis I's reign, however, Italian classicism was overwhelming, actively encouraged by a king who, according to one contemporary, was "marvelously addicted to architecture". First in the Loire valley, and then in the Ile de France, the royal châteaux were transformed. At Blois, the palace of the king's first wife, Claude de France, he enlarged one wing of the château; on the outer side he gave it a new facade of Italian loggias in the style of Bramante's Vatican; and on the courtyard side he commissioned a classical facade and a remarkable spiral staircase. Then, in the royal forests to the east of Blois, he began to build the extraordinary château at Chambord.

After 1528, Francis I began extensive works at the Louvre, Fontainebleau, St Germain-en-Laye and in

Above Charles V, king of Spain and Holy Roman Emperor, spent two months in a hastily conceived royal "progress" across France to suppress a rebellion in the Low Countries. Francis I, hoping to win concessions in Italy from the emperor in return for this evident demonstration of *entente*, greeted his great adversary warmly. Their meeting is evoked in this painting by the Italian artist Taddeo Zuccari.

Right: The Valois Renaissance
The French Renaissance was preeminently (though not exclusively) associated with the royal court. The Valois kings of France had an elaborate court that played a leading part in artistic changes, uniting the cultural values of its aristocracy as well as governing the kingdom and masterminding its military campaigns. During the reign of Francis I (1515–47) the Renaissance court was at the height of its effectiveness. The king's "progresses" round his kingdom were dictated by a complex set of strategic and political considerations. Their cultural effects were immense. In his influential book, *The Most Excellent Buildings of France*, the engraver J. Androuet du Cerceau presented architectural drawings of the buildings he most admired in the kingdom. The result showed the cultural assumptions of someone closely attached to the dominant taste at the French court of the time.

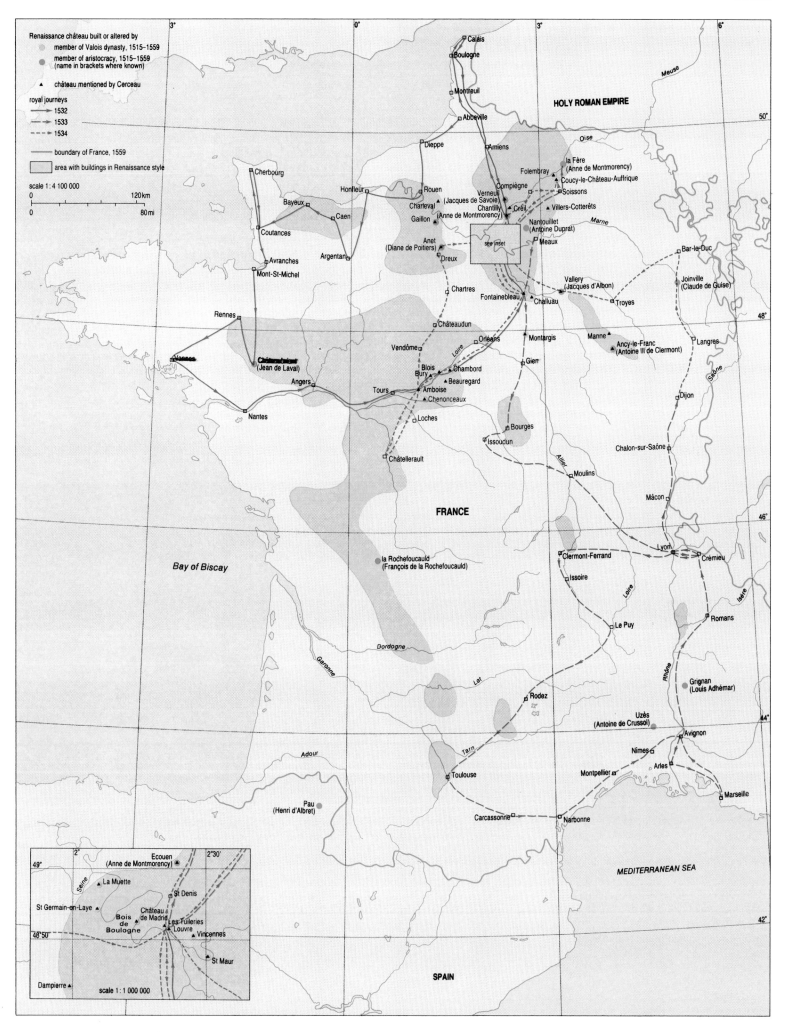

Renaissance château built or altered by
member of Valois dynasty, 1515–1559
member of aristocracy, 1515–1559
(name in brackets where known)
château mentioned by Cerceau

royal journeys
1532
1533
1534

boundary of France, 1559

area with buildings in Renaissance style

scale 1:4 100 000

0   120km
0   80 mi

Calais
Boulogne
Montreuil
Abbeville
Dieppe
Amiens
la Fère
(Anne de Montmorency)
Folembray
Coucy-le-Château-Auffrique
Compiègne
Soissons
Rouen
Honfleur
Verneuil
(Jacques de Savoie)
Cherbourg
Créil
Villers-Cotterêts
Charleval
Chantilly
Bayeux
Caen
Gaillon
(Anne de Montmorency)
Nantouillet
(Antoine Duprat)
Coutances
Anet
(Diane de Poitiers)
Meaux
Marne
Bar-le-Duc
Avranches
Dreux
see inset
Mont-St-Michel
Vallery
(Jacques d'Albon)
Joinville
(Claude de Guise)
Chartres
Fontainebleau
Challuau
Troyes
Langres
Rennes
Châteaudun
Manne
Ancy-le-Franc
(Antoine III de Clermont)
Vendôme
Orléans
Montargis
Vannes
Châteaubriant
(Jean de Laval)
Loire
Blois
Chambord
Dijon
Bury
Gien
Angers
Beauregard
Amboise
Tours
Chenonceaux
Saône
Nantes
Loches
Bourges
Issoudun
Châtellerault
Chalon-sur-Saône
Allier
Moulins
Mâcon
FRANCE
la Rochefoucauld
(François de la Rochefoucauld)
Lyon
Bay of Biscay
Clermont-Ferrand
Crémieu
Issoire
Isère
Garonne
Romans
Le Puy
Dordogne
Rhône
Lot
Grignan
(Louis Adhémar)
Rodez
Uzès
(Antoine de Crussol)
Adour
Avignon
Tarn
Nîmes
Toulouse
Arles
Montpellier
Marseille
Pau
(Henri d'Albret)
Carcassonne
Narbonne
MEDITERRANEAN SEA
SPAIN

Meuse
Oise
50°
48°
46°
44°
42°
3°
0°
3°
6°

Ecouen
(Anne de Montmorency)
49°
Seine
La Muette
St Denis
St Germain-en-Laye
Château
de Madrid
Bois
de
Boulogne
Les Tuileries
Louvre
48°50'
Vincennes
St Maur
Dampierre
scale 1:1 000 000
2°
2°30'

Chambord

In the woods to the east of Blois, Francis I built an entirely new Renaissance palace. The result, one of the most remarkable buildings of the Renaissance, survives as a unique monument to the extravagant grandeur of the French Renaissance monarchy and its court. Built on marshy ground, the huge château of Chambord needed considerable foundations though; building began in 1519, the central wings were not completed before 1533 and their internal decoration not before 1539. Work on Chambord continued into the 1550s, the outer wings were never completed.

The dimensions of the project were, by 16th-century standards, vast. So too was the interest it inspired among contemporary crowned heads. Henry VIII of England, for example, was so impressed by what he heard of Chambord that he commissioned an equivalent palace in the woods to the south of Hampton Court, making its frontage a little larger than Chambord – Nonsuch palace.

In the 17th century a drawing was made of the original wooden mock-up of the château, a model possibly constructed by Domenico da Cortona, who may have been the principal architect of Chambord.

This did not, however, mean that the eventual palace was constructed to Italian design, since we know from the accounts that the work was carried out under a succession of French master masons. In any case, the final building departed from the model in several respects, notably in the facades and the staircase in the central wing. The overall result was a triumph of Renaissance architecture.

With abundant evidence of Renaissance motifs on the facades of the building, perhaps the most striking feature of Chambord is the crowded roofline. Here extravagant use was made of the strong native traditions of royal architecture. More than 300 dormer-windows, monumental chimneys and ornamental turrets cluster around a central lantern that provides downlight to the double-spiral staircase, giving Chambord an air of medieval romance.

The 16th-century chronicler Brantôme once claimed to have seen carved in a window seat at Chambord, in Francis I's own hand, the words "Tout femme varie" ("All women are fickle"). Inconstancy was the fundamental problem of both his personal and his diplomatic relationships.

Below Even today, Chambord is imposing. Situated in a park as large as the city of Paris in the 16th century, its overall dimensions are similarly gargantuan. With 440 rooms, it could house the ever-expanding royal court.

Chambord key

1 Entrance
2 Main courtyard
3 *Donjon*
4 Guardrooms
5 Main staircase
6 Chapel
7 Apartment of Francis I
8 Place d'Armes

Below The plan of Chambord is superficially medieval: a central keep, four towers and a curtain wall. In other respects, however, it represents the application of Renaissance principles. It is the contrast between these two styles that makes Chambord so distinctive.

Bottom The most striking internal feature of Chambord is the remarkable double-spiral staircase (possibly the idea of Leonardo da Vinci). The stonework is open so that the light from above reflects onto the connecting passages.

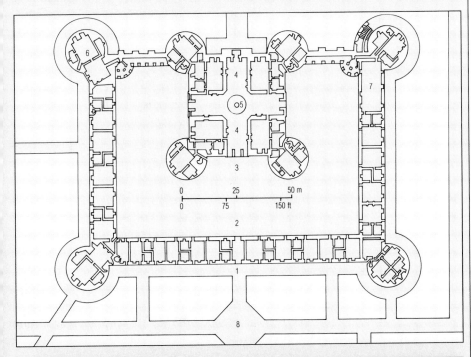

the Bois de Boulogne. The last of these, popularly known as the Château de Madrid (for reasons which are unclear), no longer exists, though sufficient of its structure and decoration can be deduced to assess its Italian influences and overall novelty. Fontainebleau, however, provides us with the most characteristic royal palace of the French Renaissance, a sustained evocation (both within and without) of the greatness of the French monarchy and state.

Beyond the confines of the royal court lay the governing equivalent of its standing army, the royal officials. France employed more officials than any other state of Renaissance Europe. Its officials had to pay for their posts in its *parlements* (sovereign law-courts) and numerous other tribunals, and kept them permanently. It has been estimated that in 1515 there were over 4,000 royal officers, the backbone of the state's program of territorial integration. The cost of the Italian campaigns in the early 16th century increased both their numbers and the importance of the contribution their payments made to the French monarchy's finances. Office-holding proved to be vital in the transmission of Renaissance culture in France.

The impact of the Renaissance was felt most clearly among the dynasties of senior royal officials. It was they who, in the forest playgrounds of the Valois in the Loire valley, built the magnificent country houses that tell us much about the combination of rivalry and emulation that forged French Renaissance classical architecture. Among the earliest was one built by Florimond Robertet at Bury in the 1510s. The founder of a dynasty of royal servants to the later Valois, he became an influential official under Louis XII and Francis I. Only the ruins of Bury now survive, but contemporaries were impressed by its arcaded gallery, its regular classical facades and its collection of antique statuary, which included a bronze *David* by Michelangelo. It is possible that Bury exercised an architectural influence over the new Francis I wing at Blois. Not far away Thomas Bohier was acquiring the lordship of Chenonceaux. A leading figure in the treasury, he made a fortune in royal service. He married Catherine Briçonnet, the daughter of one of the great royal financier families, and eventually rose to become president of the Paris Chamber of Acounts. His first step was to demolish most of the old castle at Chenonceaux in 1514 and build in its place a sumptuous fashionable Renaissance residence on the foundations of its watermill. Meanwhile at nearby Azay-le-Rideau in 1518 more than 400 workers were employed rebuilding the house of another financier and secretary to the king, Gilles Berthelot. Architecturally, it incorporated features from both Blois and Bury.

Bury, Chenonceaux, Azay-le-Rideau — other examples are not difficult to find. In their careful blend of features both classical and Gothic these buildings say something about the ambition, even snobbery, of these newer nobles. Not that the officials of the Valois state always succeeded. Government servants and financiers, suspected of profiting too much from royal service, were the first scapegoats for the failure of royal policy — as Thomas Bohier was to find when he was disgraced in 1531.

The officials of the Valois state also left a distinctive mark on the intellectual scene. Their humanist education and legal training provided them with the background essential for an appreciation of the *studia humanitatis*. The majority confined themselves to buying and reading humanist texts; a few managed to

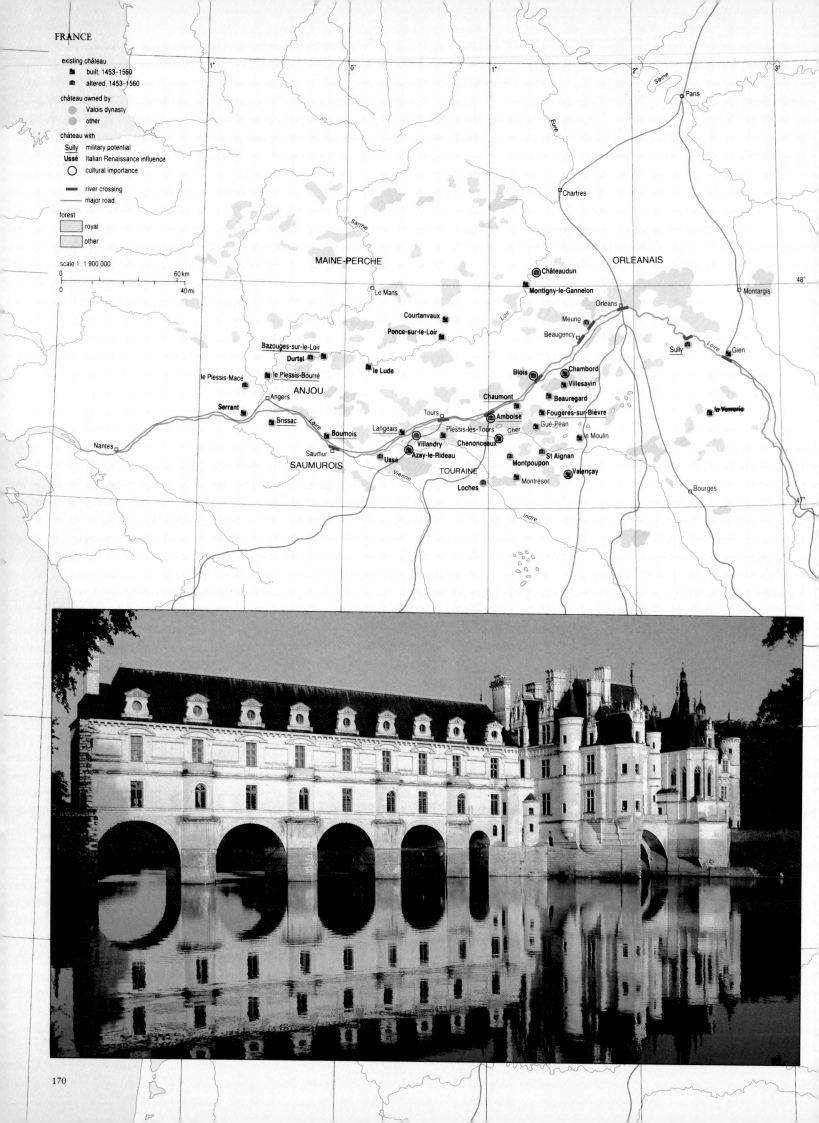

FRANCE

existing château
- built, 1453–1560
- altered, 1453–1560

château owned by
- Valois dynasty
- other

château with
- Sully — military potential
- Ussé — Italian Renaissance influence
- ○ — cultural importance

— river crossing
— major road

forest
- royal
- other

scale 1:1 900 000

0   60 km
0   40 mi

MAINE-PERCHE

ORLEANAIS

Paris

Chartres

Montargis

Le Mans

Châteaudun

Montigny-le-Gannelon

Orléans

Courtanvaux

Ponce-sur-le-Loir

Meung

Beaugency

Sully

Gien

Bazouges-sur-le-Loir

Durtal

le Lude

Blois

Chambord

Villesavin

le Plessis-Macé

le Plessis-Bourré

ANJOU

Chaumont

Beauregard

Fougères-sur-Bièvre

la Verrerie

Serrant

Angers

Tours

Amboise

Gué-Péan

Brissac

Boumois

Langeais

Plessis-lès-Tours

Chenonceaux

Cher

le Moulin

Villandry

Nantes

Saumur

Ussé

Azay-le-Rideau

St Aignan

Montpoupon

Valençay

SAUMUROIS

TOURAINE

Loches

Montrésor

Bourges

Vienne

Indre

170

combine a life of active scholarship with a devotion to busy royal service. Perhaps none achieved this more than Claude de Seyssel (c. 1450–1520). Italian by birth, he studied law at Pavia before becoming Louis XII's most trusted royal adviser, experienced administrator and active diplomat. Yet he managed to find time to use the newly assembled royal library at Blois, where he prepared translations into French of Greek and Roman historians. He aimed to provide "not merely a delectation and delight to read but an education and direction in how to govern wisely and well and manage the affairs of a kingdom". This was why, after Seyssel's death, Francis I ordered his secretary and almoner, Jacques Colin (the first translator of Castiglione's *The Courtier* into French), to edit and publish these translations, and had them read to him after his evening meal. Seyssel's political treatise *Le Grant Monarchie de France*, one of the most important examples of French political thought in the 16th century, was presented to Francis I in 1516 during his official visit to the city of Marseille, where Seyssel was bishop. It argued that the French monarchy, a careful balance of the monarchical, the aristocratic and the democratic, surpassed the greatness of the Roman Empire. Should not those subjected to its dominion (and especially those in Italy), it implied, have reason to count themselves fortunate? French humanism, in the hands of France's governing elites, easily became political propaganda of one sort or another.

The allure of Italy

The influence of the Italian Renaissance on French culture began before Charles VIII's expedition to Italy in 1494. There had been humanist teaching at some French universities from the middle of the 15th century. There was already a natural interest in things Italian, particularly among senior French clergy, an interest initially stimulated during the 14th century when the papacy was based in Avignon, but sustained by a succession of French cardinals.

Yet for the nobility who served in the royal army, the Italian campaign of 1494 (and its sequels) was a turning-point. They were dazzled by what they found. One chronicler of the campaign noted with excitement "all kinds of singularities, houses with dainty windows, great galleries, long, wide and high, delightful gardens with little lawns, paths and hedges, fountains and streams...where there are antique alabaster statues of white marble and porphyry". King Charles VIII wrote back to Pierre de Bourbon from Italy in March 1495: "You would not possibly believe the beautiful gardens I have seen...For upon my faith it seems it would only need Adam and Eve to turn them into an earthly paradise, so beautiful are they, so full of good and remarkable things... and I have discovered in this land the best artists and you will send for them to make the most beautiful panels imaginable."

Charles VIII in fact returned from Italy with 20 or so workmen who were "to construct and fashion in the Italian style". They were mainly decorators, artists and sculptors, but they also included a Neapolitan gardener, Pacello de Mercogliano. He was assisted by Domenico de Cortona, *faiseur de châteaux* – that is, a fabricator of garden pavilions as well as wooden architectural models for new buildings. Their compatriot Fra Giocondo constructed the aqueduct which brought water to the redesigned gardens at Blois.

Under Francis I the Italian influence grew greater. Leonardo da Vinci (1452–1519), whose connections with the French court went back to the reign of Louis XII, arrived in 1516 and settled at the king's invitation at the manor of Cloux (Clos-Lucé) near Amboise. There has been much speculation about what the king had in mind for him. One possibility is that he was commissioned to design a new palace for the queen mother at Romorantin. A set of sketches in the Leonardo Codex Atlanticus has been identified as belonging to this project. But by the year of his death (1519) the project was stillborn. Leonardo has also been claimed as the architect of Chambord, one of the finest châteaux of the French Renaissance, though this is unlikely as work on it began some four months after his death. It is possible, however, that the bold decision to build the central double-helix staircase may have owed something to his influence.

Many of the distinctive qualities of Fontainebleau may also be ascribed to Italian influences. The internal decorations were under the direction of Giovanni Battista Rosso (1495–1540) and Francesco Primaticcio (1504–70). Rosso was a Florentine artist who had worked under Michelangelo and Raphael while in Rome. About 1529 he moved to Venice and drew a sketch of *Mars and Venus* for the Italian writer Pietro Aretino. The composition was an allegory on the Peace of Cambrai (1529), a treaty agreed during the Italian Wars, and its presentation to Francis I may have led to Rosso's invitation to France. The following year (1532) he was joined by Primaticcio, the greatest stucco artist of his day, who was recommended to the French king by the duke of Mantua.

Left A fresco in the bedchamber of the Duchess d'Étampes, by Primaticcio. In 1540 Primaticcio, sent to Rome to purchase works of art for Francis I, came into direct contact with ancient sculpture and the work of Parmigianino. On his return to Fontainebleau he developed the distinctive style of drawing human figures seen in these bas-relief caryatids with their flatteringly long, tapering limbs, thin necks and demure heads.

Rosso and Primaticcio were the principal members of the School of Fontainebleau, a large and varied group of artists, both native and foreign, who worked at the French court from about 1530 to 1560. They included the sculptor Jean Goujon (c.1510–64) and the painters Niccolò dell' Abbate (c.1509–71), and Jean Cousin (c. 1490–1560). Rosso's bold stucco and Primaticcio's flatteringly long-limbed, thin-necked nudes can still be seen at Fontainebleau in the Francis I Gallery, the Duchess d'Étampes' bedchamber and the Ballroom. The paintings, stucco, tapestries and overmantle statuary are intricately worked into an ensemble of mythological and contemporary allusion that contributes to its overall artistic success. The style of the school as a whole is self-consciously elegant, sensuous and often erotic. Although largely Italian in inspiration, the School of Fontainebleau helped to establish France as a major artistic center and was widely influential.

The Italian influences on the two artists who created the most distinctive images of the French court – Jean Clouet and his son François – are less pronounced. The subtle and refined portraits of Jean Clouet (c.1485–c.1540) are often seen as sensitive essays in the psychology of his sitters. Although he lived in France for most of his life, he came from the southern Netherlands and his painting techniques, particularly his use of color, seem fundamentally Flemish. On the other hand his compositions seem influenced by the Italian style of Renaissance portraiture introduced to the French court by the influential Florentine painter Andrea del Sarto (1486–1531). Italian influences can be more clearly seen in the work of François Clouet

(c.1510–72), whose graphic skills match those of his father. Both father and son painted striking portraits of Francis I.

The baggage of the returning French armies from Italy contained what would become the basis of royal and private Renaissance collections of paintings, sculpture, *objets d'art* and manuscripts. But there was also an accompanying transfer of science and technology that in time would make a deep impact. French banking was transformed by the activities of the Italian merchants in Lyon. In 1465 the Medici had transferred their operations north of the Alps from Geneva to Lyon; by 1502 there were roughly 40 Florentine firms with branches in Lyon, dominating many of France's long-distance trades and, increasingly, its money-markets. Foundry techniques were improved by the imported skills of court bronze manufacturers, skills that also influenced enamel artists such as Léonard Limousin (c.1505–c.1577). At Florence Charles VIII had seen a lion menagerie: he wanted his own zoo and it was begun on his return to Amboise. In Poggio Reale an artificial egg incubator had attracted his attention: one was installed in Amboise. Italian medical skills were imported through the surgeons of the French armies. One of these, Ambroise Paré (c.1510–90), who served his apprenticeship in one of the Italian campaigns, eventually became the most accomplished and observant surgeons and anatomists of the century. Italian drainage techniques also found their way to France and agricultural innovations, based in part upon an imaginative application of classical Roman texts, were also imported. In the market gardens around Nîmes new

Above Although he began life humbly as apprentice to a barber surgeon, Ambroise Paré became surgeon to the last four Valois kings of France. His renown did much to advance the professional status of surgeons. He accompanied French troops during the Italian Wars, and his greatest contributions to surgery techniques were often the result of inspired guesswork within earshot of battles.

Above Guillaume Budé was an indefatigable advocate of humanism in France. Although he suffered regularly from severe headaches, nervous depression and illness, he was nevertheless driven by an insatiable curiosity that expanded his range of interests to include mathematics, philosophy, logic, law and the natural sciences. His profound knowledge of the classics was evident in all his publications. By the time of this portrait of him by Jean Clouet (c. 1536) he had succeeded in persuading Francis I to establish the famous Trilingual Royal College, the forerunner of the *Collège de France*.

muses..." The sentiments are those of the major French humanist Guillaume Budé (1468–1540) and they appear in his *Right and Proper Institution of the Study of Learning* published in 1532. He was expressing what by this date were humanist commonplaces echoed in the writings of Jacques Lefèvre d'Étaples and François Rabelais, the jewels in the crown of French humanism.

There had been humanism in France in the 15th century. The first known printed work in France was produced on the printing press established in the Sorbonne in 1470 – a humanist treatise by an Italian on the art of elegant Latin composition. In the hands of its leading campaigners, however, humanism set out to transform the study of law, philosophy and theology. It thus had a profound effect on the nature and conduct of public life. In the advanced urban societies of northern Italy such changes were absorbed and channeled without too much difficulty. In the more traditional society of France, however, they proved more difficult to assimilate. Those who had no power or authority in the kingdom were expressing dissent. The enthusiasms of the humanists and the growing influence of their following became controversial and divisive.

Although the humanists sometimes overstated their novelty, in some respects they did not exaggerate. Crudely speaking, they rejected scholastic learning and educational methods, both of which depended primarily on logic, and turned instead to rhetoric: the art of persuasion. Their inspiration came not just from the philosophers of antiquity but also from its orators, poets and historians. It was based on a perception of human beings as active and engaged social beings for whom language is an essential energy, a vital power. But language, they argued, is always imprisoned within a particular culture and a particular moment of history. Only through the new science of philology (the study of language and its development) would scholars be able to return to the original sources of knowledge and to the accompanying human reality.

The first decade of the 16th century was decisive for French humanism. The first shockwaves of the new learning began to make an impact. Guillaume Budé's apprenticeship as a humanist was a long one, as he later admitted, but it was carefully prepared. After a conventional education at the university of Paris and then at the law school in Orléans, he took to serious study after something approaching a "conversion" in 1490, and in 1494 began to study Greek. In 1508, in a matter of a few months, Budé wrote and published his *Annotations on the Pandects*, his passport to humanist renown.

There had been many commentaries on the texts of Roman law in the Middle Ages, but Budé's was different. It attacked the medieval commentators, urged its readers to study Roman law directly, and proclaimed the necessity of using philology to do so. Up to this date no one in France had dared to introduce humanist critical methods into one of the major professions and basic university disciplines. The result was soon to show through in the French law faculties, particularly at Orléans, Bourges and Toulouse, the finishing schools of France's royal officials. The French "legal Renaissance" is of fundamental importance, not least for its contribution to political thought. It was here that the first coherent statement of the sovereignty of the state was articulated, first by the brilliant legal humanist Jean de

salad crops were grown, while in the Cévennes and Provence mulberry-trees were planted to feed the silk-worms whose thread was turned into fashionable silk in Lyon and Tours.

But not everything imported from Italy was regarded as a benefit, and in time there was a reaction. By the reign of Henry II there was an evident dislike for the undue influence at court of the refugee Italians, particularly the ambitious relatives of his Italian wife, Catherine de Medici. There was also resentment of the numerous Italians in senior positions within the French church. Were Italians not to blame, it was said, for the indiscipline, the immorality, deceptions and dishonesty of courtly life? Dueling with rapiers, a custom which spread with alarming speed among the feuding French nobility, was perceived as a fatal Italian infection. By 1558 the French state owed almost twice its annual revenues to the Italian bankers of Lyon. Worst of all, Italian humanism appeared to some to open the door to irreligion and atheism. It was time to rediscover an independent French antiquity, a French Hercules, a French church, and a *mos gallicus* (French custom and tradition) in its laws, history and traditions of statecraft.

French humanism: the shock of the new in the rediscovery of the old

The humanists made much of their novelty. A "disastrous flood" had submerged authentic learning in the Middle Ages, burying Christendom under "the overwhelming debris of barbarism". Such was "the sorry state of many centuries past" until "this age boldly undertook to reinstitute the choirs of the ancient

Coras, and then definitively by his student Jean Bodin (1530–96) in *The Six Books of the Commonwealth* (1576).

Nor was this all. Budé also used the first 24 books of the *Pandects* as a vehicle to proclaim the need for changes of all kinds. There were passing shots at the *parlement* of Paris and its judges. He had harsh words, too, for under-aged bishops and worldly clerics, ignorant of Latin, who put the pursuit of power above the saving of souls.

Meanwhile a similar explosion was taking place in philosophy and theology. Jacques Lefèvre (c. 1455–1536) came from Étaples, a small seaport in Picardy. He became a student in Paris and remained there for most of his life. He studied with phenomenal concentration and published at a prodigious rate. His achievement was remarkable. Single-handedly he produced the first thorough and uncompromising humanist editions of the bulk of Aristotle's works. At last the greatest of the ancient philosophers could be studied directly in reliable editions and not through medieval commentators. In 1509 Lefèvre turned to biblical texts, publishing the *Fivefold Psalter*. This was a milestone in biblical studies. It was so called because it presented the five different Latin versions of the text of the Psalms in separate columns, along with their theme, an exposition, a harmonizing comparison with other passages of scripture and a set of annotations. Gone was the elaborate system of interpretation used in the Middle Ages.

In the decades that followed there was much more to come from Lefèvre and Budé and their disciples. In his book on Roman coinage (*De Asse*) of 1514, Budé demonstrated his profound knowledge of the differences between Greek and Latin civilizations, analyzed the basic rules of economic life, and voiced further outspoken opinions on politics and religion. Meanwhile Lefèvre produced his *Commentary on St Paul's Epistles* (1512), a huge folio book that attempted a clear, unadorned exposition of St Paul's beliefs based on a humanist examination of the texts. With God's assistance and with true piety, proclaimed Lefèvre, man may be led toward God's divine truth. Here Lefèvre confronted the fundamental theological issues that would lie at the heart of the Protestant Reformation: grace, human responsibility, and justification by faith. It is difficult not to imagine that there would have been a strong theological debate in France even had there been no Martin Luther.

Many other aspects of the thought of these humanists struck French contemporaries as novel. Firstly, there was a profound sense of the underlying unity of all knowledge: Budé introduced the evocative word "encyclopedia" into the French language. Secondly, there was neo-Platonic mysticism. Budé's first translations from Greek included a work on meditation, and the epilogue of *De Asse* contains a dialogue on the human and the divine. Among the recurring images of his works, that of Minerva (sometimes Hermes) stands out most strikingly, the messenger goddess and mediator of knowledge sometimes equated with Christ. Lefèvre was influenced by the Spanish philosopher and mystic Ramon Lull, and attracted by writing on magic and the cabbala (a body of Hebrew mystical speculation).

The French humanists saw themselves as a minority campaigning for truth. They sought protection in high places and Francis I was prepared to be convinced by them. After a decade-long publicity campaign in the 1520s, Budé eventually inspired him to subsidize two university chairs, one in Greek and one in Hebrew. In time additional professors were added in mathematics, Latin and Arabic, and eventually they collectively became known as the Collège Royal (later the Collège de France). The first professors included the leading lights of French humanism, disciples of Lefèvre and Budé such as the mathematician Oronce Finé (1494–1555), the encyclopedist Guillaume Postel (1510–81), and the Greek scholar Jean Dorat (1508–1588), who became known as the "Gallic Horace", the "French Pindar". Under the influence of Budé French literature absorbed the full impact of the example of antiquity.

Ronsard and the Pléiade

Before becoming professor of Greek at the Collège de France, Jean Dorat was principal of a college at the university of Paris. Few teachers could expect students of the quality of those who gathered around him in 1547. It included Pierre de Ronsard (1524–85), Joachim du Bellay (1522–60) and Jean-Antoine de Baïf (1532–89) as well as a number of others who became noted poets and writers. Under Dorat's influence they studied and translated the Greek and Roman poets as well as Dante, Boccaccio and Petrarch. Soon this "poetic brigade" (as they referred to themselves) sought to emulate antique verse forms, rhythms, vocabulary and richness in French. Their goals were expressed in du Bellay's famous *Defense and Illustration of the French Language* (1549). French poetry, he wrote, must seek to adopt the "more

Above The School of Fontainebleau often exploited all the resources of classical myth and imagery to evoke Platonic themes of sacred and profane love. In this allegorical painting – known as *Allegory of Water and Love* – the theme to profane love is evoked though sensual gestures, allusions to classical myth, and the depiction of water-loving plants that carried sexual connotations, such as marsh marigold, water violet and water forget-me-not.

older contemporary, François Rabelais (c.1483–1553), the son of a lawyer. He took holy orders in a Franciscan monastery, but later abandoned religion for the study of medicine. In 1521 he began his studies in Greek and completed his humanist credentials by engaging Budé in correspondence. He had fellow humanists close at hand in the Loire valley and enjoyed the protection of his local bishop. *Pantagruel*, the first of Rabelais's comic masterpieces, clearly reflects the strong provincial roots humanism developed in 16th-century France.

In 1532 Rabelais published three works in addition to *Pantagruel* (if that was indeed the year in which the first edition was produced) and in their various ways they reflect how widely read he was. His volume of letters of the respected Ferrara physician Giovanni Mainardi (c.1460–1513), for example, is a reminder of the deep admiration for Renaissance Italian medicine in 16th-century France. The medical faculty at Montpellier had an outstanding reputation and it was here that Rabelais received his medical doctorate in 1537.

Pantagruel was far from being just a humanist passport, however. A fantastic tale about a giant with an enormous appetite, it subjected its readers to a sustained series of unpredictable satirical detonations laid uncomfortably close to the pillars of tradition and pretension. The flavor and some of the incidental detail reflect Rabelais's wanderings around the provincial centers of humanist learning in France – not the royal court but such rapidly growing cities as Lyon, Toulouse and Montpellier. Rabelais may well have engaged in the young world of student culture. He

exalted and better style" of the ode, the elegy and the sonnet. It must enlarge the vernacular vocabulary and in its rhythms and harmonies imitate the measured verse of the ancients. Within a year of its publication, du Bellay published his first Petrarchan sonnets and Ronsard his first collection of odes. In 1556 the "poetic brigade" adopted the name of the "Pléiade" after a famous group of seven Alexandrine poets of antiquity.

The effect the Pléiade had on drama was profound. The techniques and forms of French drama had been dominated by the traditions of medieval mystery plays. Du Bellay, however, openly wrote of restoring its "former dignity". It was with Seneca and Euripides in mind that Étienne Jodelle (1532–88), another member of the Pléiade, wrote the first French humanist drama. His *Dido's Self-Sacrifice* abandoned the stylized and exaggerated theatricality of the mystery plays, with their emphasis on divine intervention. Instead, with the power of meter and the dramatic intensity of Dido's tragedy, Jodelle wrote a play that became a model for classical French theater.

By no means all the output of the Pléiade poets has stood the test of time. Their objectives often led them in the direction of ingenious word-play and complex mythological imagery at the expense of sincerity and the expression of genuine emotions. Pierre de Ronsard, inspired by a love of Homer and Pindar, is the great exception. In the gentle climate of the Loire valley, where in the 1550s he wrote his greatest poetry, he transcended antique forms and examples to convey the simple human truths of love, beauty, remorse, gaiety and the quiet life.

Rabelais and the censors

Also from the Loire valley was Ronsard's slightly

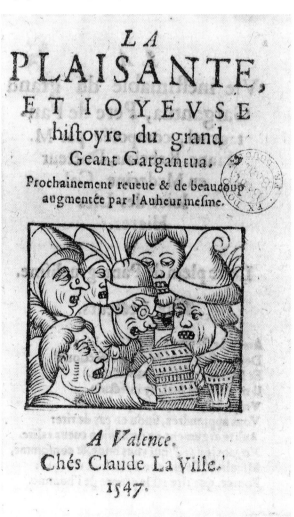

sought the company of the *basoche* (the company of lawyer's clerks involved in annual revels presided over by a Lord of Misrule) and *Pantagruel* is full of erudite and bawdy antiestablishment jokes that doubtless gave their author status among them.

But there were also classical sources for his humor, particularly Lucian of Samosata, a Greek skeptic who made fun of the ancient gods and snickered at their confused picture of the afterlife. Rabelais actually completed a translation of Lucian, though it no longer survives. The first chapter of *Pantagruel* ended with his name and even in the last firmly attributable section of *Gargantua* (Book Four), published in 1552, he was still drawing on Lucian for his comic techniques.

Satire and ridicule are dangerous weapons for those whose power lies only in persuasion and Rabelais repeatedly confronted the censors. As early as 1524, he had his Greek books seized by his Franciscan superiors. In 1533 the frank bawdiness and irreverence of *Pantagruel* met with censorship by the Sorbonne. Rabelais's instinctive reaction was to heap scorn on the *agelastes* (the nonlaughers), calling them *sophistae*, Sorbillans, Sorbonagres, Sorbonigenes, Sorboniformes. "Fly from such men, abhor them, and hate them as much as I do", ended the *Pantagruel* edition of 1534. In the various chronicles of *Gargantua*, mock-heroic adventures written in a similar vein, Rabelais exploited the surreal humor of an author writing in the shadow of the informer.

It is not difficult to understand how the emotive charge of impiety and heresy might arise in times of abrupt change to a fundamentally traditional society. Budé and Lefèvre, like Erasmus, preached the compatibility of Christian and pre-Christian culture. Yet however much humanists protested their innocence, the anxieties their activities caused were real and the debates intense.

For there were undeniably "dangerous" texts (as the 16th century perceived it) in the classics and these found their way into published editions and onto the shelves of the well-read. In the materialist natural philosophy of Lucretius, in the ideas of the ancient empirical philosophers, in the texts attacking the early Church, there was much to be anxious about if you were concerned to maintain belief in divine providence, the immortality of the soul, the divinity of Christ and the existence of the Trinity. Historians still debate the degree to which, in a century that "wanted to believe" (as the French historian Lucien Febvre put it), it was possible to be an "atheist", and the extent to which irreligion lay in the mind of the beholder. How much of a skeptic, for example, was Pierre Bunel (1499–1549)? His studies of the *Natural Theology* of Raymond Sebond led him to present a copy of it to Montaigne's father – the consequences of which are plain to read in the pages of his son's *Essays*. What sort of deist was Julius Caesar Scaliger (1484–1558), the exiled Veronese physician who took up residence in Agen and whom even Rabelais described as "an atheist if ever there was one"? What sort of faith led Bonaventure des Périers (died c. 1544) to write and publish *Cymbalum Mundi* (1538), a melange of blasphemies against orthodox Christianity that questioned God's role in creation and openly denied the divinity of Christ? In 1546 in Lyon the humanist scholar and printer Étienne Dolet (1509–1546) was burnt at the stake for impiety. And increasingly it was not just among the defenders of Catholic orthodoxy

that atheism was a real fear. Jean Calvin, the leader of France's Protestant Reformation, also felt it necessary to prepare a proper defense of the Christian religion against superstition and irreligion.

Renaissance and Reformation

By 1520, the eve of the Protestant Reformation's explosion in Germany, the French Renaissance had established strong roots. Although initially slow to adopt the new printing technology, it had caught up fast. Over 40 towns had a printing press by 1500. By 1530 nearly 300 titles are known to have been published in Paris alone, making it the rival of such printing centers as Antwerp and Venice. Among these works were many reflecting the twin influences of the "new learning" of Italian humanism and the "new devotion" of the Low Countries, a lay religious movement that stressed simple piety. Combined, these two movements raised fundamental questions about traditional Christianity.

So France was bound to be deeply affected by the Reformation in neighboring Germany. Already in 1521, more or less coinciding with the Diet of Worms, the Sorbonne decreed that 104 of Luther's theological propositions were heretical. In 1523 Lutheran books were seized from a notable Parisian humanist and scholar, Louis de Berquin (c.1490–1529). Six years later Berquin mounted the scaffold in the *place* Maubert in Paris for refusing to recant his heretical writings – the first humanist to fall victim to the forces opposing reformation. In some French provinces both heresy and its repression spread quickly. By 1530 the Strasbourg reformer Martin Bucer described part of Normandy as a "little Germany".

In the eyes of many in authority, humanism and heresy were close allies. They thought humanist printers were responsible for printing Lutheran books and Scripture in the vernacular. They suspected humanists of preparing the seedbed of dissent in their criticisms of the Church. They smelt Lutheranism among the "Meaux sect", a group of scholars and ecclesiastical reformers who gathered around Guillaume Briçonnet, the bishop of Meaux. They noticed how in 1523 Lefèvre, by this time a man in his seventies, published his translations of Scripture in French. It was a radical step for a scholar who was steeped in the refined language of Latin to translate Holy Scripture into a fluid and unformed medium such as vernacular French. Even more alarmingly, they noticed how in 1525, under the influence of the first wave of anti-Protestant repression, Lefèvre took up exile in Strasbourg, then at the heart of Reformation change.

In fact, those at the forefront of French humanism reacted in very different ways to the Protestant Reformation. Many, possibly most, hoped that by relying on royal protection and not associating themselves too closely with Lutheranism they might continue prudently to advocate a religion that stressed a personal devotion to the Gospel of Jesus Christ without resorting to the establishment of a separate church.

In reality, however, France was a very traditional society and the forces of orthodoxy proved too great. Gradually, and far from coherently, the anxieties provoked by the risks of heresy predominated. Within the powerful, privileged and immensely wealthy ecclesiastical establishment many were prepared to exploit such anxieties. The Sorbonne proclaimed itself

The French Wars of Religion
After 1559 France was engulfed by a crisis that led to the worst sectarian violence to appear anywhere in Europe during the Reformation. The crisis rapidly developed a momentum of its own, driven by the triple pressures of royal bankruptcy (the effects of the prolonged wars), a series of underage or ineffectual monarchs, and bitter aristocratic feuding. All these were exacerbated, however, by deep religious divisions. Despite the monarchy's best endeavors to eradicate it by persecution, Protestantism took root. Protestant (Huguenot) crowds engaged in iconoclastic destruction and abuse of Catholic church wealth, property and clergy. The response from the Catholic majority was to destroy anything that smacked of heresy – people, objects and ideas alike. The most dramatic effects of the so-called Wars of Religion were felt during the first decade from 1562–72, reaching their climax in the bloody massacre of St Bartholomew's Day. The conflict ended in 1598 with the Edict of Nantes, which finally granted Protestants freedom of conscience and worship.

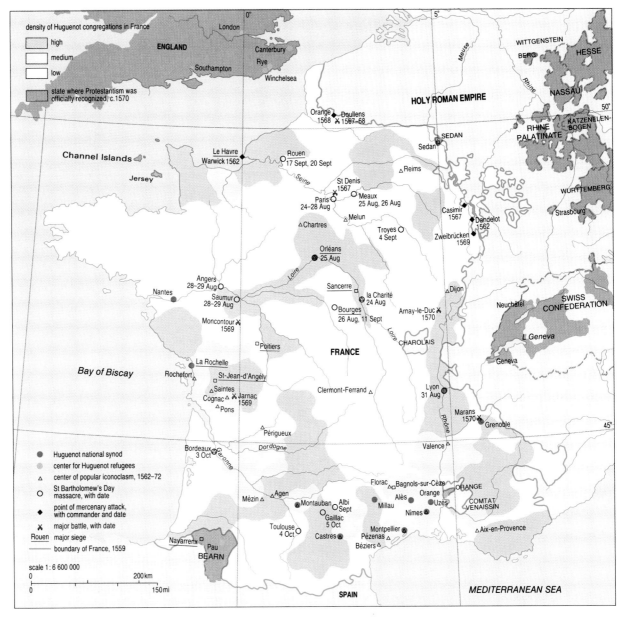

the pillar of Catholic orthodoxy. In addition, though prominent figures in the French Renaissance enjoyed royal patronage and protection, neither the king nor the judges could be seen to condone heresy. In time holding Protestant beliefs became a crime prosecutable in the royal courts. The result was that about 1540, as the repression of heresy intensified, small groups of French exiles in Strasbourg, Basel, Neuchâtel and Geneva began to organize the French Reformation from without.

John Calvin (1509–64) was among these exiles. The son of a minor ecclesiastical official, he was educated at the university of Paris and studied for a law degree at the university of Orléans. Of all the Protestant reformers he was the one most thoroughly influenced by the new learning. His first published work was in fact a humanist commentary on Seneca's *On Clemency* (1532). When he came to compose the first edition of his famous treatise the *Institutes of Christian Religion* (1536), he utilized the perceptions and language of the humanists. In the biblical commentaries and lectures he published he drew on the insights of Renaissance philology and often integrated biblical and classical knowledge. By "institute" he meant instruction, education, persuasion, indoctrination. His purpose was to set out how a total and life-changing reformation, transforming mind and con-

science, church, state and the whole of society, was to be brought about.

Resident in Geneva from 1541, he had the opportunity to put this vision into practice on a small scale. In due course, and after a good deal of opposition, Geneva became the beacon and refuge for Protestant exiles from across western Europe, but particularly from France. Among them were many printers, scholars, lawyers, physicians and clerics who would, in the normal order of things, have constituted the next generation of its Renaissance. In Geneva, however, they felt the full transforming effects of Calvin's ideology. With the example of the refugee churches before them, the French Protestants gradually congregated into a national force. In 1559, under the noses of the authorities whose repression had merely served to strengthen their resolve, they held their first national synod. This took place in an atmosphere of national crisis accompanying the Peace of Cateau-Cambrésis (1559), which required France to renounce its claims on Italian territory.

The Valois monarchy had finally run out of people to blame for its military failures. It had also run out of money. Harsher economic and political realities began to curb its grandiose ambitions. The ensuing crisis of the French monarchy also engulfed the French Renaissance.

The Wars of Religion

The sudden death of the French king Henry II in a jousting tournament in 1559 was the beginning of a prolonged period of civil wars – the Wars of Religion (1560–98). The king's death caused a weakening of the monarchy and his immediate successors could do little to restore authority – Francis II (1559–60) and Charles IX (1560–74) were minors, and Henry III (1574–89) was ineffectual. It was their mother, Catherine de Medici (1519–89), who effectively held power. Initially she adopted a tolerant attitude toward Protestants. But gradually Catholic fears over the spread of Protestant influence grew and it was almost certainly she who ordered the St Bartholomew's Day Massacre (1572). First in Paris and then in a score of provincial locations, thousands of Protestants were butchered in a furious wave of sectarianism. The popular sectarian violence of the French Wars of Religion was unlike any other in reformation Europe in its scale and intensity.

French Renaissance artists and engravers, divided by religion as was the rest of society, struggled to convey the shock and intensity of emotion of the period. In paintings such as *The Massacre of the Innocents* and *The Triumvirate* the court-painter Antoine Caron (c. 1527–99) sought to express his anguish and revulsion using classical subjects. In a preparatory sketch entitled *The Triumph of War* (completed about 1570), Caron represented the chariot of war drawn along by 'Cruelty' and 'Fury'. It was a dramatic reversal of the heroic conquering theme of the first half of the century. In their published book of engravings of 1570, the artists Tortorel and Perrissin were uncompromising in their depictions of the reality of the sectarian killings.

The French Renaissance was engulfed by the Wars of Religion, but not submerged. There was a continuing process of "vernacularization" of classical literature and styles evident among the French poets. Although unable to finance major building works and sustain patronage at its previous levels, the later Valois continued to maintain a lavish court and utilize it to promote the positive benefits of monarchy. Often uncertain of the loyalty of parts of their kingdom and bitterly attacked in print (and eventually in person – the last Valois was assassinated in 1589), they and their court developed a more introspective and elitist style of personal devotions, palace academies, masques and court ballets.

Historical writing was another way by which contemporaries could try to come to terms with what was happening to the world around them. Combining philology, French religious devotion and a love of history, Pierre Pithou (1539–96) collected the archival materials for a grand "history of France", though he never completed the task. His correspondence and vast learning, however, encouraged others. While Pithou retired to the relative quiet of Troyes, comparing the troubles of France to the fratricidal conflicts of Rome under Sulla, his friend and admirer Joseph Justus Scaliger (1540–1609) was working in another secluded corner of France on his great work rectifying the chronology of the ancient historians, the *Emendations of Chronology* (1583). It was one of the most significant contributions to historical scholarship of the century. Meanwhile another of Pithou's correspondents, Jacques-Auguste de Thou (1553–1617), who inherited part of Pithou's library of manuscripts, set about writing the greatest contemporary history

produced by the Renaissance. As the civil wars came to an exhausted close marked by the Edict of Nantes (1598), which granted Protestants a degree of religious freedom, de Thou put the conflict into a global context in his monumental *History of his Own Time*, the first volume of which appeared in 1603.

Among despairing royal officials and the increasingly vulnerable Protestant minority, the philosophy of the Stoics seemed to offer the best consolation to the conflicts afflicting France. It meant the patient acceptance of what providence decreed, acknowledging individual suffering as necessary for the greater good of the whole, and recognizing the importance of *prudentia* (prudence), the mask behind which real intellectual, religious and political loyalties could conveniently hide. If the civil wars encouraged men to

Above The sectarian violence that spilled onto the streets of France's cities during the civil wars reached its furious climax in the St Bartholomew's Day Massacre. This began in Paris on Sunday, 24 August 1572, immediately after the wedding of the Protestant Henry of Navarre (future Henry IV of France) to Catherine de Medici's daughter, Marguerite. The marriage brought the provincial leaders of French Protestantism to

Below The Italian princess Catherine de Medici, who on the unexpected death of her husband Henry II was thrust to the forefront of French politics.

Above Michel Montaigne was by turns a courtier, magistrate and traveler until, at the age of 38, he retired to his château to write. Even after completing his famous *Essays* he was typically modest: "I have directed all my energies into shaping my life. This was my craft, my work. I am no more an author than anything else."

the capital and it is possible that the fear of a Protestant *coup d'état* persuaded the French king to commit himself to the elimination of Protestant leaders. In the six days of bloody communal violence in Paris many thousands lost their lives – many thousands more died in provincial cities in the following month. This depiction of the massacre was painted by François Dubais, a Protestant who survived the bloodshed.

conceal their true political and religious commitments, Montaigne showed that there were ways in which honorable men could come to terms with the madness of the age. Michel Eyquem de Montaigne (1533–92) was descended from the newer nobility and spent the first half of his adult life as a royal magistrate in Bordeaux. In the midst of the civil wars, however, he inherited the family's estates and, though he never entirely escaped political involvement thereafter, retired to study and write. His first two books – published in 1580 and called the *Essays* – created a new literary form. As he described it, his "melancholy humor" at what he saw around him had led him to a "frenzy" of writing in which "I presented myself with myself as argument and object". For him, "all the evils of this world are engendered by those who teach us not

to be aware of our own ignorance". Self-awareness will teach tolerance, good sense and moderation. The civil wars were the "true school of treason, inhumanity and brigandage", breeding-grounds for prejudice and arrogance. Refusing to write a history of the tragic events unfolding around him, he showed how men of goodwill could, in the quiet of the study and on the basis of accurate self-knowledge, sustain the civilizing forces of friendship, love, courage and the gentle arts of living and dying gracefully. The final version of the *Essays*, published at the climax of the civil wars in 1588, was a masterpiece admired for its picture of the skeptical and honorable man (*honnête homme*). Beneath the turmoil of the Wars of Religion, the foundations of the French classical 17th century were being laid.

The Royal Collection of Francis I

Francis I was not only a great patron he was also an active and avid collector, and it was the château of Fontainebleau that, housing his remarkable collections, became the monument to his ambition to transform French art and culture. The works he amassed there were later to form the foundation of the Louvre museum.

Work began on Fontainebleau in the late 1520s. A team of the finest artistic talens of the day was assembled to work on the château, and agents were employed to obtain paintings, sculptures and *objets d'art* from those artists and craftsmen who could not work at Fontainebleau. This royal collection included paintings by Leonardo da Vinci, Raphael, Titian, Bronzino and Andrea del Sarto; sculptures by Michelangelo and Tribulo, together with bronze casts of such works as the *Belvedere Apollo* and the *Cnidian Venus* (both of which greet visitors to the Louvre today); and scores of antiques, curios and *objets d'art*, among the finest being exquisite works of craftsmanship by Raphael and Benvenuto Cellini.

The king's collection also contained many works by the School of Fontainebleau, those artists closely associated with the French court. The style of these artists, fluid, sensuous and ornate, was the first distinctive product of the king's cultural experiment and was widely imitated. Among the best of these artists were Jean Clouet and his son François (both famous for their portraits of Francis I and other members of the court) Jean Cousins, Primaticcio and Niccolò dell' Abbate.

Francis I also had a typical Renaissance passion for collecting books and manuscripts. Charles VII had deposited the books and manuscripts he had inherited, together with manuscripts brought back from Florence and Naples, at Blois. The substantial Visconti-Sforza collection was added later, so that by 1518 the royal library at Blois contained some 1,626 items. Under the eager patronage of Francis there were many important additions, particularly of Greek works, and the royal library grew rapidly. The Ordinance of Montpellier (1537) made the library a copyright collection for every book published in the kingdom; moreover, foreign books sold in France were required to be deposited for examination and were purchased if regarded as important. The royal library was transferred to Fontainbleau in 1544.

In addition, Francis appointed one of Europe's foremost printers as royal printer in Hebrew and Latin (1539) and then in Greek (1542). The letters-patent explained that this was in part to make the contents of the king's library accessible to scholars. Almost all the Greek editions of this period were published from manuscripts in the royal collection. Francis also took a personal interest in printing, paying for three special Greek typefaces – the *grec du roi* – designed by Claude Garamond and used by the publisher Robert Estienne. With the king's patronage such publishers as Estienne, Simon de Colines and Geoffroi Tory flourished and were able to produce some of the finest books of the Renaissance.

Left The Cardinal who commissioned Bevenuto Cellini to make a saltcellar rejected it because of its extravagance. It was not too extravagant for the king of France, however, who on first seeing it – according to Cellini's (often unreliable) *Autobiography* – cried out that it was "a hundred times more divine a thing than I have ever dreamed of". It is made of cast and chiseled gold, partly covered in richly colored enamels, and set on a base of ebony. The male figure represents the sea, the female figure earth. Also represented are day and night, dawn and dusk, and the seasons.

Below A French miniature (c. 1530) showing Francis I, together with his three sons and members of the court, listening to a scholar reading – an image of the king as a Renaissance man of letters. Many books were published under his patronage and he encouraged translations from Greek, Hebrew, Latin and Italian. Here he is portrayed listening to a translation of the Greek historian Diodorus. According to Guillaume Petit, court librarian, the king liked to keep a strict daily routine, and meals were often followed by readings, the king preferring histories and chivalric romances.

Left The "Horseshoe" staircase of the Château of Fontainebleau. Originally a medieval hunting lodge, the château was completely transformed by Francis I in order to be the focus of his ambition to transform French cultural life. Fontainebleau was not to be merely a place to house his collections; it was to be an embodiment of cultural values. The finest French and Italian artists of the day were employed on its reconstruction, providing not only paintings, sculptures and architectural designs, but also stucco work.

Above Bronzino's *Venus, Cupid, Folly and Time* (c. 1546) was commissioned by Cosimo I of Florence as a gift for Francis I. It is an allegory whose meaning is now unclear, though there are several ingenious interpretations – it is sometimes known as *The Vice of Luxury*. Bronzino's combination of sophisticated moral allegory and detached eroticism proved very popular at the French court.

Right Raphael's *Saint Michael* (1518) was a gift to Francis I, humanist prince and "second Charlemagne", from Pope Leo X, who was eager to promote good relations between France and the papacy. This dramatic picture, influenced by both Michelangelo and Leonardo da Vinci, had a profound effect on the development of Baroque art, particularly in sculpture.

Court Entertainments

Below Ambassadors arrived from Poland in August 1573 to offer its crown to Catherine de Medici's son, Henry of Anjou (later Henry III). This was the culmination of some of her most elaborate diplomacy. The ambassadors were treated to splendid festivities, here depicted in the Valois Tapestries.

Both political necessity and cultural potential made magnificence a supreme virtue at the Renaissance court, and nowhere was this more evident than in France. Yet though there are innumerable contemporary references to entertainments at the Valois court, detailed descriptions of its festivities are hard to find. The fullest accounts are those from the era of Catherine de Medici, whose Florentine background had taught her the value of spectacle. The programs for the magnificent royal entries into Lyon (1548), Paris (1549) and Rouen (1550), for example, testify to their lavishness. It was amid the banquets, plays and tournaments designed to celebrate a double wedding in 1559 that Catherine's husband, Henry II, met his death. At the end of a day of tournaments in a Paris street he was wounded by the lance of a Normandy nobleman and died 11 days later. This is a reminder that, for all the Renaissance novelty of such entertainments, traditional elements remained.

As Queen Mother, Catherine de Medici led her younger son, the boy-king Charles IX, on a great royal "progress". Beginning in January 1564 after the trauma of the first of the Wars of Religion, the court left Paris to travel through the kingdom for over two years. Visiting most of the provinces, the royal progress proclaimed the virtues of peace and reconciliation under royal benevolence. The climax occurred at Bayonne in June 1565. The royal printer published a detailed account of the entertainments there, which included tournaments performed by richly adorned knights in disguise, dancing, concerts, and banquets on barges and in riverside tents. The various entertainments interwove medieval romances, classical mythology and contemporary political message into a spectacle that both domesticated warfare and proclaimed the imperial greatness of the French crown. These and subsequent royal entertainments are exquisitely evoked in the famous Valois Tapestries, now in Florence. Worked to the designs of Catherine's court painter Antoine Caron (c. 1520–c. 1600), these recall specific festivities at the court of Catherine de Medici, such as the reception for the Polish ambassadors in 1573.

The climax of this tradition of royal entertainments was reached by the extraordinary fortnight of celebrations that took place in September 1581 to commemorate the weddings of the king's three *mignons*, or favorites. For these celebrations there exists both the draft sequence of events and the final program. There were banquets, musical interludes and dancing, fireworks and water festivals. Its permanent cultural value, however, came from the famous *balet comique* held in the Louvre. Here the new harmonies of Renaissance secular music were combined with the cadences of French poetry in a way that had been foreshadowed by the Royal Academy of Music and Poetry, founded 10 years earlier. To these were added spectacular scenery and delicate choreography. It is in the exquisite *balet comique*, first performed at the royal court, that the beginnings of French ballet and opera can be glimpsed.

Catherine de Medici (seated) is watching couples dancing while brilliantly attired Polish deputies look on. To her left is an empty chair symbolizing the throne in Poland awaiting her son, who is dancing close by. The gardens are the Tuileries, and the rock, draped with figures playing musical instruments alluding to Apollo and the muses, is an allusion to the ballet of the nymphs of the French provinces that has just been performed. To the left is the elegant *mignon* Anne de Joyeuse. Although not there in 1573, he was included by Caron in his designs for the Valois Tapestries a decade later.

Below The court ball, a distinctive feature of the French court, attracted numerous painters. This anonymous painting may represent the ball that accompanied the wedding of Anne de Joyeuse and Marguerite de Lorraine, the queen's sister, in 1581.

Bottom A tournament from the Bayonne festival in 1565, recreated by Flemish weavers to a design by Caron. Catherine has a protective hand on the shoulder of the young king, Charles IX. Together they watch a tournament celebrating the triumph of Virtue and Love.

SPAIN AND PORTUGAL

The Spanish empire and the Golden Age

A Bohemian visitor to the court of Henry IV of Castile at Olmedo in 1466 found the king seated on the floor surrounded by pretty young boys and dressed in Saracen clothes and a turban. The bishop of Salamanca entertained his guests with bullfights. Twenty years later in 1485 – when Renaissance humanism enjoyed enthusiastic patronage at the Castilian court – a German traveler was again struck by the "Moorish vices" of the court of Ferdinand and Isabella. The women went veiled in mantillas "in the Saracen manner", the royal officials were "mostly baptized

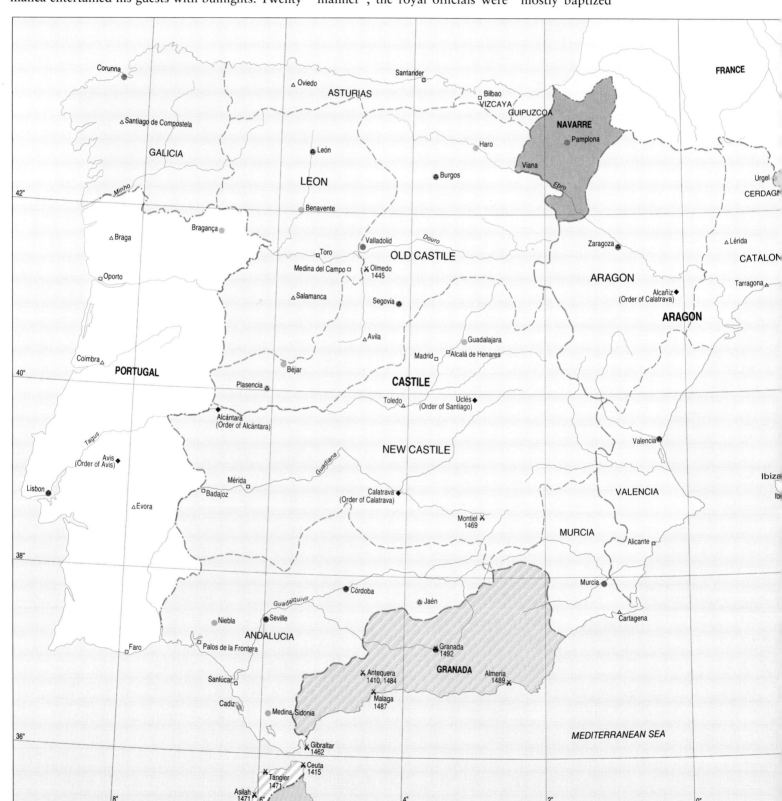

Jews or unbaptized Saracens whom the king makes no attempt to convert", and he heard courtiers refer to Ferdinand and Isabella as "those offspring of a convert Jewess". The priests spoke no Latin, the bishop of Seville was a Jew, and the Grand Cardinal spent his nights in a "harem". Another German complained that "Christianity was more mocked in Spain than in Turkey".

These observations show how hard it was for northern Europeans to comprehend the unfamiliar society of the five kingdoms of medieval Iberia: Castile, Aragon, Navarre, Portugal and Granada. For over seven centuries since the Moorish conquest in AD 711, large parts of the peninsula had been under Muslim rule. Andalucia, as the Arabs called Islamic Spain, was governed first by the caliphs of Córdoba and then, as the Christian reconquest advanced gradually south, by the princes of Granada. Muslim religious tolerance had also made Sepharad, as the Jews called Spain, the chief haven of medieval Hebrew culture. Medieval Iberian society and art were penetrated through and through with oriental influences. It was little wonder that our 15th-century travelers portrayed Spain as a land of mysterious eastern customs and marvels.

In 1469, however, Princess Isabella of Castile married Prince Ferdinand of Aragon. Their accession to their respective thrones led in 1479 to the union of the two most powerful Christian confederations in Iberia. In 1492 their armies conquered Granada and drove the last Moorish king from Spanish soil. The sovereigns were acclaimed throughout Europe as crusaders for the Faith and granted the special title "Catholic Monarchs" by the pope. Within months they decreed the expulsion of the Jews from their kingdoms. In the same year Christopher Columbus set out from the Canary Islands (which had been conquered by Castile in the 1480s) to make the Atlantic voyage that ended with his momentous landfall in the Americas. Columbus promptly claimed these vast territories as the property of the Castilian crown, and justified the "conquest" as another crusade to convert the heathen.

Portugal had been no less enterprising. The capture of the north African stronghold of Ceuta in 1415 marked the beginning of Portuguese overseas expansion. Soon the caravels of Prince Henry the Navigator were skirting the west coast of Africa beyond the equator in search of gold, slaves and converts. Under John II (1481–95) of Portugal and Manuel I of Portugal (1495–1521), Bartholomew Dias rounded the Cape of Good Hope and Vasco da Gama reached the western shores of India (1498). In 1494 a papal bull was issued dividing Asia, Africa and the American Indies between Spain and Portugal.

Left: Political divisions and centers of power in 15th-century Iberia Medieval Iberia was made up of a patchwork of independent kingdoms. Granada was ruled by Arabic-speaking Muslims. The two major confederations in the peninsula were Aragon and Castile. Aragon consisted of Catalan-speaking Barcelona, Valencia and the Balearic Islands, and the Aragonese-speaking hinterland. The largest and potentially most powerful nation was Castile. Throughout the 15th century, however, the Castilian crown was torn by dynastic struggles. These were not solved until Isabella of Castile married Ferdinand of Aragon. Their combined might was sufficient to defeat a Portuguese invasion and conquer the Moors of Granada.

Above An illuminated initial from a manuscript of 1484 portraying Ferdinand of Aragon and Isabella of Castile. Their marriage in 1469 brought about the Union of the Crowns of Spain, thus laying the basis for Iberian imperial expansion in the Golden Age of the 16th century. The political unification is symbolized by the monarchs' embrace. They are shown face-to-face to stress the strict equality of their powers – traditionally a queen would be portrayed behind her spouse and facing the same way. Isabella expressly stipulated in her marriage contract that this was to be the design used on coinage. The image thus reflects a Renaissance preoccupation with the propagandistic potential of classical imagery and symbolism in art.

Map legend (left):
- kingdom boundary, 1479
- crown boundary, 1479
- area unified under Catholic Monarchs, 1479
- area dominated by Moors, 1492

Spanish expansion
- by 1493
- by 1512

- international boundary, 1512
- ● royal court or palace
- □ noble stronghold
- ◆ major military order
- △ episcopal see
- ✕ important battle, with date

Scale 1 : 4 500 000

120 km

100 mi

Map labels: erpignan □, ROUSSILLON, Gerona △, Iona, MAJORCA to Aragon, Ciudadela □, Minorca, Palma, Majorca, Balearic Islands

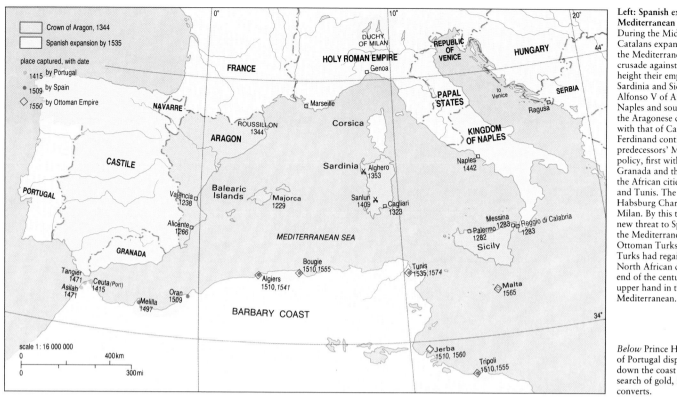

Left: Spanish expansion in the Mediterranean
During the Middle Ages the Catalans expanded eastwards to the Mediterranean as part of their crusade against the Muslims. At its height their empire included Sardinia and Sicily. In 1442 Alfonso V of Aragon conquered Naples and southern Italy. When the Aragonese crown was united with that of Castile in 1479, Ferdinand continued his predecessors' Mediterranean policy, first with the conquest of Granada and then with attacks on the African cities of Oran, Algiers and Tunis. The accession of the Habsburg Charles V in 1516 added Milan. By this time, however, a new threat to Spanish expansion in the Mediterranean had arisen, the Ottoman Turks. By the 1550s the Turks had regained control of the North African coastline and by the end of the century had gained the upper hand in the eastern Mediterranean.

Below Prince Henry the Navigator of Portugal dispatched caravels far down the coast of West Africa in search of gold, ivory, slaves and converts.

Within an astoundingly short time the old image of Iberia cut off from the rest of Christian Europe had been overturned. Spain was poised to embark upon a century of imperial expansion, religious fervor and artistic creativity. Ferdinand's patrimony included the Aragonese seaborne empire of the Balearic islands, Sardinia, Sicily and Naples; by the Treaty of Barcelona in 1493 he regained Roussillon from France. In 1512 all of Navarre south of the Pyrenees was annexed, fixing the borders of the Spanish crown where they have remained ever since. In 1516 Ferdinand was succeeded by his grandson Charles I of Spain, who became Charles V of the Holy Roman Empire in 1519, and so added to the Spanish crown his family's dominions in Flanders and the Low Countries, the Franche Comté, Austria, Styria, Carinthia, the Tyrol and various principalities in Germany; in 1535 he acquired Milan. By the time Charles's son Philip II came to the throne in 1555, Habsburg Spain was the dominant European power, ruling over large parts of the Mediterranean, Atlantic and Pacific worlds.

The century from 1480 to 1580 was also distinguished by an extraordinary flowering in the cultural and artistic life of the Iberian kingdoms that became known even within the lifetime of Ferdinand and Isabella as the Golden Age. The most magnificent manifestations of this cultural expansion are to be found in architecture and sculpture, in literature and in learning.

Spanish scholars and Italy in the 15th century

As in the rest of Europe, the chief cultural impulse for the early Spanish and Portuguese Renaissance came from Italy. Classical humanism, the scholarly study and revival of ancient Roman and Greek literature, philosophy and science, first began to influence Iberian culture during the reigns of John II of Castile (1406–54) and his cousins Alfonso V of Aragon (1416–58) and John II of Navarre and Aragon (1425/58–79). Similar developments occurred in the Portugal of Edward I (1433–38) and Alfonso V

Above A reredos from the Benedictine hermitage of Sopetrán: the donor, Don Inigo Lopez de Mendoza, duke of Infantado, son of the celebrated 15th-century poet the Marquis of Santillana and brother of Cardinal Mendoza. The immensely wealthy Mendoza family were the chief patrons of Renaissance art and architecture in Castile, amassing fine collections in their exquisite plateresque palaces. In this painting by an unknown artist, the treatment of light and perspective, the architectural details and the liveliness of the duke's portrait betray the first signs of Italian Renaissance influence.

palace at Guadalajara and commissioned treatises and classical translations from numerous scholars. As a keen amateur of letters and a talented poet who experimented with the first Petrarchan sonnets in Castilian, Santillana headed a circle of writers and noble patrons who promoted the study of Italian and classical letters at the court of John II of Castile.

Santillana's direct descendants, the grandees of the Mendoza family, were to be the chief noble patrons of Spanish arts and letters in the early Renaissance. The palace at Guadalajara of his eldest son, the Count of Infantado, is a jewel of the "plateresque" style, the architectural transition from late Gothic to Renaissance. Another son, the Count of Tendilla, a trusted lieutenant of Ferdinand and Isabella, invited the distinguished Italian humanist Pietro Martire d'Anghiera to Spain. Another, the bibliophile archbishop of Toledo, Pedro González de Mendoza, the mastermind behind Ferdinand and Isabella's early political success, was a patron of printing and learning, and founder of the College of Vera Cruz in Valladolid with its plateresque facade and patio.

The Portuguese royal house of Avis also established contacts through its bureaucrats and prelates with Florentine scholars and booksellers, as can be seen from the biographies of Portuguese clients in the *Lives* written by the famous Florentine bookseller Vespasiano da Bisticci in the 1480s. The most intriguing of these was Vasco Fernández de Lucena (c. 1410–95). Vespasiano describes Lucena's student pranks in Bologna, where he pawned his law books to devote himself to the poetry of Petrarch. Lucena served under three Portuguese kings as classical translator, chronicler and Latin orator. He corresponded with the Florentine humanist Poggio Bracciolini in the 1430s about the voyages of exploration of Prince Henry the Navigator, served as Portuguese spokesman at the Church Councils of Basel and Florence, and later made the official announcement to Pope Innocent VIII of the news that Dias had rounded the Cape of Good Hope.

The Aragonese king Alfonso V the Magnanimous (1416–58) spent almost the whole of his reign in Italy. Once installed as king of Naples (1442), Alfonso established a vast library of precious manuscripts and a humanist academy within his palace in the Castel Nuovo. A host of Italian and Spanish scholars and poets contributed their talents to the glorification of the Aragonese monarchy: Lorenzo Valla, for example, the most famous Latin scholar in 15th-century Italy, wrote the life of Alfonso's father. In Navarre humanist activity was centered on the court of the bibliophile Prince Charles of Viana, patron of the Greek scholar Theodore Gaza and the Italian scholar Angelo Decembrio, who amused himself by translating the works of Aristotle into Aragonese.

Royal patronage, printing presses and the new learning

The regional centers of the new arts and learning in 15th-century Iberia acquired a marked local character. In the Crown of Aragon, for example, there were separate circles of humanists in the provincial courts of Saragossa, Barcelona, Valencia, Majorca, Sicily and Naples. In Catalonia the humanist group led by Jeroni Pau, Joan Peyró and Pere Miquel Carbonnell was influenced by the ethos of Barcelona's chancery, the most sopisticated administrative bureaucracy in Europe. In Majorca, on the other hand, the jurist

(1438–81). During this period Castilian and Portuguese scholars who had studied at the Spanish College of Bologna, in Padua, or in Florence established personal contacts with the foremost Florentine and north Italian humanists and booksellers of the day, notably Leonardo Bruni, Piercandido and Angelo Decembrio, Poggio Bracciolini, and the Greeks George of Trebizond, and Bessarion. Meanwhile the Aragonese conquest of Naples in 1442 opened another channel of communication with Roman, Sicilian and Neapolitan scholars such as Lorenzo Valla, Bartolomeo Fazio and Antonio Becadelli.

In Castile the torchbearer of this first wave of Italian influence was Iñigo López de Mendoza, Marquis of Santillana (1398–1458). A fluent reader of Italian, he amassed a magnificent library of manuscripts in his

Ferran Vallet, who studied in Florence in the early 1440s under Leonardo Bruni, baptized his children with classical names such as Theseus, Hippolyta, Phaedra, Polyxena and Lucretia, translated Cicero's *Paradoxes* into Catalan, and composed frivolous Horatian odes for his friends. In Aragonese Saragossa, by contrast, the humanists congregated at the archbishop's palace and pursued a more regalist and spiritual range of interests. Similarly the grandiose cosmopolitan courts of Valencia, Sicily and Naples each stamped their own local character on the style of humanism practiced there.

The Union of Crowns under the Catholic Monarchs did not efface these regional centers, but their powerful royal patronage harnessed the diverse streams of the new learning in a common cause – the service of their own regime. In particular Ferdinand and Isabella gave their full support to the teaching and propagation of classical scholarship. In the late 1470s Antonio de Nebrija (1444–1522), an Andalusian scholar who had been trained in Bologna, returned to teach at Salamanca, the premier university of Iberia. With Isabella's approval he proclaimed himself "the vanquisher of barbarism" and published his *Latin Introductions* (1481), a grammar designed to replace the medieval manuals then in use in Salamanca.

The success of Nebrija's *Introductions* was immediate; the book was expanded and issued in a bilingual edition dedicated to Queen Isabella, and subsequently exported all over Europe, being republished many times in Salamanca, Barcelona, Venice, Lyon and other cities. Nebrija's grammar was used to teach Latin to Henry VIII of England and his children. The humanist message was soon taken up throughout Iberia, and Salamanca became one of the leading centers of humanist scholarship in Europe. Italian scholars accepted invitations to live at the Spanish court; Greek studies were introduced at Salamanca and Valencia; and several new universities – such as

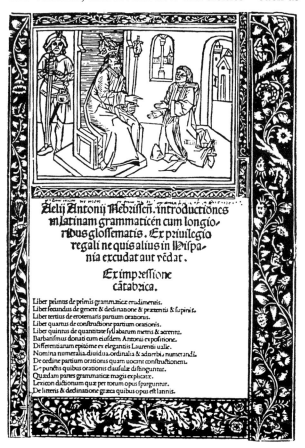

the colleges of Vera Cruz and San Gregorio in Valladolid, and the various colleges of the Complutensian University of Alcalá de Henares – were founded to uphold the new learning, all housed in fine Renaissance buildings.

In Portugal Manuel I (1495–1521) followed a similar pattern, inviting Sicilian and Flemish scholars to Portugal to teach the ancient languages. His successor, John III of Portugal (1521–57), transferred Lisbon university to Coimbra in 1537, where he inaugurated the humanist Colégio das Artes. It was staffed in 1548 by a group of distinguished scholars from Bordeaux that included the Scot George Buchanan.

Nebrija's celebrated opening oration to the university of Salamanca of 1486, in which he ridiculed his scholastic colleagues as barbarians unable to construe a sentence of Aristotle, started a revolution. However, though most of the humanists were middle-class civil servants, lawyers or teachers, their radical program reflected the political interests of their noble patrons. Indeed the humanists stressed that the new education in "liberal" or "humane" letters was particularly suited to aristocrats living the active or civil life.

Above With its profusion of classical motifs, the early 16th century plateresque facade of the university of Salamanca epitomizes the humanist aspirations of the time. Ferdinand and Isabella are seen grasping a joint scepter, and a Greek inscription aptly expresses their patronage of the new learning in Spain: "The monarchs for the university, the university for the monarchs."

Left Antonio de Nebrija's *Latin Introductions* (1481) caused an immediate sensation, revolutionizing the study of Latin along new humanist lines. The book was issued in countless editions (that of 1521 is shown here) and made its author the best-known Spanish humanist scholar in Europe. Nebrija was, in fact, one of the first scholars in Europe to exploit the immense potential for publicity offered by the new printing presses.

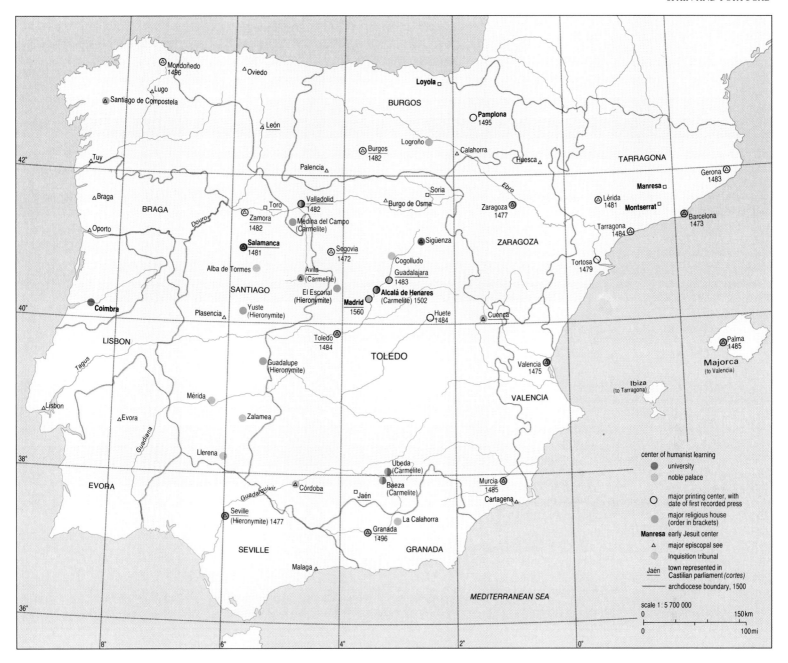

The map shows the following labelled locations:

Mondoñedo 1496, Oviedo, Lugo, Loyola, BURGOS, Santiago de Compostela, Pamplona 1495, León, Logroño, Calahorra, TARRAGONA, Tuy, Burgos 1482, Huesca, Gerona 1483, Palencia, Soria, Zaragoza 1477, Manresa, Braga, BRAGA, Toro, Valladolid 1482, Burgo de Osma, Lérida 1481, Montserrat, Oporto, Zamora 1482, Medina del Campo (Carmelite), Sigüenza, ZARAGOZA, Tarragona 1484, Barcelona 1473, Salamanca 1481, Segovia 1472, Cogolludo, Tortosa 1479, Alba de Tormes, Avila (Carmelite), Guadalajara 1483, Coimbra, SANTIAGO, El Escorial (Hieronymite), Alcalá de Henares (Carmelite) 1502, Huete 1484, Cuenca, Palma 1485, Madrid 1560, Plasencia, Yuste (Hieronymite), Toledo 1484, TOLEDO, Valencia 1475, Majorca (to Valencia), LISBON, Guadalupe (Hieronymite), Mérida, Ibiza (to Tarragona), VALENCIA, Lisbon, Evora, Zalamea, Llerena, EVORA, Ubeda (Carmelite), Murcia 1485, Córdoba, Baeza (Carmelite), Cartagena, Jaén, Seville (Hieronymite) 1477, Granada 1496, La Calahorra, SEVILLE, GRANADA, Malaga, MEDITERRANEAN SEA

Legend:

center of humanist learning
● university
● noble palace
○ major printing center, with date of first recorded press
● major religious house (order in brackets)
Manresa early Jesuit center
△ major episcopal see
 Inquisition tribunal
Jaén town represented in Castilian parliament (*cortes*)
—— archdiocese boundary, 1500

scale 1 : 5 700 000
0 — 150km
0 — 100mi

Above: Religious and cultural centers in 16th-century Iberia
The Golden Age of Spain and Portugal marked a unique upsurge of energy in every aspect of cultural, artistic and spiritual life. New universities and colleges were founded at Coimbra, Alcalá de Henares, and Valencia, while the university of Salamanca saw reforms that kept it at the forefront of European learning. The art of printing spread rapidly – the first books were printed in the early 1470s and by 1500 most great cathedral and university towns had their own presses. By mid century, as the Counter-Reformation Church closed ranks against Protestants, the Inquisition and the Jesuit order began to exert an increasingly tight stranglehold on education and intellectual speculation. Nevertheless, the second half of the century witnessed no diminution of artistic energy, and saw the foundation of new spiritual movements.

Three factors made this claim tenable: the rapid spread of literacy among the lay nobility; the great growth in bureaucracy and modern state methods of administration that provided the market for their newly acquired educational skills; and the invention of printing. For the first time the sons of the gentry began to be sent to university, where they studied Nebrija's *Introductions* and the speeches of Cicero. The number of students matriculated at Salamanca rose from 600 in the early 15th century to over 3,000 by the beginning of the 16th century, and to over 7,000 by the latter half of the century. Queen Isabella gave a powerful lead by ostentatiously taking up the study of Latin herself at the age of 31, and by instituting a grammar school for the young noblemen in her court. This publicly demonstrated that the humanist curriculum in classical culture and eloquence was considered a fitting training for any gentleman who aspired to high office and favor in the royal court.

The presses were introduced in Castile about 1472 and in Aragon by 1473. By 1500 printers were operating commercially in some 20 towns, and had published 856 known editions. A further 1,368 edi-tions survive from the period 1501–20. Ferdinand and Isabella quickly grasped the cultural importance of the invention. They personally invited German printer-booksellers to set up business in major towns such as Seville and granted them special financial privileges. When the royal lawyer Álvaro Díaz de Montalvo compiled the *Royal Ordinances* of 1480, the sovereigns instructed him to print and distribute copies to "every city, town, or village in these our said realms" at a fixed price. State licensing of printed books started in the 1490s, and was made statutory by the celebrated *Decree on Printed Books* of 1502.

So, whereas the great works of Spanish medieval literature survive in two or three manuscripts, literary works could now be printed in thousands of copies, spreading their fame far and wide. Diego de San Pedro's popular sentimental romance *Prison of Love* (1492) was printed many times in Castilian, but also in Catalan, Italian, French, English and German. Even this popularity could not compete with that of the chivalric romance *Amadis of Gaule* (1508), which became Europe's first international "bestseller", being the most widely printed vernacular work of its age. The availability of mass-produced texts, consumed by a whole class of laymen rather than a closed circle of professionals, meant that the prestige of humanist letters could be spread and appreciated by an ever-widening readership.

Chivalry and vernacular humanism in the Spanish Renaissance

The Marquis of Santillana, besides being the most important early patron of Italian humanism in Castile, was a renowned knight. After his death his nephew Gómez Manrique described him as "the first man of our times to conjoin science and chivalry, the breast-plate and the toga"; the royal chronicler Fernando del Pulgar called him "Apollo in the court, Hannibal in war". Santillana's example gave rise to that most characteristic Spanish Renaissance stereotype, the chivalrous *hidalgo* (soldier-poet). Another nephew, Jorge Manrique, author of the most famous poem in the Spanish language, *Verses on the Death of his Father* (1474), was a commander of the crusading order of Knights of Santiago who died in battle in 1479 at the age of 39. The chivalric tradition was continued in 1536 when Santillana's grandnephew, Garcilaso de la Vega, an equally celebrated poet (in Latin as well as Castilian), died a soldier's death at the age of 35. The combination of arms and letters became the most highly prized ideal in Spanish Renaissance society, celebrated in heroic literature, portrait paint-ing and sculpture, until Cervantes held it up to laughter in his immortal portrait of Don Quixote, an *hidalgo* driven mad by reading too many tales of chivalry.

The form of humanism favored by the nobility was very different from that of the professional anti-quarians and scholars. The nobles preferred to read their Roman texts in translations and imitations inspired by an idealized late-medieval vision of antiq-uity. Their vernacular or "bastard" humanism, which presented the ancients as chivalric knights, was given a strong impetus by King John II of Castile, who commissioned the bishop of Burgos, Alonso de Car-tagena (1384–1456) to produce Castilian versions of numerous works of the Spanish-born Stoic philo-sopher Seneca, and of many other classical and religious texts. During the following century and a half almost the whole range of classical Greek and Roman literature was translated into Spanish, Catalan, Italian and Portuguese at the request of Iberian noblemen.

Vernacular humanism produced not only transla-tions, but also a pungently characteristic original literature. Its first great exponent was Juan de Mena (1411–56), chronicler and secretary to John II of Castile. Mena's allegorical dream-vision *Labyrinth of Fortune* (1444) set the "labyrinth" of contemporary Castilian history against the panorama of the ancient Roman Empire. It celebrated the glorious emergence of "new Caesar" in the person of "our most prepotent king" – a patriotic boast, soon fulfilled, which ensured that Mena acquired the status of the "Homer of Spain".

An even more popular example of vernacular humanism was the *Golden Book of Marcus Aurelius* (1528) by Antonio de Guevara, bishop of Mondoñedo (c. 1480–1545). Guevara's sententious biography of Marcus Aurelius, supposedly translated from a Greek manuscript discovered in Florence, was a fake, an imaginative fiction designed as a "mirror of princes". Guevara's learning was bogus but entertaining; his

book became immensely popular, being printed in French, Italian, English, German and Latin. Its florid style was imitated all over Europe, giving rise to the Euphuism (highly elaborate classical rhetoric) of the 16th-century English writer John Lyly.

Another characteristic product of the vernacular humanists' blending of classical and chivalric forms was the birth of a national theater. Spanish noble courts in the 15th century had their own native tradition of masques and revels, which often included Nativity plays and farces played by buffoons. When humanists introduced the Italian revival of ancient Roman comedy, the fusion of the two traditions gave birth to the Spanish Renaissance comedy of manners. The musician Juan del Encina (1468–1529), a pupil of Nebrija at Salamanca, produced eight *Eclogues* – short vernacular plays imitating the shepherds and shepherdesses of classical pastoral – in the palace of his patrons the dukes of Alba de Tormes before 1496. His later plays, composed for the large Spanish community in Rome, moved further toward the full Renaissance type of romantic drama. Similar ex-

Above One of the striking features of the Spanish Renaissance was the continuing influence of chivalric ideals and medieval forms in the literature of the age. In 1508 Garci Ordóñez de Montalvo published his adaptation of a medieval romance of knight-errantry, *Amadis of Gaule*, a nostalgic tale of enchanters, damsels and knights in shining armor. The book evidently captured the spirit of the moment, for it enjoyed an astounding success. Soon translated into French, Italian, English and other languages, it became for nearly a century the most popular work of entertainment in Europe. Many other chivalric romances were written to try to emulate *Amadis*, until Cervantes wrote his immortal parody of the genre in *Don Quixote* (1605).

periments were made by Encina's rival at Salamanca, Lucas Fernández (c.1474–1542), by the prolific Portuguese court playwright Gil Vicente (c. 1465–c. 1536), and by Bartolomé de Torres Naharro (c. 1484–c. 1525), whose plays were also first performed for the Spanish colony in Rome.

The tone of noble life, with its elaborate rituals of gentility and chivalry and its luxurious tournaments, gave to Iberian vernacular humanism a strongly individual stamp. A striking example was the continuing cult of courtly love. Chivalry could not conceive of renown or nobility without the approbation of beautiful women – as Don Quixote said, "a knight without a lover is like a tree without leaves and fruit, or a body without a soul".

The successful introduction of Petrarchan love poetry into Castilian Renaissance verse is attributed to Garcilaso de la Vega (c. 1501–36) and his Catalan friend Juan Boscàn (c. 1492–1542). A chance encounter at Charles V's court in Granada brought Boscàn into contact with the Venetian ambassador Andrea Navagero, a famous humanist. Navagero encouraged him to attempt the new Italian verse forms and the iambic pentameter in Spanish; and so, to pass the time on the long and dusty return to Barcelona, Boscàn tried drafting his first sonnets. But it was the genius of the younger Garcilaso that took Iberia by storm. His dreamlike imitations of Petrarchan *canzoni*

Below Because Spain exercised political domination over several regions of Italy during the Renaissance, Iberian humanists were particularly sensitive to the frequent Italian accusations of Spanish "barbarism". Native scholars therefore determined to prove that Spaniards were just as preeminent in culture as they were in military prowess. One favored tactic was to claim that Spain could boast of a classical heritage as glorious and ancient as that of Italy itself, going back to Hercules. In defense of this absurd but important proposition Iberian scholars were stimulated first to invent, but later to study with real rigor, the ancient history and archeology of their country. The grander relics of Roman engineering and architecture in Spain, such as the celebrated aqueduct of Segovia illustrated here, were sought out afresh and discovered to be monuments of "primitive Hispanic skill and art".

and Virgilian pastorals were composed with stunning technical accomplishment. But Garcilaso wove into the texture of his verses the courtly loves of knights and damsels at the court of his patron the Duke of Alba in Naples. The result was that characteristically Spanish blend of classical form with chivalric content. In 1532 Boscàn published his translation of *The Courtier*, the classic treatise on Renaissance manners and gentle culture of another Italian ambassador to the Spanish court, Baldassare Castiglione. Garcilaso declared that Boscàn's verson was "perhaps the first work written in Spanish worthy of a learned man's attention".

Humanists and the antiquities of Spain

The advent of humanist scholarship led to a scholarly interest in antiquities and history. From the first, antiquarianism in Spain was deeply affected by patriotic and anti-Italian motives. In the 15th century it was common to give special praise and attention to those classical figures and stories that had particular connections with ancient Hispania. The Spanish-born Roman writers Lucan, Quintilian, Martial, Trogus Pompeius, Orosius, Prudentius, Isidore and above all the Stoic philosopher and orator Seneca, were singled out for study, praise and translation. The "healthy fruit" of their solid Spanish virtues contrasted with the "fool's gold" of such Italian-born writers as Virgil, Cicero and Ovid.

This chauvinistic attitude soon led to a more scholarly exploration of Spain's rich classical legacy. The Cordovan bibliophile Nuño de Guzmán eagerly informed his Florentine humanist friend Giannozzo Manetti, whom he had commissioned to write a scholarly biography of Seneca, that he had "discovered" Seneca's original house and garden in Córdoba. Meanwhile Seville and Lisbon boasted of their foundation by Hercules and Ulysses. The inhabitants of Zamora fiercely defended their city's (incorrect) claim to be the classical Numantia, whose Celtiberian inhabitants had heroically resisted the Roman conquest. According to Roman historians, when the Numantians could hold out no longer, even through cannibalism, the entire population committed mass suicide by leaping off a cliff. This stirring patriotic story of courage and resistance was a great favorite and formed the subject of one of the stage plays of Cervantes.

The most striking product of this patriotic antiquarianism was the so-called "neo-Gothic" theory, which traced the Castilian monarchy's descent in unbroken line from the 7th-century Visigothic emperors of Toledo. Presented in his Latin *Recapitulation of the Kings of Spain* by Alonso de Cartagena, this claim directly challenged the Italian humanists' view that anything Gothic was medieval and barbaric. The manufacture of the neo-Gothic thesis had a political purpose – to justify Castilian royal claims to supreme power over the whole of Iberia and north Africa. The first work of Spanish humanism to appear in print, the *Compendious Hispanic History*, published in Rome in 1470 by Rodrigo Sánchez de Arévalo, a high official in the papal curia of Paul II, publicized the Celtiberian, Roman and Gothic descent of the Castilian dynasty from the time of Hercules. His purpose was to show that Spanish civilization far from being inferior was more ancient, more glorious and more cultured than that of Italy.

The fact that the ancient geography and archeology of pre-Muslim Iberia had become a topic of importance to kingly propaganda opened humanists' eyes to Spain's abundant antique remains. A Sicilian visitor, Luca di Marinis, was stunned by the spectacular Roman aqueduct of Segovia and the theater of Mérida. Nebrija recorded his excitement at an archeological excursion near the palace of his patron the Grand Master of Alcántara in 1495, and subsequently planned a four-volume book on Spanish antiquities; only the Castilian "sampler" sent to Queen Isabella was published. Alfonso de Palencia (1423–90) described the fruit of his archeological and topographical researches in the 10 lost books of his *Antiquities of Hispania* and the surviving *Little Compendium of the Ancient Sites of Hispania*. The *Forgotten Chronicles of Hispania* of Juan Margarit, the Catalan bishop of Gerona, still unfinished after 20 years of work when he died in Rome in 1484, was based on personal measurements of the ancient sites as well as the accounts of Strabo, Ptolemy, Diodorus Siculus, Appian, Plutarch, Pomponius Mela, Solinus, and the Antonine *Itinerary*. Jeroni Pau studied the ancient inscriptions of Barcelona in the course of his researches into classical legends about Spain, and Cardinal Mendoza collected the first great museum of antique artifacts in Iberia – coins, bronzes, cameos, and jewels, as well as Renaissance imitations by Italian craftsmen such as Pisanello.

The rise and fall of Spanish Erasmianism

When the Habsburg Charles I (later Emperor Charles V) came to the Spanish throne in 1516 a new element was introduced into Spanish humanism. Charles was brought up in Flanders (he spoke no Spanish) and his courtiers brought with them the culture of their homeland. The importance of the Flemish connection was the extra impulse it gave to the spread in Spain of the spiritual ideals and classical scholarship of Erasmus of Rotterdam. Erasmianism already enjoyed a high reputation in Spain and Portugal, where a vigorous movement for religious reform had been instituted by the Catholic Monarchs' greatest statesman Francisco Jiménez de Cisneros (1436–1517), cardinal-archbishop of Toledo.

Cisneros was particularly sympathetic to Erasmus's brand of Christian humanism, with its emphasis on the scholarly study of Scripture and the Church Fathers. In 1498 he petitioned Pope Alexander VI for permission to found a new university at Alcalá de Henares, where the teaching would be humanist but the emphasis would be on theological and ecclesiastical studies. As the centerpiece there would be a college devoted to the study of the three languages of Christian learning, Hebrew, Greek and Latin. The Complutensian University, as it was called after the Roman name of Alcalá, opened its doors to students in 1509. Its inauguration was triumphantly marked by the greatest project of Spanish scholarship of the century, the *Complutensian Polyglot*, the first edition of the Bible in which the text was presented in the original languages arranged in adjacent columns. The first printing was in 1514–17, and there were many other editions, the best-known being published by Plantin in Antwerp in the 1570s.

With the arrival of Charles's court, Christian humanism spread beyond the confines of academic scholarship to become the leading intellectual movement at court. The bureaucracy of Charles's court was

full of men who had been educated in humanist Latin, and who now pressed Erasmus's Ciceronian style and satirical verve into the service of imperial ideology and social and religious reform. Erasmus's works were turned into elegant Castilian, and his ideas were adopted to comment on a variety of political and social questions, from the Sack of Rome by German mercenaries in Charles's pay (1527) to legislation on the treatment of the poor and unemployed.

The satire of the Spanish Erasmians was perhaps more influenced by the ironic and pointed style of Erasmus's controversial works than by his theology. Their criticisms were often so sharp that the authors preferred to remain anonymous. This was the case of *The Rattle*, a series of dialogues between a cobbler and his worldly-wise cockerel designed to wake an audience out of their smug complacency. The author owed much to the paradoxical and sarcastic manner of Erasmus's *In Praise of Folly*. His use of a supposedly dumb animal as a mouthpiece was typical of Erasmian irony, and inspired Cervantes's beautifully crafted short story *The Colloquy of the Dogs* (1613). Another anonymous work of great verve was *The Turkish Voyage*, whose author has been identified as Andrés Laguna (1499–1560), a medical scholar. The work claimed to be the autobiography of a disreputable rogue who spent several years as a slave in Constantinople. In fact, Laguna's book is a work of utopian fiction, but full of such lifelike detail and based on such reliable sources that even expert orientalists have been fooled into thinking it a genuine firsthand account of Ottoman society. By a paradox subtly hinted rather than heavily underlined, the Muslim society of the Turks emerges as more civilized and virtuous than its Christian counterpart. Since the Turks were the terror and nightmare of Europe during the 16th century, the point was a brutal one. Nevertheless, *The Turkish Voyage* testified to the energetic and well-informed spirit of open inquiry, as well as the spiritual seriousness, of this brilliant generation of scholars and writers.

However, the glorious Indian summer of Erasmianism was not destined to last for long. All over Europe war-clouds were gathering as Luther's Ninety-five Theses sparked off the bitter schism between the Catholic hierarchy and the Protestants in which Charles V, as Holy Roman Emperor, had no choice but to become involved. Erasmus tried to remain aloof, but the conservatives in the Spanish Church had realized that the enthusiasm of his followers, if unchecked, would lead to the dismantling of their powers. They therefore mounted a campaign to discredit Erasmus by accusing him of holding heretical Lutheran ideas. Even before the publication of the *Complutensian Polyglot*, Cardinal Cisneros dismissed Nebrija for his revolutionary ideas on the textual criticism of the Bible, which were closely parallel to those of Erasmus.

The Inquisition found a useful ally for its attacks in the impressive intellectual reform of Catholic theology by the Dominican theologians of Salamanca, Francisco de Vitoria and his followers Domingo de Soto and Melchor Cano. Their first public clash with the Erasmians came at the *junta* of Valladolid, convened to judge Erasmus's orthodoxy in 1527. Although no decision was reached because of an outbreak of plague, the *junta* (official committee) sealed the fate of Iberian Erasmianism. A savage backlash followed, in which the Inquisition rooted out the "Lutherans" (as

Above The Virgin of the Catholic Monarchs (c. 1490), attributed to Michael Sittow. It shows Ferdinand and Isabella in the traditional medieval posture of donors and benefactors of a religious house – in this case the Dominican friary of St Thomas in Ávila, the first tribunal of the Spanish Inquisition. Behind the monarchs stand St Thomas, the patron saint of the convent, and St Dominic, the

founder of the Dominican order.
What differentiates this
composition from medieval
devotional images is the presence
of various influential court figures
portrayed with the same life-like
realism as the monarchs: the
infants Don Juan and Doña Juana,
and behind them the first Grand
Inquisitor Torquemada and the
Italian humanist Pietro Martire
d'Anghiera.

was written after the downfall of Erasmianism as an intellectual and spiritual movement. Its author prudently preserved a strict anonymity that has never been unmasked, despite strenuous attempts. The book purports to be the autobiography of a *pícaro* (a professional rogue). Lázaro, the disreputable narrator, confesses to a series of amusing adventures with various masters, from a blind beggar and mean country curate to the rich archpriest of Toledo, who bribes Lázaro to let him sleep with his wife. Although severely censored by the Inquisition for its anticlericalism, *Lazarillo de Tormes* was printed in Antwerp and Spain. In an expurgated form the work later inspired the Baroque genre of the picaresque novel.

Art and learning in service of state and empire

The reign of Ferdinand and Isabella saw a thorough reform of the administrative organization of government. The sovereigns challenged the medieval feudal jurisdictions of the nobility, the towns and the Church, gradually gathering absolute power into their own hands. Machiavelli took Ferdinand as a model of the new Renaissance despot in his treatise *The Prince*: "He may rightly be called a new prince because he has transformed himself from insignificance into the greatest monarch in Christendom." Contemporaries often claimed that the greatness of Ferdinand and Isabella was the direct cause of the cultural flowering of Spain's Golden Age. In part they were right, because the sovereigns' strong support of learning and art was based on the understanding that in return the humanists' public role would be to glorify and justify the absolutism of the new Spanish monarchy. Nebrija expressed this idea tersely: "language is the companion of empire."

Humanist writers were thus expected to fashion an image designed to support Spanish imperialism. They invented parallels with the Roman empire under Augustus Caesar, and with the Golden Age of Virgil, Horace and Livy. They claimed that, like Augustus, Ferdinand and Isabella had pacified a country split and ravaged by civil war, routed an oriental and barbarian enemy, restored the state and instituted a "new order". They glorified the legends of the ancient Gothic empire and the age-long Christian crusade against the Spanish Moors. They affirmed that the victory of the Catholic Monarchs had been prophesied in the Bible, and that the kings of Spain had a divine universal mission to defeat idolatry and heresy, to conquer the holy city of Jerusalem, and rule over a Christian world empire in peace and harmony before the Second Coming of Christ, which was expected imminently.

The triumphal note of the literature of the age of the Catholic Monarchs was expressed in hyperbole. Poets blasphemously compared the sovereigns to gods, or addressed Queen Isabella with the metaphors of courtly love. On her accession to the throne in 1474, for example, Antón de Montoro wrote: "High sovereign queen, if you had lived before the daughter of St Anne [the Virgin Mary], the Son of God would have been incarnated in you." The chorus of official propaganda in chronicles, hymns and architectural monuments formed one of the most successful publicity campaigns in history. At state marriages poems of praise made extravagant comparisons with classical mythology. Royal entries and pageants were accompanied by allegorical masques with Roman themes. Latin epigrams and epistles, comedies and epics were

Erasmians were now regarded) and burnt them at the stake or drove them into exile. Their intellectual leadership was taken over by the sternly orthodox and papist Jesuit order founded by St Ignatius Loyola. The Jesuits and Salamancan Dominicans were to be the chief architects of Spanish Counter-Reformation ideology at the Council of Trent (1545–63), which condemned Erasmus's works and also issued a series of restrictive canons against profanity and irreverence in art that were to have a profound effect on the nature of Spanish literary and cultural life.

Nevertheless, the crowning legacy of the Erasmian tradition, the novella *Lazarillo de Tormes* (c. 1549),

The New Learning and the Inquisition

The new learning of humanism arose as scholars began to look to the ancient world for inspiration in philosophy, literature and art. The center of man's concern was shifting from the divine to the human. As part of this process, scholars turned to the close study of language in order to establish authentic texts: first of classical works and then of the Bible. The new learning was introduced to Spain and Portugal from Italy during the 14th century, and quickly became part of their cultural background. A new spirituality, the "modern devotion", which began in the Low Countries in the 14th century, developed alongside the new learning. Those who followed the modern devotion sought the essential message of the Scriptures – hidden under the theological accretions of the Middle Ages – in order to live simply and piously.

These intellectual and religious strands of thought united in Erasmus, and in Spain his ideas received a more enthusiastic acceptance than in any other country. Alfonso de Valdés, for instance, wrote two Erasmian dialogues to show that the pope, not Charles V, was responsible for the Sack of Rome in 1527. There was, however, a stubborn resistance from those who felt themselves to be the targets of Erasmian satire, and it was they who finally prevailed. The Inquisition was established by Ferdinand and Isabella in 1478 to examine the sincerity of the often forcibly converted Jews and Muslims. In due course it was to prove a useful instrument both in the censorship of books, thus impeding the spread of the new learning and new religious ideas, and also in the fight against the movement that inspired the Reformation. The early manifestations of Protestant sentiment were so effectively crushed that – largely through Dutch and English propaganda based on the writings of exiled Spanish reformers – Spain became a byword for religious persecution. At spectacular autos-da-fé (ceremonies accompanying the pronouncement of judgment by the Inquisition) the Catholic faith was exalted and heresy condemned. Those found guilty by the Inquisition were handed over to the secular authorities for punishment – flogging, internal exile, prison, the galleys, or the stake. The victims of the Inquisition wore the *sanbenito* (a long, loose garment in the Inquisition's colors) as an unmistakable warning to others. The machinery of repression was all pervasive. By 1570 Spain had retreated behind a religious and cultural *cordon sanitaire*.

Far right A painting by Pedro Berruguete showing St Dominic presiding over the burning of heretics in 1215. Parallels with recent autos-da-fé would have been inescapable when this picture was painted (c. 1500).

Right A page from the *Complutensian Polyglot*, a Bible printed in its original languages, together with translations. Produced (1514–17) at the personal expense of Cardinal Cisneros.

Right *Cardinal Cisneros* by Juan de Borgona. Although the Inquisition was decisive in rooting out Protestant influence, Cisneros lessened its impact by printing devotional literature and restoring discipline to the Church (though leaving its structure and doctrine untouched). A resolute and informed opponent of Islam as Inquisitor-General, he was also a humanist open to Erasmian piety.

Philip II

Philip II (1527–98) was the son of the Holy Roman Emperor Charles V and Isabella of Portugal. He inherited a vast and ever-growing empire. Between 1554 and 1556 Philip became ruler of Milan, Sicily, Naples, the Low Countries, Franche-Comte, Spain and the Spanish possessions in the New World. In 1580 he annexed Portugal. He worked ceaselessly to hold his empire together. Making his capital Madrid, at the very center of Spain, he had the palace of the Escorial built not far away. It was from the seclusion of the Escorial – which in its combination of palace, monastery and library was an expression of Philip's complex personality – that he increasingly exercised control over his empire. Officials were required to submit long and detailed reports often, reports he read attentively, covering them with copious comments in his own scarcely legible handwriting.

He faced many problems. Silver and gold poured in from the New World, but expensive wars (such as those fought against France, Portugal, England, the Ottoman Empire, and rebels in the Low Countries, wars often fought for religious rather than purely political reasons) drained the exchequer and caused progressive inflation. Finding an heir to continue the dynasty – while at the same time forging foreign alliances – also proved difficult. In 1543 he married Mary of Portugal. She died three years later giving birth to their son Don Carlos, who at the age of 23 was found guilty of conspiring to kill his father. As part of his plan to keep England Catholic Philip married Mary Tudor in 1554. When she died childless three years later he tried, unsuccessfully, to marry her sister and successor, Elizabeth. His policy toward England reached its final expression 30 years later with the launch of the ill-fated Armada. His marriage to Isabella of France (the daughter of Henry II) produced two daughters on whom he doted; but it was his final marriage, to Anne of Austria, the daughter of emperor Maximilian II, that produced a male heir – the future Philip III of Spain.

For Philip II, a deeply pious, even fanatical Catholic, matters of religion and matters of state were deeply interwoven: policy was ultimately an expression of faith. He saw himself as a loyal son of the Church and his letters of state often devoted long sections to relatively minor matters of piety, with only a perfunctory consideration of political affairs. Under Philip the Inquisition reached the high point of its influence and power. He used the inquisition not merely to combat heresy but also to extend his control over his dominions. A series of spectacular autos-da-fé in Seville and Valladolid marked the start of a ruthless campaign against Protestants. Literature and art flourished – Philip himself patronized Titian, El Greco and Alonso Berruguete – but they were harnessed to the defense of orthodoxy. But his Catholic Majesty was no servant of the Church, and he challenged both the papacy and the Council of Trent, the chief instrument of Catholic reform, when his own policies dictated. It was Philip II's commitment to policies based on faith that helped to bankrupt Spain.

Left Portrait of Philip II by Titian. Inheriting the huge Habsburg empire, Philip ruled from 1555 to 1598 as the Renaissance prince – ruler of an empire, devout Catholic and faithful son of the Church (within certian limits), and patron of the arts. By the time of his death, however, Spain had passed its zenith.

Above Adoration of the Name of Jesus by El Greco. This picture's usual title, *Philip II's Dream*, is misleading since Philip appears in it merely as one of the people worshipping Jesus (Philippians 2: 10, "in the name of Jesus every knee shall bow"). Philip's apparently genuine religious humility contrasts strikingly with his proud Habsburg ambition.

Right The Duke of Alba Overcoming Philip II's Enemies, an anonymous polychrome wooden statue in conscious imitation of statues of the Archangel Michael slaying Satan, or St George and the Dragon. The serpents are Queen Elizabeth of England, the pope, and the Elector of Saxony.

composed in classical style to celebrate important events such as the capture of Granada or the failure of an attempt to assassinate King Ferdinand. Alfonso de Valdés, a secretary to Charles V, composed witty imitations of Erasmian dialogues or Ciceronian epistles in defense of the Sack of Rome (1527).

After the crisis and downfall of Erasmianism, scholars and writers were forced to toe the official line with ever greater subservience, especially in questions of imperial policy and religious orthodoxy. During Philip II's reign Spain's most classical poet, the Augustinian professor of biblical studies at Salamanca, Luis de León, was imprisoned by the Inquisition on the grounds that his study of Hebrew and advocacy of vernacular versions of the Bible were heretical. Not even the primate of Toledo was immune: when Archbishop Bartolomé Carranza was denounced, the king himself was summoned to testify before the inquisitors.

Such censorship withered the early promise of Spanish learning and promoted obscurantism, anti-intellectualism, and religious mysticism (though this too was viewed with suspicion). The rigorous Latin training of the Jesuits, who increasingly controlled secondary and university education, continued to produce classical scholars and theologians, but did not encourage free speculation on political or spiritual matters.

The only challenge that remained for the humanists was the description and justification of Spain's immense overseas empire. In the 1430s, when the Italian scholar Poggio Bracciolini dubbed the early voyages of Iberian navigators "discoveries", he meant that they had charted seas unknown to classical geographers. In 1489 the Florentine humanist Angelo Poliziano prophesied the discovery of "new lands, new seas, new worlds and even new stars". When Columbus fulfilled the prophecy in 1493, European intellectuals devoured the news avidly. Columbus's brief *Letter on the New-Found Isles of the Ocean Sea* (1493) was immediately printed in Latin and other languages. Although Columbus insisted to his dying breath that he had discovered nothing more than a sea route to China and India, Italian and German cosmographers immediately deduced that he had stumbled upon a "new world".

The first humanist work on the discoveries written in Spain were the *Decades on the New World* of Pietro Martire d'Anghiera (1459–1526), an Italian friend of Nebrija who had been invited to teach Latin at the court of Ferdinand and Isabella. In 1510 he was appointed chronicler of the Council of the Indies. An installment of the *Decades* was printed with its famous woodcut map of the West Indies at Seville in 1511. Martire's account of America was strongly colored by his humanist education; knowing the native Arawak only at secondhand, Martire portrayed them as fair-skinned classical nymphs and shepherds living in a state of nature. Reported cannibals and tribes of women warriors were identified as Homer's long-lost Laestrygonians and Amazons, strange marine creatures as Tritons or Sirens. It was just such imaginary descriptions that inspired Thomas More to base his account of Utopia on the New World.

The brutality and greed of the conquistadors of Mexico and Peru soon put an end to these dreams, and sparked off a debate on the justice of the Castilian crown's imperial policy in the Indies. In 1513 the lawyer Juan López de Palacios Rubios drew up a *Brief*

Above This woodcut of Ferdinand and Isabella receiving the dedication of a book by its author is based on a common medieval motif in manuscript illumination. It was published, however, in 1502, the year in which it was decreed that no book should be printed, priced or marketed in Spain without a crown license.

on the Islands of the Ocean Sea, in which he used Aristotle's argument that barbarians were "natural slaves" to prove that the Indians were so primitive that they could legally be enslaved by superior Europeans. This expedient argument was demolished, however, when Charles V submitted the question to a committee of Salamancan theologians. They demonstrated that Aristotle's doctrine was incompatible with Christianity, and proved that the Spanish crown had no rights in the Indies other than those of peaceful evangelization. When the Dominican bishop of Chiapas in Mexico, Bartolomé de las Casas (1474–1566), began his great campaign against the slavery of the Indians, this academic debate became a matter of state.

The theologians' rebuttal of Aristotle posed a direct challenge to the humanists. Juan Ginés de Sepúlveda (1490–1573), an Italian-trained expert on Aristotelian ethics, had managed to avoid the Inquisition during their persecution of the Erasmians by publicly attacking any form of humanist activity that might spread "the pernicious plague of Lutheran heresy". In 1547 he submitted to the royal censors his dialogue *Second Democrates on the Just Conquest of the Indians*, a defense of the Aristotelian doctrine of natural slavery. A committee of theologians was again convened to adjudicate a public debate between Sepúlveda and Las Casas in Valladolid in 1550–51. Inevitably the theologians passed sentence against Sepúlveda, condemning his humanist arguments as amateurish. It was to be the last important occasion on which humanist learning was used in an attempt to determine royal policy; from that time on, the role of Renaissance classicism was purely ornamental.

Art and literature in the Golden Age

The formal literature of the Golden Age is distinguished by two things: the decorum of its style, based on the figures of speech and thought of classical Latin; and its profound concern for the system of genres of Greek and Roman literary theory. The two aspects were subsumed in the Renaissance theory of *imitatio* ("imitation"), without which the writing of the age cannot be understood. *Imitatio* meant more than mere copying of classical models. It signified an imaginative recreation in which skillful allusion and inventive adaptation played more part than paraphrase.

The first triumph of *imitatio* was the *Tragicomedy of Calisto and Melibea* (1502) by Fernando de Rojas (c. 1475–1541). Taking as his model the Roman comedies of Plautus and Terence about masters, slaves and courtesans, Rojas boldly transposed the story to the contemporary world of courtly love and set it against a realistic Spanish underworld of cheating servants and sweaty bordellos. He kept the traditional Latin repertoire of stock names, but made the characters speak in a racy vernacular prose. Above all he flaunted the classical rules of decorum by giving the erotic comedy a tragic end. Contemporaries immediately grasped the point and praised Rojas for having "surpassed" his ancient models by this remarkable innovation. The book achieved instant fame, being printed, translated and adapted in Italian, French, German, English and Latin.

The vernacular humanism of Antonio de Guevara Garcilaso, the early playwrights, and the prose satire of the Erasmians were further stages on the inventive road of imitation. After 1550 the technical mastery of Spanish poets attained such harmonious brilliance

Left The palace built by Charles V beside the Alhambra of the Moorish kings of Granada was the first truly classical monument of Renaissance architecture to be raised in Iberia. It was designed in 1527 by Pedro Machuca, who had studied with Michelangelo in Italy. Its circular court was based on the ground-plan of the classic Roman villa as described in the letters of Pliny the Younger and constructed according to the dimensions of the villa of the Roman emperor Hadrian at Tivoli near Rome. The pure and elegant line of Charles's Granadine palace is emphasized by a restrained decoration of antique medallions and bas-reliefs of classical motifs whose symbolism is designed to express the imperial grandeur of Charles V as the Ceasar of his age.

that the classic Petrarchan and Horatian veins of imitation were exhausted. The last, and as it happens the greatest, exponent of pure classical *imitatio* was the Salamancan scholar Luis de León (1527–91), who in a mere handful of odes achieved a ravishing harmony of meter and purity of diction.

In the 1580s *imitatio* began to be replaced by a different principle, *admiratio* ("amazement"), the introduction of ingenious conceits and special effects of subtle wit and complex imagery designed to surprise readers who thought they knew what to expect from the classical patterns. *Admiratio* heralded the end of Renaissance style and the beginning of the Baroque.

The same development can be traced in Portugal. The greatest literary triumph of the Iberian Renaissance, *The Lusiads* by Luís de Camões (1524–80), was an epic imitation of Virgil's *Aeneid*, yet Baroque elements are already present. Camões took as his narrative subject Vasco da Gama's epoch-making sea voyage to India, but his theme was the glorification of Portuguese heroism. What is remarkable about this poem, published in 1572, is the way in which the simple and comparatively uneventful story is made to contain the whole past, present and future of the Portuguese imperial identity. To achieve this, Camões employed the gods and supernatural machinery of classical epic. Prophetic and visionary devices not only allowed him to encompass a vast sweep of narrative, they also enabled him to endow the surface narrative with great ethical and emotional subtlety. No other European response to the astounding geographical discoveries of the age came close to Camões's poem in imaginative brilliance and maturity.

Not all the literature of the Golden Age belonged to the Renaissance canon of formal imitation. The abundant popular works of edification and entertainment proved equally creative, especially in the field of prose fiction. Medieval romance was transformed by Garci Rodríguez de Montalvo's elegant reworking of *Amadis of Gaule*. Montalvo's *Amadis* (1508) spawned numerous continuations and imitations, and became the most widely read work of adventure in Europe. The so-called "sentimental" romances were a variation that cut out knight errantry and jousts to concentrate only on the delicious torments of chivalric love. They too enjoyed a European vogue for nearly two centuries. These works were later to contribute to the rise of the realist novel. The greatest Spanish work of fiction of this or any other age, however, was *Don Quixote* by Cervantes (1547–1616). *Don Quixote* began as a comic parody of the chivalric romances. Its hero, an aging and shabby country *hidalgo*, is driven mad by reading *Amadis of Gaule*, and sets out to emulate his hero's adventures as a knight errant, accompanied by the foolish bumpkin Sancho Panza.

The full triumph of the Renaissance style in art and architecture came relatively late to Iberia. This was not for lack of interest – the first treatise on Renaissance architecture to be printed outside Italy was published in Toledo in 1526 – but because Ferdinand and Isabella, who were among the greatest builders in the Europe of their day, continued to observe a strict division between ecclesiastical architecture, which remained Gothic, and domestic and public buildings, in which the classical style was gradually being introduced – "plateresque".

A parallel development occurred in painting and sculpture. The same eclectic blend of Gothic and

The Escorial

Built 50 kilometers from Madrid in the Guadarrama mountains, the Escorial is a vast complex comprising a mausoleum, monastery, church, library and palace. Remote, austere and forbidding, it stands as a fitting symbol of the Spanish monarchy during the 16th century. Commissioned by Philip II, who was keenly interested in all aspects of its design and construction, it took 21 years to build (1563–84). The initial design – based on the biblical description of Solomon's temple – was by Juan Bautista de Toledo, who had studied under Michelangelo in Rome. The work later passed to his assistant, Juan de Herrera, who stamped on it his own austerely purified form of the classical architecture of Renaissance Italy. The absence of decoration, a style encouraged by Philip II, marked a complete break with the ornateness of earlier Spanish architecture. A large group of Spanish and Italian artists worked on the interior, including the sculptors Leo and Pompeo Leoni, and the painters Titian and El Greco.

The Escorial became Philip's preferred residence, and increasingly the work of overseeing his expanding empire was carried out there. The combination of monastery, palace and library reflects the difficulty facing Spain in the 16th century – the coming together of medieval religiosity and Renaissance humanism. Philip was commited to the former.

Below A site-plan of the Escorial. The severe lines of the Escorial's grid plan may refer to the martyrdom of St Lawrence, who was put to death on a gridiron.

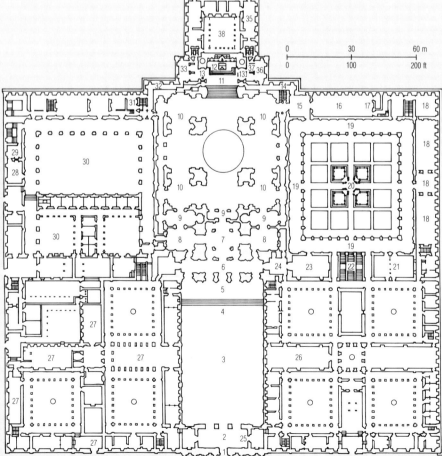

1. Door and Main Entrance
2. Porch, the Library on the first floor
3. Courtyard of the Kings
4–5. Staircases which lead to the Basilica and its facade
6. Porch or vestibule of the Basilica
7. Atrium of the Temple or Low Choir
8. Courtyard
9. Choirs of the Seminaries
10. Basilica
11–12. Presbitery and High Altar
13. Royal Oratories
14. Staircase which leads to the Choir and entrance to Pantheon
15. Antesacristy
16. Sacristy
17. Altar of the Sacred Form
18. Capitulary Halls
19. Main Lower Cloister
20. Court of the Evangelist
21. Old Church
22. Main Staircase
23. Hall of the Trinity
24. Hall of Secrets, ancient porter's lodge
25. Entrance and ascent to the Main Library through Porch No.2
26. Library of manuscripts
27. College
28. Entrance to the Palace of the Bourbons

Right The Burial of the Count of Orgaz (1586–88), painted for the church of Santo Tomé in Toledo displays the peculiar genius of the Cretan painter, El Greco. It illustrates the miraculous appearance of St Stephen and St Augustine at the burial in 1323 of the church's principal benefactor. So bold was El Greco's originality in this picture that the ecclesiastical authorities withheld a quarter of the agreed payment because the artist had modified their instructions. Although many of the heads in the lower half of the painting are portraits of El Greco's contemporaries, the artist's power to convey inner emotion through facial expression and gesture, coupled with the spiritual idealization and otherworldliness of its startlingly bold composition, transform the picture into a mystical vision.

Above In this early picture both the grandeur and the stern formality of the Escorial are evident. The dome of the church was based on Italian models. The royal apartments are next to the church, and the mausoleum below it. The distinctive spires on the corner towers became a common feature in Spanish architecture.

Left Emperor Charles V and his family at prayer. These larger-than-life gilded bronzes by Pompeo Leohi are in the church of the Escorial. A similar memorial to Philip II is not far away in the church.

29. Staircase of the Palace
30. Rooms of the Palace
31. Door which leads out of the Palace and ascent to that of the XVI Century
32. Hall of Battles
33. Apartments of the Infant Isabel Clara Eugenia
34. Gallery of the Royal Chambers
35. The throne Room
36. Apartments of Philip II
37. Bedroom and Oratory of the King
38. Courtyard of the Masks
39. College Entrance
40. Convent Entrance

Florentine influence is detectable in several of the talented masters working for Ferdinand and Isabella, notably in portrait painting and in the magnificent reredoses (carved and painted multipanelled altarpieces) that were the chief artistic glory of the age. The best-known master of the period was Pedro Berruguete (active 1483–1504). Although he received his early training in the fashionable Flemish style, he spent several years in Urbino, where he was one of the artists who worked on the ducal palace of Federigo da Montefeltro in the 1480s.

Outstanding among Portuguese artists was Nuño Gonçalves (active 1450–72), who was court painter to Alfonso V. His paintings display a realism strongly influenced by Flemish painting, but also the decorativeness of tapestry. His finest work is the *St Vincent Polyptych* (c. 1465), in which he depicts – almost lifesize and with astonishing inventiveness of composition and brilliance of color – a crowded panorama of Portuguese society, including King Alfonso, Prince Henry the Navigator, churchmen, soldiers and the humblest fishermen.

In painting, the peculiar genius of the Greek iconpainter Domenikos Theotokopoulos, nicknamed "El Greco", stands out. After working in Venice and Rome, El Greco (1541–1614) was attracted to Spain, probably by Philip II's great plans for the decoration of the Escorial, and settled in Toledo in 1577. Despite constant battles with patrons who tried to impose strict requirements upon the artist in the execution of his commissions, El Greco remained wholly original and hardly touched by convention.

Conclusion

By the end of the 16th century Spanish was recognized worldwide as one of the four languages of literature, along with Latin, French and Italian. But no Italian prose work of the century could compete in European fame and popularity with *Amadis of Gaule* or *Don Quixote*. Iberian drama, which had been dependent on Italian theater, was revolutionized in the 1580s by the building of permanent public playhouses in Madrid and other cities, and by the rise of professional native companies of actors, as well as by the genius of Spain's greatest playwright, Lope de Vega, and his many followers such as Pedro Calderón. By the 1640s Spain could boast of one of the richest and most original theaters in European history. In poetry, too, the period deserved to be called the Golden Age.

In all these forms, as well as in art and architecture, the original Renaissance style had been overlaid by a strong and distinctive Iberian character. In Spain and Portugal the lessons of the Italian Renaissance were fully absorbed, and in most cases transcended.

Plateresque Architecture

In Spain, the influence of Renaissance architectural ideals, when combined with older Flemish traditions, gave rise to the lavish style known as "plateresque" (from the resemblance of its surface ornament to the intricate filigree work of silversmiths, *platería*). A meticulous refinement of realistic detail can be seen in the flamboyant medieval ogee arches, fretted canopies and sculptural decorative screens and surfaces of the great public buildings erected during the reign of Ferdinand and Isabella by Juan Guas. His works include San Juan de los Reyes (1478–92) in Toledo, built to commemorate the Monarchs' victory over Portugal at the battle of Toro; and the Patio de los Leones in the Infantado Palace (1480–83), built for the Mendoza at Guadalajara. The work of the sculptor Gil de Siloé shows a similar refinement of detail. But it was the Segovian architect Lorenzo Vásquez, a follower of Brunelleschi, who introduced simple classical pilasters and rounded arches into the Gothic patio and facade of the College of Santa Cruz at Valladolid (1484–91). In the beautiful palace of the dukes of Medinaceli in Cogolludo (1495–1500) Vásquez designed the first building with a truly Renaissance plan.

The high point of plateresque was reached in the work of master builders of the second quarter of the 16th century such as Juan and Rodriqo Gil de Hontañón, architects of the New Cathedral and Palace of Monterrey in Salamanca, of Segovia cathedral, and (with Pedro Gumiel of Toledo) of Cisneros' new university of Alcalá de Henares. High plateresque, even when constructed entirely out of classical motifs, continued to display delight in symbolic or ornamental decoration that overspilled the framework dictated by Renaissance principles of harmony and order. In the work of Alonso Covarrubias and Diego de Siloé, the architects summoned to supervise the design of the new cathedral of Granada in 1528, the final refinement of plateresque can be seen, purified of exuberant ornament.

Below The Batalha monastery, Portugal. In Portugal a distinctive form of plateresque known as Manueline developed. Manueline was a transitional style combining medieval elements modified by Renaissance influences. What made Manueline distinctive was its highly ornate decoration. Typical motifs are twisted ropes, knots, branches and corals, all in great profusion and arranged in sinuous lines – the overall effect evokes the sculpture and architecture of Hindu and Jain temples in newly colonized Portuguese India. The monastery of Batalha is one of the finest examples of Manueline.

Above left The patio of the College of San Gregorio at Valladolid. Founded in 1488, the college was one of the first Renaissance foundations of learning in Castile, and one of the finest examples of early plateresque. The exuberant patio is the work of the German master Simon of Cologne. The facade shows the royal arms in a pomegranate tree (symbolizing the capture of Granada).

Above This medallion of Ferdinand and Isabella on the plateresque facade of Salamanca university symbolized royal patronage of the new learning. The sheaf of arrows and the yoke above the sovereigns' heads, and their hands jointly grasping the scepter, denote the Union of the Crowns of Castile and Aragon.

Left The patio of the archbishop's palace in Alcalá de Henares, destroyed by fire in 1940, was commissioned in 1524 by Cardinal Fonseca from Alonso de Covarrubias. The delicately carved stone balustrade of the open-newel staircase and the details of the doorway, arches and upper gallery are characteristic of the more restrained classical style of high plateresque.

ENGLAND AND SCOTLAND

The Renaissance in Britain occurred in two kingdoms whose histories are closely interwoven: England and Scotland. Their relationship changed significantly during the 130 years covered by this chapter. Henry VII, the founder of the Tudor dynasty, married his daughter to James IV of Scotland in 1503. Thereafter England tried to impose its will on Scotland – often by force. From mid century onward, however, the initiative shifted. When the unmarried Elizabeth came to the English throne in 1558, Mary Queen of Scots became the heir to the English crown by virtue of her descent from Henry VII. Her son, James VI of Scotland, succeeded to the English crown as James I of England with the death of Elizabeth I in 1603. The Tudor dynasty was at an end.

The brutality that tended to characterize English policy toward Scotland remained a constant in Wales and Ireland. Wales, a cultural backwater, was ruled from Ludlow Castle by the Lord President of the Marches. Similarly, Ireland was ruled from Dublin Castle by a Lord Deputy, his principal task being to put down revolts and to prevent foreign powers from using Ireland as a base from which to launch an invasion of England. This drained the English exchequer disastrously and Ireland itself remained irredeemably barbarous. In England and Scotland there were signs of change from the early decades of the 15th century. But a fully developed Renaissance court only came into being, in London, during the reign of Henry VIII (1509–47). Thus the emphasis of this chapter will be on the culture of the south of England. The Renaissance in Scotland, splendid enough in embryo, was severely damaged when the English massacred James IV and the Scottish nobility at the battle of Flodden Field in 1513. Things slowly recovered, only to be checked again by the social disintegration that followed the death of James V in 1542. In England the impetus Henry VIII had given to cultural growth was checked at exactly the same time by religious divisions. A late flowering at the end of the reign of Elizabeth gave way to the influx of cultural traditions from Scotland when the Stuarts came to the English throne in 1603.

One theme in particular dominates the Renaissance in England and Scotland – the close relationship between culture and politics. Henry VIII demanded cultural propaganda that would proclaim his splendor and righteousness in building, music and book. The wartime culture of the Elizabethan regime required miniaturist and poet alike to extol the virtues of Elizabeth with contrived allegories plundered from both pagan and sacred literature. This intimate connection between politics and culture in Britain continued beyond the Renaissance. Rubens, the greatest artist ever to be commissioned by a British sovereign, created a fantasy portraying James VI and I as *Rex Pacificus*, and as a monarch who saw himself as a second Solomon. Rubens's ceiling of 1635, for Inigo Jones's Banqueting House, London, is the first and the greatest monument to the Union of the Crowns of England and Scotland.

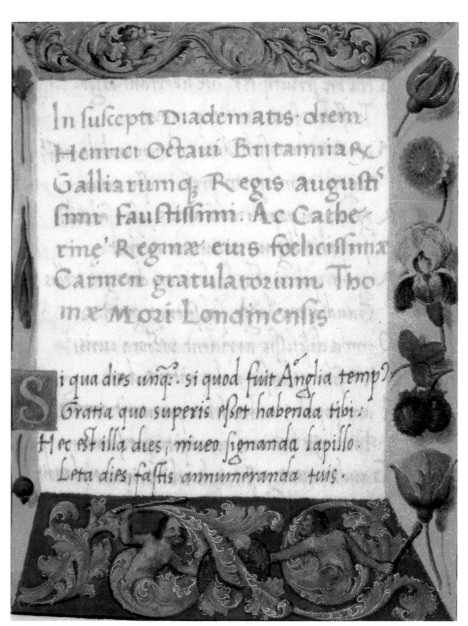

Beginnings

The 15th century in England was a period of political instability when those who in settled times would have been patrons became caught up in the Wars of the Roses, the civil war between the houses of York and Lancaster. It began in 1455 and ended with the defeat and death of Richard III at the battle of Bosworth Field in 1485. The victor, the Lancastrian Henry Tudor, became Henry VII and reconciled the warring factions by marrying Elizabeth of York (the niece of Richard III) the next year. But though the lives of patrons were disrupted, the conflict was intermittent and extensive areas were untouched. Neither Oxford nor Cambridge was involved and the middle years of the 15th century saw important colleges founded at both universities – at Cambridge, King's (1441) and Queens' (1448); at Oxford, All Souls (1437) and Magdalen (1458). In addition, Oxford benefited from the generosity of Humfrey, Duke of Gloucester

Above A presentation copy of Thomas More's *Epigrams* (c. 1509). More's epigrams were largely written when he was a young man, though not published until he was about 40. This richly decorated copy, commissioned by More himself, was given to Henry VIII to celebrate his marriage to Catherine of Aragon. There is a tragic irony about this gift, for it was More's refusal to countenance Henry's divorce from Catherine that led to his execution for treason.

(1391–1447), Regent to the one-year-old Henry VI, who came to the throne in 1422. Duke Humfrey's donations, beginning in 1411, first gave Oxford University an important library of its own. The duke left his collection of manuscript books, which included Latin versions of Plato and Aristotle, as well as poetry by Dante and Latin prose works by Petrarch and Boccaccio, to the university: this donation became the nucleus of the Bodleian Library, built between 1598 and 1613.

Although civil war dominated the reign of Edward IV (1461–83) there was cultural growth, much of it promoted by the king himself. Edward IV was on friendly terms with the printer Caxton, who in 1474 published in Bruges the *Recuyell of the Historyes of Troye*, the first book printed in English. In painting the reign saw the completion of an ambitious series of wall paintings at Eton College Chapel (1479); Eton College itself had been founded by Henry VI in 1440. Edward was succeeded by his brother Richard III (1483–85), whose reign was too short for him to accomplish much.

Henry VII (1485–1509) began by eliminating rival claimants to the throne before devoting his energies to putting crown finances on a firm footing. Thus in the first decade of his reign there was little patronage of the arts. But he became a keen builder and between 1494 and his death in 1509 he spent £28,000 on his principal residences. An assessment of his achievement, however, starts with a consideration of his ecclesiastical buildings, many of which have survived. He restarted work on the chapel of King's College, Cambridge (begun by Henry VI in 1446) so that by his death the fabric of the building was complete; the interior furnishings were completed under Henry VIII. Other projects of the period include an almshouse at Westminster (1500–02); a friary at Richmond (1501–02); the Savoy Hospital (1508–19); and the most famous extant building of his reign, his own memorial chapel in Westminster Abbey (1503–12). Henry VII and his executors spent over £40,000 on these five church buildings, the Westminster memorial chapel costing most. Here, as at King's College, Cambridge, Henry Tudor was following the precedent of his Lancastrian and Yorkist forebears by embellishing the church in which English kings were always crowned, and frequently buried. The Henry VII Chapel at Westminster was designed by the King's master masons, Robert and William Vertue, Robert Janyns and John Lebons. Henry also began a program of secular building, adding a tower to Windsor Castle and new buildings to the palaces at Woodstock and Woking; at Richmond and Greenwich he created entirely new palaces.

His death provided the impetus for important work by the Florentine sculptor Pietro Torrigiano: the tombs of Henry VII and his wife, Elizabeth of York, in the Henry VII Chapel; and, in the same location, the tomb of Henry's mother, Lady Margaret Beaufort. Torrigiano (1472–1528), who had been a studio rival of Michelangelo under Ghirlandaio in Florence, gave the English monarchy an Italian Renaissance iconography. The chapel also contained a tabernacle altar designed by Torrigiano in 1517–20 (destroyed in 1644) that, in its combination of Italianate design and English heraldic ornamentation, set the tone of much English Renaissance classicism.

The royal family also patronized scholarship, and the reorganization of the Royal scriptorium may have given an impetus to illumination. This led indirectly to the development of "limners" – painters of miniatures – who were to do so much to create the character of Elizabethan culture in the next generation. Lady Margaret Beaufort (c. 1441–1509), had founded Christ's College in Cambridge in 1505; in 1511 she went on to found St John's College, also in Cambridge. As the adopted home of the humanists John Fisher (1469–1535) and Erasmus (c. 1467–1536), St John's made the most significant contribution to the new learning in Cambridge during the 16th century. In 1517 Bishop Fox of Winchester founded Corpus Christi College, Oxford. The statutes specified that a search for good teachers must not be confined to England, but extended, if necessary, to "Greece or Italy, beyond the Po".

In the reign of Henry VII scholars in England made a remarkable contribution to humanist letters. Duke Humfrey had been the first conspicuous English example of a princely patron; men such as Robert Flemmyng (d. 1483), for the most part ecclesiastics and university figures, formed the next generation. Flemmyng traveled to Italy, where he became friendly

Below A woodcut from *Aesop's Fables* (1484), translated and printed by William Caxton. Caxton, who was England's first printer, probably learned his trade in Cologne in the early 1470s. He set up his first press in Bruges and then moved to London. He published about 100 titles, among the most important being Chaucer's *Canterbury Tales* and Malory's *Morte d'Arthur*.

with Guarino da Verona, professor of Greek and Latin at Ferrara. In Rome he met Platina, the papal librarian, and Pope Sixtus IV, a great patron of humanist studies. Flemmyng would retire to Tivoli in the summer, where he wrote Latin poems dedicated to Sixtus. But it was men of the third generation who brought English scholarship into the heart of the Italian Renaissance. Of these the most distinguished were Thomas Linacre, William Grocyn and William Latimer. It was largely they who formed the minds of diplomats and lawyers at the Inns of Court and the scholars and churchmen at Oxford.

Thomas Linacre (c.1460–1524) set out from Oxford in 1485 to study in Italy under the humanist scholar Poliziano; one of his fellow students was Giovanni de' Medici, later to become Pope Leo X. Many years later Linacre remembered his time in Florence by dedicating his edition of Galen to Leo X because, as he wrote in his dedication, he wished to "recall the common studies of their youth". Meanwhile William Grocyn (c. 1446–1519), the intimate of Linacre, had the distinction of delivering the first public lectures on Greek at Oxford in 1491. Erasmus, More and Colet were to study under Grocyn, whose example had a profound effect on scholarship.

English scholars made two important contributions to the new learning. The first was in the editing of texts. This work by Englishmen in Italy was concentrated at Venice, and in particular at the printing presses of Aldus Manutius, first established in that city in the 1490s. The second was in the task of ridding the Bible of spurious additions and corruptions. This was undertaken once the scholarly traveler had returned to England, though using methods acquired in Italy. John Colet's Oxford lectures on St Paul's Epistle to the Romans, delivered in the autumn of 1497, were the fruits of experience gained in Italy between 1493 and

Left A portrait of the churchman John Colet by Hans Holbein. John Colet, one of the most important and influential scholars of the early English Renaissance, studied and later lectured at Oxford, where he met Erasmus. He is best known for his lectures on the Scriptures and for his attacks on ecclesiastical abuses. He was dead by the time Holbein visited England, so this portrait must have been based on a bust of Colet by Torrigiano.

Bottom left The tomb of Henry VII and Elizabeth of York (1512–18) by Pietro Torrigiano. This tomb, one of the finest works of the English Renaissance, is in the Henry VII Chapel, Westminster Abbey. It was commissioned by Henry VIII. According to Cellini, on his return to Florence Torrigiano had a wealth of stories about his adventures among "those brutes, the English".

1496. His lectures were a decisive moment in English biblical scholarship, for he abandoned an interpretation of the text in scholastic terms, and offered instead a straightforward and wide-ranging exposition that included an account of the culture of ancient Rome. This he achieved by comparing the words of St Paul with the accounts of the Roman historian Suetonius. Colet was the central figure in the history of English learning at the end of the reign of Henry VII, and his influence was far reaching. He founded St Paul's School in 1509, giving it enlightened and progressive statutes and an up-to-date curriculum. He was the spiritual son of Thomas Linacre, but also, through his influence as a teacher and writer, father to a new community of scholars of extraordinary distinction. Of these Sir Thomas More – disciple of Colet, intimate of Erasmus and tragic victim of Henry VIII – was the finest example.

The last decade of the reign of Henry VII saw many advances in the spread of humanism. In 1498 Erasmus visited Oxford because, as he said, it was no longer necessary to make the journey to Italy – England could provide the best in classical education. In 1511 he was appointed to a Greek lectureship at Cambridge, another benefaction of Lady Margaret Beaufort, the greatest royal patron of humanism of the early Tudor period. In 1516 he published his Greek version of the New Testament, a version that laid the foundation of modern biblical scholarship.

Henry VII created the settled conditions necessary for a court culture. But he had to face a number of revolts. In 1487 a revolt led by Lambert Simnel was crushed at Stoke-on-Trent. In 1497 a more serious rising led by Perkin Warbeck, who claimed to be the son of Edward IV, ended when Warbeck, having persuaded Cornish rebels to march on London, was defeated and captured at Blackheath. Despite intermittent crises, Henry VIII inherited a prosperous realm and a court with much enhanced status, both at home and abroad. Henry VII had concentrated on binding together a kingdom weakened by 30 years of civil war. Although venturing into a number of ambitious foreign alliances in Europe, he proceeded cautiously. By contrast, Henry VIII was a more

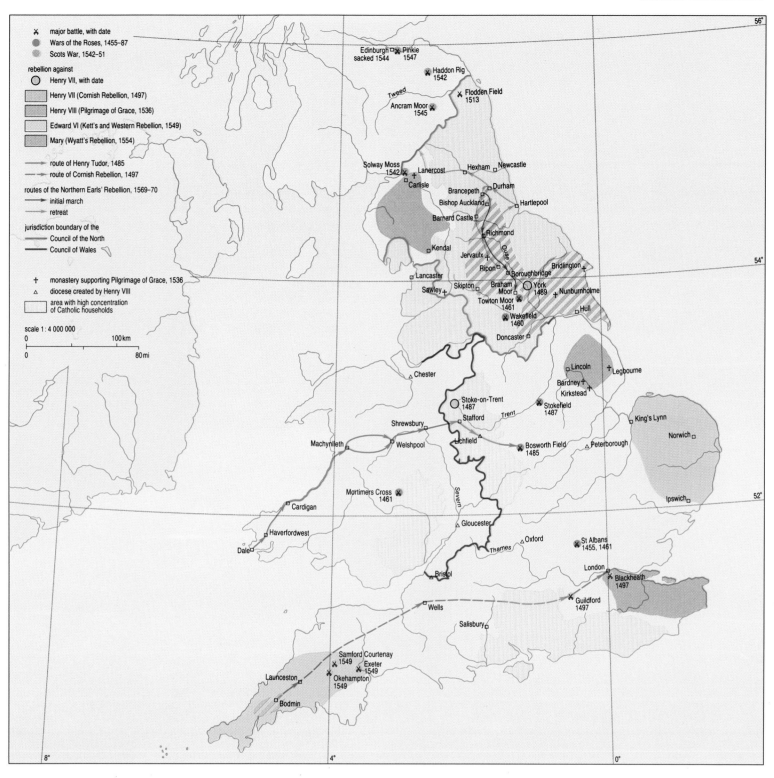

Legend:

✗ major battle, with date
● Wars of the Roses, 1455–87
● Scots War, 1542–51

rebellion against
○ Henry VII, with date

Henry VII (Cornish Rebellion, 1497)
Henry VIII (Pilgrimage of Grace, 1536)
Edward VI (Kett's and Western Rebellion, 1549)
Mary (Wyatt's Rebellion, 1554)

→ route of Henry Tudor, 1485
→ route of Cornish Rebellion, 1497
routes of the Northern Earls' Rebellion, 1569–70
→ initial march
→ retreat

jurisdiction boundary of the
— Council of the North
— Council of Wales

✝ monastery supporting Pilgrimage of Grace, 1536
△ diocese created by Henry VIII
area with high concentration of Catholic households

scale 1 : 4 000 000
0   100km
0   80mi

Map labels:

Edinburgh sacked 1544 — Pinkie 1547
Haddon Rig 1542
Tweed
Flodden Field 1513
Ancram Moor 1545
Solway Moss 1542 — Lanercost — Hexham — Newcastle
Carlisle — Brancepeth — Durham
Bishop Auckland — Hartlepool
Barnard Castle
Richmond
Kendal
Jervaulx — Ouse
Ripon — Boroughbridge — Bridlington
Lancaster — Skipton — Braham Moor — York 1489 — Nunburnholme
Sawley — Towton Moor 1461
Wakefield 1460 — Hull
Doncaster
Chester
Lincoln — Legbourne
Bardney — Kirkstead
Stoke-on-Trent 1487 — Stokefield 1487
Shrewsbury — Stafford — Trent
Machynlleth — Welshpool — Lichfield — Bosworth Field 1485 — Peterborough
King's Lynn — Norwich
Cardigan — Mortimers Cross 1461 — Severn
Haverfordwest — Ipswich
Dale — Gloucester
Oxford — St Albans 1455, 1461
Thames — London — Blackheath 1497
Bristol — Guildford 1497
Wells
Salisbury
Samford Courtenay 1549 — Exeter 1549
Launceston — Okehampton 1549
Bodmin

Above: Political unrest in Britain, 1461–1509

The geographical and chronological distribution of rebellions in Tudor England suggests how hard the dynasty worked to sustain dominance and political equilibrium. Henry VII established the Tudors on a firm financial and administrative footing; nevertheless, he had to contend with serious threats to his authority. Even in the last years of Elizabeth I, her favorite the Earl of Essex challenged her rule by inciting open revolt. By contrast, the Stuarts enjoyed years of internal peace until the 1640s. This was in part because of the union of the crowns of England and Scotland in 1603, the first and greatest achievement of the Stuart dynasty.

spontaneous and volatile figure on the international stage. The difference between father and son was at its most striking over the question of marriage. Henry Tudor accomplished an adroit but insular alliance with the house of York. Henry VIII looked for wives from the plains of Aragon to the shores of the Baltic. Henry VII established the claims of the Tudor dynasty to the crown of England. Henry VIII expanded those horizons until he made a bid for the title of Holy Roman Emperor.

Henry VIII

Henry VIII (1509–47) pursued a confident, expansionist policy of self-aggrandizement. For this he demanded a supportive cultural network dedicated to the production of an imperial image – he claimed and

sought equality with Emperor Charles V and King Francis I of France. There was a royal building program unlike any seen before or since in England. Hampton Court, above all, has come to be associated with Henry VIII, though it had been conceived and much of it built by Cardinal Wolsey (c. 1474–1530), who in 1527 offered it to Henry. Henry spent prodigious amounts on his palaces. He built Whitehall from new, thus breaking with the centuries-old tradition of the monarch residing in the old Palace of Westminster. Royal residences required embellishment and a program of royal glorification on a scale unimagined before.

In 1526 the German artist Hans Holbein the Younger (c. 1497–1543) came to work in England. This was through the intervention of Erasmus who

Hampton Court

Hampton Court is the best preserved Renaissance palace in Britain, giving the most vivid sense of the splendor of Henry VIII's court. It was begun in 1515 by Cardinal Wolsey, the Lord Chancellor. He intended it as a Thames-side residence to complement his other palace of Whitehall in London. When he began to lose favor with the king, Wolsey gave both palaces to Henry in 1525. Wolsey built the Outer Court and what is now known as the Fountain Court. The work that survives from Wolsey's building program shows that he was the most sophisticated art patron in England. Especially notable are the terra-

cotta roundels on the main gate by the Italian sculptor, Benedetto da Maiano, and the chamber known as Wolsey's Closet. This has a frieze of paintings showing the Passion of Christ that can be favorably compared with contemporary work in Italy. Henry built a new and larger Great Hall (1532–34) and remodeled the Chapel (1535–36). He also greatly expanded the lay-out of Hampton Court as a whole by building The King's Lodgings and The Queen's Lodgings (1534–37), besides creating a range of chambers for the courtiers known as the Gentlemen of the Privy Chamber.

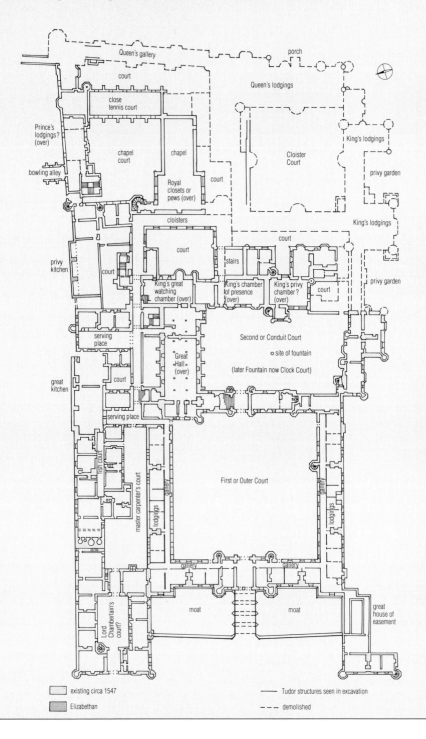

Right This aerial view shows how Hampton Court was sited next to the river Thames – journeys by road were slow compared with those by river. This was typical of Renaissance palace design, and a number of the other 50 or so royal residences owned by Henry VIII were also on the Thames, including Greenwich to the east of London, and Richmond close to Hampton Court itself. The palace was surrounded by a great moat originally excavated by Wolsey as part of the first building program. In addition there were extensive gardens and Henry built a famous "tilt yard" for jousting and horsemanship, popular pursuits at a Renaissance court.

Far right The red-brick main gateway with the arms of Henry VIII under the principal stone window. This creates a lively contrast to the red of the walls. The formula of a facade pierced with a great gate topped with pepper-pot turrets was typical of the English Renaissance palace. The staircase turrets, flanking the gate left and right, contain two of the terracotta roundels ordered by Wolsey. In front is the moat, with a drawbridge supporting the king's personal emblems in the form of heraldic beasts. The rows of magnificent Tudor chimney stacks are evidence of the skill of English native craftsmanship during the Renaissance.

gave him an introduction to More. Holbein worked in London until 1528, when he returned to Basel, but in 1532 returned to England, where he was to die of the plague. The finest achievement of Holbein's first visit was the portrait group *Sir Thomas More and his Family*, now destroyed (though a fine preparatory drawing for it still exists). The most ambitious royal portrait he undertook was painted during his second visit of 1532–43. It was a dynastic fresco painted on the wall of the Privy Chamber at Whitehall in 1537. It portrayed Henry VIII and his wife Jane Seymour standing on either side of a classical altar front with a Latin inscription proclaiming the legitimacy of the Tudors: behind Henry VIII and his wife stood Henry VII and Margaret of York. The fresco was destroyed in a fire at Whitehall in 1698. Holbein also produced the remarkable full-length image of Henry VIII as a Herculean colossus astride the world. He painted or drew many leading figures at the English court, one of his most beautiful portraits being that of the astronomer Nicholas Kratzer, painted in 1528. Kratzer was the royal astronomer and "deviser of the king's horologies" – a manufacturer of sundials and scientific instruments. He was introduced to Holbein by More, and struck up a friendship with the artist. At a banqueting house erected at Greenwich in 1527 they combined their talents to produce a "cosmological ceiling" depicting the universe. In his many sensitive and closely observed portraits, Holbein created an image of the English Renaissance comparable in artistry and sophistication with Bronzino's presentation of the Medici court, or the Clouets' depiction of the Valois dynasty.

As a patron Henry VIII emulated Renaissance princes in Europe. He was interested in astronomy, literature and music; he himself wrote theology and composed music of real quality. In 1520 he met the French king Francis I near Calais at an encounter that came to be known as "The Field of the Cloth of Gold". The two monarchs tried to outshine each other in the splendor of their retinues and the gorgeousness of their tents. The meeting was decisive, for it gave Henry a vision of himself as a Renaissance prince, a vision extending far beyond the narrower horizons of his father's ambitions. The Tudors now vied with the Valois and the Habsburgs.

The life and work of "the King's good servant", Sir Thomas More (1478–1535), best exemplify the European character of the English Renaissance. By his example a new emphasis was given to the humanities, and Italian Renaissance scholarship was gradually incorporated into education in Britain. More's first publication, printed in Paris in 1506, was a translation of the Greek satirist, Lucian. His first English book was his *Life of Picus* (1510), a biography of the Italian humanist Pico della Mirandola together with an abridgement of his writings. More's most celebrated work, however, was his *Utopia*, published in Louvain in 1516. In the first part of *Utopia*, More offered a keen analysis of contemporary evils; in the second, better-known, part, influenced by accounts of Vespucci's voyages to South America, More depicted an ideal world in which evils such as poverty, crime and political corruption did not exist, and religious tolerance was practiced. More's outlook was essentially international rather than narrowly English, and under a European-minded monarchy Englishmen were able to feel an integral part of the intellectual and religious life of Europe.

Much of this changed, however, with the judicial murder of More and John Fisher, the Bishop of Rochester, in 1535. They were executed for their refusal to support the divorce of Henry VIII from Catherine of Aragon. Henry followed that divorce by breaking his allegiance to Rome, a break made final by the passing of the Act in Restraint of Appeals of 1533. The preamble to this act stated that "this realm of England is an empire": England was a law unto itself and so no longer answerable to an external force such as the papacy. The Act in Restraint of Appeals embodied a view of the relations between church and state upon which all subsequent English legislation down to modern times has been based. It was followed a year later by the Act of Supremacy, which made Henry the "Supreme Head of the Church of England". Although England remained firmly Catholic until Edward VI came to the throne, easy communication between England and Rome ceased.

One of the most important consequences of the break with Rome was the Dissolution of the Monasteries. This began in 1536 and brought about the destruction of the great monastic houses such as Fountains and Rievaulx, the romantic ruins of which remain to this day. They, however, were only among the largest of many hundreds of monasteries and abbeys that had for centuries played a central role in the social, economic, educational and medical welfare of medieval communities from the wilderness of the Scottish borders to the teeming parishes of London.

During the Dissolution huge areas of land and a great number of buildings were absorbed by the

crown, and then rapidly granted or sold. Old buildings were quickly put to new uses. Some London monasteries were turned into markets; others into tenements built to deal with the sharp rise in population during the 16th century. Farther afield they were reshaped to accommodate families whose assets had been swollen by this glut. The impact can be clearly seen in a small area of Hampshire and Sussex. At Titchfield Abbey in Hampshire in 1538, Thomas Wriothesley, Lord Chancellor, built a massive gatehouse at right angles to the nave of the church, but otherwise simply converted what existed within the walls of the monastic buildings. Only a few miles away, William Paulet, Treasurer of the Household, converted Netley Abbey, while about 25 miles beyond

Above The family of Henry VIII by an unknown artist (c. 1545). Henry VIII is seated with his heir Edward VI to his right and Edward's mother, Jane Seymour, to his left. His two daughters, the future monarchs Mary I and Elizabeth I, are also shown. What is remarkable about this family portrait is that when it was painted Henry was married to his last wife, Catherine Parr. Henry may have wanted to give Jane Seymour prominence because she was the mother of his only son.

Left This remarkable armored helmet was given to Henry VIII by Emperor Maximilian. It testifies to the significance of Henry in European at a time when the Habsburgs, the Valois and the Tudors vied with one another for dominance. It also indicates the prestige attached to royal armories during the Renaissance.

Mid-century: Edward VI and Mary

With the death of Henry VIII and the accession of Edward VI (1547–53), England became significantly more isolated as the country turned increasingly Protestant. Edward was dominated first by the Duke of Somerset, known as Protector Somerset (1547–49), and then by the Duke of Northumberland (1549–53). In 1549 there was a rising in Norfolk led by Jack Cade, the consequence of sharp price rises and acute rural unemployment. This was ruthlessly suppressed by Northumberland, who then ousted Somerset. Northumberland encouraged a new, more severe Protestant regime. Before, the destruction of religious images aimed only at what had encouraged the cult of the saints – in 1538 Henry VIII had ordered the destruction of the shrine of Thomas à Becket in Canterbury Cathedral, one of the great sights of medieval England.

Now, however, under Northumberland, the first wave of destruction began, with widespread loss of medieval ecclesiastical art. Far more was destroyed in these four years than during the Civil War and Oliver Cromwell's Commonwealth in the 17th century. And yet there was cultural growth too. Somerset built Somerset House, the first major London building displaying an understanding of the principles of classical design. Before this time the application of Renaissance ornament taken from a "pattern book" had been the norm in English Renaissance building. Northumberland, too, was an enlightened patron of architecture, despite his hatred of church furnishings. John Shute prefaced his *First and Chief Grounds of Architecture* (1563), the first English Renaissance treatise on architecture, with a dedication to Queen Elizabeth in which he stated that he had been to Italy to confer with the "skillful masters in architecture".

Right A portrait of Nicholas Kratzer (1527) by Hans Holbein. Kratzer, German by birth, lectured at Oxford before becoming Henry VIII's astronomer and maker of scientific instruments. The fascinating array of instruments in the picture is evidence of the increasing importance of science and technology during the Renaissance – though it is significant that Kratzer was an astrologer as well as an astronomer. He was for a time a tutor to the children of Thomas More.

that William Fitzwilliam, Lord Admiral, completed the more ambitious conversion of Cowdray House in Sussex. So much building naturally led to an increase in the numbers of masons and craftsmen, but these men were ingenious adapters rather than creators of new architectural styles. At Newstead Abbey, Nottinghamshire, the ancestral home of the poet Lord Byron, the cloisters were converted to a corridor leading to the public rooms. It was from such ad hoc arrangements that the traditional plan of the English country house developed – in general, British architecture is characterized by gradual adaptation. Only rarely were monastic buildings taken down and the stone used to create a house from new.

The "new" men who had helped dismantle the apparatus of English papal Catholicism did very well. However, like most revolutions, Henry's break with Rome was carried out by a few, for a few, and the vast majority opposed it. In the northern counties and in Lincolnshire, conservative areas where the loss of monasteries and abbeys had been keenly felt, there was open rebellion in what historians have called "The Pilgrimage of Grace" (1536). The leaders were pardoned, only to be executed a year later when a new uprising began.

The harm caused by the Dissolution of the Monasteries and England's growing isolation from the rest of Europe – the execution of Sir Thomas More is a telling symbol of this – makes an assessment of the cultural significance of Henry's reign complex, for he was without doubt one of the most important patrons in early modern Britain.

major 16th-century building
+ converted ecclesiastical building
🏛 country house
🏯 royal palace
🏰 tower house
× other

date construction begun
○ before 1500
○ 1500–1525
○ 1526–1550
● 1551–1575
● 1576–1600
● after 1600

● more than one building,
  see list opposite
— international boundary, 1500
--- boundary of the Pale, 1550

scale 1 : 4 000 000

0   100km
0   80mi

Aberdeen
⊗ King's College Chapel
⊗ St Machaw's Cathedral

Cambridge
⊗ Christ's College
⊗ Emmanuel College
● Gonville and Caius College
⊗ King's College Chapel
⊗ Queen's College
⊗ St John's College
⊗ Trinity College

Edinburgh
⊗ Edinburgh Castle
⊗ Heriots Hospital
🏛 Holyroodhouse
🏛 Moray House

London
🏛 Bridewell
+ Charlton House
+ Charterhouse
● Eastbury House
🏛 Eltham Palace
🏛 Greenwich Palace
🏛 Holland House
🏛 Richmond Palace
🏛 St James's Palace
● Somerset House
🏛 Syon House
🏛 Whitehall

Ludlow
⊗ The Feathers Hotel
⊗ Ludlow Castle

Oxford
⊗ Bodleian Library
⊗ Cardinal College, Christchurch
⊗ Corpus Christi College
⊗ Wadham College

Birsay
Bishop's Palace

Huntly Castle   Craigston Castle
Fyvie Castle
Castle Fraser
Craigievar Castle   Aberdeen
Midmar   Tweed
Crathes Castle

Edzell Castle

Tay

Falkland Palace
Stirling Castle
Culross Palace   St Columba's
Linlithgow Palace   Pinkie
                  Edinburgh
                  Crichton Castle

Tyne
Naworth Castle

Sizergh Castle   Ouse
Levens Hall
Fountains Hall   Burton Agnes Hall
King's Manor
Burton Constable

Dublin Castle

Jigginstown House

Barrow

Bolsover Castle   Worksop
Haddon Hall   Hardwick Hall
Crewe Hall   Little Moreton Hall
                   Newstead Abbey
                   Wollaton Hall   Stiffkey Hall
                   Trent
Shrewsbury   Tixall
Powis Castle
Condover Hall   Burghley House
Dudley Castle   Kirby Hall Deene Park Hall
                            Rushton   Lyveden New Bield
Ludlow   Kenilworth Castle Rothwell Hinchingbrooke House
Llanidloes   Lord Leycester Hospital Holdenby Castle Ashby Hengrave Hall
               Charlecote Park   House   Cambridge   Framlingham Church
               Canons Ashby   Audley End House
               Compton Wynyates

Severn

Sudeley Castle   Hatfield   New Hall
Ditchley Park Gorhambury House   Layer Marney Tower
Woodstock Oxford House   Leez Priory
Thornbury   Thame   Theobalds
               Park
Hanworth   London
Windsor Castle   Hampton Court   Reigate Priory
Oatlands   Nonsuch
Lacock Abbey Bramshill   Knole Canterbury
The Vyne   Sutton Place Penshurst Walmer Castle
Basing House   Guildford Hever Place
Longleat House Wilton House   Castle Sissinghurst
Wardour Castle Longford Castle
Poundisford Park Sherborne Castle Cowdray House
Barrington Court Clifton Maybank Titchfield Abbey
Montacute House

Cotehele House   Buckland Abbey
Mount Edgcumbe

56°
54°
52°
8°
4°
0°

While statues of the Virgin Mary came down, houses of a refined classicism went up, Longleat and Lacock Abbey, both in Wiltshire, being the most conspicuous examples.

In 1531 Sir Thomas Elyot (c. 1490–1546) published *The Book Named the Governor*, an educational homily addressed to those who wished to equip their sons for government service. Elyot was heavily dependent on Castiglione's *The Courtier*, which first appeared in English in 1561 in a translation by Sir Thomas Hoby. Between the appearance of Elyot's treatise and Hoby's translation, the poet Henry Howard, Earl of Surrey (1517–47), had published sonnets inspired by Italian Renaissance writers. Sir Thomas Wyatt, an English diplomat at the court of Emperor Charles V, combined the penning of Petrarchan verse with a successful public career.

Mary Tudor (1553–58), Catholic daughter of Henry VIII and Catherine of Aragon, tried to root out Protestantism in England and restore papal supremacy. Her persecution of Protestants, which included executing bishops Cranmer, Latimer and Ridley, earned her the nickname "Bloody Mary". Little of any cultural significance took place in her short reign, though she was painted by the Flemish artist Anthonis Mor (c. 1519–c. 1576), one of the great northern portraitists of the time. Furthermore, she was married to Philip II of Spain, the greatest living art patron of the day, who was himself painted by Mor. Mary was succeeded by her half-sister, the Protestant Elizabeth, daughter of Henry VIII and Anne Boleyn.

Elizabeth I

Stephen Gardiner, Catholic Bishop of Winchester and Mary Tudor's Lord Chancellor, had recommended that Mary execute Elizabeth so that the crown would then pass to Mary Queen of Scots. Faced in early life with threats of this kind, Elizabeth (1558–1603) favored a policy of cautious consolidation. Believing that the speculations of theologians were "ropes of sand or sea-slime leading to the Moon", she sought a middle path in affairs of church and state, and allowed greater religious tolerance.

Early in her reign relations with Spain became strained when in 1563 Sir John Hawkins' ships and goods were seized by the Spanish. A year later the Revolt of the Netherlands began. The United Provinces, who were trying to drive the Spanish out of the Netherlands, saw in Elizabeth a Protestant savior, and she became drawn into a conflict that was to have a most decisive effect on Britain. In 1568 she ordered the seizure of the fleet carrying the pay for the Spanish armies fighting in the Netherlands; in return the Dutch offered her the regency of their new state. Elizabeth declined, but lent large sums of money and encouraged the dispatch of English mercenaries to the rebels.

Elizabeth was a reluctant champion of religion. Nevertheless, England became bound up with the larger issues of the struggle between a Protestantism often strongly influenced by an unyielding and authoritarian Calvinism, and a Catholicism newly invigorated by the Counter-Reformation. England became directly threatened by the issue of the Papal Bull *Regnans in Excelsis*, issued by Pius V in 1570. This excommunicated Elizabeth and invited Catholic princes to overthrow her. Elizabeth had been vulnerable to an alliance of European Catholic

powers. In the 1580s the struggle between European Protestantism and Habsburg Catholicism became intense, and what happened in Europe had consequences within England. A Cheshire gentleman, Francis Throckmorton conspired against Elizabeth with Mendoza, the Spanish ambassador in London; and in 1584 Pope Gregory XIII launched the "Enterprise of England", designed to restore Roman Catholicism. After the assassination of William of Orange in 1584, the leader of the Dutch struggle for independence, Elizabeth sent the Earl of Leicester to the Netherlands to make open war on Spain. The following year Sir Francis Drake was sent to plunder the West Indies, then held by Spain, and sacked Cartagena, Santiago and Santo Domingo. Two years later he raided Cadiz, destroying the Spanish fleet and delaying the launch of the Spanish Armada, a full-scale attack on England that Philip II of Spain had planned for many years. The struggle with Spain came to a head in 1588 with the failure of the Armada, defeated as much by the weather and the technical problems of the Spanish ships as by the good seamanship of the English. A continental, Catholic threat to Elizabeth and England was now effectively at an end. She spent the last 15 years of her reign trying to control a more vocal and critical parliament and to suppress extreme forms of Puritanism.

The Elizabethan age was a war culture. It focused on Elizabeth and served to make a virtue out of her vulnerability. Elizabeth herself was uninterested in the arts. She built little. She bought only official portraits, acquired with as much enthusiasm as a pair of bed hangings. Nevertheless, within a wider courtly circle painting developed an extreme refinement and an emphasis on heraldry that made it quite idiosyncratic in 16th century Europe. It reached its fullest expression in the miniature, the finest exponent of which was Nicholas Hilliard. The Elizabethan miniature tends to be a portrait confined to the head and shoulders, with

emphasis on ruffs and jewelry, the face described with little shadow, and the clothes in brilliant colors. They were frequently conceived as a jeweled ornament and hung as a pendant within an elaborate jeweled case. The indivisible connection between the miniaturist and the jeweler is seen to best effect in the so-called *Armada Jewel* of about 1600 (possibly by Hilliard). This is a profile portrait of Elizabeth I conceived in the style of an antique cameo. It was presented by Elizabeth to Sir Thomas Heneage to commemorate the defeat of the Spanish Armada.

Elizabeth turned her back on her father's magnificent building program, but went far beyond him in developing the "royal progress" and the tournament, highly sophisticated means of nurturing her own image. Elizabeth became a skilled manipulator of her own image as she deflected criticism and distracted her court from the urgent problems facing the kingdom – the threat from Spain, the unsettled nature of Ireland, the increasing financial difficulties of the crown, the lack of a direct heir, the rise of Puritanism, and the loss of control over the House of Commons. The image grew more and more important.

On the progress the Queen was an enchantress, weaving a spell around her own image at the expense of her star-struck courtiers. In summer she would tour the South and the Midlands as the guest of courtiers who would rebuild or extend their properties hoping to ensure a worthy reception. Her Lord Chancellor, Sir Christopher Hatton, made a disastrous miscalculation. At Holdenby, on the Northamptonshire-Lincolnshire border, Hatton built at huge expense and reckless extravagance, but the Queen never came. By

contrast, the Earl of Hertford made himself famous as the host of an entertainment at his estate at Elvetham, Hampshire in September 1591. Hertford created a lake shaped like a crescent-moon and set with islands, in which was enacted a spectacle centered upon the person of Diana, virgin goddess of the moon – a clear allusion to Elizabeth.

The Elizabethan tournament was closely linked with the royal progress. In a conscious revival of medievalism, Elizabethan courtiers, such as Sir Henry Lee of Ditchley, Queen's Champion at the Tilt, adopted the characters of Arthurian knights. In romantic guises they competed in defense of the Queen's honor, or in pretended pursuit of her hand. Elizabeth encouraged these elaborate revivals of medieval chivalry by allowing herself to be cast in the role of the Virgin Queen. She succeeded in arousing the competitive, ambitious and romantic instincts of her courtiers. The chivalry of Elizabethan England was best expressed through the cultivation of the St George's Day Feast (St George being the patron saint of England), when the Queen progressed with her Knights of the Garter. This world of escapist fantasy, mock romance and over-refined chivalry is captured most evocatively in Hilliard's miniatures – in particular his portrait of *George, 3rd Earl of Cumberland*, in which the Earl is dressed as the Knight of Pendragon Castle.

In the intensely competitive world of Elizabethan England it was the court rather than the crown that brought about a flowering of the arts. There was, for example, the development of the "prodigy house", with its emphasis upon eye-catching and spectacular features. At Hardwick Hall, "more glass than wall", the great windows seem to hang suspended like galleon sails from the battlemented initials crowning the skyline – *E* and *S*, for Elizabeth Shrewsbury, better known as Bess of Hardwick, the patroness responsible for it all.

Courtiers took an active interest in painting. It may have been Robert Dudley, Earl of Leicester (c. 1532–88), one-time favorite of the Queen and hero of the Dutch Wars, who brought Federico Zuccaro to England for six months in 1575. Zuccaro (1543–1609) was a talented Italian artist who painted a full-length portrait of Leicester, and one of Elizabeth. The portrait of Elizabeth no longer exists, but a preparatory drawing for it shows that its interest must have lain less in the vivacity of likeness than in its symbolism: pillar (constancy and fortitude); serpent (wisdom); ermine (chastity); dog (fidelity). The priority given to a subtle message over a palpable likeness was characteristically Elizabethan. John, Lord Lumley (d.1609), was the first Englishman to assemble a collection of portraits which might be termed a "gallery of worthies". Lumley had *cartellini*, or illusionistic labels, painted on his portraits to identify sitters. Additionally, he amassed a famous library, which was later acquired by Henry, Prince of Wales, to form the basis of the Royal Library at the beginning of the 17th century. But the most famous late Renaissance library in England, formed during the Elizabethan era at Nonsuch Palace by Henry Fitzalan, Earl of Arundel, was raised upon the dispersal of monastic collections.

Education and writing were the glories of the Elizabethan era. Elizabeth herself had had a superb education at the hands of the humanist Roger Ascham (1515–68), and she could speak Greek, Latin, French

Top left A portrait of Sir Francis Drake by an unknown artist. Drake is the epitome of the popular Elizabethan hero – a navigator and adventurer, he was the first Englishman to circumnavigate the world (1577–80), returning with his ship the *Golden Hind* laden with treasure. He is perhaps best known for fighting the Spanish – "singeing the king of Spain's beard" at Càdiz and playing a leading role in the defeat of the Armada.

Above The *Blackfriars Portrait* (c. 1600) by Robert Peake. This is one of the most celebrated portraits of Elizabeth I and her court. Carried in a canopy of state borne by her favorite courtiers, Elizabeth is dressed in silver-white to symbolize her status as the Virgin Queen. Such lavish spectacles played an important role in fashioning an image of royal splendor and power.

and Italian. In Elizabethan England education flourished as never before. Roger Ascham wrote *The Schoolmaster* (published posthumously in 1570), a manual on the teaching of children that enjoyed an international popularity. The Queen herself founded Westminster School in 1560. This school, resting under the shadow of the Houses of Parliament, immediately brought about a change in the pattern of education for many young gentlemen. Boys would not always be confined to the schoolroom of a great house: a public element came into the teaching of future courtiers. Many of those who would wield influence in the late Elizabethan and Jacobean eras had been taught by William Camden, first headmaster of Westminster School.

Besides being the greatest teacher of his age, Camden (1551–1623) was the most creative antiquarian England had seen. The Tudors knew the value of historians. Henry VII had employed the Italian

historian Polydore Vergil (c. 1470–1555) to write a history of England, while the last years of the reign of Henry VIII witnessed John Leyland's ambitious but unfinished survey of the antiquities and topography of England. Taking up Leyland's unfinished work, Camden proved altogether more productive. His *Britannia* of 1586 was the first systematic account of the history of Britain, though it was based as much upon classical writers, inscriptions and artifacts as it was on monastic chroniclers. It was Camden's larger achievement to establish history as a respected discipline, and antiquarianism as an intellectual pursuit. History became an interest that appealed as much to the man of affairs as to the university scholar. The diplomat, soldier and adventurer Sir Walter Raleigh, a typical Elizabethan popular hero, for example, spent the last years of his life, while imprisoned in the Tower of London, writing his *History of the World* (1616). The pursuit of history was given institutionalized

The Portrait in Miniature

The history of miniature painting in England begins with Henry VII's establishment of a Royal Library at Richmond Palace at the end of the 15th century. For this he recruited artists from the court of Burgundy who had been trained as illuminators of manuscripts. "Limners", as miniature painters were called, recalls the roots of this art form in the medieval illuminated book. Henry VIII invited the Hornebolte family from the Low Countries, who became the leading miniaturists at court during the 1530s. Hans Holbein is known to have painted at least 15 miniatures, which took the form of reduced versions of life-size portraits. After the death of Lucas Hornebolte and Holbein in the 1540s, Henry VIII persuaded the female miniaturist Levina Teerlinc to settle in London. Teerlinc was responsible for training Nicholas Hilliard, the greatest of all English miniaturists.

Hilliard, like all miniaturists of the 16th century, practiced other arts too: he was a painter of life-size portraits, a jeweler, medalist and engraver. It was Hilliard's versatility that allowed him to evolve the jeweled miniature, in which the exquisite craftsmanship of the silver or gold surround, often studded with precious stones or overlaid with filigree enameling, complemented the delicacy of the miniature itself. After a period of several years at the Valois court in France, Hilliard emerged by the 1580s as the queen's favored portraitist, and it was Hilliard who created the most famous images of Elizabeth. By the 1590s Hilliard faced competition at court, particularly from Isaac Oliver, whose exquisite works record the precious and fantastic world of the Jacobean masque. Oliver died in 1617, Hilliard in 1619. Thereafter the art of miniature, so peculiarly an English one, began to

decline. This decline coincided with the emergence of artists who specialized in miniature painting alone, and it may well be that the connection is no coincidence. Most of what is known about the technical aspects of the painting of miniatures derives from Hilliard's account, *A Treatise Concerning the Art of Limning* (c. 1598).

In Shakespeare's *The Merchant of Venice*, Bassanio discovers Portia's portrait as "counterfeit":

Fair Portia's counterfeit! What demi-god
Hath come so near creation? Move these eyes?
Or whether riding on the balls of mine
Seem they in motion? Here are sever'd lips,
Parted with sugar breath; so sweet a bar
Should sunder such sweet friends. Here in her hairs
The painter plays the spider, and hath woven
A golden mesh t' entrap the hearts of men
Faster than gnats in cobwebs. But her eyes —
How could he see to do them? Having made one,
Methinks it should have power to steal both his,
And leave itself unfurnish'd.

Above In this self-portrait (1577), painted when he was 30 and working in France, Hilliard appears as a dandified courtier. It shows the influence of Jean Clouet, the leading painter at the Valois court. It is characteristic of Hilliard's miniatures in being circular, using minimal shading, having a cursive gold-leaf script in Latin, and in showing only the head and shoulders. Like most Tudor miniatures it is painted on vellum stuck to a playing card.

Left Sir Christopher Hatton (c. 1588) by Nicholas Hilliard. This is a rare example of a miniature showing the sitter at full length – in this case one of Elizabeth I's most important statesmen. It reveals a very poor grasp of perspective and because of this Hilliard soon abandoned the full-length, reverting to his successful formula of showing just head and shoulders. It is a fine example of the brilliant colors miniaturists could achieve.

Left Edward Herbert, 1st Baron Herbert of Cherbury (c. 1614) by Isaac Oliver. This is Oliver's most famous miniature and it is unusual in having the sitter set in a landscape. It is archaic for the time, recalling the romance of Elizabethan chivalry. Herbert poses as philosopher, poet, and knight-at-arms.

Above James I by Nicholas Hilliard. This is one of a large number of miniatures Hilliard painted of James I. Originally it would have been framed in a jeweled case for presentation by the sitter to a court favorite or foreign ambassador. It would have been worn as a pendant around the neck, breast or upper arm.

Left Anne of Cleves (1539) by Hans Holbein. Anne of Cleves was the fourth wife of Henry VIII. This portrait was painted when Holbein was sent abroad to paint Anne, who was then a prospective bride. The need to give the king an indication of the sitter's precise appearance explains the intensity of the image. This has a monumental quality quite distinct from the exquisite finesse of Hilliard's work.

expression with the foundation of The Society of Antiquaries in 1573.

Camden was researching the history of Britain during a remarkable period for literature in London. *The Chronicles of England, Scotland and Ireland* (1577) by Raphael Holinshed (d. 1580), later provided the principal source for Shakespeare's history plays. The translation of Plutarch's *Lives* (1579) by Sir Thomas North (c. 1535–c. 1601) stimulated a revival of interest in Italian literature. The finest expression of that revival came not in the epic, but in the pastoral – Edmund Spenser's *The Shepherd's Calendar* appeared in 1579, and Sir Philip Sidney's *Arcadia* in 1590. Spenser's *Faerie Queene*, which also appeared in 1590, was a popular romance set in the court of Gloriana, a thinly veiled and flattering allusion to the aged Queen Elizabeth. The literary output of Sir Philip Sidney (1554–86) and Edmund Spenser (c. 1552–99) had an immeasurable influence on the later development of the court masque by Ben Jonson and Inigo Jones – they collaborated on *The Masque of Blacknesse* (1605). Before then, London witnessed the first staging of plays by Marlowe and Shakespeare: Marlowe's *Tamburlaine* in 1587, and Shakespeare's *Richard III* in the early 1590s in the house of Sir Edward Hoby, the son of Castiglione's translator.

Shakespeare (1564–1616) is the greatest literary figure of the English Renaissance – a man described by Jonson as "not of an age but for all time". Shakespeare made an impact on the literary world of London in the early 1590s and soon established himself as a leading member of the Lord Chamberlain's Men, a company of actors who played at the Globe and Blackfriars theaters, and also at court. His poems *Venus and Adonis* and *The Rape of Lucrece* appeared at about that time, while his sonnets, largely composed during the late 1590s, appeared in print in 1609. His first Roman tragedy, *Titus Andronicus*, was performed in 1594 and *Two Gentlemen of Verona*, his first comedy, at the same time. The next six or seven years saw the appearance of his greatest works. *Hamlet* was probably first performed in about 1601, *Othello* in 1604, *King Lear* in 1605, and finally *The Tempest* in 1611. Shakespeare died in 1616, aged 52. His literary output was gathered together and published as the "First Folio" in 1623.

The last years of the reign of Elizabeth I were confident and expansive. The geographer Richard Hakluyt (c. 1552–1616) provided the epitaph to what had been the heroic era of English exploration, *The Principal Navigations of the English Nation* (1589). In music, philosophy and theology major works appeared during that last, golden decade of the Tudors. Thomas Morley (c. 1557–1602), the organist of St Paul's Cathedral, published his *Madrigals* in 1593, John Dowland (1563–1626) published his *First Book of English Airs* in 1597. Meanwhile the Anglican Church, which had been given permanent definition by the Elizabethan Church Settlement, received its finest expression in *Of the Laws of Ecclesiastical Politie* (1594) by Richard Hooker (c. 1554–1600). This was a persuasive and reasoned defense of the genius of Anglicanism as a system of belief that drew nourishment from Catholic and Puritan alike, while avoiding the extremes of both.

Science and commerce were intimately connected in the Elizabethan era. As England extended its markets through its explorations, a more rational approach to the pure and applied sciences began to express itself in

The English Theater

The English Renaissance reached its finest expression in literature, and particularly in drama, which was dominated by such figures as Christopher Marlowe, William Shakespeare, Ben Jonson and John Webster. In the early Renaissance, plays were performed by small companies of actors in the houses of the nobility or (under the control of the Lord Chamberlain) at court. In time, some of these companies – usually with the patronage of a nobleman – set up public playhouses. The first, built by the actor James Burbage, opened in 1576 in the London suburb of Shoreditch, far from the prying eyes of the court censors. The Rose opened in 1587 in Southwark, much nearer to the center of London life, and it was followed by the Swan (c. 1595) and the Globe (c. 1599), all within sight of each other. The Globe was the theater most often associated with Shakespeare. According to one tradition, *Hamlet* was once performed there with Shakespeare playing the role of the Ghost and Richard Burbage (the leading actor of his day and the son of James Burbage) playing Hamlet. The Globe could house over 2,000 people, and plays were seen by every social class, for admission was extremely cheap for those prepared to stand; those who could pay more sat in the galleries or even on the side of the stage. Performances were often crowded and boisterous – Southwark was famous for its bear-baiting pits and brothels as well as its theaters – but it is clear from the plays themselves that audiences were able to appreciate plays of great subtlety, wit and depth.

the foundation of educational establishments and the writings of philosophers. In the 1570s the entrepreneur and patron Sir Thomas Gresham (1519–79) founded Gresham's College, seen by some as a forerunner of the Royal Society. In 1605 Sir Francis Bacon (1561–1626), the most distinguished philosopher in England at the time, and later Lord Chancellor to James I, published *The Advancement of Learning*. In this he appealed for scientific endeavor to be based on the discovery of rational laws accessible to all. In *The Advancement of Learning* and his *The New Atlantis* (1627), which describes a Utopia established on scientific principles, Bacon foreshadowed the work of the great scientists and philosophers of the later Stuart period, including Newton, Boyle and Locke.

Scotland

Two great paintings stand as symbols of Scottish Renaissance culture of the 15th century, of which very little survives. The first is a fresco from the Pinturicchio cycle in the Piccolomini Library, Siena. It depicts the distinguished Italian humanist Enea Sylvio Piccolomini, later Pope Pius II, visiting James I of Scotland in 1435. James (1424–37) was a man of some culture. He had been a prisoner in England, where he had composed one of the most celebrated poem of the period *The Kingis Quair* (The King's Book). Written in a mixture of Scots and Chaucerian English, it describes his love of the English noblewoman who would become his bride.

The second painting, by the Flemish artist Hugo van der Goes, shows James III (1460–88) and his wife Margaret of Denmark. Their portraits appear separately on opposite wings of the mutilated *Trinity Altarpiece*, a triptych almost certainly commissioned by James himself. Not only did James commission great works of art, he also issued coinage bearing a Renaissance portrait. His tutor Archibald Whitelaw possessed editions of Lucan, Horace and Sallust. There are parallels between James III of Scotland and Henry VI of England: both were pious, bookish and keen to patronize the arts.

The reign of James IV (1488–1513) has been described as a "golden age". A Spanish visitor to Scotland, Pedro de Ayala, noted the brilliance of James IV, who was at ease with Latin, French, German, Flemish, Italian and Spanish. He also knew Gaelic and was the last Scottish king to master the old language of the remote north and west of the kingdom. He was passionately interested in education. In 1495 he founded Aberdeen University, the first in Britain to have a chair of medicine, and he was the moving force behind the foundation of The Royal College of Surgeons in Edinburgh in 1505. A royal charter of 1507 established the first Scottish printing press under Walter Chepman and Andrew Myllar at the Cowgate in Edinburgh. The earliest book to survive from this first printing press is a volume of poetry that includes poems by William Dunbar (c. 1460–c. 1530) and Robert Henryson (c. 1425–c. 1508), principal poets of the Scottish Renaissance. The high point of Renaissance splendor in Scotland was the wedding in 1503 of James IV to Margaret Tudor, daughter of Henry VII. From this union sprang the claim of the Scottish house of Stuart to the English crown. The festivities for the wedding would not be equaled in Scotland until the masque enacted at Stirling Castle to celebrate the baptism of James VI in 1566. The wedding is the subject of William Dunbar's

poem *The Thistle and the Rose*. But such a high point lasted only 10 years. At Flodden in 1513 the flower of the Scottish nobility was destroyed by the English. The battle of Flodden Field was the greatest cultural disaster in the history of Scotland. Although there was revival under James V, the promise of the court of James IV was never to be fulfilled.

James V (1513–42) came to the throne as a minor, and his short personal reign (1528–42) was not long enough to recreate a vigorous court culture. However, by his second marriage, to Mary of Guise in 1538 following his own visit to France in 1536–7, he strengthened those Scottish links with France which have come to be described as the "The Old Alliance". After this Scotland benefited greatly from its cultural links with France.

At home, James was the first to support George Buchanan, who would dominate Scottish learning toward the end of the century. A satirist who was much encouraged by James V was Sir David Lindsay (c. 1490–c. 1555), whose play *A Satire of the Three Estates*, first performed in 1540 at Linlithgow Palace, became one of the most popular statements of the anticlericalism that was then prevalen in Scotland. An important consequence of the visit James V made to France was that for the last four years of his reign he became the most active and inspired royal builder in the history of Scotland. Following upon the work of his father, who had given shape to the castles at Edinburgh and Stirling, he erected a number of ebullient and florid buildings. The best was the King's Range at Stirling Castle, which was influenced by the French royal chateau of Azay-le-Rideau. Stirling included the so-called "Stirling Heads", roundels depicting a mix of antique heroes and Renaissance courtiers and originally mounted on the ceiling of the King's Presence Chamber. By the end of the 16th century, the principal royal residences in Scotland were Linlithgow

Above Shakespeare from the frontispiece of the First Folio (1623). This is one of the best-known images of Shakespeare and it was much admired by the playwright Ben Jonson.

Top Macbeth and Banquo Meet the Witches, a woodcut from *The Chronicles of England, Scotland and Ireland* (1571) by Ralph Holinshed. Shakespeare drew heavily on Holinshed's *Chronicles*, at times using Holinshed's own words.

Left Henry Wriothesley, 3rd Earl of Southampton (1603) by John de Critz. The 3rd Earl of Southampton was Shakespeare's greatest patron, and the subject of some of his sonnets. This striking portrait was painted while he was imprisoned in the Tower of London for his part in the Essex Rebellion of 1599. Most writers – and theaters – needed the support of aristocratic patrons.

Far left The Swan theater. This sketch (c. 1596) by a Dutch visitor is the only surviving contemporary drawing of the interior of an Elizabethan theater.

Palace, Dunfermline (birthplace of Charles I, 1600), Edinburgh (Palace of Holyroodhouse, and Edinburgh Castle), Stirling Castle (birthplace of James VI of Scotland and I of England, 1566), and Falkland Palace. James died at Falkland Palace in December 1542 after the English inflicted a humiliating defeat on the Scots, this time on the Solway. He was succeeded by his daughter Mary, who was less than a week old.

Two things prevented the full flowering of the Renaissance in Scotland. First, because an exceptional number of monarchs came to the throne as children, the country was often governed by regents. Second, there were periodic invasions by the English. Henry VIII wanted his son Edward VI to be married to Mary Queen of Scots. But Mary's mother Mary of Guise, helped by Cardinal David Beaton, took her to France. Henry's response was to send the Earl of Hertford north in 1544 with instructions from the Privy Council to "put all to fire and sword...." The city was sacked a second time, three years later, by the Earl of Somerset, who inflicted another disastrous defeat on the Scots at Pinkie Cleugh.

Born in 1542, Mary Queen of Scots was entirely French by culture and upbringing. She assumed personal responsibility for her kingdom when she was eighteen. Between the death of her father and her assumption of sovereignty, she lived in France. In 1558 she married François, Dauphin of France, who succeeded his father Henry II in July 1559, only to die himself in December 1560. In August 1561 Mary returned to Scotland to play out her future as Queen. She reigned from 1561 to 1567.

Mary did not significantly influence the development of Scottish culture. She had patronized the great French poets Joachim du Bellay (1522–60) and Pierre de Ronsard (c. 1524–85), and had been painted by François Clouet (c. 1515–72). But such literature as was addressed to her in Edinburgh tended to be strident Protestant broadsides denouncing her for her Catholicism and her dulcet ways at Holyrood. There she refurbished rooms that still survive as important examples of a Scottish Renaissance interior. However, with battle lines drawn up between Catholic and Protestant, by the time she assumed sovereignty more buildings had been destroyed than embellished, with houses and castles ransacked, and churches pilaged. The cultural high point of Mary's reign came with the masque enacted at Stirling Castle following the birth of her son, James VI, in the winter of 1566. The festivities reflected much of the sophistication of the French court. Allegories in praise of the Stuart monarchy anticipated the propaganda that would later be employed to bolster the Elizabethan regime in England.

As the grand-daughter of Henry VII, Mary was a claimant to the English throne in the event of Elizabeth dying childless. When Mary married Lord Darnley, and gave birth to the future James VI of Scotland, her claims became pressing and she herself the focus of disaffection against Elizabeth. Mary began to lose control. She lacked decisiveness when presented with a warring and factious nobility, and her difficulties were aggravated by the domination in Scotland of John Knox (c. 1513–72), an extreme Calvinist who grudgingly conceded her intelligence, even her charm, while vilifying her for how she lived and what she believed. Her marriage to Darnley, a turbulent and scandalous character, did nothing for her standing. In 1566 Darnley was assassinated – blown up by the Earl of Bothwell, possibly with the connivance of Mary

Previous page A portrait of James I by Daniel Mytens (1621). In 1603 the Scottish Stuart dynasty succeeded that of the Tudors, James uniting the two crowns as James VI of Scotland and James I of England. Here James appears in his robes as a Knight of the Garter, the oldest English chivalric order. With the passing of the Tudor dynasty, the Renaissance in England was rapidly drawing to a close.

Below The execution of Mary Queen of Scots, 1587. This vivid Dutch drawing is evidence of the fierce international controversy that followed the execution of the Scottish queen by her English cousin, Elizabeth I. Within months of the event prints were being circulated claiming to show the execution in detail. This drawing was probably a preliminary drawing for such a print.

Above Glamis Castle, Angus, Scotland. Glamis, made famous by Shakespeare in his play *Macbeth*, is the most splendid example of that peculiarly Scottish contribution to the Renaissance in Britain, the fortified tower house. A richly turreted skyline became characteristic of the Renaissance palace in Scotland.

herself. Mary then married Bothwell and had to abdicate, largely because of the disreputable character of Bothwell, and the jealousy his marriage provoked among the Scottish nobility. Bothwell attempted to place her back on the throne, but his army was defeated at Langside in 1568. She was forced to flee to England and throw herself on the mercy of her embarrassed cousin, Elizabeth, who imprisoned her. Mary's position became hazardous with the rising of the Northern Earls in 1569, when an attempt was made to depose Elizabeth and replace her with Mary. Two years later the Ridolfi plot was discovered. This had centered on an attempt by the catholic Duke of Norfolk, a powerful member of the English aristocracy, to become her fourth husband. Mary's position finally become hopeless with the failure of the Babington plot, which had involved the assassinating Elizabeth. The degree to which Mary was a party to

these conspiracies has long exercised historians and inspired poets. But for Elizabeth and her secretary, Lord Burleigh, the time to act had arrived. In February 1587 Mary was executed at Fotheringhay Castle in Northamptonshire. So passed the greatest threat to Protestantism in England.

After years of instability in Scotland due to the void left by the abdication of Mary, a more settled pattern of life began to be established after James VI assumed personal government in 1578. James had been given a rigorous but masterly Protestant education at the hands of George Buchanan, friend of Roger Ascham, and sometime professor at universities in Europe as far afield as Bordeaux and Coimbra. It was through his influence that James himself wrote poetry and political theory. In 1599 James published *Basilikon Doron*, an important and influential book on the education of princes.

New Colleges

The universities of both Oxford and Cambridge benefited from new college foundations during the Renaissance. The most ambitious were Christ Church in Oxford (initially called Cardinal College), founded by Cardinal Wolsey in 1525, and Trinity College, Cambridge, founded by Henry VIII in 1546. At Oxford, Corpus Christi (1517) was set up with a curriculum based upon Latin, Greek and Divinity, and with encouragement to look to Italy for the best teachers. Many Oxford scholars obtained positions at the courts of Italian city-states; others made important contributions to the cultural revolution brought about by the printing houses of Europe. At Cambridge, St John's (1511) became renowned throughout Europe when Erasmus joined the college. By the reign of Elizabeth it was normal for statesmen to have been educated at Oxford or Cambridge – a revolution in social attitudes within the ruling class.

New disciplines were encouraged: the historian William Camden established a professorship of "civil history" at Oxford in 1622. Oxford remained in tune with the court while Cambridge became radicalized. The Puritan Sir Walter Mildmay had founded Emmanuel College in Cambridge in 1584 because the Puritans at the university opposed the established Anglican Church. Oxford became the headquarters of Charles I during the Civil War, Cambridge one of the staunchest supporters of Oliver Cromwell.

Right An anonymous portrait of Cardinal Wolsey, painted on panel. It is the most famous likeness, revealing the heavy features of the cardinal wearing his robes as a prince of the Church.

Below Christ Church, Oxford. Cardinal Wolsey had only four years to build his new college before he was disgraced by Henry VIII in 1529. He finished most of the great quadrangle, which he had wanted cloistered, the hall, and the lower part of the main gate, later completed by Sir Christopher Wren.

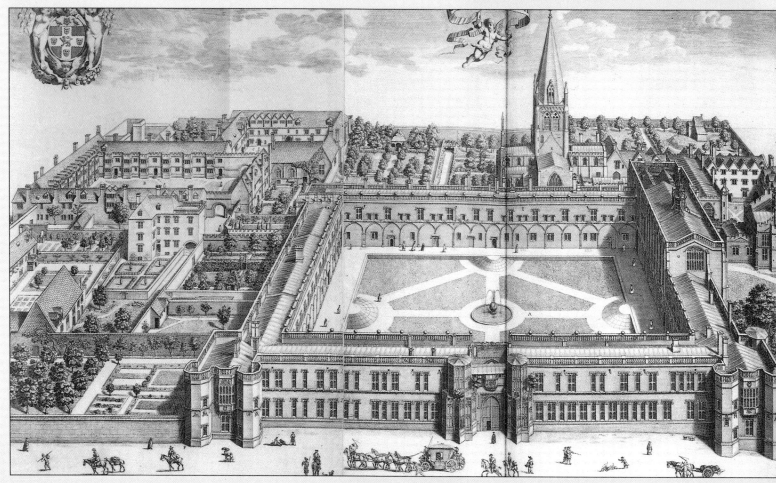

Below A woodcut taken from a manual on astronomy published in Oxford in 1519. It symbolizes a new sophistication in the curriculum of Oxford and Cambridge by the early 16th century. Mathematics, astronomy, map-making and ancient philosophy were challenging the old dominance of theology.

Right Gate of Virtue, Gonville and Caius College, Cambridge. Dr John Caius, a distinguished English doctor who had worked with Vesalius at Padua, refounded Gonville College in 1557. He designed the Gates of Humility, Virtue and Honour to signify the three stages of a university education.

Above Cardinal John Fisher by Hans Holbein. Fisher, a close friend of Erasmus, was the greatest Cambridge humanist of the Renaissance. He was the only English bishop to denounce the divorce of Henry VIII and Catherine of Aragon and for this he was beheaded in 1535.

Right The Schools Quad, Bodleian Library, Oxford. The Bodleian Library, was founded in 1598 by the scholar-diplomat Sir Thomas Bodley. The quadrangle has doorways on all sides with the names of the various "schools" to which they give access.

Buchanan (1506–82) was the most influential figure in late 16th-century Scottish culture. Distinguished as an educationalist, he has been described as "far and away the finest Latin poet in Europe". Buchanan saw to important reforms at St Andrews University. But he died in 1582, as his protégé, James VI, inspired by Buchanan's belief in humanist education, granted a charter to the "town's college" in Edinburgh, an action that encouraged the establishment of a university. One of the great early benefactors of Edinburgh University was William Drummond of Hawthornden (1585–1649). Drummond was the outstanding poet of the Scottish Renaissance and celebrated for his satires, a genre that was one of the peculiar strengths of Scottish writers.

Prestongrange, the first of the great painted ceilings of Scotland, was finished in 1581. For the next five decades there was continuous embellishment of both town houses such as Culross Palace in Fife, and tower-houses such as Craigston Castle. The last significant painted ceiling in Scotland, Skelmorlie Aisle at Largs, was painted in 1638. When religious differences between Scotland and England led to war, this most vigorous and colorful – and much neglected – aspect of the Scottish Renaissance died out. Many of these ceilings, depicting either the virtues or the arms and crests of the owners, were inspired by Renaissance emblem books such as Geoffrey Whitney's *Choice of Emblems* (1586).

The Stuarts came to the English throne in the person of the peace-loving James VI of Scotland: he became James I of England at the death of Elizabeth I in 1603 because of his direct descent from Margaret Tudor,

sister of Henry VII of England. This change of dynasty resulted in much more contact with Europe than had been possible in the embattled times of Henry VIII and of Elizabeth. James's wife, Anne of Denmark, came from a highly sophisticated court in northern Europe. After years of isolation men were encouraged to travel again. Both Inigo Jones and the composer Dowland worked for a time in Denmark, and the style of Jones was formed by his contact with Italy.

Jones (1573–1652), the first great Renaissance architect in England, began to design buildings for the Cecil family about 1607. His travels in Italy with the Earl of Arundel in 1613–14 was both a revival of English humanist practice, as it had existed before the break with Rome, and an anticipation of the Grand Tour. During his travels in Italy Jones became familiar with the architecture of Andrea Palladio, which strongly influenced him. He was the royal architect from 1615 to 1642 (the outbreak of the English Civil War). Among his finest works are the Queen's House, Greenwich (begun 1616), the Banqueting House, Whitehall, London (1619–22) and the Double Cube Room at Wilton House (1649–52). The influence of the neo-classicism of Jones would in time dominate British architecture.

The British East India Company was formed in 1600. Shakespeare died in 1616 and the First Folio appeared in 1623. The Renaissance in Britain drew to a close when the art-loving Charles I came to the throne in May 1625. Charles was not a Renaissance monarch, but he shares with Henry VIII the distinction of being the most magnificent patron of culture in early modern Britain.

Above The Queen's House, Greenwich, designed by Inigo Jones in 1616 but not completed until 1635, was the first English building in the classical style. At Greenwich the park and the gardens were separated by a public road. Jones therefore built the house as two blocks, one in the park and the other in the garden, the two connected by a covered bridge. In the 1660s the two blocks were joined to form a single building. The colonnades on either side of the house, following the line of the former road, were added in the 19th century. Jones, the finest architect of the English Renaissance, drew heavily on Italian designs, particularly those of Palladio. The neo-classical style he fashioned from these sources was to exert a profound influence on British architecture.

LIST OF CONTRIBUTORS

C.F. Black, Lecturer at the Department of Modern History, University of Glasgow, has written on the High Renaissance.

Dr Richard Goy, chartered architect and architectural historian, has contributed on the Venice Arsenal.

Dr Mark Greengrass, lecturer in the Department of History, University of Sheffield, has written on the French Renaissance.

Dr David Howarth, of the Department of Fine Art, University of Edinburgh, has written on the Renaissance in England and Scotland.

Dr Gordon Kinder, of the Department of Spanish and Portuguese Studies, University of Manchester (retired) has contributed on aspects of the Renaissance in Spain.

Dr Jeremy Lawrance, of the Department of Spanish and Portuguese Studies, University of Manchester, has written on the Renaissance in Spain and Portugal.

Dr Richard Mackenney, of the Department of History, University of Edinburgh, has written on the Diffusion of the Renaissance.

Linda Proud, writer and researcher, has written on various aspects of Renaissance learning.

Dr Martin Rady, of the School of Slavonic and East European Studies, University of London, has written on the meaning of Renaissance, and the Renaissance in Germany and the Low Countries.

Angela Voss, astrologer and musician, has contributed on Renaissance music.

Dr Evelyn Welch, of Birkbeck College, University of London, has contributed text and photographic captions on the Early Italian Renaissance and the Classical Renaissance.

CONSULTANT

Professor Nicholas Mann, Director of The Warburg Institute, University of London, has contributed a Foreword.

LIST OF ILLUSTRATIONS

Abbreviations: t = top, tl = top left, tr = top right, c = center, b = bottom etc.

BAL = Bridgeman Art Library, London; JF = John Fuller; M = Erich Lessing, Magnum, London; S = Scala, Florence.

Endpapers: World map by Mercator (Mary Evans Picture Library, London).

1–7 *Primavera*, 1478, and *Birth of Venus*, 1485, tempera on panel by Botticelli: Uffizi, Florence (S).
8–9 artwork: JF
13 Borgia emblem, ceiling decoration, stucco: Borgia apartments, Vatican (S).
14 *Procession of the Magi* detail showing Lorenzo de' Medici, fresco by Gozzoli, c.1460: Palazzo Medici-Riccardi, Florence (S).
17 *St. Augustine teaching rhetoric and philosophy,* fresco by Gozzoli: San Agostino, San Gimignano (S).
18 *Arnolfini Marriage*, oil painting by Jan van Eyck: National Gallery, London (BAL).
19 Medallion portrait of Giovanni Pico della Mirandola: JF.
19 tr *The Appearance of the Angel to Zaccharia,* detail showing portraits of Marsilio Ficino, Cristoforo Landino, Angelo Poliziano and Gentile de Becchi fresco by Ghirlandaio: Santa Maria Novella, Florence (S).
20 *Primavera*, fresco by Botticelli, 1478: Uffizi, Florence (S).
21 Panoramic plan of Genoa by A. Danti: Gallery of Maps, Vatican (S).
23 *Arianna abbandonata*, detail, by Gerolamo del Pacchia: Collection Chigi Saracini, Siena (S).
25 *Portrait of a lady*, oil painting by Robert Campin c.1430: National Gallery, London.
26 c Apollo Belvedere, marble, Greek: Vatican Museum, Rome.
26 bl Tazza Farnese, *Fertility of Egypt,* Graeco-Egyptian, sardonyx: Museo Nazionale, Naples.
26 br *Birth of Venus*, tempera on panel by Botticelli, 1485: Uffizi, Florence (S).
26–27 *Taddeo Zuccari copying antique statues in Rome,* drawing by Federico Zuccari: Gabinetto dei Disegni e delle Stampe, Uffizi, Florence (S).
27 bl *St. James before Herod* by Mantegna, 1454: previously in Eremitania, Padua, but destroyed (Mansell Collection, London).
27 br Petrarch's copy of Virgil, painted by Simone Martini: Biblioteca Ambrosiana, Milan (S).
29 San Gimignano: Zefa Ltd, London.
30 Corso Donati, the day of Calendimaggio, detail from contemporary manuscript: Biblioteca Nazionale, Florence (Arnoldo Mondadori s.p.a.).
31 Campo, Siena: Kina Italia, Milan.
32 tr *St Bernardino of Siena preaching in the Campo*, by Sano di Pietro: Cathedral, Siena (S).
32 bl Palazzo Pubblico, Siena: S.
32–33 b *Maesta* by Simone Martini: Palazzo Pubblico, Siena (S).
35 Florence at dusk: Zefa, London.
36–37 *Massacre of the Innocents*, detail from Pistoia pulpit by Giovanni Pisano: Sant' Andrea, Pistoia 1297–1301 (S).
37 b *Maesta*, detail of the Virgin Mary, by Duccio: Cathedral, Siena (S).
38 *Good Government*, fresco by Lorenzetti, 1339, detail: Palazzo Pubblico, Siena (S).
39 *The death of St Francis of Assisi*, fresco by Giotto c. 1315–20: Bardi chapel, Santa Croce, Florence (S).
40–41 Illustration from Boccaccio's *Decameron*,

14th century: Bibliotheque Nationale, Paris, Italian 482, fol. 4v.
42–43 *Dante standing before the city of Florence*, fresco by Domenico di Michelino, 1465: Cathedral, Florence (S).
44 Portinari altarpiece, oil painting by Hugo van der Goes: (BAL).
45 *Deposition*, oil painting by Fra Angelico: (S).
46tr *Flight into Egypt*, fresco by Giotto: Arena Chapel, Padua (S).
47 Arena Chapel, Padua: S.
48 *Sir John Hawkwood*, fresco by Uccello, 1436: Cathedral, Florence (S).
48 Medallion of Sigismondo Malatesta by Pisanello, c. 1445: JF.
50 *The meeting of Solomon and Sheba*, fresco by Piero della Francesca, 1452: San Francesco, Arezzo (S).
51 Medallion self-portrait by Leon Battista Alberti: JF.
51 tr Malatesta temple, 1450–62: Rimini (Mansell Collection).
52 cl Poggio Bracciolini, from MS Urb. lat. 224 fol. 2r: Biblioteca Apostolica Vaticana.
52 t A page from Petrarch's copy of Horace, Plut. 34.1: Biblioteca Medicea Laurenziana, Florence.
53 *Saint Jerome*, detail of fresco by Ghirlandaio: Chiesa di Ognissanti, Florence (S).
54 tl *Dialogues of Plato* translated by Marsilio Ficino, titlepage, Plut. 82.6, c.1: Biblioteca Medicea Laurenziana, Florence (Photo Pineider).
54 tr *Judith and Holofernes*, sculpture by Donatello, 1457: Piazza della Signoria, Florence (S).
54 b *Annunciation* by Fra Filippo Lippi, 1448–50: National Gallery, London.
55 tl Photo of the Palazzo Medici, 1444: Alinari Archives, Florence.
55 b Cosimo de' Medici, marble relief portrait by Verrocchio c. 1464: Andromeda archive.
56 Lorenzo de' Medici, terracotta bust by Verrocchio: Alinari Archives, Florence.
57 Medals commemorating Pazzi conspiracy, by Bertoldo di Giovanni: JF.
57 b Poliziano and the Medici children, detail from *Life of St Francis*, fresco by Ghirlandaio: Sassetti chapel, Santa Trinita, Florence (S).
59 *Parnassus* by Mantegna: Louvre, Paris (S).
60–61 *Scene from the life of Enea Silvano*, fresco by Pinturricchio, 1508: Piccolomini Library, Siena Cathedral (S).
62 *Adoration of the Magi*, fresco by Fra Angelico, 1438–45: Cosimo's cell at San Marco, Florence (S).
64 *Zuccone* by Donatello: Museo dell' Opera del Duomo, Florence (S).
65 t *Holy Trinity* by Masaccio: Cathedral, Florence (S).
65 b *The Tribute Money* fresco by Masaccio c. 1424–25: Brancacci chapel, Church of the Carmines, Florence (S).
67 *The dream of St Ursula*, from *The Legend of St Ursula*, fresco by Carpaccio, 1490–95: Accademia, Venice (S).
68 *The Gonzaga family and court* by Mantegna, 1472: Camera degli Sposi, Palazzo Ducale, Mantua (S).
69–70 Diagrams by John Brennan, Oxford.
69 br Perspective drawing of a chalice by Uccello, c. 1430: Uffizi, Gabinetto dei Disegni e delle Stampe (S).
70 l A Music Teacher, woodcut from *Regule Florum Musices* by Petrus de Canuntus, 1510: Andromeda archive.

70 tc Plan of a church with the figure of a man, drawing by Francesco di Giorgio: Biblioteca Nazionale, Florence Andromeda archive).
70 r Pazzi chapel, drawing by Dick Barnard, London.
72 t *Federico and Guidobaldo da Montefeltro*, oil painting by Justus of Ghent or Pedro Berruguete: Galleria Nazionale, Urbino (S).
72 b *Flagellation*, oil painting on wood panel by Piero della Francesca: Palazzo Ducale, Urbino (S).
73 t Photo of Federico's studiolo: Palazzo Ducale, Urbino (M).
73 bl *Calumny of Apelles*, majolica dish by Nicola da Urbino, Urbino c. 1520: Ashmolean Museum, Oxford.
73 br *Baldassare Castiglione*, oil painting by Raphael: Louvre, Paris (S).
74–75 Map of Florence c. 1480: Museo di Firenze Com'era, Florence (S).
76 Siege of Padua from *Li Successi Bellici* by Niccolo degli Agostini, 1521: Andromeda archive.
80 *Madonna with the Yarn-Winder*, oil painting by Leonardo, c.1501: Collection of the Duke of Buccleuch, KT, Drumlanrig Castle, Dumfriesshire, Scotland (National Gallery, London).
81 l *David*, marble sculpture by Michelangelo, 1501–4: Galleria dell'Accademia, Florence (S).
81 r Terracotta bust of Machiavelli: Palazzo Vecchio, Florence (S).
82 *Luca Pacioli*, oil painting by Jacopo de' Barbari, c.1495: Museo di Capodimonte, Naples (S).
83 *Lady with an Ermine*, oil painting by Leonardo, c.1483: Czartorisky Museum, Cracow (S).
84 l *Pope Leo X and Cardinals Luigi de' Rossi and Giulio de' Medici*, c.1518: Uffizi, Florence (S).
84 r Medallion of Michelangelo 1560–1: JF.
85 *Pietà*, marble sculpture by Michelangelo, 1497–1500: Vatican Museums.
86 The Sistine ceiling, frescoes by Michelangelo: Vatican Museums.
88 View from Piazza San Marco, Venice: Zefa, London.
89 *Portrait of a lady*, oil painting by Lorenzo Lotto, c.1533: National Gallery, London.
90 *Bacchus and Ariadne*, oil painting by Titian, 1523: National Gallery, London.
92 bl St Peter's from the Vatican gardens: Fred Mayer/M.
92 br Pope Sixtus V, frontispiece to *Invicti quinarii numeri series quae summatim a superioribus pontificibus et maxime a Sixto Quinto res praeclare quadrienni gestas ecc.* of Giovanni Pinadelli, Romae 1589: British Library.
92–93 t Campidoglio: Photo by Edwin Smith.
93 b Map of Rome by A. Danti, 16th century: Gallery of Maps, Vatican (S).
94 Medallion of Clement VII by Cellini: Museo Nazionale, Bargello, Florence JF.
97 Stairs designed by Michelangelo: Laurentian Library, Florence (S).
98 *Cosimo I*, bronze bust by Cellini, 1545: Museo Nazionale, Bargello, Florence (S).
99 *Feast at the House of Levi*, oil painting by Veronese, 1573: Gallerie dell'Accademia, Venice (S).
100 t *Temple facade surviving in Assisi*, drawing by Palladio: Royal Institute of British Architects, London.
100 b Villa Rotunda, Vicenza, by Palladio: M.
101 t Villa Barbaro di Maser, Treviso, by Palladio: S.
101 br Teatro Olimpico, Vicenza, by Palladio: M.

102 l *Star of Bethlehem*, drawing by Leonardo: by gracious permission of HM Queen Elizabeth II, Royal Library, Windsor Castle.

102 r *Sketches of cats*, drawing by Leonardo: by gracious permission of HM Queen Elizabeth II, Royal Library, Windsor Castle.

103 tl *The larynx, trachea, and muscles of the left leg*, drawing by Leonardo: by gracious permission of HM Queen Elizabeth II, Royal Library, Windsor Castle.

103 tr *Study of horse*, drawing by Leonardo: Gabinetto dei Disegni e delle Stampe, Uffizi, Florence (S).

103 br *Landscape*, drawing by Leonardo: Gabinetto dei Disegni e delle Stampe, Uffizi, Florence (S).

104 t Effigy of Lady Margaret Beaufort by Torrigiano: Westminster Abbey, London.

104 b Medal of Cecilia Gonzaga by Pisanello, 1447: Victoria and Albert Museum, London JF.

105 tl Margaret Roper, detail from *Thomas More and his family*, after Holbein: National Portrait Gallery, London.

105 tr Marguerite of Navarre, mss illuminated by Robinet Testard showing her playing chess, c.1504, from *Livres des Echecs Amoureaux*, 1504: Bibliotheque Nationale, Paris.

105 cr Medal of Vittoria Colonna, anonymous, c. 1533: Kunsthistorisches Museum, Vienna JF.

105 bl Correspondence between Isabella d'Este and Cesare Borgia: M.

106 *The Ambassadors*, oil painting by Holbein, detail: National Gallery, London (BAL)

107 Catalan map c. 1450–60: Biblioteca Estense, Modena (S).

109 World map drawn in a fool's head, c. 1590: Bibliotheque Nationale, Paris.

112 *Salvator Mundi*, oil painting by Antonello da Messina, 1465: National Gallery, London.

113 *Procession of the True Cross*, oil painting by Gentile Bellini, 1496: Accademia Venezia (S).

114 t *Doge Andrea Gritti*, oil on canvas by Titian, c. 1535: Samuel H. Kress Collection, (c) National Gallery of Art, Washington.

114 b *Sacred and Profane Love*, oil painting by Titian, c. 1515: Galleria Borghese, Rome (S).

116 tc Page from *Hypnerotomachia Poliphili*, 1499: Biblioteca Marciana, Venice (S).

116 tr Medal of Aldus Manutius: Victoria and Albert Museum, London JF.

116 c Page from *Psalterium graecum*, Venice c. 1497: Biblioteca Marciana, Venice (S).

116 bl Aldine pressmark: Andromeda archive.

116–7 b Reconstruction of the Aldine printing shop: (M).

117 t *Death and the printers*, Lyon, 1499: Andromeda archive.

118 *Charles V on horseback*, oil painting by Titian, 1533: Prado, Madrid (BAL).

118 Anatomical drawing by Vesalius: Andromeda archive.

120 t Venice Arsenal: Chris Donahue, Oxford.

121 *Panoramic view of Venice*, by A. Danti: Gallery of Maps, Vatican (S).

120 b *The leave-taking of the betrothed* from *The Legend of St Ursula*, fresco by Carpaccio, 1490–95: Accademia, Venice (S).

124 t Columbus's ship, *Santa Maria*, woodcut from his letter printed in Basel, 1494, after the second voyage: Bibliotheque Nationale, Paris, Reserve Imprimes.

124 b *Battle of Lepanto*, oil painting by unknown artist, 16th century: National Maritime Museum, London.

126–7 Map by Willem Blaeu: British Museum, London (photo Derek Bayes).

128 bl Detail from the Ghent Altarpiece by Jan van Eyck: S.

128 tr 'Le Benedictus', an excerpt from Mouton's 'Messe d'Allemaigne', *Viginti Missarum Musicalium* printed by Pierre Attaignant, 1532: Boston Athenaeum.

128 br *Music Party*, painting by Lorenzo Costa: National Gallery, London (BAL).

129 *Pastoral concert* by Unbekannter Meister, 16th century: Musee du Berry, Bourges (BAL).

129 br Title page woodcut from *Viginti Missarum Musicalium* printed by Pierre Attaignant, 1532: Boston Athenaeum.

130–1 *The Sense of Hearing*, oil painting by Jan Velvet Brueghel: Prado, Madrid (S).

132 tl *Sole*, Table VIII from *De Sphaera Estense*, 15th century: Biblioteca Estense, Modena.

133 tl *Hermes Trismegistus with armillary sphere*, fresco by Pinturicchio, 15th century: Borgia apartments, Vatican.

133 tr Terrestrial globe by Martin Behaim, 1492: Germanisches Nationalmuseum, Nuremberg.

133 cl Diagram of the universe from *On the Revolution of the Celestial Spheres* by Copernicus, 1543: Bodleian Library, Oxford.

133 cr Portrait of Galileo, chalk drawing by Ottavio Leone: Biblioteca Marucelliana, Florence (S).

132 b Music of the spheres from *Harmony of the World* by Kepler, 1619: Bodleian Library, Oxford.

133 br Man and zodiacal influence, from *Kalender* by Guy Marchant: Cambridge University Library.

134 l Horse of San Marco: M.

134 br The taking of Constantinople by the Turks, 22 April 1453, from *Voyage d'Outremer* by Bertrand de la Broquiere, MS fr. 9087 f. 207: Bibliotheque Nationale, Paris (Sonia Halliday Photographs).

135 t *Venetian embassy in the east* by Bellini: Louvre, Paris (M).

135 b Suleyman riding to the Friday prayer, anonymous woodcut in 9 sheets published/engraved by Domenico de' Franceschi, c.1563: British Museum, London.

136 *Country of Cockaigne* by Bruegel, Pieter the Elder, 1567: Alte Pinakothek, Munich (S).

137 Woodcut of Deventer: Andromeda archive.

138 *The Stag Hunt* by Lucas Cranach the Elder, 1544: Prado, Madrid (S).

139 Bible of King Matthias Corvinus, Laur. Plut. 15, 17 f. 2r: Biblioteca Medicea Laurenziana, Florence (Photo Pineider).

141 Medallion of Willibald Pirkheimer designed by Durer: JF.

142–3 *Triumphus Doctoris Reuchlin*, Hagenau 1518: Archiv fur Kunst und Geschichte, Berlin.

144 t The Cabalist Alchemist from *Amphitheater of Eternal Wisdom* by H. Khunrath, 1609: Bodleian Library, Oxford.

144 b Alchemy and Geometry from *Atalanta Fugiens* by Michael Maier, 1618: Bodleian Library, Oxford.

145 t The Cave of the Illuminati from *Amphitheater of Eternal Wisdom* by H. Khunrath, 1609: Bodleian Library, Oxford.

145 b Frederick V and Princess Elizabeth, engraving, 16th century: Ashmolean Museum, Oxford.

146 Erasmus doodle: Offentliche Bibliothek der Universitat, Basel.

147 b Portrait of Erasmus by Holbein: Louvre, Paris (S).

147 t Frontispiece to Froben's edition of the *Adagia* of Erasmus, 1523: Bodleian Library, Oxford

148–9 t *Luther preaching against the Pope*, woodcut by Cranach, c. 1545: Kupferstichkabinett, Berlin.

148 bl Portrait of Luther by Cranach: Germanisches Nationalmuseum, Nuremberg (S).

148 br Title of the *New Testament* translated into German by Martin Luther, Wittenberg, 1522: Andromeda archive.

149 br *Luther with seven heads*, woodcut from *Lutherus septiceps* by Johannes Cochlaus, 1529: Andromeda archive.

150 Self-portrait, oil painting by Durer, 1500: Alte Pinakothek, Munich (Artothek).

152 *Portrait of a woman* by Lucas Cranach the Elder, 1526: Hermitage Museum, St Petersburg (S).

153 *St George and the Dragon*, oil painting by Altdorfer, 1525: Alte Pinakothek, Munich (S).

155 l Portrait of Melancthon by Lucas Cranach the Elder: Uffizi, Florence (S).

155 *Massacre of the Innocents* by Bruegel, Pieter the Elder, 1565–7: by gracious permission of HM Queen Elizabeth II, Royal Collection, Hampton Court.

156–7 b Alchemical treatise from ms. Voss. Chym. Q.51, f. 6v-7r: Universiteitsbibliotheek, Leiden.

157 *Portrait of Rudolf II as Vertumnus* by Arcimboldo, 1590: Skoklosters Slott, Stockholm.

158–9 Ghent Altarpiece, oil on wood, Jan and Hubert van Eyck, 1432: St Bavo Cathedral, Ghent (photo Paul M. R. Maeyeart).

158 bl *Man in a red turban*, oil on wood by Jan van Eyck, 1433: National Gallery, London.

160 *The Lime Tree*, woodcut from *Kreuter Buch* by Hieronymous Bock, Strasbourg, 1551: Plant Sciences Library, Oxford University.

160–161 Artwork of wood-sculptures: JF.

162 tr *Temptation of St Anthony*, wood engraving after Schongauer, c. 1485: Ashmolean Museum, Oxford.

162 bl *Christ ascendant* from the *Isenheim altarpiece* by Gruenwald c. 1512–15: Unterlinden Museum, Colmar, France (BAL).

162 br *Temptation of St Anthony*, oil painting by Bosch, detail: Museu d'Art Ancien, Lisbon (BAL).

163 r *Melancolia* wood engraving by Durer, 1514: Guildhall Library, London (BAL).

164 tr Constable Anne de Montmorency, enamel by Limousin: Louvre, Paris.

164 bl *Francis I meets Julius Caesar* from *Commentaries on Caesar's Gallic Wars* by Godefroy le Batave, ms fr. 13429 f. 5v: Bibliotheque Nationale, Paris.

164 br Medallion of Francis I celebrating victory at Marignano: Bibliotheque Nationale, Paris JF.

166 *Francis I receiving Charles V and Cardinal Alessandro Farnese at Paris* by Taddeo Zuccari: Palazzo Farnese, Rome (S).

168 Chateau Chambord: Robert Harding Picture Library, London.

169 Chambord staircase: Olive Smith, Saffron Walden, Essex (photo Edwin Smith).

170 Château Chenonceaux: Robert Harding Picture Library, London.

171 Blois staircase: A. F. Kersting, London.

172 Fresco in the bedroom of Mme d'Etampes by Primaticcio: Robert Harding Picture Library, London.

172 c Amboise Pare, wood engraving: Hulton Picture Company, London.
173 tr Portrait of Bude by Jean Clouet, c. 1536: Metropolitan Museum of Art, New York.
174 *Allegory of Water and Love*, School of Fontainebleau, 16th century: Louvre, Paris (Giraudon).
175 t Frontispiece of *Pantagruel and Gargantua* by Rabelais, woodcut, Valence edition, 1547: Bodleian Library, Oxford.
175 b Woodcut illustration from *Pantagruel and Gargantua* by Rabelais, Valence edition, 1547: Bodleian Library, Oxford.
178–9 *St Bartholomew's Day Massacre* by Francois Dubois: Musee Cantonal des Beaux-Arts, Lausanne (Andre Held).
178 t Portrait of Catherine de Médicis, miniature by Francois Clouet: Victoria and Albert Museum, London (BAL).
178 c Portrait of Montaigne, anonymous, 16th century: Musee Conde, Chantilly (Giraudon).
180 t Salt cellar, gold, by Cellini: M.
180 b Fontainebleau stairs: Robert Harding Picture Library, London.
181 tl *Allegory of Venus, Cupid, Folly and Time* by Bronzino, c. 1546: National Gallery, London (BAL).
181 tr *Francis I being presented with a translation of the first three books of Diodorus of Sicily by Anthony Macault*, c. 1530: Musee Conde, Chantilly (Giraudon/BAL).
181 br *St Michael* by Raphael, 1518: Louvre, Paris (Giraudon/BAL).
182–3 Polish ambassadors, Valois tapestry: Louvre, Paris (S).
183 tr Court Ball, anonymous, 16th century: Louvre, Paris.
183 br Tournament, Valois tapestry: Louvre, Paris (S).
185 d Ferdinand and Isabella, illuminated initial from a manuscript of 1484: University of Valladolid Library (MAS).
186 Portrait of Henry the Navigator by Goncalves: Museu Nacional de Arte Antiga, Lisbon (MAS).
187 *Lopez de Mendoza, Marquis of Santillana* by the Master of Sopetran, from the Sopetran reredos: Prado Museum, Madrid (MAS).
188 t Facade of Salamanca University: AGE Fotostock, Barcelona.
188 b Title page of Nebrija's *Latin Introductions*, edition of 1510: Andromeda archive.
190 Frontispiece to *Amadis of Gaule*, Seville, 1509: Andromeda archive.
191 Aqueduct of Segovia: AGE Fotostock, Barcelona.
192–3 *Virgin of the Catholic Monarchs* by Michael Sittow, c. 1490: Prado, Madrid (MAS).
194–5 *Auto da Fe* by Pedro Berruguete: Prado, Madrid (S).

195 tr Complutensian Polyglot Bible: Bibliotheque Nationale, Paris.
195 b Cardinal Cisneros by Juan de Borgona: MAS.
196 t *Adoration of the Name of Jesus* by El Greco: Escorial, Madrid (S).
196 bl Portrait of Philip II by Titian: Galleria Barberini, Rome (S).
197 *The Duke of Alba overcoming Philip II's enemies*, anonymous polychrome wooden statue: Palacio de Lina, Madrid (MAS).
198 Charles V Palace, Alhambra: AGE Fotostock, Barcelona.
199 *Ferdinand and Isabella receiving author's work*, woodcut, 1502: Andromeda archive.
201 t *Civitates Orbis L'Escorial* by Braun: Biblioteca Nazionale, Florence (S).
201 c Monument of Charles V: Escorial, Madrid (S).
201 *Burial of Count Orgaz* by El Greco, 1568–88: Toledo, S. Tome (BAL).
202 b Batalha Monastery, Portugal: Robert Harding Picture Library, London.
203 tl Patio of the College of San Gregorio: AGE Fotostock, Barcelona.
203 tr University facade, medallion of Ferdinand and Isabella, Salamanca: AGE Fotostock, Barcelona.
203 b Patio of the Archbishop's Palace, Alcala de Henares: MAS.
204 Presentation copy of *Epigrams* by Thomas More, c. 1509, Cotton MS Titus D IV: British Library, London.
205 *The Frog and the Ox*, woodcut from *Aesop's Fables*, translated and printed by Caxton, 1484: British Library, London.
206 t Portrait of John Colet, drawing by Holbein: by gracious permission of HM Queen Elizabeth II, Royal Library, Windsor Castle.
206 b Tomb of Henry VII and Elizabeth of York by Torrigiano: Westminster Abbey (A. Kersting).
209 tr Aerial view of Hampton Court: Zefa, London
208–9 b Hampton Court: Zefa, London
210–211 *Henry VIII and family* by unknown artist c. 1545: by gracious permission of HM Queen Elizabeth II, the Royal Collection, Hampton Court.
210 Helmet of Henry VIII: the Armories, HM Tower of London (JF).
211 Portrait of Nikolaus Kratzer by Holbein, 1527: Louvre, Paris (S).
213 Portrait of Mary I by Anthonis Mor: Prado Museum, Madrid (S).
214 Portrait of Sir Francis Drake, panel by unknown artist, 1580–85: National Portrait Gallery, London.
215 *Blackfriars Portrait of Elizabeth I* by Robert Peake c. 1600: Sherborne Castle, Wiltshire, Simon Wingfield Digby Esq.

216–7 t Edward Herbert by Isaac Oliver, 7 1/8 x 9": The Earl of Powis, Powis Castle (National Trust).
216 bl Sir Christopher Hatton by Nicholas Hilliard, 2 1/4 x 1 3/4": Victoria and Albert Museum, London.
216 cr Self-portrait by Nicholas Hilliard, diam 1 5/8", 1577: Victoria and Albert Museum, London.
217 tr James I of England and VI of Scotland by Nicholas Hilliard, 2 1/8 x 1 5/8": Victoria and Albert Museum, London.
217 br Anne of Cleves by Holbein, c. 1539: Louvre, Paris.
219 cl Shakespeare portrait from First Folio: Mansell Collection, London.
218 bl Swan Theater by Johannes de Witt c. 1596: Bibliotheta der Rijksuniversiteit, Utrecht (Fotomas Index, London).
218–9 t *Macbeth and the Witches* from Holinshed's *Chronicles of England, Scotland and Ireland*, 1571: Cambridge University Library.
218 br Henry Wriothesley, Third Earl of Southampton by John de Critz the Elder, c. 1603: Boughton House, Northamptonshire, by permission of the Duke of Buccleuch and Queensberry.
219 tr James I of England and VI of Scotland, oil on canvas by Daniel Mytens, 1621: National Portrait Gallery, London.
220 *Execution of Mary Queen of Scots*, Dutch drawing, 16th century: Robert Harding Picture Library, London.
221 Glamis Castle: Zefa, London.
222 tr Cardinal Wolsey, panel by unknown artist: National Portrait Gallery, London.
222–3 b Christ Church from *Oxiensis* by David Loggan: Central Library Reference Collection, Oxford.
223 tl *Tutor and class at Oxford*, woodcut from a manual on astronomy and calendar calculation published at Oxford in 1519: Cambridge University Library.
223 tr Gate of Virtue, Cambridge: Wimm Swaan, New York.
223 c St. John Fisher, drawing by Holbein: by gracious permission of HM Queen Elizabeth II, Royal Collection.
223 br School's quad, Bodleian Library: Linda Proud, Oxford.
224 Queen's House, Greenwich, by Inigo Jones: John Bethell, St. Albans.

Maps drafted by Euromap, Pangbourne; Lovell Johns, Oxford; Alan Mais, Hornchurch.

Artwork and site plans drawn by John Brennan, John Fuller.

BIBLIOGRAPHY

Chapter One
H. Baron, *The Crisis of the Early Italian Renaissance*, Princeton, 1966.
C. Brooke, *The Twelfth Century Renaissance*, London, 1969.
A. Brown, *The Renaissance*, London, 1988.
P. Burke, *The Renaissance*, London, 1987.
P. Burke, *The Renaissance Sense of the Past*, London, 1969.
D. Hay, *The Italian Renaissance in its Historical Background*, Cambridge, 1977.
D. Hay, *Renaissance Essays*, London, 1988.
P. and L. Murray, *The Art of the Renaissance*, London, 1963.
F. Yates, *Giordano Bruno and the Hermetic Tradition*, Chicago, 1964.

Chapter Two
D. Bomford, J. Dunkerton, D. Gordon and A. Roy, *Art in the Making: Italian Painting before 1400*, London, 1990.
E. Borsook, *The Mural Painters of Tuscany*, Oxford, 1980.
W.M. Bowsky, *A Medieval Italian Commune: Siena under the Nine, 1287–1355*, Berkeley, 1981.
C. Brandi, *Palazzo Pubblico di Siena*, Siena, 1983.
J. Dunkerton, S. Foister, D. Gordon, and N. Penny, *Giotto to Dürer: Early Renaissance Painting in the National Gallery*, London, 1991.
G. Holmes, *Florence, Rome and the Origins of the Renaissance*, Oxford, 1986.
J. Hook, *Siena: A City and its History*, London, 1980.
J.K. Hyde, *Society and Politics in Medieval Italy: The Evolution of the Civil Life, 1000–1380*, London, 1973.
J. Larner, *Culture and Society in Italy, 1290–1420*, London 1971.
J. Larner, *Italy in the Age of Dante and Petrarch, 1216–1380*, London, 1980.
N. Mann, *Petrarch*, Oxford, 1984.
M. Meiss, *Painting in Florence and Siena after the Black Death*, Princeton, 1951.
J. Pope-Hennessy, *Italian Gothic Sculpture*, London, 1955.
B. Pullan, *A History of Early Renaissance Italy from the Mid-thirteenth to the Mid-fifteenth Century*, London, 1973.
J.H. Stubblebine, (ed.), *Giotto: The Arena Chapel Frescoes*, New York, 1969.
D. Waley, *The Italian City Republics*, London and New York, 1988.
J. White, *Art and Architecture in Italy, 1250–1400*, London, 1987.

Chapter Three
M. Baxandall, *Painting and Experience in Fifteenth-century Italy*, Oxford, 1972.
F. Borsi, *Leon Battista Alberti: The Complete Works*, New York, 1977.
G. Brucker, *Renaissance Florence*, New York, 1969.
P. Burke, *The Italian Renaissance: Culture and Society in Italy*, Oxford, 1972.
B. Cole, *The Renaissance Artist at Work from Pisano to Titian*, London, 1983.
D. Chambers, *The Imperial Age of Venice, 1380–1580*, London, 1970.
R. Goldthwaite, *The Building of Renaissance Florence*, Baltimore and London, 1980.
W.L. Gundersheimer, *Ferrara: The Style of a Renaissance Despotism*, Princeton, 1973.
L.H. Heydenreich and W. Lotz, *Architecture in Italy, 1400–1600*, London, 1974.
H.W. Janson, *The Sculpture of Donatello*, Princeton, 1957.
R. Krautheimer, *Lorenzo Ghiberti*, Princeton, 1956.
F.C. Lane, *Venice: A Maritime Republic*, Baltimore and London, 1973.
M. Mallett, *The Borgias*, London, 1969.
L. Martines, *The Social World of Florentine Humanism*, Princeton, 1963.
I. Origo, *The World of San Bernardino*, London, 1963.
J. Pope-Hennessy, *Italian Renaissance Sculpture*, London, 1958.
F.D. Prager and G. Scaglia, *Brunelleschi*, Cambridge, 1970.

C. Trinkaus, *In Our Image and Likeness: Humanity and Divinity in Italian Humanist Thought*, 2 vols, Chicago, 1970.
J. White, *The Birth and Rebirth of Pictorial Space*, Cambridge, Mass, 1987.
W.H. Woodward, *Studies in Education during the Age of the Renaissance, 1400–1600*, Cambridge, 1906.

Chapter Four
J. S. Ackerman, *Palladio*, London, 1966.
D. Arnold, *Giovanni Gabrieli and the Music of the Venetian High Renaissance*, London, 1979.
T.S.R. Boase, *Giorgio Vasari: The Man and the Book*, Princeton, 1978.
S. Bramly, *Leonardo: The Artist and the Man*, London, 1992.
S. De Grazia, *Machiavelli in Hell*, London and New York, 1989.
L.D. and H.S. Ettlinger, *Raphael*, Oxford, 1987.
H. Hibbard, *Michelangelo*, London, 1975.
C. Hope (ed.), *The Autobiography of Benvenuto Cellini*, Oxford, 1983.
H. Huse and W. Wolters, *The Art of Renaissance Venice: Architecture, Sculpture and Painting 1460–1590*, Chicago and London, 1990.
M. Kemp, *Leonardo da Vinci: The Marvellous Works of Nature and Man*, London, 1981.
C. Lazzaro, *The Italian Renaissance Garden*, New Haven and London, 1990.
M. Levey, *High Renaissance: Style and Civilization*, London, 1975.
O. Logan, *Culture and Society in Venice 1470–1790*, London, 1972.
C. McCorquodale, *Bronzino*, London, 1981.
L. Murray, *The High Renaissance and Mannerism*, London, 1990.
J. Pope-Hennessy, *Cellini*, London, 1985.
C. Robertson, *"Il Gran Cardinale": Alessandro Farnese Patron of the Arts*, New Haven and London, 1992.
J.M. Saslow, *The Poetry of Michelangelo: An Annotated Translation*, New Haven and London, 1991.
J.H. Whitfield, *A Short History of Italian Literature*, London, 1960.
T. Wilson, *Ceramic Art of the Italian Renaissance*, London, 1987.

Chapter Five
F. Braudel, *The Mediterranean and the Mediterranean World in the Age of Philip II* (2 vols), London, 1972–73.
P. Burke, *The Renaissance*, London, 1964.
D.S. Chambers, *The Imperial Age of Venice, 1380–1580*, London, 1970.
A. Debus, *Nature and Man in the Renaissance*, Cambridge, 1978.
A.G. Dickens, *The Age of Humanism and Reformation*, Eaglewood Cliffs, 1972.
S. Dresden, *Humanism in the Renaissance*, London, 1968.
J.H. Elliott, *The Old World and the New*, Cambridge, 1970.
D. Hay, *The Italian Renaissance in its Historical Background*, Cambridge, 1961.
D. Hay (ed.), *The Age of the Renaissance*, London, 1967.
G. Holmes, *The Florentine Enlightenment, 1400–1450*, London, 1969.
M. Kemp, *The Science of Art*, London, 1990.
R. Mackenney, *Sixteenth-Century Europe*, London, 1993.
R. Porter and T. Mikulas (eds.), *The Renaissance in National Context*, Cambridge, 1992.
P. Rossi, *Philosophy, Technology and the Arts in the Early Modern Era*, New York, 1970.
G.V. Scammell, *The First Imperial Age*, London, 1989.

Chapter Six
M. Baxandall, *The Limewood Sculptors of Renaissance Germany*, New Haven and London, 1980.
O. Benesch, *The Art of the Renaissance in Northern Europe*, Harvard, 1945.
E.M. Butler, *The Fortunes of Faust*, Cambridge, 1979.
J.K. Cameron, "Humanism in the Low Countries", in A. Goodman and A. Mackay (eds.), *The Impact of*

Humanism on Western Europe, London, 1990.
Erasmus, *Praise of Folly and Letter to Martin Dorp 1515*, translated by Betty Radice, London, 1971.
Erasmus, *The Adages*, Cambridge, 1964.
R.J.W.Evans, *Rudolf II and His World: A Study in Intellectual History, 1576–1612*, Oxford, 1973.
R.H. Fuchs, *Dutch Painting*, London, 1978.
J. Huizinga, *Erasmus of Rotterdam*, London, 1924.
J. McConica, *Erasmus*, Oxford, 1991.
T. Kaufmann, *The School of Prague*, Chicago, 1988.
L.W. Spitz, *Conrad Celtis: The German Arch-Humanist*, Harvard, 1957.
L.W. Spitz, *The Northern Renaissance*, New York, 1972.
H. Trevor-Roper, *Princes and Artists: Patronage and Ideology at Four Habsburg Courts, 1517–1633*, London, 1976.

Chapter Seven
E. Armstrong, *Ronsard and the Age of Gold*, Cambridge, 1968.
A. Blunt, *Art and Architecture in France, 1400–1500*, London, 1953.
P. Burke, *Montaigne*, Oxford, 1981.
D.G. Coleman, *Rabelais*, Cambridge.
I. Dunlop, *Royal Palaces of France*, London, 1985.
M. Greengrass, *France in the Age of Henri IV*, London and New York, 1984.
R.J. Knecht, *French Renaissance Monarchy: Francis I and Henry II*, London and New York, 1984.
C. de Nicolay-Mazery and J.B. Naudin, *French Chateaux: Life, Style, Tradition*, London, 1991.
M. Rady, *France: Renaissance, Religion and Recovery, 1494–1610*, London, 1988.
G. Ring, *A Century of French Painting, 1400–1500*, London, 1949.
D. Seward, *Prince of the Renaissance: The Life of François I*, London, 1973.

Chapter Eight
M. Alper (ed.), *Two Spanish Picaresque Novels*, London, 1969.
G. Brenan, *The Literature of the Spanish People*, Cambridge, 1953.
L. Bronstein, *El Greco*, London, 1991.
J.H. Elliott, *Imperial Spain, 1469–1716*, London, 1963.
J. Gudiol, *The Arts of Spain*, London, 1964.
J.H. Harvey, *The Cathedrals of Spain*, London, 1957.
H. Kamen, *The Spanish Inquisition*, London, 1965.
H. Kamen, *Golden Age Spain*, London, 1988.
J. Lassaigne, *Spanish Painting from the Catalan Frescoes to El Greco*, New York, 1952.
T. Miller, *The Castles and the Crown*, London, 1963.
S. Morison, *Admiral of the Ocean: Christopher Columbus*, Oxford, 1942.
P. Pierson, *Philip II of Spain*, London, 1975.
E. Prestage, *The Portuguese Pioneers*, London, 1933.
F. de Rojas, *La Celestina*, translated by James Mabbe, London, 1972.
P.E. Russell, *Cervantes*, Oxford, 1985.
B. Smith, *Spain: A History in Art*, London, 1966.

Chapter Nine
E. Auerback, *Hilliard*, London, 1961.
A. Cherry, *Princes Poets and Patrons: The Stuarts and Scotland*, Edinburgh, 1987.
S. Greenblatt, *Renaissance Self-Fashioning: From More to Shakespeare*, Chicago, 1980.
J.R. Hale, *England and the Italian Renaissance*, London, 1954.
P. Johnson, *Elizabeth I: A Study in Power and Intellect*, London, 1974.
E. Mercer, *English Art, 1563–1625*, Oxford, 1962.
G.B. Parks, *The English Traveler to Italy*, Rome, 1954.
G. Parry, *The Golden Age Restor'd*, Manchester, 1981.
F. Saxl and R. Wittkomer, *British Art and the Mediterranean*, London, 1948.
S. Schoenbaum, *Shakespeare: The Globe and the World*, New York, 1980.
D. Starkey (ed.), *Henry VIII: A European Court in England*, London, 1991.
R. Strong, *The English Renaissance Miniature*, London, 1984.
N. Williams, *Henry VIII and His Court*, London, 1971.

GAZETTEER

An entry includes a descriptive term if it is a physical feature and the modern country name, eg Rhodes (*isl*), (*Greece*). An entry followed by an asterisk indicates a territorial unit, eg a province, kingdom or region. Modern place names, including some not shown on the map, are cross-referenced to the ancient name for the full entry.

Abbeville (*France*), 50°06′N 1°51′E, 167
Aberdeen (*UK*), 57°10′N 2°04′W, 110, 212
Abruzzi*, 58
Acapulco (*Mexico*), 16°51′N 99°56′W, 122
Acre (*Israel*), 32°58′N 35°06′E, 23
Adda (*r*), 58
Aden (*Yemen*), 12°46′N 45°45′E, 123
Adige (*r*), 15, 28, 34, 41, 49, 58, 91
Adour (*r*), 167
Adriatic Sea, 10, 15, 28, 34, 56, 66, 77, 79, 94, 95, 112, 142
Aegean Sea, 11
Agde (*France*), 43°19′N 3°29′E, 22
Agen (*France*), 44°12′N 0°38′E, 177
Agnadello (*Italy*), 45°27′N 9°42′E , 77
Agrigento (*Italy*), 37°19′N 13°35′E, 22
Agropoli (*Italy*), 40°21′N 14°59′E, 22
Aigues-Mortes (*France*), 43°34′N 4°11′E, 108
Aix-en-Provence (*France*), 43°31′N 5°27′E, 110, 165, 177
Ajaccio (*France*), 41°55′N 8°43′E, 58
Alba de Tormes (*Spain*), 40°50′N 5°30′W, 189
Albi (*France*), 43°56′N 2°08′E, 177
Ålborg (*Denmark*), 57°03′N 9°56′E, 138
Alcalá de Henares (*Spain*), 40°28′N 3°22′W, 110, 184, 189
Alcañiz (*Spain*), 41°03′N 0°09′W, 184
Alcántara (*Spain*), 39°44′N 6°53′W, 184
Alençon (*France*), 48°25′N 0°05′E, 165
Alès (*France*), 44°08′N 4°05′E, 177
Alessandria (*Italy*), 44°55′N 8°37′E, 22, 28, 56, 58
Alexandria (*Egypt*), 31°12′N 29°55′E, 23, 108
Alghero (*Italy*), 40°34′N 8°19′E, 186
Algiers (*Algeria*), 36°50′N 3°00′E, 10, 22, 108, 186
Alicante (*Spain*), 38°21′N 0°29′W, 184, 186
Allier (*r*), 10, 167
Almeria (*Spain*), 36°50′N 2°26′W, 22, 108, 184
Alost (*Belgium*), 50°57′N 4°03′E, 140
Alps (*mts*), (*France/Switzerland*), 46°01′N 7°00′E, 10, 77
Altoluogo (*Turkey*), 37°38′N 27°22′E, 23
Amazon (*r*), 122
Amboise (*France*), 47°25′N 1°01′E, 82, 167, 170
Amiens (*France*), 49°54′N 2°18′E, 167
Amsterdam (*Netherlands*), 52°21′N 4°54′E, 10, 110, 115
Ancona (*Italy*), 43°37′N 13°31′E, 15, 22, 34, 56, 58, 108
Ancona*, 58
Ancram Moor (*UK*), 55°32′N 2°39′W, 207
Ancy-le-Franc (*France*), 47°47′N 4°10′E, 167
Andalucia*, 184
Anet (*France*), 48°51′N 1°26′E, 167
Angers (*France*), 47°29′N 0°32′W, 110, 165, 167, 170, 177
Angoulême (*France*), 45°40′N 0°10′E, 165
Angoumois*, 165
Anhalt*, 154
Anjou*, 165, 170
Ankara (*Turkey*), 39°55′N 32°50′E, 11
Ansbach*, 154
Antequera (*Spain*), 37°01′N 4°34′W, 184
Antioch (*Turkey*), 36°12′N 36°10′E, 23
Antwerp (*Belgium*), 51°13′N 4°25′E, 108, 115, 138, 140, 146
Aosta (*Italy*), 45°43′N 7°19′E, 58
Appenines (*mts*), (*Italy*), 10, 77
Apulia*, 34
Aquila (*Italy*), 42°22′N 13°24′E, 58
Aquileia (*Italy*), 45°47′N 13°22′E, 56, 58
Aragon*, 16, 17, 165, 184, 186
Archangel (*Russia*), 64°32′N 40°40′E, 125
Archduchy of Austria*, 140
Ardennes*, 10
Arequipa (*Peru*), 16°25′S 71°32′W, 122
Arezzo (*Italy*), 43°28′N 11°53′E, 15, 22, 28, 34, 41, 49, 58, 66, 77, 79, 110, 112
Argentan (*France*), 48°32′N 4°45′W, 167
Arica (*Chile*), 18°30′S 70°20′W, 122
Arles (*France*), 43°41′N 4°38′E, 22, 167
Arnay-le-Duc (*France*), 47°08′N 4°30′E, 177
Arno (*r*), 28, 34, 49, 56, 58, 66, 77, 79, 95, 112
Arquà (*Italy*), 45°01′N 11°44′E, 41
Arras (*France*), 50°17′N 2°46′E, 22, 165
Artois*, 154, 165
Arzew (*Algeria*), 35°50′N 0°19′W, 22
Asilah (*Morocco*), 35°38′N 6°02′W, 184, 186
Asolo (*Italy*), 45°48′N 11°55′E, 95
Assisi (*Italy*), 43°04′N 12°37′E, 15, 58
Asti (*Italy*), 44°54′N 8°13′E, 58, 77, 79
Astrakhan (*Russia*), 46°22′N 48°04′E, 125
Asturias*, 184
Asunción (*Paraguay*), 25°15′S 57°40′W, 122
Athens (*Greece*), 38°00′N 23°44′E, 11
Atlantic Ocean, 10, 16, 17, 108, 110, 119, 122, 125
Audley End House (*UK*), 52°01′N 0°10′E, 212
Augsburg (*Germany*), 48°21′N 10°54′E, 108, 115, 138, 140, 142, 154
Augsburg*, 119
Austria*, 119, 154
Auvergne*, 165
Aversa (*Italy*), 40°58′N 14°13′E, 77
Avignon (*France*), 43°56′N 4°48′E, 16, 17, 22, 41, 52, 110, 165, 167
Avila (*Spain*), 40°39′N 4°42′W, 184, 189
Avis (*Portugal*), 39°14′N 8°12′W, 184
Avranches (*France*), 48°42′N 1°21′W, 167
Axim (*Ghana*), 4°53′N 2°14′W, 122
Axios (*r*), 11
Azay-le-Rideau (*France*), 47°16′N 0°28′E, 170
Azores (*isls*), (*Portugal*), 38°30′N 28°00′W, 122
Azov, Sea of, 11

Badajoz (*Spain*), 38°53′N 6°58′W, 184
Baden*, 154
Bad Schussenried (*Germany*), 50°55′N 9°12′E, 140
Baeza (*Spain*), 38°00′N 3°28′W, 189
Bagnaia (*Italy*), 42°25′N 12°09′W, 95
Bagnols-sur-Cèze (*France*), 44°10′N 4°36′E, 177
Bahia (*Brazil*), 12°58′S 38°29′W, 122
Balearic Islands (*Spain*), 39°00′N 2°30′E, 10, 22, 108, 110, 115, 119, 185, 186
Balkan Mts (*Bulgaria*), 42°30′N 25°00′E, 11
Baltic Sea, 10, 110, 119, 138
Bamberg (*Germany*), 49°54′N 10°54′E, 110, 115, 140, 154
Barbary Coast*, 186
Barcelona (*Spain*), 41°25′N 2°10′E, 10, 16, 22, 108, 110, 115, 184, 189
Bardney (*UK*), 53°12′N 0°21′W, 207
Bari (*Italy*), 41°07′N 16°52′E, 22, 58, 79
Bari*, 58
Bar-le-Duc (*France*), 48°46′N 5°10′E, 167
Barletta (*Italy*), 41°20′N 16°17′E, 22
Barnard Castle (*UK*), 54°33′N 1°55′W, 207
Barrington Court (*UK*), 50°58′N 2°52′W, 212
Barrow (*r*), 212
Bar-sur-Aube (*France*), 48°14′N 4°43′E, 22
Basel (*Switzerland*), 47°33′N 7°36′E, 16, 110, 115, 119, 138, 140, 142, 146, 154
Basing House (*UK*), 51°16N 1°03′W, 212
Bavaria*, 119, 154
Bayeux (*France*), 49°16′N 0°42′W, 167
Bayreuth*, 154
Bazouges-sur-le-Loir (*France*), 47°42′N 0°11′W, 170
Bearn*, 177
Beaugency (*France*), 47°47′N 1°38′E, 170
Beauregard (*France*), 47°31′N 1°24′E, 167, 170
Beauvais (*France*), 49°26′N 2°05′E, 110
Bec (*France*), 49°22′N 1°04′E, 110
Beirut (*Lebanon*), 33°52′N 35°28′E, 11, 108
Béjar (*Spain*), 40°24′N 5°45′W, 184
Belgrade (*Yugoslavia*), 44°50′N 20°30′E, 11, 115, 138
Belluno (*Italy*), 46°08′N 12°13′E, 58
Ben Nevis (*mt*), (*UK*), 56°48′N 5°00′W, 10
Benavente (*Spain*), 42°00′N 5°40′W, 184
Benevento (*Italy*), 41°08′N 14°46′E, 58, 79
Berg*, 154, 177
Bergamo (*Italy*), 45°42′N 9°40′E, 41, 56, 58, 66, 77, 79, 112
Bergen (*Norway*), 60°23′N 5°20′E, 108
Berlin (*Germany*), 52°32′N 13°25′E, 10, 115, 154
Bern (*Switzerland*), 46°57′N 7°26′E, 10, 115, 119
Bernina Pass (*Switzerland*), 46°25′N 10°02′E, 77
Beromünster (*Switzerland*), 47°13′N 8°12′E, 140
Berry*, 165
Besançon (*France*), 47°14′N 6°02′E, 22, 108, 110, 140, 165
Beysehir, Lake (*Turkey*), 37°45′N 31°45′E, 11
Béziers (*France*), 43°21′N 3°13′E, 177
Bicocca (*Italy*), 45°30′N 9°13′E, 77
Bilbao (*Spain*), 43°15′N 2°56′W, 184
Birmingham (*UK*), 52°30′N 1°50′W, 10
Birsay (*UK*), 59°08′N 3°18′W, 212
Biscay, Bay of, 10, 146, 165, 167, 177
Bishop Auckland (*UK*), 54°40′N 1°40′W, 207
Bishop's Palace (*UK*), 58°59′N 2°58′W, 212
Black Forest (*Germany*), 48°00′N 8°00′E, 10
Blackheath (*UK*), 51°28′N 0°01′W, 207
Blanc, Mont (*France/Italy*), 45°50′N 6°52′E, 10
Blaubeuren (*Germany*), 48°25′N 9°47′E, 140
Blois (*France*), 47°36′N 1°20′E, 167, 170
Bobbio (*Italy*), 44°46′N 9°23′E, 52, 58
Bodmin (*UK*), 50°29′N 4°43′W, 207
Bohemia*, 16, 119, 140, 154
Bologna (*Italy*), 44°30′N 11°20′E, 15, 16, 22, 28, 34, 41, 49, 56, 58, 66, 77, 79, 82, 94, 95, 108, 110, 138, 142, 146
Bolsover Castle (*UK*), 53°14′N 1°18′W, 212
Bolzano (*Italy*), 46°30′N 11°22′E, 142
Bône (*Algeria*), 36°55′N 7°45′E, 22, 108
Bonn (*Germany*), 50°44′N 7°06′E, 10, 115
Bordeaux (*France*), 44°50′N 0°34′W, 110, 165, 177
Bornholm (*isl*), (*Denmark*), 55°02′N 15°00′E, 10
Boroughbridge (*UK*), 54°05′N 1°24′W, 207
Bosworth Field (*UK*), 52°40′N 1°23′W, 207
Bougie (*Algeria*), 36°49′N 5°03′E, 22, 186
Boulogne (*France*), 50°43′N 1°37′E, 165, 167
Boumois (*France*), 47°19′N 0°08′W, 170
Bourbon*, 165
Bourges (*France*), 47°05′N 2°23′E, 110, 165, 167, 170, 177
Brabant*, 154, 165
Brac (*isl*), (*Croatia*), 43°20′N 16°45′E, 34
Bracciano (*Italy*), 42°06′N 12°11′E, 77
Braga (*Portugal*), 41°32′N 8°26′W, 184, 189
Braga*, 189
Bragança (*Portugal*), 41°47′N 6°46′W, 184
Braham Moor (*UK*), 53°56′N 1°22′W, 207
Bramshill (*UK*), 51°20′N 0°56′W, 212
Brancepeth (*UK*), 54°44′N 1°39′W, 207
Brandenburg*, 140, 154
Brasov (*Romania*), 45°39′N 25°35′E, 138
Bratislava (*Slovakia*), 48°10′N 17°08′E, 10, 138, 140
Bremen (*Germany*), 53°05′N 8°48′E, 108, 138, 154
Brenner Pass (*Austria/Italy*), 47°02′N 11°32′E, 77
Brescia (*Italy*), 45°33′N 10°13′E, 28, 58, 66, 77, 79, 108
Breslau (*Poland*), 51°05′N 17°00′E, 108, 138, 140, 142
Bresse*, 165
Bridlington (*UK*), 54°05′N 0°12′W, 207
Brindisi (*Italy*), 40°37′N 17°57′E, 58
Brissac (*France*), 47°22′N 0°26′W, 170
Bristol (*UK*), 51°27′N 2°35′W, 125, 207
Brittany*, 165
Brixen (*Austria*), 47°27′N 12°15′E, 154
Brno (*Czech Republic*), 49°11′N 16°39′E, 138, 140
Bruges (*Belgium*), 51°13′N 3°14′E, 22, 108, 138, 140
Brunswick (*Germany*), 52°15′N 10°30′E, 108, 138
Brunswick*, 154
Brussels (*Belgium*), 50°50′N 4°21′E, 10, 22, 108, 115, 138, 140, 154, 165
Bucharest (*Romania*), 44°25′N 26°07′E, 11
Buckland Abbey (*UK*), 50°25′N 4°05′W, 212
Buda *see* Budapest
Budapest (Buda), (*Hungary*), 47°30′N 19°03′E, 10, 22, 138, 140, 142
Bug (*r*), 11
Bugey*, 165
Buggiano (*Italy*), 43°49′N 10°48′E, 49
Burgdorf (*Switzerland*), 47°09′N 7°38′E, 140
Burghley House (*UK*), 52°40′N 0°21′W, 212
Burgo de Osma (*Spain*), 41°35′N 3°04′W, 189
Burgos (*Spain*), 42°21′N 3°41′W, 184, 189
Burgos*, 189
Burgundy*, 165
Burton Agnes Hall (*UK*), 54°03′N 0°19′W, 212
Burton Constable (*UK*), 53°46′N 0°06′W, 212
Bury (*France*), 47°35′N 1°15′E, 167

Cadiz (*Spain*), 36°32′N 6°18′W, 108, 184
Caen (*France*), 49°11′N 0°22′W, 108, 110, 165, 167
Cafaggiolo (*Italy*), 43°58′N 11°21′E, 95
Cagli (*Italy*), 43°33′N 12°38′E, 66
Cagliari (*Italy*), 39°13′N 9°08′E, 22, 58, 110, 186
Cahors (*France*), 44°28′N 0°26′E, 110
Calabria*, 58
Calahorra (*Spain*), 42°19′N 1°58′W, 189
Calais (*France*), 50°57′N 1°52′E, 165, 167
Calaisis*, 165
Calatrava (*Spain*), 38°54′N 4°05′W, 184
Calicut (*India*), 11°15′N 75°45′E, 123
Callao (*Peru*), 12°05′S 77°08′W, 122
Calvi Risorta (*Italy*), 41°13′N 14°09′E, 77
Cambrai (*France*), 50°10′N 3°14′E, 146, 165
Cambridge (*UK*), 52°12′N 0°07′E, 110, 146, 212
Camerino (*Italy*), 43°08′N 13°04′E, 95
Canary Islands (*Spain*), 28°30′N 15°10′W, 122
Candia (*Greece*), 35°20′N 25°08′E, 108
Cannamore (*India*), 11°53′N 75°23′E, 123
Canons Ashby (*UK*), 52°09′N 1°09′W, 212
Cantabrian Mts (*Spain*), 43°00′N 6°00′W, 10
Canterbury (*UK*), 51°17′N 1°05′W, 110, 177, 212
Cantiano (*Italy*), 43°28′N 12°38′E, 66
Cape Breton Island (*Canada*), 46°00′N 61°00′W, 125
Capitanata*, 58
Capranica (*Italy*), 42°15′N 12°11′E, 41
Caprarola (*Italy*), 42°20′N 12°15′E, 66, 95
Carcassonne (*France*), 43°13′N 2°21′E, 167
Cardigan (*UK*), 52°06′N 4°40′W, 207
Careggi (*Italy*), 43°50′N 11°14′E, 95
Carinthia*, 119
Carlisle (*UK*), 54°54′N 2°55′W, 207
Carniola*, 119
Carpathian Mts (*Romania/Ukraine*), 48°00′N 28°00′E, 11
Carpentras (*France*), 44°03′N 5°03′E, 41
Carpi (*Italy*), 44°47′N 10°53′E, 95
Cartagena (*Columbia*), 10°24′N 75°33′W, 122
Cartagena (*Spain*), 37°36′N 0°59′W, 184, 189
Casablanca (*Morocco*), 33°39′N 7°35′W, 10
Casale (*Italy*), 43°03′N 11°18′E, 95
Caspian Sea, 125
Cassino (San Germano), (*Italy*), 41°30′N 13°50′E, 77
Castel Durante (*Italy*), 43°40′N 12°31′E, 95
Castel Fiorentino (*Italy*), 43°36′N 10°58′E, 77
Castelfranco (*Italy*), 45°40′N 11°56′E, 112
Castellammare (*Italy*), 40°47′N 14°29′E, 22
Castiglione del Lago (*Italy*), 43°07′N 12°03′E, 15
Castile*, 16, 17, 165, 184, 186
Castle Ashby (*UK*), 52°13′N 1°36′W, 212
Castle Fraser (*UK*), 57°12′N 2°29′W, 212
Castres (*France*), 43°46′N 2°14′E, 177
Catalonia*, 165, 184
Catania (*Italy*), 37°31′N 15°06′E, 58, 95, 110
Catanzaro (*Italy*), 38°54′N 16°36′E, 79
Cateau-Cambrésis (*France*), 50°05′N 3°20′E, 165
Cattaro (*Yugoslavia*), 42°27′N 18°46′E, 58
Central Massif (*mts*), (*France*), 45°00′N 3°00′E, 10
Central Russian Uplands (*Russia*), 54°00′N 36°00′E, 11
Cerdagne*, 165, 184
Cerignola (*Italy*), 41°16′N 15°54′E, 77
Cesena (*Italy*), 44°09′N 12°15′E, 58
Ceuta (*Morocco*), 35°53′N 5°19′W, 22, 184, 186
Challuau (*France*), 48°22′N 2°50′E, 167
Chalon-sur-Saône (*France*), 46°47′N 4°51′E, 167
Chambord (*France*), 47°37′N 1°32′E, 167, 170
Champagne*, 165
Chang (*r*), 123
Channel Islands (*UK*), 49°00′N 2°00′W, 10, 177
Chantilly (*France*), 49°12′N 2°28′E , 167
Charlecote Park (*UK*), 52°13′N 1°36′W, 212
Charleval (*France*), 49°22′N 1°23′E, 167
Charolais*, 165, 177
Chartres (*France*), 48°27′N 1°30′E, 52, 110, 165, 167, 170, 177
Châteaubriant (*France*), 47°43′N 1°22′W, 167
Chateau de Madrid (*France*), 48°52′N 2°20′E, 167
Châteaudun (*France*), 48°04′N 1°20′E, 167, 170
Châtellerault (*France*), 46°49′N 0°33′E, 167
Chaumont (*France*), 47°29′N 1°11′E, 170
Chenonceaux (*France*), 47°20′N 1°04′E, 167, 170
Cher (*r*), 10, 170
Cherbourg (*France*), 49°38′N 1°37′W, 167
Chester (*UK*), 53°12′N 2°54′W, 207
Chiemsee (*Germany*), 48°02′N 12°20′E, 154
Chieri (*Italy*), 45°01′N 7°49′E, 77
Chioggia (*Italy*), 45°13′N 12°17′E, 34, 56, 58
Chios (*isl*), (*Greece*), 38°23′N 26°07′E, 23
Chiusi (*Italy*), 43°02′N 11°57′E, 58
Cisa Pass (*Italy*), 44°28′N 9°55′E, 77
Citeaux (*France*), 47°10′N 4°52′E, 110
Citta di Castello (*Italy*), 43°27′N 12°14′E, 15
Ciudadela (*Spain*), 40°00′N 3°50′E, 185
Cividale (*Italy*), 46°06′N 13°25′E, 22, 58
Civita Castellana (*Italy*), 42°17′N 12°25′E, 66, 77
Civitavecchia (*Italy*), 42°05′N 11°47′E, 22, 41, 58, 66, 77
Clairvaux (*France*), 48°09′N 4°47′E, 110
Clermont-Ferrand (*France*), 45°47′N 3°05′E, 167, 177
Cleves*, 154
Clifton Maybank (*UK*), 50°57′N 2°35′W, 212
Cluj-Napoca (*Romania*), 46°47′N 23°37′E, 138
Cluny (*France*), 46°25′N 4°39′E, 52, 110, 115
Cochin (*India*), 9°56′N 76°15′E, 123
Cognac (*France*), 45°42′N 0°19′W, 177
Cogolludo (*Spain*), 40°56′N 3°06′W, 189
Coimbra (*Portugal*), 40°12′N 8°25′W, 110, 184, 189
Colle di Val d'Elsa (*Italy*), 43°25′N 11°08′E, 49
Cologne (*Germany*), 50°56′N 6°57′E, 10, 16, 22, 52, 108, 110, 115, 138, 140, 142, 154
Colombo (*Sri Lanka*), 6°55′N 79°52′E, 123
Comacchio (*Italy*), 44°42′N 12°11′E, 58
Comminges*, 165
Como (*Italy*), 45°49′N 9°06′E, 56, 58
Como, Lake (*Italy*), 46°00′N 9°10′E, 15, 28, 34, 56, 66, 95
Compiègne (*France*), 49°25′N 2°50′E, 167
Compton Wynates (*UK*), 52°04′N 1°31′W, 212
Comtat Venaissin*, 165, 177
Condover Hall (*UK*), 52°39′N 2°46′W, 212
Congo (*r*), 122
Constance (*Germany*), 47°40′N 9°10′E, 16, 52
Constance, Lake (*Germany/Switzerland*), 47°30′N 9°00′E, 10, 140, 154
Constantinople *see* Istanbul
Copa (*Russia*), 45°02′N 37°28′E, 23

Copenhagen (*Denmark*), 55°41′N 12°34′E, 10, 110, 115
Córdoba (*Spain*), 37°53′N 4°46′W, 108, 184, 189
Corinth (*Greece*), 37°56′N 22°55′E, 23
Corsica (*isl*), (*France*), 42°00′N 8°00′E, 10, 15, 16, 17, 22, 28, 34, 41, 52, 66, 77, 79, 82, 94, 95, 108, 110, 115, 119, 186
Cortona (*Italy*), 43°17′N 11°59′E, 15, 58
Corunna (*Spain*), 43°22′N 8°24′W, 184
Corvey (*Germany*), 51°47′N 9°24′E, 52, 110
Cosenza (*Italy*), 39°17′N 16°16′E, 79, 95
Cotehele House (*UK*), 50°26′N 4°10′W, 212
Coucy-le-Château-Auffrique (*France*), 49°32′N 3°20′E, 167
Courland*, 119
Courtanvaux (*France*), 47°51′N 0°45′E, 170
Coutances (*France*), 49°03′N 1°29′W, 167
Cowdray House (*UK*), 51°00′N 0°45′W, 212
Cracow (*Poland*), 50°04′N 19°57′E, 10, 108, 110, 138, 140, 142
Craigievar Castle (*UK*), 57°10′N 2°44′W, 212
Craigston Castle (*UK*), 57°32′N 2°27′W, 212
Crathes Castle (*UK*), 57°04′N 2°30′W, 212
Creil (*France*), 49°16′N 2°29′E, 167
Crema (*Italy*), 45°22′N 9°41′E, 56, 58, 66, 77, 79
Crémieu (*France*), 45°43′N 5°15′E, 167
Cremona (*Italy*), 45°08′N 10°01′E, 28, 56, 58, 77, 79, 95, 108, 138
Cres (*isl*), (*Croatia*), 44°58′N 14°25′E, 34
Crete (*isl*), (*Greece*), 35°10′N 25°00′E, 11, 23, 108
Crewe Hall (*UK*), 53°05′N 2°27′W, 212
Crichton Castle (*UK*), 55°49′N 3°10′W, 212
Crotone (*Italy*), 39°05′N 17°08′E, 108
Cuenca (*Spain*), 40°04′N 1°28′E, 189
Culemborg (*Netherlands*), 51°58′N 5°14′E, 140
Culross Palace (*UK*), 56°03′N 3°35′W, 212
Cuzco (*Peru*), 13°32′S 71°57′W, 122
Cyprus (*isl*), (*Cyprus*), 35°00′N 32°30′E, 23, 108

Dal (*r*), 10
Dale (*UK*), 51°43′N 5°11′W, 207
Dalmatia*, 58, 119
Dampierre (*France*), 48°44′N 1°59′E, 167
Danube (*r*), 10, 11, 23, 52, 108, 110, 115, 119, 125, 138, 140, 142, 146, 154
Danzig *see* Gdansk
Dauphine*, 58, 165
Deene Park Hall (*UK*), 52°32′N 0°36′W, 212
Delft (*Netherlands*), 52°01′N 4°21′E, 140
Demirkazik (*mt*), (*Turkey*), 37°50′N 35°10′E, 11
Denmark*, 16, 17
Denmark-Norway*, 115, 119
Derbent (*Russia*), 42°03′N 48°18′E, 125
Deruta (*Italy*), 42°58′N 12°25′E, 95
Desna (*r*), 11
Deventer (*Netherlands*), 52°15′N 6°10′E, 16, 108, 115, 138, 140, 146
Dieppe (*France*), 49°55′N 1°05′E, 167
Dijon (*France*), 47°20′N 5°02′E, 22, 165, 167, 177
Dillngen (*Germany*), 48°33′N 10°30′E, 110, 140
Ditchley Park (*UK*), 51°54′N 1°24′W, 212
Diu (*India*), 20°41′N 71°03′E, 123
Dnepropetrovsk (*Ukraine*), 48°29′N 35°00′E, 11
Dnieper (*r*), 11, 108
Dniester (*r*), 11, 23
Dôle (*France*), 47°05′N 5°30′E, 110, 140
Dolomites (*mts*), (*Italy*), 46°20′N 12°30′E, 10
Don (*r*), 11, 108
Doncaster (*UK*), 53°32′N 1°01′W, 207
Donets (*r*), 11
Donetsk (*Ukraine*), 48°00′N 37°50′E, 11
Dordogne (*r*), 10, 41, 165, 167, 177
Dortmund (*Germany*), 51°32′N 7°27′E, 138
Douai (*France*), 50°22′N 3°05′E, 165
Doullens (*France*), 50°09′N 2°21′E, 177
Douro (*r*), 10, 110, 115, 119, 184, 189
Dover (*UK*), 51°08′N 1°19′E, 22
Drava (*r*), 10, 22, 52, 79, 108, 110, 115, 119, 138, 140, 142
Dresden (*Germany*), 51°03′N 13°45′E, 154
Dreux (*France*), 48°44′N 1°23′E, 167
Drina (*r*), 10
Dublin (*Ireland*), 53°20′N 6°15′W, 10, 110, 115
Dublin Castle (*Ireland*), 53°20′N 6°15′W, 212
Dubrovnik (Ragusa), (*Croatia*), 42°40′N 18°07′E, 22, 58, 108, 138, 186
Duchy of Ferrara*, 56, 58, 79
Duchy of Mantua*, 79
Duchy of Milan*, 56, 58, 79, 186
Duchy of Modena*, 56, 58, 79
Duchy of Parma*, 79
Duchy of Savoy*, 56, 58
Duchy of Tuscany*, 79
Duchy of Urbino*, 79
Dudley Castle (*UK*), 52°30′N 2°00′W, 212
Durance (*r*), 10, 58
Durham (*UK*), 54°47′N 1°34′W, 207
Durmitor (*mt*), (*Yugoslavia*), 42°38′N 19°01′E, 10
Durtal (*France*), 47°40′N 0°13′W, 170
Dvina (*r*), 11

Ebro (*r*), 10, 16, 17, 108, 110, 115, 119, 184, 189
Ecouen (*France*), 49°01′N 2°22′E, 167
Edinburgh (*UK*), 55°57′N 3°13′W, 108, 110, 115, 207, 212
Edzell Castle (*UK*), 56°49′N 2°40′W, 212
Egridir, Lake (*Turkey*), 38°00′N 31°00′E, 11
Eichstätt (*Germany*), 48°54′N 11°13′E, 140
Elba (*isl*), (*Italy*), 42°40′N 11°20′E, 28, 34, 66, 77, 79
Elbe (*r*), 10, 16, 17, 22, 108, 110, 115, 119, 138, 140, 142, 154
Elbing (*Poland*), 54°10′N 19°25′E, 138
El Escorial (*Spain*), 40°34′N 4°08′E, 189
Elmina (*Ghana*), 5°09′N 1°19′W, 122
Eltville (*Germany*), 50°02′N 8°08′E, 140
Emden (*Germany*), 53°23′N 7°13′E, 115
Emilia*, 28, 58
Empoli (*Italy*), 43°43′N 10°57′E, 15, 49
Ems (*r*), 154
England*, 16, 17, 115, 119, 140, 165, 177
Erfurt (*Germany*), 50°58′N 11°02′E, 110, 138, 140, 142
Esslingen (*Germany*), 48°45′N 9°19′E, 140
Este (*Italy*), 45°13′N 11°40′E, 58
Esztergom (*Hungary*), 47°46′N 18°44′E, 154
Etna, Mt (*Italy*), 37°45′N 15°00′E, 10
Eure (*r*), 170
Evora (*Portugal*), 38°34′N 7°54 W, 110, 184, 189
Evora*, 189
Exeter (*UK*), 50°43′N 3°31′W, 207

Faenza (*Italy*), 44°17′N 11°53′E, 15, 58, 77, 95
Falkland Palace (*UK*), 56°15′N 3°13′W, 212
Famagusta (*Cyprus*), 35°07′N 33°57′E, 23, 108
Faro (*Portugal*), 37°01′N 7°56′W, 184
Faroe Islands (*Denmark*), 62°00′N 7°00′W, 125
Feodosiya (Kaffa), (*Ukraine*), 45°03′N 35°23′E, 23
Fermo (*Italy*), 43°09′N 13°44′E, 58
Fernando Po (*isl*), (*Equatorial Guinea*), 3°30′N 8°42′E, 122
Ferrara (*Italy*), 44°50′N 11°38′E, 15, 22, 28, 41, 49, 56, 58, 66, 79, 94, 95, 110, 142
Finland, Gulf of, 11
Fiorenzuola (*Italy*), 44°56′N 9°54′E, 77
Fivizzano (*Italy*), 44°14′N 10°07′E, 77
Flanders*, 16, 17, 125, 165
Fleury (*France*), 47°50′N 2°56′E, 110
Flodden Field (*UK*), 55°38′N 2°10′W, 207
Florac (*France*), 44°02′N 3°35′E, 177
Florence (*Italy*), 43°47′N 11°15′E, 15, 16, 22, 28, 34, 41, 49, 52, 56, 58, 66, 77, 79, 82, 94, 95, 108, 110, 112, 115, 142, 146
Foix*, 165
Folembray (*France*), 49°35′N 3°18′E, 167
Foligno (*Italy*), 42°57′N 12°43′E, 79
Fontainebleau (*France*), 48°24′N 2°42′E, 94, 167
Forez*, 165
Forli (*Italy*), 44°13′N 12°02′E, 22, 58, 77
Fornovo (*Italy*), 44°42′N 10°07′E, 77
Fougères-sur-Bièvre (*France*), 47°26′N 1°24′E, 170
Fountains Hall (*UK*), 54°04′N 1°42′W, 212
Framlingham Church (*UK*), 52°13′N 1°21′E, 212
France*, 16, 17, 77, 79, 115, 119, 140, 154, 165, 167, 177, 184, 186
Franche-Comte*, 140, 154, 165
Franeker (*Netherlands*), 53°11′N 5°33′E, 110, 140
Frankfurt (*Germany*), 52°20′N 14°32′E, 138, 140
Frankfurt (*Germany*), 50°06′N 8°41′E, 10, 108, 138, 154
Frascati (*Italy*), 41°48′N 12°41′E, 95
Freiberg (*Germany*), 50°55′N 13°21′E, 140
Freiburg (*Germany*), 48°00′N 7°52′E, 110, 140, 142, 146
Freising (*Germany*), 48°24′N 11°45′E, 140
Friesland*, 154
Fulda (*Germany*), 50°33′N 9°41′E, 52, 110
Fürstenwalde (*Germany*), 52°22′N 14°04′E, 154
Fyvie Castle (*UK*), 57°56′N 2°24′W, 212

Gaeta (*Italy*), 41°13′N 13°36′E, 22, 108
Gaillac (*France*), 43°54′N 1°53′E, 177
Gaillon (*France*), 49°10′N 1°19′E, 167
Galicia*, 184
Ganges (*r*), 123
Garda, Lake (*Italy*), 45°30′N 10°50′E, 15, 28, 34, 56, 66, 91, 95
Garigliano (*Italy*), 41°15′N 13°40′E, 77
Garonne (*r*), 10, 41, 110, 115, 119, 165, 167, 177
Gdansk (Danzig), (*Poland*), 54°22′N 18°38′E, 108, 138, 140, 142
Gediz (*r*), 11
Geldern*, 154
Geneva (*Switzerland*), 46°13′N 6°09′E, 22, 58, 108, 110, 115, 119, 138, 140, 154, 177
Geneva, Lake (*France/Switzerland*), 46°30′N 6°13′E, 10, 77, 79, 82, 94, 140, 154, 165, 177
Genoa (*Italy*), 44°24′N 8°56′E, 15, 16, 22, 28, 34, 41, 49, 56, 58, 77, 79, 95, 108, 138, 186
Genoa*, 77
Gerlachovsky (*mt*), (*Slovakia*), 49°06′N 20°14′E, 10
German Empire*, 16, 17, 115
Gerona (*Spain*), 41°59′N 2°49′E, 16, 184, 189
Gevaudan*, 165
Gex*, 165
Ghent (*Belgium*), 51°02′N 3°42′E, 108, 138, 140
Giblet (*Lebanon*), 34°08′N 35°38′E, 23
Gibraltar (*UK*), 36°09′N 5°21′W, 184
Gien (*France*), 47°41′N 2°37′E, 167, 170
Giessen (*Germany*), 50°35′N 8°42′E, 110
Glasgow (*UK*), 55°53′N 4°15′W, 10, 110
Gloucester (*UK*), 51°53′N 2°14′W, 207
Gniezno (*Poland*), 52°32′N 17°32′E, 154
Goa (*India*), 15°31′N 73°56′E, 123
Good Hope, Cape of (*South Africa*), 35°00′S 20°00′E, 122
Gorhambury House (*UK*), 51°45′N 0°20′W, 212
Gorizia (*Italy*), 45°47′N 13°37′E, 58
Gorky (Nizhniy Novgorod), (*Russia*), 56°20′N 44°00′E, 11, 125
Gotland (*isl*), (*Sweden*), 57°00′N 18°00′E, 10, 108
Gouda (*Netherlands*), 52°01′N 4°43′E, 140, 146
Grado (*Italy*), 45°40′N 13°23′E, 58
Granada (*Spain*), 37°10′N 3°35′W, 108, 110, 184, 189
Granada*, 16, 17, 184, 186, 189
Grand St Bernard, Col du (*Italy/Switzerland*), 45°52′N 7°11′E, 165
Graz (*Austria*), 47°05′N 15°22′E, 110, 140
Greenland (*isl*), (*Denmark*), 70°00′N 40°00′W, 125
Greifswald (*Germany*), 54°06′N 13°24′E, 110, 140
Grenoble (*France*), 45°11′N 5°43′E, 110, 165, 177
Grignan (*France*), 44°25′N 4°55′E, 167
Groningen (*Netherlands*), 53°13′N 6°35′E, 110
Groonendaal (*Belgium*), 50°50′N 5°30′E, 16
Gross Glockner (*mt*), (*Austria*), 47°05′N 12°44′E, 10
Grottaferrata (*Italy*), 41°49′N 12°41′E, 66
Guadalajara (*Mexico*), 20°30′N 103°20′W, 122
Guadalajara (*Spain*), 40°37′N 3°10′W, 184, 189
Guadalquivir (*r*), 10, 110, 184, 189
Guadalupe (*Spain*), 39°27′N 5°19′W, 189
Guadiana (*r*), 10, 184, 189
Guayaquil (*Ecuador*), 2°13′S 79°54′W, 122
Gubbio (*Italy*), 43°21′N 12°35′E, 95
Gué-Péan (*France*), 47°22′N 1°21′E, 170
Guildford (*UK*), 51°14′N 0°35′W, 207, 212
Guipuzcoa*, 184

Haarlem (*Netherlands*), 52°23′N 4°38′E, 140
Haddon Hall (*UK*), 53°08′N 1°45′W, 212
Haddon Rig (*UK*), 55°49′N 2°41′W, 207
Hagenau (*France*), 48°49′N 7°47′E, 140, 154
Hague, The (*Netherlands*), 52°05′N 4°16′E, 22
Hainault*, 165
Halle (*Germany*), 51°28′N 11°58′E, 110
Hamburg (*Germany*), 53°33′N 10°00′E, 10, 108, 115, 138, 140, 154
Hampole (*UK*), 53°34′N 1°14′W, 16
Hampton Court (*UK*), 51°24′N 0°19′W, 212
Hanworth (*UK*), 51°26′N 0°23′W, 212
Harderwijk (*Netherlands*), 52°21′N 5°37′E, 110
Hardwick Hall (*UK*), 53°09′N 1°20′W, 212
Haro (*Spain*), 42°34′N 2°52′W, 184
Hartlepool (*UK*), 54°42′N 1°11′W, 207
Harz (*mts*), (*Germany*), 51°45′N 10°30′E, 10
Hasselt (*Belgium*), 50°56′N 5°20′E, 140
Hatfield House (*UK*), 51°46′N 0°13′W, 212
Hatteras, Cape (*USA*), 35°14′N 75°31′W, 125
Hauts Plateaux (*Algeria*), 34°00′N 1°30′W, 10
Havana (*Cuba*), 23°07′N 82°25′W, 122
Haverfordwest (*UK*), 51°49′N 4°58′W, 207
Heidelberg (*Germany*), 49°25′N 8°42′E, 110, 140, 142, 154
Heilsberg (*Poland*), 54°08′N 20°35′E, 154
Helmstedt (*Germany*), 52°14′N 11°01′E, 110, 140
Helsingborg (*Sweden*), 56°03′N 12°43′E, 138
Helsinki (*Finland*), 60°08′N 25°00′E, 11
Hengrave Hall (*UK*), 52°15′N 0°39′W, 212
Herborn (*Germany*), 50°41′N 8°19′E, 110, 140
Hersfeld (*Germany*), 50°53′N 9°43′E, 50
Hesse*, 154, 177
Hever Castle (*UK*), 51°11′N 0°06′W, 212
Hexham (*UK*), 54°58′N 2°06′W, 207
Hildesheim (*Germany*), 52°09′N 9°58′E, 110
Hinchingbrooke House (*UK*), 52°15′N 0°11′W, 212
Holdenby House (*UK*), 52°18′N 0°59′W, 212
Holland*, 154
Holstein*, 140
Holy Roman Empire*, 28, 77, 79, 119, 154, 165, 167, 177, 186
Honein (*Morocco*), 35°02′N 2°27′W, 22
Honfleur (*France*), 49°25′N 0°14′E, 167
Hooghly (*India*), 23°19′N 88°02′E, 123
Hormuz (*Iran*), 27°31′N 54°56′E, 123
Huang (*r*), 123
Huesca (*Spain*), 42°08′N 0°25′W, 110, 189
Huete (*Spain*), 40°09′N 2°42′W, 189
Hull (*UK*), 53°45′N 0°20′W, 108, 207
Hungary*, 16, 17, 77, 141, 154, 186
Huntly Castle (*UK*), 57°27′N 2°47′W, 212
Hvar (*isl*), (*Croatia*), 43°11′N 16°28′E, 34

Ibiza (*isl*), (*Spain*), 39°00′N 1°30′E, 184, 189
Ibiza (*Spain*), 38°54′N 1°26′E, 184
Iceland (*isl*), (*Iceland*), 65°00′N 20°00′E, 125
Ile de France*, 165
Imola (*Italy*), 44°22′N 11°43′E, 41, 56, 58
Imperial Hungary*, 115, 119
Incisa (*Italy*), 43°40′N 11°27′E, 41
Indian Ocean, 123
Indre (*r*), 170
Indus (*r*), 123
Ingolstadt (*Germany*), 48°46′N 11°27′E, 110, 140, 142
Inn (*r*), 10
Innsbruck (*Austria*), 47°17′N 11°25′E, 138, 154
Ionian Sea, 10
Ipswich (*UK*), 52°04′N 1°10′E, 207
Ireland*, 17, 115, 119
Isère (*r*), 58, 167
Issoire (*France*), 45°33′N 3°15′E, 167
Issoudun (*France*), 46°57′N 1°59′E, 167
Istanbul (Constantinople), (*Turkey*), 41°02′N 28°57′E, 11, 23, 49, 108, 115
Istria*, 34, 56, 58
Italy*, 16, 17
Ivrea (*Italy*), 45°28′N 7°52′E, 58

Jacmel (*Haiti*), 18°18′N 72°32′W, 122
Jaén (*Spain*), 37°46′N 3°48′W, 184, 189
Jarnac (*France*), 45°41′N 0°10′W, 177
Jarrow (*UK*), 54°59′N 1°29′W, 110
Jerba (*isl*), (*Tunisia*), 33°54′N 10°56′E, 108, 186
Jersey (*isl*), (*UK*), 49°13′N 2°07′W, 177
Jerusalem (*Israel/Jordan*), 31°47′N 35°13′E, 108
Jervaulx (*UK*), 54°14′N 1°34′W, 207
Jigginstown House (*Ireland*), 52°58′N 6°45′W, 212
Joinville (*France*), 48°27′N 5°08′E, 167
Jura Mts (*France*), 47°25′N 6°30′E, 10

Kaffa *see* Feodosiya
Kalenberg*, 154
Kalinin (Tver), (*Russia*), 56°49′N 35°57′E, 125
Kaliningrad (Königsberg), (*Russia*), 54°40′N 20°30′E, 108, 110, 138, 140
Kamien (*Poland*), 53°58′N 14°49′E, 154
Katzenelenbogen*, 177
Kazan (*Russia*), 55°45′N 49°10′E, 125
Kendal (*UK*), 54°20′N 2°45′W, 207
Kenilworth Castle (*UK*), 52°21′N 1°34′W, 212
Kharkov (*Ukraine*), 50°00′N 36°15′E, 11
Kiel (*Germany*), 54°20′N 10°08′E, 110, 138
Kiev (*Ukraine*), 50°28′N 30°29′E, 11, 108
Kilwa (*Tanzania*), 8°55′S 39°34′E, 123
Kingdom of Hungary*, 79
Kingdom of Naples*, 15, 29, 34, 56, 58, 77, 79, 186
Kingdom of Sicily*, 79
King's Lynn (*UK*), 52°45′N 0°24′E, 108, 207
King's Manor (*UK*), 53°58′N 1°05′W, 212
Kirby Hall (*UK*), 52°35′N 0°39′W, 212
Kirchheim (*France*), 48°40′N 7°30′E, 140
Kirkstead (*UK*), 53°09′N 0°16′W, 207
Kishinev (*Moldavia*), 47°01′N 28°20′E, 11
Klar (*r*), 10
Knole (*UK*), 51°29′N 0°10′W, 212
Königsberg *see* Kaliningrad
Korcula (*isl*), (*Croatia*), 42°57′N 17°08′E, 34
Kosice (*Slovakia*), 48°43′N 21°14′E, 138
Krk (*isl*), (*Croatia*), 45°02′N 14°34′E, 34
Kutna Hora (*Czech Republic*), 49°58′N 15°18′E, 140

La Calhorra (*Spain*), 37°11′N 3°03′W, 189
La Chaise Dieu (*France*), 45°19′N 3°42′E, 110
la Charité (*France*), 47°11′N 3°01′E, 177
Lacock Abbey (*UK*), 51°25′N 2°08′W, 212
la Fère (*France*), 49°40′N 3°22′E, 167
Lagny (*France*), 48°53′N 2°43′E, 22
La Malcontenta (Villa Foscari), (*Italy*), 45°26′N 12°05′E, 91
La Marche*, 165
La Muette (*France*), 48°57′N 2°07′E, 167
Lancaster (*UK*), 54°03′N 2°48′W, 207
Lanercost (*UK*), 54°57′N 2°54′W, 207
Langeais (*France*), 47°21′N 0°26′E, 170
Langres (*France*), 47°53′N 5°20′E, 52, 167
Languedoc*, 165
Laon (*France*), 49°34′N 3°37′E, 110
Lapland*, 125
la Rochefoucauld (*France*), 45°44′N 0°24′E, 167
La Rochelle (*France*), 46°10′N 1°10′W, 165, 177
La Rotonda (*Italy*), 45°30′N 11°30′E, 91
La Spezia (*Italy*), 44°07′N 9°48′E, 77
Latium*, 28
Lauingen (*Germany*), 48°33′N 10°26′E, 140
Launceston (*UK*), 50°38′N 4°21′W, 207
Lausanne (*Switzerland*), 46°32′N 6°39′E, 94, 140
Lavant (*Austria*), 47°26′N 14°32′E, 154
la Verrerie (*France*), 47°26′N 2°31′E, 170
Layer Marney Tower (*UK*), 51°50′N 0°48′E, 212
Lecce (*Italy*), 40°21′N 18°11′E, 79, 95
Leez Priory (*UK*), 51°49′N 0°21′E, 212
Legbourne (*UK*), 53°21′N 0°03′E, 207
Legnago (*Italy*), 45°12′N 11°18′, 77
Le Havre (*France*), 49°30′N 0°06′E, 165, 177
Leiden (*Netherlands*), 52°10′N 4°30′E, 110, 140
Leipzig (*Germany*), 51°20′N 12°20′E, 10, 108, 110, 115, 138, 140, 142, 154
le Lude (*France*), 47°38′N 0°13′E, 170
Le Mans (*France*), 47°59′N 0°13′E, 165, 170
le Moulin (*France*), 47°21′N 1°42′E, 170
León (*Spain*), 42°35′N 5°34′W, 184, 189
Leon*, 184
le Plessis-Bourré (*France*), 47°33′N 0°32′W, 170
le Plessis-Macé (*France*), 47°31′N 0°45′W, 170

Le Puy (*France*), 45°03′N 3°53′E, 167
Lerici (*Italy*), 44°04′N 9°55′E, 41
Lérida (*Spain*), 41°37′N 0°38′E, 110, 184, 189
Les Tuileries (*France*), 48°52′N 2°19′E, 167
Levens Hall (*UK*), 54°16′N 2°47′W, 212
Licata (*Italy*), 37°07′N 13°57′E, 22
Lichfield (*UK*), 52°42′N 1°48′W, 207
Liège (*Belgium*), 50°38′N 5°35′E, 50
Liguria*, 28
Ligurian Sea, 10, 15, 28, 34, 49, 66, 77, 79, 95
Lille (*France*), 50°39′N 3°05′E, 10, 165
Lima (*Peru*), 12°06′S 77°03′W, 122
Limburg*, 165
Limoges (*France*), 45°50′N 1°15′E, 165
Limousin*, 165
Lincoln (*UK*), 53°14′N 0°33′W, 207
Linlithgow Palace (*UK*), 55°59′N 3°37′W, 212
Linz (*Austria*), 48°19′N 14°18′E, 110, 138, 142
Lions, Gulf of, 10
Lippe*, 154
Lisbon (*Portugal*), 38°44′N 9°08′W, 10, 108, 110, 115, 125, 184, 189
Lisbon*, 189
Lithuania*, 119
Little Moreton Hall (*UK*), 53°06′N 2°17′W, 212
Livonia*, 119
Livorno (*Italy*), 43°33′N 10°18′E, 56, 58, 94
Ljubljana (*Slovenia*), 46°04′N 14°30′E, 10
Llanidloes (*UK*), 52°27′N 3°32′W, 212
Llerena (*Spain*), 38°14′N 6°00′W, 189
Loches (*France*), 47°08′N 0°58′E, 167, 170
Lodi (*Italy*), 45°19′N 9°30′E, 28, 52, 56, 58, 66
Lodz (*Poland*), 51°49′N 19°28′E, 10
Logroño (*Spain*), 42°28′N 2°26′W, 189
Loir (*r*), 170
Loire (*r*), 10, 16, 17, 41, 52, 82, 94, 108, 110, 115, 119, 146, 165, 167, 170, 177
Lombardy*, 28
Lombez (*France*), 43°29′N 0°54′E, 41
London (*UK*), 51°30′N 0°10′W, 10, 22, 108, 115, 125, 146, 177, 207, 212
Longford Castle (*UK*), 51°02′N 1°52′W, 212
Longleat House (*UK*), 51°12′N 2°13′W, 212
Lord Leycester Hospital (*UK*), 52°12′N 1°43′W, 212
Loreto (*Italy*), 43°26′N 13°36′E, 15, 66, 79, 94
Lorraine*, 154
Lorsch (*Germany*), 49°39′N 8°35′E, 50
Losna (*r*), 10
Lot (*r*), 41, 167
Louvain (*Belgium*), 50°53′N 4°42′E, 110, 140, 146
Louvre (*France*), 48°51′N 2°20′E, 167
Low Countries*, 140
Loyola (*Spain*), 43°15′N 2°20′W, 189
Luanda (*Angola*), 8°50′S 13°15′E, 122
Lübeck (*Germany*), 53°52′N 10°40′E, 22, 108, 138, 140, 142, 154
Lucca (*Italy*), 43°50′N 10°30′E, 15, 16, 22, 28, 34, 49, 56, 58, 77, 79
Lucca*, 15, 56, 58
Lucmanier Pass (*Switzerland*), 46°34′N 8°48′E, 77
Ludlow (*UK*), 52°22′N 2°43′W, 212
Lugo (*Spain*), 43°00′N 7°33′W, 189
Lund (*Sweden*), 55°42′N 13°10′E, 110
Lüneburg (*Germany*), 53°15′N 10°24′E, 138, 140
Lusatia*, 140, 154
Luxembourg (*Luxembourg*), 49°37′N 6°08′E, 10, 165
Luxembourg*, 140, 154, 165
Luxeuil (*France*), 47°49′N 6°24′E, 52
Lvov (*Ukraine*), 49°50′N 24°00′E, 138
Lyon (*France*), 45°46′N 4°50′E, 10, 22, 41, 94, 108, 115, 138, 165, 167, 177
Lyveden New Bield (*UK*), 52°26′N 0°30′W, 212

Macao (*Portugal*), 22°10′N 113°33′E, 123
Macerata (*Italy*), 43°18′N 13°27′E, 95
Machynlleth (*UK*), 52°35′N 3°51′W, 207
Mâcon (*France*), 46°18′N 4°50′E, 167
Madrid (*Spain*), 40°25′N 3°43′W, 10, 115, 184, 189
Magdeburg (*Germany*), 52°08′N 11°37′E, 110, 140, 154
Magellan, Strait of, 122
Maggiore, Lake (*Italy*), 46°00′N 8°45′E, 15, 28, 34, 56, 66
Main (*r*), 10
Maine*, 165
Maine-Perche*, 170
Mainz (*Germany*), 50°00′N 8°16′E, 22, 52, 110, 115, 140, 154
Majorca (*isl*), (*Spain*), 39°30′N 3°00′E, 185, 186, 189
Majorca*, 184
Makri (*Turkey*), 36°42′N 29°10′E, 23
Malacca (*Malaysia*), 2°14′N 102°14′E, 123
Malaga (*Spain*), 36°43′N 4°25′W, 22, 108, 184, 189
Malindi (*Kenya*), 3°14′S 40°08′E, 123
Malmö (*Sweden*), 55°35′N 13°00′E, 138
Malta (*isl*), (*Malta*), 35°58′N 14°00′E, 119, 186
Manila (*Philippines*), 14°36′N 120°59′E, 123
Manne (*France*), 47°58′N 3°45′E, 167
Manresa (*Spain*), 41°43′N 1°50′E, 189
Mantua (*Italy*), 45°10′N 10°47′E, 15, 16, 28, 41, 49, 58, 66, 79, 82, 91, 94, 95, 112, 138
Mantua*, 15, 56, 58
Marans (*France*), 46°19′N 1°01′W, 177
Marburg (*Germany*), 50°49′N 8°36′E, 110, 140
March of Ancona*, 28
Marienburg (*Poland*), 54°02′N 19°01′E, 138, 140
Marienthal (*Germany*), 50°01′N 7°38′E, 140
Marienwerder (*Poland*), 53°44′N 18°53′E, 154
Marignano (*Italy*), 45°22′N 9°19′E, 77
Maritime Alps (*mts*), (*France*), 44°00′N 6°45′E, 10
Maritime Atlas (*mts*), (*Algeria*), 36°00′N 5°30′E, 10
Mark*, 154
Marne (*r*), 10, 167
Marsala (*Italy*), 37°48′N 12°27′E, 22
Marseille (*France*), 43°18′N 5°22′E, 10, 16, 22, 41, 108, 165, 167, 186
Massa (*Italy*), 43°54′N 10°45′E, 58
Meaux (*France*), 48°58′N 2°54′E, 167, 177
Mecklenburg (*Germany*), 53°52′N 11°27′E, 154
Mecklenburg*, 154
Medina del Campo (*Spain*), 41°18′N 4°55′W, 184, 189
Medina Sidonia (*Spain*), 36°28′N 5°55′W, 184
Mediterranean Sea, 10, 16, 17, 22, 41, 52, 82, 94, 108, 110, 119, 122, 125, 165, 167, 177, 184, 186, 189
Meissen (*Germany*), 51°10′N 13°28′E, 140, 154
Melilla (*Morocco*), 35°17′N 2°57′W, 108, 186
Melun (*France*), 48°32′N 2°40′E, 177
Memmingen (*Germany*), 47°59′N 10°11′E, 140
Menderes (*r*), 11
Mérida (*Mexico*), 20°59′N 89°39′W, 122
Mérida (*Spain*), 38°55′N 6°20′W, 184, 189
Merseburg (*Germany*), 51°22′N 12°00′E, 140
Messina (*Italy*), 38°13′N 15°33′E, 22, 108, 110, 186
Metz (*France*), 49°07′N 6°11′E, 110, 138, 140, 154, 165
Meung (*France*), 47°50′N 1°42′E, 170
Meuse (*r*), 10, 22, 52, 154, 165, 167, 177
Mézin (*France*), 44°04′N 0°16′E, 177
Middle Atlas (*mts*), (*Morocco*), 33°00′N 5°00′W, 10
Midmar (*UK*), 57°07′N 2°30′W, 212
Milan (*Italy*), 45°28′N 9°12′E, 10, 15, 22, 28, 34, 41, 49, 56, 58, 66, 77, 79, 82, 95, 108, 110, 112, 115, 138
Milan*, 15
Miletus (*Turkey*), 37°30′N 27°18′E, 23
Millau (*France*), 44°06′N 3°05′E, 177
Minho (*r*), 184
Minorca (*isl*), (*Spain*), 40°00′N 4°00′E, 185
Minsk (*Belorussia*), 53°51′N 27°30′E, 11
Modena (*Italy*), 44°39′N 10°55′E, 28, 41, 58, 79
Modena*, 15
Modon (*Greece*), 36°49′N 21°42′E, 108
Moldoveanu (*mt*), (*Romania*), 45°37′N 24°59′E, 11
Mombasa (*Kenya*), 4°04′S 39°40′E, 123
Monaco (*Monaco*), 43°46′N 7°23′E, 41, 58
Moncastro (*Ukraine*), 46°01′N 30°21′E, 23
Moncontour (*France*), 46°53′N 0°01′W, 177
Mondavio (*Italy*), 43°41′N 12°59′E, 66
Mondoñedo (*Spain*), 43°26′N 7°22′W, 189
Mondovi (*Italy*), 44°23′N 7°49′E, 58
Monreale (*Italy*), 38°05′N 13°17′E, 110
Mons (*Belgium*), 50°28′N 3°58′E, 22
Monselice (*Italy*), 45°41′N 11°46′E, 41
Montacute House (*UK*), 50°57′N 2°43′W, 212
Montalcino (*Italy*), 43°03′N 11°29′E, 77
Montargis (*France*), 48°00′N 2°44′E, 167, 170
Montauban (*France*), 44°01′N 1°20′E, 177
Mont Cenis, Col du (*France*), 45°15′N 6°55′E, 77, 94, 165
Monte Cassino (*Italy*), 41°29′N 13°50′E, 5, 110
Montecatini (*Italy*), 43°53′N 10°47′E, 49
Montefiascone (*Italy*), 42°32′N 12°03′E, 66
Montemurlo (*Italy*), 43°56′N 11°03′E, 77
Montepulciano (*Italy*), 43°05′N 11°46′E, 15, 66
Monte San Giovanni Campano (*Italy*), 41°38′N 13°32′E, 77
Montferrat*, 15, 58, 79
Mont Genèvre, Col de (*France*), 44°56′N 6°45′E, 77, 165
Montiel (*Spain*), 38°42′N 2°52′W, 184
Montigny-le-Gannelon (*France*), 48°01′N 1°15′E, 170
Montpellier (*France*), 43°36′N 3°53′E, 22, 41, 110, 165, 167, 177
Montpoupon (*France*), 47°15′N 1°10′E, 170
Montrésor (*France*), 47°09′N 1°12′E, 170
Montreuil (*France*), 50°28′N 1°46′E, 167
Mont-St-Michel (*France*), 48°38′N 1°30′W, 110, 167
Montserrat (*Spain*), 41°36′N 1°48′E, 189
Morava (*r*), 11
Moravia*, 119, 140, 154
Mortimers Cross (*UK*), 52°16′N 2°50′W, 207
Moscow (*Russia*), 55°45′N 37°42′E, 11, 108, 125
Moselle (*r*), 165
Moulins (*France*), 46°34′N 3°20′E, 167
Moulouya (*r*), 10
Mount Edgcumbe (*UK*), 50°15′N 4°11′W, 212
Mozambique (*Mozambique*), 15°00′S 40°44′E, 123
Mulhacén (*mt*), (*Spain*), 37°04′N 3°19′W, 10
Munich (*Germany*), 48°08′N 11°35′E, 10, 115, 138, 140, 154
Münster (*Germany*), 51°58′N 7°37′E, 138, 140, 154
Murbach (*France*), 47°43′N 7°50′E, 50
Murcia (*Spain*), 37°59′N 1°08′W, 184, 189
Murcia*, 184
Mures (*r*), 11
Musala (*mt*), (*Bulgaria*), 42°10′N 23°40′E, 11

Nagasaki (*Japan*), 32°45′N 129°52′E, 123
Namur*, 165
Nantes (*France*), 47°14′N 1°35′W, 110, 167, 170, 177
Nantouillet (*France*), 49°02′N 2°48′E, 167
Naples (*Italy*), 40°50′N 14°15′E, 10, 15, 16, 22, 34, 41, 58, 77, 79, 94, 95, 108, 110, 186
Naples*, 16, 17, 115, 119
Narbonne (*France*), 43°11′N 3°00′E, 165, 167
Narni (*Italy*), 42°31′N 12°31′E, 22, 41, 66
Nassau*, 154, 177
Navarre*, 16, 17, 165, 184, 186
Navarrenx (*France*), 43°20′N 0°45′W, 177
Naworth Castle (*UK*), 54°52′N 2°46′W, 212
Neman (*r*), 11
Nepi (*Italy*), 42°14′N 12°21′E, 66, 77
Nettuno (*Italy*), 41°27′N 12°20′E, 66
Neuchâtel (*Switzerland*), 46°60′N 6°56′E, 177
New Castile*, 184
Newcastle (*UK*), 54°59′N 1°35′W, 108, 207
Newfoundland (*isl*), (*Canada*), 49°20′N 6°40′W, 125
New Hall (*UK*), 51°50′N 0°30′E, 212
Newstead Abbey (*UK*), 53°04′N 1°13′W, 212
Nice (*France*), 43°42′N 7°16′E, 41, 108
Nicosia (*Cyprus*), 35°11′N 33°23′E, 11
Niebla (*Spain*), 37°22′N 6°40′W, 184
Niger (*r*), 122
Nijmegen (*Netherlands*), 51°50′N 5°52′E, 140
Nile (*r*), 123
Nîmes (*France*), 43°50′N 4°21′E, 167, 177
Nis (*Yugoslavia*), 43°20′N 21°54′E, 138
Nivernais*, 165
Nizhniy Novgorod *see* Gorky
Nonsuch (*UK*), 51°21′N 0°15′W, 212
Nördlingen (*Germany*), 48°51′N 10°31′E, 108
Normandy*, 165
Norway*, 16, 17
Norwich (*UK*), 52°38′N 1°18′E, 207
Novara (*Italy*), 45°27′N 8°37′E, 28, 58, 77, 79
Novgorod (*Russia*), 58°30′N 31°20′E, 108
Nunburnholme (*UK*), 53°56′N 0°42′W, 207
Nuremberg (*Germany*), 49°27′N 11°05′E, 108, 115, 138, 140, 142, 154

Oatlands (*UK*), 51°22′N 0°25′W, 212
Oder (*r*), 10, 110, 115, 119, 138, 142
Odessa (*Ukraine*), 46°30′N 30°46′E, 11
Offenburg (*Germany*), 48°29′N 7°57′E, 140
Offida (*Italy*), 42°56′N 13°41′E, 66
Oise (*r*), 167
Oka (*r*), 11
Okehampton (*UK*), 50°44′N 4°00′W, 207
Old Castile*, 184
Olinda (*Brazil*), 8°00′S 34°51′W, 122
Olmedo (*Spain*), 41°17′N 4°41′W, 184
Olomouc (*Czech Republic*), 49°38′N 17°15′E, 110, 138, 140, 142
Olt (*r*), 11
Olympus (*mt*), (*Greece*), 40°05′N 22°21′E, 11
Oporto (*Portugal*), 41°09′N 8°37′W, 10, 184, 189
Oppenheim (*Germany*), 49°52′N 8°22′E, 140
Oran (*Algeria*), 35°45′N 0°38′W, 22, 108, 186
Orange (*France*), 44°08′N 4°48′E, 110, 177
Orange*, 165, 177
Orkney Islands (*UK*), 59°00′N 3°00′W, 10, 125
Orleanais*, 165, 170
Orléans (*France*), 47°54′N 1°54′E, 110, 165, 167, 170, 177
Orte (*Italy*), 42°27′N 12°23′E, 22
Orthez (*France*), 43°29′N 0°46′W, 110
Orvieto (*Italy*), 42°43′N 12°06′E, 15, 34, 58, 66, 79
Oslo (*Norway*), 59°56′N 10°45′E, 10, 108
Osnabrück (*Germany*), 52°17′N 8°03′E, 110
Ostia (*Italy*), 41°46′N 12°18′E, 66
Otranto (*Italy*), 40°08′N 18°30′E, 22, 58
Otranto*, 58
Ottoman Empire*, 77, 79, 115, 119, 141, 154
Oudenaarde (*Belgium*), 50°50′N 3°37′E, 140
Ouse (*r*), 207, 212
Oviedo (*Spain*), 43°21′N 5°50′W, 110, 184, 189
Oxford (*UK*), 51°46′N 1°15′W, 110, 115, 146, 207, 212

Pacific Ocean, 122, 123
Paderborn (*Germany*), 51°43′N 8°44′E, 110
Padua (*Italy*), 45°24′N 11°53′E, 15, 22, 28, 34, 41, 49, 58, 77, 79, 91, 94, 95, 110, 112, 138, 142
Palatinate*, 154
Palencia (*Spain*), 42°01′N 4°32′W, 110, 189
Palermo (*Italy*), 38°08′N 13°23′E, 10, 22, 58, 79, 108, 110, 186
Palestrina (*Italy*), 41°50′N 12°54′E, 41
Palma (*Spain*), 39°34′N 2°31′E, 108, 110, 185, 189
Palos de la Frontera (*Spain*), 37°14′N 6°53′W, 184
Pamplona (*Spain*), 42°49′N 1°39′W, 184, 189
Papal States*, 15, 16, 17, 28, 34, 56, 58, 77, 79, 115, 119, 186
Paphos (*Cyprus*), 34°45′N 32°23′E, 108
Paris (*France*), 48°52′N 2°20′E, 10, 22, 49, 52, 94, 108, 110, 115, 140, 146, 165, 170, 177
Parma (*Italy*), 44°48′N 10°19′E, 28, 41, 56, 58, 77, 79, 82, 94, 95, 110, 138
Parma*, 15
Passau (*Germany*), 48°35′N 13°28′E, 140, 154
Patrimony of St Peter*, 58
Pau (*France*), 43°18′N 0°22′W, 167, 177
Pavia (*Italy*), 45°12′N 9°09′E, 22, 28, 41, 49, 58, 66, 77, 79, 82, 95, 110
Peipus, Lake, 11
Peñíscola (*Spain*), 40°22′N 0°24′E, 16
Penshurst Place (*UK*), 51°11′N 0°11′E, 212
Pera (*Turkey*), 41°05′N 28°58′E, 23
Perigord*, 165
Périgueux (*France*), 45°12′N 0°44′E, 177
Perpignan (*France*), 42°42′N 2°54′E, 16, 110, 184
Perugia (*Italy*), 43°07′N 12°23′E, 15, 22, 34, 41, 56, 58, 77, 79, 95, 110
Pesaro (*Italy*), 43°45′N 12°54′E, 15, 79, 95
Pescara (*Italy*), 42°27′N 14°13′E, 58
Peschiera (*Italy*), 45°26′N 10°41′E, 77
Pescia (*Italy*), 43°54′N 10°41′E, 49
Peterborough (*UK*), 52°35′N 0°15′W, 110, 207
Pézenas (*France*), 43°28′N 3°25′E, 177
Pforzheim (*Germany*), 48°53′N 8°41′E, 140
Phocaea (*Turkey*), 38°39′N 26°46′E, 23
Piacenza (*Italy*), 45°03′N 9°41′E, 28, 34, 56, 58, 77, 79, 94, 95, 110, 138
Piave (*r*), 15, 58, 77, 91
Picardy*, 165
Picco St Bernard, Col du (*France/Italy*), 45°40′N 6°53′E, 165
Piedmont*, 15, 28
Pietracupa (*Italy*), 44°03′N 11°57′E, 66
Pieve di Cadore (*Italy*), 46°27′N 12°23′E, 77
Pindus Mts (*Greece*), 39°00′N 21°00′E, 11
Pinkie (*UK*), 55°49′N 3°09′W, 207
Piobbico (*Italy*), 43°35′N 12°30′E, 79
Piombino (*Italy*), 42°56′N 10°32′E, 56, 58, 66, 77, 82, 108
Piombino*, 15
Pisa (*Italy*), 43°43′N 10°24′E, 15, 16, 22, 28, 34, 41, 56, 58, 66, 77, 94, 95, 108, 110
Pistoia (*Italy*), 43°56′N 10°55′E, 15, 34, 49, 56, 58, 66
Plasencia (*Spain*), 40°02′N 6°05′W, 184, 189
Plessis-lès-Tours (*France*), 47°20′N 0°43′E, 170
Plzen (*Czech Republic*), 49°45′N 13°22′E, 140
Po (*r*), 15, 17, 22, 28, 34, 41, 49, 56, 58, 77, 79, 82, 91, 94, 95, 110, 112, 115, 119, 140, 146
Poggibonsi (*Italy*), 43°28′N 11°09′E, 77
Poggio a Caiano (*Italy*), 43°48′N 11°03′E, 95
Poggio Imperiale (*Italy*), 43°45′N 11°12′E, 66, 77, 95
Poggio Reale (*Italy*), 40°52′N 14°17′E, 95
Poitiers (*France*), 46°35′N 0°20′E, 110, 165, 177
Poitou*, 165
Poland*, 16, 17, 115, 119, 141, 154
Pomerania*, 154
Pomposa (*Italy*), 45°02′N 12°19′E, 52
Ponce-sur-le-Loir (*France*), 47°47′N 0°43′E, 170
Pons (*France*), 45°35′N 0°32′W, 177
Pont-à-Mousson (*France*), 48°55′N 6°03′E, 110
Pontecorvo (*Italy*), 41°27′N 13°40′E, 58
Pontine Mts (*Turkey*), 41°00′N 41°30′E, 11
Pontremoli (*Italy*), 44°23′N 9°53′E, 77
Port 'Ercole (*Italy*), 42°23′N 11°13′E, 77
Portico di Romagna (*Italy*), 44°01′N 11°47′E, 49
Porto Maurizio (*Italy*), 43°54′N 7°59′E, 41
Porto Recanati (*Italy*), 43°26′N 13°39′E, 16
Porto Torres (*Italy*), 40°51′N 8°24′E, 108
Portugal*, 16, 17, 115, 119, 122, 184, 186
Potosí (*Bolivia*), 19°34′S 65°45′W, 122
Poundisford Park (*UK*), 50°59′N 3°15′W, 212
Powis Castle (*UK*), 52°40′N 3°20′E, 212
Poznan (*Poland*), 52°25′N 16°53′E, 138
Prague (*Czech Republic*), 50°05′N 14°25′E, 10, 108, 110, 115, 138, 140, 142, 154
Prato (*Italy*), 43°53′N 11°06′E, 15, 34, 66, 77
Pratolino (*Italy*), 43°51′N 11°17′E, 95
Principate of Piedmont*, 79
Promenthoux (*Switzerland*), 46°20′N 6°13′E, 140
Provence*, 16, 17, 41, 58, 165
Provins (*France*), 48°34′N 3°18′E, 22
Prussia*, 119, 140, 154
Prut (*r*), 11
Puebla (*Mexico*), 19°03′N 98°10′W, 122
Pula (*Croatia*), 44°52′N 13°52′E, 16
Puy de Sancy (*mt*), (*France*), 45°32′N 2°48′E, 10
Pyrenees (*mts*), (*France/Spain*), 42°56′N 0°12′E, 10

Quercy*, 165

Rabat (*Morocco*), 34°02′N 6°51′W, 10
Ragusa *see* Dubrovnik
Rapallo (*Italy*), 44°21′N 9°13′E, 77
Ravenna (*Italy*), 44°25′N 12°12′E, 15, 28, 49, 56, 58, 77, 79, 110
Regensburg (*Germany*), 49°01′N 12°07′E, 110, 140, 142, 154
Reggio (*Italy*), 44°42′N 10°37′E, 28, 34, 58, 79, 110
Reggio di Calabria (*Italy*), 38°06′N 15°39′E, 58, 66, 77, 79, 115, 186
Reichenau (*Germany*), 47°42′N 9°05′E, 52
Reigate Priory (*UK*), 51°14′N 0°13′W, 212
Reims (*France*), 49°15′N 4°02′E, 110, 165, 177
Rennes (*France*), 48°06′N 1°40′W, 108, 165, 167
Reno (*r*), 58, 77
Republic of Florence*, 15, 56, 58
Republic of Genoa*, 15, 56, 58, 79
Republic of Lucca*, 79
Republic of Siena*, 15, 56, 58

Republic of Venice*, 15, 28, 56, 58, 77, 79, 140, 154, 186
Resia Pass (*Italy*), 46°50′N 10°31′E, 77
Reuss*, 154
Reutlingen (*Germany*), 48°30′N 9°13′E, 140
Reval *see* Tallinn
Rheinstein (*Germany*), 49°59′N 7°41′E, 140
Rhine (*r*), 10, 16, 17, 22, 52, 94, 108, 110, 115, 119, 138, 140, 142, 146, 154, 165, 177
Rhine Palatinate*, 177
Rhodes (*isl*), (*Greece*), 36°25′N 28°16′E, 11, 23, 108
Rhodes (*Greece*), 36°26′N 28°14′E, 23
Rhodope Mts (*Bulgaria*), 41°30′N 24°30′E, 11
Rhône (*r*), 10, 16, 17, 22, 41, 58, 82, 94, 108, 110, 115, 119, 142, 146, 165, 167, 177
Richmond (*UK*), 54°24′N 1°44′W, 207
Rieti (*Italy*), 42°24′N 12°51′E, 79
Rievaulx (*UK*), 54°15′N 1°07′W, 110
Riga (*Latvia*), 56°53′N 24°08′E, 11, 108, 138
Rimini (*Italy*), 44°03′N 12°34′E, 15, 16, 22, 28, 34, 41, 49, 58, 66, 77, 79
Ripon (*UK*), 54°08′N 1°31′W, 207
Rochefort (*France*), 45°57′N 0°28′W, 177
Rodez (*France*), 44°21′N 2°34′E, 167
Rodosto *see* Tekirdag
Romagna*, 28, 58
Romans (*France*), 45°03′N 5°03′E, 167
Rome (*Italy*), 41°53′N 12°30′E, 10, 15, 16, 17, 22, 28, 34, 41, 49, 58, 66, 77, 79, 82, 94, 95, 108, 110, 115, 142
Rostock (*Germany*), 54°06′N 12°09′E, 110, 138, 140, 142, 154
Rothwell (*UK*), 52°25′N 0°48′W, 212
Rotterdam (*Netherlands*), 51°55′N 4°29′E, 10
Rouen (*France*), 42°26′N 1°05′E, 108, 165, 167, 177
Rouergue*, 165
Rougemont (*Switzerland*), 46°30′N 7°13′E, 140
Roussillon*, 165, 184, 186
Rushton (*UK*), 52°26′N 0°40′W, 212
Ryazan (*Russia*), 54°37′N 39°43′E, 125
Rye (*UK*), 50°57′N 0°44′E, 177

Sabbioneta (*Italy*), 45°00′N 10°29′E, 95
Saharan Atlas (*mts*), (*Algeria*), 34°00′N 2°00′E, 10
St Agostín (*USA*), 29°45′N 81°19′W, 122′W
St Aignan (*France*), 47°16′N 1°22′E, 170
St Albans (*UK*), 51°46′N 0°21′W, 207
St Andrews (*UK*), 56°20′N 2°48′W, 110
St Columba's (*UK*), 56°05′N 3°12′W, 212
St Denis (*France*), 48°56′N 2°21′E, 167, 177
St Dizier (*France*), 48°38′N 4°58′E, 165
Saintes (*France*), 45°44′N 0°38′W, 177
St Gall (*Switzerland*), 47°25′N 9°23′E, 52, 110
St Germain-en-Laye (*France*), 48°53′N 2°04′E, 167
St Gotthard (*Switzerland*), 46°34′N 8°31′E, 77
St-Jean-d'Angély (*France*), 45°47′N 0°31′W, 177
St Lawrence (*r*), 125
St Maur (*France*), 48°48′N 2°30′E, 167
Saintonge*, 165
St Petersburg (*Russia*), 59°55′N 30°25′E, 11
St Quentin (*France*), 49°51′N 3°17′E, 165
Salamanca (*Spain*), 40°58′N 5°40′W, 110, 184, 189
Salé (*Morocco*), 34°04′N 6°50′W, 22
Salerno (*Italy*), 40°40′N 14°46′E, 22, 34, 79, 95, 110
Salins (*France*), 46°56′N 5°53′E, 140
Salisbury (*UK*), 51°05′N 1°48′W, 207
Salonika (*Greece*), 40°38′N 22°58′E, 23, 115
Saltillo (*Mexico*), 25°30′N 101°00′W, 122
Saluzzo (*Italy*), 44°39′N 7°29′E, 58
Saluzzo*, 58, 79, 165
Salzburg (*Austria*), 47°54′N 13°03′E, 110, 154
Salzburg*, 119
Samford Courtenay (*UK*), 50°45′N 3°58′W, 207
San Bernardino Pass (*Switzerland*), 46°30′N 9°11′E, 77
Sancerre (*France*), 47°20′N 2°50′E, 177
San Germano *see* Cassino
San Gimignano (*Italy*), 43°28′N 11°02′E, 15, 28
San Juan (*Puerto Rico*), 18°29′N 66°08′W, 122
San Leo (*Italy*), 43°54′N 12°20′E, 66
Sanlúcar (*Spain*), 37°23′N 6°13′W, 184
Sanluri (*Italy*), 39°34′N 8°54′E, 186
Sansepolcro (*Italy*), 43°34′N 12°08′E, 15, 66, 77
San Stefano (*Italy*), 43°51′N 10°27′E, 77
Santa Fé de Bogotá (*Colombia*), 4°38′N 74°05′W, 122
Santa Maria de Capellis (*Italy*), 41°19′N 14°18′E, 41
Santa Marta (*Columbia*), 11°18′N 74°10′W, 122
Santander (*Spain*), 43°28′N 3°48′W, 184
Santiago (*Chile*), 33°30′S 70°40′W, 122
Santiago de Compostela (*Spain*), 42°52′N 8°33′W, 110, 184, 189
Santiago*, 189
Santo Domingo (*Dominican Republic*), 18°30′N 69°57′W, 122
Saône (*r*), 10, 167
Sarajevo (*Bosnia and Hercegovina*), 43°52′N 18°26′E, 10
Sardinia (*isl*), (*Italy*), 40°00′N 9°30′E, 10, 15, 16, 17, 22, 41, 66, 77, 79, 95, 108, 110, 115, 119, 186
Saronno (*Italy*), 45°38′N 9°02′E, 66
Sarthe (*r*), 170
Sarzanello (*Italy*), 44°07′N 9°57′E, 77
Sassocorvara (*Italy*), 42°47′N 12°30′E, 66
Sassoferrato (*Italy*), 43°26′N 12°51′E, 66
Saumur (*France*), 47°16′N 0°05′W, 170, 177
Saumurois*, 170
Sava (*r*), 10, 22, 52, 79, 95, 108, 115, 119, 138, 140, 142
Savigny (*France*), 48°33′N 1°00′W, 110
Savoy*, 16, 17, 79, 140, 165
Sawley (*UK*), 53°55′N 2°20′W, 207
Saxony*, 140, 154
Schiedam (*Netherlands*), 51°55′N 4°25′E, 140
Schleswig (*Germany*), 54°32′N 9°34′E, 140
Schoonhoven (*Netherlands*), 51°57′N 4°51′E, 140
Scotland*, 16, 17, 115, 119
Seckau (*Austria*), 47°14′N 14°50′E, 154
Sedan (*France*), 49°42′N 4°57′E, 177
Sedan*, 177
Segovia (*Spain*), 40°57′N 4°07′W, 184, 189
Seine (*r*), 10, 16, 17, 22, 52, 94, 110, 115, 119, 140, 142, 146, 165, 167, 170
Serbia*, 186
Serego (*Italy*), 45°29′N 10°49′E, 91
Serrant (*France*), 47°23′N 0°45′W, 170
Severn (*r*), 207, 212
Seville (*Spain*), 37°24′N 5°59′W, 22, 108, 110, 184, 189
Seville*, 189
Seyhan (*r*), 11
Sherborne Castle (*UK*), 50°57′N 2°31′W, 212
's-Hertogenbosch (*Netherlands*), 51°41′N 5°19′E, 140, 146
Shetland Islands (*UK*), 61°00′N 1°30′W, 10, 125
Shrewsbury (*UK*), 52°43′N 2°45′W, 207, 212
Sibiu (*Romania*), 45°46′N 24°09′E, 138
Sicily (*isl*), (*Italy*), 37°30′N 13°00′E, 10, 16, 17, 22, 77, 79, 95, 108, 110, 115, 119, 186
Siena (*Italy*), 43°19′N 11°19′E, 15, 16, 22, 28, 34, 41, 49, 56, 58, 77, 79, 94, 95, 110, 146
Sierra Morena (*mts*), (*Spain*), 38°00′N 4°00′W, 10
Sierra Nevada (*mts*), (*Spain*), 37°25′N 2°30′W, 10
Signa (*Italy*), 43°47′N 11°06′E, 77
Sigüenza (*Spain*), 41°04′N 2°38′W, 110, 189
Silesia*, 119, 140, 154
Sint Maartensdijck (*Netherlands*), 52°17′N 5°04′E, 140
Sissinghurst (*UK*), 51°07′N 0°35′E, 212
Sizergh Castle (*UK*), 54°20′N 2°46′W, 212
Skipton (*UK*), 53°58′N 2°01′W, 207
Skopje (*Macedonia*), 42°00′N 21°28′E, 11
Sluis (*Netherlands*), 51°18′N 3°23′E, 22
Smolensk (*Russia*), 54°49′N 32°04′E, 108
Sofala (*Mozambique*), 20°09′S 34°43′E, 123
Sofia (*Bulgaria*), 42°40′N 23°18′E, 11
Soissons (*France*), 49°23′N 3°20′E, 167
Solway Moss (*UK*), 54°58′N 2°56′W, 207
Soria (*Spain*), 41°46′N 2°28′W, 189
Sorrento (*Italy*), 40°37′N 14°23′E, 79
Southampton (*UK*), 50°55′N 1°25′W, 177
Spain*, 115, 119, 122, 165, 167, 177
Spanish Netherlands*, 119
Speyer (*Germany*), 49°18′N 8°26′E, 110, 138, 140, 154
Split (*Croatia*), 43°31′N 16°28′E, 58
Spoleto (*Italy*), 42°44′N 12°44′E, 15, 22, 58, 66
Spoleto*, 58
Sponheim (*Germany*), 49°49′N 7°52′E, 142
Stafford (*UK*), 52°48′N 2°07′W, 207
Stendal (*Germany*), 52°36′N 11°52′E, 140
Stettin *see* Szczecin
Steyn (*Netherlands*), 51°52′N 4°49′E, 146
Stiffkey Hall (*UK*), 52°57′N 0°56′E, 212
Stignano (*Italy*), 43°48′N 10°42′E, 49
Stirling Castle (*UK*), 56°07′N 3°57′W, 212
Stockholm (*Sweden*), 59°20′N 18°05′E, 10, 108, 115
Stoke-on-Trent (*UK*), 53°00′N 2°10′W, 207
Stokefield (*UK*), 52°59′N 0°52′W, 207
Stora (*Algeria*), 36°57′N 7°06′E, 22
Stralsund (*Germany*), 54°18′N 13°06′E, 138
Strasbourg (*France*), 48°55′N 7°45′E, 110, 115, 138, 140, 154, 165, 177
Stuttgart (*Germany*), 48°47′N 9°12′E, 140
Styria*, 119
Subiaco (*Italy*), 41°56′N 13°06′E, 66, 115
Sudeley Castle (*UK*), 51°54′N 2°01′W, 212
Sunderland (Wearmouth), (*UK*), 54°55′N 1°23′E, 110
Sully (*France*), 47°46′N 2°22′E, 170
Sursee (*Switzerland*), 47°11′N 8°07′E, 140
Susa (*Italy*), 45°08′N 7°02′E, 58, 77
Sutri (*Italy*), 42°14′N 12°14′E, 58
Sutton Place (*UK*), 51°19′N 0°30′W, 212
Sweden*, 16, 17, 115, 119
Swiss Confederation*, 119, 140, 154, 177
Syracuse (*Italy*), 37°04′N 15°18′E, 22, 58, 108
Szczecin (Stettin), (*Poland*), 53°25′N 14°32′E, 108, 138

Tagus (*r*), 10, 22, 110, 115, 119, 184, 189
Talamone (*Italy*), 42°33′N 11°08′E, 22, 58
Tallinn (Reval), (*Estonia*), 59°22′N 24°48′E, 11, 108
Tana (*Russia*), 47°11′N 39°24′E, 23
Tanaro (*r*), 28, 34, 66
Tangier (*Morocco*), 35°48′N 5°45′W, 184, 186
Tarasçon (*France*), 43°48′N 4°39′E, 22
Tarn (*r*), 167
Taro (*r*), 77
Tarragona (*Spain*), 41°07′N 1°15′E, 184, 189
Tarragona*, 189
Tauern*, 10
Taurus Mts (*Turkey*), 37°00′N 33°00′E, 11
Tay (*r*), 212
Tekirdag (Rodosto), (*Turkey*), 40°59′N 27°31′E, 23
Tenda (*France*), 44°09′N 7°34′E, 58
Ténès (*Algeria*), 36°34′N 1°18′E, 22
Tenochtitlán (*Mexico*), 19°25′N 99°08′W, 122
Termini (*Italy*), 37°59′N 13°42′E, 22
Terni (*Italy*), 42°34′N 12°39′E, 22, 66
Terra di Lavoro*, 58
Terracina (*Italy*), 41°17′N 13°15′E, 58
Terranuova (*Italy*), 43°38′N 11°35′E, 49
Thame Park (*UK*), 51°45′N 0°59′W, 212
Thames (*r*), 10, 207, 212
Theobalds (*UK*), 51°44′N 0°02′W, 212
Thornbury (*UK*), 51°37′N 2°32′W, 212
Thurgarton (*UK*), 53°02′N 0°58′W, 16
Tiber (*r*), 10, 15, 28, 34, 49, 52, 56, 58, 66, 77, 79, 82, 94, 95
Ticino (*r*), 58
Timor (*Indonesia*), 9°42′S 124°40′E, 123
Tiranë (*Albania*), 41°20′N 19°49′E, 10
Tisza (*r*), 11
Titchfield Abbey (*UK*), 50°51′N 1°13′W, 212
Tivoli (*Italy*), 41°58′N 12°48′E, 66, 95
Tixall (*UK*), 52°48′N 2°01′W, 212
Tlemcen (*Algeria*), 34°53′ 1°21′W, 22
Todi (*Italy*), 42°47′N 12°24′E, 34, 41, 49, 66, 79
Toledo (*Spain*), 39°52′N 4°02′W, 110, 184, 189
Toledo*, 189
Tolentino (*Italy*), 43°12′N 13°17′E, 49
Toro (*Spain*), 41°31′N 5°24′W, 184, 189
Tortona (*Italy*), 44°54′N 8°52′E, 58
Tortosa (*Spain*), 40°49′N 0°31′E, 22, 189
Toscanella (*Italy*), 42°28′N 11°51′E, 77
Toul (*France*), 48°41′N 5°54′E, 165
Toulon (*France*), 43°07′N 5°55′E, 165
Toulouse (*France*), 43°37′N 1°26′E, 41, 108, 110, 165, 167, 177
Touraine*, 170
Tournai (*Belgium*), 50°36′N 3°24′E, 110, 165
Tours (*France*), 47°23′N 0°42′E, 110, 165, 167, 170
Towton Moor (*UK*), 53°51′N 1°16′W, 207
Transylvanian Alps (*mts*), (*Romania*), 41°00′N 25°00′E, 11
Trapani (*Italy*), 38°02′N 12°32′E, 22
Trent (*r*), 207, 212
Trent (*Italy*), 46°04′N 11°08′E, 58
Trent*, 58
Treviso (*Italy*), 45°40′N 12°15′E, 28, 34, 58, 77, 110
Trier (*Germany*), 49°45′N 6°39′E, 110, 140, 154
Trieste (*Italy*), 45°39′N 13°47′E, 34, 56, 58, 142
Tripoli (*Libya*), 32°53′N 13°12′E, 22, 108, 186
Tristan da Cunha (*isl*), (*UK*), 37°15′S 12°30′W, 122
Troyes (*France*), 48°18′N 4°05′E, 22, 108, 165, 167, 177
Tübingen (*Germany*), 48°32′N 9°04′E, 110, 140
Tunis (*Tunisia*), 36°50′N 10°13′E, 10, 22, 108, 186
Turin (*Italy*), 45°04′N 7°40′E, 10, 58, 77, 79, 110, 146, 165
Tuscany*, 28
Tuy (*Spain*), 42°03′N 8°39′W, 189
Tuz, Lake (*Turkey*), 38°00′N 33°00′E, 11
Tver *see* Kalinin
Tweed (*r*), 207, 212
Tyne (*r*), 212
Tyrnau (*Slovakia*), 48°22′N 17°36′E, 110
Tyrol*, 10, 119, 140, 154
Tyrrhenian Sea, 10, 15, 28, 34, 66, 77, 79, 95

Ubeda (*Spain*),38°01′N 3°22′W, 189
Uclés (*Spain*), 39°58′N 2°52′W, 184
Udine (*Italy*), 46°04′N 13°14′E, 15, 22, 91
Ulm (*Germany*), 48°24′N 10°00′E, 138, 140, 154
Umbria*, 28, 58
Upper Palatinate*, 154
Uppsala (*Sweden*), 59°55′N 17°38′E, 110
Urach (*Germany*), 48°30′N 9°25′E, 140
Urbino (*Italy*), 43°43′N 12°38′E, 15, 58, 66, 79, 95, 110
Urgel (*Spain*), 42°16′N 1°26′E, 184
Ussé (*France*), 47°14′N 0°18′E, 170
Utrecht (*Netherlands*), 52°06′N 5°07′E, 110, 115, 140
Uvek (*Russia*), 51°27′N 45°58′E, 125
Uzès (*France*), 44°01′N 4°25′E, 167, 177

Vadstena (*Sweden*), 58°26′N 14°55′E, 16
Valençay (*France*), 47°10′N 1°33′E, 170
Valence (*France*), 44°56′N 4°54′E, 110, 177
Valencia (*Spain*), 39°29′N 0°24′W, 10, 22, 108, 110, 184, 186, 189
Valencia*, 184, 189
Valenciennes (*France*), 50°22′N 3°32′E, 140
Valladolid (*Spain*), 41°39′N 4°45′W, 110, 184, 189
Vallery (*France*), 48°24′N 3°10′E, 167
Valmontone (*Italy*), 41°47′N 12°55′E, 77
Vanern, Lake (*Sweden*), 58°00′N 13°00′E, 10
Vannes (*France*), 47°40′N 2°44′W, 167
Varna (*Bulgaria*), 43°12′N 27°57′E, 23
Vattern, Lake (*Sweden*), 57°30′N 14°00′E, 10
Vaucluse*, 41
Velikiy Ustyug (*Russia*), 60°48′N 46°15′E, 125
Vellano (*Italy*), 43°57′N 10°43′E, 49
Velletri (*Italy*), 41°41′N 12°47′E, 77
Vendôme (*France*), 47°48′N 1°04′E, 167
Venetia*, 28
Venice (*Italy*), 45°26′N 12°20′E, 15, 22, 28, 34, 41, 49, 56, 58, 66, 77, 79, 82, 91, 94, 95, 108, 112, 115, 125, 138, 140, 142, 146
Venice*, 16, 17, 115, 119
Ventoux, Mt (*France*), 44°09′N 5°16′E, 41
Vera Cruz (*Brazil*), 19°29′S 40°01′W, 122
Veracruz (*Mexico*), 19°11′N 96°10′W, 122
Vercelli (*Italy*), 45°19′N 8°26′E, 22, 28, 34, 52, 56, 58, 79, 110
Verdun (*France*), 49°10′N 5°24′E, 165
Verneuil (*France*), 49°20′N 2°28′E, 167
Veroli (*Italy*), 41°41′N 13°26′E, 77
Verona (*Italy*), 45°26′N 11°00′E, 15, 22, 28, 34, 41, 49, 52, 56, 58, 77, 79, 91, 95, 208, 112, 138
Vesuvius (*mt*), (*Italy*), 40°49′N 14°26′E, 10
Viana (*Spain*), 42°31′N 2°22′W, 184
Vibo Valentia (*Italy*), 38°40′N 16°06′E, 22
Vicenza (*Italy*), 45°33′N 11°33′E, 22, 34, 56, 58, 79, 91, 95, 110, 112
Vich (*Spain*), 41°56′N 2°16′E, 184
Vicovaro (*Italy*), 42°01′N 12°54′E, 66
Vienna (*Austria*), 48°13′N 16°22′E, 10, 110, 115, 138, 140, 142, 154
Vienne (*France*), 45°32′N 4°54′E, 16
Vigevano (*Italy*), 45°19′N 8°51′E, 82
Villa Badoer (*Italy*), 45°03′N 11°37′E, 91
Villa Caldogno (*Italy*), 45°35′N 11°30′E, 91
Villa Chiericati (*Italy*), 45°29′N 11°37′E, 91
Villa Cornaro (*Italy*), 45°35′N 12°00′E, 91
Villa Emo (*Italy*), 45°39′N 12°02′E, 91
Villa Farnesina (*Italy*), 41°49′N 12°27′E, 95
Villa Garzoni (*Italy*), 45°12′N 11°59′E, 91
Villa Gazzotti (*Italy*), 45°53′N 11°34′E, 91
Villa Giulia (*Italy*), 41°56′N 12°31′E, 95
Villa Giustinian (*Italy*), 45°35′N 12°21′E, 91
Villa Godi (*Italy*), 45°44′N 11°32′E, 91
Villa Maser (Villa Barbaro), (*Italy*), 45°47′N 11°57′E, 91
Villandry (*France*), 47°21′N 0°30′E, 170
Villa Pisani (*Italy*), 45°13′N 11°27′E, 91
Villa Pisani-Ferri (*Italy*), 45°18′N 11°19′E, 91
Villa Poiana (*Italy*), 45°16′N 11°30′E, 91
Villa Trissino (*Italy*), 45°34′N 11°34′E, 91
Villa Valmarana-Bressan (*Italy*), 45°35′N 11°34′E, 91
Villa Valmarana-Scagnaroli (*Italy*), 45°34′N 11°36′E, 91
Villa Vescovile (*Italy*), 45°19′N 11°41′E, 91
Villers-Cotterêts (*France*), 49°15′N 3°06′E, 167
Villesavin (*France*), 47°35′N 1°31′E, 170
Vilna *see* Vilnius
Vilnius (Vilna), (*Lithuania*), 54°40′N 25°19′E, 11, 141
Vimperk (*Czech Republic*), 49°03′N 13°45′E°, 140
Vincennes (*France*), 48°51′N 2°27′E, 167
Visby (*Sweden*), 57°37′N 18°20′E, 108
Vistula (*r*), 10, 22, 109, 110, 115, 119, 138, 140, 142
Viterbo (*Italy*), 42°24′N 12°06′E, 15, 16, 58, 77, 79, 94, 95
Vivarais*, 165
Vizcaya*, 184
Volga (*r*), 11, 108, 125
Vologda (*Russia*), 59°10′N 39°55′E, 125
Volterra (*Italy*), 43°24′N 10°52′E, 15, 58
Vosges (*mts*), (*France*), 48°20′N 6°50′E, 10
Vyne, The (*UK*), 51°30′N 1°21′W, 212

Wakefield (*UK*), 53°42′N 1°29′W, 207
Wales*, 115, 119
Walmer Castle (*UK*), 51°13′N 1°24′E, 212
Wardour Castle (*UK*), 51°04′N 2°07′W, 212
Warsaw (*Poland*), 52°15′N 21°00′E, 10, 115
Warta (*r*), 10
Wearmouth *see* Sunderland
Wells (*UK*), 51°13′N 2°39′W, 207
Welshpool (*UK*), 52°40′N 3°09′W, 207
Weser (*r*), 10
Westphalia*, 154
Wiener Neustadt (*Austria*), 47°49′N 16°15′E, 154
Wilton House (*UK*), 51°05′N 1°52′W, 212
Winchelsea (*UK*), 50°55′N 0°42′E, 177
Windsor Castle (*UK*), 51°29′N 0°38′W, 212
Wittenberg (*Germany*), 51°53′N 12°39′E, 110, 140, 154
Wittgenstein*, 177
Wolfenbuttel*, 154
Wollaton Hall (*UK*), 52°56′N 1°14′W, 212
Woodstock (*UK*), 51°52′N 1°21′W, 212
Worksop (*UK*), 53°18′N 1°07′W, 212
Worms (*Germany*), 49°38′N 8°23′E, 110
Wurttemberg*, 154, 177
Würzburg (*Germany*), 49°48′N 9°57′E, 110, 140, 142

Yaroslavl (*Russia*), 57°34′N 39°52′E, 125
York (*UK*), 53°58′N 1°05′W, 110, 207
Yuste (*Spain*), 40°09′N 5°45′W, 189

Zagreb (*Croatia*), 45°48′N 15°58′E, 10, 22, 138, 140
Zalamea (*Spain*), 38°40′N 5°39′E, 189
Zambesi (*r*), 123
Zamora (*Spain*), 41°30′N 5°45′W, 189
Zara (*Croatia*), 44°07′N 15°14′E, 108
Zaragoza (*Spain*), 41°39′N 0°54′W, 110, 184, 189
Zaragoza*, 189
Zeyla (*Somalia*), 11°21′N 43°30′E, 123
Zinna (*Germany*), 51°59′N 12°43′E, 140
Zurich (*Switzerland*), 47°23′N 8°33′E, 10, 94, 115, 119, 140, 154
Zweibrücken (*Germany*), 49°15′N 7°22′E, 140
Zwolle (*Netherlands*), 52°31′N 6°06′E, 140

INDEX

Italic page numbers refer to picture captions.

A

Aachen, Charlemagne's palace 15
Abbate, Niccolò dell' 172, 180
  Palazzo Poggi frescoes 96
Aberdeen university 219
Academies 78, *94*
  Platonic Academy *19*; *see also* sodalities
Act in Restraint of Appeals 210
Act of Supremacy 210
Adam, Robert 100
adept *19*, 132
admiratio 199
Adrian I, Pope 18
Adrian VI, Pope 83
Aduard
  abbey 141; Academy 141
Africa 121, 122, 125, 185
  Ottoman Empire 134; papal bull granting land 185; Portuguese conquests *186*; Spanish conquests *186*
Agen 176
Agricola, Rudolf 139, 146
agricultural innovations 172
Alba, Duke of
  The Duke of Alba Overcoming Philip II's Enemies 196
Alba de Tormes, dukes of 190, 191
Alberti, Leon Battista 21, 24, 49, 51, 68, 69, 70, 72, 96, 100, 151
  architectural commissions 63, 68, 74; classical influences 27; Malatesta Temple *51*, 67–68; medallion self-portrait *51*; treatise on architecture 60, 62; treatise on perspective 21, 27, 69
Albertus Magnus 16
Albizzi family 53
Alcalá de Henares
  archbishop's palace *203*; university (Complutensian University) 188, *189*, 192, 202
Alcántara, Grand Master of 192
Alcazarquivir, Battle of 122
alchemy 19, 144, *144*, 145, 162
  Book of Great Alchemy 156
Alexander VI, Pope 60, 76, 80, 83, 87, 92, 192
Alexandria 120
Alfonso V (the Magnanimous), king of Aragon 67, 186, *186*, 187
Alfonso, king of Naples 48, *55*
Alfonso V, king of Portugal 186–87, 201
Algiers *186*
Alhambra *199*
Almerico, Paolo *101*
Alonso de Cartagena, bishop of Burgos 190
  Recapitulation of the Kings of Spain 191
Alsace
  humanism 145–46; visual arts 151
altarpieces 44, *44*, *45*
Altdorfer, Albrecht 151, 153
  Battle of Issus 153; *St George and the Dragon* 153, *153*
Alva, Duke of *136*
Amboise *82*, 171
  château 166, 172
America 109, 111, 121, 122, *124*, 125, 127, 185
  Decades on the New World (Martire) 197; papal bull granting land 185; Spanish possessions 196
anatomy, study of 78, 89, *103*, *118*, 119

Andreoli, Giorgio 96
Angelico, Fra
  Deposition 45; Observant monastery of San Marco 63
Anglican Church 217
Anjou 164
Anne of Austria 196
Anne of Cleves *217*
Anne of Denmark 224
antica script 52
antiquarianism and the pursuit of history 16, 17, 51, 141, 146, 191–92, *191*, 215, 217
Antonine *Itinerary* 192
Antwerp *109*, 111, 141, 156
  printing 111, 112, 154, 192; sack 154
Apocalypse, premonitions of 162
Apollo Belvedere 26
Appian 192
Aquinas, Thomas 16
Aragon 20, 185, *185*;
  humanism 187–88; printing 189
Archangel 127
architecture
  classical influence 21, 27, *27*, 63, 70, *70*, 84, *91*, *97*, *100*, *199*; England and Scotland 208, *208*, 211, *213*, 219–20, 221, 224; *First and Chief Grounds of Architecture* (Shute) 211; Florence 71; fortifications 76, 123–24; France 166, *166*, 168–69, *168*, *169*, 171, *171*; Germany 156; High Renaissance 81, 98; Italy 29, 30–33, *31*, *32*, *33*; Manueline 33; marble 33; neo-classicism 100, *100*, *101*; Northern Renaissance 156; patronage 23, 24; plateresque 187, *188*, 199, 202, *202*, *203*; rebuilding of Rome 92, *92*; Spain 199, *199*, 200, *200*, *201*, 202, *202*, *203*; spatial relationships and proportion 70–71, *70*, *71*, 78; Venice 113, 125
Arcimboldo, Giuseppe 156
  portrait of Rudolf II *157*
Arco dei Gavo 26
Aretino, Pietro 78, 87, 91, 93, 99, 171
  The Courtesan 91; *Orazia* 91; *Ragionamenti* 91; *Sonetti lussuriosi* 91
Arévalo, Rodrigo Sánchez de
  Compendious Hispanic History 191
Arezzo *34*, *51*
Ariosto, Ludovico 93, 96, 98
  Orlando Furioso 96
Aristophanes 141'
Aristotle 16, *39*, 49, 58, 85, 113, 132, 141, 187
  "natural slavery" doctrine 199; *Poetics* 155; *Politics* 23
Armada Jewel 214
Armagnac 164
Arnolfini, Giovanni 18, *18*
Arnolfini family 149
Arquà *40*
Artois 164
Arundel, Henry Fitzalan, Earl of 214, 224
Ascham, Roger 153, 221
  The Schoolmaster 215
Asia, papal bull granting land 185
Assisi, Basilica of St Francis 36
astrology 19, 83, 132, *133*, 144, 162
astronomy 109, 119, 121, 132, *133*, 155, 156
Athens, Walter, Duke of 29
Atlantic, opening of 121–25, 127
atlases, printed 89
Attaingnant, Pierre *128*
Augsburg 141
Augustine, St *16*, 17, 40

Augustinian order 146, 148
Aurispa, Giovanni 49, 52
Austria 139, 186
  Habsburg dynasty 24; visual arts 151
autos-da-fé 194, *194*, 196
Autun cathedral 16
Avelli, Francesco Xanto 96
Avignon papacy 16, 20, 40, 171
Ávila, friary of St Thomas *192*
Avis dynasty 187
Ayala, Pedro de 219
Azay-le-Rideau, chateau 169, 219

B

Babington plot 221
Bacon, Sir Francis 219
  The Advancement of Learning 219; *The New Atlantis* 219
Baduel, Claude 153
Baglioni, Atalanta 84
Baïf, Jean–Antoine de 174–75
Baldovinetti, Alessio 43
Balearic Islands 186
balet comique 182
Baltic trading zone 111, *139*
Balzac, Honoré de 14
Banco, Nanni di 63
banking 39, 172
Barbari, Jacopo de' 89
  portrait of Luca Pacioli *82*
Barbaro, Daniele 101
Barbaro, Marcantonio 101
Barbera of Brandenberg 68
Barcelona 187, 188, 192
Barcelona, Treaty of 186
Bardi family 39
Barocci, Federico 78, 79, 96
Baroque style 99, 156, 157, *181*, 199
  picaresque novel 193
Bartolommeo, Fra (Bartolommeo della Porta) 80, 84
Basel 141, 177
Basel, Council of 137, 187
Basinio da Parma 68
Batalha monastery *202*
Batave, Godefroy le *164*
Bautista de Toledo, Juan 200
Bayonne 182
Bazzi, Giovanni *see* Sodoma
Beaton, Cardinal David 220
Beaufort, Henry, bishop of Winchester 49
Beaufort, Lady Margaret 104, *104*, 205
Becadelli, Antonio 187
Becchi, Gentile de' *19*
Behaim, Martin *133*
Beirut 120
Bellay, Joachim du 174–75, 220
  Defense and Illustration of the French Language 174–75
Bellini, Gentile 65, 66
  Procession of the True Cross 113; *Venetian Embassy in the East* 135
Bellini, Giovanni 20, 65, 66
Bellini, Jacopo 65
Belvedere Apollo 180
Bembo, Cardinal Pietro 93
Benedictines 41
Bernardino of Siena, St 62–63
Berquin, Louis de 176
Berruguete, Alonso 196
Berruguete, Pedro 201
  Federigo da Montefeltro with his son Guidobaldo (attributed) *73*; *St Dominic Presiding over the Burning of Heretics* 194
Berthelot, Gilles 169
Bertoldo di Giovanni
  medallion commemorating Pazzi conspiracy *56*

Bessarion 123, 187
Bible 40
  application of humanist scholarship 117; *Commentary on St Paul's Epistles* (Lefèvre) 174; *Complutensian Polyglot* 154, 192, *194*; English biblical scholarship 206; *Fivefold Psalter* (Lefèvre) 174; publication and study in original languages 145, 146, 154, 156, 192; vernacular editions 117, 137, *149*, 154, 176, 197
Biondo, Flavio 15
  Italy Illustrated 26; *Roman Restored* 26
Bisticci, Vespasiano da 49, *55*
  Lives 187
Black Death 30, *32*, 33, 39, *40*, 41
Blaeu, Willem
  World Map 124
Blois, château 168, 169, 171, *171*, 180
Boccaccio, Giovanni 37, 40, 41, 174
  biography of Dante 41; censorship of 99; *Decameron* 40, 41; *On Famous Women* 41; *On the Fates of Famous Men* 41
Bock, Hieronymus
  The Lime Tree 161
Bodin, Jean
  The Six Books of the Commonwealth 174
Bodleian Library 205, *223*
Bodley, Sir Thomas *223*
Bohemia 24
  Charles IV 136–37; election of Holy Roman Emperor *141*; humanism 137; Hussites 16, 137, *154*; "modern devotion" 137; Northern Renaissance 136–37
Bohier, Thomas 169
Bois de Boulogne 169
Boleyn, Anne 104, 213
Bologna 30, *34*, 48, *49*
  Palazzo Poggi 96; Spanish College 187; university 16, 78, *94*
Bologna, Concordat of 118
Bonacolsi, Pinamonte 29
Bonfini, Antonio 139
Boniface VIII, Pope 33
Borgia, Cesare 59, 60, 81, *82*
Borgia, Lucrezia 60
Borgona, Juan de
  Cardinal Cisneros 194
Boscàn, Juan 191
Bosch, Hieronymus 14, 24, *44*, *136*, 149, 151, 162
  Temptation of St Anthony 162
Bosworth Field, Battle of 204
botany, printed illustrations 89
Bothwell, James Hepburn, Earl of 220–21
Botticelli, Sandro 14, *56*
  Birth of Venus 26; *Primavera* 16, 20, *20*
Bourbon, Charles de 164
Bourbon, Pierre de 171
Bourges, law faculty *173*
Bracciolini, Poggio 49, *49*, 51, 52, *52*, 53, 138, 187, 197
Brahe, Tycho 155, 156
Bramante, Donato 21, 81, 82, 97, 98, 100
  St Peter's 84; Santa Maria delle Grazie 81; Santa Maria San Satiro 81; Sant'Ambrogio 81; Tempietto at San Pietro 84
Brancacci, Felice 53
Brandenburg, election of Holy Roman Emperor *141*
Brant, Sebastian 145, 147
  The Ship of Fools 145
Brantôme, Pierre de Bourdeilles 168

Brescia, sack 76
Brethren of the Common Life 136–37, *137*, 141, 145, 146
Breugel, Jan
  The Sense of Hearing 129
Briçonnet, Catherine 169
Briçonnet, Guillaume, bishop of Meaux 176
Bristol 127
Brittany 164, *165*
Bronzino, Agnolo 96, 97, 99, 180
  Christ in Limbo 97; *Venus, Cupid, Folly and Time* (*The Vice of Luxury*) 97, *181*
Brotherhood of the Rosie Cross 144
Bruegel, Pieter, the Elder 151
  Landscape with the Fall of Icarus 153; *The Land of Cockaigne* 136
Bruges 158
Brunelleschi, Filippo 51, 53, 63, 121
  biography by Manetti 69;. classical influence 27; Florence cathedral 21, 53, 64, 70, 71, 121; Innocenti Hospital 64, 70; Old Sacristy San Lorenzo 71, *71*; Pazzi Chapel 71; perspective 21, 27, 64, 69, *69*, 71; proportion 70–71, *70*, *71*; San Lorenzo 54, 64
Bruni, Leonardo 49, 52, 53, 187, 188
Brunswick 156
Brussels 156
Bucer, Martin 112, 176
Buchanan, George 188, 219, 221, 224
Buda 139
Budé, Guillaume 173–74, *173*, 175, 176
  Annotations on the Pandects 173–74; *De Asse* 174; portrait by Jean Clouet *173*; *Right and Proper Institution of the Study of Learning* 173
Bunel, Pierre 176
Buontalenti, Bernardo 98
Burbage, James 218
Burbage, Richard 218
Burckhardt, Jacob 24
  The Civilization of the Renaissance in Italy 14
Burgundy 164
Burgundy, Philip the Good, Duke of *128*, 158
Burleigh, William Cecil, 1st Baron 221
Burlington, Lord 100
Bury 169
Byzantine Greek scholars 19
Byzantium 123, 134

C

Ca' da Mosto, Alvise da 125
Cabot, John *124*, 125
Cabot, Sebastian *124*, 125, 127
Cabral, Pedro 121
Cade, Jack 211
Càdiz, English raid 213, *214*
Caesar
  Gallic Wars 164, *164*
Calabria, Carlo, Duke of 29
Calderón, Pedro 201
Calvin, John 117–18, 176, 177
  commentary on Seneca's *On Clemency* 117, 177; *Institutes of the Christian Religion* 117–18, 177
Calvinism *119*, 153, 220
Cambrai, League of 78, 113, 114
Cambrai, Peace of 171

Cambridge university 104, 112, 204, 205, 206, 222, 223
Camden, William 26, 215, 217, 222
  Britannia 215
Camões, Luís de
  The Lusiads 199
campanilismo 23
Campbell, Colen 100
Campin, Robert 24
  Portrait of a Lady 24
Canary Islands 125, 185
Cano, Melchor 192
canonista 16
Canterbury Cathedral, shrine of Thomas à Becket 211
Cape Blanco 125
Cape of Good Hope 185, 187
Caprarola, Villa Farnese 93
Carbonnell, Pere Miquel 187
Carinthia 186
Carolingian minuscule 16, 52
Carolingian Renaissance 15–16
Caron, Antoine
  The Massacre of the Innocents 178; *The Triumph of War* 178; *The Triumvirate* 178; Valois Tapestries 182, 182, 183
Carpaccio, Vittore
  The Legend of St Ursula 66–67, 66, 121
Carranza, Bartolomé, archbishop of Toleda 197
Carrara, Francesco 37, 51
Cartagena 213
cartellini 214
Cartier, Jacques 165
Casale 78
Caspian Sea 127
Castiglione, Baldassare 93, 98
  censorship of 99; *The Courtier* 17, 72, 73, 94–95, 104, 171, 191, 213; portrait by Raphael 73
Castile 185, 185, 186, 187
  humanism 190; "neo-Gothic" theory 191; printing 189
Catalana 24, 186
Catalonia 187
Catara 123
Cateau-Cambrésis, Peace of 76, 78, 177
Catherine of Aragon 213
  divorce 210, 223; marriage to Henry VIII 204, 210
Catherine de Medici 173, 178, 178, 179, 182, 182, 183
Catherine of Siena 16
Catholic Church
  Council of Florence 123; Council of Trent 99, 119; Counter-Reformation *see* Counter-Reformation; and education 153; "Enterprise of England" 213; and humanism 19, 60, 62–63, 111; indulgences 62, 148, 149, 162; Inquisition 36, 99, 118, 189, 192–93, 192, 193, 194, 194, 196, 197; Jesuits 93, 193, 197; monasticism 36, 40, 117; papacy *see* papacy; pilgrimage 62, 162; preaching and pulpits 33, 36, 36, 62; relic worship 162; sack of Rome 78; schism 20, 60; and science 109, 111; Spain 24; Venice 87
Catullus 90
Cavalieri, Emilio de' 98
Caxton, William 116
  Aesop's Fables 205; *Canterbury Tales* (Chaucer) 205; *Morte d'Arthur* (Malory) 205; *Recuyell of the Historyes of Troye* 205
Cecil family 224
Cellini, Benvenuto 82, 93, 94, 96, 180
  Autobiography 181; *Perseus* 97; portrait bust of Cosimo de' Medici 97; saltcellar 93, 181

Celtis, Conrad 26, 142–43, 153, 154
  College of Poets 142; editions of Seneca 142; *The Four Loves* 142; sodalities 141, 142; travels of 143; treatise on Latin verse 142
Cenami, Giovanna 18, 18
censorship 99, 114, 176, 197
Cerceau, J. Androuet du
  The Most Excellent Buildings of France 171
Cerines 123
Certaldo 41
Cervantes Saavedra, Miguel de
  The Colloquy of the Dogs 192; *Don Quixote* 190, 190, 191, 199; stage plays 191
Ceuta 185
Cévennes 173
Chambers of Rhetoric 141
Chambord, chateau 166, 168, 168, 169, 171
Chancellor, Richard 127
Charles V, Emperor 90, 118, 119, 134, 139, 166, 186, 191, 199
  abdication 118; Counter-Reformation 154, 192; palace at Alhambra 199; patronage 153; sack of Rome 192, 194, 197; Spanish Erasmianism 192; succession 196; tomb 200, 201
Charles IV, king of Bohemia 40, 136–37
Charles I, king of England 224
Charles VII, king of France 180
Charles VIII, king of France 164, 166, 171, 172
  Italian Wars 20, 57, 76, 76
Charles IX, king of France 178, 182, 183
Charles I, king of Spain *see* Charles V, Emperor
Charles of Anjou 28
Charles of Viana 187
Charlemagne 15–16
Chaucer, Geoffrey 205
Chenonceaux 169
Chepman, Walter 219
Chigi, Agostino 87
Chile 122
China 120
chivalry and medievalism 190–91, 190, 199, 214
Christian I, king of Denmark 68
Christianity
  Aristotelian philosophy 16; Christian iconography 16, 18, 18; classical and Christian traditions 16, 20; heretical movements 16; and humanism 19, 24; and Islam 123; medieval western Christendom 16; mysticism 16; *see also* Catholic Church; Orthodox Church; papacy; Protestant Reformation; religion and theology
Christine of Lorraine 98
Chrysoloras, Manuel 49
Cicero 17, 40, 140, 151, 188, 189
Cimabue, Giovanni 14, 37
Cipango 109
circumnavigations of the world 121, 123, 127, 214
Cisneros, Cardinal 192, 194
city-states 23, 23, 28
classical culture, influence of 16, 21, 34, 58–60, 62, 70, 70, 97, 98, 100, 186–88, 191–92
  admiratio 199; antiquarianism 51; architecture 21, 63, 84, 91, 199; city-states 23–24; education 104, 137, 138; fall of Constantinople 49; Greek language 116, 116, 137; High Renaissance 78; humanism

16–17, 19, 26, 48–49, 146; *imitatio* 199; impact of printing 116, 141; italic and roman scripts 49, 52; Latin language 48–49; literature 16, 17, 19, 26, 40, 41, 52, 52, 78, 146, 175–76, 199; mathematics 16; neo-Platonism *see* neo-Platonism; philosophy 16; Reformation 153; rhetoric 48, 141; universities 16; visual arts 14, 16, 20, 26–27, 26, 27, 36, 41, 63, 64, 90, 90, 151
Claude de France 166, 171
Clement VII, Pope 83, 91, 93, 94, 94, 97
Clouet, François 24, 172, 180, 220
Clouet, Jean 172, 173, 180, 216
Clovio, Giulio
  Farnese Hours 93
Cnidian Venus 180
Cogolludo 202
Coimbra university 188, 189
Colet, John 112, 145, 146, 146, 206, 206
Colin, Jacques 171
Colines, Simon de 180
Cologne 141, 145; archbishopric 141; university 139, 141
Colonna, Cardinal Giovanni 40
Colonna, Vittoria 93–94
Columbus, Christopher 20, 109, 121, 124, 185
  Letter (1494) 124; *Letter on the New-Found Isles of the Ocean Sea* (1493) 197
Complutensian University (Alcalá de Henares) 188, 189, 192, 202
condottieri 20, 48, 48, 58, 59, 60, 67–68, 72
confraternities (*scuole*) 66, 78, 82–83, 87, 89
Conrad IV 28
Conradin of Swabia 28
Constance, Council of 137
Constantinople, fall of 19, 49, 55, 62, 123, 134, 134
Contarini, Cardinal Gasparo 76
  On the Commonwealth and Government of Venice 113
Copernicus, Nicholas 121, 155, 156
  On the Revolutions of the Celestial Spheres 119, 132, 133, 155; translation of Simocatta 155
Coras, Jean de 173–74
Córdoba 185, 191
Corfu, siege of 123–24
Cornish Rebellion 207
Coron 123
Correggio, Antonio Allegri da 59
Corsignano 62
Cortés, Hernán 111, 121
Cortona, Domenico da 168, 171
Cosenza 78
Costa, Lorenzo 59, 129
Counter-Reformation 24, 78, 93, 98–99, 109, 111, 119, 119, 154, 156, 196
  Council of Trent 119; literature 96; visual arts 89, 90, 97
court entertainments 182, 182, 183
Cousin, Jean 172, 180
Covarrubias, Alonso 202, 203
Cowdray House 211
Cracow 139, 142
  sodality 141; university 142; Wawel castle 139
Craigston castle 224
Cranach, Lucas, the Elder 149, 151, 152, 152
  portrait of Luther 149; *The Stag Hunt* 139
Cranmer, Thomas 213
Cromwell, Oliver 222
Crusades 16
Culross palace 224

Cumberland, George, 3rd Earl of 214
Cyprus, Turkish capture 123, 125
Czech, Bible translated into 137

D

Daddi, Bernardo 33
Dante Alighieri 19, 40, 137, 174
  biography by Boccaccio 41; *Dante Standing Before the City of Florence* (Domenico di Michelino) 43; *Divine Comedy* 16, 37, 40, 42, 46, 121
Danti, Ignazio
  view of Genoa 20; view of Rome 92; view of Venice 121
Darnley, Henry Stewart, Lord 220
Decembrio, Angelo 187
Decembrio, Piercandido 187
Dee, John 156
Delft 141
Della Torre 29
Demosthenes 143
Demoulins, François
  commentary on Caesar's *Gallic Wars* 164, 164
Deruta 96
Deventer 141
  Brethren of the Common Life 137, 137, 145, 146; trade and commerce 137
Dias, Bartholomew 121, 185, 187
Diet of Worms 176
Diodorus 181, 192
diplomacy 135
diptychs 44
Dolet, Étienne 176
Domenico di Michelino
  Dante Standing Before the City of Florence 43
Dominican order 36, 40
Don Carlos 196
Don Juan 193
Doña Juana 193
Donatello 54, 64–65, 69, 71
  David 64; equestrian statue of Erasmo da' Narni 64; *Gattamelata* 21; *Judith and Holofernes* 55, 64; Orsanmichele statues 63; shrine to St Anthony 64; *Zuccone* 65
Donation of Constantine (papal fraud) 19, 48, 117, 118, 143
Dorat, Jean 174
dossal 44
Dowland, John 217, 224
Drake, Sir Francis 127, 213, 214
Drummond, William, of Hawthornden 224
Dubais, François 178
Dublin castle 204
Duccio di Buoninsegna
  Maestà 36–37, 36, 45
Dufay, Guillaume
  Nuper rosarum flores 70
Dunbar, William 219
  The Thistle and the Rose 219
Dunfermline 220
Dürer, Albrecht 113, 139, 141, 149, 151, 153, 158
  The Apocalypse of St John 151; *Great Piece of Turf* 152; *Hare* 152; *The Knight, the Devil and Death* 151; medallion designed by 141; *Melancolia* 163; *Self-Portrait* 149

E

Eckhardt, Meister 16
economy 23, 30

Edinburgh
  castle 220; Holyroodhouse 220; Royal College of Surgeons 219; university 224
education
  Brethren of the Common Life 136–37, 137, 141, 145, 146; Catholic Church 153; England 214–15; Germany 142, 156–57; Holy Roman Empire 140; humanist 51, 108, 111, 138, 140–41, 142, 153; humanities (*studia humanitatis*) 16, 17, 48; Italy 40; Jesuits 156; literacy 40, 189; Low Countries 156–57; monastic orders 40, 141; Poland 155–56; printing *see* printing; Reformation 153–54; Scotland 224; Spain 189, 193, 197; study of Greek 137; *trivium* 139–40; women 51; *see also* Academies; sodalities; universities
Edward IV, king of England 205
Edward VI, king of England 210, 211, 213, 220
  Jack Cade 211; Kett's Rebellion 207; Reformation 210; Western Rebellion 207
Edward I, king of Portugal 186
Egypt 122
El Greco (Domenikos Theotokopoulos) 196, 200, 201
  Adoration in the Name of Jesus (Philip II's Dream) 196; *The Burial of the Count of Orgaz* 201
Elcano, Juan 121
Eleanor of Aragon 62
Elizabeth I, queen of England 104, 153, 210, 213–15, 217, 219
  Babington plot 221; *Blackfriars Portrait* 215; chivalry and medievalism 214; Church Settlement 217; education 214–15; Essex Rebellion 207, 219; execution of Mary Queen of Scots 220, 221; patronage 213; and Philip II of Spain 196; propaganda 214; *Regnans in Excelsis* Papal Bull 213; religious tolerance 213; Revolt of the Netherlands 213, 214; Ridolfi plot 221; rising of the Northern Earls 207, 221; and Spain 196, 213; state policy 213; succession 204, 224; Throckmorton Plot 213; war culture 204, 213
Elizabeth of York 204, 205
Elvetham 214
Elyot, Sir Thomas 213
enameling 164, 172
Encina, Juan del
  Eclogues 190
England 24
  Act in Restraint of Appeals 210; Act of Supremacy 210; Anglican Church 217; antiquarianism and the pursuit of history 215, 217; Armada 196; Babington plot 221; Battle of Bosworth Field 204; Battle of Flodden Field 219; Battle of Pinkie Cleugh 220; biblical scholarship 206; Catholic Church 207, 210, 213, 213; civil war 21, 207, 222; Council of the North 207; Council of Wales 207; culture and politics 204; Dissolution of the Monasteries 210–11, 213, 214; Dutch Wars 213, 214; education 104, 204–05, 206, 214–15, 222; "Enterprise of England" 213; exploration 124, 125, 127, 214, 217; House of Commons 214; humanism 146, 146, 205–06, 224; Hundred Years War 21; and Ireland 204; Lollards 16; printing and

publishing 116, 205, *205*; Puritanism 213, 214, 217, 222; rebellions and political unrest 206, *207*, 211; Reformation 24, 118, 210, 211, 213; *Regnans in Excelsis* Papal Bull 213; religion 16; Ridolfi plot 221; rising of the Northern Earls *207*, 221; Royal Society 219; St George's Day Feast 214; science 109, 217, 219; and Scotland 204, *207*; Society of Antiquaries 217; and Spain 196, 213; Stuart dynasty 204, *207*, *219*, 224; trade and commerce 120, *124*, 127, 217, 219; Tudor dynasty 196, 204, *207*, *207*, 209, *210*; Union of Crowns 204, *207*, *219*; and Wales 204; Wars of the Roses 204, *207*

Erasmus, Desiderius *105*, 115, 143, 145, 146–47, *146*, 152, 154, 156, 176, 194, 206
Adagia 114, 146, *147*; *Antibarbari* 146, 147; *Colloquies* 147; commentary on the *Christmas Hymn of Prudentius* 105; education 137, *137*, 146; England 205, 206, *206*, 207, 209, 222; Greek edition of New Testament 146; *In Praise of Folly* 147, 192; letters 146; and Manutius 114; *Paraclesis* 146–47; portrait by Holbein *147*; and printing 112; Spanish Erasmianism 192–93; travels of 112, 146, *146*

Erfurt
monastery 148; university 139
eroticism 87, 90, 91, 93, 96, 98
Escorial 196, 200, *200*, 201, *201*
Essex, Robert Devereux, 2nd Earl *207*
Essex Rebellion *219*
Este, Alfonso d' *90*
Este, Azzo VII d' 29
Este, Beatrice d' 81, 82
Este, Borso d' 67
Este, Isabella d' *59*, 96, *129*
studiolo 59
Este, Cardinal Luigi d' 96
Este, Niccolò d' 67
Este, d', family 24, 30, 96
Estienne, Robert 116, 180
Esztergom 139
Eton College 205
Euboea 123
Euclid 85
Eugenius IV, Pope 51, 60, 62, 63
Euphuism 190
Euripides 175
exploration and expansionism 121–25, *124*, 127
circumnavigations of the world 121, *123*, 127, *214*; English *214*, 217; northeast passage 127; Portuguese 185; slavery *186*, 199; Spanish 185, 197, 199
Eyck, Hubert van 158, *158*
Eyck, Jan van *44*, *59*, 149, 151, 158
Angels *128*; *Arnolfini Marriage* 16, 18, *18*, 151; Ghent altarpiece 151, 158, *158*, *159*; *Madonna with Chancellor Rolin* 151; *Man in a Red Turban* 158; treatment of space 151

F

Fabriano, Gentile da 66
Falkland palace 220
Famagusta 123
Farnese, Cardinal Alessandro 93
Faroe Islands 125

Faustus, Doctor 141
Fazio, Bartolommeo 158, 187
Book of Famous Men 149
Febvre, Lucien 176
Fedele, Cassandra 104
Feltre, Vittorino da 51, 58, 72, 104, *104*
Ferdinand of Aragon *see* Ferdinand and Isabella
Ferdinand I, Emperor 156
Ferdinand II, Emperor 139
Ferdinand and Isabella (Catholic Monarchs) 104, *124*, 184–85, *184*, *185*, 186, *186*, 187, *188*, 192, *192*, 197, *199*
humanism, classical scholarship and education 188, 189, 193; Inquisition 194; patronage 199, 201, 202, *203*
Fernández, Lucas 191
Fernández de Lucena, Vasco 187
Ferrara 56, 59, 67, 96
civic government 29; d'Este 24, 29, 67; League of Cambrai 76
Ficino, Marsilio 15, *19*, 49, 53, 55, 60, 72, 116, 143
translation of Plato 54
Field of the Cloth of Gold 209
Fiesole 53, 54
Finé, Oronce 174
Fisher, John, bishop of Rochester 205
execution 210, *223*; portrait by Holbein *223*
fisheries 125
Fitzwilliam, William 211
Flanders 186
Flemish artists 24, *24*, *44*, 151; *see also* Low Countries
Flemmyng, Robert 205–06
Flodden Field, Battle of 204, 219
Florence 21, 23, 28, *34*, 41, 74, 76, *94*
Accademia del Disegno 78; Accademia della Crusca 78; Baptistery 21, 23, 31, 63, 69, *69*; Bargello 30; Black Death 33; Brancacci Chapel 64, 65, *65*; cathedral 21, 23, 31, 33, 39, 42, *43*, 53, 64, 65, 70, 71, 74; Charles VIII of France 76; civic government 28, 29–30, 31; civic humanists 53; *Dante Standing Before the City of Florence* (Domenico di Michelno) *43*; education 40; expansionism 48, 56; Ghibellines 30; "Golden Age" 74; Guelfs 28, 30, 40; guilds 23, 113; High Renaissance 79–81, 96–98; humanism 48–49, 49, 53, 57, 111; Innocenti Hospital 64, *70*; Laurentian Library 97, *97*; Medici 21, 23, *23*, 24, 51, 53–57, 54, 55, 56, 58, 76, 79, 81, 96–98, 111; and Milan 111; oratory 23; Orsanmichele 23, 33, 63–64; Palazzo Medici 54, *55*, 63; *Palazzo Pubblico* 30; Palazzo Vecchio 97; patronage 23, 53, 54, *54*, 55, 63, 111; Pazzi Chapel 71; Peace of Lodi 55, 123; Pitti 21, *23*; *podestà* 30; Poggio a Caiano 57; Ponte Vecchio *34*; population 21, 30; public architecture 30; Republic 79–81; revolt of *Ciompi* 30; San Lorenzo 53, 54, 64; Santa Croce 39, 53, 54, 71; Santa Maria Novella 57, 63, 64, 69, 74, *74*; Sassetti Chapel 56; Savonarola 80, 96; siege 76, 96; *signoria* 30, 40, 41; Strozzi palace 63; Uffizi 97; Venice compared 113
Florence, Council of 123, 187
Fonseca, Cardinal 203
Fontainebleau 166, 169, 171, 172, *172*, 180, *181*

School of 172, *172*, *174*, 180
Fontana, Domenico 92
Fotheringhay castle 221
Fountains Abbey 210
Fox, Richard, bishop of Winchester 205
France 24, *164ff*
Avignon papacy 16, 20, 60, 171; banking 172; Catholic Church 177; church and state 118; civil war 21; Collège Royal (*Collège de France*) 173, 174; constitution 165; Counter Reformation 24; court 166; Edict of Nantes 177, 178; expansionism 164–65, *165*; *gendarmerie* 165, *165*; historical writing 178; Huguenots 177; humanism 169, 171, 173–74, *173*, 176; Hundred Years War 21; Italian influence 171–73, 175; Italian Wars 20, 56, 57, 76, 76, 78, 111, 164–65, *165*, 166, 171, *172*, 172, 177; League of Cambrai 76; "legal Renaissance" 173–74; Meaux sect 176; Naples 111; Old Alliance 219; Ordinance of Montpellier 180; *parlements* 165, *165*, 169, 174; Peace of Cateau-Cambrésis 177; Pléiade poets 175; "poetic brigade" 174–75; printing and publishing 116, 173, 176, 180; Reformation 24, 176–79, *177*; royal officials 169; St Bartholomew's Day Massacre *177*, 178, *178*–79; theological debate 174; Treaty of Barcelona 186; universities 173, 174; Valois dynasty 164, 165–66, *166*, 171, 177, 178, 182; Wars of Religion *177*, 178–79, *178*, 179, 182
Franche-Comté 186, 196
Francis of Assisi, St 34, 36, *39*
Francis I, king of France 82, *93*, *94*, *105*, 119, 164, *164*, *165*, 166, *166*, 169, 171, *171*, *181*
châteaux 166, 171; Collège Royal (*Collège de France*) 173, 174; Field of the Cloth of Gold 209; French humanism 174; Italian Wars 164–65, *165*, 166; Ottoman alliance 134; patronage 171, 172, 180, *181*
Francis II, king of France 178
Franciscans 36, 39, 63
Conventuals 63; *fraticelli* 36; *Meditations on the Life of Christ* 40; Observants 63
Franco, Matteo 56
Franco, Veronica 87
François, Dauphin 220
Frankfurt 141
Frascati 87
Frederick II (*Stupor Mundi*), Emperor 28
Frederick III, Emperor 62, 138, 142
Frederick of the Palatinate 145, *145*
Frederick the Wise of Saxony 139, 152
Froben 116
Fugger bank 141

G

Gabrieli, Andrea 79
Gabrieli, Giovanni 79
galeass 124
Galen 206
Galileo Galilei 109, 111, 119, 121, 132, *133*, 155
Dialogue Concerning Two New

Sciences 121; *Starry Messenger* 133
Gallerani, Cecilia 82, *83*
Gama, Vasco da 121, 185, 199
Gambello, Antonio 125
Garamond, Claude 180
garden design 93, 171
Gardiner, Stephen, bishop of Winchester 213
Gascony 164
Gaza, Theodore 187
Geertgen tot Sint Jans 151
The Holy Kindred 151; *The Man of Sorrows* 151; *Nativity at Night* 151
Geneva 177
Genoa 20, 21, *23*, 28
Holy League 125, 134
George of Trebizond 187
Gerbel, Nicolas 136
Gerhaert, Nikolaus 160
Bust of a Man *161*
Germany *136ff*
Christian humanism 24; *cuius regio, eius religio* 118; education 139–41, 142, 153, 156–57; Habsburg dynasty 156; historical studies 141, 146; humanism 136, 140, 142, 153, 156; Italian Wars 111; literature 145; mercenaries 76, 111; patronage 156; printing and publishing 116, *140*, 141, 146; Reformation 24, 109, 118, 142–43, 148, *149*, 153; semi-independent principalities 139; universities 139–40, *140*; *see also* Holy Roman Empire
Gesualdo, Carlo 79, 96
Ghibellines 28, 30, *30*
Ghiberti, Lorenzo 64, 71, 121
Baptistery doors 21, 63; *Commentarii* 69; *Gates of Paradise* 63, 69; Orsanmichele statues 63
Ghirlandaio, Domenico 205
Appearance of the Angel to Zaccharia 19; *St Jerome* 52; *Sassetti Chapel* 56; Tornabouni Chapel 74
Gil de Hontañón, Juan 202
Gil de Hontañón, Rodriqo 202
Gil de Siloé 202
Giocondo da Verona, Fra 76, 171
Giorgio, Francesco di 70
Giorgione 78
Giotto di Bondone 14, 37, 39, 41, 68
Arena Chapel frescoes 39, 46, *46*, 47; *The Death of St Francis of Assisi* 39; Florence Cathedral bell tower 39; Santa Croce frescoes 39
Giudecca 100
Glamis castle 221
Gloucester, Humfrey, Duke of 204–05
Goes, Hugo van der
Portinari Altarpiece 44; *Trinity Altarpiece* 219
Golden Hind 127, *214*
Gomes, Fernão 121
Gonçalves, Nuño 201
St Vincent Polyptych 201
Gonzaga, Cecilia *104*
Gonzaga, Elisabetta 72, *73*, 104
Gonzaga, Francesca 59
Gonzaga, Guglielmo 96
Gonzaga, Lodovico 68, *68*
González de Mendoza, Pedro, archbishop of Toledo 187
Gothic culture in Italy *34*
Gouda 141
Goujon, Jean 172
Gozzoli, Benozzo
The Procession of the Magi 14; *St. Augustine teaching Rhetoric and Philosophy* 16

Granada 185, *185*, *186*, 199; cathedral 202
Greenland 125
Greenwich
palace 205; Queen's House 224, *224*
Gregory XIII, Pope 92
"Enterprise of England" 213
Gresham, Sir Thomas 219
Gresham's College 219
Gritti, Doge Andrea 78, 113, *114*
Grocyn, William 206
Groote, Gerard
Bretheren of the Common Life 137, *137*
Grotius, Hugo 155
The Law of War and Peace 155
Grünewald, Mathis 24, *44*, 151, 153, 162
Isenheim alterpiece 151, 153, 162; Protestantism 153; *The Temptation of St Anthony* 151
Guadalajara 187, 202
Guarini, Giovanni Battista 96
The Faithful Shepherd 96
Guarino, Battista 104
Guas, Juan 202
Gubbio 96
Guelphs 28–29, 30, *30*, 36, 40
Guevara, Antonio de, bishop of Mondoñedo
Golden Book of Marcus Aurelius 190
Guevara Garcilaso, Antonio de 199
Guicciardini, Ludovico
Description of the Netherlands 154
guild system 23, 30
Gutenberg, Johannes 116
Guzmán, Nuño de 191

H

Habsburg dynasty 24, 139, 156, 157, *186*, 192, 196
Italian Wars 111, *165*; patronage 156
Hague 158
Hakluyt, Richard
The Principal Navigations of the English Nation 217
Hammer of Witches 162
Hampton Court 208, *208*
Hanseatic League 111, *137*, *139*
Hardwick Hall 214
Hatton, Sir Christopher 214, *216*
Hawkins, Sir John 213
Hawkwood, Sir John 48, *48*
Hebrew cabbala *19*, 20, 143, 145, 153, 156, 174
Hegius, Alexander 146
Heidelberg 139
castle 156; sodality 141; university 139, 140, 145
Heinsius, Daniel 155
edition of Aristotle's *Poetics* 155; *Nederduytsche Poemata* 155
Heneage, Sir Thomas 214
Henry IV, king of Castile 184
Henry VI, king of England 205
Henry VII, king of England *104*, 125, 204, *207*, *207*, 209, 215, 216
building program 205; Cornish Rebellion *207*; Lambert Simnel 206; Perkin Warbeck 206
Henry VIII, king of England 119, 152, *188*, 204, 206–07, 209–11, *210*, 215
bid for title of Holy Roman Emperor 207; break with Rome 210, 211; Dissolution of Monasteries 210–11, *213*; divorce from Catherine of

Aragon 204, 210, 223; expansionism 207; Field of the Cloth of Gold 209; marriage to Anne Boleyn 213; marriage to Anne of Cleves 217; marriage to Catherine of Aragon 204; marriage to Catherine Parr 210; marriage to Jane Seymour 209, 210; Nonsuch palace 168; patronage and cultural propaganda 204, 205, 207, 209, 216, 222; Pilgrimage of Grace 207, 211; Reformation 118
Henry II, king of France 173, 178, 179, 182, 196
Henry III, king of France 178, 182
Henry IV, king of France 178
Henry, Prince of Wales 214
Henry of Anjou see Henry III, king of France
Henry of Navarre see Henry IV, king of France
Henry the Navigator 185, 186, 187, 201
Henryson, Robert 219
hermeticism 132, 133
Herrera, Juan de 200
Hertford, Earl of 214, 220
Hesse 156
hidalgo 190, 199
Hilliard, Nicholas 213–14, 216
Armada Jewel (attributed) 214; George, 3rd Earl of Cumberland 214; James I 217; Self-portrait 216; Sir Christopher Hatton 216; A Treatise Concerning the Art of Limning 216
Hippocrates 143
Hoby, Sir Edward 217
Hoby, Sir Thomas 213
Hohenstaufen emperors 28
Holbein, Hans, the Younger 147, 151–52, 153, 207, 209, 216; Anne of Cleves 217; Cardinal John Fisher 223; "cosmological ceiling" 209; portrait of Colet 206; portrait of Erasmus 147; portrait of Kratzer 209, 211; Sir Thomas More and his Family 209; Whitehall fresco 209
Holdenby House 214
Holinshed, Raphael 217, 219
Holy League 125, 134
Italian Wars 76
Holy Roman Empire 21, 28, 140 confederate nature 140–41; Emperor 141; Italy 28, 76; Spain 186; see also Germany
Homer 49, 58, 143, 175
Hooker, Richard 217
Horace 17, 52, 155, 219
Hornebolte, Lucas 216
Hornebolte family 216
Howard, Henry, Earl of Surrey 213
Huguenots 177
humanism 16–17, 19, 41, 48, 51, 72, 100
Alberti 69; Alsace school 145–46; Brethren of the Common Life 137, 137, 146; and the Catholic Church 60, 62–63, 111; Christian 24; civic 53; classical influence 26, 146; collecting and copying ancient texts 52, 52; and education 51, 104, 108, 111, 138, 140–41, 142, 153; England 205–06, 224; Florence 48–49, 49, 111; France 169, 171, 173–74, 173, 176; Germany 140; High Renaissance 78, 83, 84; Italy 48, 57; Low Countries 146; and the "modern devotion" 194; music 128; Northern Renaissance 136, 137, 137, 138, 141, 142, 145–47, 153, 155, 156; and printing 108, 116, 140, 141, 154, 173, 176; and the Reformation 19, 117,

177; social implications 114; sodalities 141, 142, 145; Spain and Portugal 187–91, 188, 192–94, 194, 197, 199; transmission from Italy 108; and the universities 112; Venice 114–15; vernacular (bastard) 190–91, 199; and the visual arts 114
humanities (studia humanitatis) 16, 17, 48
Hundred Years War 21, 164
Hungary 24, 138, 139, 144 Corvina library 139, 139; defeat by Turkey 134; Habsburg Empire 139
hunting 139
Hussites 16, 137, 154
Hutten, Ulrich von 136, 143, 147, 154
edition of Valla's Donation of Constantine 143; Letters of Obscure Men 143, 145

I

Iceland 125
Ignatius, St 111
Ile de France 165
illuminated manuscripts 54, 54, 139, 164, 204, 205
imitatio theory 199
India 120, 185
Indies, Council of the 197
indulgences 62, 148, 149, 162
Infantado, Count of 187
Infantado, Don Iñigo Lopez de Mendoza, Duke of 187
Ingolstadt, university 142, 143
Innocent III, Pope 33–34
Innocent VIII, Pope 187
Innsbruck 141
Inquisition 36, 99, 118, 189, 192–93, 192, 193, 194, 194, 196, 197
Ireland 204
Isabella of Castile see Ferdinand and Isabella
Isabella of France 196
Isabella of Portugal 196
Isidore 191
Islam 122, 123, 135 Spain 184–85, 185, 186, 194; see also Ottoman Empire
Italian Wars 20, 56, 57, 76, 76, 78, 111, 164–65, 165, 166, 171, 172, 172 Peace of Cambrai 171; Peace of Cateau-Cambrèsis 177
italic and roman scripts and typefaces 16, 49, 52, 116
Italy 20ff, 58 Black Death 32, 33, 39, 40, 41; Catholic Church 119; church and state 31; city life and civic values 21, 23, 24, 28, 29; city-states 20, 23–24, 23, 28; classical influence 34; communes 28; condottieri 20, 48, 48, 58, 59, 60, 67–68, 72; Counter-Reformation 111; cultural and artistic centers 15, 34, 67, 94; diffusion of Renaissance culture within 111; Donation of Constantine (papal fraud) 19, 48, 117, 118, 143; education 40; family loyalties 28; and France see Italian Wars; German empire 28; Ghibellines 28, 30, 30; Gothic culture 34; Guelphs 28–29, 30, 30, 36, 40; Hohenstaufen emperors 28; humanism 48, 51, 57; monastic orders 36; and the Ottoman Empire 62; patronage 67, 78;

Peace of Lodi 123; principalities and princely courts 20, 29, 67–68; printing and publishing 67; Roman ruins 21; and Spain 56, 186; territorial wars 48; trade and commerce 21, 23, 108; transmission of Renaissance culture to other parts of Europe 111–15; wealth 21; women 104

J

James I, king of England see James VI, king of Scotland and I of England
James I, king of Scotland 219 The Kingis Quair 219; marriage 219
James III, king of Scotland 219
James IV, king of Scotland Battle of Flodden Field 204; marriage to Margaret Tudor 204, 219
James V, king of Scotland 204, 219 marriage to Mary of Guise 219
James VI, king of Scotland and I of England 145, 219, 219, 220, 221, 224 Basilikon Doron 221; portrait by Hilliard 217; succession to English crown 204
Jannequin, Clément 164
Janyns, Robert 205
Japan 109
Jefferson, Thomas 100
Jenkinson, Anthony 124, 127
Jesuit order 93, 111, 153, 156, 193, 197
Jews Spain 185, 194; Venice 122, 135
Jiménez de Cisneros, Francisco, cardinal–archbishop of Toledo 192
Jodelle, Étienne 175
Johannes of Neumarkt 137
Johannes of Štibor 137
John II, king of Castile 186, 187, 190
John II, king of Navarre and Aragon 186
John II, king of Portugal 185
John III, king of Portugal 188
John of Austria, Don 124
John de Critz 219
John Palaeologus 62
Jones, Inigo 100, 100, 224 Banqueting House Whitehall 204, 224; Double Cube Room Wilton House 224; The Masque of Blacknesse 217; Queen's House Greenwich 224, 224
Jonson, Ben 218, 219 The Masque of Blacknesse 217
Joyeuse, Anne de 183
Julius II, Pope 76, 83, 84–85, League of Cambrai 78, 113, 114; St Peter's 84; Sistine Chapel ceiling 86; Vatican museum of antiquities 26; Villa Farnesina 87
jurisprudence 85
Justus of Ghent 73
Juvenal 23

K

Kepler, Johann 132, 133, 155, 156 Harmony of the World 133
Kett's Rebellion 207
Khania 123
Khunrath, Heinrich Amphitheater of Eternal Wisdom 144, 145

Knights' Revolt 143
Knights of St John 134
Knights of Santiago 190
Knox, John 220
Kölderer 139
Kratzer, Nicholas 209, 211 "cosmological ceiling" 209; portrait by Holbein 209, 211
Krumlov 156

L

Lacock Abbey 213
Laguna, Andrés 192
Landshut, Stadtresidenz 156
Laocoon 26
Las Casas, Bartolomé de, bishop of Chiapas 199
Las Navas de Tolosa, Battle of 122
Latimer, Hugh 213
Latimer, William 206
Latin 36, 40, 116
Laudino, Cristoforo 19
Laurana, Francesco 72
Lazarillo de Tormes 193
Lebons, John 205
Lecce 78
Lee, Sir Henry 214
Lefèvre d'Etaples, Jacques 145, 173, 174, 176 Commentary on St Paul's Epistles 174; editions of Aristotle 174; Fivefold Psalter 174
legista 16–17
Leicester, Robert Dudley, Earl of 213, 214
Leiden 141 university 155
Leo X, Pope 83, 87, 143, 145, 181, 206 portrait by Raphael 84
León, Luis de 197, 199
Leonardo da Vinci 20, 78, 81–83, 82, 84, 98, 121, 180 architecture 169, 171; The Battle of Anghiari 81, 102; chiaroscuro 82; classical influence 26; drawings and notebooks 102, 102, 103; fortification designs 124; France 82, 171; illustrations to Pacioli's Divine Proportion 82; Lady with an Ermine 82, 83; The Last Supper 82; Leda and the Swan 102; Leonardo Codex Atlanticus 171; Madonna and Child with St Anne 81; Madonna with the Yarn-Winder 80, 81; Mona Lisa 81; sfumato 80, 81, 82; theatrical set designs 82; travels of 82, 111; Virgin of the Rocks 82–83
Leoni, Leone 85
Lepanto, Battle of 124–25, 125, 134
Leto, Pomponio 51
Leyland, John 215
Limousin, Léonard 172 enameled medallion 164
Linacre, Thomas 206
Lindsay, Sir David 219
Linlithgow palace 219–20
Lippi, Fra Filippo The Annunciation 54
Lipsius, Justus 155, 156 edition of Tacitus's Annals 155; On Constancy 155
Lisbon 191 university 188
literacy 40, 189
literature 16, 17, 85 admiratio 199; Baroque styles 199; censorship 176; classical influence 19, 26, 40, 41, 48–49,

52, 52, 116, 146, 175–76, 199; Counter-Reformation 96; England 214–15, 217, 218, 219; Euphuism 190; France 174–76, 178, 182; Germany 145; High Renaissance 78; humanist 16–17, 19; imitatio 199; italic and roman scripts and typefaces 16, 49, 52, 116; Italy 40–41, 78, 96; Latin verse 142; picaresque novel 193; Pléiade poets 175; "poetic brigade" 174–75; Portugal 199; printing see printing; Reformation 154; Scotland 224; Spain 189–90, 190, 193, 197, 199, 201; teaching 16, 17; Venice 76, 87, 91; vernacular (bastard) humanism 190; vernacular languages 155
Livy 17
Lodi, Peace of 55, 123
Loire Valley 165, 166, 169
Lollards 16
Lombardy 28 city-states 20; civic government 28; plague epidemic 76
London 111 Banqueting House 204; theaters 217, 218, 219; trade and commerce 124, 127
Longleat 213
López de Palacios Rubios, Juan Brief on the Islands of the Ocean Sea 197, 199
Lord Chamberlain's Men 217
Lord President of the Marches 204
Lorenzetti, Ambrogio Good and Bad Government 32, 37, 39
Lotto, Lorenzo 89 Portrait of a Lady 89
Louis II, king of Hungary and Bohemia 139
Louis XII, king of France 76, 164, 169, 171 Italian Wars 57
Louvain 141 university 141, 155
Lovati, Lovato di 40
Low Countries 24, 136ff, 139 Brethren of the Common Life 136–37, 137, 141, 145, 146; Chambers of Rhetoric 141; Christian humanism 24; education 141, 155, 156–57; Holy Roman Empire 186; humanism 24, 136, 141, 146, 154, 155; "modern (new) devotion" 114, 137, 176, 194; patronage 156; printing and publishing 116, 141; Reformation 24, 153; religion 16; Revolt 119, 154, 196, 213; science 109; sodalities 141, 145; Spanish occupation 119, 136, 154, 156, 196; trade 120; visual arts 18, 18, 149, 151, 153, 156
Loyola, St Ignatius 193
Lübeck 142 sodality 141
Lucan 191, 219
Lucian of Samosata 176, 209
Lucretius 176
Luder, Peter 140
Ludlow castle 204
Ludwig of Bavaria 156
Lull, Ramon 174
Lumley, John, Lord 214
Luna, Francesco della 70
Luther, Martin 24, 112, 142, 143, 145, 148, 149, 176 Bible translation 117, 149; Ninety-Five Theses 148, 192; portrait by Cranach 149
Luzzaschi, Luzzasco 96
Lyly, John Euphuism 190

Lyon *109*, 172, 173, 182, 188
Lyons 111, 112

M

Machiavelli, Niccoló 59–60, 81, *81*, 98, 118
  The Art of War 81; *Clizia* 81; declared heretical 99; *The Discourses* 81; *Mandragola* 81; *The Prince* 81, *81*, 118, 193
Machuca, Pedro 199
Maderno, Carlo 84
Madonna of the Big Eyes 36
Madrid, Château de 169
Madrid, created captial 196
Magdeburg 141
Magellan, Ferdinand 121, *123*
magic, practice of 19–20, 144, *144*, *145*, 156, *156*, *162*, 174
magus (magician) 19–20, 132, 144
Maiano, Benedetto 208
Maier, Michael *144*
Mainardi, Giovanni 175
Mainz 116, *140*, 142
  archbishopric *141*
majolica ware 72, *94*, 96
Majorca 187–88
Malatesta, Sigismondo Pandolfo 48, *51*, 67–68
Malory, Sir Thomas *205*
Malta
  fortifications 124; siege 134
Malvezzi, Cristofano 98
Manetti, Antonio 69
Manetti, Giannozzo 191
Manfred, king of Sicily 28
Mannerism 99
Manrique, Gómez 190
Manrique, Jorge 190
Mantegna, Andrea 24, 26, 59, 68, 96, 151
  camera picta Castello di San Giorgio 68, *68*; classical influence 26; *Parnassus* 59; *St. James Before Herod* 26
Mantua 56, 58, 59, *59*, 67, 94, *94*, 96
  Castello di San Giorgio 68, *68*; civic government 29; Gonzaga 24, 51, 68, 96; League of Cambrai 76; Palazzo del Tè 156; San Sebastiano 68; Sant'Andrea 68
Manuel I, king of Portugal 185, 188
Manueline style *202*
Manutius, Aldus 78, 89, 114, 116, *116*, 206
maps, printed 89, *109*, *124*
Marcus Aurelius, equestrian statue of 16, 21
Marenzio, Luca 96, 98
Margaret of Denmark 219
Margaret Tudor 219
Margaret of York 209
Margarit, Juan, bishop of Gerona
  Forgotten Chronicles of Hispania 192
Marguerite d'Angouleme 104, *105*
  Heptameron 105
Marguerite de Lorraine *183*
Marguerite of Valois *178*
Marignano (Melegnano), Battle of 164, 165
Marinis, Luca di 192
Marlowe, Christopher 218
  Tamburlaine 217
Martial 191
Martin V, Pope 60
Martini, Simone
  illustration to Virgil *27*, 40–41; *Maestà 32*; Siena town hall fresco 37
Martire d'Anghiera, Pietro 187, *193*

Decades on the New World 197
Mary I, queen of England *210*, 213
  marriage to Philip II of Spain 196, 213; persecution of Protestants 213, *213*; portrait by Mor 213, *213*; Wyatt's Rebellion 207
Mary Queen of Scots 213, 220
  abdication 221; Babington plot 221; claim to English throne 204, 219, 220; execution *220*, 221; marriages 220–21; Ridolfi plot 221; rising of the Northern Earls 221
Mary of Guise 219, 220
Mary of Portugal 196
Masaccio 64–65, 149
  Brancacci Chapel 64, *65*, *65*; *Holy Trinity* 64, *65*, 69
Maser, Villa Barbaro *101*
Masolino 65
Master of Flémalle *24*
mathematics 16, 82, *82*
Matthias Corvinus, king of Hungary 139, *139*
Mauch, Daniel 160, *161*
Maurice of Saxony 118
Maximilian I, Emperor 139, 142, 145, 146, *210*;
  League of Cambrai 78; *Teuerdank* 139; *Weisskunig* 139
Maximilian II, Emperor 156, 196
Meaux sect 176
Medici, Alexander de' 96
Medici, Cosimo de' 53, 54, *54*, 55, 58, 63, 64
  bust by Verrocchio *55*
Medici, Duke Cosimo I de' 96–98, 166
  portrait by Cellini 97
Medici, Grand Duke Ferdinando de' 98
Medici, Giovanni de' 54
Medici, Giovanni de' *see* Leo X, Pope
Medici, Giuliano de' 56, *56*, 97
Medici, Cardinal Giulio de' *84*
Medici, Lorenzino 96
Medici, Lorenzo de' 14, 56–57, *56*, 74, 97, 104
  bust by Verrocchio *56*; patronage 26, 56; Platonic Academy 19
Medici, Lucrezia de' 104
Medici, Piero de' 54, *55*, 56, 57, 58
Medici family 21, 23, *23*, 24, *44*, 51, 53–57, *54*, *55*, *56*, 58, 84, 96–98, 149
  anti-Medici plots 56, *56*; banking interests 55, 57, 172; driven from Florence 76, 79; Laurentian Library 97, *97*; Medici Chapel San Lorenzo 96; Palazzo Medici 54, *54*, *55*, 63;.papacy 96; patronage *14*, 23, 53, 54, *54*, 55, 63, 64, 78, 96–98, 111; Peace of Lodi 55; return to Florence 81
medicine and surgery 172, *172*, 175, 219
Mediterranean, Spanish expansionism *186*
Mehmed the Conqueror 62, 134
Melancthon, Philipp 153
Memmi, Lippo 32
Mena, Juan de 190
Mendoza, Cardinal *187*, 192
Mendoza (Spanish ambassador to England) 213
Mendoza family 187, *187*, 202
Mercator, Gerhardus *124*
mercenaries 48, *48*, 162, *165*
  condottieri 20, 48, *48*, 58, 59, 60, 67–68, 72
Mercogliano, Pacello de 171
Mérida 192
Messina, Antonello da *113*
  Salvator Mundi 113
Metternich, Prince 20
Mexico 111, 121, 197, 199

Michelangelo 14, 78, 82, *85*, 90, *90*, *96*, 98, 100, 169, 171, 180, 200, 205
  The Battle of Cascina 81; Christianity 93–94, 96; classical influence 26; *Cupid* 59; *David* 81, *81*; *The Deposition of Christ* 84; fortification designs 124; *Last Judgment* 94, 99; Laurentian Library 97, *97*; Medici Chapel 96; *Moses* 84; Pauline Chapel frescoes 94; *Pietà* 84, *85*; poetry 94; Porta Pia 92; *Rondanini Pietà* 84; St Peter's dome 84, 92, *92*; Sistine Chapel 20, 76, 84, 86, *86*, 94, 99; *Slaves* 84; tomb for Julius II 84; and Vittoria Colonna 93–94
Michelet, Jules 14
Michelozzo 65
  Palazzo Medici 54, *55*, 63
middle ages 15
  European economy 23; medieval renaissances 15–16; medieval western Christendom 16
Milan 28, 67, 94
  civic government 29; Della Torre 29; education 40; expansionism 48, 56; and Florence 111; High Renaissance 81–83; Holy Roman Empire 186; Italian Wars 57, 76, 111, 164; Peace of Lodi 55, 123; population 21; Santa Maria delle Grazie 81, 82; Sant'Ambrogio 81; Sforza 24, 48, 55–56, 57, 67, 81, 82, 139; Spanish rule 76, 186, 196; Visconti 23, 24, 29, 30, 48, *58*, 111
Mildmay, Sir Walter 222
Milič of Kroměříž 137
"modern (new) devotion" 114, 137, 176, 194
Modon 123
Mohacs, Battle of 134
Mohacs, Battle of 134
Monemvasia 123
Montaigne, Michel Eyquem de 179, *179*
  Essays 176, 179, *179*
Montalvo, Alvaro Díaz de
  Royal Ordinances 189
Montalvo, Garci Ordóñez de
  Amadis of Gaule 189, 190, 199
Montanus, Benedictus Arias 154
Monte Cassino 41
Montefeltro, Federigo da 58, 72, 73, 201
  studiolo 58, 72
Montefeltro, Guidobaldo 72, 73
Monteverdi, Claudio *113*
  The Battle of Tancredi and Clorinda 96
Montmorency, Anne de *164*, 165
Montone, Braccio da 60
Montorio 60
Montoro, Antón de 193
Montpellier, medical faculty 175
Mor, Anthonis
  portrait of Mary I 213, *213*
Moravia 139
More, Sir Thomas 105, *146*, 152, 206, 209;
  Epigrams 204; execution 204, 210, 211; *Life of Picus* 209; *Sir Thomas More and his Family* (Holbein) 209; translation of Lucian 209; *Utopia* 197, 209
Morea 134
Morley, Thomas 217
Moscow 127
Mouton, Jean 128
Mugello 39
Mühlberg, Battle of *118*, *154*
music 128, *128*, *129*
  chanson 129; England 217; Florentine *Intermedi* 96; France 182; *frottola* 129; harmonic proportions 70; High

Renaissance 98; Italy 96; musical drama *19*; printed 89, *128*; religious 128, *128*, *129*; secular 128; Venice *113*
Mussato, Alberto 40
Musurus, Marcus 116, *116*
Myllar, Andrew 219
Mytens, Daniel ; portrait of James I *219*

N

Nantes, Edict of *177*, 178
Naples 20, 67, 94, 187, 188
  expansionism 48; Italian Wars 57, 76, *76*, 164; Peace of Lodi 55, 123; Spanish rule 76, 186, *186*, 187, 196
Narni, Erasmo da' (Gattamelata) 64
Nauplia 123
Navagero, Andrea 191
Navarre 185, 186, 187
Nebrija, Antonio de 188, 192
  Latin Introductions 188, *188*, 189
neo-classicism 100, *100*, *101*
neo-Platonism 19–20, *19*, 60, 74, 84, 86, 91, 111, 112, 117, 132, *133*, 153
  adept 19, 132; High Renaissance 78; music 128; visual arts 20, *85*
Netherlands *see* Low Countries
Netley Abbey 210
Neuchâtel 177
New World 109, 111, 114, 196, 197
Newfoundland 125
Newstead Abbey 211
Niccoli, Niccolo 49, 52, *52*
Nicholas of Custa 137
Nicholas V, Pope 60, 62
Nicola da Urbino 72
Nijmegen 141
Nîmes 153, 172
Nogarola, Isotta 104
Nonsuch palace 168, 214
Norfolk, Thomas Howard, 4th Duke 221
Normandy 165
North, Council of the *207*
North, Sir Thomas 217
northeast passage 127
Northern Earls' Rebellion *207*, 221
Northern European vision 162, *162*, *163*
Northumberland, Duke of 211
Nuremberg 141, *141*

O

occult, interest in 19–20, 144, *144*, *145*, 153, 156, 157
Ojeda, Alonso de 121
Oliver, Isaac 216
Olomouc 139
Oran 186
Orcagna, Andrea 33
Ordinance of Montpellier 180
Orkney 125
Orléans, law faculty *173*
Orosius 191
Orsini, Clarice 56
Ortelius 154
Orthodox Church *51*, 62, 123
Osman dynasty 134
Otranto, Battle of 123, 134
Otto Heinrich of the Palatinate 156
Ottoman Empire 19, 76, 111, 123, 127, *134*, *134*, *135*, 139
  Africa 134; alliance with Francis I 134; capture of Constantinople

Renaissance 98; Italy 96;
19, 49, *55*, 62, 123, 134, *134*; and Italy 62, 76, *76*; and Spain 196; and Venice 123–25, *125*, 134
Ouwater, Albert 149, 151
  Raising of Lazarus 151
Ovid 78, 90, *90*, 98, 140;
  Metamorphoses 87
Oxford university 16, *104*, 112, 204–05, 206, 222, *222*
  Bodleian Library 205, *223*

P

Pacher, Michael 151
Pacioli, Luca 82, *82*
Padua 30, *34*, 40, 49, 51, 64, 87, 113
  Arena Chapel 39, 46, *46*, *47*; *Infiammati* 78; siege 76; university 16, 40, 78, *94*, 155
painting *see* visual arts
Palatinate 156
  election of Holy Roman Emperor 141
Palencia, Alfonso de
  Antiquities of Hispania 192; *Little Compendium of the Ancient Sites of Hispania* 192
Palestrina, Giovanni 96
Palio 33
Palladio, Andrea 21, 78, 91, *91*, 100, *100*, *101*, 113, 224, *224*
  buildings of *91*; classical influences *100*; *Four Books of Architecture* 91, 100, *100*; Il Redentore 100, *100*; Olympian Academy *101*; Palazzo Valmarana *100*; San Giorgio Maggiore 100; Santa Maria della Presentazione 100; Teatro Olimpico *101*; theater and set design *101*; translation of and comment on Vitruvius *101*; Villa Barbaro *101*; Villa La Malcontenta *100*; Villa La Rotonda *101*
Pannonia 139
Panofsky, Erwin *18*, 158
Pantheon 21
papacy 2, 60, 83–84, 87
  Avignon papacy 16, 20, 60, 171; Borgia 24; Donation of Constantine (papal fraud) 19, 48, 117, 118, 143; Guelphs 28–29, 30, *30*, 36; Holy League 125, 134; Index of Prohibited Books 99; Italian Wars 76, 78; Medici 96; patronage 62, 83–84, 92, *92*; *Regnans in Excelsis* Papal Bull 213; schism 20, 60
Papal State 28, *56*, 76, 82, 84
  constitution *58*; Peace of Lodi 55, 123
Paré, Ambroise 172, *172*
Parentucelli, Tommaso *see* Nicholas V, Pope
Paris 182
  Louvre 166, 180, 182; printing and publishing 176; Royal Academy of Music and Poetry 182; St Bartholomew's Day Massacre 178, *178*, *179*; Sorbonne 111, 112, 146, 173, 176–77; university 16, 174
Parmigianino 172
Parr, Catherine *210*
Paruta, Paolo 76
Pasti, Matteo de
  Malatesta Temple *51*
patronage 23, 24
  confraternities 78, 82–83, 87, 89
Pau, Jeroni 187, 192
Paul III, Pope 83, 92, 93, 94
Paulet, William 210

Pavia 30
Pavia, Battle of 165
Pazzi, Jacopo dei 56
Pazzi family 56, 56
Peake, Robert 215
Périers, Bonaventure des 176
Perrissin 178
perspective 14, 27, 64, 69, 71, 78, 98, 111
  Alberti's treatise on 69; Brunelleschi 69, 69; Uccello 69, 69
Peru 111, 121, 197
Perugia 30, 48, 84
Perugino, Piero 59, 84, 85
Peruzzi, Baldassare 87
Peruzzi family 39
Pesaro, Lucrezia 89
Petit, Guillaume 181
Petrarch, Francesco 15, 37, 40–41, 48, 49, 51, 52, 60, 137, 174, 187
  Africa 40; copy of Virgil 27, 40–41; Scipio 26; travels of 40
Peyro, Joan 187
Pfefferkorn, Johannes 143
Pforzheim 143
Philip II, king of Spain 90, 118, 125, 154, 186, 196, 196
  Catholic Church and Inquisition 196, 197; Dutch Revolt 154; and England 196, 213; Escorial 196, 200, 200, 201, 201; Holy League 125, 134; marriages 196, 213; patronage 196; Peace of Cateau–Cambrésis 76; succession 196
Philip III, king of Spain 196
philology 173
philosopher's stone 144
philosophy 85
  and Christianity 16; classical influence 16; neo-Platonism see neo-Platonism
piazze 30
Picardy 165
Piccolomini, Enea Silvio 123, 138: see also Pius II, Pope
Piccolomini, Cardinal Francesco 62
Pico della Mirandola, Giovanni 19, 56, 60, 116, 143
  biography by More 209; Oration on the Dignity of Man 17
Piero della Francesca 26, 82
  Flagellation 73; Legend of the True Cross fresco cycle 51; treatise on mathematics and perspective 72
Pigghe, Albert 164
pilgrimage 162
  Roman jubilee years 62
Pilgrimage of Grace 207, 211
Pindar 175
Pinkie Cleugh, Battle of 220
Pinturricchio 62
Pirckheimer, Willibald 139, 141, 141
Pirckheimer family 141
Pisa 28, 30, 34, 48
  Baptistery 36; Campo Santo 31; cathedral 31, 33; sieges 76; university 78, 94
Pisanello 66, 192
Pisano, Giovanni 33, 36, 36, 37, 39, 41, 68
  Arena Chapel sculptures 39
Pisano, Nicola 33, 34, 36, 37, 39, 41, 68
Pistoia 30
  Sant'Andrea 36, 36
Pithou, Pierre 178
Pitti, Buonacorso 21
Pitti family 21, 23, 56
Pius II, Pope 62, 62, 123, 125, 219: see also Piccolomini, Enea Silvio
Pius III, Pope 83

Pizarro, Francisco 111, 121
plague 23, 30, 76, 162; Black Death 30, 32, 33, 39, 40, 41
Plantin, Christopher 111, 154
  Complutensian Polyglot 154, 192
plateresque architecture 187, 188, 199, 202, 202, 203
Platina 206
Plato 19, 19, 49, 52, 55, 58, 72, 85, 132
  Ficino's translation 54; theory of forms 20; see also neo-Platonism
Platonic Academy 19
Plautus 17, 78, 81, 140, 142, 199
Pléiade poets 175
Plethou 123
Pliny the Younger 199
Plotinus 49
Plutarch 141, 192
  Lives 217
podestà 30, 32
poetry see literature
Poland 139, 155–56, 157
Pole, Cardinal Reginald 93
Poliziano, Angelo 49, 52, 56, 57, 104, 116, 197, 206
  Miscellanea 116; Orfeo 19
Polo, Marco 109
polyptychs 44, 45
Pompeius 191
Pomponius Mela 192
population 21, 30, 33
Porte d'Arroux 16
Portinari, Tommaso 44
Portinari family 149
Portugal 185, 185
  Avis dynasty 187; exploration and expansionism 121–25, 123, 127, 185; humanism 186–87, 194; Italian influence 187; Manueline architecture 202; printing and publishing 187–90; religious and cultural centers 189; and Spain 196, 202; trade 122
Postel, Guillaume 174
Prague 137, 156
  Hradčany castle 156; St Vitus's cathedral 137; university 137
Prato, sack of 76
preaching and pulpits 33, 36, 36, 62
predella 44, 45
Prestongrange 224
Prevesa, Battle of 134
Primaticcio, Francesco 171–72, 172, 180
printing 19, 24, 109, 111–12, 114, 116, 116, 117
  centers of 114; classical works 141; devotional works 141; England 205; engravings 118, 119, 121; France 173, 176, 180; Germany 141, 146; Greek language and typefaces 87, 116, 180; Holy Roman Empire 140; and humanism 108, 116, 140, 141, 154, 173, 176; Iberian peninsula 187–90, 192, 199; italique (Aldino) typefaces 116; Italy 67; Low Countries 141; maps 124; music 128; printer's device (kolophon) 116; Reformation 140; roman typefaces 16; Scotland 219; Venice 89, 121, 121; woodcuts 121
Protestant Reformation 24, 99, 109, 111, 114, 117–19, 119, 142–43, 149, 154, 157
  Brethren of the Common Life 136–37, 137, 141, 146; church and state 118–19; eastern Europe 24; Edict of Nantes 177, 178; England 210, 211, 213; France 176–79, 177, 182;

Germany 142–43; and humanism 19, 117, 177; Hussites 16, 137, 154; impact of printing 114, 117; learning and education 153–54; literature 154; Luther 148; Meaux sect 176; "modern (new) devotion" 114, 137, 176, 194; printing 140; St Bartholomew's Day Massacre 177, 178, 178–79; salvation by faith alone 148; Venice 114–15; vernacular translations of the Bible 117, 137, 149, 154, 176, 197; visual arts 153
Provence 164, 165, 173
Prudentius 191
Ptolemy of Egypt 85, 132, 192
Pulci, Luigi 56, 57
Pulgar, Fernando del 190
Pythagoras 85, 145

Q

Quintilian 151, 191

R

Rabelais, François 173, 175, 175
  censorship of 176; Gargantua 175, 176; Pantagruel 175–76, 175
Raleigh, Sir Walter 215
Raphael 20, 72, 76, 78, 80, 82, 83, 84–85, 87, 90, 98, 100, 171, 180
  classical influence 26; The Entombment 84; Galatea 87; Portrait of Baldassare Castiglione 73; Portrait of Leo X 84; Saint Michael 181; St Peter's 87; Stanze 85, 87; Villa Farnesina fresco cycle 87
Rattle, The 192
Ravenna 43
Rees, Abbot Henry van 141
Reformation see Protestant Reformation
Regensburg 142
relics, worship of 162
religion and theology 85
  altarpieces 44, 44, 45; anticlericalism 114; church and state 31, 118–19; Concordat of Bologna 118; confraternities 78, 82–83; Council of Basil 137, 187; Council of Constance 137; Council of Florence 123, 187; Council of Trent 99, 119; Counter-Reformation see Counter-Reformation; cuius regio, eius religio 118; education 40; France 176; Hebrew cabbala 19, 20, 143, 145, 153, 156, 174; "modern (new) devotion" 114, 137, 176, 194; monasticism 36, 40, 117, 141; music 128, 128, 129; paganism and Christianity 16, 20; papacy see papacy; premonitions of Apocalypse 162; Protestant Reformation see Protestant Reformation; sects 33; see also Bible; Catholic Church; Christianity; Islam; Orthodox Church
Rembrandt Harmensz van Rijn 158
retable 44
Reuchlin, Johannes 143, 143, 145
  On the Art of the Cabbala 145; On the Wonder–Making Word 145

rhetoric 48, 141
  Chambers of Rhetoric 141
Rhineland 141
Rhodes 134
Richard III, king of England 204, 205
Richmond 205
Ridley, Nicholas 213
Ridolfi plot 221
Riemenschneider, Tilman 160
  Statue of St Paul 161
Rienzo, Cola di 23, 137
Rievaulx Abbey 210
Rimini 51, 67–68
Rinuccini, Ottavio 98
Robert, king of Anjou 37
Robert, king of Naples 29
Robertet, Florimond 80, 169
Rojas, Fernando de 199
Roman culture, influence of see classical culture, influence of
Romano, Giulio 78, 83, 96
  illustrations to Aretino's Sonetti lussuriosi 91
Rome 60, 62, 112
  Capitoline Hill (Campidoglio) 92; Castel Sant'Angelo 92; High Renaissance 83–85, 87, 91, 93–94; Il Gesù 93; jubilee years 62; Pantheon 21; papacy see papacy; population 84, 92; Porta Pia 92; rebuilding 92, 92; Rienzo's republic 23; sack 76, 78, 91, 97, 111, 192, 194, 197; St Peter's 62, 84, 87, 92, 92; Vatican see Vatican; Villa Farnesina 87
Ronsard, Pierre de 174–75, 220
Roper, Margaret 105
Rosa, Salvator 96
Rosicrucians 144, 145
Rossellino, Bernardo 53, 62
Rossi, Cardinal Luigi 84
Rosso, Giovanni Battista 171–72
Rouen 182
Roussillon 186
Roussillon 186
Rovere, della 95–96
Royal College of Surgeons (Edinburgh) 219
Royal Society 219
Rožmberk family 156
Rubens, Peter Paul 158
  Banqueting House ceiling 204; portrait of James VI and I 204
Rucellai, Giovanni 63, 64
Rudolf II, Emperor 156, 157, 157
Ruskin, John 69

S

St Andrews university 224
St Bartholomew's Day Massacre 177, 178, 178–79
St Germain–en–Laye 166
St Malo 165
St Paul's School 206
Salamanca 188
  New Cathedral 202; Palace of Monterrey 202; university 188, 188, 189, 189, 192–93, 203
Sallust 219
Salutati, Coluccio 41, 48, 49, 52, 52, 53
Saluzzo, bishop of 166
Samos 123
San Gimignano 29
San Lorenzo 71, 71, 96
San Marco 53, 54, 58, 63
San Pedro, Diego de
  Prison of Love 189
San Satiro 81
Sangallo, Antonio, the Younger 87
Sangallo, Antonio da 76, 100
Sangallo, Guiliano da 71, 76, 100
Sanmicheli, Michele 123–24

Sano di Pietro
Sansovino, Jacopo 76, 91, 98, 100, 113, 114
  Mars and Neptune 91; Venetian buildings 89, 91
Santa Maria 124
Santiago 213
Santiago in Estrema 122
Santillana, Iñigo López de Mendoza, Marquis of 187, 187
Santillana, Marquis of 190
Santo Domingo 213
Saragossa 187, 188
Sardinia 186, 186
Sarto, Andrea del 76, 172, 180
Sassetti, Francesco 56
Satutati 49
Savonarola, Fra Girolamo 60, 80
Savoy Hospital 205
Saxony 139, 139, 153
  election of Holy Roman Emperor 141
Scaliger, Joseph Justus 178
Scaliger, Julius Caesar 176
Scamozzi, Vincenzo 101
Scandinavia, Protestant Reformation 24
Schongauer, Martin 151
  Temptation of St Anthony 163
science 119, 121, 217, 219; Catholic Church's attitude toward 109, 111; Scientific Revolution 109, 111, 111, 117
Scotland 219–21; anticlericalism 219; Battle of Flodden Field 219; Battle of Pinkie Cleugh 220; Calvinism 119, 220; culture and politics 204; defeat on the Solway 220; education 224; and England 204, 207, 220; Old Alliance 219; printing and publishing 219; Protestant Reformation 24; Union of Crowns 204, 207, 219
scriptoria 16
Scrovegni, Enrico 39, 46, 47
sculpture see visual arts
scuole see confraternities
Sebastian, prince of Portugal 122
Sebond, Raymond 176
Segovia 191, 192, 202
Seljuk Turks 134
Seneca 40, 140, 142, 155, 175, 190, 191
  On Clemency 117
Senegal 125
Sepharad 185
Sepúlveda, Juan Ginés de 199
  Second Democrates on the Just Conquest of the Indians 199
Seville 109, 111, 191, 196
Seymour, Jane 209, 210
Seyssel, Claude de 171
  Le Grant Monarchie de France 171; translations of classical texts 171
Sforza, Francesco 48, 55, 57
Sforza, Galeazzo Maria 55–56
Sforza, Gian Galeazzo 81
Sforza, Lodovico (il Moro) 81, 82, 83, 94, 102
Sforza, Lodovico Maria 57
Sforza family 24, 48, 55–56, 67, 82, 139
Shakespeare, William 217, 218, 219, 224
  First Folio 217, 219, 224; Hamlet 217, 218; history plays 217; King Lear 217; Macbeth 221; The Merchant of Venice 216; A Midsummer Night's Dream 108; Othello 217; The Rape of Lucrece 217; Richard III 217; sonnets 217, 219; The Tempest 217; Titus Andronicus 217; Two Gentlemen of Verona 217; Venus and Adonis 217
s'Hertogenbosch 146

ships and shipping
Atlantic routes 121–25, 127; circumnavigations of the world 121, 123, 127, 214; galeass 124; Golden Hind 127; northeast passage 127; Santa Maria 124; Venice Arsenal 121; warfare 123
Shrewsbury, Elizabeth (Bess of Hardwick) 214
Shute, John 211
Sicily 20, 28, 187, 188
Spanish rule 186, 186, 196
Siculus 192
Sidney, Sir Philip 217
Siena 30, 33, 36–37, 48
Campo 30, 31, 32, 33; Cappella della Piazza 32; cathedral 31, 36–37; contrade 33; Great Council 32; the Nine 30, 32, 33, 37; Palazzo Pubblico 31, 32–33, 32, 33, 39; Palio 33; Pinturicchio fresco cycle 219; podestà 32; public art and architecture 30, 31, 36–37; Tower of the Mangia 32
Sigismund I, king of Poland 139
silk industry 173
Siloé, Diego 202
Simnel, Lambert 206
Simocatta 155
Sittow, Michael 192
Sixtus IV, Pope 56, 56, 62, 86, 206
Sixtus V, Pope 92, 92
Skelmorlie Aisle 224
slavery 186, 199
Sluter, Klaus 149
Society of Antiquaries 217
sodalities 141, 142, 145
Sodoma (Giovanni Bazzi) 87
Solinus 192
Solway 220
Somerset, Duke of 211
Somerset, Earl of 220
Sopetrán, Benedictine hermitage 187
Soto, Domingo de 192
Spain 21, 184ff
administrative organization 193; America 111, 185; antiquarianism 191–92, 191; Armada 196; Catholic Monarchs see Ferdinand and Isabella; censorship 197; chivalric ideals 190–91, 190, 199; church and state 118, 194; Council of the Indies 197; Counter-Reformation 24, 111, 189, 192–93, 194, 196; Decree on Printed Books 189; education and literacy 187, 188, 189, 193, 197; and England 196, 213; Erasmianism 192–94, 197; exploration and expansionism 121, 122–23, 123, 124, 125, 185, 186, 186, 197; Golden Age 185, 186, 189, 193; Habsburg dynasty 24, 186, 192, 196; hidalgo 190, 199; Holy League 125, 134; humanism 186–91, 188, 192–94, 194, 197, 199; Inquisition 118, 189, 192–93, 192, 193, 194, 194, 196, 197; Islam 16, 184–85, 185, 186, 194; and Italy 56, 76, 76, 186–87, 196; Jesuits 193, 197; Jewish community 185, 194; League of Cambrai 76; and the Low Countries 119, 136, 154, 156, 196; Madrid as capital 196; Naples 111; and the Ottoman Empire 196; patronage 187; Peace of Cateau–Cambrésis 76; plateresque architecture 188, 199, 202, 202, 203; and Portugal 196, 202; printing and publishing 187–90, 192, 199; religion 24, 111, 119, 185, 189, 196; religious and cultural

centers 189; Revolt of the Netherlands 154, 213; Royal Ordinances 189; theater 190–91, 201; trade 120; Treaty of Barcelona 186; Union of Crowns 188
Spenser, Edmund 217
Sponheim, abbey of 141
Spranger, Bartholomeus 156
Statius 139
Steyn monastery 146
Stirling castle 219, 220
Stoics 155, 178, 190
Stoss, Veit 160
St Roche 161
Strabo 192
Strasbourg 141, 145, 153, 176, 177
Strozzi family 53, 60, 63
Stuart, Princess Elizabeth 145
Stuart dynasty 204, 207, 219, 219, 224
studioli 58, 59
Sturm, Johannes 153, 155
Styria 186
Suetonius 206
Suleiman I, sultan of Ottoman Empire 76
Swiss Confederation 76, 81, 141, 165
Italian Wars 76, 76; Protestant Reformation 109, 119
symbolism and allegory 18, 18, 20, 214
syphilis 76, 142, 143

T

Taccone, Baldassare
Tacitus
Annals 155; Germania 138, 146
Tasso, Torquato 79, 96
Tazza Farnese 26
Teerlinc, Levina 216
telescope 119, 121
Tendilla, Count of 187
Terence 17, 140, 142, 155, 199
Terraferma 87, 121
theater
England 217, 218, 219; France 175; Leonardo's set designs 82; Pléiade poets 175; Spain 190–91, 201
Thirty Years War 156
Thou, Jacques-Auguste de 178
Throckmorton, Francis 213
Thucydides 141
Thurzó, Bishop Stanislas 139
Tiepolo, Giambattista 96
Tintoretto, Jacopo 89, 115
Titchfield Abbey 210
Titian (Tiziano Vecellio) 78, 82, 87, 89, 90–91, 98, 115, 180, 196
The Assumption of the Virgin (Assunta) 90; Bacchus and Ariadne 90; Charles V on Horseback 118; portrait of Andrea Gritti 114; Portrait of Philip II 196; Sacred and Profane Love 114
Tivoli 87
Hadrian's villa 199
Toledo 202
Tornabuoni, Giovanni 57
Toro, Battle of 202
Torquemada, Grand Inquisitor 193
Torres Naharro, Bartolomé de 191
Torrigiano, Pietro 94, 205, 206
Tortorel 178
Tory, Geoffroi 180
Toscanelli, Paolo 71
Toulouse, law faculty 173
Tours 173
trade and commerce 108, 109,

111, 127
effect of plagues 23; Hanseatic League 137, 139; Italy 21, 23; London 124; Portugal 122; trade routes 121–25, 124, 127, 139; Venice 120, 122, 125
Trent, Council of 99, 119, 193
Tribulo 180
triptychs 44, 44, 45
Trier, archbishopric 141
Trissino, Giangiorgio 100
Trithemius, Abbot Johannes 141
Trogus 191
Troyes 178
Tubingen, university 143
Tudor, Edmund 104
Tudor dynasty 196, 204, 207, 207, 209, 210
Tunis 186
Turkey see Ottoman Empire
Turkish Voyage, The 192
Tuscany 15, 28, 29–30, 34, 76
city-states 20; communes 28; Medici 96
Tyrol 186

U

Uccello, Paolo
perspective 69, 69; Sir John Hawkwood 48
Umbria 28
universities 16, 40, 78, 94, 108, 111, 112, 139–40, 140, 187, 188, 205, 206, 222, 222, 223
Urbino 58, 67, 72, 72, 73, 94, 95–96
usury 39, 46
Utrecht 137, 141

V

Valdés, Alfonso de 194, 197
Valencia 187, 188, 189
Valla, Lorenzo 117, 187
investigation of Donation of Constantine 48, 117, 143
Valladolid 192, 196, 199
College of San Gregorio 188, 203; College of Santa Cruz 202; College of Vera Cruz 187, 188
Vallet, Ferran 188
Valois dynasty 24, 164, 165–66, 166, 171, 177, 178, 182
Italian Wars 111; patronage 165–66
Valois Tapestries 182, 182, 183
Varchi, Benedetto 94
Vasari, Giorgio 14–15, 26, 78, 81, 94, 96, 160, 161
on Bronzino 97; Chancellery Palace frescoes 93; Lives of the Artists 15, 78, 93, 97, 111; on Michelangelo 94, 97; Palazzo Vecchio 97; Perseus and Andromeda 97; on Raphael 87; on Uccello 69; Uffizi 97; on the Venetian school 89, 90
Vásquez, Lorenzo
College of Santa Cruz 202; Medináceli palace 202
Vatican 92, 92, 94
architecture 27; library 62; museum of antiquities 26; Pauline Chapel frescoes 94; Sistine Chapel 20, 62, 76, 84, 86, 86, 94, 99; Stanze 85
Vega, Garcilaso de la 190, 191
Vega, Lope de 201
Venetia, plague epidemic 76
Venetian Republic 76, 113
Italian Wars 76, 78; League of

Cambrai 113, 114
Venice 28, 188
Arsenal 120, 120, 121, 121, 124, 125; Catholic Church 87, 114–15; civic government 28, 29; Commission of Spices 122; constitution 58, 113; as cultural center 113; doge 29, 65; doge's palace 65; eastern influence 89; exploration and expansionism 48, 56, 125; Florence compared 113; Great Council 29; High Renaissance 87, 89–91; Holy League 125, 134; humanism 114–15; Jewish community 122, 135; library 89, 91; Lion of St Mark 89; Loggetta 91; manufacturing 120, 121; Mint 91; "myth of" 76, 113; On the Commonwealth and Government of Venice (Contarini) 113; Palladio 91, 100; papal interdicts 114, 115; patronage and the arts 65–66, 78, 87, 89–91; Peace of Lodi 55, 123; population 21, 87; printing and publishing 89, 112, 116, 116, 121, 121; St Mark's 91; San Giorgio Maggiore 89; Santa Maria dei Frari 90; Scuola Grande of San Rocco 89; Terraferma 87, 121; trade and communications 120, 122, 125; transmission of Renaissance culture to other parts of Europe 111–15; and the Turks 123–25, 125, 134
Venier, Sebastian 125
Vergerio, Pietro 138
Vergil, Polydore 215
Verona 26, 29, 30, 87
Verona, Guarino da 206
Veronese, Paolo 78, 91
depictions of the Battle of Lepanto 125; Feast in the House of Levi (Last Supper) 99, 99, 125; Villa Barbaro 101
Verrocchio, Andrea del
bust of Lorenzo d'Medici 56; bust of Cosimo d'Medici 55
Vertue, Robert and William 205
Vesalius, Andreas 118, 119
Vespucci, Amerigo 109, 121, 209
Vicente, Gil 191
Vicenza 30, 56, 87, 91, 100
Olympian Academy 101; Palazzo Valmarana 100; Teatro Olimpico 82, 101; Villa La Rotonda 101
Vienna 139, 142
College of Poets 142; fortifications 124; sodality 141; university 139, 142
Vigevano 82
Vignola, Jacopo
Il Gesù 93; Villa Farnese 93
Villa Barbaro 101
Villa Farnese 93
Villa Farnesina 87
Villa La Malcontenta 101
Villa La Rotonda 101
Villani, Giovanni 40
Villiers, Cardinal Jean 84
Virgil 42, 58, 140
Aeneid 199; Petrarch's copy 27, 40–41
Visconti, Lord Azzone 37
Visconti, Bernabò 29, 30
Visconti, Duke Filippo Maria 48
Visconti, Gian Galeazzo 30, 48, 57
Visconti, Archbishop Giovanni 40
Visconti family 23, 24, 29, 48, 58, 111
Visconti–Sforza collection 180
Visigrád, palace 139
Viterbo, Egidio da 84
Vitéz, Archbishop Jànos 139
Vitoria, Francisco de 192

Cambrai 113, 114
Venice 28, 188
Vitruvius 27, 70, 70, 81, 100
Ten Books of Architecture 101
Voragine, Jacopo da 40, 46
Vries, Adriaen de 156

W

Waldseemüller, Michael 109
Wales 204
Wales, Council of 207
Warbeck, Perkin 206
Warham, Archbishop 146
Wars of the Roses 204, 207
wars and warfare 76
condottieri 20, 48, 48, 58, 59, 60, 67–68, 72; fortifications 76, 123–24; mercenaries 48, 48, 162, 165; naval 123
Webster, John 218
Welser 141
West Indies 197, 213
Western Rebellion 207
Westminster
abbey, Henry VII Chapel 205, 206; almshouse 205
Westminster School 215
Weyden, Rogier van der 44, 149
Deposition of Christ 149
Whitehall palace 208, 209
Whitelaw, Archibald 219
Whitney, Geoffrey
Choice of Emblems 224
Widmanstetter, Johann 156
Willaert, Adrian 113
William of Orange 154
assassination 213
Willoughby, Sir Hugh 127
Wilton House 224
Wimpfeling, Jacob 137, 145–46
Epitome of German Affairs 146; On Integrity 146
Windsor castle 205
witchcraft 162
Wittenberg 141
university 139, 142, 148
Woking palace 205
Wolsey, Cardinal Thomas 222, 222
Hampton Court 208, 208
women
courtiers 95; education 51, 104
Woodstock palace 205
Wotton, Sir Henry 114
Wren, Sir Christopher 222
Wriothesley, Henry, 3rd Earl of Southampton 219
Wriothesley, Thomas 210
Württemberg 145, 156
Württemberg, Ulrich, Duke of 143
Wyatt, Sir Thomas 213
Wyatt's Rebellion 207

X

Xenophon 141

Z

Zadar 123
Zamora 191
Zeno, Antonio 125
Zeno, Niccolò 125
Zonchio, Battle of 123
Zuccaro, Federico 27, 93, 214
Zuccaro, Taddeo 93, 166
Zurich 141
Zwingli, Ulrich 147
Zwinglianism 153
Zwolle 141

AMERICA SIVE INDIA NOVA

Anno 1492 à Christophoro Columbo nomine Regis
Castilia primum detecta

Circulus Aequinoctialis

Tropicus Capricorni

MAR

PACIFICO

Archipelago

minore

Estrecho de Magellanes

TERRA

AUSTRALIS.

Circulus Antarcticus

Tropicus Cancri

DEL

ZUR

Brasil

Terra del fuego